PENGUIN

D0020543

HISTORY OF THE PEL~~~~~~~~~~

ADVISORY EDITOR: BETTY RADICE

THUCYDIDES the son of Olorus was born probably about 460 B.C. and died about the year 400 B.C. When the Peloponnesian War broke out in 431 B.C. Thucydides probably took part in some of its early actions. Some time between 430 and 427 he fell ill of the plague, but recovered. In 424 he was appointed general, but his small squadron of ships arrived too late to save the important Athenian colony of Amphipolis from the Spartan commander Brasidas, though he successfully held the nearby port of Eion against Brasida's attacks. In consequence he was exiled, not returning until twenty years had passed, only to die a few years later.

For much of the period he describes *The Peloponnesian War* is the only source that survives. The verity of his reports and the justice of his perceptions have been the cause of controversy amongst scholars for centuries. But it is certain that he used his historical imagination to reconstruct only as a last resort. When the various parts of the history were composed, which of these he revised, and whether their chronological inconsistencies are due to later editing – these questions are still unsolved.

REX WARNER was University Professor of the University of Connecticut from 1964 until his retirement in 1974. He was born in 1905 and was a classical scholar of Wadham College, Oxford. He wrote poems, novels and critical essays, and translated many works, of which Xenophon's *History of My Time* and *The Persian Expedition*, Plutarch's *Lives* (under the title *Fall of the Roman Republic*) and *Moral Essays* have been published in Penguin Classics. Rex Warner died in 1986.

M. I. FINLEY took his M.A. and Ph.D. at Columbia University and was appointed a lecturer in Classics at Cambridge in 1955. From 1970 to 1979 he was Professor of Ancient History at Cambridge, and from 1976 to 1982 Master of Darwin College, Cambridge. He received a knighthood in 1979. Among his books the following are published in Penguin: *The World of Odysseus*, *The Ancient Greeks*, *Aspects of Antiquity*, *Ancient Slavery and Modern Ideology* and *Economy and Society in Ancient Greece*. He died in 1986.

THUCYDIDES

*

HISTORY OF THE
PELOPONNESIAN
WAR

*

*Translated by Rex Warner
with an Introduction and Notes
by M. I. Finley*

PENGUIN BOOKS

PENGUIN BOOKS

Published by the Penguin Group
Penguin Books Ltd, 27 Wrights Lane, London W8 5TZ, England
Penguin Putnam Inc., 375 Hudson Street, New York, New York 10014, USA
Penguin Books Australia Ltd, Ringwood, Victoria, Australia
Penguin Books Canada Ltd, 10 Alcorn Avenue, Toronto, Ontario, Canada M4V 3B2
Penguin Books (NZ) Ltd, Private Bag 102902, NSMC, Auckland, New Zealand

Penguin Books Ltd, Registered Offices: Harmondsworth, Middlesex, England

This translation first published 1954
Revised with a new introduction and appendices 1972
39 40

Translation copyright 1954 by Rex Warner
Introduction and appendices copyright © M. I. Finley, 1972
All rights reserved

Printed in England by Clays Ltd, St Ives plc
Filmset in Monotype Bembo

CONTENTS

BOOK IV

BOOK V

BOOK VI

BOOK VII

BOOK VIII

INTRODUCTION*

THE fame of ancient wars is commonly fashioned by myth and romance. Helen of Troy, the pass of Thermopylae, Alexander, Hannibal – these are the people and the incidents that keep wars alive in popular imagination. But not so the Peloponnesian War (as we call it), fought between Athens and Sparta from 431 to 404, with a scarcely honoured seven-year 'peace' in the middle. That war lives on not so much for anything that happened or because of any of the participants, but because of the man who wrote its history, Thucydides the Athenian. No other historian can match this achievement; no other war, or for that matter no other historical subject, is so much the product of its reporter.

That is achievement enough. It becomes even greater when we look more closely at the man and his book. All that we know about Thucydides is found in the few scraps he tells us himself, and in a short, eccentric and unreliable biography from late antiquity credited to someone named Marcellinus. Clearly he was a humourless man, pessimistic, sceptical, highly intelligent, cold and reserved, at least on the surface, but with strong inner tensions which occasionally broke through the impersonal tone of his writing in savage whiplash comments, such as 'Hyperbolus, a wretched character, who had been ostracized, not because anyone was afraid of his power and prestige, but because he was a thoroughly bad lot and a disgrace to the city' (VIII, 73). He wrote in a complicated style, overloaded and lacking in charm. Not that he was indifferent to language and its nuances; on the contrary, correct use of language was for him a moral question, its debasement a symptom of moral breakdown. Summing up the consequences of *stasis* (civil war), he wrote:

To fit in with the change of events, words, too, had to change their usual meanings. What used to be described as a thoughtless act of aggression was now regarded as the courage one would expect to find in a party member; to think of the future and wait was merely another way of saying

*Chatto & Windus and the Viking Press, the English and American publishers, respectively, of my book, *Aspects of Antiquity* (1968), have kindly given me permission to draw freely on the chapter on Thucydides.

one was a coward; any idea of moderation was just an attempt to disguise one's unmanly character; ability to understand a question from all sides meant that one was totally unfitted for action (III, 82).

In his struggle to convey the sense of an action or a statement precisely, Thucydides juggled tenses in a sophisticated way, piled up subordinate clauses and resorted to other devices that are often the despair of modern readers. (A surprising proportion of commentaries is given over to sorting out just what Thucydides was trying to say in any particular passage.) Neither in style nor in treatment of his subject did he make the slightest concession to his audience. Nothing mattered but the events and the issues; these he would get right by dedicated effort, by devotion to accuracy and understanding, and he would report his findings without adornment.

And it may well be that my history will seem less easy to read because of the absence in it of a romantic element (*to mythodes*). It will be enough for me, however, if these words of mine are judged useful by those who want to understand clearly the events which happened in the past and which (human nature being what it is) will, at some time or other and in much the same ways, be repeated in the future. My work is not a piece of writing designed to meet the needs of an immediate public, but was done to last for ever (I, 22).

Thucydides was a young man, probably in his late twenties, when the war began. It is a guess that he was born about 460 B.C., but a good guess. He had to be old enough to hold the office of *strategos* (general) in 424, for which the minimum age was probably thirty, and at the same time young enough to warrant the rather defensive remark he inserted in what is now conventionally known as the 'Second Introduction':

I myself remember that all the time from the beginning to the end of the war it was being put about by many people that the war would last thrice nine years. I lived through the whole of it, *being of an age to understand what was happening* (V, 26).

As soon as the war began, he tells us, he perceived that this would be a conflict on a scale without precedent, and he resolved to become its historian. As an able-bodied Athenian citizen from the propertied – indeed, aristocratic – class, he was of course not free to give all his time to his project. He had to fight, too. But in 424 he was exiled on a charge of failure to carry out properly an assignment as commander in the north-east. It is characteristic of him that he reports this fact briefly and without comment, except to add that he was in a better position thereafter to obtain information from both sides (IV, 104–7 and V, 26). Mining property in Thrace provided him with the necessary income. His exile presumably came to an end with the Athenian defeat in 404, and he died in Athens soon after, though the exact date is unknown.

How Thucydides went about his self-assigned task is also unknown, for he says very little about his methods apart from a passage on the unreliability of eye-witness testimony, which turns out to be less informative than modern praise of it might suggest:

> And with regard to my factual reporting of the events of the war I have made it a principle not to write down the first story that came my way, and not even to be guided by my own general impressions; either I was present myself at the events which I have described or else I heard them from eye-witnesses whose reports I have checked with as much thoroughness as possible. Not that even so the truth was easy to discover: different eye-witnesses gave different accounts of the same events, speaking out of partiality for one side or the other or else from imperfect memories (I, 22).

As a declaration of intent these sentences are irreproachable, in Thucydides' own day even revolutionary (and it is anachronistic to complain that nothing is said about documents[1]), but the performance is for us, at least, most frustrating. Unlike Herodotus, Thucydides never names his informants, and on only two occasions does he say that he was a direct participant: he suffered from the plague and he was a general at Amphipolis. Occasionally there is a pointer: the detailed knowledge of developments in 413 and 412 as seen from Chios implies heavy reliance on a Chiot source (or sources) for one stretch in Book VIII. But was he himself present in the Assembly when Cleon and Diodotus debated the fate of Mytilene (III, 36–49)? Who informed him about the curious discussion of strategy among the three Athenian generals after they landed in Sicily (VI, 46–50)? We do not know and we cannot even make a reasonable guess. We ask not out of idle curiosity but in order to assess the account intelligently. In the end, we can only conjure up an imaginary picture of Thucydides the 'hedgehog' (Sir Isaiah Berlin's phrase for Tolstoi from his book, *The Hedgehog and the Fox*), tirelessly seeking out a vast number of witnesses from both sides, cross-questioning them closely, deciding on their veracity, piling up notes, sorting out the data, selecting and thinking and writing. He read what was available in books, but that would have been very little. Basically, everything – the debates in the assemblies, the behind-the-scenes manoeuvres, the battles – had to be reconstructed from what he was told or had

1. See below, pp. 19–20.

personally witnessed. And he achieved his announced objective: he created a *ktema es aei*, a possession for all time.

When he died, someone published the manuscript as he left it, and there are some very puzzling aspects about the shape of the work at that stage. The whole of the last book (discussed in Appendix 4) is utterly unlike the preceding seven: it has the look of a collection of notes, organized but not worked up.[2] It breaks off abruptly in the year 411 B.C., nearly seven years before the war ended. One might reasonably surmise that Thucydides had stopped writing when he reached that point in his story. However, there are important sections early in the volume that could not have been written until after 404, such as the discussion (V, 26) of the exact dating of the war and its duration. Thucydides was obviously working away at his *History* long after 411.

Indeed, one school of modern scholars hold that the *History* 'was composed not at widely scattered times but essentially at one time after 404 when the outcome of events had become clear.'[3] There are objections, not least the psychological improbability that Thucydides, or any man, would patiently assemble material for more than twenty-seven years but refrain from actual composition until he was satisfied that the conflict was at last ended, not even being tempted by the peace of 421 B.C. to try his hand at writing down the first decade of the war. The view adopted in this introduction is that, on the contrary, the *History* reveals that in the course of the war Thucydides altered his views and had fresh insights about such central topics as empire and political leadership – it is really impossible to believe that twenty-seven years left him untouched – and that he also wrestled constantly with the technique of historical composition. It may be hazardous, and often impossible, to 'date'

2. In Thucydides' time, books consisted of papyrus rolls. The conventional division of a work into a number of separate 'books' was an innovation by scholars in the Hellenistic Age, after Alexander the Great, in particular those working in the great library of Alexandria. Although the division of Thucydides' *History* into eight books goes back to that period, Marcellinus refers to a thirteen-book edition, Diodorus (XIII, 37, 2 and XIII, 42, 5) to one in nine books. One must therefore not assume that Thucydides himself thought of each of the eight books as a unit (like a chapter in a modern work). The only 'breaks' he indicated were chronological: 'So the winter ended and the nth year of this war recorded by Thucydides.' As for the chapters within each book, as they appear in modern editions, they were introduced for the first time in the Oxford edition of 1696.

3. John H. Finley, Jr, *Thucydides* (Harvard University Press, 1942), p. 77.

sections of the book as we have it, but the sustained narrative of the Sicilian expedition in Books VI and VII, for example, gives the strong impression that it was composed in one burst not long after 413. On the other hand, both the Funeral Oration (II, 34–46), delivered by Pericles in the first year of the war, and his last speech, in 430 (II, 60–64), were, it can be argued, worked up by Thucydides not contemporaneously but nearly thirty years later: they are the old historian's retrospective views of the strength and great possibilities of Athens when the war began, written in the light of his city's complete, and unnecessary, defeat.[4] And even earlier, in the first book with its detailed account of the incidents leading up to the war, there are sentences that look very much like marginal notes Thucydides made for himself, much later, for still further recasting and rewriting. In Book VIII, finally, there is an implicit suggestion that he had come late to a realization of the importance of Persia in the conflict. Who can say that, had he lived on, the inadequate earlier references to Persia would not have been supplemented in the light of this new appreciation?

We shall never know what was going on in Thucydides' mind in those final years; what it was that drove him back to the earlier years at the cost of a complete neglect of the ending. It is necessary to make some sort of reasonable guess, however, in order to get at his thinking in general. There is not a sentence in the book – this cannot be stressed enough – that states explicitly what Thucydides thought history was about, why it was worth a lifetime of very hard effort to write a detailed and accurate history of the war, or why that history could lay claim to being a possession for all time. These were far from obvious questions in his day, for the simple reason that the writing of history had scarcely begun. The Greeks were deeply attached to their past, but it was the distant timeless past, the age of gods and heroes, which attracted them and which they never tired of learning about from Homer and the tragic poets. For the rest, for the post-heroic centuries, a few popular traditions served well enough – stories about Solon and the tyrants and a handful of other figures. No doubt these stories were not very accurate, but what did that matter? Myths and half-truths performed the necessary functions: they selected important bits out of the enormous, unintelligible mass of past happenings and fixed them; they gave the Greeks a feeling of continuity from time immemorial to their own

4. This view of the time when Thucydides worked up the two speeches rests on another controversial position, about the authenticity of the speeches, explained below, pp. 25–9.

day; they strengthened the sense of nationhood; they were a source of religious and moral teaching. None of these purposes required precise chronology: 'once upon a time' served well enough. Nor did they require accurate detail or complete documentation. In short, there seemed to be no need for history as the modern world understands it, or as Thucydides understood it.

To be sure, there were sceptics and rationalists who were dissatisfied. They neither believed in the philandering of Zeus and the savage jealousies of Hera nor approved a moral code with so unreliable a foundation. By Thucydides' time a considerable line of philosophers had been challenging the whole mythical structure and developing newer and more advanced systems of metaphysics and ethics on rational bases. What they were challenging, however, was not the *history* in the old myths, not the facts of the Trojan War, for example, but the morals of the heroes, the beliefs about the gods, the universe and man. It was not from such interests that the impulse came for the writing of history. The explanation must be sought elsewhere, in the political life and the political situation of fifth-century Greece. Politics, like philosophy, was a Greek 'invention'. Never before, at least in the west, had there been a society in which ordinary men, lacking either inherited authority or divine sanction, openly debated and decided on such vital matters as war and peace, public finance, or crime and punishment. Political activity had become accepted not only as a legitimate activity but even as the highest form of social activity. And the defeat of the great Persian Empire proved that this new way of running society was effective and valuable. That it was a *new* way was recognized; so was the fact that even now there were among the Greeks powerful opponents of the city-state system, whereby free men organized their lives under the rule of law. An *inquiry* into the past (as distinct from a mere re-telling of the accepted tales) was thus stimulated, as a complement to the inquiries into ethics and philosophy.

The word for 'inquire' in Greek is *historein*, and the man who was first responsible for a sustained inquiry, a *historia*, into the past was Herodotus. He was born and brought up in the opening years of the fifth century B.C. in Halicarnassus, across the Aegean Sea from Athens, in that part of the Greek world which was in closest touch with the 'barbarians', and which for many years had been subject to the Persians and before them to the Lydians. To satisfy Greek curiosity about these people, not only the 'barbarians' near by but also those more distant, none of whom had a place in the Greek stock of myths and traditions, a body of writing had grown up consisting of descriptions of manners and customs, geography, and fragments of history, much of it wholly or partly fictitious. Herodotus apparently planned another such work and travelled widely to collect the necessary information. Eventually he came to Athens and was inspired to an altogether new vision of his vocation. It was during his childhood that the Persians had twice been driven back, against all the odds, thanks, he now realized, largely to the moral and political leadership provided by the Athenians. This was a heroic tale, not only of heroic individuals, as in the Trojan War, but of the city-state, and it would soon be lost from memory unless it was fixed in writing. And so Herodotus wrote the first book about Greek history.

Thucydides never mentions Herodotus by name, but there are enough indirect indications that he had read his predecessor with care. Although we can never be certain that the considerable number of divergences between the two on particular details reflect conscious corrections on the part of Thucydides, and although we cannot be absolutely certain (probable though it is) that the explicit rejection of a 'romantic element' points to Herodotus in particular, there can be no doubt about the reference in an early, programmatic passage (I, 20):

> The rest of the Hellenes, too, make many incorrect assumptions not only about the dimly remembered past, but also about contemporary history. For instance, there is a general belief that the kings of Sparta are each entitled to two votes, whereas in fact they have only one: and it is believed, too, that the Spartans have a company of troops called 'Pitanate'. Such a company has never existed. Most people, in fact, will not take trouble in finding out the truth, but are much more inclined to accept the first story they hear.

Both these errors appear in Herodotus (VI, 57 and IX, 53), and these are surely the passages Thucydides had in mind: it is hard to imagine that there was a 'general belief' or even general interest in whether or not the Spartans called one company 'Pitanate', or, for that matter, in the precise details of the voting procedure in the Spartan Gerousia (Council of Elders).

We may well think that only a humourless pedant would draw the brutal judgement of the final sentence from two such small details. But it would be wrong to go on from there to suggest that this represents the real judgement of Thucydides about the achievement of Herodotus. After all, he paid his predecessor the high compliment of beginning where Herodotus had left off, implying that there was no need to go over that ground again. It was necessary only to bridge the period between the Persian and Peloponnesian wars; and Thucydides did that by writing a brief digression (I, 89–118), in which he singled out some important events that occurred between 479 B.C. and the beginning of the Corcyra affair in 435. Following a late commentator in antiquity, this digression is now conventionally, if imprecisely, referred to as the Pentecontaetia (the 'Fifty-Year Period').

Further, Thucydides paid Herodotus the even higher compliment of grasping and accepting, as virtually no other contemporary had done, the great discovery the Father of History had made, namely, that it was possible to analyse the political and moral issues of the time by a close study of events, of the concrete day-to-day experiences of society, thereby avoiding the abstractions of the philosophers on the one hand and the myths of the poets on the other. Thucydides proceeded to dedicate his life to a similar enterprise, though with a number of fundamental departures from the Herodotean model. One or two have already been mentioned, but we must now consider them more fully.

Herodotus, we must remember, tried to re-create, for the most part, the atmosphere and the events of the past, some of it so remote that he would not have been able to interview anyone who had been alive at the time. Thucydides, on the contrary, was a contemporary of, and for a time a direct participant in, his war; indeed, when he decided to write his *History*, the subject matter lay in the future. His choice was not a free one: after the Persian wars there had been, by his standards, no subject worthy of sustained historical inquiry until the Peloponnesian War broke out. But there is more to it. The past cannot be cross-examined, and Thucydides made it plain at the outset that only the most patient checking and double-checking could reach the truth. Therefore the past can never be really known (and, as we shall see, contemporary history is anyway sufficient for all important purposes). 'I have found it impossible,' he wrote in his opening paragraph (I, 1),

because of its remoteness in time, to acquire a really precise knowledge of the distant past *or even of the history preceding our own period*, yet, after looking back into it as far as I can, all the evidence leads me to conclude that these periods were not great periods either in warfare or in anything else.

Nevertheless, there are in Thucydides a number of significant excursuses into the past. Each has its own specific reason for being there. It is not possible to examine them all in this introduction, but three merit consideration. The first comes at the beginning (I. 2–21) and is designed to support the assertion that nothing in the past was as great as the Peloponnesian War, and therefore to justify Thucydides' *History*. Some of the evidence adduced comes from Herodotus; for the rest, Thucydides had nothing to go on other than Homer, other poets, a few prose chroniclers (whom he himself contemptuously dismissed in I, 21), and the application of his powerful and disciplined mind to the evidence of his own world. The result is a brilliant sweeping theory, namely, that Hellenic power and greatness emerged only in consequence of the systematic development of navigation and commerce, which were followed by an accumulation of resources, stable community organization, empires, and finally the greatest of all Greek power struggles, the Peloponnesian War. Although this theory is historical in the sense that Thucydides made the bold suggestion that there was continuity and development in Greece from the most ancient times to his own, it is fundamentally a sociological theory derived from prolonged meditation about the world in which Thucydides lived, not from a systematic study of history.

The whole excursus includes very few concrete events, and only four of those are dated: the migration of the Boeotians to Boeotia sixty years after the Trojan War and of the Dorians into the Peloponnese twenty years after that; the construction of four ships by the Corinthian Ameinocles for the Samians three hundred years before the end of the Peloponnesian War (i.e. about 700 B.C.); forty years later, the first recorded naval battle, between Corinth and Corcyra. He does not date the Trojan War, so that two of the events are fixed in time only relatively, not absolutely. If, however, Thucydides accepted Herodotus' chronology, the Boeotian migration took place about 1190 B.C., the Dorian migration about 1170. The following 470 years lack a single dated event, a period equal in length to that between the accession of Henry VII and our own day. Everything that fell between could only be fixed as 'later' or 'much later'.

It should be noted that Thucydides' extreme scepticism did not extend to the myths and poems as a whole. The poets may 'exaggerate the importance of their themes' and the chroniclers 'are less interested in telling the truth than in catching the attention of their public', but their main narratives are accepted as historical fact. Even Hellen son of Deucalion, the mythological ancestor of the Hellenes (as the Greeks called themselves), appears as a genuinely historical personage. In another context (III, 104) Thucydides quotes at length from the so-called 'Homeric Hymn' to Apollo as evidence not only for ancient rites on the island of Delos but also for the biography of

Homer. No doubt creeps in, unlike, for example, I, 10: 'if we can believe the evidence of Homer', and probably no contemporary of the historian had any doubts. Today, however, it is universally agreed that these hymns were not composed by 'Homer', whatever else they may be.[5]

This kind of difficulty did not face Thucydides in the second major excursus, the Pentecontaetia. There were not a few men alive in his own circle of friends and relations who had participated in these events, and who could have been questioned and cross-questioned. Despite the statement already quoted, that it is impossible to 'acquire a really precise knowledge of the distant past or even of the history preceding our own period', Thucydides could not have meant in a literal sense that the period following the Trojan War and the Pentecontaetia were equally inaccessible. If this second excursus is not a history of the half century, if it is as empty of exact dates as the opening digression, that was a deliberate decision by the historian. This time he merely strung out a series of selected events, reported with little comment and without any broad generalizations, in order to show, by example rather than by explicit formulation, how the Delian League became an empire, thereby setting the stage for the war. The result is not very satisfactory, as is apparent from any commentary on Thucydides or any modern history of the period. That Thucydides could have written a more systematic account cannot be doubted. We therefore conclude that he chose not to, presumably because of his conviction that contemporary history alone was valid.

Third, there is the short section, at the beginning of the story of the Sicilian expedition, summarizing the colonization of Sicily by Greeks and non-Greeks (VI, 2–5). For this excursus Thucydides adopted yet another style of presentation, and it is altogether an odd digression. It is led into by the critical remark that the Athenians decided to invade Sicily despite the fact that 'they were for the most part ignorant of the size of the island and of the numbers of its inhabitants'. However, instead of going on to supply this vital information, he continued with pure antiquarianism of little relevance to the war, set out in a series of flat statements, beginning with the mythological Cyclopes and Laestrygonians of Homer. Again the chronology is relative and often vague, except for the foundation of Megara Hyblaea 245 years before the inhabitants were driven out by Gelon, tyrant of Syracuse, a date that works out to about 728 B.C. Why did

5. The 'Homeric Hymns' are available in the Loeb Classical Library together with Hesiod, in a translation by H. G. Evelyn-White.

Thucydides bother with these pages, and where did he get his information? As usual, he does not say, but the probability is that his source was a history of Sicily by Antiochus of Syracuse, which, we know from Diodorus (XII, 71, 2), began with the mythical King Cocalus of the Sicanians and ended with the events of 424 B.C. Presumably the work had only recently become available and was not well known, so that not even the austere Thucydides could resist the opportunity to parade a bit of learning about the distant past.

Essentially, then, the Thucydidean manner, as we may call it, was reserved for what mattered to him, for the contemporary history that makes up the bulk of his work. For this he set himself a standard of accuracy which, commonplace as it may seem today, was quite extraordinary in the fifth century B.C.[6] The only possible models were among a few philosophers and among the medical writers of the school of Hippocrates of Cos. But the mere existence of parallels will not explain why Thucydides transferred their passion for accuracy to the field of history. Like all such manifestations of individual psychology, the question defies explanation. Whatever the reason, it left him an exceedingly lonely figure in the history of ancient historical writing, for not one man after him, among either the Greek historians or the Roman, felt this passion to the same degree, much as some of them protested that they did. In this sense, Thucydides' kind of history was a dead-end street. Only among scientists, such as Aristotle and his disciples, do we find anything comparable in later generations, and they never took history seriously.

The modern reader, however, is puzzled, and perhaps disturbed, by the fact that the passionate search for truth did not take Thucydides to documents, the foundation of all modern historical writing. He quotes only a few at any length; those fall almost entirely in Books V and VIII, the two which appear to be in an unworked state, so that it is at least plausible that the full quotations would have disappeared in the final revision, had Thucydides lived long enough. In the digression on the Athenian tyrannicides (VI, 54–9) there is effective use of an obliterated Athenian inscription and another from Lampsacus. Thucydides was clearly not unaware of the possibilities of documentary evidence. Yet he rarely took advantage of it, and we must not assume, when he mentions an alliance or the Athenian decree excluding the Megarians from all ports within the Athenian empire (I, 67), that he personally consulted the actual texts every time. The contents would have been common

6. The speeches pose a problem that is discussed below, pp. 25–9.

knowledge among the politically active citizens, and we are bound to think that Thucydides' failure to include scrutiny of documents in his statement of his methods was deliberate, not an oversight. Like Herodotus before him, his research was among people, not among papers.

For Thucydides, history was in the most fundamental sense a strictly human affair, capable of analysis and understanding entirely in terms of known patterns of human behaviour, without the intervention of the supernatural. It is impossible to say what his religious beliefs were, but it is clear that his piety, if he possessed any, did not extend to faith in the soothsayers and purveyors of oracles, who were particularly numerous and aggressive in time of war. As a historian, he recorded incidents in which action was determined or held up by omens and oracles, but he also went out of his way to denigrate popular trust in them. The neatest example comes near the end of the account of the plague (II, 54):

> At this time of distress people naturally recalled old oracles, and among them was a verse which the old men claimed had been delivered in the past and which said: *War with the Dorians comes, and a death will come at the same time.* There had been a controversy as to whether the word in this ancient verse was 'dearth' (*limos*) rather than 'death' (*loimos*); but in the present state of affairs the view that the word was 'death' naturally prevailed; it was a case of people adapting their memories to suit their suffering. Certainly I think that if there is ever another war with the Dorians after this one, and if a dearth results from it, then in all probability people will quote the other version.[7]

The mode of thinking is reminiscent of the opening of the famous Hippocratic treatise on epilepsy:

> I am about to discuss the disease called 'sacred'. It is not, in my opinion, any more divine or more sacred than other diseases, but has a natural cause, and its supposed divine origin is due to men's inexperience, and to their wonder at its peculiar character.[8]

Like the best Hippocratic writings, Thucydides' *History* unfolds without gods or oracles or omens. This was perhaps his greatest break from Herodotus.

Not that men could always control their actions and their circumstances, not even ideally. Chance played its part, as in the storm

7. A more complex example of Thucydides' treatment of oracles is noted in Appendix 3.

8. Translated by W. H. S. Jones in Volume II of the Loeb Classical Library edition of the Hippocratic writings.

that first brought Demosthenes and his fleet to Pylos (IV, 3) or in the accidental fire that was so important a prelude to the Athenian capture of Sphacteria (IV, 30). Thucydides recorded these things but he drew no conclusions; he was not tempted to muse about divine intervention or the like, not even in his account of the plague (II, 47–54). That was the most shattering and influential 'accident' of the whole war; it moved Thucydides to an unsurpassed piece of dramatic and emotional writing (utterly unlike the first book of the Hippocratic *Epidemics* with which it has been mistakenly compared). But he explicitly refrained from considering the causes, and he made the point, with equal explicitness, that, 'as for the gods, it seemed to be the same thing whether one worshipped them or not, when one saw the good and the bad dying indiscriminately'.

The various aspects I have been discussing were matters of fundamental outlook, and they gave Thucydides' work its tone. But they could not provide the techniques. How does one go about writing the history of a long war fought in many theatres? Thucydides had no precedent to fall back on, no book, no teacher from whom he could learn the business of being a historian. Not even Herodotus, for he was too diffuse, interested in too many things, while Thucydides proposed to concentrate very narrowly on the war and the surrounding politics. Even his digressions did not depart from his single theme. Neither war nor politics were to be understood in the superficial sense of battle tactics or rudimentary manoeuvres in political assemblies, though they were part of the story. For Thucydides, as for any serious Greek thinker, moral issues and conflicts were an integral element in politics, and also what we should call social psychology. Again the account of the plague provides a clear indication. Any historian of the Peloponnesian War would have discussed the plague because it killed off so many Athenians. To make that point, however, Thucydides did not need to build up the horrifying picture he did, as detail is piled on detail with superb artistry. Nor was he aiming at cheap emotional effects, at what some later historians contemptuously called 'tragic history'. The objective, for which the details laid the necessary basis, was the long final peroration on the moral and social breakdown brought about by the plague, the section beginning, 'For the catastrophe was so overwhelming that men, not knowing what would happen next to them, became indifferent to every rule of religion and law.' One is reminded of the section on the consequences of civil strife that I quoted at the beginning.

Thinking about technique, Thucydides was soon brought up

against the elementary problem of dates. We say that the Peloponnesian War began in 431 B.C. An Athenian had to say that it began in the archonship of Pythodorus, which was meaningless to non-Athenians, and indeed to Athenians twenty or thirty years later, unless they had a list of the annual archons before them as they read. In a large-scale war, furthermore, with many things happening in different places at the same time, dating by years alone would not give the right kind of picture for Thucydides. All the little connections and sequences, the day-to-day causes and consequences, would be lost. As he said (V, 20), if one were to 'trust any reckoning based on the names of magistrates in the various states', there could 'be no accuracy, since a particular event may have taken place at the beginning or the middle or at any time during their periods of office'. He might have added that he would have found it difficult to pinpoint his informants about chronology as well, coming, as they did, from many different Greek states.

Introducing months would not have helped. Every city had its own calendar: the names of the months were not all alike – more than 300 names are known today – nor was the order nor even the time of the new year. The peace treaty of 421, according to the official text quoted by Thucydides (V, 19) 'comes into effect from the 27th day of the month of Artemisium at Sparta, Pleistolas holding the office of ephor; and at Athens from the 25th day of the month of Elaphebolium, in the archonship of Alcaeus'. To write a coherent narrative, therefore, Thucydides had to invent his own system. After fixing the beginning of the war, he dated all subsequent events first by counting the number of (solar) years that elapsed from the start, and then by dividing each war year into 'winter' and 'summer'. Simple enough, yet the scheme was unique and Thucydides was openly proud of it. It was also incomplete: he does not say whether winters and summers began on a fixed date nor does he narrow the time within each season beyond 'early', 'middle' or 'late'.

Fixing the beginning of the war was almost the hardest problem of all. Wars do not erupt out of nothing on one particular day. The first shot or the formal declaration of war can conveniently be called the beginning of a war, but it cannot be the beginning of its history. How far back must the historian go? That is a most critical decision for him; on it depends the interpretation he presents to his readers. In the two decades between 1919 and 1939, three radically different views of the causes of the First World War prevailed, in turn, among students of modern history. Each required its own account

of the prehistory of the war. No doubt there were similar disagree-
ments in Athens and elsewhere in the Greek world about the causes
of the Peloponnesian War. And Thucydides was the man who first
attempted a serious analysis of that question, not only for the Peloponnesian War but for any war.

Thucydides sorted out the essential from the casual, the primary
causes from the more immediate grievances and the pretexts. The
latter he wrote up in great detail, devoting the whole of the first book
to the background. The result is clear, brilliant, and yet somehow
incomplete. Thucydides himself, I believe, was never satisfied with
it. Ideas which seemed right early in the war lost some of their
persuasiveness twenty or twenty-five years later. From that distance
in time the grievances of Corinth over Corcyra and Potidaea, for
example, no longer loomed so large. The Athenian empire had a
different look, retrospectively, after it was broken apart; so did
Pericles after a succession of leaders like Cleon and Hyperbolus, for
whom Thucydides felt a contempt and an anger that he did not
disguise. More and more it was power, the morality of power, the
rights and wrongs, which seemed the only important and permanent
elements in the picture, with the concrete details mere exemplifica-
tions. 'The real reason for the war', he came to believe, was this:
'What made war inevitable was the growth of Athenian power and
the fear which this caused in Sparta' (I, 23). No one can prove that
this sentence was a late insertion, and many scholars deny it. Yet it is
a fact that in the detailed narrative that follows, beginning with the
quarrel between Epidamnus and Corcyra, Spartan fear of Athens is
notably absent.

Sorting out, selecting what goes into the account and what is to
be excluded from the mass of available data, highlighting and under-
scoring – these are of course what the historian, any historian, does
all the time. Consciously or not, he is applying his personal canons
of relevance, and that means his ideas about the nature of politics, of
social behaviour, in a word, about history. Even when a historian is
explicit and tells us what he thinks history is about, he is judged not
so much by his theoretical remarks as by the work itself. Thucydides
tells us nothing, so that only the work in the form in which he left it
reveals his thinking. And the work is, in a sense, self-contradictory;
the historian seems to be pulling, and to be pulled, in opposite
directions all the time.

On the one hand there is the passion for the most minute detail –
minor commanders, battle alignments, bits of geography and
the like – so that the proper names alone occupy about twelve

double-column pages in the index to the present edition. On the other hand, there are astonishing gaps and silences, whole chunks of history that are left out altogether or dismissed in a phrase or odd sentence. This may sometimes reflect a weakness in Thucydides' knowledge or appreciation; as in the insufficient attention to Persia already noticed. But Thucydides certainly knew that in 425 B.C. the Athenians, running short of funds, made a radical re-assessment of the tribute from the empire, more than trebling the total demanded; and it is impossible to believe that he thought the action less significant than thousands of minor details he rescued from oblivion. Yet there is not even a hint of the decree in the book.[9] In a different vein, there is the way he deals with civil strife. It played a large role in the war, affecting the strength of many states and determining their relations with the two protagonists, now one way, now the other. That is obvious to us, if for no other reason because Thucydides himself has made it so clear. However, after the magnificent account of the Corcyraean civil war of 427 B.C., *stasis* is treated almost casually, though mentioned frequently, until the oligarchic coup of 411 in Athens itself. How many did he fail to mention at all? It is impossible to know.

Thucydides was a genius, and he was a dedicated man. Easy explanations therefore will not do. His difficulties lay very deep; to this day they remain a major problem of historical writing, and it is the mark of Thucydides' greatness that he appreciated it so early, at the very beginning of historiography. The historian's data are individual events and persons; the sum total of their interrelationships is the historical process. Unlike the poet, he must get the events and the relationships right, exactly as they were, and not, in Aristotle's phrase about tragedy (*Poetics*, 9), as they might or ought to have been 'from probability or necessity'. But then what? A mere retelling of individual events in sequence, no matter how accurate and precise, would just be that and nothing more. It could be exciting, moving, scandalous, entertaining – but would it be important, would it be worth the pain and effort of a lifetime? Greek intellectuals like Thucydides were in dead earnest about their conviction that man is a rational being. As a corollary, they believed that knowledge for its own sake was meaningless, its mere accumulation a waste of time. Knowledge must lead to understanding. In the field of history, even

9. A large fragment of the original text of this decree has been found. See the edition, with commentary, in R. Meiggs and D. Lewis, eds., *A Selection of Greek Historical Inscriptions to the End of the Fifth Century B.C.* (Oxford, 1969), no. 69.

when largely restricted to contemporary history, that meant trying to grasp general ideas about human behaviour, in war and politics, in revolution and government. Thucydides' problem, in short, was to move from the particular to the universal, from the concrete and unique event to the underlying patterns and generalities, from a single revolution (such as the one in Corcyra) to revolution in essence, from a demagogue like Cleon to the nature of demagogues, from specific instances of power politics to power itself.

Undoubtedly, Thucydides did not grasp the complexity of the problem right at the start, nor did he ever find a solution that fully satisfied him. He was constantly probing and experimenting, trying out techniques and refining them. To ensure maximum accuracy, he kept his narrative sections rather impersonal, making infrequent (though very telling) comments and allowing the story to unfold itself. Then, to lay bare what stood behind the narrative, the moral and political issues, the debates and disagreement over policy, the possibilities, the mistakes, the fears and the motives, his main device was the speech. It was a device he employed with variety and artistry: sometimes he chose only one speech out of a number made at an assembly or conference; sometimes a pair, which by their diametrical opposition presented the sharpest possible choice of actions: sometimes an address to his troops by a commander before an engagement. The total impact is overwhelming. The reader is quite carried away; not only does he feel that he has seen the Peloponnesian War from the inside, but he is certain that he knows exactly what the issues were, why things happened as they did. More than that, his understanding seems to come from the actors themselves, without the intervention of the historian, as it were.

The speeches are reproduced in direct discourse, and they are very much abridged – a perfectly legitimate procedure. But they are also, without exception, written in the language and style of Thucydides, and that begins to give the modern reader twinges of discomfort. In fact, doubts were raised by ancient critics, and there is a noted ambivalence on the subject among subsequent historians. No people have elevated talk and debate into a way of life as did the ancient Greeks. They talked all the time, in public and private, and they talked with enthusiasm and persuasiveness. Their literature was filled with talk, from the long speeches of the *Iliad* and *Odyssey* through the monologues of the tragedians to the equally long speeches and debates in Herodotus. We may assume that it did not occur to Herodotus to argue with himself at length before deciding to incorporate speeches into his *History*, but that he did so as a matter of course. What does human behaviour consist of, after all, but talk and action?

The first man, so far as we know, to suggest that speeches were a problem in historical writing was, surprisingly enough, Thucydides himself. In the brief section on method already quoted in part, he went out of his way to distinguish the reporting of speeches from the reporting of actions (I, 22):

I have found it difficult to remember the precise words used in the speeches which I listened to myself and my various informants have experienced the same difficulty; so my method has been, while keeping as closely as possible to the general sense of the words used, to make the speakers say what, in my opinion, was called for by each situation.

There is no way to get round the incompatibility of the two parts of that statement. If all speakers said what, in Thucydides' opinion, the situation called for, the remark becomes meaningless. But if they did not always say what was called for, then, insofar as Thucydides attributed such sentiments to them, he could not have been 'keeping as closely as possible to the general sense of the words used'. It is also worth remembering that he never claimed to make generals, for example, conduct themselves in a manner called for by each situation, as distinct from what they actually did.

All historians after Thucydides continued to quote speeches, but they tended to go on the defensive about the practice. We are even told that a younger contemporary named Cratippus said that Thucydides himself saw the error of his ways and finally abandoned speeches, but that is surely nothing more than an argument *post factum*, not based on knowledge but inferred from the absence of speeches in the unfinished Book VIII. This information comes to us from Dionysius, a native of Halicarnassus who became perhaps the greatest authority on literature and rhetoric in the Rome of Augustus and who wrote the most extensive critical analysis of the ancient historians that survives today.[10] Dionysius himself did not object to speeches as such, and he wrote very long fictitious ones for his own *Roman Antiquities*, but he disapproved of Thucydides' procedure on grounds of structure. Why this particular Funeral Oration, he asked? The occasion was neither glorious nor significant. The

10. So far as I know, Dionysius' essay on Thucydides is not available in English; the best edition, with Italian translation and commentary, is that of G. Pavano (Palermo, 1958). There is also interesting material about the historians in the *Three Literary Letters*, edited with English translation and notes by W. Rhys Roberts (Cambridge, 1901). The reference to Cratippus appears in Chapter 16 of the essay.

answer, he suggested, is that Thucydides wanted a Funeral Oration by Pericles, at any price. Or why, he asked, are we given the long debate on the *reconsideration* of the decision to put all Mytilenian males to death, when we properly ought to have had the original debate? And anyway Thucydides ought to have finished his book rather than allow himself to be constantly sidetracked by his obsession with speeches.[11]

It is impossible to present all the ancient discussions here, though it is difficult to resist mentioning the unedifying example of Polybius, writing in the second century B.C., who was very free with his criticism of predecessors who invented speeches and whose surviving work includes thirty-seven speeches, a fair number of which he could not possibly have had accurate reports about, if any. Nor is it possible to examine the vast, unending discussions among modern scholars, who naturally raise different questions, stimulated by modern ideas of what is and what is not proper in historical writing. I can only present the point of view I share, and indicate some of the reasons for it.

The Mytilene debate is a good point of departure. Thucydides introduces it by saying that 'there was a sudden change of feeling and people began to think how cruel and unprecedented such a decision was – to destroy not only the guilty, but the entire population of a state' (III, 36). A second assembly was therefore summoned, at which 'various opinions were expressed on both sides'. Thucydides chose two to summarize, one by Cleon and the other by the otherwise unknown Diodotus. These antithetical speeches, as presented, never depart from tough arguments of practical necessity and expediency – this is the case regularly with debates in Thucydides – never refer to the revulsion which brought about the debate in the first place, never make or reject the obvious pleas to decency and morality that, we should think, were called for by the situation. If Diodotus in fact refrained from such an appeal, he would have been virtually unique in the annals of political oratory. All extant genuine Athenian speeches are replete with precisely that sort of rhetoric. Even assuming, therefore, that Thucydides added nothing (an assumption my argument cannot accept), his omissions are inconsistent with the claim of 'keeping as closely as possible to the general sense of the words used'.

Another kind of omission appears in the first book. When the Spartans sent an embassy to Athens in 431 with an ultimatum, an assembly was summoned at which 'many speakers came forward

11. See Chapters 16–18 of the essay.

and opinions were expressed on both sides, some maintaining that war was necessary and others saying that the Megarian decree should be revoked and should not be allowed to stand in the way of peace' (I, 139). Pericles then went to the rostrum, and his speech stands alone, without a paired opposite, in stark contrast to the brilliant series of debates on the Spartan side to which we have just been treated. We are given no indication of the arguments presented by the anti-war speakers, or of what they ought to have said. There is, furthermore, too much 'telepathy' in the speech. On one occasion (I, 69) the Corinthians had said in Sparta: 'you know that there have been many occasions when, if we managed to stand up to Athenian aggression, it was more because of Athenian mistakes than because of any help we got from you'; Pericles now echoes them in Athens (I, 144), 'What I fear is not the enemy's strategy, but our own mistakes.' At another meeting in Sparta the Corinthians suggested (I, 121) that 'if we borrow money' from Olympia and Delphi, 'we shall be able to attract the foreign sailors in the Athenian navy by offering higher rates of pay. For the power of Athens rests on mercenaries rather than on her own citizens.' And again Pericles replies in Athens (I, 143): 'Suppose they lay their hands on the money at Olympia or Delphi and try to attract the foreign sailors in our navy by offering higher rates of pay: that would be a serious thing if we were not still able to be a match for them by ourselves and with our resident aliens serving on board our ships.'

The conclusion is that the speeches are not what we should call historical reporting in the same sense as the narrative. It is not suggested that Cleon and Diodotus did not actually address the Assembly in the second Mytilenian debate (though it is relevant to note that individual speakers are not always named), nor that they did not say, in their own words, some of the things Thucydides has them say in his words. But they could not have said everything attributed to them, and they said important things the historian omitted. Our trouble is that it is normally impossible to distinguish, though my credulity stops short of believing that Pericles ever said in the Athenian Assembly that 'your empire is now like a tyranny' (II, 63, echoed by Cleon in III, 37 without the word 'like'). The notice Thucydides gave in I, 22 was, I think, a warning he wrote early in his life, and I also think that as the years went on he cared less and less about 'keeping as closely as possible to the general sense of the words used'. His search for the mainsprings of political behaviour, his struggle to escape from the tyranny of the concrete and the unique, to understand and then to communicate the real and the universal, would have been the driving force in the direction he took.[12]

Nothing in this Introduction is intended in any way to denigrate Thucydides the historian. To criticize or judge him by contemporary standards of historical inquiry would be wholly fallacious (though no more so than some of the more extravagant claims for his modernity). What has to be stressed, instead, is that we are compelled to take Thucydides on faith. He left no ground for re-examination or alternative judgement. We cannot control the reliability of his informants, since they are not named. We cannot check his judgement of what was irrelevant, since he omitted it ruthlessly; or of what he decided was a false report or a wrong explanation, since he left that out too.

An occasional inscription confirms one or another statement or fills out a gap in the information he supplied. Sometimes he casts doubt on himself: perhaps the strangest example is the way the narrative of the Sicilian expedition in Books VI and VII fails to support, and even belies, the conclusion (II, 65) that 'the mistake was not so much an error of judgement . . . as a failure on the part of those who were at home to give proper support to their forces overseas'. Sometimes other Greek writers cast a different light on a situation. For example, there were Athenian opponents of the war in 431 who resorted not only to policy arguments but also to slurs on Pericles' private life and on his motives for dragging Athens into the war. Thucydides was right to reject such scurrilous rumours, but he proceeded to ignore them so completely (along with the more serious arguments) that we should be unaware of their existence were it not for a few remarks in Aristophanes, Diodorus and Plutarch.[13]

Apart from such rare glimpses, we have no alternative history of the Peloponnesian War to compare. Ephorus, a pupil of Isocrates, disliked the Thucydidean account and wrote his own, as part of a *Universal History* (in thirty books) coming down to the year 341 B.C. But Ephorus did no original research into the war; he merely

12. The Melian Dialogue marks the furthest departure and is discussed in Appendix 3.

13. See Aristophanes, *Peace*, 619–24; Diodorus, XII, 38–41; Plutarch, *Pericles*, 29–33. Cleon was a different matter: Thucydides had no hesitation in commenting, in his own name, not merely as a report of what others were saying, that Cleon blocked peace moves 'because he thought that in time of peace and quiet people would be more likely to notice his evil doings and less likely to believe his slander of others' (V, 16).

reinterpreted the material Thucydides had collected, and the abridged version preserved by Diodorus (in Books XII and XIII) suggests that we do far better to hold fast to the Thucydidean history.

What is most remarkable is that we in fact do take Thucydides on faith, though a sharper distinction might be drawn between Thucydides the reporter and Thucydides the interpreter. He probably has more readers in any single year today than in the whole of antiquity: this translation by Rex Warner, first published in 1954, has been reprinted many times. More significant, he has more authority today than in antiquity. A number of writers in the fourth century B.C. continued the story where he broke off. The one surviving example, Xenophon's *History*, begins exactly at the point at which Book VIII of Thucydides stops. But Thucydides had no genuine successors. True, the serious Greek and Roman historians who came after him shared his belief in the primacy of contemporary history and his concentration on war and politics. They also followed him, and Herodotus before him, in their reliance on oral tradition and eye-witness reports in preference to documentary research. However, they departed on precisely those aspects of his work that are his most characteristic, his passion for accuracy and his austerity, his rejection of the irrelevant and the 'romantic'. In a long passage, Dionysius of Halicarnassus wrote of him:

The first, and one may say the most necessary, task for writers of any kind of history is to choose a noble subject and one pleasing to their readers. In this Herodotus seems to me to have succeeded better than Thucydides . . . (who) writes of a single war, and that neither glorious nor fortunate; one which, best of all, should not have happened, or (failing that) should have been ignored by posterity and consigned to silence and oblivion. In his Introduction he makes it clear that he has chosen a bad subject, for he says that many cities of the Greeks were desolated because of the war . . . The natural consequence is that readers of the Introduction feel an aversion to the subject, for it is of the misfortunes of Greece that they are about to hear.[14]

This shocks modern readers, who tend to dismiss it as silly and contemptible. Dionysius, however, was neither, and his judgement has the value of summing up for us an attitude that was widely prevalent in antiquity among the educated classes to whom the historians addressed themselves.

From the beginning, the modern world has had a different judgement. The great humanist Lorenzo Valla published a Latin translation between 1450 and 1452 (followed by a translation of Herodotus

14. *Letter to Pompeius*, section 3, translated by W. Rhys Roberts.

that remained incomplete). The first vernacular translation appeared in French in 1527 (made from Valla's Latin, not from the original Greek), the first in English in 1550. By that time Thucydides was established among the major authors in English classical education. And it was not only classicists who showed an interest. Thomas Hobbes's first publication, at the age of forty, was a translation of Thucydides, in his own beautiful muscular style, issued in 1628, foreshadowing the high status the Greek historian acquired in political education in Victorian England.

It must be admitted that Thucydides was not an original thinker. The general ideas with which he was obsessed were few and simple. He had a pessimistic view of human nature and therefore of politics. Some individuals and some communities, by their moral qualities, are entitled to positions of leadership and power. But power is dangerous and corrupting, and in the wrong hands it quickly leads to immoral behaviour, and then to civil strife, unjust war and destruction. These were familiar themes among poets and philosophers. The genius and originality of Thucydides lay in his effort to present them in a new way, by writing contemporary history, and in the artistry of the presentation.

How successful he was is shown, for example, by the fact that to this day the image of Pericles or Cleon that the world preserves is the one Thucydides created by calculated, economical means. Cleon led Athens for several years after the death of Pericles, but Thucydides gives him four appearances only, one of them restricted to a single sentence and one a speech. The picture that emerges is rounded and dramatic; more than that, it is intended to represent not only Cleon but the demagogue as a type, the kind of leader who took over when Pericles died and, in the historian's judgement, led Athens to folly and ruin. Having summed Cleon up, Thucydides ignored the other demagogues, just as he summed up civil strife in general by one example, that of Corcyra.

No historian has ever surpassed Thucydides in the ability to portray a typical figure or situation, and to do so without seeming to intervene in any significant measure. Pericles' Funeral Oration, the plague, the civil war in Corcyra, the debate between Cleon and Diodotus over the fate of Mytilene, the account of the oligarchic coup of 411 B.C. – these are what makes the book a possession for all time. The continuous war narrative in which they are embedded has another quality and another interest. Without it the big scenes and the main ideas would lose their persuasiveness. It is the painstaking accuracy of the narrative that makes the rest seem so real and convincing. On the other hand, Thucydides was right in his feeling that the mere piling up of details, no matter how carefully chosen and described, would eventually lose its interest. The combination he discovered survives because it is particular and universal at the same time, and because it is in the last analysis a moralist's work.

August 1970   M. I. F.

TRANSLATOR'S NOTE

IT is difficult, pleasurable, and bold to attempt to translate Thucydides into English. There are difficulties of many kinds. Not only is it a question of working long hours, since the work is long. It is also the fact that, though the meaning of Thucydides is usually (though not always) clear enough, it is expressed in a style which is extremely hard to turn into another language. To begin with one is sometimes repelled by what seems an overdoing of antitheses or an unnecessary roughness in the transitions of the syntax. Soon one comes to respect these qualities, for they are the marks of a really great mind expressing itself in a manner that has never been used before and grappling with ideas which are novel, unexpected, and illuminating. But it is a style which, in its sudden illuminations and in its abrupt strength, can never, I think, be reproduced in English. Even Plato would be easier.

As for the pleasures of translation, it is sufficient to say that, if one loves one's author, one loves being in his company.

The boldness of the attempt demands some words of apology. There already exist in English at least two excellent versions of Thucydides. The translation of Hobbes has already been mentioned. He, above all men, had an intellect equipped to understand and to enjoy the greatness of his original; nor is there anything in his style that is not exact, masculine, and emphatic. There is no nonsense about Hobbes. His only defect is inaccuracy, a thing that was, to a large extent, unavoidable, considering the advances in textual criticism which have been made since his day. Some modern readers also will be repelled rather than attracted by English that was written in the early part of the seventeenth century. It is therefore, perhaps, legitimate to sidle in where Hobbes has not feared to tread; but, in doing so, one cannot but express one's deference to a great philosopher, a great stylist, and one of the greatest of translators.

Then there is Crawley, whose very fine translation first appeared in 1876. He, too, has evidently felt the spell of Hobbes. I know that often, after cudgelling my brains to find a phrase that would be, not better than one of Crawley's phrases, but at least adequate, I have referred to Hobbes and found that Crawley himself must have been in the same dilemma, since he has taken over for himself the words of the great seventeenth-century philosopher. On such occasions I have usually followed his lead, and I have taken something from him, too, in the knowledge that he would probably wish me to do so, just as my own ambitions would be gratified if some future translator were to see fit to employ some words or phrases of my own. Certainly I would not pretend that in this translation I have improved on Crawley. He is accurate, where Hobbes is not; he has a zeal and a love for his author; he has a clear, flowing, and distinguished style. I owe much to him and much to Hobbes, and for my own translation can claim no merit other than the questionable one of modernity. For it is more than three hundred years since Hobbes wrote and nearly eighty since the publication of Crawley's version. Thucydides himself is alive, and it would be a pity if any reader were deterred from studying him by any misapprehension about his antiquity.

Finally I must express my gratitude to Professor Kitto, of Bristol University, for his great kindness in reading the proofs, in detecting error, and in making many valuable suggestions.

R. W.

BOOK ONE

INTRODUCTION

1 THUCYDIDES the Athenian wrote the history of the war fought between Athens and Sparta, beginning the account at the very outbreak of the war, in the belief that it was going to be a great war and more worth writing about than any of those which had taken place in the past. My belief was based on the fact that the two sides were at the very height of their power and preparedness, and I saw, too, that the rest of the Hellenic world was committed to one side or the other; even those who were not immediately engaged were deliberating on the courses which they were to take later. This was the greatest disturbance in the history of the Hellenes, affecting also a large part of the non-Hellenic world, and indeed, I might almost say, the whole of mankind. For though I have found it impossible, because of its remoteness in time, to acquire a really precise knowledge of the distant past or even of the history preceding our own period, yet, after looking back into it as far as I can, all the evidence leads me to conclude that these periods were not great periods either in warfare or in anything else.

2 It appears, for example, that the country now called Hellas[1] had no settled population in ancient times; instead there was a series of migrations, as the various tribes, being under the constant pressure of invaders who were stronger than they were, were always prepared to abandon their own territory. There was no commerce, and no safe communication either by land or sea; the use they made of their land was limited to the production of necessities; they had no surplus left over for capital, and no regular system of

1. In the Greek language, ancient as well as modern, the name of the country is 'Hellas', of the people 'Hellenes'. 'Hellas' included all Greek communities, wherever they were established, but here Thucydides is referring more narrowly to the Greek peninsula.

agriculture, since they lacked the protection of fortifications and at any moment an invader might appear and take their land away from them. Thus, in the belief that the day-to-day necessities of life could be secured just as well in one place as in another, they showed no reluctance in moving from their homes, and therefore built no cities of any size or strength, nor acquired any important resources. Where the soil was most fertile there were the most frequent changes of population, as in what is now called Thessaly, in Boeotia, in most of the Peloponnese (except Arcadia), and in others of the richest parts of Hellas. For in these fertile districts it was easier for individuals to secure greater powers than their neighbours: this led to disunity, which often caused the collapse of these states, which in any case were more likely than others to attract the attention of foreign invaders.

It is interesting to observe that Attica, which, because of the poverty of her soil, was remarkably free from political disunity, has always been inhabited by the same race of people. Indeed, this is an important example of my theory that it was because of migrations that there was uneven development elsewhere; for when people were driven out from other parts of Greece by war or by disturbances, the most powerful of them took refuge in Athens, as being a stable society; then they became citizens, and soon made the city even more populous than it had been before, with the result that later Attica became too small for her inhabitants and colonies were sent out to Ionia.

3   Another point which seems to me good evidence for the weakness of the early inhabitants of the country is this: we have no record of any action taken by Hellas as a whole before the Trojan War. Indeed, my view is that at this time the whole country was not even called 'Hellas'. Before the time of Hellen, the son of Deucalion, the name did not exist at all, and different parts were known by the names of different tribes, with the name 'Pelasgian' predominating. After Hellen and his sons had grown powerful in Phthiotis and had been invited as allies into other states, these states separately and because of their connections with the family of Hellen began to be called 'Hellenic'. But it took a long time before the name ousted all the other names. The best evidence for this can be found in Homer, who, though he was born much later

than the time of the Trojan War,[2] nowhere uses the name 'Hellenic' for the whole force. Instead he keeps this name for the followers of Achilles who came from Phthiotis and were in fact the original Hellenes. For the rest in his poems he uses the words 'Danaans', 'Argives', and 'Achaeans'. He does not even use the term 'foreigners',[3] and this, in my opinion, is because in his time the Hellenes were not yet known by one name, and so marked off as something separate from the outside world. By 'Hellenic' I mean here both those who took on the name city by city, as the result of a common language, and those who later were all called by the common name. In any case these various Hellenic states, weak in themselves and lacking in communications with one another, took no kind of collective action before the time of the Trojan War. And they could not have united even for the Trojan expedition unless they had previously acquired a greater knowledge of seafaring.

4   Minos, according to tradition, was the first person to organize a navy. He controlled the greater part of what is now called the Hellenic Sea;[4] he ruled over the Cyclades, in most of which he founded the first colonies, putting his sons in as governors after having driven out the Carians. And it is reasonable to suppose that he did his best to put down piracy in order to secure his own revenues.

5   For in these early times, as communication by sea became easier, so piracy became a common profession both among the Hellenes and among the barbarians who lived on the coast and in the islands. The leading pirates were powerful men, acting both out of self-interest and in order to support the weak among their own people. They would descend upon cities which were unprotected by walls and indeed consisted only of scattered settlements; and by plundering such places they would gain most of their livelihood. At this time such a profession, so far from being regarded as disgraceful, was considered quite honourable. It is an attitude that can be

2. As is pointed out in the Introduction, p. 17, Thucydides gives no date for the Trojan War.

3. Rex Warner regularly translates the Greek *barbaroi* by 'foreigners'. It should be noted that the Athenians, for example, would call other Greeks, such as Spartans or Corinthians, *xenoi*, which is also commonly rendered by 'foreigners'.

4. We now say 'Aegean Sea'.

illustrated even today by some of the inhabitants of the mainland among whom successful piracy is regarded as something to be proud of; and in the old poets, too, we find that the regular question always asked of those who arrive by sea is 'Are you pirates?' It is never assumed either that those who were so questioned would shrink from admitting the fact, or that those who were interested in finding out the fact would reproach them with it.

The same system of armed robbery prevailed by land; and even up to the present day much of Hellas still follows the old way of life – among the Ozolian Locrians, for instance, and the Aetolians and the Acarnanians and the others who live on the mainland in that area. Among these people the custom of carrying arms still
6 survives from the old days of robbery; for at one time, since houses were unprotected and communications unsafe, this was a general custom throughout the whole of Hellas and it was the normal thing to carry arms on all occasions, as it is now among foreigners. The fact that the peoples I have mentioned still live in this way is evidence that once this was the general rule among all the Hellenes.

The Athenians were the first to give up the habit of carrying weapons and to adopt a way of living that was more relaxed and more luxurious. In fact the elder men of the rich families who had these luxurious tastes only recently gave up wearing linen undergarments and tying their hair behind their heads in a knot fastened with a clasp of golden grasshoppers: the same fashions spread to their kinsmen in Ionia, and lasted there among the old men for some time. It was the Spartans who first began to dress simply and in accordance with our modern taste, with the rich leading a life that was as much as possible like the life of the ordinary people. They, too, were the first to play games naked, to take off their clothes openly, and to rub themselves down with olive oil after their exercise. In ancient times even at the Olympic Games the athletes used to wear coverings for their loins, and indeed this practice was still in existence not very many years ago. Even today many foreigners, especially in Asia, wear these loincloths for boxing matches and wrestling bouts. Indeed, one could point to a number of other instances where the manners of the ancient

Hellenic world are very similar to the manners of foreigners to-day.

7 Cities were sited differently in the later periods; for, as seafaring became more general and capital reserves came into existence, new walled cities were built actually on the coasts, and isthmuses were occupied for commercial reasons and for purposes of defence against neighbouring powers. Because of the wide prevalence of piracy, the ancient cities, both in the islands and on the mainland, were built at some distance from the sea, and still remain to this day on their original sites. For the pirates would rob not only each other but everyone else, seafaring or not, who lived along the coasts.

8 Piracy was just as prevalent in the islands among the Carians and Phoenicians, who in fact colonized most of them. This was proved during this present war, when Delos was officially purified by the Athenians and all the graves in the island were opened up. More than half of these graves were Carian, as could be seen from the type of weapons buried with the bodies and from the method of burial, which was the same as that still used in Caria.[5] But after Minos had organized a navy, sea communications improved; he sent colonies to most of the islands and drove out the notorious pirates, with the result that those who lived on the sea-coasts were now in a position to acquire wealth and live a more settled life. Some of them, on the strength of their new riches, built walls for their cities. The weaker, because of the general desire to make profits, were content to put up with being governed by the stronger, and those who won superior power by acquiring capital resources brought the smaller cities under their control. Hellas had already developed some way along these lines when the expedition to Troy took place.

9 Agamemnon, it seems to me, must have been the most powerful of the rulers of his day; and it was for this reason that he raised the force against Troy, not because the suitors of Helen were bound to

5. In III, 104 Thucydides explains more fully: burials were henceforth prohibited on Delos because it was declared sacred ground. The archaeological evidence suggests that Thucydides, or his source, incorrectly identified early (Geometric) Greek pottery as Carian; see R. M. Cook in *Annual of the British School at Athens*, 50 (1955), 266–70.

follow him by the oaths which they had sworn to Tyndareus.[6]
Pelops, according to the most reliable tradition in the Peloponnese,
came there from Asia. He brought great wealth with him, and,
settling in a poor country, acquired such power that, though he
was a foreigner, the whole land was called after him. His descendants became still more prosperous. Eurystheus was killed in Attica
by the sons of Heracles, and before setting out he had entrusted
Mycenae and its government to his relative Atreus, the brother of
Eurystheus's mother, who had been exiled by his father because of
the death of Chrysippus. When Eurystheus failed to return, Atreus,
who had the reputation of a powerful man and who had made
himself popular with the Mycenaeans, took over at their request,
since they were frightened of the sons of Heracles, the kingship of
Mycenae and of all the land that Eurystheus had ruled. So the
descendants of Pelops became more powerful than the descendants
of Perseus. It was to this empire that Agamemnon succeeded, and
at the same time he had a stronger navy than any other ruler; thus,
in my opinion, fear played a greater part than loyalty in the raising
of the expedition against Troy. It appears, if we can believe the
evidence of Homer, that Agamemnon himself commanded more
ships than anyone else and at the same time equipped another fleet
for the Arcadians. And in describing the sceptre which Agamemnon had inherited, Homer calls him:

Of many islands and all Argos King.

As his power was based on the mainland, he could not have ruled
over any islands, except the few that are near the coast, unless he
had possessed a considerable navy. And from this expedition we
can make reasonable conjectures about other expeditions before
that time.

10   Mycenae certainly was a small place, and many of the towns of
that period do not seem to us today to be particularly imposing;
yet that is not good evidence for rejecting what the poets and what
general tradition have to say about the size of the expedition.

6. The tradition was that Helen was wooed by many leading Greek
kings and nobles, that she was allowed to make her own choice, and that
all the suitors swore on oath to her father Tyndareus to abide by her decision.

Suppose, for example, that the city of Sparta were to become deserted and that only the temples and foundations of buildings remained, I think that future generations would, as time passed, find it very difficult to believe that the place had really been as powerful as it was represented to be. Yet the Spartans occupy two-fifths of the Peloponnese and stand at the head not only of the whole Peloponnese itself but also of numerous allies beyond its frontiers. Since, however, the city is not regularly planned and contains no temples or monuments of great magnificence, but is simply a collection of villages, in the ancient Hellenic way, its appearance would not come up to expectation. If, on the other hand, the same thing were to happen to Athens, one would conjecture from what met the eye that the city had been twice as powerful as in fact it is.

We have no right, therefore, to judge cities by their appearances rather than by their actual power, and there is no reason why we should not believe that the Trojan expedition was the greatest that had ever taken place. It is equally true that it was not on the scale of what is done in modern warfare. It is questionable whether we can have complete confidence in Homer's figures, which, since he was a poet, were probably exaggerated. Even if we accept them, however, it appears that Agamemnon's force was smaller than forces are nowadays. Homer gives the number of ships as 1,200, and says that the crew of each Boeotian ship numbered 120, and the crews of the ships of Philoctetes were fifty men for each ship. By this, I imagine, he means to express the maximum and the minimum of the various ships' companies. In any case he gives no other figures for the crews in his catalogue of the ships. The men not only rowed in the ships but also served in the army, as is made clear by the passage about the ships of Philoctetes, when he states that the rowers were all archers. Apart from the kings and the very highest officers, it is unlikely that there were many men aboard who were not sailors; especially as they had to cross the open sea, carrying all their equipment with them, in ships that had no decks but were built in the old fashion of the pirate fleets. If, therefore, we reckon the numbers by taking an average of the biggest and the smallest ships, they will not appear very great, considering that this was a force representing the united effort of the whole of Hellas.

11 The reason for this was not so much shortage of man-power as shortage of money. Lack of supplies made them cut down their numbers to the point at which they expected they would be able to live off the country in which they were fighting. Even after the victory which they won on landing (it is clear that there must have been a victory: otherwise they could not have put up the fortifications round their camp), it does not appear that they brought the whole of their force into action; instead they cultivated the soil of the Chersonese and went on plundering expeditions because of their shortage of supplies. It was because of this dispersal of their forces that the Trojans managed to hold out for ten years of warfare, since they were always strong enough to deal with that fraction of the Greek army which at any one time remained in the field. If, however, Agamemnon had had plenty of supplies with him when he arrived, and if they had used their whole force in making war continuously, without breaking off for plundering expeditions and for cultivating the land, they would have won easily, as is obvious from the fact that they could contain the Trojans when they were not in full force but employing only whatever portion of their army happened to be available. If, therefore, they had all settled down to the siege at once, they would have taken Troy in a shorter time and with less trouble.

12 As it was, just as lack of money was the reason why previous expeditions were not really considerable, so in the case of this one, which was more famous than any others before it, we shall find, if we look at the evidence of what was actually done, that it was not so important as it was made out to be and as it is still, through the influence of the poets, believed to have been.

Even after the Trojan War Hellas was in a state of ferment; there were constant resettlements, and so no opportunity for peaceful development. It was long before the army returned from Troy, and this fact in itself led to many changes. There was party strife in nearly all the cities, and those who were driven into exile founded new cities. Sixty years after the fall of Troy, the modern Boeotians were driven out of Arne by the Thessalians and settled in what is now Boeotia, but used to be called Cadmeis. (Part of the race had settled in Boeotia before this time, and some of these joined in the expedition to Troy.) Twenty years later the Dorians with the descendants of Heracles made themselves masters of the Peloponnese.

Thus many years passed by and many difficulties were encountered before Hellas could enjoy any peace or stability, and before the period of shifting populations ended. Then came the period of colonization. Ionia and most of the islands were colonized by the Athenians. The Peloponnesians founded most of the colonies in Italy and Sicily, and some in other parts of Hellas. All of them were founded after the Trojan War.

13 The old form of government was hereditary monarchy with established rights and limitations; but as Hellas became more powerful and as the importance of acquiring money became more and more evident, tyrannies were established in nearly all the cities, revenues increased, shipbuilding flourished, and ambition turned towards sea-power.

The Corinthians are supposed to have been the first to adopt more or less modern methods in shipbuilding, and it is said that the first triremes ever built in Hellas were laid down in Corinth. Then there is the Corinthian shipwright, Ameinocles, who appears to have built four ships for the Samians. It is nearly 300 years ago (dating from the end of this present war) that Ameinocles went to Samos. And the first naval battle on record is the one between the Corinthians and the Corcyraeans: this was about 260 years ago.

Corinth, planted on its isthmus, had been from time immemorial an important mercantile centre, though in ancient days traffic had been by land rather than by sea. The communications between those who lived inside and those who lived outside the Peloponnese had to pass through Corinthian territory. So Corinth grew to power by her riches, as is shown by the adjective 'wealthy' which is given to her by the ancient poets. And when the Greeks began to take more to seafaring, the Corinthians acquired a fleet, put down piracy, and, being able to provide trading facilities on both the land and the sea routes, made their city powerful from the revenues which came to it by both these ways.

Later the Ionians were a great naval power. This was in the time of Cyrus, the first King of the Persians, and of his son Cambyses. Indeed, when they were fighting against Cyrus, they were for some time masters of all the sea in their region.

Then Polycrates, the tyrant of Samos, made himself powerful by means of his navy. He conquered a number of the islands, among which was Rhenea, which he dedicated to the Delian Apollo.

The Phocaeans, too, when they were founding Marseilles, defeated the Carthaginians in a naval engagement.

14 These were the greatest navies of the past, and even these navies, though many generations later than the Trojan War, do not seem to have possessed many triremes, but to have been still composed, as in the old days, of long-boats and boats of fifty oars. Triremes were first used in any numbers by the Sicilian tyrants and by the Corcyraeans. This was just before the Persian War and the death of Darius, who was King of Persia after Cambyses. There were no other navies of any importance in Hellas before the time of the expedition of Xerxes. Athens and Aegina and a few other states may have had navies of a sort, but they were mainly composed of fifty-oared boats. It was at the very end of this period, when Athens was at war with Aegina and when the foreign invasion was expected, that Themistocles persuaded his fellow-citizens to build the ships with which they fought at Salamis. Even these ships were not yet constructed with complete decks.

15 All the same these Hellenic navies, whether in the remote past or in the later periods, although they were as I have described them, were still a great source of strength to the various naval powers. They brought in revenue and they were the foundation of empire. It was by naval action that those powers, and especially those with insufficient land of their own, conquered the islands. There was no warfare on land that resulted in the acquisition of an empire. What wars there were were simply frontier skirmishes; no expedition by land was sent far from the country of its origin with the purpose of conquering some other power. There were no alliances of small states under the leadership of the great powers, nor did the smaller states form leagues for action on a basis of equality among themselves. Wars were simply local affairs between neighbours. The nearest approach to combined action was in the ancient war between Chalcis and Eretria. On this occasion the rest of the Hellenic world did join in with one side or the other.

16 Different states encountered different obstacles to the course of

their development. The Ionians, for instance, were a rapidly rising power; but King Cyrus and his Persians, having eliminated Croesus, invaded the country between the river Halys and the sea, and brought the Ionian cities on the mainland into the Persian Empire. Later Darius, with the aid of the Phoenician navy, conquered the islands as well.

17 And in the Hellenic states that were governed by tyrants, the tyrant's first thought was always for himself, for his own personal safety, and for the greatness of his own family. Consequently security was the chief political principle in these governments, and no great action ever came out of them – nothing, in fact, that went beyond their immediate local interests, except for the tyrants in Sicily, who rose to great power. So for a long time the state of affairs everywhere in Hellas was such that nothing very remarkable could be done by any combination of powers and that even the individual cities were lacking in enterprise.

18 Finally, however, the Spartans put down tyranny in the rest of Greece, most of which had been governed by tyrants for much longer than Athens. From the time when the Dorians first settled in Sparta there had been a particularly long period of political disunity; yet the Spartan constitution goes back to a very early date, and the country has never been ruled by tyrants. For rather more than 400 years, dating from the end of the late war, they have had the same system of government, and this has been not only a source of internal strength, but has enabled them to intervene in the affairs of other states.

Not many years after the end of tyrannies in Hellas the battle of Marathon was fought between the Persians and the Athenians. Ten years later the foreign enemy returned with his vast armada for the conquest of Hellas, and at this moment of peril the Spartans, since they were the leading power, were in command of the allied Hellenic forces. In face of the invasion the Athenians decided to abandon their city; they broke up their homes, took to their ships, and became a people of sailors. It was by a common effort that the foreign invasion was repelled; but not long afterwards the Hellenes – both those who had fought in the war together and those who later revolted from the King of Persia – split into two divisions, one group following Athens and the other Sparta. These were clearly the two most powerful states, one being supreme on land, the other on the sea. For a short time the war-time alliance held together, but it was not long before quarrels took place and Athens and Sparta, each with her own allies, were at war with each other, while among the rest of the Hellenes states that had their own differences now joined one or other of the two sides.[7] So from the end of the Persian War till the beginning of the Peloponnesian War, though there were some intervals of peace, on the whole these two Powers were either fighting with each other or putting down revolts among their allies. They were consequently in a high state of military preparedness and had gained their military experience in the hard school of danger.

19   The Spartans did not make their allies pay tribute, but saw to it that they were governed by oligarchies who would work in the Spartan interest. Athens, on the other hand, had in the course of time taken over the fleets of her allies (except for those of Chios and Lesbos) and had made them pay contributions of money instead. Thus the forces available to Athens alone for this war were greater than the combined forces had ever been when the alliance was still intact.

20   In investigating past history, and in forming the conclusions which I have formed, it must be admitted that one cannot rely on every detail which has come down to us by way of tradition. People are inclined to accept all stories of ancient times in an uncritical way – even when these stories concern their own native countries. Most people in Athens, for instance, are under the impression that Hipparchus, who was killed by Harmodius and Aristogiton, was tyrant at the time, not realizing that it was Hippias who was the eldest and the chief of the sons of Pisistratus, and that Hipparchus and Thessalus were his younger brothers. What happened was this: on the very day that had been fixed for their attempt, indeed at the very last moment, Harmodius and Aristogeiton had reason to believe that Hippias had been informed of the plot by some of the conspirators. Believing him to have been forewarned, they kept away from him, but, as they wanted to perform some daring exploit before they were arrested themselves, they killed Hipparchus when they

7. See Appendix 1.

found him by the Leocorium organizing the Panathenaic procession.[8]

The rest of the Hellenes, too, make many incorrect assumptions not only about the dimly remembered past, but also about contemporary history. For instance, there is a general belief that the kings of Sparta are each entitled to two votes, whereas in fact they have only one; and it is believed, too, that the Spartans have a company of troops called 'Pitanate'. Such a company has never existed. Most people, in fact, will not take trouble in finding out the truth, but are much more inclined to accept the first story they hear.[9]

21   However, I do not think that one will be far wrong in accepting the conclusions I have reached from the evidence which I have put forward. It is better evidence than that of the poets, who exaggerate the importance of their themes, or of the prose chroniclers, who are less interested in telling the truth than in catching the attention of their public, whose authorities cannot be checked, and whose subject-matter, owing to the passage of time, is mostly lost in the unreliable streams of mythology. We may claim instead to have used only the plainest evidence and to have reached conclusions which are reasonably accurate, considering that we have been dealing with ancient history. As for this present war, even though people are apt to think that the war in which they are fighting is the greatest of all wars and, when it is over, to relapse again into their admiration of the past, nevertheless, if one looks at the facts themselves, one will see that this was the greatest war of all.

22   In this history I have made use of set speeches some of which were delivered just before and others during the war. I have found it difficult to remember the precise words used in the speeches which I listened to myself and my various informants have experienced the same difficulty; so my method has been, while keeping as closely as possible to the general sense of the words that were actually used, to make the speakers say what, in my opinion, was called for by each situation.[10]

8. In vi, 53–9 there is a lengthy digression on the assassination of Hipparchus in 514 B.C.

9. See the Introduction, p. 15.

10. See the Introduction, pp. 25–9.

And with regard to my factual reporting of the events of the war I have made it a principle not to write down the first story that came my way, and not even to be guided by my own general impressions; either I was present myself at the events which I have described or else I heard of them from eye-witnesses whose reports I have checked with as much thoroughness as possible. Not that even so the truth was easy to discover: different eye-witnesses give different accounts of the same events, speaking out of partiality for one side or the other or else from imperfect memories. And it may well be that my history will seem less easy to read because of the absence in it of a romantic element. It will be enough for me, however, if these words of mine are judged useful by those who want to understand clearly the events which happened in the past and which (human nature being what it is) will, at some time or other and in much the same ways, be repeated in the future. My work is not a piece of writing designed to meet the taste of an immediate public, but was done to last for ever.

23   The greatest war in the past was the Persian War; yet in this war the decision was reached quickly as a result of two naval battles and two battles on land. The Peloponnesian War, on the other hand, not only lasted for a long time, but throughout its course brought with it unprecedented suffering for Hellas. Never before had so many cities been captured and then devastated, whether by foreign armies or by the Hellenic powers themselves (some of these cities, after capture, were resettled with new inhabitants); never had there been so many exiles; never such loss of life – both in the actual warfare and in internal revolutions. Old stories of past prodigies, which had not found much confirmation in recent experience, now became credible. Wide areas, for instance, were affected by violent earthquakes; there were more frequent eclipses of the sun than had ever been recorded before; in various parts of the country there were extensive droughts followed by famine; and there was the plague which did more harm and destroyed more life than almost any other single factor. All these calamities fell together upon the Hellenes after the outbreak of war.

War began when the Athenians and the Peloponnesians broke the Thirty Years Truce which had been made after the capture of

Euboea.[11] As to the reasons why they broke the truce, I propose first to give an account of the causes of complaint which they had against each other and of the specific instances where their interests clashed: this is in order that there should be no doubt in anyone's mind about what led to this great war falling upon the Hellenes. But the real reason for the war is, in my opinion, most likely to be disguised by such an argument. What made war inevitable was the the growth of Athenian power and the fear which this caused in Sparta. As for the reasons for breaking the truce and declaring war which were openly expressed by each side, they are as follows.

THE DISPUTE OVER EPIDAMNUS

24 The city of Epidamnus is on the right of the approach to the Ionic Gulf. It is in foreign territory that is inhabited by an Illyrian race called the Taulantians. The place is a colony of Corcyra and it was founded by Phalius, the son of Eratocleides, a Corinthian of the family of the Heraclids. In accordance with the old custom, the founder had been invited from the mother city. Among the colonists there were also a certain number of Corinthians and some other Dorians.

As time went on Epidamnus became both powerful and populous; but there followed many years of political unrest, caused, they say, by a war with the foreign inhabitants of the country. As a result of this Epidamnus declined and lost most of her power. Finally, just before the war between Athens and Sparta, the democratic party drove out the aristocratic party, who then went over to the foreign enemies of the city and joined them in making piratical attacks on it both by sea and by land. The democrats inside the city now found themselves in difficulties and sent an embassy to Corcyra, begging their mother country not to allow them to perish, and asking for help both in making some settlement with the exiled party and in putting an end to the war with the foreigners. The ambassadors took up their position in the temple of Hera in Corcyra, and there made their requests, but the

11. In 446–5 B.C.

people of Corcyra refused to receive the ambassadors and sent them back without having achieved anything.

25   When the people in Epidamnus realized that no help was forthcoming from Corcyra, they were at a loss how to deal with the situation. They therefore sent to Delphi to inquire from the god whether they should hand over their city to the Corinthians, who had founded it, and so get help from that quarter. The reply from Delphi was that they should hand over their city and accept the leadership of Corinth. So, in obedience to the oracle, they sent to Corinth, and made over the colony to the Corinthians. They pointed out that the original founder had come from Corinth; they made public the reply which they had received from Delphi, and they begged the Corinthians to come to their help and not allow them to be destroyed.

The Corinthians agreed to come to their assistance. They felt they had a good right to do so, since they regarded the colony as belonging just as much to them as to Corcyra; and at the same time they hated the Corcyraeans because they failed to show to Corinth the respect due from a colony to the mother city. Unlike their other colonies, the Corcyraeans did not give to Corinthians the usual rights and honours at public festivals or allow them the correct facilities for making sacrifices. Instead they looked down upon their mother city, claiming that their financial power at this time made them equal with the richest states in Hellas and that their military resources were greater than those of Corinth. In particular they boasted of their naval superiority, sometimes even basing this claim on the ground that those famous sailors the Phaeacians had inhabited Corcyra before them. This belief did in fact encourage them to give particular attention to their navy, which was by no means an inconsiderable one. They had, at the outbreak of war, a fleet of 120 triremes.

26   All this caused ill feeling, and so the Corinthians were glad enough to send to Epidamnus the help required. They advertised for volunteers to settle there, and sent out a force consisting of Ambraciots, Leucadians, and their own citizens. This force marched by land to Apollonia, a Corinthian colony, avoiding the sea route out of fear that they might be intercepted by the Corcyraeans.

When the Corcyraeans discovered that the settlers and the

troops had arrived at Epidamnus and that the colony had been handed over to Corinth, they reacted violently. As soon as the news arrived they put to sea with twenty-five ships, which were soon followed by another fleet. Sailing up to Epidamnus, they demanded in the most threatening and abusive language first that the Epidamnians should reinstate the exiled party. These exiles, meanwhile, had come to Corcyra, had appealed to the claims of their family connections (pointing out the tombs of their own ancestors there), and begged for help in being brought back. Secondly they demanded that the Epidamnians should send away the troops and settlers that had come from Corinth.

The Epidamnians rejected both demands, and the Corcyraeans began operations against them with a fleet of forty ships. They had with them the exiles, whom they promised to restore to power, and also the Illyrian army. Taking up their positions in front of the city, they proclaimed an offer of immunity to all, whether citizens or not, who would abandon the city; those who failed to take advantage of the opportunity would be treated as enemies. Then, since there was no response to this offer, they began to besiege the city, which stands on an isthmus.

27   Messengers soon arrived at Corinth with the news that Epidamnus was being besieged, and the Corinthians began to equip a relief force. At the same time they advertised for volunteers to form a new colony at Epidamnus. Those who went out there were to have absolutely equal rights, and those who were not prepared to sail at once, but still wanted to have a share in the colony, could buy this share, together with the right of remaining behind, by putting down the sum of fifty Corinthian drachmae. There was a wide response to this offer both from people who wanted to sail at once and from people who paid the deposit. Various cities were asked to help with ships to escort the convoy in case the Corcyraeans attempted to intercept it. Megara provided eight ships; Pale, the Cephallenian city, provided four; five ships came from Epidaurus, one from Hermione, two from Troezen, ten from Leucas, and eight from Ambracia. The Thebans and Phliasians were asked to provide money, the Eleans were asked for money and also for hulls. The Corinthians themselves equipped a fleet of thirty ships and 3,000 hoplites.

28   When the Corcyraeans heard of these preparations they sent an embassy to Corinth, accompanied by some envoys from Sparta and Sicyon to support them. There they demanded that Corinth should withdraw her troops and colonists from Epidamnus, since Epidamnus was no concern of hers. They were prepared, however, if Corinth wished to put in a counter claim, to accept arbitration. Cities in the Peloponnese should be chosen by mutual agreement to act as arbitrators, and the colony should go to whichever side the arbitrators awarded it. Alternatively, they proposed referring the matter to the oracle at Delphi. They urged Corinth not to start a war, saying that, if she did, they themselves, through no fault of their own, would be forced in sheer self-defence to make friends elsewhere and in quarters where they had no wish to make friends.

The Corinthian reply to this was that if Corcyra withdrew the fleet and the foreign army from Epidamnus, then discussion might be profitable; but it was quite absurd to talk of arbitration while the city was still being besieged.

The Corcyraeans countered by saying that if the Corinthians also withdrew their forces from Epidamnus, they would do as was suggested. Or, they were prepared to let both sides stay in their present positions and to arrange an armistice to remain in operation until the result of the arbitration was declared.

29   None of these proposals was acceptable to the Corinthians. By this time their ships were manned and their allies were ready. They sent in front of them a herald to declare war, and then set sail with a force of seventy-five ships and 2,000 hoplites to fight against the Corcyraeans at Epidamnus. The fleet was under the command of Aristeus, the son of Pellichas, Callicrates, the son of Callias, and Timanor, the son of Timanthes. The land forces were commanded by Archetimus, the son of Eurytimus, and Isarchidas, the son of Isarchus.

They sailed on as far as Actium in Anactoria, at the mouth of the Ambracian Gulf, where the temple of Apollo stands. Here they were met by a herald from the Corcyraeans who had sailed out in a light boat with instructions to urge them not to attack. At the same time the Corcyraeans were manning their ships; they had fitted new crossbeams in the old vessels to make them sea-worthy and had seen to it that the rest of their fleet was ready for action.

By the time their herald had returned and reported that his offers of peace had been rejected, the ships, eighty of them in all, were manned (forty were still engaged in the siege of Epidamnus). They then put out to sea against the enemy, formed line, and went into action. The result of the engagement was a decisive victory for the Corcyraeans, who destroyed fifteen Corinthian ships. It happened that on the very same day the besiegers of Epidamnus had forced the city to surrender, the terms being that all foreign troops and settlers in the garrison should be sold as slaves and that Corinthian citizens should be held as prisoners pending a further decision.

30   After the battle the Corcyraeans put up a trophy on Leukimme, a headland of Corcyra. They then put all their prisoners to death, with the exception of the Corinthians, whom they still kept in custody.

The Corinthians and their allies went back home after their defeat in the sea battle, and now Corcyra had complete control of the seas in her own area. A Corcyraean fleet descended on Leucas, a colony of Corinth, and laid its territory waste. They also burnt Cyllene, the Elean port, because the Eleans had provided Corinth with ships and money. So for most of the time after the battle the Corcyraeans kept control of the sea and sent fleets to attack the allies of Corinth. Finally, however, at the beginning of the following summer, Corinth, seeing the difficulties in which her allies were placed, sent out a fleet and an army. This force, in order to protect Leucas and the other friendly cities, held and fortified positions at Actium and round Chimerium in Thesprotis. The Corcyraeans, also with naval and land forces, took up positions opposite them at Leukimme. Here they stayed for the rest of the summer, neither side making any move, and it was not until the beginning of winter that they both retired to their home bases.

THE DISPUTE OVER CORCYRA

31 In Corinth tempers were running high over the war with Corcyra. All through the year following the sea battle and in the year after that the Corinthians were building ships and doing everything possible to increase the efficiency of their navy. Rowers were

collected from the Peloponnese itself, and good terms were offered to bring them also from the rest of Hellas.

In Corcyra the news of the preparations provoked alarm. They had no allies in Hellas, since they had not enrolled themselves either in the Spartan or in the Athenian league. They decided therefore to go to Athens, to join the Athenian alliance, and see whether they could get any support from that quarter.

When the news of this move reached Corinth, the Corinthians also sent representatives to Athens, fearing that the combined strength of the navies of Athens and Corcyra would prevent them from having their own way in the war with Corcyra. An assembly was held and the arguments on both sides were put forward. The representatives of Corcyra spoke as follows:

32   'Athenians, in a situation like this, it is right and proper that first of all certain points should be made clear. We have come to ask you for help, but cannot claim that this help is due to us because of any great services we have done to you in the past or on the basis of any existing alliance. We must therefore convince you first that by giving us this help you will be acting in your own interests, or certainly not against your own interests; and then we must show that our gratitude can be depended upon. If on all these points you find our arguments unconvincing, we must not be surprised if our mission ends in failure.

'Now Corcyra has sent us to you in the conviction that in asking for your alliance we can also satisfy you on these points. What has happened is that our policy in the past appears to have been against our own present interests, and at the same time makes it look inconsistent of us to be asking help from you. It certainly looks inconsistent to be coming here to ask for help when in the past we have deliberately avoided all alliances; and it is because of this very policy that we are now left entirely alone to face a war with Corinth. We used to think that our neutrality was a wise thing, since it prevented us being dragged into danger by other people's policies; now we see it clearly as a lack of foresight and as a source of weakness.

'It is certainly true that in the recent naval battle we defeated the Corinthians single-handed. But now they are coming against us with a much greater force drawn from the Peloponnese and from the rest of Hellas. We recognize that, if we have nothing but our own national resources, it is impossible for us to survive, and we can imagine what lies in store for us if they overpower us. We are therefore forced to ask for assistance, both from you and from everyone else; and it should not be held against us that now we have faced the facts and are reversing our old policy of keeping ourselves to ourselves. There is nothing sinister in our action; we merely recognize that we made a mistake.

33   'If you grant our request, you will find that in many ways it was a good thing that we made it at this particular time. First of all, you will not be helping aggressors, but people who are the victims of aggression. Secondly, we are now in extreme peril, and if you welcome our alliance at this moment you will win our undying gratitude. And then, we are, after you, the greatest naval power in Hellas. You would have paid a lot of money and still have been very grateful to have us on your side. Is it not, then, an extraordinary stroke of good luck for you (and one which will cause heartburning among your enemies) to have us coming over voluntarily into your camp, giving ourselves up to you without involving you in any dangers or any expense? It is a situation where we, whom you are helping, will be grateful to you, the world in general will admire you for your generosity, and you yourselves will be stronger than you were before. There is scarcely a case in history where all these advantages have been available at the same time, nor has it often happened before that a power looking for an alliance can say to those whose help it asks that it can give as much honour and as much security as it will receive.

'In case of war we should obviously be useful to you, but some of you may think that there is no immediate danger of war. Those who think along those lines are deceiving themselves; they do not see the facts that Sparta is frightened of you and wants war, that Corinth is your enemy and is also influential at Sparta. Corinth has attacked us first in order to attack you afterwards. She has no wish to make enemies of us both at once and find us standing together against her. What she wants is to get an initial advantage over you in one of two ways – either by destroying our power or by forcing us to use it in her interests. But it is our policy to be one move ahead, which is why we want you to accept the alliance

which we offer. It is better to have the initiative in these matters –
to take our own measures first, rather than be forced to counter
the intrigues that are made against us by others.

34   'If the Corinthians say that you have no right to receive one of
their colonies into your alliance, they should be told that every
colony, if it is treated properly, honours its mother city, and only
becomes estranged when it has been treated badly. Colonists are
not sent abroad to be the slaves of those who remain behind, but
to be their equals. And it is quite clear that Corinth was in the
wrong so far as we are concerned. We asked them to settle the
affair of Epidamnus by arbitration; but they chose to prosecute
their claims by war instead of by a reasonable settlement. Indeed,
the way in which they are treating us, their kinsmen, ought to be a
warning to you and ought to prevent you from falling into their
deceitful traps or listening to what may appear to be their straightforward demands. When one makes concessions to one's enemies,
one regrets it afterwards, and the fewer concessions one makes the
safer one is likely to be.

35   'It is not a breach of your treaty with Sparta if you receive us
into your alliance. We are neutrals, and it is expressly written down
in your treaty that any Hellenic state which is in this condition is
free to ally itself with whichever side it chooses. What is really
monstrous is a situation where Corinth can find sailors for her ships
both from her own allies and from the rest of Hellas, including in
particular your own subjects, while we are shut off from a perfectly
legitimate alliance, and indeed from getting help from anywhere:
and then, on top of that, they will actually accuse you of behaving
illegally if you grant our request. In fact it is we who shall have
far greater reasons to complain of you if you are not willing to
help us; you will be rejecting us, who are no enemies of yours, in
the hour of our peril, and as for the others, who are enemies of
yours and are also the aggressors, you will not only be doing
nothing to stop them, but will actually be allowing them to build
up their strength from the resources of your own empire. Is this
right? Surely you ought either to stop them from engaging troops
from your own subjects, or else to give us, too, whatever assistance
you think proper. Best of all would be for you to receive us in
open alliance and help us in that way.

'We have already suggested that such a course would be very much in your own interests. Perhaps the greatest advantage to you is that you can entirely depend on us because your enemies are the same as ours, and strong ones, too, quite capable of doing damage to those who revolt from them. And then it is quite a different matter for you if you reject alliance with a naval power than if you do the same thing with a land power. Your aim, no doubt, should be, if it were possible, to prevent anyone else having a navy at all: the next best thing is to have on your side the strongest navy that there is.

36   'Some of you may admit that we have shown that the alliance would be in your interests, and yet may still feel apprehensive about a breach of your treaty with Sparta. Those who think in this way should remember that, whether you feel apprehensive or not, you will certainly have become stronger, and that this fact will make your enemies think twice before attacking you; whereas if you reject us, however confident you may feel, you will in fact be the weaker for it, and consequently less likely to be treated with respect by a strong enemy. Remember, too, that your decision is going to affect Athens just as much as Corcyra. At the moment your thoughts are on the coming war – a war, in fact, which has almost broken out already. Certainly you will not be showing very much foresight for your own city if, at this time, you are in two minds whether to have on your side a power like Corcyra, whose friendship can be so valuable and whose hostility so dangerous to you. Apart from all other advantages, Corcyra lies in an excellent position on the coastal route to Italy and Sicily, and is thus able to prevent naval reinforcements coming to the Peloponnese from there, or going from the Peloponnese to those countries.

'The whole thing can be put very shortly, and these few words will give you the gist of the whole argument why you should not abandon us. There are three considerable naval powers in Hellas – Athens, Corcyra, and Corinth. If Corinth gets control of us first and you allow our navy to be united with hers, you will have to fight against the combined fleets of Corcyra and the Peloponnese. But if you receive us into your alliance, you will enter upon the war with our ships as well as your own.'

After this speech from the Corcyraean side, the representative of
37 Corinth spoke as follows: 'These Corcyraeans have not confined
their argument to the question of whether or not you should accept their alliance. They have named us as aggressors and have
stated that they are the victims of an unjust war. Before, therefore,
we go on to the rest of our argument, we must deal first with these
two points. Our aim will be to give you a clear idea of what exactly
we are claiming from you, and to show that there are good reasons
why you should reject the appeal of Corcyra.

' "Wisdom" and "Moderation" are the words used by Corcyra
in describing her old policy of avoiding alliances. In fact the motives were entirely evil, and there was nothing good about them at
all. She wanted no allies because her actions were wrong, and she
was ashamed of calling in others to witness her own misdoings.
The geographical situation of Corcyra gives its inhabitants a certain
independence. The ships of other states are forced to put in to their
harbours much more often than Corcyraean ships visit the harbours
of other states. So in cases where a Corcyraean has been guilty of
injuring some other national, the Corcyraeans are themselves their
own judges, and there is no question of having the case tried by
independent judges appointed by treaty. So this neutrality of theirs,
which sounds so innocent, was in fact a disguise adopted not to
preserve them from having to share in the wrong-doings of others,
but in order to give them a perfectly free hand to do wrong themselves, making away with other people's property by force, when
they are strong enough, cheating them, whenever they can manage to do so, and enjoying their gains without any vestige of shame.
Yet if they really were the honourable people they pretend to be,
this very independence of theirs would have given them the best
possible opportunity of showing their good qualities in the relations of common justice.

38 'In fact they have not acted honourably either towards us or towards anyone else. Though they are colonists of ours, they have
never been loyal to us and are now at war with us. They were not
sent out in the first place, they say, to be ill treated. And we say
that we did not found colonies in order to be insulted by them, but
rather to retain our leadership and to be treated with proper respect.
At all events our other colonies do respect us, and indeed they treat

us with great affection. It is obvious, then, that, if the majority are pleased with us, Corcyra can have no good reason for being the only one that is dissatisfied; and that we are not making war unreasonably, but only as the result of exceptional provocation. Even if we were making a mistake, the right thing would be for them to give in to us, and then it would be a disgrace to us if we failed to respect so reasonable an attitude. As it is, their arrogance and the confidence they feel in their wealth have made them act improperly towards us on numerous occasions, and in particular with regard to Epidamnus, which belongs to us. When this place was in distress, they took no steps towards bringing it under their control; but as soon as we came to relieve it, they forcibly took possession of it, and still hold it.

39 'They actually say that they were prepared in the first place to submit the matter to arbitration. The phrase is meaningless when used by someone who has already stolen an advantage and makes the offer from a safe position; it should only be used when, before opening hostilities, one puts oneself on a real and not an artificial level with one's enemies. And in their case there was no mention of this excellent idea of arbitration before they started to besiege Epidamnus; they only brought the word forward when they began to think that we were not going to let them have their own way.

'And now, being in the wrong themselves over Epidamnus, they have come to you and are asking you not so much for alliance as for complicity in their crime. They are asking you to welcome them at a time when they are at war with us. What they should have done was to have approached you in the days when they were really secure, not at this present moment, when they have wronged us and when danger threatens them. Under present circumstances you will be giving aid to people who never gave you a share in their power, and you will force us to hold you equally responsible with them, although you took no part in their misdeeds. Surely, if they expect you to join fortunes with them now, they should have shared their power with you in the past.

40 'We have shown, I think, that we have good reasons for complaint, and that the conduct of Corcyra has been both violent and grasping. Next we should like you to understand that it would

not be right or just for you to receive them as allies. Though there may be a clause in the treaty stating that any city not included in the original agreement is free to join whichever side it likes, this cannot refer to cases where the object of joining an alliance is to injure other powers; it cannot refer to a case where a city is only looking for security because it is in revolt, and where the result of accepting its alliance, if one looks at the matter dispassionately, will be, not peace, but war. And this is what may well happen to you, if you will not take our advice. You would not only be helping them, but making war on us, who are bound to you by treaty. If you join them in attacking us, we shall be forced to defend ourselves against you as well as against them.

'The right course, surely, is either for you to preserve a strict neutrality or else to join us against them. At least you have treaty obligations towards Corinth, whereas you have never even had a peace treaty with Corcyra. What you ought not to do is to establish a precedent by which a power may receive into its alliance the revolted subjects of another power. At the time when Samos revolted from you and when the Peloponnesian states were divided on the question whether to help them or not, we were not one of those who voted against you; on the contrary, we openly opposed the others and said that every power should have the right to control its own allies. Now, if you are going to welcome and assist people who have done wrong to us, you will find just as many of your own people coming over to our side, and you will be establishing
41 a precedent that is likely to harm you even more than us. All this we have a perfect right to claim from you by Hellenic law and custom. We should like also to give you some advice and to mention that we have some title to your gratitude. We are not enemies who are going to attack you, and we are not on such friendly terms that such services are quite normal. We say, therefore, that the time has come for you to repay us for what we did for you in the past.

'You were short of warships when you were fighting Aegina, just before the Persian invasion. Corinth then gave you twenty ships. As a result of this act of kindness you were able to conquer Aegina, and as a result of our other good turn to you, when we prevented the Peloponnesian states from helping Samos, you were able to punish that island. And these acts of ours were done at critical periods, periods when people are very apt to turn upon their enemies and disregard every other consideration except victory. At such times people regard even former enemies as their friends, so long as they are on their side, and even genuine friends as their enemies, if they stand in their way; in fact their overmastering desire for victory makes them neglect their own best interests.

42   'We should like you to think carefully over these points; we should like your young men to ask their elders about them, and for you to decide that you ought to behave towards us as we have behaved towards you. Do not think: "the Corinthians are quite right in what they say, but in the event of war all this is not in our interest." It is generally the best policy to make the fewest errors of judgement, and you must remember that, though Corcyra is trying to frighten you into doing wrong by this idea of a coming war, there is no certainty that a war will come. You may think that Corinth will be your enemy in the future, but it is not worth your while to be carried away by this idea and to make open enemies of us now. A much wiser course would be to remove the suspicions which we already feel towards you in connection with Megara. And you will find that an act of kindness done at the right moment has a power to dispel old grievances quite out of proportion to the act itself.

'Do not be influenced by the fact that they are offering you a great naval alliance. The power that deals fairly with its equals finds a truer security than the one which is hurried into snatching
43   some apparent but dangerous advantage. We ourselves are now in the position that you were in at the time when, during the discussions at Sparta, we laid down the principle that every power should have the right to punish its own allies. We claim that you should uphold this principle, and, since our vote helped you then, you should not injure us now by voting against us. No, you should deal with us as we have dealt with you, and you should be conscious that we are in one of those critical situations where real friendship is to be gained from helping us and real hostility from opposing us. Do not go against us by receiving these Corcyraeans into your alliance. Do not aid and abet them in their crimes. Thus

you will be acting as you ought to act and at the same time you will be making the wisest decision in your own interests.'

44   This was the speech of the Corinthian delegation. The Athenians, after listening to both sides, discussed the matter at two assemblies. At the first of these, opinion seemed to incline in favour of the Corinthian arguments, but at the second there was a change, and they decided on entering into some kind of alliance with Corcyra. This was not to be a total alliance involving the two parties in any war which either of them might have on hand; for the Athenians realized that if Corcyra required them to join in an attack on Corinth, that would constitute a breach of their treaty with the Peloponnese. Instead the alliance was to be of a defensive character and would only operate if Athens or Corcyra or any of their allies were attacked from outside.

The general belief was that, whatever happened, war with the Peloponnese was bound to come. Athens had no wish to see the strong navy of Corcyra pass into the hands of Corinth. At the same time she was not averse from letting the two Powers weaken each other by fighting together; since in this way, if war did come, Athens herself would be stronger in relation to Corinth and to the other naval Powers. Then, too, it was a fact that Corcyra lay very conveniently on the coastal route to Italy and Sicily.

45   So, with these considerations in mind, Athens made her alliance with Corcyra. The Corinthian representatives returned to Corinth, and soon afterwards Athens sent ten ships as a reinforcement to Corcyra. These ships were under the command of Lacedaimonius, the son of Cimon, Diotimus, the son of Strombichus, and Proteas, the son of Epicles. Their instructions were to avoid battle with the Corinthians except under the following circumstances. If the Corinthians sailed against Corcyra with the intention of landing on the island itself or at any point in Corcyraean territory, then they were to do whatever they could to prevent it. These instructions were given in order to avoid breaking the existing treaty.

46   The ten ships reached Corcyra, and now the Corinthians had completed their preparations and sailed for the island with a fleet of 150 ships. Ten of these came from Elis, twelve from Megara, ten from Leucas, twenty-seven from Ambracia, one from Anactorium, and ninety from Corinth herself. Each contingent had its

own officers; the Corinthian admiral, who had four subordinate commanders, was Xenoclides, the son of Euthycles.

This fleet sailed out from Leucas to the mainland opposite Corcyra and came to anchor at Chimerium in the territory of Thesprotis. There is a harbour here, and above it, at some distance from the sea, is the city of Ephyre in the Elean district. Near Ephyre the waters of the Acherusian Lake flow into the sea. It gets its name from the river Acheron, which flows through Thesprotis and falls into the lake. The other river in the district is the Thyamis, which forms the boundary between Thesprotis and Cestrine. Between the mouths of these two rivers is the high promontory of Chimerium. It was at this point of the mainland that the Corinthians came to anchor and made an encampment.

47   The Corcyraeans, as soon as they heard of their enemies' approach, manned 110 ships, commanded by Miciades, Aisimides, and Eurybatus, and made a camp on one of the group of islands which are called 'Sybota'. The ten Athenian ships were with them. Their land forces were posted on the headland of Leukimme and had been reinforced by a contingent of 1,000 hoplites from Zacynthus. The Corinthians, too, on the mainland received considerable reinforcements from the natives of those parts, who had always been on friendly terms with them.

48   When the Corinthians had finished their preparations, they took with them rations for three days and put out to sea by night from Chimerium with the intention of engaging the enemy. At dawn they came in sight of the Corcyraean ships already in the open sea and bearing down upon them. As soon as they saw each other, both sides took up their positions for battle. The Athenian ships were on the right of the Corcyraean line, which otherwise consisted of their own ships in three squadrons, each under the command of one of their admirals. This was the Corcyraean order of battle. On the other side the ships of Megara and of Ambracia were on the right, the other allies were variously distributed in the centre, and the Corinthians themselves, with the best ships at their disposal, held the left of the line, facing the Athenians and the right wing of the Corcyraeans.

49   Then, after the signals had been hoisted on both sides, they joined battle. The fighting was of a somewhat old-fashioned kind,

since they were still behindhand in naval matters, both sides having numbers of hoplites[12] aboard their ships, together with archers and javelin throwers. But the fighting was hard enough, in spite of the lack of skill shown: indeed, it was more like a battle on land than a naval engagement. When the ships came into collision it was difficult for them to break away clear, because of the number engaged and of their close formation. In fact both sides relied more for victory on their hoplites, who were on the decks and who fought a regular pitched battle there while the ships remained motionless. No one attempted the manoeuvre of encirclement; in fact it was a battle where courage and sheer strength played a greater part than scientific methods. Everywhere in the battle confusion reigned, and there was shouting on all sides.

The Athenian ships would come up in support of the Corcyraeans whenever they were hard pressed and would so help to alarm their enemies, but they did not openly join the battle, since the commanders were afraid of acting contrary to the instructions they had received at Athens.

The right of the Corinthian line was in the greatest difficulties. Here a Corcyraean squadron of twenty ships routed their enemies and drove them back in confusion to the mainland. Sailing right up to their camp, they landed, set fire to the empty tents, and plundered the property they found there. Here, then, the Corcyraeans won a victory and the Corinthians and their allies suffered a defeat. But on the left, where the Corinthians themselves were, things went very differently. The Corcyraeans were in any case in inferior numbers, and they also lacked the support of the twenty ships engaged in the pursuit. And now the Athenians, seeing that the Corcyraeans were in difficulties, began to support them more openly. At first they refrained from actually ramming any Corinthian ship; but finally, when there was no doubt about the defeat and the Corinthians were still pressing on, there came a point where everyone joined in and nothing was barred. Thus a situation inevitably came about where Corinthians and Athenians were openly fighting with each other.

12. The hoplites were the heavily accoutred infantry. Since they were responsible for providing their own arms and armour, they were drawn solely from the wealthier sections of the population.

50   After their victory, the Corinthians, instead of taking into tow
and dragging away the ships that they had put out of action,
turned their attention to the men. They sailed in and out of the
wreckage, killing rather than taking prisoners. Thus they unknow-
ingly killed some of their own friends, since they did not realize
that those on the right of their line had been defeated. Many ships
had been engaged on both sides and the action had been an extensive one, so that, once battle was joined, it was not easy to make
out who were winning and who were being defeated. Indeed, so
far as numbers of ships were concerned, this was the biggest battle
that had ever taken place between two Hellenic states.

After they had driven the Corcyraeans to the land, the Corinthians gave their attention to the wrecks and to their own dead,
most of whom they were able to recover and bring back to Sybota,
not an inhabited place, but a harbour in Thesprotis, where the land
army of their native allies was stationed in their support. They then
formed up again and sailed out against the Corcyraeans.

The Corcyraeans, fearing that they might attempt to make a
landing on their island, came out to meet them with every available ship, including the ten Athenian ships as well as the remainder
of their own fleet.

It was already late in the day, and both sides had sung the paean
before attacking, when suddenly the Corinthian ships began to
back water. They had seen in the distance twenty more Athenian
ships approaching. These had been sent out later from Athens to
reinforce the original ten, since the Athenians feared (quite rightly,
as it turned out) that the Corcyraeans might be defeated and that
51   their own ten ships would not be enough to support them. It was
this new force that the Corinthians saw. They suspected that they
came from Athens, and thought that there might be still more
behind the ships that were visible. Therefore they began to retire.

The Corcyraeans were making their attack from a direction
where visibility was not so good, and had not sighted the ships.
They were amazed when they saw the Corinthians backing water.
Finally someone sighted them and shouted out that there were
ships ahead. Then they also retired, since it was already getting
dark and the Corinthians had turned and broken off contact with
them. The Corcyraeans went back to their camp on Leukimme,

and the twenty Athenian ships, which were under the command of Glaucon, the son of Leagrus, and Andocides, the son of Leogoras, sailed up to their camp, making their way through the wrecks and the dead bodies. They arrived not very long after they had originally been sighted, but it was now night and the Corcyraeans feared that they might be enemy ships. However, they were recognized and came safely to anchor.

52   Next day the thirty Athenian ships with all the Corcyraean ships that could put to sea sailed out to the harbour of Sybota, where the Corinthians lay at anchor, to see whether they were prepared to fight. The Corinthians put out from shore and formed a line in the open sea. There they remained, having no intention of starting an engagement. They saw that a fresh fleet had arrived from Athens, and they were conscious of their own difficulties: the prisoners whom they had aboard their ships had to be guarded, and in the desolate place where they were there were no facilities for repairing their vessels. What particularly worried them was the thought of how they were to make their voyage home. They feared that the Athenians might consider that the treaty had been broken by the recent fighting and might intercept them on their way back.

53   They therefore decided to put some of their men, not carrying a herald's wand, on board a boat and to send them to the Athenians to find out how matters stood.

This was done, and the Corinthian messengers made the following speech: 'Athenians, you are putting yourselves in the wrong. You are starting a war and you are not abiding by the treaty. We are here in order to deal with our own enemies, and now you are standing in our path and have taken up arms against us. Now if your intention is to prevent us from sailing against Corcyra or anywhere else that we wish, if, in other words, you intend to break the treaty, then make us who are here your first prisoners, and treat us as enemies.'

After this speech of the Corinthians, all those in the Corcyraean forces who had been within hearing shouted out in favour of making prisoners of them at once and then putting them to death. The Athenians, however, replied as follows: 'Peloponnesians, we are not starting a war and we are not breaking the treaty. These Corcyraeans are our allies, and we came here to help them. We shall do nothing to stop you if you wish to sail in any other direction; but if you sail against Corcyra or against any part of her territory, then we shall do our best to prevent you.'

54   When they received this reply from the Athenians, the Corinthians began to prepare for their voyage home. They also put up a trophy to commemorate their victory on the part of Sybota that is on the mainland. Meanwhile the Corcyraeans salvaged the wreckage of their ships and took up the bodies of their own dead. These had been washed towards them by the current and by a wind which got up during the night and scattered them in all directions. They then put up a trophy on the island of Sybota, claiming that the victory had been theirs.

The reasons that each side had for claiming the victory and setting up a trophy were as follows. The Corinthians had had the upper hand in the fighting until nightfall: thus they had brought in most of the disabled ships and their own dead: they held at least 1,000 prisoners and they had sunk about seventy enemy ships. The Corcyraeans had destroyed about thirty ships and, after the arrival of the Athenians, they had recovered off their coast their own dead and their disabled vessels. Then on the day after the battle the Corinthians, on seeing the Athenian fleet, had backed water and retired before them, and after the Athenians had arrived, had not come out from Sybota to fight. So both sides claimed the victory.

55   On their voyage home the Corinthians took Anactorium, at the mouth of the Ambracian Gulf. It was a place in which both Corinth and Corcyra had rights and it was given up to the Corinthians by treachery. Before sailing home the Corinthians put settlers of their own into Anactorium. They sold 800 of the Corcyraean prisoners who were slaves, and they kept in captivity 250 whom they treated with great consideration, hoping that a time would come when they would return and win over the island to Corinth. Most of them were in fact people of great power and influence in Corcyra.

So Corcyra remained undefeated in her war with Corinth and the Athenian fleet left the island. But this gave Corinth her first cause for war against Athens, the reason being that Athens had fought against her with Corcyra although the peace treaty was still in force.

THE DISPUTE OVER POTIDAEA

56 Almost immediately afterwards it happened that there was another dispute between Athens and the Peloponnese. This also contributed to the breaking out of the war. It concerned the people of Potidaea who live on the isthmus of Pallene, and who, though colonists of Corinth, were allies of Athens in the tribute-paying class. Corinth was searching for means of retaliation against Athens, and Athens had no illusions about the hatred felt for her by Corinth. She therefore made the following demands of Potidaea: they were to pull down the fortifications looking towards Pallene, to send hostages to Athens, to banish their Corinthian magistrates, and in future not to receive those who were sent out annually from Corinth to replace them. These demands were made because Athens feared that, under the influence of Perdiccas and of the Corinthians, Potidaea might be induced to revolt and might draw
57 into the revolt the other allied cities in the Thracian area. It was directly after the sea battle off Corcyra that the Athenians took these precautions with regard to Potidaea. Corinth was now quite openly hostile, and though Perdiccas, the son of Alexander and King of Macedonia, had in the past been a friend and an ally, he had now been made into an enemy. This had come about because the Athenians had entered into an alliance with his brother Philip and with Derdas, who had joined forces together against Perdiccas. Perdiccas was alarmed by these moves and not only sent his agents to Sparta in order to try to involve Athens in a war with the Peloponnese, but also was approaching Corinth in order to get support for a revolt in Potidaea. He was also in communication with the Chalcidians in Thrace and with the Bottiaeans, and was urging them to revolt at the same time. All these places bordered on his own country, and his idea was that if he had them as his allies, their support would make his own military position easier.

The Athenians knew what he was doing and wished to anticipate the revolt of these cities. They were just on the point of sending out to Macedonia a force of thirty ships and 1,000 hoplites under the command of Archestratus, the son of Lycomedes, with other commanders. Now, these officers were instructed to take hostages from the Potidaeans, to destroy the fortification, and to keep a close watch on the neighbouring cities so as to prevent any movement of revolt.

58　Meanwhile the Potidaeans had sent representatives to Athens in the hope of persuading the Athenians not to make any alterations in the existing state of affairs. They also sent representatives with the Corinthians to Sparta in order to win support there in case it should be necessary. After long negotiations at Athens nothing valuable was achieved; in spite of all their efforts, the fleet for Macedonia was ordered to sail against them too. The Spartan authorities, however, promised to invade Attica if the Athenians attacked Potidaea. This, then, seemed to the Potidaeans to be the moment: they made common cause with the Chalcidians and the Bottiaeans and revolted from Athens.

Perdiccas, at this point, persuaded the Chalcidians to pull down and abandon their cities on the coast, and to settle inland at Olynthus, making that into one big city. To those who left their homes in this way he offered the use for the duration of the war with Athens of some of his own territory in Mygdonia round Lake Bolbe. The Chalcidians therefore, after destroying their cities,
59　settled inland and prepared for war. When the thirty Athenian ships arrived in Thrace they found that Potidaea and the other cities were already in a state of revolt. Their commanders considered that with the forces at their disposal it was impossible to make war both against Perdiccas and against the league of revolted cities; they therefore turned their attention to Macedonia, which had been their original objective. They established themselves on the coast and made war in cooperation with Philip and the brothers of Derdas, who had invaded the country from the interior.

60　Now that Potidaea had revolted and the thirty Athenian ships were off the coast of Macedonia, the Corinthians feared that the place might be lost and regarded its safety as their own responsibility. They therefore sent out a force of volunteers from Corinth itself and of mercenaries from the rest of the Peloponnese. Altogether this force amounted to 1,600 hoplites and 400 light troops. It was under the command of Aristeus, the son of Adeimantus, who had always been a staunch friend to the people of Potidaea. And it was largely because of his personal popularity that most of the Corinthian volunteers joined the expedition. This force reached Thrace forty days after the revolt of Potidaea.

61   The Athenians also had received the news immediately after the revolt of the cities. They heard, too, of the reinforcements under Aristeus, and they sent out against the places in revolt an army of 2,000 citizen hoplites and a fleet of forty ships. This force was commanded by Callias, the son of Calliades, with four other commanders. First they arrived at Macedonia, where they found that the original force of 1,000 had just captured Therme and were now besieging Pydna. They therefore joined in the operations against Pydna. The siege lasted for a time, but finally they came to an agreement with Perdiccas and made an alliance with him. They were forced into doing this by the need to hurry on with the campaign at Potidaea and by the arrival there of Aristeus.

Leaving Macedonia, then, they came to Beroea and from there went on to Strepsa. After making an unsuccessful attempt at capturing the place, they marched on by land to Potidaea. They had 3,000 hoplites of their own, apart from a large force of allies and 600 Macedonian cavalry from the army of Philip and Pausanias. The seventy ships sailed with them along the coast. Proceeding by short marches, they reached Gigonus on the third day and camped there.

62   The people of Potidaea and the Peloponnesian army under Aristeus had been expecting the Athenians and had made their camp on the isthmus facing Olynthus; a market for the troops had been established outside the city. The allies had chosen Aristeus as commander-in-chief of all the infantry, and given the command of the cavalry to Perdiccas. The latter had immediately once again broken his treaty of alliance with Athens and was now fighting on the side of the Potidaeans. Instead of being there in person, he sent Iolaus as deputy commander.

The plan of Aristeus was as follows: he would be on the isthmus with his own force and would there wait for an Athenian attack; the Chalcidians, the other allies from outside the isthmus, and the 200 cavalry of Perdiccas were to stay in Olynthus; this force, when the Athenians attacked the positions on the isthmus, was to take them in the rear and thus place the enemy between the two armies.

However, the Athenian general Callias and his colleagues sent out to Olynthus their Macedonian cavalry and a small force of allied troops to prevent reinforcements coming from there. They then broke up their camp and marched on Potidaea. Arriving at the isthmus, they saw the enemy making ready for battle. They, too, formed up in battle order, and soon the forces were engaged. The wing commanded by Aristeus, where the Corinthians and other picked troops were fighting, routed the troops in front of it and went after them for some distance in pursuit. But the rest of the army of Potidaeans and Peloponnesians was defeated by the Athenians and fled back behind their fortifications. Thus, when

63 Aristeus turned back from the pursuit and saw that the other part of his army had been defeated, it was difficult for him to decide which was the safest direction in which to go, whether to Olynthus or into Potidaea. In the end he decided to concentrate his troops into as small a space as possible and to force his way through into Potidaea at the double. He managed to do this by going along by the breakwater through the sea; but it was not an easy operation, as arrows and javelins were falling among his men and, though he got most of them through safely, he lost a certain number.

At the beginning of the battle, signals were shown, and those who were meant to reinforce the Potidaeans from Olynthus (which is about seven miles away and in sight of Potidaea) advanced a little way with the object of joining in. At the same time the Macedonian cavalry took up their positions to intercept them. But victory soon went to the Athenians, and the signals were lowered. The troops from Olynthus thereupon fell back again and the Macedonians rejoined the Athenians. There was therefore no cavalry in action on either side.

After the battle the Athenians put up a trophy and granted an armistice to the Potidaeans so that they could recover their dead. Nearly 300 of the Potidaeans and their allies had been killed; the Athenians had lost 150 of their own citizens, including their general, Callias.

64 The Athenians at once built and manned a counter wall to the north of the wall across the isthmus. They did not build fortifications opposite Pallene, since they did not think they were strong enough both to man their wall on the isthmus and also to cross over to Pallene and build a wall there; they were afraid that, if they

divided their force in two, the Potidaeans and their allies would attack them.

When it was reported in Athens that no fortifications had been raised against Pallene, the Athenians sent out some time later a force of 1,600 citizen hoplites under the command of Phormio, the son of Asopius. Phormio arrived at Pallene and, basing himself at Aphytis, moved slowly forward towards Potidaea, ravaging the country on his way. The Potidaeans did not come out to fight, and so he built a counter wall cutting them off from Pallene. Now, therefore, Potidaea was firmly invested by land on both sides, and at the same time Athenian ships were blockading the place from 65 the sea. Cut off as it was, Aristeus had no hope that it could survive unless some miracle happened or else events in the Peloponnese took a different turn. The advice he gave to the Potidaeans was to watch for a favourable wind and then sail away, leaving behind a garrison of 500, amongst whom the food would last longer. He himself volunteered to stay with those who were left behind. His advice, however, was not taken, and, wishing to do what he thought was best under the circumstances and at the same time to organize help from outside, he slipped through the Athenian blockade and sailed out of the town. He then lived with the Chalcidians and helped them in the fighting. Among his other actions, he organized an ambush near the city of Sermyle and destroyed a number of men there. He was also in touch with the Peloponnese and was trying to arrange for help from that quarter.

Phormio, now that the blockade had been completed, used his 1,600 troops in laying waste the country of Chalcidice and Bottiaea. He also captured some of their towns.

THE DEBATE AT SPARTA AND
DECLARATION OF WAR

66 Both the Athenians and the Peloponnesians had already grounds of complaint against each other. The grievance of Corinth was that the Athenians were besieging her own colony of Potidaea, with Corinthians and other Peloponnesians in the place: Athens, on the other hand, had her own grievances against the Pelopon-

nesians; they had supported the revolt of a city which was in alliance with her and which paid her tribute, and they had openly joined the Potidaeans in fighting against her. In spite of this, the truce was still in force and war had not yet broken out. What had been done so far had been done on the private initiative of Corinth.

67   Now, however, Corinth brought matters into the open. Potidaea was under blockade, some of her own citizens were inside, and she feared that the place might be lost. She therefore immediately urged the allies to send delegates to Sparta.[13] There her own delegates violently attacked the Athenians for having broken the truce and committed acts of aggression against the Peloponnese. The people of Aegina were on her side. Out of fear of Athens they had not sent a formal delegation, but behind the scenes they played a considerable part in fomenting war, saying that they had not been given the independence promised to them by the treaty. The Spartans also issued an invitation to their own allies and to anyone else who claimed to have suffered from Athenian aggression. They then held their usual assembly, and gave an opportunity there for delegates to express their views. Many came forward with various complaints. In particular the delegates from Megara, after mentioning a number of other grievances, pointed out that, contrary to the terms of the treaty, they were excluded from all the ports in the Athenian empire and from the market of Athens itself. The Corinthians were the last to come forward and speak, having allowed the previous speakers to do their part in hardening Spartan opinion against Athens. The Corinthian speech was as follows:

68   'Spartans, what makes you somewhat reluctant to listen to us others, if we have ideas to put forward, is the great trust and confidence which you have in your own constitution and in your own way of life. This is a quality which certainly makes you moderate in your judgements; it is also, perhaps, responsible for a kind of ignorance which you show when you are dealing with foreign affairs. Many times before now we have told you what we were likely to suffer from Athens, and on each occasion, instead of taking to heart what we were telling you, you chose instead to suspect our motives and to consider that we were speaking only about our own grievances. The result has been that you did not call together

13. On the procedure, see Appendix 1.

this meeting of our allies before the damage was done; you waited until now, when we are actually suffering from it. And of all these allies, we have perhaps the best right to speak now, since we have the most serious complaints to make. We have to complain of Athens for her insolent aggression and of Sparta for her neglect of our advice.

'If there were anything doubtful or obscure about this aggression on the whole of Hellas, our task would have been to try to put the facts before you and show you something that you did not know. As it is, long speeches are unnecessary. You can see yourselves how Athens has deprived some states of their freedom and is scheming to do the same thing for others, especially among our own allies, and that she herself has for a long time been preparing for the eventuality of war. Why otherwise should she have forcibly taken over from us the control of Corcyra? Why is she besieging Potidaea? Potidaea is the best possible base for any campaign in Thrace, and Corcyra might have contributed a very large fleet to the Peloponnesian League.

69   'And it is you who are responsible for all this. It was you who in the first place allowed the Athenians to fortify their city and build the Long Walls after the Persian War. Since then and up to the present day you have withheld freedom not only from those who have been enslaved by Athens but even from your own allies. When one is deprived of one's liberty one is right in blaming not so much the man who puts the fetters on as the one who had the power to prevent him, but did not use it – especially when such a one rejoices in the glorious reputation of having been the liberator of Hellas.

'Even at this stage it has not been easy to arrange this meeting, and even at this meeting there are no definite proposals. Why are we still considering whether aggression has taken place instead of how we can resist it? Men who are capable of real action first make their plans and then go forward without hesitation while their enemies have still not made up their minds. As for the Athenians, we know their methods and how they gradually encroach upon their neighbours. Now they are proceeding slowly because they think that your insensitiveness to the situation enables them to go on their way unnoticed; you will find that they will develop their full strength once they realize that you do see what is happening and are still doing nothing to prevent it.

'You Spartans are the only people in Hellas who wait calmly on events, relying for your defence not on action but on making people think that you will act. You alone do nothing in the early stages to prevent an enemy's expansion; you wait until your enemy has doubled his strength. Certainly you used to have the reputation of being safe and sure enough: now one wonders whether this reputation was deserved. The Persians, as we know ourselves, came from the ends of the earth and got as far as the Peloponnese before you were able to put a proper force into the field to meet them. The Athenians, unlike the Persians, live close to you, yet still you do not appear to notice them; instead of going out to meet them, you prefer to stand still and wait till you are attacked, thus hazarding everything by fighting with opponents who have grown far stronger than they were originally.

'In fact you know that the chief reason for the failure of the Persian invasion was the mistaken policy of the Persians themselves; and you know, too, that there have been many occasions when, if we managed to stand up to Athenian aggression, it was more because of Athenian mistakes than because of any help we got from you. Indeed, we can think of instances already where those who have relied on you and remained unprepared have been ruined by the confidence they placed in you.

'We should not like any of you to think that we are speaking in an unfriendly spirit. We are only remonstrating with you, as is natural when one's friends are making mistakes. Real accusations must be kept for one's enemies who have actually done one harm.

70 'Then also we think we have as much right as anyone else to point out faults in our neighbours, especially when we consider the enormous difference between you and the Athenians. To our minds, you are quite unaware of this difference; you have never yet tried to imagine what sort of people these Athenians are against whom you will have to fight – how much, indeed how completely different from you. An Athenian is always an innovator, quick to form a resolution and quick at carrying it out. You, on the other hand, are good at keeping things as they are; you never originate an idea, and your action tends to stop short of its aim. Then again,

Athenian daring will outrun its own resources; they will take risks against their better judgement, and still, in the midst of danger, remain confident. But your nature is always to do less than you could have done, to mistrust your own judgement, however sound it may be, and to assume that dangers will last for ever. Think of this, too: while you are hanging back, they never hesitate; while you stay at home, they are always abroad; for they think that the farther they go the more they will get, while you think that any movement may endanger what you have already. If they win a victory, they follow it up at once, and if they suffer a defeat, they scarcely fall back at all. As for their bodies, they regard them as expendable for their city's sake, as though they were not their own; but each man cultivates his own intelligence, again with a view to doing something notable for his city. If they aim at something and do not get it, they think that they have been deprived of what belonged to them already; whereas, if their enterprise is successful, they regard that success as nothing compared to what they will do next. Suppose they fail in some undertaking; they make good the loss immediately by setting their hopes in some other direction. Of them alone it may be said that they possess a thing almost as soon as they have begun to desire it, so quickly with them does action follow upon decision. And so they go on working away in hardship and danger all the days of their lives, seldom enjoying their possessions because they are always adding to them. Their view of a holiday is to do what needs doing; they prefer hardship and activity to peace and quiet. In a word, they are by nature incapable of either living a quiet life themselves or of allowing anyone else to do so.

71   'That is the character of the city which is opposed to you. Yet you still hang back; you will not see that the likeliest way of securing peace is this: only to use one's power in the cause of justice, but to make it perfectly plain that one is resolved not to tolerate aggression. On the contrary, your idea of proper behaviour is, firstly, to avoid harming others, and then to avoid being harmed yourselves, even if it is a matter of defending your own interests. Even if you had on your frontiers a power holding the same principles as you do, it is hard to see how such a policy could have been a success. But at the present time, as we have just pointed out to you, your

whole way of life is out of date when compared with theirs. And it is just as true in politics as it is in any art or craft: new methods must drive out old ones. When a city can live in peace and quiet, no doubt the old-established ways are best: but when one is constantly being faced by new problems, one has also to be capable of approaching them in an original way. Thus Athens, because of the very variety of her experience, is a far more modern state than you are.

'Your inactivity has done harm enough. Now let there be an end of it. Give your allies, and especially Potidaea, the help you promised, and invade Attica at once. Do not let your friends and kinsmen fall into the hands of the bitter enemies. Do not force the rest of us in despair to join a different alliance. If we did so, no one could rightly blame us – neither the gods who witnessed our oaths nor any man capable of appreciating our situation. The people who break a treaty of alliance are the ones who fail to give the help they swore to give, not those who have to look elsewhere because they have been left in the lurch. But if you will only make up your minds to act, we will stand by you. It would be an unnatural thing for us to make a change, nor could we find other allies with whom we have such close bonds. You have heard what we have to say. Think carefully over your decision. From your fathers was handed down to you the leadership of the Peloponnese. Maintain its greatness.'

72   This was the speech of the Corinthians. There happened to be already in Sparta some Athenian representatives who had come there on other business. When they heard the speeches that had been made, they decided that they, too, ought to claim a hearing. Not that they had any intention of defending themselves against any of the charges that had been made against Athens by the various cities, but they wished to make a general statement and to point out that this was an affair which needed further consideration and ought not to be decided upon at once. They wanted also to make clear how powerful their city was, to remind the elder members of the assembly of facts that were known to them, and to inform the younger ones of matters in which they were ignorant. In this way they hoped to divert their audience from the idea of war and make them incline towards letting matters rest. They therefore

approached the Spartans and said that, if there was no objection, they, too, would like to make a speech before the assembly. The Spartans invited them to do so, and they came forward and spoke as follows:

73   'This delegation of ours did not come here to enter into a controversy with your allies, but to deal with the business on which our city sent us. We observe, however, that extraordinary attacks have been made on us, and so we have come forward to speak. We shall make no reply to the charges which these cities have made against us. Your assembly is not a court of law, competent to listen to pleas either from them or from us. Our aim is to prevent you from coming to the wrong decision on a matter of great importance through paying too much attention to the views of your allies. At the same time we should like to examine the general principles of the argument used against us and to make you see that our gains have been reasonable enough and that our city is one that deserves a certain consideration.

'There is no need to talk about what happened long ago: there our evidence would be that of hearsay rather than that of eyewitnesses amongst our audience. But we must refer to the Persian War, to events well known to you all, even though you may be tired of constantly hearing the story. In our actions at that time we ventured everything for the common good; you have your share in what was gained; do not deprive us of all our share of glory and of the good that it may do us. We shall not be speaking in the spirit of one who is asking a favour, but of one who is producing evidence. Our aim is to show you what sort of a city you will have to fight against, if you make the wrong decision.

'This is our record. At Marathon we stood out against the Persians and faced them single-handed. In the later invasion, when we were unable to meet the enemy on land, we and all our people took to our ships, and joined in the battle at Salamis. It was this battle that prevented the Persians from sailing against the Peloponnese and destroying the cities one by one; for no system of mutual defence could have been organized in face of the Persian naval superiority. The best proof of this is in the conduct of the Persians themselves. Once they had lost the battle at sea they realized that their force was crippled and they immediately withdrew most of

74 their army. That, then was the result, and it proved that the fate of Hellas depended on her navy. Now, we contributed to this result in three important ways: we produced most of the ships, we provided the most intelligent of the generals, and we displayed the most unflinching courage. Out of the 400 ships, nearly two-thirds were ours: the commander was Themistocles, who was mainly responsible for the battle being fought in the straits, and this, obviously, was what saved us. You yourselves in fact, because of this, treated him with more distinction than you have ever treated any visitor from abroad. And the courage, the daring that we showed were without parallel. With no help coming to us by land, with all the states up to our frontier already enslaved, we chose to abandon our city and to sacrifice our property; then, so far from deserting the rest of our allies in the common cause or making ourselves useless to them by dispersing our forces, we took to our ships and chose the path of danger, with no grudges against you for not having come to our help earlier. So it is that we can claim to have given more than we received. There were still people living in the cities which you left behind you, and you were fighting to preserve them; when you sent out your forces you feared for yourselves much more than for us (at all events, you never put in an appearance until we had lost everything). Behind us, on the other hand, was a city that had ceased to exist; yet we still went forward and ventured our lives for this city that seemed so impossible to recover. Thus we joined you and helped to save not only ourselves but you also. But if we, like others, had been frightened about our land and had made terms with the Persians before you arrived, or if, later, we had regarded ourselves as irretrievably ruined and had lacked the courage to take to our ships, then there would no longer have been any point in your fighting the enemy at sea, since you would not have had enough ships. Instead things would have gone easily and quietly just as the Persians wished.

75 'Surely, Spartans, the courage, the resolution, and the ability which we showed then ought not to be repaid by such immoderate hostility from the Hellenes – especially so far as our empire is concerned. We did not gain this empire by force. It came to us at a time when you were unwilling to fight on to the end against the Persians. At this time our allies came to us of their own accord and

begged us to lead them. It was the actual course of events which first compelled us to increase our power to its present extent: fear of Persia was our chief motive, though afterwards we thought, too, of our own honour and our own interest. Finally there came a time when we were surrounded by enemies, when we had already crushed some revolts, when you had lost the friendly feelings that you used to have for us and had turned against us and begun to arouse our suspicion: at this point it was clearly no longer safe for us to risk letting our empire go, especially as any allies that left us would go over to you. And when tremendous dangers are involved no one can be blamed for looking to his own interest.

76   'Certainly you Spartans, in your leadership of the Peloponnese, have arranged the affairs of the various states so as to suit yourselves. And if, in the years of which we were speaking, you had gone on taking an active part in the war and had become unpopular, as we did, in the course of exercising your leadership, we have little doubt that you would have been just as hard upon your allies as we were, and that you would have been forced either to govern strongly or to endanger your own security.

'So it is with us. We have done nothing extraordinary, nothing contrary to human nature in accepting an empire when it was offered to us and then in refusing to give it up. Three very powerful motives prevent us from doing so – security, honour, and self-interest. And we were not the first to act in this way. Far from it. It has always been a rule that the weak should be subject to the strong; and besides, we consider that we are worthy of our power. Up till the present moment you, too, used to think that we were; but now, after calculating your own interest, you are beginning to talk in terms of right and wrong. Considerations of this kind have never yet turned people aside from the opportunities of aggrandizement offered by superior strength. Those who really deserve praise are the people who, while human enough to enjoy power, nevertheless pay more attention to justice than they are compelled to do by their situation. Certainly we think that if anyone else was in our position it would soon be evident whether we act with moderation or not. Yet, unreasonably enough, our very consideration for others has brought us more blame than

77   praise. For example, in law-suits with our allies arising out of con-

tracts we have put ourselves at a disadvantage, and when we arrange to have such cases tried by impartial courts in Athens, people merely say that we are overfond of going to law. No one bothers to inquire why this reproach is not made against other imperial Powers, who treat their subjects much more harshly than we do: the fact being, of course, that where force can be used there is no need to bring in the law. Our subjects, on the other hand, are used to being treated as equals; consequently, when they are disappointed in what they think right and suffer even the smallest disadvantage because of a judgement in our courts or because of the power that our empire gives us, they cease to feel grateful to us for all the advantages which we have left to them: indeed, they feel more bitterly over this slight disparity than they would feel if we, from the first, had set the law aside and had openly enriched ourselves at their expense. Under those conditions they would certainly not have disputed the fact that the weak must give in to the strong. People, in fact, seem to feel more strongly about their legal wrongs than about the wrongs inflicted on them by violence. In the first case they think they are being outdone by an equal, in the second case that they are being compelled by a superior. Certainly they put up with much worse sufferings than these when they were under the Persians, but now they think that our government is oppressive. That is natural enough, perhaps, since subject peoples always find the present time most hard to bear. But on one point we are quite certain: if you were to destroy us and to take over our empire, you would soon lose all the goodwill which you have gained because of others being afraid of us – that is, if you are going to stick to those principles of behaviour which you showed before, in the short time when you led Hellas against the Persians. Your own regulated ways of life do not mix well with the ways of others. Also it is a fact that when one of you goes abroad he follows neither his own rules nor those of the rest of Hellas.

78 'Take time, then, over your decision, which is an important one. Do not allow considerations of other people's opinions and other people's complaints to involve you in difficulties which you will feel yourselves. Think, too, of the great part that is played by the unpredictable in war: think of it now, before you are actually committed to war. The longer a war lasts, the more things tend to

depend on accidents. Neither you nor we can see into them: we
have to abide their outcome in the dark. And when people are
entering upon a war they do things the wrong way round. Action
comes first, and it is only when they have already suffered that
they begin to think. We, however, are still far removed from such
a mistaken attitude; so, to the best of our belief, are you. And so
we urge you, now, while we are both still free to make sensible
decisions, do not break the peace, do not go back upon your oaths;
instead let us settle our differences by arbitration, as is laid down in
the treaty. If you will not do so, we shall have as our witnesses the
gods who heard our oaths. You will have begun the war, and we
shall attempt to meet you in any and every field of action that you
may choose.'

79   The Athenians spoke as I have described. Now the Spartans had
heard the complaints made by their allies against Athens and also
the Athenian reply. They therefore requested all outsiders to leave
and discussed the situation among themselves. Most people's views
tended to the same conclusion – namely, that Athens was already
acting aggressively and that war should be declared without delay.
However, the Spartan King Archidamus, a man who had a reputation for both intelligence and moderation, came forward and
made the following speech:

80   'Spartans, in the course of my life I have taken part in many
wars, and I see among you people of the same age as I am. They
and I have had experience, and so are not likely to share in what
may be a general enthusiasm for war, nor to think that war is a
good thing or a safe thing. And you will find, if you look carefully
into the matter, that this present war which you are now discussing
is not likely to be anything on a small scale. When we are engaged
with Peloponnesians and neighbours, the forces on both sides are
of the same type, and we can strike rapidly where we wish to
strike. With Athens it is different. Here we shall be engaged with
people who live far off, people also who have the widest experience of the sea and who are extremely well equipped in all other
directions, very wealthy both as individuals and as a state, with
ships and cavalry and hoplites, with a population bigger than that
of any other place in Hellas, and then, too, with numbers of allies
who pay tribute to them. How, then, can we irresponsibly start a

war with such a people? What have we to rely upon if we rush into it unprepared? Our navy? It is inferior to theirs, and if we are to give proper attention to it and build it up to their strength, that will take time. Or are we relying on our wealth? Here we are at an even greater disadvantage: we have no public funds, and it is

81 no easy matter to secure contributions from private sources. Perhaps there is ground for confidence in the superiority which we have in heavy infantry and in actual numbers, assets which will enable us to invade and devastate their land. Athens, however, controls plenty of land outside Attica and can import what she wants by sea. And if we try to make her allies revolt from her, we shall have to support them with a fleet, since most of them are on the islands. What sort of war, then, are we going to fight? If we can neither defeat them at sea nor take away from them the resources on which their navy depends, we shall do ourselves more harm than good. We shall then find that we can no longer even make an honourable peace, especially if it is thought that it was we who began the quarrel. For we must not bolster ourselves up with the false hope that if we devastate their land, the war will soon be over. I fear that it is more likely that we shall be leaving it to our children after us. So convinced am I that the Athenians have too much pride to become the slaves of their own land, or to shrink back from warfare as though they were inexperienced in it.

82 'Not that I am suggesting that we should calmly allow them to injure our allies and should turn a blind eye to their machinations. What I do suggest is that we should not take up arms at the present moment; instead we should send to them and put our grievances before them; we should not threaten war too openly, though at the same time we should make it clear that we are not going to let them have their own way. In the meantime we should be making our own preparations by winning over new allies both among Hellenes and among foreigners – from any quarter, in fact, where we can increase our naval and financial resources. No one can blame us for securing our own safety by taking foreigners as well as Greeks into our alliance when we are, as is the fact, having our position undermined by the Athenians. At the same time we must put our own affairs in order. If they pay attention to our diplomatic

protests, so much the better. If they do not, then, after two or three
years have passed, we shall be in a much sounder position and can
attack them, if we decide to do so. And perhaps when they see that
our actual strength is keeping pace with the language that we use,
they will be more inclined to give way, since their land will still
be untouched and, in making up their minds, they will be thinking
of advantages which they still possess and which have not yet been
destroyed. For you must think of their land as though it was a
hostage in your possession, and all the more valuable the better it
is looked after. You should spare it up to the last possible moment,
and avoid driving them to a state of desperation in which you will
find them much harder to deal with. If now in our present state of
unpreparedness we lay their land waste, hurried into this course
by the complaints of our allies, I warn you to take care that our
action does not bring to the Peloponnese still more shame and still
greater difficulties. As for complaints, whether they come from
cities or from private individuals, they are capable of arrangement;
but when war is declared by our whole confederacy for the sake
of the interests of some of us, and when it is impossible to foresee
the course that the war will take, then an honourable settlement is
not an easy thing at all.

83   'Let no one call it cowardice if we, in all our numbers, hesitate
before attacking a single city. They have just as many allies as we
have, and their allies pay tribute. And war is not so much a matter
of armaments as of the money which makes armaments effective:
particularly is this true in a war fought between a land power and
a sea power. So let us first of all see to our finances and, until we
have done so, avoid being swept away by speeches from our allies.
It is we who shall bear most of the responsibility for what happens
later, whether it is good or bad; we should therefore be allowed
the time to look into some of these possibilities at our leisure.

84   'As for being slow and cautious – which is the usual criticism
made against us – there is nothing to be ashamed of in that. If you
take something on before you are ready for it, hurry at the beginning will mean delay at the end. Besides, the city in which we live
has always been free and always famous. "Slow" and "cautious"
can equally well be "wise" and "sensible". Certainly it is because
we possess these qualities that we are the only people who do not

become arrogant when we are successful, and who in times of stress are less likely to give in than others. We are not carried away by the pleasure of hearing ourselves praised when people are urging us towards dangers that seem to us unnecessary; and we are no more likely to give in shamefacedly to other people's views when they try to spur us on by their accusations. Because of our well-ordered life we are both brave in war and wise in council. Brave, because self-control is based upon a sense of honour, and honour is based on courage. And we are wise because we are not so highly educated as to look down upon our laws and customs, and are too rigorously trained in self-control to be able to disobey them. We are trained to avoid being too clever in matters that are of no use – such as being able to produce an excellent theoretical criticism of one's enemies' dispositions, and then failing in practice to do quite so well against them. Instead we are taught that there is not a great deal of difference between the way we think and the way others think, and that it is impossible to calculate accurately events that are determined by chance. The practical measures that we take are always based on the assumption that our enemies are not unintelligent. And it is right and proper for us to put our hopes in the reliability of our own precautions rather than in the possibility of our opponent making mistakes. There is no need to suppose that human beings differ very much one from another: but it is true that the ones who come out on top are the ones who have been trained in the hardest school.

85   'Let us never give up this discipline which our fathers have handed down to us and which we still preserve and which has always done us good. Let us not be hurried, and in one short day's space come to a decision which will so profoundly affect the lives of men and their fortunes, the fates of cities and their national honour. We ought to take time over such a decision. And we, more than others, can afford to take time, because we are strong. As for the Athenians, I advise sending a mission to them about Potidaea and also about the other cases where our allies claim to have been ill treated. Especially is this the right thing to do since the Athenians themselves are prepared to submit to arbitration, and when one party offers this it is quite illegal to attack him first, as though he was definitely in the wrong. And at the same time

carry on your preparations for war. This decision is the best one you can make for yourselves, and is also the one most likely to inspire fear in your enemies.'

After this speech of Archidamus, Sthenelaidas, one of the ephors of that year, came forward to make the final speech, which was as follows:

86 'I do not understand these long speeches which the Athenians make. Though they said a great deal in praise of themselves, they made no attempt to contradict the fact that they are acting aggressively against our allies and against the Peloponnese. And surely, if it is the fact that they had a good record in the past against the Persians and now have a bad record as regards us, then they deserve to pay double for it, since, though they were once good, they have now turned out bad. We are the same then and now, and if we are sensible, we shall not allow any aggression against our allies and shall not wait before we come to their help. They are no longer waiting before being ill treated. Others may have a lot of money and ships and horses, but we have good allies, and we ought not to betray them to the Athenians. And this is not a matter to be settled by law-suits and by words: it is not because of words that our own interests are suffering. Instead we should come to the help of our allies quickly and with all our might. And let no one try to tell us that when we are being attacked we should sit down and discuss matters; these long discussions are rather for those who are meditating aggression themselves. Therefore, Spartans, cast your votes for the honour of Sparta and for war! Do not allow the Athenians to grow still stronger! Do not entirely betray your allies! Instead let us, with the help of heaven, go forward to meet the aggressor!'

87 After this speech he himself, in his capacity of ephor, put the question to the Spartan assembly. They make their decisions by acclamation, not by voting, and Sthenelaidas said at first that he could not decide on which side the acclamations were the louder. This was because he wanted to make them show their opinions openly and so make them all the more enthusiastic for war. He therefore said: 'Spartans, those of you who think that the treaty has been broken and that the Athenians are aggressors, get up and stand on one side. Those who do not think so, stand on the other side,' and he pointed out to them where they were to stand. They

then rose to their feet and separated into two divisions. The great majority were of the opinion that the treaty had been broken.

They then summoned their allies to the assembly and told them that they had decided that Athens was acting aggressively, but that they wanted to have all their allies with them when they put the vote, so that, if they decided to make war, it should be done on the basis of a unanimous resolution.

Afterwards the allied delegates, having got their own way, returned home. Later the Athenian representatives, when they had finished the business for which they had come, also returned. This decision of the assembly that the treaty had been broken took place in the fourteenth year of the thirty years' truce which was made 88 after the affair of Euboea. The Spartans voted that the treaty had been broken and that war should be declared not so much because they were influenced by the speeches of their allies as because they were afraid of the further growth of Athenian power, seeing, as they did, that already the greater part of Hellas was under the control of Athens.

THE PENTECONTAETIA [14]

89 The following is an account of how Athens came to be in the position to gain such strength.

After the Persians had retreated from Europe, defeated by the Hellenes on sea and land, and after those of them who had fled by sea to Mycale had been destroyed, the Spartan king Leotychides, who had commanded the Hellenes at Mycale, returned home, taking with him the allies from the Peloponnese. The Athenians, however, with the allies from Ionia and the Hellespont who had already revolted from the king of Persia, stayed behind and besieged the city of Sestos, which was occupied by the Persians. They spent the winter there and finally took the place after the Persians had evacuated it. They then sailed out of the Hellespont and dispersed to their own cities.

Meanwhile the Athenian people, as soon as their land was free from foreign occupation, began to bring back their children and

14. On this digression, see the introduction, pp. 15-16, 18.

wives and what property they had left from the places where they had hidden them away. They also started on the rebuilding of their city and their fortifications; for only small portions of their surrounding wall were still standing, and most of their houses were in ruins, the few remaining ones being those in which important Persian officers had had their quarters.

90   When the Spartans heard of what was going on they sent an embassy to Athens. This was partly because they themselves did not like the idea of Athens or any other city being fortified, but chiefly because they were urged on by their allies, who were alarmed both by the sudden growth of Athenian sea-power and by the daring which the Athenians had shown in the war against the Persians. The Spartans proposed that not only should Athens refrain from building her own fortifications, but that she should join them in pulling down all the fortifications which still existed in cities outside the Peloponnese. In making this suggestion to the Athenians they concealed their real meaning and their real fears; the idea was, they said, that if there was another Persian invasion, the Persians would have no strong base from which to operate, such as they had in Thebes; and that the Peloponnese was capable of serving the needs of everyone, both as a place of refuge and as a place from which to attack.

After this speech from the Spartans, the Athenians, on the advice of Themistocles, immediately sent them away with the reply that they would send an embassy to discuss the points that had been raised. Themistocles then proposed that they should send him to Sparta at once, but should not for the time being send the other delegates elected to go with him; instead they should wait until they had built their fortifications high enough to be able to be defended. Meanwhile the whole population of the city was to work at building the walls; no private house or public building which might be of any use to the work was to be spared, but must in every case be demolished.

So Themistocles set off, leaving these instructions behind him and indicating that he himself would arrange everything else that needed arranging in Sparta. When he arrived there he did not approach the Spartan government, but kept on putting things off on various excuses. If anyone in authority asked him why he did not come before the Assembly, he replied that he was waiting for his colleagues, that they had not been able to leave Athens because of urgent business, but that he expected them to come soon and 91 was surprised that they had not arrived already. The Spartans believed what Themistocles said because of the respect in which they held him; but as other people kept on arriving, all positively asserting that the fortifications were being built and had already reached a certain height, they did not see how they could reject such information. Themistocles, realizing this, told them that instead of being led astray by rumours they ought to send some reliable people of their own who could go and see for themselves and come back with a correct report. This the Spartans did, and Themistocles sent secretly to Athens, telling the Athenians to keep the Spartan envoys there, to avoid, if possible, putting them under open constraint, but not to let them go until he and his colleagues had got back. For his fellow delegates – Abronichus, the son of Lysicles, and Aristides, the son of Lysimachus – had now arrived, and had told him that the fortifications were now sufficiently far advanced. Themistocles therefore was afraid that the Spartans might now refuse to let them go, once they received accurate information about what had happened.

The Athenians followed his instructions and detained the Spartan delegates. Themistocles approached the Spartan authorities and at last spoke to them openly. He said that Athens was now fortified, and fortified sufficiently well to be able to protect her people: that if the Spartans or their allies wanted to send embassies to Athens on any subject, they should in future go there prepared to recognize that the Athenians were capable of making up their own minds both about their own interests and about the interests of the rest of Hellas. He pointed out that when the Athenians decided to abandon their city and take to their ships, it was not in consultation with Sparta that they adopted that daring resolution, and that whenever they had joined in counsel with the Spartans it was clear that no one else had offered better advice. And now they thought it better that their city should be fortified; it was better for their own citizens and also would be an advantage to the whole alliance; for it was only on the basis of equal strength that equal and fair discussions on the common interest could be held. This meant either that no city in the alliance should be fortified or else that what the Athenians had done should be approved.

92   After listening to this, the Spartans showed no open signs of displeasure towards Athens. The fact was that their original embassy to the Athenian people had not stated any intention to prevent the action but had only appeared to offer advice. Also this was a time when Sparta was particularly friendly to Athens, because of the courage displayed by Athens against the Persians. All the same the Spartans had not got their own way and secretly they felt aggrieved because of it. The delegates from both states returned home without making any complaints.

93   In this way the Athenians fortified their city in a very short time. Even today one can see that the building was done in a hurry. The foundations are made of different sorts of stone, sometimes not shaped so as to fit, but laid down just as each was brought up at the time; there are many pillars taken from tombs and fragments of sculpture mixed in with the rest. For the city boundaries were extended on all sides, and so in their haste they used everything that came to hand, sparing nothing.

Themistocles also persuaded them to complete the walls of Piraeus, which had been begun previously during his year of office as archon. He liked the position of the place, with its three natural harbours, and he considered that if the Athenians became a seafaring people they would have every advantage in adding to their power.[15] Indeed it was he who first ventured to tell the Athenians that their future was on the sea. Thus he at once began to join in laying the foundations of their empire.

In breadth the wall was built according to his specifications, just as one can see it today around Piraeus. There was room for two wagons to pass each other with their stones for the building, and the space in between the outer surfaces was not filled in with rubble or clay; instead large blocks of stone were cut and fitted together, with clamps of iron and lead on the outside. The height of the finished wall was about half what he planned. With these great and thick walls he intended to repulse all enemy attacks, and

15. Earlier, the Greek practice was to beach their ships, so that the main Athenian 'harbour' was at Phalerum. It was only now that the great natural harbour of the Piraeus came to the fore.

he considered that they could be perfectly well defended by a few troops of inferior quality, so that the rest would be able to serve in the navy. It was particularly on the navy that his thoughts were concentrated. He realized, I imagine, that it was easier for a Persian force to approach Athens by sea than by land, and in his view Piraeus was a more valuable place than the main city of Athens. Indeed, the advice that he constantly gave to the Athenians was that if ever they should be hard pressed on land they should go down to Piraeus, take to their ships, and defy all comers.

It was in this way, directly after the Persian withdrawal, that the Athenians fortified their city and generally strengthened their position.

94   Soon afterwards Pausanias, the son of Cleombrotus, was sent out from Sparta in command of the Hellenic forces. He had with him twenty ships from the Peloponnese; the Athenians joined his force with thirty ships and there were a number more from the other allies. They went first to Cyprus and won over most of the island; later they went against Byzantium, which was in Persian occupation, and, still under the command of Pausanias, forced the place
95   to surrender. But Pausanias had already begun to reveal the arrogance of his nature, and was becoming unpopular with the Hellenes, particularly so with the Ionians and those who had just recently been liberated from Persian domination. These states approached the Athenians, asking them, since they were their own kinsmen, to take them under their protection and, if Pausanias acted in a dictatorial manner, not to allow it. These approaches were welcomed by the Athenians, who made up their minds to put a check on Pausanias and to arrange matters generally in a way that would best suit their own interests.

Meanwhile the Spartans recalled Pausanias to face a court of inquiry in connection with various reports that they had received. Serious charges had been made against him by Hellenes arriving at Sparta: instead of acting as commander-in-chief, he appeared to be trying to set himself up as a dictator. It happened that he was recalled just at the time when, because of his unpopularity, the allies, apart from the soldiers from the Peloponnese, had gone over to the side of the Athenians.

At Sparta Pausanias was condemned for various acts of injustice against individuals, but he was acquitted on all the main counts: one of the most serious charges was that he was collaborating with the Persians, and there seemed to be very good evidence for this. Instead of sending him out again as commander-in-chief, they sent Dorcis and other officers with quite a small force. But by this time the allies were no longer willing to accept them as supreme commanders. Realizing this, the Spartans went back, and afterwards Sparta sent out no other commanders. They feared that when their officers went overseas they would become corrupted, as they had seen happen in the case of Pausanias, and at the same time they no longer wanted to be burdened with the war against Persia. They regarded the Athenians as being perfectly capable of exercising the command and as being also at that time friendly to themselves.

96   So Athens took over the leadership, and the allies, because of their dislike of Pausanias, were glad to see her do so. Next the Athenians assessed the various contributions to be made for the war against Persia, and decided which states should furnish money and which states should send ships – the object being to compensate themselves for their losses by ravaging the territory of the King of Persia. At this time the officials known as 'Hellenic Treasurers' were first appointed by the Athenians. These officials received the tribute, which was the name given to the contributions in money. The original sum fixed for the tribute was 460 talents.[16] The treasury of the League was at Delos, and representative meetings were held in the temple there.

97   The leadership of the Athenians began with allies who were originally independent states and reached their decision in general congress. I shall now describe the use they made of it, both in war and in their management of the League, during the period from the end of the Persian until the beginning of the Peloponnesian War. Some of these actions were against the Persians, some against their own allies when they revolted, some against the Peloponnesian Powers with whom on various occasions they became involved. I am giving this account and making this digression from my main narrative because this is a period that has not been dealt with by previous writers, whose subjects have been either Hellenic

16. See Appendix 2.

history before the Persian Wars or else the Persian Wars themselves. The only one of them who has touched upon this period is Hellanicus, in his *Attic History*, but he has not given much space to the subject and he is inaccurate in his dates. At the same time the history of these years will show how the Athenian Empire came into being.

98 The first action of the Athenians was the siege of Eion, a town on the Strymon occupied by the Persians.[17] Under the command of Cimon, the son of Miltiades, they captured this place and made slaves of the inhabitants. Then they turned to the island of Scyros in the Aegean, which was populated by Dolopians. They enslaved the inhabitants and colonized the island themselves. Next there was a war with the Carystians, who were not supported by the rest of Euboea. In the end Carystus surrendered on terms. After this Naxos left the League and the Athenians made war on the place. After a siege Naxos was forced back to allegiance. This was the first case when the original constitution of the League was broken and an allied city lost its independence, and the process was continued in the cases of the other allies as various circumstances

99 arose. The chief reasons for these revolts were failures to produce the right amount of tribute or the right numbers of ships, and sometimes a refusal to produce any ships at all. For the Athenians insisted on obligations being exactly met, and made themselves unpopular by bringing the severest pressure to bear on allies who were not used to making sacrifices and did not want to make them. In other ways, too, the Athenians as rulers were no longer popular as they used to be: they bore more than their fair share of the actual fighting, but this made it all the easier for them to force back into the alliance any state that wanted to leave it. For this position it was the allies themselves who were to blame. Because of this reluctance of theirs to face military service, most of them, to avoid serving abroad, had assessments made by which, instead of producing ships, they were to pay a corresponding sum of money. The result was that the Athenian navy grew strong at their expense, and when they revolted they always found themselves inadequately armed and inexperienced in war.

100 Next came the battles of the river Eurymedon in Pamphylia,

17. In 476-5 B.C.

fought on land and on sea by the Athenians and their allies against the Persians. In both battles the Athenians won the victory on the same day under the command of Cimon, the son of Miltiades, and they captured or destroyed the entire Phoenician fleet of 200 triremes.

Some time later occurred the revolt of Thasos.[18] This was caused by a dispute over the markets on the mainland opposite in Thrace, and over the mine under the control of the Thasians. The Athenians sailed to Thasos with their fleet, won a naval engagement, and landed on the island. About the same time they sent out to the river Strymon 10,000 colonists from their own citizens and from allied states to settle in the place then known as Nine Ways, but now called Amphipolis. They occupied Nine Ways, driving out the Edonians who held the place, but when they advanced farther into the interior of Thrace their force was cut to pieces at the Edonian town of Drabescus by a combined army of Thracians, who regarded the founding of a colony at Nine Ways as an act of hostility against themselves.

101   Meanwhile the people of Thasos, who had been defeated in battle and were now besieged, appealed to Sparta and urged her to come to their help by invading Attica. The Spartans, without informing Athens of their intentions, promised to do so, and would have done so if they had not been prevented by the earthquake which happened then and by the simultaneous revolt and secession to Ithome of the helots and of some of the perioeci,[19] the Thuriats and the Aethaeans. The helots were mostly descendants of the ancient Messenians, who had been enslaved in the famous war. Thus they all came to be called Messenians. So Sparta had a war on her hands against the rebels in Ithome, and the Thasians, in the third year of the siege, had to accept the Athenian terms: their walls were demolished and their navy surrendered; they were ordered to pay an indemnity immediately and to pay tribute in future;

18. About 465 B.C.

19. The helots were the servile population, first of Laconia and later also of Messenia, assigned to individual Spartans for work on the land and other services. The perioeci, in contrast, were free Greeks, living in their own Laconian communities, but subject to Spartan control in external affairs and obligated to provide military contingents to the Spartan armics.

they surrendered their rights on the mainland and also the mine there.

102   And now the Spartans, finding that their war in Ithome showed no signs of ending, appealed for help to their allies, including Athens, and the Athenians came to Sparta with a considerable force under the command of Cimon. The chief reason that they asked for Athenian help was that the Athenians had the reputation of being good at siege operations, and, after a long siege, it became clear to the Spartans that they themselves lacked experience in this department of warfare; for otherwise they would have succeeded in taking the place by assault. This expedition was the occasion for the first open quarrel between Athens and Sparta. The Spartans, failing to capture Ithome by assault, grew afraid of the enterprise and the unorthodoxy of the Athenians; they reflected, too, that they were of a different nationality and feared that, if they stayed on in the Peloponnese, they might listen to the people in Ithome and become the sponsors of some revolutionary policy. So, while keeping the rest of their allies, they sent the Athenians home again, not saying openly what their suspicions were, but merely declaring that they had no further need of Athenian help. The Athenians, however, realized that they were not being sent away for any such honourable reason as this, and saw that in fact they had become in some way suspect. They were deeply offended, considering that this was not the sort of treatment that they deserved from Sparta, and, as soon as they had returned, they denounced the original treaty of alliance which had been made against the Persians and allied themselves with Sparta's enemy, Argos. At the same time both Argos and Athens made an alliance on exactly the same terms with the Thessalians.

103   Meanwhile the rebels in Ithome after ten years' fighting[20] were unable to hold out longer, and came to terms with Sparta, the terms being that they should have a safe conduct to leave the Peloponnese and should never set foot in it again: if any of them was caught there in future, he should be the slave of whoever caught him. There was also an oracle from Delphi which the

20. This figure has been the cause of endless controversy. One plausible solution is to read 'four' for 'ten' in the manuscripts: the evidence that the revolt did not last ten years is firm.

Spartans had and which instructed them to let go the suppliant of
Zeus at Ithome. So they left the country with their wives and
children, and the Athenians, because of the ill feeling against Sparta
which had already developed, received the exiles and settled them
in the town of Naupactus, which they had recently taken from the
Ozolian Locrians.

At this time Megara also joined the Athenian alliance, abandoning her alliance with Sparta because the Corinthians were attacking
her in a war concerning the frontier boundaries. Thus the Athenians held Megara and Pegae, and built for the Megarians their long
walls from the city to Nisaea, garrisoning them with Athenian
troops. It was chiefly because of this that the Corinthians began to
conceive such a bitter hatred for Athens.

104   About this time Inaros, the son of Psammetichus, a Libyan and
the King of the Libyans bordering on Egypt, starting out from
Marea, the town south of Pharos, organized the revolt of nearly the
whole of Egypt from the Persian King Artaxerxes. After taking
over power himself he called in the Athenians to help him. The
Athenians happened to be engaged in a campaign against Cyprus
with 200 ships of their own and of their allies; they abandoned this
campaign, came to Egypt, and sailed from the sea up the Nile.
They gained control of the river and of two-thirds of Memphis,
and then attempted to subdue the remaining third, which was
called the White Castle and inside which were the Persians and
Medes who had escaped and those of the Egyptians who had not
joined in the revolt.

105   At this time, too, the Athenians sent out a fleet and made a landing at Haliae. Here they were engaged by a force of Corinthians
and Epidaurians, and the Corinthians were victorious. Later there
was a sea battle of Cecryphalia between the Athenian and Peloponnesian fleets, and the Athenians were victorious.

After this war broke out between Athens and Aegina, and there
was a big battle at sea off Aegina between the Athenians and the
Aeginetans, with the support of allies on both sides. The battle was
won by the Athenians, who captured seventy enemy ships. They
then landed on Aegina and started to besiege the place, under the
command of Leocrates, the son of Stroebus. At this point the
Peloponnesians, wishing to relieve Aegina, made a landing in the

island with 300 hoplites who had previously been serving with the Corinthians and Epidaurians. At the same time the Corinthians and their allies seized the heights of Geraneia and moved down into the Megarid, believing that it would be impossible for the Athenians to come to the relief of Megara, since they had two large forces already serving abroad in Aegina and in Egypt; and, they thought, if Athens did manage to relieve Megara, she would have to withdraw her troops from Aegina. The Athenians, however, did nothing of the kind. They raised in the city a force out of the old men and the very young who had been left behind and marched to Megara under the command of Myronides. Here an indecisive battle was fought between them and the Corinthians, and when the battle was broken off, each side considered that it had had the advantage. However, after the Corinthians had withdrawn, the Athenians, who had in fact done best in the fighting, set up a trophy. About twelve days later the Corinthians, who had had to suffer the taunts of the older people in their own city, made their preparations, marched out, and put up a trophy of their own to prove that the victory had been theirs. The Athenians came out against them from Megara, overwhelmed the contingent that was

106 setting up the trophy, and then engaged and defeated the rest of their enemy. As the defeated Corinthians were retreating, quite a large section of their army, coming under severe pressure and being uncertain of its route, plunged into an enclosure on someone's estate which had a deep ditch all round it so that there was no way out. Seeing what had happened, the Athenians closed up the main entrance with their hoplites and, surrounding the rest of the enclosure with light-armed troops, stoned to death all who were inside. This was a very severe blow to the Corinthians. The main body of their army fell back on Corinth.

107 At about this time the Athenians began to build their two long walls down to the sea, one to Phalerum and one to Piraeus. And at the same time the Phocians started a campaign against Doris, the original homeland of the Spartans, containing the towns of Boeum, Cytinium, and Erineum. When they had captured one of these places the Spartans came to the assistance of the Dorians with a force of 1,500 hoplites of their own and 10,000 of their allies. This force was commanded by Nicomedes, the son of Cleombrotus,

acting as deputy for the Spartan King Pleistoanax, who was still under age. The Spartans compelled the Phocians to come to terms and to give back the town which they had taken. They then began to think of their return journey. If they went by sea, across the Gulf of Crisa, the Athenians would be able to sail up with their fleet and stop them; nor did the route across Geraneia appear to be a safe one, since the Athenians held Megara and Pegae. The passes over Geraneia are difficult ones and were always guarded by the Athenians; moreover, on this occasion the Spartans had information that the Athenians had every intention of preventing them from taking this route. It seemed best, therefore, to stay in Boeotia and wait and see what the safest line of march would be. In this course they were also influenced by the fact that there was a party in Athens who were secretly negotiating with them in the hope of putting an end to democratic government and preventing the building of the Long Walls.

108   The Athenians marched out against them with their whole army, supported by 1,000 troops from Argos and by contingents from their other allies, making up altogether a force of 14,000 men. They made this attack partly because they thought that the Spartans were in difficulties about their way back, and partly because they had some suspicions of the plot to overthrow the democracy.

The battle was fought at Tanagra in Boeotia, and, after great losses on both sides, the Spartans and their allies were victorious. The Spartans then marched down into the Megarid, and, after cutting down some of the plantations of trees, returned home through Geraneia and past the Isthmus. The Athenians, on the sixty-second day after the battle, marched into Boeotia under the command of Myronides. They defeated the Boeotians in battle at Oenophyta and conquered the whole of Boeotia and Phocis. They pulled down the fortifications of Tanagra and took as hostages a hundred of the richest people among the Opuntian Locrians. Meanwhile they finished the building of their own Long Walls. Shortly afterwards Aegina surrendered, and was forced to destroy her fortifications, to hand over her fleet, and to agree to pay tribute in the future. Then, too, the Athenians, under the command of Tolmides, the son of Tolmaeus, sailed round the Peloponnese, burnt the Spartan dockyards, captured the Corinthian city of

Chalcis, and, after making a landing at Sicyon, defeated the Sicyonians in battle.

109   Meanwhile the Athenian and allied force in Egypt was still engaged, and suffered all the chances and changes of war. At first the Athenians were masters of Egypt, and the King of Persia sent to Sparta a Persian named Megabazus with money to bribe the Spartans to invade Attica and so force the Athenians to recall their fleet from Egypt. These negotiations, however, were unsuccessful, and as the money was being spent without any results, Megabazus and what remained of it were recalled to Asia. The King then sent out to Egypt another Persian, Megabazus, the son of Zopyrus, with a large army. He arrived by land, defeated the Egyptians and their allies in battle, and drove the Hellenes out of Memphis. In the end he penned them up on the island of Prosopitis and besieged them there for eighteen months. Finally he drained the channels round the island by diverting the water elsewhere. The ships were thus left high and dry; most of the island was connected with the mainland,

110 and he captured it by marching across to it on foot. So, after six years of war, this great venture of the Hellenes came to nothing. Out of the whole great force a few managed to make their way through Libya and find safety in Cyrene, but nearly all were destroyed. Egypt once more passed into the control of the King of Persia, except that Amyrtaeus, the King in the marshes, still kept his independence. Because of the size of the marshes it was impossible to capture him: also the Egyptians who live in the marshes are the most warlike of their race. Inaros, the King of the Libyans, who had been the person responsible for the Egyptian revolt, was betrayed to the Persians and crucified. Meanwhile fifty triremes from Athens and the rest of the League had sailed out to relieve the forces in Egypt. They put in at the Mendesian mouth of the Nile, having no idea of what had happened. Here they were under attack from the land by the Persian army and from the sea by the Phoenician fleet. Most of the ships were lost, though a few managed to escape. This was the end of the great expedition against Egypt made by the Athenians and their allies.

111   Meanwhile Orestes, the son of the King of Thessaly Echecratides, was exiled from his country and persuaded the Athenians to restore him. The Athenians took with them a force of Boeotians and

Phocians, who were now their allies, and marched to Pharsalus in Thessaly. Here they dominated the country – though without being able to go far from their camp, being prevented by the Thessalian cavalry – but they failed to capture the town or to secure any other of the objects of the expedition, and they returned home again with Orestes, not having achieved any results.

Shortly afterwards a force of 1,000 Athenians embarked at Pegae (which was now in Athenian control) and sailed along the coast to Sicyon. This force was under the command of Pericles, the son of Xanthippus. They made a landing at Sicyon and defeated in battle the troops who opposed them. Immediately afterwards they took with them the Achaeans, sailed across the gulf, and made an attack on the Acarnanian town of Oeniadae. They besieged this place, but failed to capture it. They then returned home.

112   Three years later a five years' truce was made between Athens and the Peloponnese. Having no Hellenic war on their hands, the Athenians, under the command of Cimon, made an expedition against Cyprus with 200 ships of their own and of their allies. Sixty of these were detached to go to Egypt at the request of Amyrtaeus, the King in the marshes; with the rest they laid siege to Citium. Cimon's death, however, and also a shortage of provisions made them leave Citium. Then, when they were sailing off Salamis in Cyprus, they fought both by land and sea with an army and a fleet of Phoenicians, Cyprians, and Cilicians. They were victorious in both battles, and then went home together with the sixty ships which had returned from Egypt.

After this the Spartans engaged in the campaign known as the sacred war. They took over the temple at Delphia and give it back to the Delphians. As soon as they had retired, the Athenians marched out, took the temple again, and gave it back to the Phocians.

113   Some time after this the exiled party among the Boeotians gained possession of Orchomenus, Chaeronea, and some other Boeotian towns. The Athenians, under the command of Tolmides, the son of Tolmaeus, marched against these enemy strongholds with a force of 1,000 of their own hoplites and contingents from their allies. They captured Chaeronea, made slaves of the inhabitants, and left a garrison in the town before retiring. On their way back

they were attacked at Coronea by the Boeotian exiles from Orchomenus supported by Locrians, by exiles from Euboea, and by others who shared their political views. This force defeated the Athenians, killing some of them and taking others alive. The Athenians then made a treaty by which they got back their prisoners at the price of evacuating the whole of Boeotia. The exiled party among the Boeotians came back into power and the other states also regained their independence.

114   Not long after this, Euboea revolted from Athens. Pericles had already crossed over to the island with an Athenian army when he received the news that Megara had revolted, that the Peloponnesians were on the point of invading Attica, and that the Megarians had destroyed the Athenian garrisons except for a few who had managed to escape to Nisaea; in making this revolt Megara had called in the aid of Corinth, Sicyon, and Epidaurus. Pericles hurriedly brought the army back from Euboea, and soon afterwards the Peloponnesians, under the command of the Spartan King Pleistoanax, the son of Pausanias, invaded Attica, laying waste the country as far as Eleusis and Thria. Then, without advancing any farther, they returned home.

The Athenians, under the command of Pericles, crossed over again into Euboea and subdued the whole island. Its future status was defined by the peace terms, except in the case of Hestiaea, where they drove out the inhabitants and occupied their land themselves.

115   Soon after they had returned from Euboea the Athenians made a thirty years' truce with Sparta and her allies: Athens gave up Nisaea, Pegae, Troezen, and Achaea – all places which they had seized from the Peloponnesians.

In the sixth year of the truce war broke out between Samos and Miletus over the question of Priene. After having had the worst of the fighting the Milesians came to Athens and lodged violent protests against the Samians. Their cause was supported by various private individuals from Samos itself who wished to set up there a different form of government. So the Athenians sailed to Samos with forty ships and established a democracy there. They took fifty boys and fifty men as hostages and kept them in Lemnos. Then, leaving a garrison behind in Samos, they returned home.

However, some of the Samians, instead of staying on the island, had fled to the mainland. These entered into communications with the leading oligarchs still in the city and also made an alliance with Pissuthnes, the son of Hystaspes, who at that time was the Persian Governor at Sardis. They raised a force of about 700 mercenaries, and passed over into Samos under cover of night. First they made an attack on the democratic party and imprisoned most of the leaders; then they rescued the hostages from Lemnos and declared themselves independent. They handed over to Pissuthnes the troops in the Athenian garrison and the Athenian officials who had been left in Samos, and at once made preparations for an attack on Miletus. At the same time Byzantium joined them in revolting from Athens.

116   When the Athenians heard of this they sailed against Samos with a fleet of sixty ships. Sixteen of these were not brought into action: some had been sent to Caria to watch the movements of the Phoenician fleet; others had gone to Chios and Lesbos with orders to send reinforcements. The remaining forty-four, under the command of Pericles and nine other commanders, fought, off the island of Tragia, with a Samian fleet of seventy ships which was returning from Miletus and included twenty transports. The result was a victory for the Athenians.

Later they were reinforced by forty ships from Athens and twenty-five from Chios and Lesbos. Having landed on the island and established their superiority with their ground forces, they built three walls to blockade the city, which was already blockaded from the sea. Pericles then took sixty ships from the fleet anchored off Samos and sailed away at full speed for Caunus and Caria, since news had arrived that the Phoenician fleet was on its way against them. Stesagoras and others, with five ships, had actually left

117 Samos and gone to enlist the aid of the Phoenicians. During Pericles' absence the Samians put out to sea in a surprise attack; they fell upon the Athenian camp, which had not been fortified, destroyed the ships that were posted to keep a look-out, and defeated in battle the other ships that were launched to meet them. So for about fourteen days they controlled the sea round their island and were free to bring in or take out what they wanted. But when Pericles returned they were once more under naval blockade. Later

the Athenian fleet was reinforced from Athens with forty ships under the command of Thucydides, Hagnon, and Phormio, and twenty more under the command of Tlepolemus and Anticles; also thirty ships from Chios and Lesbos. The Samians made a brief effort at resistance by sea, but were unable to hold their own and were forced to accept terms of surrender after a nine months' siege: they pulled down their walls, gave hostages, handed over their fleet, and agreed to pay reparations in instalments at regular intervals. Byzantium also agreed to return to its status of a subject city.

THE ALLIED CONGRESS AT SPARTA

118 It was only a few years later that there took place the events already described – the affair of Corcyra, the affair of Potidaea, and the other occurrences which served as causes for the war between Athens and Sparta. The actions of the Hellenes against each other and against foreign Powers which I have just related all took place in a period of about fifty years between the retreat of Xerxes and the beginning of this present war. In these years the Athenians made their empire more and more strong, and greatly added to their own power at home. The Spartans, though they saw what was happening, did little or nothing to prevent it, and for most of the time remained inactive, being traditionally slow to go to war, unless they were forced into it, and also being prevented from taking action by wars in their own territory. So finally the point was reached when Athenian strength attained a peak plain for all to see and the Athenians began to encroach upon Sparta's allies. It was at this point that Sparta felt the position to be no longer tolerable and decided by starting this present war to employ all her energies in attacking and, if possible, destroying the power of Athens.

Though the Spartans had already decided that the truce had been broken by Athenian aggression, they also sent to Delphi to inquire from the god whether it would be wise for them to go to war. It is said that the god replied that if they fought with all their might, victory would be theirs, and that he himself would be on
119 their side, whether they invoked him or not. Still, however, the

Spartans called together their allies once more, since they wished
to take their votes on the question of whether war should be declared. Representatives came from the allied states and, in a general
conference, put forward their views, in most cases attacking the
Athenians and advocating a declaration of war. The Corinthians,
who feared that any further delay might cost them Potidaea, had
already sent embassies on their own account to all the allies, urging
them to vote for war. They, too, were present at this conference,
and their representative made the final speech, which was as
follows:

120   'Fellow allies, there is no occasion now for us to make any complaints about the Spartans. They have already voted for war
themselves, and they have summoned us here to do the same thing.
Indeed, this is what a leader should do – to look after his own interests as everyone else does, but also, in return for all the honour
he receives from others, to give a special consideration to the
general interest.

'Now, all those of us who have already had dealings with the
Athenians do not need to be told that we have to be on our guard
against them; but those who live inland or off the main trade routes
ought to recognize the fact that, if they fail to support the maritime
powers, they will find it much more difficult to secure an outlet for
their exports and to receive in return the goods which are imported
to them by sea; they should therefore consider carefully what is
being said now, and not regard it as something in which they are
not concerned; they must be prepared to see that, if the maritime
powers are sacrificed, it will not be long before the danger spreads
farther, until they, too, are threatened, and that thus this discussion
affects them just as much as it affects us. Therefore they should not
shrink from the prospect of choosing war instead of peace. Wise
men certainly choose a quiet life, so long as they are not being attacked; but brave men, when an attack is made on them, will reject
peace and will go to war, though they will be perfectly ready to
come to terms in the course of the war. In fact they will neither
become over-confident because of their successes in war, nor,
because of the charms and blessings of peace, will they put up with
acts of aggression. He who thinks of his own pleasures and shrinks
from fighting is very likely, because of his irresolution, to lose

those very delights which caused his hesitation; while he who goes too far because of a success in war fails to realize that the confidence in which he goes forward is a hollow thing. Many badly planned enterprises have had the luck to be successful because the enemy has shown an even smaller degree of intelligence; and even more frequently has it happened that what seemed to be an excellent plan has ended not in victory, but in disaster. No one can alike conceive and dare in the same spirit of confidence; we are in perfect security when we make our estimates; but in the test of action, when the element of fear is present, we fall short of our ideal.

121 'Now, on this present occasion it is because we are the victims of aggression and because we have adequate reasons that we are going to war; and once we have made ourselves secure from the Athenians we shall at the proper time return to peace. There are many reasons why victory should be ours. First, we are superior in numbers and in military experience; secondly, one and all and all together we obey the orders that we receive. As for sea-power, in which they are strong, we shall build ours up both from the existing resources of our alliance and also from the funds in Olympia and in Delphi. If we borrow money from there we shall be able to attract the foreign sailors in the Athenian navy by offering higher rates of pay.[21] For the power of Athens rests on mercenaries rather than on her own citizens; we, on the other hand, are less likely to be affected in this way, since our strength is in men rather than in money. The chances are that, if they once lose a battle at sea, it will be all over with them. And supposing they do manage to hold out, then that will give us more time in which to improve our own naval tactics, and once our skill is on a level with theirs, there can be little doubt about our superiority so far as courage is concerned. They cannot acquire by education the good qualities that are ours by nature: we, on the other hand, by taking pains can abolish the advantage they hold over us in point of skill. It will require money to carry out these projects, and we will contribute money. What an appalling thing to imagine that, while their allies never stop bringing in contributions to maintain their own slavery,

21. See Pericles' 'reply' in I, 143, and the comment in the Introduction, p. 28.

we, whose aims are vengeance and survival, should hesitate to incur expense in order to prevent this very money that we are saving from being taken from us by the Athenians and then used to make us suffer!

122   'There are also other ways open to us for carrying on the war. We can foster revolts among their allies – and this is the best means of depriving them of the revenues on which their strength depends. Or we can build fortified positions in their country. And there will be other ways and means which no one can foresee at present, since war is certainly not one of those things which follow a fixed pattern; instead it usually makes its own conditions in which one has to adapt oneself to changing situations. So, when one enters upon a war, one will be all the safer for keeping one's self-possession: the side that gets over-excited about it is the most likely side to make mistakes.

'And here is another point to consider. If this was merely a question of boundary disputes between equals and affecting individual states separately, the situation would not be so serious; as it is, we have Athens to fight, and Athens is so much stronger than any single state in our alliance that she is capable of standing up to all of us together. So unless we go to war with her not only in full force but also with every city and every nationality inspired by the same purpose, she will find us divided and will easily subdue us. And let us be sure that defeat, terrible as it may sound, could mean nothing else but total slavery. To the Peloponnese the very mention of such a possibility is shameful, or that so many cities should suffer the oppression of one. If that were to happen, people would say either that we deserved our sufferings or that we were putting up with them through cowardice and showing ourselves much inferior to our fathers; for they brought freedom to the whole of Hellas, while we not only failed to safeguard our own freedom, but also allowed a dictator state to be set up in Hellas, although in individual states we made it a principle to put down despots. Such a policy, in our view, cannot be held to be exempt from three of the greatest mistakes that can be made – lack of intelligence, lack of resolution, or lack of responsibility. Nor do we imagine that you can escape these imputations by claiming that you feel superior to your enemies. This feeling of superiority has done much harm before now; indeed, from the number of cases where it has proved disastrous it has come to be known as something quite different – not superiority, but plain stupidity.

123   'But there is no need to bring up these complaints from the past except in so far as they may help us in the present. As for the future, you must look to that by safeguarding what you have now and by being willing to face sacrifices. It is in your blood to regard all kinds of excellence as the prizes of toil and sweat, and you ought not to change that way of looking at things even if you have at the moment some advantages in wealth and in power; for it would be wrong to lose because of plenty what was gained because of abstinence. Instead we must go forward into this war, in the knowledge that we have many reasons for feeling confident: we are acting on the authority of the god, who has himself promised to support us; and all the rest of Hellas will be with us in the struggle, either through fear of slavery or through hope of liberation. It is not you who will be the first to break the treaty, since the god, in ordering us to make war, regards the treaty as already broken. It is rather a case of enforcing a treaty whose terms have been contravened. What constitutes the breach of a treaty is the first act of aggression, not measures taken in self-defence.

124   'From every point of view, therefore, you have good reason to go to war, and this course is what we recommend as being in the interests of all of us, remembering that identity of interest both among cities and among individuals is the surest of all guarantees. Let there be no delay, therefore, in coming to the help of the people of Potidaea. They are Dorians and are being besieged by Ionians – a very different state of affairs from what used to happen in the past. Let there be no delay either in claiming liberty for all the rest. It is out of the question to wait any longer, with some of us already suffering from aggression, and the rest of us certain to suffer before long in the same way, if it should once be known that we have met in conference and did not dare to take measures to defend ourselves. No, fellow allies, you must recognize instead that the crucial moment has come, that the advice we give you is the best possible advice, and you must vote for war. Do not be afraid of the terrors of the moment, but set your minds instead on the enduring peace

that will follow war. War gives peace its security, but one is still not safe from danger if, for the sake of quiet, one refuses to fight. As for that dictator city which has been established in Hellas, let us make up our minds that it is there to dominate all alike and is planning to subdue what has not been subdued already. Let us then go forward against it and destroy it, let us be able to live our own lives in the future without fear, and let us liberate the Hellenes who are now enslaved!'

125　This was the speech of the Corinthians. The Spartans had now heard everyone's opinion, and put the vote city by city to all their allies who were present, both great and small. The majority voted for war. They decided, however, that in their present state of unpreparedness it would be impossible to attack immediately, but it was agreed that each state should make its own preparations and that there should be no delay. All the same, while they were occupied in these necessary preliminaries, a year, or rather less, went by before Attica was invaded and war openly broke out.

THE STORIES OF PAUSANIAS AND THEMISTOCLES

126　The period before the outbreak of war was spent in sending embassies to Athens with various complaints, so that there should be a good pretext for making war if the Athenians paid no attention to them.

The first embassy from Sparta to Athens was instructed to demand that the Athenians should 'drive out the curse of the goddess'. The meaning of this was as follows: In former times there was an Athenian called Cylon, a victor in the Olympic Games, belonging to a noble family, and a powerful man himself. He had married the daughter of Theagenes, a Megarian, who at that time was dictator of Megara. Cylon went to Delphi to consult the god, and the reply he received was that he was to seize the Acropolis of Athens during the great festival of Zeus. Theagenes gave him some troops and, summoning his own friends to join him, when the time came for the Olympic festival in the Peloponnese, he seized the Acropolis with the intention of making himself dictator, believing that the Olympic festival must be 'the great festival of Zeus' and also that there was something appropriate in it to his own case, since he had won a victory at the Olympic Games. Whether perhaps the festival referred to was meant to be in Attica or somewhere else he never even considered, nor did the oracle offer any enlightenment. In fact the Athenians have a festival, the Diasia, which is called the great festival of Zeus the Gracious. This takes place outside the city, and the whole people make a number of sacrifices not including blood sacrifices, but traditional offerings of the country. However, imagining that his view of the matter was correct, he attempted to seize power. However, when the Athenians discovered what had happened they all came in from the country in full force to resist Cylon's party and surrounded and blockaded them on the Acropolis.[22] After some time had passed the Athenians grew tired of the siege, and most of them withdrew, leaving the nine archons, in those times the chief political power in Athens, with absolute authority both for carrying on the siege and for settling the whole affair as seemed best to them. Meanwhile the besieged party of Cylon and his supporters were suffering badly from lack of food and water. Cylon and his brother managed to escape, but the rest, who were now in great straits, some of them actually dying of hunger, took their places as suppliants in front of the altar on the Acropolis. When they saw that they were dying in the temple, the Athenians who had been set there on guard persuaded them to leave their position on the understanding that they would not he harmed, took them out, and put them to death. They also killed some of them who, on their way past, took refuge at the altars of the Dread Goddesses. It was because of this that the men who killed them and their families after them were called accursed and guilty before the goddess. Certainly these guilty men were driven out by the Athenians, and driven out again later by the Spartan Cleomenes with the Athenian party who backed him: they exiled the living and dug up and cast out the bones of the dead. Nevertheless they came back later, and their descendants still live in Athens.

127   It was this curse that the Spartans now demanded should be

22. Cylon made an unsuccessful attempt to establish a tyranny in Athens about 630 B.C.

driven out. Their first aim, so they said, was to do honour to the
gods, but of course they knew that Pericles, the son of Xanthippus,
was connected with the curse on his mother's side, and they
thought that if he were exiled they would be more likely to get
their own way with the Athenians. Not that they really expected
this to happen to him, but they did hope to make him unpopular
in Athens on the ground that the war would be partly laid down
to his account. He was the most powerful man of his times, and in
his leadership of the state he invariably opposed Sparta, allowing
no concessions and urging Athens on to war.

128   The Athenians countered the Spartan demand by demanding
that the Spartans should drive out the curse of Taenarus. For the
Spartans had in the past raised up some helot suppliants from the
altar of Poseidon, and had taken them away and killed them. They
believe that the great earthquake in Sparta was the result of this.
The Athenians also demanded that they should drive out the curse
of the goddess of the Brazen House. The meaning of this was as
follows:

After the Spartan Pausanias had been recalled by his government
for the first time from his command in the Hellespont and had been
tried and acquitted, he was not sent out again in an official capacity.
However, on his own initiative and without Spartan authority he
took a trireme from the town of Hermione and sailed to the
Hellespont. He pretended that his intention was to join in the
national struggle against Persia, but in fact he went in order to intrigue with the King of Persia, as he had already begun to do
before, with the aim of becoming ruler of Hellas. The first occasion when he was able to put the King under an obligation to him
was as follows, and it was from this that the whole plot began.
When he was in the area before, after the return from Cyprus, he
captured Byzantium, which had been held by the Persians and in
which some friends and relations of the King had been taken
prisoner. At that time he sent back these prisoners to the King,
hiding his action from the other allies and making out that the
prisoners had escaped. This was done through the agency of Gongylus of Eretria, whom he had put in charge of the prisoners and of
Byzantium itself. He also sent Gongylus to the King with a letter,
the text of which, as was afterwards revealed, was as follows:

'Pausanias, the commander-in-chief of Sparta, wishing to do you a favour, sends you these men whom he has taken prisoner in war. And I propose also, if you agree, to marry your daughter and to bring both Sparta and the rest of Hellas under your control. I consider that, if we make our plans together, I am quite able to achieve this. If therefore you are attracted by this idea, send down to the coast a reliable person through whom we may in future communicate with each other.'

129 So much was revealed in the written message, and Xerxes was pleased with the letter. He sent down to the coast Artabazus, the son of Pharnaces, with orders to take over the satrapy of Dascylium from its present governor Megabates. He gave Artabazus a letter in reply to Pausanias in Byzantium and told him to send it across with all speed, to show him the King's seal, and, if Pausanias made any suggestions about the King's affairs, to support him faithfully and to the best of his ability.

Artabazus on his arrival carried out his orders and sent the letter across to Byzantium. The King's reply was as follows: 'These are the words of King Xerxes to Pausanias. Your act in saving the men whom you have sent to me across the sea from Byzantium will be laid up for you in gratitude, recorded for ever in our house. With the words also which you sent to me I am pleased. Let neither night nor day keep you idle in the performance of your promises to me, nor let them be hindered for want of gold or silver to spend, nor for numbers of troops, should they be needed anywhere. I have sent you a good man in Artabazus. With him go forward confidently and advance your interests and mine in the way that will be best and most successful for us both.'

130 Even before this Pausanias had had a great reputation among the Hellenes because of his generalship at the battle of Plataea, and now, when he received this letter, he thought even more of himself and could no longer bear to live in the ordinary way. Instead he used to go out of Byzantium dressed in the Persian style of clothing; he was escorted on his journeys through Thrace by a bodyguard of Persians and Egyptians; he held banquets in the Persian manner, and was so far incapable of concealing his purpose that in small matters he made it quite clear what he intended to do later and on a grander scale. He shut himself off from normal contacts and

behaved towards everyone alike in such a high-handed way that no one was able to come near him. This was one of the chief reasons why the allied forces turned towards the Athenians.

131   It was because they had heard that he was behaving like this that the Spartans had recalled him once already. Now he had gone out again, without their authority, in a ship from Hermione, and appeared to be acting in just the same way as before. Then, too, when, after a siege, he was driven out of Byzantium by the Athenians, he did not return to Sparta; instead he was reported to have established himself at Colonae in the Troad, to be carrying on intrigues with Persia, and to be prolonging his stay abroad for no good reason. A point was now reached where the ephors could wait no longer. They sent out to him a herald with a scytale,[23] instructing him to return with the herald on pain of being declared a public enemy by the Spartans.

Pausanias particularly wished to avoid becoming suspected, and at the same time felt confident of being able to clear himself by means of bribery. So for the second time he returned to Sparta. On his arrival he was thrown into prison by the ephors (who have the power to imprison the King), but later he managed to have himself released, and offered to answer any complaints that might be made of him at an inquiry.

132   The Spartans – neither his private enemies nor the state as a whole – had no direct evidence against him, nothing definite enough to justify condemning a man who belonged to the royal family and who at that time held so high an office, acting as Regent for his cousin, King Pleistarchus, the son of Leonidas, who was still under age. On the other hand, by his contempt for the laws and his imitation of foreign ways he had made himself very widely suspected of being unwilling to abide by normal standards, and there was an examination into the various occasions when he had departed from the accepted rules of behaviour. There was the case of the tripod in Delphi, dedicated by the Hellenes as the first fruits of the Persian spoils, on which Pausanias, entirely on his own responsibility, had thought fit to have inscribed the following couplet:

23. A 'scytale' was a staff or rod used for sending messages in cipher by means of strips of leather.

Leader of Hellenes in war, victorious over the Persians,
Pausanias to the god Phoebus erected the trophy.

As for this couplet, the Spartans had immediately had it erased, and had inscribed by name all the cities who had joined in defeating the Persians and who were making the dedication. Nevertheless, this action, which even at the time was held against Pausanias, now, in view of his recent activities, appeared to be not at all inconsistent with his present way of thought. It was also reported that Pausanias was intriguing with the helots, and this was in fact the case. He was offering them their freedom and full rights as citizens if they would join him in revolt and help him to carry out all his schemes.

Not even then, when they were receiving information from some of the helots, would the ephors believe this information and take action against Pausanias. This was in accordance with their usual practice in matters that concerned their own people, which is never to act hastily in the case of a Spartan citizen and never to come to any irrevocable decision except on the basis of absolutely cast-iron evidence. They say, however, that finally the man who was going to take to Artabazus the last letter for the King of Persia, a man from Argilus who had once been the boy friend of Pausanias, and very faithful to him, turned informer. He had become frightened because he had observed that none of the previous messengers had ever come back again. He therefore forged the seal, so that he would not be found out if either his suspicions proved false or if Pausanias were to ask for the letter in order to make some alteration to it. He then opened the latter and found just what he had expected to find – namely, a postscript to the effect that he should be put to death.

133   When he showed this letter to the ephors, they certainly found this to be more convincing evidence, but still they wanted to have the proof of their own ears in listening to Pausanias commit himself in some way. They therefore made an arrangement with the man, who went away as a suppliant to the temple at Taenarus and took up his quarters in a hut which was divided in two by a partition. On one side of this partition he hid some of the ephors, and when Pausanias came to him and asked him why he was there

as a suppliant, the ephors heard the whole story. The man first complained to Pausanias of the instructions given about him in the letter; he then went into all the other details, pointing out that in all the negotiations with the King he had never once compromised Pausanias's interests, and that now his only reward was to be put on a level with the rest of the servants and killed. All this Pausanias admitted, and then begged him not to be angry at what he had done. By raising him up from his position of suppliant he pledged his word for his safety and urged him to set off as soon as possible, and not to delay the negotiations.

134   The ephors listened carefully to all this. For the moment they went away, but, since they were now perfectly sure of things, they planned to arrest Pausanias in the city. It is said that just when he was about to be arrested in the street, he saw from the expression of one of the ephors who was approaching him why it was that he was coming; and that another one of the ephors out of friendship to him gave him a secret sign to show him his danger; he then took to flight and escaped them by running to the temple of the Goddess of the Brazen House, the precinct of which was quite close. There, so that he should not suffer from exposure to the weather, he found a small room inside the temple and stayed in it without making a sign of his presence. For the time being the ephors had been left behind in their pursuit of him, but they afterwards removed the roof of the room, and, having made sure that he was caught inside, they walled up the doors, put sentries round the place, and proceeded to starve him out. When they found that he was on the point of dying, just as he was, in the room, they brought him out of the temple while he was still just breathing, and, as soon as he was brought out, he died. They first intended to throw his body into the Caeadas, where criminals are disposed of, but later they decided to bury him somewhere nearby. Afterwards the god in Delphi commanded the Spartans to move his tomb to the place where he died (his body now lies in the ground in front of the sacred precinct, as is shown by an inscription on the pillars there) and, since what had been done was bringing a curse on them, to give back two bodies instead of one to the Goddess of the Brazen House. So the Spartans made two bronze statues and dedicated

35   them so as to take the place of Pausanias. Since the god himself

had declared that this event constituted a curse the Athenians replied to the Spartan embassy by telling them to drive it out.

With regard to Pausanias's collaboration with Persia, the Spartans sent an embassy to Athens and, on the basis of evidence which they had discovered at the inquiry, accused Themistocles also of the same crime. They urged the Athenians to punish him in the same way, and the Athenians agreed to do so. At the time, however, he had been ostracized and was living in Argos, though he often travelled about in the rest of the Peloponnese. The Athenians therefore sent back with the Spartans, who were quite willing to help in tracing him, some of their own officers with orders to arrest Themistocles where they found him and bring him to
136 Athens. Themistocles realized what was afoot and fled from the Peloponnese to Corcyra, which honoured him as a benefactor. But the Corcyraeans said that they did not dare to risk the hostility of Sparta and Athens by giving him shelter, and so they sent him across to the mainland opposite. Here, with the officers from Athens on his heels as they found out the route he took, he was on one occasion so hard pressed that he had to rest at the house of Admetus, the King of the Molossi, who was no friend of his. Admetus happened not to be there at the time, and Themistocles was instructed by the King's wife, to whom he applied as a suppliant, to take their child in his arms and to sit down by the hearth. Before long Admetus returned and Themistocles told him who he was. 'It is true,' he said, 'that when you were asking for Athenian help I opposed you, but it would be wrong for you to revenge yourself on me now that I am in exile. At the present time I am at the mercy of people much less strong than you are, and it is not a generous thing to do to avenge oneself on one's equals when they are at a disadvantage. Then, too, when I opposed you it was not on a matter of life and death, but only on a question of a request that you were making; but, if you give me up' (and he told him who his pursuers were and what they intended to do with him) 'you will most certainly be depriving me of my life.'
137   Admetus listened to him and then raised him to his feet, together with his own child, whom Themistocles had been holding in his arms as he sat there – and this indeed had had the greatest effect on the success of his supplication. Not long afterwards the Spartans

and Athenians arrived, and in spite of all that they said Admetus refused to give him up. Since he wished to go to the King of Persia, he sent him by land to Alexander's city of Pydna on the Aegean. There he found and took passage in a merchant ship which was sailing for Ionia, but was carried by a storm towards the Athenian fleet that was besieging Naxos. He was unknown to the people on the ship, and fearing what might happen, he informed the captain who he was and why he was escaping, saying that, if the captain refused to save him, he would accuse him of having taken a bribe to secure his escape. Their safety, he said, depended on no one being allowed to leave the ship until it was possible to set sail again, and he promised the captain a suitable reward if he followed his instructions. The captain did so, and, after lying to for a day and a night at a distance from the Athenian fleet, they arrived later at Ephesus.

Here Themistocles rewarded the captain by giving him a sum of money. (Money had reached him after his arrival from his friends in Athens and from what he had put away in Argos.) He then travelled inland with one of the Persians living on the coast and sent a letter to Artaxerxes, the son of Xerxes, who had recently come to the throne. The letter was as follows: 'I, Themistocles, have come to you. More than any of the Hellenes I did harm to your house during the time when I was forced to defend myself against your father's invasion; yet during the retreat, when I was safe and he was in danger, the good I did then was more than the harm I did before. I deserve to be repaid for the help I gave then' (here he gave an account of the warning to retreat which he had sent from Salamis and of the preservation of the bridges over the Hellespont which he pretended, quite untruly, was due to him), 'and at the present time I am here with the power to do you important services, pursued by the Hellenes because of my friendship for you. I wish, however, to wait for one year and then to explain to you myself the reasons for my coming.'

138   It is said that the King was greatly struck by this resolution of his and ordered him to do as he wished. In the time that he was waiting Themistocles learned as much as he could of the Persian language and of the manners of the country. Then after a year he arrived at Court and became a person of importance, indeed more

influential there than any Hellene has ever been, partly because of
the great reputation he had already, partly because of the hopes he
held out of conquering Hellas for the King, but chiefly because he
gave constant proof of the ability and intelligence which he possessed.

Indeed, Themistocles was a man who showed an unmistakable
natural genius; in this respect he was quite exceptional, and beyond
all others deserves our admiration. Without studying a subject in
advance or deliberating over it later, but using simply the intelligence that was his by nature, he had the power to reach the right
conclusion in matters that have to be settled on the spur of the
moment and do not admit of long discussions, and in estimating
what was likely to happen, his forecasts of the future were always
more reliable than those of others. He could perfectly well explain
any subject with which he was familiar, and even outside his own
department he was still capable of giving an excellent opinion. He
was particularly remarkable at looking into the future and seeing
there the hidden possibilities for good or evil. To sum him up in a
few words, it may be said that through force of genius and by
rapidity of action this man was supreme at doing precisely the
right thing at precisely the right moment.

His death came as a result of an illness; though there are some
people who say that he committed suicide by taking poison, when
he found that it was impossible to keep the promises that he had
made to the King. In any case, there is a monument to him in the
market-place of Magnesia in Asia. This was the district over which
he ruled; for the King gave him Magnesia for his bread (and it
brought in fifty talents a year), Lampsacus for his wine (which was
considered to be at the time the best wine district of all), and Myos
for his meat. It is said that his bones were, at his desire, brought
home by his relations and buried secretly in Attica. The secrecy
was necessary since it is against the law to bury in Attica the bones
of one who has been exiled for treason.

So ended the careers of the Spartan Pausanias and the Athenian
Themistocles, who were the most famous people of their day in
Hellas.

THE SPARTAN ULTIMATUM AND PERICLES' REPLY

39 The first embassy of the Spartans was as I have described: they demanded that those under the curse should be driven out, and they received a counter demand from Athens in the same terms. Later they sent another embassy to demand that Athens should abandon the siege of Potidaea and should give Aegina her independence. But the chief point and the one that they made most clear was that war could be avoided if Athens would revoke the Megarian decree which excluded the Megarians from all ports in the Athenian Empire and from the market in Attica itself.

The Athenians would not give in on the first points, nor would they revoke the decree. They accused Megara of cultivating consecrated ground, of cultivating land that did not belong to them, and of giving shelter to slaves who had escaped from Athens.

Finally an embassy arrived with the Spartan ultimatum. The Spartan representatives were Ramphias, Melesippus, and Agesander. They made no reference to any of the usual subjects that had been spoken of before, but said simply: 'Sparta wants peace. Peace is still possible if you will give the Hellenes their freedom.'

The Athenians then held an assembly in order to debate the matter, and decided to look into the whole question once and for all and then to give Sparta her answer. Many speakers came forward and opinions were expressed on both sides, some maintaining that war was necessary and others saying that the Megarian decree should be revoked and should not be allowed to stand in the way of peace. Among the speakers was Pericles, the son of Xanthippus, the leading man of his time among the Athenians and the most powerful both in action and in debate. His advice was as follows:

40 'Athenians,' he said, 'my views are the same as ever: I am against making any concessions to the Peloponnesians, even though I am aware that the enthusiastic state of mind in which people are persuaded to enter upon a war is not retained when it comes to action, and that people's minds are altered by the course of events. Nevertheless I see that on this occasion I must give you exactly the same advice as I have given in the past, and I call upon those of you who are persuaded by my words to give your full support to these

resolutions which we are making all together, and to abide by them even if in some respect or other we find ourselves in difficulty; for, unless you do so, you will be able to claim no credit for intelligence when things go well with us. There is often no more logic in the course of events than there is in the plans of men, and this is why we usually blame our luck when things happen in ways that we did not expect.

'It was evident before that Sparta was plotting against us, and now it is even more evident. It is laid down in the treaty that differences between us should be settled by arbitration, and that, pending arbitration, each side should keep what it has. The Spartans have never once asked for arbitration, nor have they accepted our offers to submit to it. They prefer to settle their complaints by war rather than by peaceful negotiations, and now they come here not even making protests, but trying to give us orders. They tell us to abandon the siege of Potidaea, to give Aegina her independence, and to revoke the Megarian decree. And finally they come to us with a proclamation that we must give the Hellenes their freedom.

'Let none of you think that we should be going to war for a trifle if we refuse to revoke the Megarian decree. It is a point they make much of, and say that war need not take place if we revoke this decree; but, if we do go to war, let there be no kind of suspicion in your hearts that the war was over a small matter. For you this trifle is both the assurance and the proof of your determination. If you give in, you will immediately be confronted with some greater demand, since they will think that you only gave way on this point through fear. But if you take a firm stand you will make it clear to them that they have to treat you properly as equals.

141 And now you must make up your minds what you are going to do – either to give way to them before being hurt by them, or, if we go to war – as I think we should do – to be determined that, whether the reason put forward is big or small, we are not in any case going to climb down nor hold our possessions under a constant threat of interference. When one's equals, before resorting to arbitration, make claims on their neighbours and put those claims in the form of commands, it would still be slavish to give in to them, however big or however small such claims may be.

'Now, as to the war and to the resources available to each side,

I should like you to listen to a detailed account and to realize that we are not the weaker party. The Peloponnesians cultivate their own land themselves; they have no financial resources either as individuals or as states; then they have no experience of fighting overseas, nor of any fighting that lasts a long time, since the wars they fight against each other are, because of their poverty, short affairs. Such people are incapable of often manning a fleet or often sending out an army, when that means absence from their own land, expense from their own funds and, apart from this, when we have control of the sea. And wars are paid for by the possession of reserves rather than by a sudden increase in taxation. Those who farm their own land, moreover, are in warfare more anxious about their money than their lives; they have a shrewd idea that they themselves will come out safe and sound, but they are not at all sure that all their money will not have been spent before then, especially if, as is likely to happen, the war lasts longer than they expect. In a single battle the Peloponnesians and their allies could stand up to all the rest of Hellas, but they cannot fight a war against a power unlike themselves, so long as they have no central deliberative authority to produce quick decisive action, when they all have equal votes, though they all come from different nationalities and every one of these is mainly concerned with its own interests – the usual result of which is that nothing gets done at all, some being particularly anxious to avenge themselves on an enemy and others no less anxious to avoid coming to any harm themselves. Only after long intervals do they meet together at all, and then they devote only a fraction of their time to their general interests, spending most of it on arranging their own separate affairs. It never occurs to any of them that the apathy of one will damage the interests of all. Instead each state thinks that the responsibility for its future belongs to someone else, and so, while everyone has the same idea privately, no one notices that from a general point of view things are going downhill.

142   'But this is the main point: they will be handicapped by lack of money and delayed by the time they will have to take in procuring it. But in war opportunity waits for no man.

'Then we have nothing to fear from their navy, nor need we be alarmed at the prospect of their building fortifications in Attica.

So far as that goes, even in peace time it is not easy to build one city strong enough to be a check upon another; and this would be a much harder thing to accomplish in enemy territory and faced with our own fortifications, which are just as strong as anything that they could build. While if they merely establish some minor outpost, they could certainly do some harm to part of our land by raiding and by receiving deserters, but this could by no means prevent us from retaliating by the use of our sea-power and from sailing to their territory and building fortifications there. For we have acquired more experience of land fighting through our naval operations than they have of sea fighting through their operations on land. And as for seamanship, they will find that a difficult lesson to learn. You yourselves have been studying it ever since the end of the Persian wars, and have still not entirely mastered the subject. How, then, can it be supposed that they could ever make much progress? They are farmers, not sailors, and in addition to that they will never get a chance of practising, because we shall be blockading them with strong naval forces. Against a weak blockading force they might be prepared to take a risk, bolstering up their ignorance by the thought of their numbers, but if they are faced with a large fleet they will not venture out, and so lack of practice will make them even less skilful than they were, and lack of skill will make them even less venturesome. Seamanship, just like anything else, is an art. It is not something that can be picked up and studied in one's spare time; indeed, it allows one no spare time for anything else.

143 'Suppose they lay their hands on the money at Olympia or Delphi and try to attract the foreign sailors in our navy by offering higher rates of pay: that would be a serious thing if we were not still able to be a match for them by ourselves and with our resident aliens serving on board our ships. As it is, we can always match them in this way. Also – which is a very important point – we have among our own citizens more and better steersmen and sailors than all the rest of Hellas put together. Then, too, how many of our foreign sailors would, for the sake of a few days' extra pay, fight on the other side at the risk not only of being defeated but also of being outlawed from their own cities?

'I have given, I think, a fair enough account of the position of

the Peloponnesians. As for our own position, it has none of the
weaknesses which I have noticed in theirs, and it also has a strength
entirely of its own. If they invade our country by land, we will
invade theirs by sea, and it will turn out that the destruction of a
part of the Peloponnese will be worse for them than the destruction of the whole of Attica would be for us. For they can get no
more land without fighting for it, while we have plenty of land
both in the islands and on the continent.

'Sea-power is of enormous importance. Look at it this way.
Suppose we were an island, would we not be absolutely secure
from attack? As it is we must try to think of ourselves as islanders;
we must abandon our land and our houses, and safeguard the sea
and the city. We must not, through anger at losing land and homes,
join battle with the greatly superior forces of the Peloponnesians. If we won a victory, we should still have to fight them
again in just the same numbers, and if we suffered a defeat, we
should at the same time lose our allies, on whom our strength
depends, since they will immediately revolt if we are left with
insufficient troops to send against them. What we should lament
is not the loss of houses or of land, but the loss of men's lives. Men
come first; the rest is the fruit of their labour. And if I thought I
could persuade you to do it, I would urge you to go out and lay
waste your property with your own hands and show the Peloponnesians that it is not for the sake of this that you are likely to give
in to them.

144   'I could give you many other reasons why you should feel confident in ultimate victory, if only you will make up your minds
not to add to the empire while the war is in progress, and not to go
out of your way to involve yourselves in new perils. What I fear
is not the enemy's strategy, but our own mistakes. However, I
shall deal with all this on another occasion when words and action
will go together. For the present I recommend that we send
back the Spartan ambassadors with the following answer: that we
will give Megara access to our market and our ports, if at the same
time Sparta exempts us and our allies from the operation of her
orders for the expulsion of aliens (for in the treaty there is no clause
forbidding either those orders of hers or our decree against
Megara); that we will give their independence to our allies if they

had it at the time that we made the treaty and when the Spartans also allow their own allies to be independent and to have the kind of government each wants to have rather than the kind of government that suits Spartan interests. Let us say, too, that we are willing, according to the terms of the treaty, to submit to arbitration, that we shall not start the war, but that we shall resist those who do start it. This is the right reply to make and it is the reply that this city of ours ought to make. We must realize that this war is being forced upon us, and the more readily we accept the challenge the less eager to attack us will our opponents be. We must realize, too, that, both for cities and for individuals, it is from the greatest dangers that the greatest glory is to be won. When our fathers stood against the Persians they had no such resources as we have now; indeed, they abandoned even what they had, and then it was by wisdom rather than by good fortune, by daring rather than by material power, that they drove back the foreign invasion and made our city what it is today. We must live up to the standard they set: we must resist our enemies in any and every way, and try to leave to those who come after us an Athens that is as great as ever.'

145   This was Pericles' speech. The Athenians considered that his advice was best and voted as he had asked them to vote. Their reply to the Spartans was the one that he had suggested, both on the main issue and on the separate points: that they would do nothing under duress, but that they were willing, according to the terms of the treaty, to reach a settlement on the various complaints on a fair and equal basis. The ambassadors returned to Sparta, and no further embassy was sent.

146   These, then, were the causes of complaint and the differences which occurred between the two powers before the outbreak of war and which arose immediately from the affairs of Epidamnus and of Corcyra. There was still communication between the two states, and people travelled to and fro without heralds, though with considerable suspicion, since events were going on which amounted to a cancellation of the treaty and an excuse for open war.

BOOK TWO

OUTBREAK OF WAR

1 WE now come to the actual outbreak of war between Athens and her allies on the one side and the Peloponnesians and their allies on the other. There was now no further communication between the two sides except through heralds. Once the war began it continued without intermission. I have recorded the events as they occurred each summer and each winter.

2 The thirty years' truce which was entered into after the reconquest of Euboea lasted for fourteen years. In the fifteenth year, the forty-eighth year of the priestess-ship of Chrysis at Argos, the year when Aenesias was ephor at Sparta, and two months before the end of the archonship of Pythodorus at Athens,[24] six months after the battle at Potidaea, just at the beginning of spring, a Theban force of rather over 300 men, commanded by the Boeotarchs Pythangelus, the son of Phylides, and Diemporus, the son of Onetorides, came at about the first watch of the night and made an armed entry into Plataea, a town in Boeotia and an ally of Athens. They came at the invitation of a Plataean party, led by Nauclides and his friends, who opened the gates to them. The aim of this party was to gain power for themselves by getting rid of their own political opponents and bringing Plataea over into the Theban alliance. The plan had been arranged with Eurymachus, the son of Leontiades, one of the most important people in Thebes. For, realizing that war was certain to come, the Thebans were anxious to get control of Plataea first (since Plataea had always been hostile to them) while it was still peace time and war had not yet actually broken out. This, indeed, was the reason why they got in so easily without being noticed, since no sentries were on guard.

Now the Theban troops marched into the market-place and grounded arms there. They did not, however, follow the advice

24. On the difficulties in dating events, see the Introduction, pp. 21-2.

of the party who had called them in, which was to set to work at once by going to the houses of their own enemies. Instead they decided to issue a proclamation in reasonable terms, since they preferred to come to a friendly arrangement and thought that in this way it would be quite easy to win the city over to their side. Their herald therefore proclaimed that all who were willing to return to their proper traditional place in the League of all Boeotia should come and fall in with them in the market-place.

3   As for the Plataeans, when they realized that the Thebans were inside their gates and that their city had been taken over in a moment, they were ready enough to come to an agreement. This was partly through terror and partly because they thought that many more had entered the city than was in fact the case; since in the night they could not see what had really happened. So they accepted the proposals and made no move against the Thebans, especially as the Thebans themselves took no violent measures against anyone.

But while negotiations were going on they became aware that the Thebans were not there in great force and came to the conclusion that, if they attacked them, they could easily overpower them. And the majority of the people was not at all in favour of leaving the Athenian alliance. They decided therefore that the attempt should be made, and, to avoid being seen going through the streets, they cut passages through the connecting walls of their houses and so gathered together in numbers. They made barricades by dragging wagons into the streets, and arranged everything else in the way that seemed likely to be most useful in their present position. When their preparations were as complete as could be, they waited for the time just before dawn, when it was still dark, and then sallied out from their houses against the Thebans. Their idea was that if they attacked in daylight their enemies would be more sure of themselves and would be able to meet them on equal terms, whereas in the night they would not be so confident and would also be at a disadvantage through not knowing the city so well as the Plataeans did. They therefore attacked at once, and fighting broke out immediately.

4   As soon as the Thebans realized that they had fallen into a trap, they closed their ranks and fought back whenever they were

attacked. Twice and three times they succeeded in beating off the assault, and all the while there was a tremendous uproar from the men who were attacking them, and shouting and yelling from the women and slaves on the roofs, who hurled down stones and tiles; at the same time it had been raining hard all night. Finally they lost heart and turned and fled through the city, most of them having no idea, in the darkness and the mud, on a moonless night at the end of the month, of which way to go in order to escape, while their pursuers knew quite well how to prevent them from escaping. The result was that most of them were destroyed. The gate by which they had entered, and which was the only one that was open, had been closed by one of the Plataeans, who used a javelin spike as a pin and drove it into the bar; so that there was no way out for them even here. In their flight through the city some got on the wall and threw themselves down on the other side: most of these lost their lives in doing so. One party managed to find a gate that was unguarded. A woman gave them an axe and they cut through the bar; but they were soon observed and only a few of them got away. Others were cut down here and there in different parts of the city. The largest detachment, which had kept itself more together than the rest, rushed into a big building which formed part of the city wall. The doors of this building happened to be open, and the Thebans thought that they were the city gates and that there was a way right through to the outside. When the Plataeans saw that their enemies were caught in this way, they discussed whether to set fire to the building and burn them just as they were, or whether there was anything else that could be done with them. Finally the Thebans in the building and all other survivors wandering about in the city handed over their arms and surrendered unconditionally to the Plataeans. Such was the fate of those who entered the town.

5   Meanwhile the rest of the Thebans, who should have been there in full force while it was still night, in case anything went wrong with those who were inside, had, while they were on their way, received news of what had happened, and were hurrying on to relieve them. But Plataea is nearly eight miles from Thebes, and the rain that had fallen in the night impeded their progress, since the river Asopus was in flood and not at all easy to cross. So, march-

ing in the rain and having had great difficulty in crossing the river, they did not arrive until the whole of the advance party had been killed or taken prisoner.

When they realized what had happened, they considered making a move against the Plataeans who were outside the city. For there were still both men and property out in the fields, since the attack had been made in peace time and had been quite unexpected. The Thebans therefore wanted, if possible, to take some prisoners, so as to have them to exchange, in case any of their own people had been made prisoner. This was their plan, but while they were still discussing it the Plataeans suspected that this was what they might do and, being anxious for the safety of those who were outside the walls, sent a herald to the Thebans. They pointed out that this attempt to seize their city in time of peace was absolutely unjustifiable and warned them not to do any harm to those who were outside. If they did, they said that they, too, would put to death the Thebans whom they had taken prisoners. If, on the other hand, the Thebans would withdraw from their land, they would give the prisoners back to them. This is the Theban account of the matter; and they claim that the agreement was ratified by oath. The Plataeans, however, do not admit that they promised to give back the prisoners immediately, but only if agreement was reached after negotiation; they also deny that there was any oath. Whatever the truth may be, the Thebans did retire from Plataean territory without doing any harm, and the Plataeans, after they had hurriedly brought into the city all their property from outside, immediately put the prisoners to death. There were 180 of them, including Eurymachus, with whom the Plataean traitors had been negotiating.

6   After this they sent a messenger to Athens, arranged an armistice for giving back the dead bodies to the Thebans, and in their own city took whatever measures seemed best to them in the existing circumstances. News had reached Athens immediately of what was happening in Plataea and the Athenians had at once arrested all Boeotians in Attica, and had sent a herald to Plataea with instructions to tell the Plataeans not to do anything irrevocable about the prisoners until Athens also had given her advice about them. The Athenians had not yet heard that they were dead; for the first

messenger had left the town at the time that the Thebans first entered it, and the second messenger had left just after the Thebans had been defeated and taken prisoner. They knew nothing of what had happened later. Thus the Athenians sent their instructions in ignorance of what the situation was, and when the herald arrived he found that the prisoners had already been put to death. Afterwards the Athenians marched to Plataea, brought provisions into the place, and left a garrison there, taking away with them the women and children and all the men who were unfit for fighting.

7   In this affair of Plataea the treaty had quite obviously been broken, and now the Athenians made ready for war, as did the Spartans and their allies. They planned to send embassies to the King of Persia and to any other foreign Power from whom they hoped to obtain support, and they tried to ally themselves with other Hellenic states who were not yet committed to either side. The Spartans, in addition to the fleet they had already, ordered more ships to be built by the states in Italy and Sicily who were on their side: the number ordered was in proportion to the size of each city, and the total was to be a fleet of 500 ships.[25] These cities were also asked each to provide a certain sum of money. Meanwhile, and until their preparations were complete, they were to remain neutral and to allow single Athenian ships to enter their harbours. The Athenians, on their side, tightened their hold on their existing allies and, in particular, sent embassies to places in the neighbourhood of the Peloponnese – to Corcyra, Cephallenia, Acarnania, and Zacynthus – realizing that they could carry on the war all round the Peloponnese if they could establish firm and friendly relations with these places.

8   Nothing in their designs was on a small or mean scale: both sides put everything into their war effort. This was natural enough. At the beginning of an undertaking the enthusiasm is always greatest, and at that time both in the Peloponnese and in Athens there were great numbers of young men who had never been in a war and were consequently far from unwilling to join in this one. Meanwhile all the rest of Hellas hung poised on the event, as the two leading cities came together in conflict. There were all kinds of prophecies and all kinds of oracular utterances being made both

25. In the event, Sparta never received this naval assistance; see III, 86.

in the cities that were about to go to war and in other places as well. Then, too, there was an earthquake in Delos just before this time – a thing that had never happened before in the memory of the Hellenes. This was said and thought to be a sign of impending events; and if anything else of the same kind happened to occur, its meaning was always carefully examined.

People's feelings were generally very much on the side of the Spartans, especially as they proclaimed that their aim was the liberation of Hellas. States and individuals alike were enthusiastic to support them in every possible way, both in speech and action, and everyone thought that unless he took a personal share in things the whole effort was being handicapped. So bitter was the general feeling against Athens, whether from those who wished to escape from her rule or from those who feared that they would come under it.

9   These were the preparations and this the state of mind at the outbreak of war. Each of the two states had her own allies, which were as follows: On the side of Sparta were all the Peloponnesian states inside the isthmus except the Argives and the Achaeans, who maintained friendly relations with both sides. Pellene was the only Achaean state that joined Sparta at the beginning, though later all the others followed her example. The Spartan allies outside the Peloponnese were the Megarians, the Boeotians, the Locrians, the Phocians, the Ambraciots, and the Leucadians and Anactorians. The allies who provided ships were the following: Corinth, Megara, Sicyon, Pellene, Elis, Ambracia, and Leucas. Cavalry was provided by the Boeotians, the Phocians, and the Locrians; and the other states contributed infantry.

This was the Spartan alliance. On the side of Athens were Chios, Lesbos, Plataea, the Messenians in Naupactus, most of Acarnania, Corcyra, Zacynthus, and other cities in the tribute-paying class in the following areas: the Carian coast (including the Dorian cities nearby), Ionia, the Hellespont, Thrace, the islands between the Peloponnese and Crete towards the east, and all the Cyclades except Melos and Thera. Chios, Lesbos, and Corcyra provided ships, the others infantry and money.

These were the allies on each side and these their resources for the war.

10   Immediately after the affair at Plataea, Sparta sent messengers through the Peloponnese and to her allies outside. The instructions were to prepare the troops and the supplies necessary for a foreign campaign, the object of which was to be the invasion of Attica. These measures were carried out, and, at the appointed time, they assembled at the isthmus, each state bringing two-thirds of its total force. When the whole army was gathered together, the Spartan King Archidamus, who led this expedition, summoned the generals of all the states and the most important and influential people in them, and made the following address to them:

11   'Peloponnesians and allies, our fathers have engaged in many campaigns both in and outside the Peloponnese, and the elder men in this army of ours are not inexperienced in war. Yet we have never marched out in greater strength than now. And, just as we are in greater numbers and in better spirit than ever before, so the city against which we are moving is at the height of her power. We must not, then, fall short of our fathers' standards, nor fail to live up to our own reputation. For the whole of Hellas is eagerly watching this action of ours, and, because of the general hatred against Athens, wishing us success in our undertakings. Therefore, even though it may seem that we are invading in tremendous force and that there is little risk of our enemy coming out to meet us in battle, this must not be made an excuse for relaxing our precautions while we are on the march: officers and soldiers of every individual state should constantly be prepared to find their own particular positions threatened. There is much that is unpredictable in war, and attacks are usually made as the result of a sudden impulse. Very often, too, a numerically inferior force, fearing for its own safety, has beaten off the superior numbers of an enemy who, through over-confidence, has relaxed his precautions. Certainly one ought to march forward confidently in an enemy country, but one should also take practical measures based on the idea of security. In this way armies are likely to be most courageous in attack and most reliable in defence.

'And the city against which we are marching is very far from being incapable of defending herself. She is extraordinarily well equipped in every respect, so that we ought to consider it very likely that they will come and meet us in battle; and that, if they have not yet set out against us before we are there, they will do so when they see us in their own country laying waste and destroying their property. People grow angry when they suffer things that they are quite unused to suffer and when these things go on actually in front of their own eyes. They do not wait to think, but plunge into action on the spur of their impulse. And the Athenians are especially likely to act in this way, since they think that they have a right to supremacy and are much more used to invading and destroying other people's land than seeing this happening to their own land. Remember, then, that you are marching against a very great city. Think, too, of the glory, or, if events turn out differently, the shame which you will bring to your ancestors and to yourselves, and, with all this in mind, follow your leaders, paying the strictest attention to discipline and to security, giving prompt obedience to the orders which you receive. The best and safest thing of all is when a large force is so well disciplined that it seems to be acting like one man.'

12 After making this short speech, Archidamus dismissed the assembly. Before making any further move he sent Melesippus, the son of Diacritus, a Spartan, to Athens to see if the Athenians were any more likely to come to terms now that they saw that their enemies were already on the march. But the Athenians refused him admission to the city or access to their assembly. This was because of a resolution of Pericles, which had previously been carried, not to receive any herald or embassy from the Spartans once they had marched out from their own country. They therefore sent Melesippus back again without giving him a hearing, and told him to be beyond the frontier that same day, adding that if in future the Spartans had anything they wanted to say they should retreat inside their own boundaries and then send an embassy. They gave Melesippus an escort to prevent him making contacts with anyone, and, when he was on the frontier and about to go his own way, he said, as he was going: 'This day will be the beginning of great misfortunes to Hellas.'

After his return to the army Archidamus realized that the Athenians were still resolved to make no concessions, and now at last he moved forward and advanced into Attica. The Boeotians had provided their contingent and also cavalry for the main force, and with their remaining troops went out against Plataea and laid waste the land there.

13   While the Peloponnesians were either still mustering at the isthmus or on their march before the invasion of Attica, Pericles, the son of Xanthippus, one of the ten Athenian generals, realizing that the invasion was coming, suspected that Archidamus, who happened to be a friend of his, might possibly pass by his estates and leave them undamaged. This might be either from a personal wish to do him a favour, or as the result of instructions given by the Spartans in order to stir up prejudice against him, just as it had been because of him that they had previously made the proclamation about driving out the curse. He therefore came forward first and made a statement to the Athenians in the assembly, saying that, though Archidamus was his friend, this fact was certainly not going to be harmful to Athenian interests, and, in case the enemy should not lay waste his estates and houses, like those of other people, he proposed to give them up and make them public property, so that no one should have any suspicions against him on their account. Then, with regard to the present situation, he gave just the same advice as he had given before. This was that they were to prepare for war and bring into the city their property in the country. They were not to go out and offer battle, but were to come inside the city and guard it. Their navy, in which their strength lay, was to be brought to the highest state of efficiency, and their allies were to be handled firmly, since, he said, the strength of Athens came from the money paid in tribute by her allies, and victory in war depended on a combination of intelligent resolution and financial resources. Here Pericles encouraged confidence, pointing out that, apart from all other sources of revenue, the average yearly contribution from the allies to Athens amounted to 600 talents,[26] then there still remained in the Acropolis a sum of 6,000 talents of coined silver. This reserve fund, at its maximum, had been 9,700 talents. It had been drawn on to pay for the Propylaea and other public buildings, and for Potidaea. In addition to this there was the uncoined gold and silver in offerings made either by individuals or by the state; there were the sacred vessels and furniture used in the processions and in the games; there were the spoils taken from the

26. See Appendix I.

Persians, and other resources of one kind or another, all of which would amount to no less than 500 talents. To this he added the money in the other temples which might be used and which came to a considerable sum, and said that, if they were ever really reduced to absolute extremities, they could even use the gold on the statue of Athene herself. There was, he informed them, a weight of forty talents of pure gold on this statue, all of which was removable. But he pointed out that if they did use this gold for their own preservation they must restore it again afterwards in the same or in a greater quantity.

Thus he reassured them about their financial position. As for their army, they had 13,000 hoplites in addition to the 16,000 others who were in various garrisons and those engaged in the actual defence of the city. This was the number originally detailed for defence in case of invasion, and the force was drawn from the eldest and the youngest of the citizens in the army together with the resident aliens who were qualified as hoplites. The wall of Phalerum ran for four miles from the sea to the city circuit; and nearly five miles of the wall surrounding the city was guarded, though part of it (the section between the Long Walls and the wall of Phalerum) was left without a guard. Then there were the four and a half miles of the Long Walls to Piraeus, the outer one of which was garrisoned. Then, too, there were seven and a half miles of fortifications surrounding Piraeus and Munychia, half of which distance was guarded. There were also 1,200 cavalry, including mounted bowmen; 1,600 unmounted bowmen, and 300 triremes ready for active service. This was an accurate, or perhaps a conservative, estimate of the resources in each department available to Athens at the time when the Peloponnesian invasion was expected and at the beginning of the war. Pericles also used his usual arguments to show that they should feel confident of final victory.

14   The Athenians took the advice he gave them and brought in from the country their wives and children and all their household goods, taking down even the wood-work on the houses themselves. Their sheep and cattle they sent across to Euboea and the islands off the coast. But the move was a difficult experience for them, since most of them had been always used to living in the country.

15   Indeed, from very early times this way of life had been especially
characteristic of the Athenians. From the time of Cecrops and the
first kings down to the time of Theseus the inhabitants of Attica
had always lived in independent cities, each with its own town
hall and its own government. Only in times of danger did they
meet together and consult the King at Athens; for the rest of the
time each state looked after its own affairs and made its own decisions. There were actually occasions when some of these states
made war on Athens, as Eleusis under Eumolpus did against King
Erechtheus. But when Theseus became King he showed himself
as intelligent as he was powerful. In his reorganization of the
country one of the most important things he did was to abolish
the separate councils and governments of the small cities and to
bring them all together into the present city of Athens, making
one deliberative assembly and one seat of government for all.
Individuals could look after their own property just as before, but
Theseus compelled them to have only one centre for their political
life – namely, Athens – and, as they all became Athenian citizens,
it was a great city that Theseus handed down to those who came
after him. From him dates the feast of the Union of Attica which
the Athenians still hold today in honour of Athene and pay for out
of public funds. Before this time the city consisted of the present
Acropolis and the part below it facing southwards.

16   Evidence for this is to be found in the fact that in the Acropolis
itself are the temples of the other gods as well as of Athene; and
the temples outside the Acropolis are, in the main, situated in this
part of the city – for instance, the temple of Olympian Zeus, of
Pythian Apollo, of Earth, and of Dionysus in the Marsh, in whose
honour the more ancient Dionysia are still held in the month of
Anthesterion, a custom which is also preserved up to the present
day by the Ionians who came from Athens. Other ancient temples
also are in this part of the city. Then there is the spring of water
which is now called 'The Nine Fountains', since the tyrants had
the fountains made, but used to be called Callirhoe or 'Fair
Stream' when the water came straight out of the earth. The
people in those days used to use this spring for all purposes since it
was so close to them, and, from this ancient habit of theirs is derived the custom of using it for ceremonies before marriage and

in other religious ceremonies. Then, too, the Acropolis is still called 'the city' by the Athenians. This is because they used to live there in the past.

For a long time, therefore, the Athenians had lived in independent communities throughout Attica. And even after the unification of Attica the old habits were retained, most Athenians, both in earlier generations and right down to the time of this present war, being born and bred in the country. So they were far from pleased at having to move with their entire households, especially as they had only recently re-established themselves after the Persian War. It was sadly and reluctantly that they now abandoned their homes and the temples time-honoured from their patriotic past, that they prepared to change their whole way of life, leaving behind them what each man regarded as his own city.

17   When they arrived at Athens a few had houses of their own to go to and a few were able to find shelter with friends or relations; but most of them had to settle down in those parts of the city that had not been built over and in the temples and in the shrines of the heroes – except in the Acropolis, in the temple of Eleusinian Demeter, and some other places that were strictly forbidden. Below the Acropolis is some land called 'the Pelasgian ground', and this land was under a curse that it should not be inhabited; also there was a fragment of a Pythian oracle forbidding anything of the kind, which said: 'Better for Athens to leave the Pelasgian quarter alone.' Nevertheless, owing to the sudden pressure of events, this quarter was now built over. It appears to me that the oracle came true in a way that was opposite to what people expected. It was not because of the unlawful settlement in this place that misfortune came to Athens, but it was because of the war that the settlement had to be made. The war was not mentioned by the oracle, though it was foreseen that if this place was settled, it would be at a time when Athens was in difficulties. A number of people also took up their quarters in the towers along the walls and, in fact, wherever they could find space to live in. For when they all came into the city together there was not enough room for them, though later they shared out sections of the Long Walls and most of Piraeus and settled there.

Meanwhile everything was being put on a war basis. Allies were being approached, and a fleet of 100 ships was equipped to sail to the Peloponnese. So Athens made ready for war.

THE FIRST YEAR OF THE WAR

18 Meanwhile the Peloponnesian army was moving forward. The first place they came to in Attica was Oenoe, and it was from this point that they intended to march farther into the country. Settling down here, they prepared to assault the wall with siege engines and by other methods. Oenoe is on the frontier between Attica and Boeotia. It had been made into a fortress, and was used by the Athenians to guard the frontier in time of war. Here the Peloponnesians prepared to make an assault and spent much time with nothing to show for it. For this Archidamus was severely criticized. Even during the period leading up to the war people had thought him weak and sympathetic to Athens, because he had not spoken in favour of a full-scale war effort. And in the period after mobilization his reputation had suffered still further because of the delay at the Isthmus, and the slow progress of the march afterwards. The present hold-up in front of Oenoe seemed worst of all; for during this time the Athenians were bringing their property into the city, and the Peloponnesians considered that, if it had not been for the delaying tactics of Archidamus, they might have made a rapid advance and found all this property still outside the walls. Thus, during the siege of Oenoe, there was bitter feeling in the army against Archidamus. The reason why he still held back was, they say, because he expected that the Athenians would not face the idea of letting their land be devastated and would make some conciliatory gesture while it was still untouched.

19   However, after an unsuccessful assault had been made on Oenoe, and after all other attempts to take the place had failed, and no herald appeared from Athens, then finally they moved forward and invaded Attica. The invasion began about eighty days after the affair of Plataea, at mid-summer, when the corn was ripe. The invading army was commanded by the Spartan King, Archidamus, the son of Zeuxidamus. First they camped near Eleusis and ravaged the neighbourhood of Eleusis and the Thriasian Plain. Here, too,

they defeated a detachment of Athenian cavalry at a place called Rheiti or 'The Streams'. Then, keeping Mount Aegaleus on their right, they moved forward through Cropia and came to Acharnae, which is the biggest of the Attic demes, or districts. Here they made their camp and, settling down in the place, continued for a long time to devastate the whole area.

20   They say that Archidamus had a planned policy in remaining at Acharnae with his army all ready for battle, and not on this invasion descending into the plain. His hope was that the Athenians, with a population of young men that had never been exceeded and prepared for war as they never had been, might quite possibly come out to battle and not allow their land to be laid waste. So when they had made no move against him at Eleusis or in the Thriasian Plain, he wanted to see whether they would come out against him if he made a camp at Acharnae. Acharnae itself seemed to him a good position for a camp, and at the same time he thought it likely that the Acharnians, who, with their 3,000 hoplites, were an important element in the state, would not allow their own property to be destroyed, but would force all the others as well to come out and fight for it. If, on the other hand, the Athenians did not come out and fight during this invasion, the Peloponnesians would in future invasions have all the more confidence in laying waste the plain and advancing right up to the walls of Athens. By that time the Acharnians would have lost their own property and would be much less willing to risk their lives for the property of other people; consequently there would be a lack of unity in the counsels of Athens. This was the policy of Archidamus which accounted for his remaining at Acharnae.

21   As for the Athenians, so long as the enemy's army was at Eleusis and in the Thriasian Plain, they still hoped that it would not advance any nearer to them. They remembered the case of the Spartan King Pleistoanax, the son of Pausanias, who, fourteen years previously, had invaded Attica with a Peloponnesian army, and, after reaching Eleusis and Thria, had gone back again without coming any farther. (In fact this resulted in his being exiled from Sparta, since it was thought that he had been bribed to go back.) But when they saw the army at Acharnae, only seven miles from Athens, they could no longer put up with the situation. Their land

was being laid waste in front of their very eyes – a thing that the young men had never seen happen and that the old men had seen only at the time of the Persian invasion. Naturally enough, therefore, they felt outraged by this and wanted, especially the young, to march out and stop it. There were constant discussions with violent feelings on both sides, some demanding that they should be led out to battle, and a certain number resisting the demand. Professional prophets came forward with prophecies of all kinds, which were eagerly listened to by the various parties. The Acharnians, seeing that they formed an important part of the whole state and considering that it was their land that was being laid waste, brought particular pressure to bear in favour of marching out. Thus the city was in a thoroughly excited state; they were furious with Pericles and paid no attention at all to the advice which he had given them previously; instead they abused him for being a general and not leading them out to battle, and put on him the whole responsibility for what they were suffering themselves.

22   Pericles was convinced of the rightness of his own views about not going out to battle, but he saw that for the moment the Athenians were being led astray by their angry feelings. So he summoned no assembly or special meeting of the people, fearing that any general discussion would result in wrong decisions, made under the influence of anger rather than of reason. Meanwhile he saw to the defences of the city and kept things as quiet as he could. He did, however, constantly send out cavalry in order to stop enemy patrols from breaking into the country near the city and doing harm. One minor cavalry battle took place at Phrygia between a squadron of Athenians with Thessalian support and the Boeotian cavalry. The Athenians and Thessalians had the better of this engagement until the hoplites came up in support of the Boeotians, when the Athenians and Thessalians retreated, leaving a few dead behind. However, they recovered the bodies on the same day without asking for an armistice. On the next day the Peloponnesians put up a trophy. The help that Athens received from Thessaly was in accordance with the terms of the old treaty. The following Thessalian peoples came: the Larissaeans, the Pharsalians, the Cranonians, the Pyrasians, the Gyrtonians, and the Pheraeans. The contingent from Larissa was commanded by

Polymedes and Aristonous, each leading one division. Menon was the commander of the Pharsalians, and the other cities also each had their own commanders.

23   Finally, since the Athenians did not come out to offer battle, the Peloponnesians left their camp at Acharnae and laid waste some of the other demes lying between Mount Parnes and Mount Brilessus. While they were still in Attica the Athenians sent off round the Peloponnese the fleet of 100 ships which they had equipped. On board the ships there were 1,000 hoplites and 400 bowmen. The commanders were Carcinus, the son of Xenotimus, Proteas, the son of Epicles, and Socrates, the son of Antigenes. This expeditionary force set off on its voyage, and the Peloponnesians, after staying in Attica for as long as their supplies lasted, went back again by way of Boeotia, though not by the route on which they had come. As they passed by Oropus they laid waste the land known as the Graean territory, which was cultivated by the people of Oropus who were dependants of Athens.

24   When the Peloponnesians had retired, the Athenians established and garrisoned positions both by land and sea, with the intention of keeping these positions up for the duration of the war. They also decided to set aside and keep intact a special fund of 1,000 talents from the money in the Acropolis. The expenses of the war were to be paid out of other funds, and the death penalty was laid down for anyone who should suggest or should put to the vote any proposal for using this money in any other way except to defend the city in the case of their enemies coming to attack them with a fleet by sea. To go with this money they set aside a special fleet of 100 triremes, the best ones of each year, with their captains. These, too, were only to be used in the same way as the money and to meet the same danger, if it should ever arise.

25   Meanwhile the Athenian fleet of 100 ships which was sailing round the Peloponnese continued its voyage. The Athenians had been reinforced by fifty ships from Corcyra and others from their allies in that area. After doing damage at various places they landed in Spartan territory at Methone and made an attack on the fortifications there, which were weak and had been left without a garrison. However, Brasidas, the son of Tellis, a Spartan officer, happened to be in this district with a special detachment of men.

When he realized what was happening he came to the support of the defenders of the place with 100 hoplites. Finding the Athenian army dispersed over the country and with its attention occupied on the fortifications, he charged right through it and forced his way into Methone, losing a few of his men in the action, but saving the city. Because of this exploit he was the first person in the war to receive official congratulation at Sparta.

After this the Athenians set sail and continued their voyage round the coast. They landed at Pheia, in Elis, spent two days in laying waste the land and defeated in battle a picked force of 300 men who had come out against them from the vale of Elis and from other places in the neighbourhood. However, as a gale began to get up and there were dangers in remaining in a place without a harbour, most of them re-embarked and sailed round the head-land known as 'the Fish' into the harbour at Pheia. Meanwhile the Messenians and some of the others who had not been able to embark marched overland to Pheia and captured it. Later the ships that were sailing up the coast picked them up there. They then put to sea again, abandoning Pheia, since by this time the main army of the Eleans had come up to resist them. The Athenians continued their cruise, laying waste other places as they went.

26   At about the same time they sent out thirty ships to sail round Locris and also to keep a watch on Euboea. The commander of this fleet was Cleopompus, the son of Clinias. He made landings at various places on the coast, laid waste the country, captured Thronium and took hostages from it. Also he defeated at Alope the Locrians who came out to oppose him.

27   In this same summer the Athenians expelled the Aeginetans with their wives and children from Aegina, accusing them of having been largely responsible for the war. Also, since Aegina lies off the Peloponnesian coast, they thought that it would be safer if they sent out colonists of their own to hold it, and not long afterwards they did send out people to occupy it. The exiles from Aegina received from Sparta the town of Thyrea to live in, with land to cultivate. This was partly because of their hostility to Athens and partly because the people of Aegina had given valuable support to Sparta at the time of the earthquake and the revolt of the helots. The land of Thyrea is on the boundary between Argolis and

Laconia, and stretches down to the sea. While some of the Aeginetans settled there, others were scattered about throughout the rest of Hellas.

28 The same summer, at the beginning of a new lunar month (which seems to be the only time when such a thing is possible), there was an eclipse of the sun after midday. The sun took on the appearance of a crescent and some of the stars became visible before it returned to its normal shape.

29 In the same summer Nymphodorus, the son of Pythes, a man of Abdera, whose sister was married to Sitalces and who himself had great influence with him, was appointed by the Athenians as their representative in Thrace and was sent for to Athens, although previously he had been regarded as hostile to them. The plan was to secure the alliance of Sitalces, the son of Teres and King of Thrace. Teres, the father of Sitalces, was the founder of the great Kingdom of the Odrysae, which extends over the greater part of Thrace, though a considerable portion of Thrace is independent. This Teres has no connection with the Tereus who married Procne, the daughter of Pandion, from Athens. The two did not even come from the same part of Thrace. Tereus lived in Daulis, which is in what is now called Phocis, but used then to be inhabited by Thracians. It was in this land that the women committed the famous crime in connection with Itys, and many of the poets, in referring to the nightingale, call it 'the Daulian bird'. Also it is likely that Pandion in making an alliance for his daughter would have had an eye on the possibilities of mutual aid. This would be more practicable in the case of such a short distance than in the case of the many days' journey between Athens and the Odrysae. Then, too, the names are different; and this Teres was the first King to gain power among the Odrysae. In working for his alliance the Athenians wanted to gain his help in controlling Perdiccas and the towns in Thrace. When Nymphodorus came to Athens he arranged an alliance with Sitalces, had his son Sadocus made an Athenian citizen and promised to settle the war in Thrace by persuading Sitalces to send the Athenians a Thracian army of cavalry and peltasts. He also brought Perdiccas over to the Athenian side and persuaded the Athenians to give Therme back to him. Immediately after this Perdiccas joined the Athenians under

Phormio in a campaign against the Chalcidians. In this way Athens secured the alliance of Sitalces, the son of Teres, King of Thrace, and Perdiccas, the son of Alexander, King of Macedonia.

30   Meanwhile the Athenian fleet of 100 ships was still in Peloponnesian waters. They captured the Corinthian town of Sollium and gave the town together with its land to the Acarnanians of Palaera. Then they stormed Astacus, where Evarchus was dictator, and, after driving Evarchus out, brought the place over into their alliance. They next sailed to Cephallenia, which faces towards Acarnania and Leucas, and consists of four cities inhabited by the Paleans, the Cranians, the Samaeans, and the Pronaeans, and won the island over without having to fight a battle. Soon after this the fleet returned to Athens.

31   In the autumn of this year the whole Athenian army, including the resident aliens, invaded the Megarid under the command of Pericles, the son of Xanthippus. The fleet of 100 ships that had been round the Peloponnese happened just at this time to have reached Aegina on their way home, and when they heard that the whole army from Athens was at Megara, they sailed over and joined forces with them. This was certainly the biggest Athenian army that had ever yet taken the field. Athens was then at the height of her power and had not yet suffered from the plague. There were at least 10,000 hoplites from the citizen body (not counting the 3,000 at Potidaea); no fewer than 3,000 hoplites from the resident aliens joined in the invasion; and there was also a considerable number of light armed troops. After laying waste most of the Megarid they returned to Athens. Other invasions of the Megarid, either with cavalry or with the whole army, were made each year during the war up to the time when Nisaea was captured by the Athenians.

32   Also at the end of this summer the Athenians established a fortified post at Atalanta, an island, previously uninhabited, lying off the coast of Opuntian Locris, in order to prevent pirates from sailing out from Opus and other parts of Locris and doing damage in Euboea.

33   All these actions took place in the summer after the Peloponnesians had withdrawn from Attica. In the winter of the same year Evarchus the Acarnanian, wanting to get back to Astacus, per-

suaded the Corinthians to sail there with forty ships and 1,500 hoplites and restore him to power. He himself hired a certain number of mercenaries. The commanders of this expedition were Euphamidas, the son of Aristonymus, Timoxenus, the son of Timocrates, and Eumachus, the son of Chrysis. After sailing to Astacus and restoring Evarchus they made some unsuccessful attempts at winning over other places which they wanted to secure on the coast of Acarnania. They then returned home and on their way down the coast put in at Cephallenia, landing in the territory of the Cranians. Here they lost some men, as the Cranians deceitfully pretended to make a pact with them and then suddenly set upon them. Thus they embarked with some difficulty and returned to Corinth.

PERICLES' FUNERAL ORATION

34 In the same winter the Athenians, following their annual custom, gave a public funeral for those who had been the first to die in the war. These funerals are held in the following way: two days before the ceremony the bones of the fallen are brought and put in a tent which has been erected, and people make whatever offerings they wish to their own dead. Then there is a funeral procession in which coffins of cypress wood are carried on wagons. There is one coffin for each tribe, which contains the bones of members of that tribe. One empty bier is decorated and carried in the procession: this is for the missing, whose bodies could not be recovered. Everyone who wishes to, both citizens and foreigners, can join in the procession, and the women who are related to the dead are there to make their laments at the tomb. The bones are laid in the public burial-place, which is in the most beautiful quarter outside the city walls. Here the Athenians always bury those who have fallen in war. The only exception is those who died at Marathon, who, because their achievement was considered absolutely outstanding, were buried on the battlefield itself.

When the bones have been laid in the earth, a man chosen by the city for his intellectual gifts and for his general reputation makes an appropriate speech in praise of the dead, and after the speech all depart. This is the procedure at these burials, and all through the war, when the time came to do so, the Athenians followed this ancient custom. Now, at the burial of those who were the first to fall in the war Pericles, the son of Xanthippus, was chosen to make the speech. When the moment arrived, he came forward from the tomb and, standing on a high platform, so that he might be heard by as many people as possible in the crowd, he spoke as follows:

35   'Many of those who have spoken here in the past have praised the institution of this speech at the close of our ceremony. It seemed to them a mark of honour to our soldiers who have fallen in war that a speech should be made over them. I do not agree. These men have shown themselves valiant in action, and it would be enough, I think, for their glories to be proclaimed in action, as you have just seen it done at this funeral organized by the state. Our belief in the courage and manliness of so many should not be hazarded on the goodness or badness of one man's speech. Then it is not easy to speak with a proper sense of balance, when a man's listeners find it difficult to believe in the truth of what one is saying. The man who knows the facts and loves the dead may well think that an oration tells less than what he knows and what he would like to hear: others who do not know so much may feel envy for the dead, and think the orator over-praises them, when he speaks of exploits that are beyond their own capacities. Praise of other people is tolerable only up to a certain point, the point where one still believes that one could do oneself some of the things one is hearing about. Once you get beyond this point, you will find people becoming jealous and incredulous. However, the fact is that this institution was set up and approved by our forefathers, and it is my duty to follow the tradition and do my best to meet the wishes and the expectations of every one of you.

36   'I shall begin by speaking about our ancestors, since it is only right and proper on such an occasion to pay them the honour of recalling what they did. In this land of ours there have always been the same people living from generation to generation up till now, and they, by their courage and their virtues, have handed it on to us, a free country. They certainly deserve our praise. Even more so do our fathers deserve it. For to the inheritance they had received

they added all the empire we have now, and it was not without blood and toil that they handed it down to us of the present generation. And then we ourselves, assembled here today, who are mostly in the prime of life, have, in most directions, added to the power of our empire and have organized our State in such a way that it is perfectly well able to look after itself both in peace and in war.

'I have no wish to make a long speech on subjects familiar to you all: so I shall say nothing about the warlike deeds by which we acquired our power or the battles in which we or our fathers gallantly resisted our enemies, Greek or foreign. What I want to do is, in the first place, to discuss the spirit in which we faced our trials and also our constitution and the way of life which has made us great. After that I shall speak in praise of the dead, believing that this kind of speech is not inappropriate to the present occasion, and that this whole assembly, of citizens and foreigners, may listen to it with advantage.

37   'Let me say that our system of government does not copy the institutions of our neighbours. It is more the case of our being a model to others, than of our imitating anyone else. Our constitution is called a democracy because power is in the hands not of a minority but of the whole people. When it is a question of settling private disputes, everyone is equal before the law; when it is a question of putting one person before another in positions of public responsibility, what counts is not membership of a particular class, but the actual ability which the man possesses. No one, so long as he has it in him to be of service to the state, is kept in political obscurity because of poverty. And, just as our political life is free and open, so is our day-to-day life in our relations with each other. We do not get into a state with our next-door neighbour if he enjoys himself in his own way, nor do we give him the kind of black looks which, though they do no real harm, still do hurt people's feelings. We are free and tolerant in our private lives; but in public affairs we keep to the law. This is because it commands our deep respect.

We give our obedience to those whom we put in positions of authority, and we obey the laws themselves, especially those which are for the protection of the oppressed, and those unwritten laws which it is an acknowledged shame to break.

38   'And here is another point. When our work is over, we are in a
position to enjoy all kinds of recreation for our spirits. There are
various kinds of contests and sacrifices regularly throughout the
year; in our own homes we find a beauty and a good taste which
delight us every day and which drive away our cares. Then the
greatness of our city brings it about that all the good things from
all over the world flow in to us, so that to us it seems just as natural
to enjoy foreign goods as our own local products.

39   'Then there is a great difference between us and our opponents,
in our attitude towards military security. Here are some examples:
Our city is open to the world, and we have no periodical deporta-
tions in order to prevent people observing or finding out secrets
which might be of military advantage to the enemy. This is because
we rely, not on secret weapons, but on our own real courage and
loyalty. There is a difference, too, in our educational systems. The
Spartans, from their earliest boyhood, are submitted to the most
laborious training in courage; we pass our lives without all these
restrictions, and yet are just as ready to face the same dangers as
they are. Here is a proof of this: When the Spartans invade our
land, they do not come by themselves, but bring all their allies
with them; whereas we, when we launch an attack abroad, do the
job by ourselves, and, though fighting on foreign soil, do not
often fail to defeat opponents who are fighting for their own
hearths and homes. As a matter of fact none of our enemies has
ever yet been confronted with our total strength, because we have
to divide our attention between our navy and the many missions
on which our troops are sent on land. Yet, if our enemies engage a
detachment of our forces and defeat it, they give themselves credit
for having thrown back our entire army; or, if they lose, they
claim that they were beaten by us in full strength. There are
certain advantages, I think, in our way of meeting danger voluntarily, with an easy mind, instead of with a laborious training,
with natural rather than with state-induced courage. We do not
have to spend our time practising to meet sufferings which are
still in the future; and when they are actually upon us we show
ourselves just as brave as these others who are always in strict
training. This is one point in which, I think, our city deserves to be
admired. There are also others:

40   'Our love of what is beautiful does not lead to extravagance; our love of the things of the mind does not make us soft. We regard wealth as something to be properly used, rather than as something to boast about. As for poverty, no one need be ashamed to admit it: the real shame is in not taking practical measures to escape from it. Here each individual is interested not only in his own affairs but in the affairs of the state as well: even those who are mostly occupied with their own business are extremely well-informed on general politics – this is a peculiarity of ours: we do not say that a man who takes no interest in politics is a man who minds his own business; we say that he has no business here at all. We Athenians, in our own persons, take our decisions on policy or submit them to proper discussions: for we do not think that there is an incompatibility between words and deeds; the worst thing is to rush into action before the consequences have been properly debated. And this is another point where we differ from other people. We are capable at the same time of taking risks and of estimating them beforehand. Others are brave out of ignorance; and, when they stop to think, they begin to fear. But the man who can most truly be accounted brave is he who best knows the meaning of what is sweet in life and of what is terrible, and then goes out undeterred to meet what is to come.

'Again, in questions of general good feeling there is a great contrast between us and most other people. We make friends by doing good to others, not by receiving good from them. This makes our friendship all the more reliable, since we want to keep alive the gratitude of those who are in our debt by showing continued good-will to them: whereas the feelings of one who owes us something lack the same enthusiasm, since he knows that, when he repays our kindness, it will be more like paying back a debt than giving something spontaneously. We are unique in this. When we do kindnesses to others, we do not do them out of any calculations of profit or loss: we do them without afterthought, relying on our free liberality. Taking everything together then, I declare that our

41 city is an education to Greece, and I declare that in my opinion each single one of our citizens, in all the manifold aspects of life, is able to show himself the rightful lord and owner of his own person, and do this, moreover, with exceptional grace and

exceptional versatility. And to show that this is no empty boasting for the present occasion, but real tangible fact, you have only to consider the power which our city possesses and which has been won by those very qualities which I have mentioned. Athens, alone of the states we know, comes to her testing time in a greatness that surpasses what was imagined of her. In her case, and in her case alone, no invading enemy is ashamed at being defeated, and no subject can complain of being governed by people unfit for their responsibilities. Mighty indeed are the marks and monuments of our empire which we have left. Future ages will wonder at us, as the present age wonders at us now. We do not need the praises of a Homer, or of anyone else whose words may delight us for the moment, but whose estimation of facts will fall short of what is really true. For our adventurous spirit has forced an entry into every sea and into every land; and everywhere we have left behind us everlasting memorials of good done to our friends or suffering inflicted on our enemies.

'This, then, is the kind of city for which these men, who could not bear the thought of losing her, nobly fought and nobly died. It is only natural that every one of us who survive them should be 42 willing to undergo hardships in her service. And it was for this reason that I have spoken at such length about our city, because I wanted to make it clear that for us there is more at stake than there is for others who lack our advantages; also I wanted my words of praise for the dead to be set in the bright light of evidence. And now the most important of these words has been spoken. I have sung the praises of our city; but it was the courage and gallantry of these men, and of people like them, which made her splendid. Nor would you find it true in the case of many of the Greeks, as it is true of them, that no words can do more than justice to their deeds.

'To me it seems that the consummation which has overtaken these men shows us the meaning of manliness in its first revelation and in its final proof. Some of them, no doubt, had their faults; but what we ought to remember first is their gallant conduct against the enemy in defence of their native land. They have blotted out evil with good, and done more service to the commonwealth than they ever did harm in their private lives. No one of these men weakened because he wanted to go on enjoying his wealth: no one put off the awful day in the hope that he might live to escape his poverty and grow rich. More to be desired than such things, they chose to check the enemy's pride. This, to them, was a risk most glorious, and they accepted it, willing to strike down the enemy and relinquish everything else. As for success or failure, they left that in the doubtful hands of Hope, and when the reality of battle was before their faces, they put their trust in their own selves. In the fighting, they thought it more honourable to stand their ground and suffer death than to give in and save their lives. So they fled from the reproaches of men, abiding with life and limb the brunt of battle; and, in a small moment of time, the climax of their lives, a culmination of glory, not of fear, were swept away from us.

43   'So and such they were, these men – worthy of their city. We who remain behind may hope to be spared their fate, but must resolve to keep the same daring spirit against the foe. It is not simply a question of estimating the advantages in theory. I could tell you a long story (and you know it as well as I do) about what is to be gained by beating the enemy back. What I would prefer is that you should fix your eyes every day on the greatness of Athens as she really is, and should fall in love with her. When you realize her greatness, then reflect that what made her great was men with a spirit of adventure, men who knew their duty, men who were ashamed to fall below a certain standard. If they ever failed in an enterprise, they made up their minds that at any rate the city should not find their courage lacking to her, and they gave to her the best contribution that they could. They gave her their lives, to her and to all of us, and for their own selves they won praises that never grow old, the most splendid of sepulchres – not the sepulchre in which their bodies are laid, but where their glory remains eternal in men's minds, always there on the right occasion to stir others to speech or to action. For famous men have the whole earth as their memorial: it is not only the inscriptions on their graves in their own country that mark them out; no, in foreign lands also, not in any visible form but in people's hearts, their memory abides and grows. It is for you to try to be like them. Make up your minds that happiness depends on being free, and

freedom depends on being courageous. Let there be no relaxation in face of the perils of the war. The people who have most excuse for despising death are not the wretched and unfortunate, who have no hope of doing well for themselves, but those who run the risk of a complete reversal in their lives, and who would feel the difference most intensely, if things went wrong for them. Any intelligent man would find a humiliation caused by his own slackness more painful to bear than death, when death comes to him unperceived, in battle, and in the confidence of his patriotism.

44   'For these reasons I shall not commiserate with those parents of the dead, who are present here. Instead I shall try to comfort them. They are well aware that they have grown up in a world where there are many changes and chances. But this is good fortune – for men to end their lives with honour, as these have done, and for you honourably to lament them: their life was set to a measure where death and happiness went hand in hand. I know that it is difficult to convince you of this. When you see other people happy you will often be reminded of what used to make you happy too. One does not feel sad at not having some good thing which is outside one's experience: real grief is felt at the loss of something which one is used to. All the same, those of you who are of the right age must bear up and take comfort in the thought of having more children. In your own homes these new children will prevent you from brooding over those who are no more, and they will be a help to the city, too, both in filling the empty places, and in assuring her security. For it is impossible for a man to put forward fair and honest views about our affairs if he has not, like everyone else, children whose lives may be at stake. As for those of you who are now too old to have children, I would ask you to count as gain the greater part of your life, in which you have been happy, and remember that what remains is not long, and let your hearts be lifted up at the thought of the fair fame of the dead. One's sense of honour is the only thing that does not grow old, and the last pleasure, when one is worn out with age, is not, as the poet said, making money, but having the respect of one's fellow men.

45   'As for those of you here who are sons or brothers of the dead, I can see a hard struggle in front of you. Everyone always speaks well of the dead, and, even if you rise to the greatest heights of

heroism, it will be a hard thing for you to get the reputation of having come near, let alone equalled, their standard. When one is alive, one is always liable to the jealousy of one's competitors, but when one is out of the way, the honour one receives is sincere and unchallenged.

46 'Perhaps I should say a word or two on the duties of women to those among you who are now widowed. I can say all I have to say in a short word of advice. Your great glory is not to be inferior to what God has made you, and the greatest glory of a woman is to be least talked about by men, whether they are praising you or criticizing you. I have now, as the law demanded, said what I had to say. For the time being our offerings to the dead have been made, and for the future their children will be supported at the public expense by the city, until they come of age. This is the crown and prize which she offers, both to the dead and to their children, for the ordeals which they have faced. Where the rewards of valour are the greatest, there you will find also the best and bravest spirits among the people. And now, when you have mourned for your dear ones, you must depart.'

THE PLAGUE[27]

47 In this way the public funeral was conducted in the winter that came at the end of the first year of the war. At the beginning of the following summer the Peloponnesians and their allies, with two-thirds of their total forces as before, invaded Attica, again under the command of the Spartan King Archidamus, the son of Zeuxidamus. Taking up their positions, they set about the devastation of the country.

They had not been many days in Attica before the plague first broke out among the Athenians. Previously attacks of the plague had been reported from many other places in the neighbourhood of Lemnos and elsewhere, but there was no record of the disease being so virulent anywhere else or causing so many deaths as it did in Athens. At the beginning the doctors were quite incapable of treating the disease because of their ignorance of the right methods.

27. See the Introduction, pp. 20–21.

In fact mortality among the doctors was the highest of all, since they came more frequently in contact with the sick. Nor was any other human art or science of any help at all. Equally useless were prayers made in the temples, consultation of oracles, and so forth; indeed, in the end people were so overcome by their sufferings that they paid no further attention to such things.

48   The plague originated, so they say, in Ethiopia in upper Egypt, and spread from there into Egypt itself and Libya and much of the territory of the King of Persia. In the city of Athens it appeared suddenly, and the first cases were among the population of Piraeus, where there were no wells at that time, so that it was supposed by them that the Peloponnesians had poisoned the reservoirs. Later, however, it appeared also in the upper city, and by this time the deaths were greatly increasing in number. As to the question of how it could first have come about or what causes can be found adequate to explain its powerful effect on nature, I must leave that to be considered by other writers, with or without medical experience. I myself shall merely describe what it was like, and set down the symptoms, knowledge of which will enable it to be recognized, if it should ever break out again. I had the disease myself and saw others suffering from it.

49   That year, as is generally admitted, was particularly free from all other kinds of illness, though those who did have any illness previously all caught the plague in the end. In other cases, however, there seemed to be no reason for the attacks. People in perfect health suddenly began to have burning feelings in the head; their eyes became red and inflamed; inside their mouths there was bleeding from the throat and tongue, and the breath became unnatural and unpleasant. The next symptoms were sneezing and hoarseness of voice, and before long the pain settled on the chest and was accompanied by coughing. Next the stomach was affected with stomach-aches and with vomitings of every kind of bile that has been given a name by the medical profession, all this being accompanied by great pain and difficulty. In most cases there were attacks of ineffectual retching, producing violent spasms; this sometimes ended with this stage of the disease, but sometimes continued long afterwards. Externally the body was not very hot to the touch, nor was there any pallor: the skin was rather reddish

and livid, breaking out into small pustules and ulcers. But inside there was a feeling of burning, so that people could not bear the touch even of the lightest linen clothing, but wanted to be completely naked, and indeed most of all would have liked to plunge into cold water. Many of the sick who were uncared for actually did so, plunging into the water-tanks in an effort to relieve a thirst which was unquenchable; for it was just the same with them whether they drank much or little. Then all the time they were afflicted with insomnia and the desperate feeling of not being able to keep still.

In the period when the disease was at its height, the body, so far from wasting away, showed surprising powers of resistance to all the agony, so that there was still some strength left on the seventh or eighth day, which was the time when, in most cases, death came from the internal fever. But if people survived this critical period, then the disease descended to the bowels, producing violent ulceration and uncontrollable diarrhoea, so that most of them died later as a result of the weakness caused by this. For the disease, first settling in the head, went on to affect every part of the body in turn, and even when people escaped its worst effects, it still left its traces on them by fastening upon the extremities of the body. It affected the genitals, the fingers, and the toes, and many of those who recovered lost the use of these members; some, too, went blind. There were some also who, when they first began to get better, suffered from a total loss of memory, not knowing who they were themselves and being unable to recognize their friends.

50　　Words indeed fail one when one tries to give a general picture of this disease; and as for the sufferings of individuals, they seemed almost beyond the capacity of human nature to endure. Here in particular is a point where this plague showed itself to be something quite different from ordinary diseases: though there were many dead bodies lying about unburied, the birds and animals that eat human flesh either did not come near them or, if they did taste the flesh, died of it afterwards. Evidence for this may be found in the fact that there was a complete disappearance of all birds of prey: they were not to be seen either round the bodies or anywhere else. But dogs, being domestic animals, provided the best opportunity of observing this effect of the plague.

51   These, then, were the general features of the disease, though I
have omitted all kinds of peculiarities which occurred in various
individual cases. Meanwhile, during all this time there was no
serious outbreak of any of the usual kinds of illness; if any such
cases did occur, they ended in the plague. Some died in neglect,
some in spite of every possible care being taken of them. As for a
recognized method of treatment, it would be true to say that no
such thing existed: what did good in some cases did harm in
others. Those with naturally strong constitutions were no better
able than the weak to resist the disease, which carried away all
alike, even those who were treated and dieted with the greatest
care. The most terrible thing of all was the despair into which
people fell when they realized that they had caught the plague; for
they would immediately adopt an attitude of utter hopelessness,
and, by giving in in this way, would lose their powers of resistance.
Terrible, too, was the sight of people dying like sheep through
having caught the disease as a result of nursing others. This indeed
caused more deaths than anything else. For when people were
afraid to visit the sick, then they died with no one to look after
them; indeed, there were many houses in which all the inhabitants
perished through lack of any attention. When, on the other hand,
they did visit the sick, they lost their own lives, and this was
particularly true of those who made it a point of honour to act
properly. Such people felt ashamed to think of their own safety
and went into their friends' houses at times when even the members of the household were so overwhelmed by the weight of their
calamities that they had actually given up the usual practice of
making laments for the dead. Yet still the ones who felt most pity
for the sick and the dying were those who had had the plague
themselves and had recovered from it. They knew what it was
like and at the same time felt themselves to be safe, for no one
caught the disease twice, or, if he did, the second attack was never
fatal. Such people were congratulated on all sides, and they themselves were so elated at the time of their recovery that they fondly
imagined that they could never die of any other disease in the
future.

52   A factor which made matters much worse than they were already was the removal of people from the country into the city,

and this particularly affected the incomers. There were no houses for them, and, living as they did during the hot season in badly ventilated huts, they died like flies. The bodies of the dying were heaped one on top of the other, and half-dead creatures could be seen staggering about in the streets or flocking around the fountains in their desire for water. The temples in which they took up their quarters were full of the dead bodies of people who had died inside them. For the catastrophe was so overwhelming that men, not knowing what would happen next to them, became indifferent to every rule of religion or of law. All the funeral ceremonies which used to be observed were now disorganized, and they buried the dead as best they could. Many people, lacking the necessary means of burial because so many deaths had already occurred in their households, adopted the most shameless methods. They would arrive first at a funeral pyre that had been made by others, put their own dead upon it and set it alight; or, finding another pyre burning, they would throw the corpse that they were carrying on top of the other one and go away.

53   In other respects also Athens owed to the plague the beginnings of a state of unprecedented lawlessness. Seeing how quick and abrupt were the changes of fortune which came to the rich who suddenly died and to those who had previously been penniless but now inherited their wealth, people now began openly to venture on acts of self-indulgence which before then they used to keep dark. Thus they resolved to spend their money quickly and to spend it on pleasure, since money and life alike seemed equally ephemeral. As for what is called honour, no one showed himself willing to abide by its laws, so doubtful was it whether one would survive to enjoy the name for it. It was generally agreed that what was both honourable and valuable was the pleasure of the moment and everything that might conceivably contribute to that pleasure. No fear of god or law of man had a restraining influence. As for the gods, it seemed to be the same thing whether one worshipped them or not, when one saw the good and the bad dying indiscriminately. As for offences against human law, no one expected to live long enough to be brought to trial and punished: instead everyone felt that already a far heavier sentence had been passed on him and was hanging over him, and that before the time for its

execution arrived it was only natural to get some pleasure out of life.

54   This, then, was the calamity which fell upon Athens, and the times were hard indeed, with men dying inside the city and the land outside being laid waste. At this time of distress people naturally recalled old oracles, and among them was a verse which the old men claimed had been delivered in the past and which said:

War with the Dorians comes, and a death will come at the same time.

There had been a controversy as to whether the word in this ancient verse was 'dearth' rather than 'death'; but in the present state of affairs the view that the word was 'death' naturally prevailed; it was a case of people adapting their memories to suit their sufferings. Certainly I think that if there is ever another war with the Dorians after this one, and if a dearth results from it, then in all probability people will quote the other version.

Then also the oracle that was given to the Spartans was remembered by those who knew of it: that when they inquired from the god whether they should go to war, they received the reply that, if they fought with all their might, victory would be theirs and that the god himself would be on their side. What was actually happening seemed to fit in well with the words of this oracle; certainly the plague broke out directly after the Peloponnesian invasion, and never affected the Peloponnese at all, or not seriously; its full force was felt at Athens, and, after Athens, in the most densely populated of the other towns.

55   Such were the events connected with the plague. Meanwhile the Peloponnesians, after laying waste the Attic plain, moved on into the Paralian district as far as Laurium, where the Athenian silver-mines are. First they laid waste the side that looks towards the Peloponnese, and then the other side facing Euboea and Andros.

THE POLICY OF PERICLES

Pericles was still general, and, just as in the previous invasion, he remained convinced that the Athenians should not march out and

56 offer battle. But he was organizing an expeditionary force of 100 ships against the Peloponnese, while the invaders were still in the plain and before they had moved into the Paralia. When everything was ready, this expedition put to sea. On board the ships Pericles took 4,000 citizen hoplites and also 300 cavalry. Old vessels were converted into transports, which on this occasion were used for the first time for carrying horses. Fifty ships from Chios and Lesbos also joined the expedition, and when this Athenian force put to sea they left the Peloponnesians behind them in Attica, in the Paralian district. Landing at Epidaurus, in the Peloponnese, they devastated most of the land and made an assault on the city. There was a moment when they seemed likely to capture the place, but in the end the attack was unsuccessful. Putting to sea again from Epidaurus they devastated the land of Troezen, Haliae, and Hermione, all places on the Peloponnesian coast. Then, sailing on, they came to Prasiae, a fortified place on the coast of Laconia. Here they devastated the land and took and sacked the place itself. After this they returned home, and found that the Peloponnesians had also retired and were no longer in Attica.

57 All the time that the Peloponnesians had been in Attica and that the Athenians had been engaged in this naval expedition, men kept dying of the plague, both in the army and in the city. Indeed, it was said that the Peloponnesians left Attica earlier than they had intended because they were afraid of the infection (they heard from deserters that it was in the city, and at the same time they could see the funerals taking place). Yet this invasion lasted longer than any other, and they laid waste the whole country, remaining in Attica for about forty days.

58 In the same summer Hagnon, the son of Nicias, and Cleopompus, the son of Clinias, who were Pericles' colleagues in the higher command, took over the force which Pericles had used against the Peloponnese and started immediately upon a campaign in Thrace against the Chalcidians and against Potidaea, which was still besieged. When they arrived there, they brought up siege engines against Potidaea and did everything they could to capture it. Nothing, however, went right. They neither captured the city nor accomplished anything else that might have been expected from such a force. This was due to the fact that here also the plague

broke out among them, with the most disastrous effects on the army. Even the Athenian troops who were there previously and who up to this time had been perfectly healthy now caught the disease from Hagnon's men. Phormio and his 1,600 men were luckily no longer in the area of the Chalcidians. In the end Hagnon returned with his ships to Athens, having lost by the plague in the space of about forty days 1,050 hoplites out of his original force of 4,000. The troops who had been there before remained in their old positions and went on with the siege of Potidaea.

59   After the second invasion of the Peloponnesians there had been a change in the spirit of the Athenians. Their land had been twice devastated, and they had to contend with the war and the plague at the same time. Now they began to blame Pericles for having persuaded them to go to war and to hold him responsible for all the misfortunes which had overtaken them; they became eager to make peace with Sparta and actually sent ambassadors there, who failed to achieve anything. They were then in a state of utter hopelessness, and all their angry feelings turned against Pericles.

Pericles himself saw well enough how bitterly they felt at the situation in which they found themselves; he saw, in fact, that they were behaving exactly as he had expected that they would. He therefore, since he was still general, summoned an assembly with the aim of putting fresh courage into them and of guiding their embittered spirits so as to leave them in a calmer and more confident frame of mind. Coming before them, he made the following speech:

60   'I expected this outbreak of anger on your part against me, since I understand the reasons for it; and I have called an assembly with this object in view, to remind you of your previous resolutions and to put forward my own case against you, if we find that there is anything unreasonable in your anger against me and in your giving way to your misfortunes. My own opinion is that when the whole state is on the right course it is a better thing for each separate individual than when private interests are satisfied but the state as a whole is going downhill. However well off a man may be in his private life, he will still be involved in the general ruin if his country is destroyed; whereas, so long as the state itself is secure, individuals have a much greater chance of recovering

from their private misfortunes. Therefore, since a state can support individuals in their suffering, but no one person by himself can bear the load that rests upon the state, is it not right for us all to rally to her defence? Is it not wrong to act as you are doing now? For you have been so dismayed by disaster in your homes that you are losing your grip on the common safety; you are attacking me for having spoken in favour of war and yourselves for having voted for it.

'So far as I am concerned, if you are angry with me you are angry with one who has, I think, at least as much ability as anyone else to see what ought to be done and to explain what he sees, one who loves his city and one who is above being influenced by money. A man who has the knowledge but lacks the power clearly to express it is no better off than if he never had any ideas at all. A man who has both these qualities, but lacks patriotism, could scarcely speak for his own people as he should. And even if he is patriotic as well, but not able to resist a bribe, then this one fault will expose everything to the risk of being bought and sold. So that if at the time when you took my advice and went to war you considered that my record with regard to these qualities was even slightly better than that of others, then now surely it is quite unreasonable for me to be accused of having done wrong.

61   'If one has a free choice and can live undisturbed, it is sheer folly to go to war. But suppose the choice was forced upon one – submission and immediate slavery or danger with the hope of survival: then I prefer the man who stands up to danger rather than the one who runs away from it. As for me, I am the same as I was, and do not alter; it is you who have changed. What has happened is this: you took my advice when you were still untouched by misfortune, and repented of your action when things went badly with you; it is because your own resolution is weak that my policy appears to you to be mistaken. It is a policy which entails suffering, and each one of you already knows what this suffering is; but its ultimate benefits are still far away and not yet clear for all to see. So, now that a great and sudden disaster has fallen on you, you have weakened in carrying out to the end the resolves which you made. When things happen suddenly, unexpectedly, and against all calculation, it takes the heart out of a man; and this certainly

has happened to you, with the plague coming on top of everything else. Yet you must remember that you are citizens of a great city and that you were brought up in a way of life suited to her greatness; you must therefore be willing to face the greatest disasters and be determined never to sacrifice the glory that is yours. We all look with distaste on people who arrogantly pretend to a reputation to which they are not entitled; but equally to be condemned are those who, through lack of moral fibre, fail to live up to the reputation which is theirs already. Each of you, therefore, must try to stifle his own particular sorrow as he joins with the rest in working for the safety of us all.

62   'And if you think that our war-time sufferings may grow greater and greater and still not bring us any nearer to victory, you ought to be satisfied with the arguments which I have often used on other occasions to show that there is no good reason for such fears. But there is this point also which I shall mention. In thinking of the greatness of your empire there is one advantage you have which, I think, you have never yet taken into consideration, nor have I mentioned it in my previous speeches. Indeed, since it sounds almost like boasting, I should not be making use of this argument now if it were not for the fact that I see that you are suffering from an unreasonable feeling of discouragement. Now, what you think is that your empire consists simply of your allies: but I have something else to tell you. The whole world before our eyes can be divided into two parts, the land and the sea, each of which is valuable and useful to man. Of the whole of one of these parts you are in control – not only of the area at present in your power, but elsewhere too, if you want to go further. With your navy as it is today there is no power on earth – not the King of Persia nor any people under the sun – which can stop you from sailing where you wish. This power of yours is something in an altogether different category from all the advantages of houses or of cultivated land. You may think that when you lose them you have suffered a great loss, but in fact you should not take things so hardly; you should weigh them in the balance with the real source of your power and see that, in comparison, they are no more to be valued than gardens and other elegances that go with wealth. Remember, too, that freedom, if we preserve our freedom by our own efforts, will

easily restore us to our old position; but to submit to the will of others means to lose even what we still have. You must not fall below the standard of your fathers, who not only won an empire by their own toil and sweat, without receiving it from others, but went on to keep it safe so that they could hand it down to you. And, by the way, it is more of a disgrace to be robbed of what one has than to fail in some new undertaking. Not courage alone, therefore, but an actual sense of your superiority should animate you as you go forward against the enemy. Confidence, out of a mixture of ignorance and good luck, can be felt even by cowards; but this sense of superiority comes only to those who, like us, have real reasons for knowing that they are better placed than their opponents. And when the chances on both sides are equal, it is intelligence that confirms courage – the intelligence that makes one able to look down on one's opponent, and which proceeds not by hoping for the best (a method only valuable in desperate situations), but by estimating what the facts are, and thus obtaining a clearer vision of what to expect.

63   'Then it is right and proper for you to support the imperial dignity of Athens. This is something in which you all take pride, and you cannot continue to enjoy the privileges unless you also shoulder the burdens of empire. And do not imagine that what we are fighting for is simply the question of freedom or slavery: there is also involved the loss of our empire and the dangers arising from the hatred which we have incurred in administering it. Nor is it any longer possible for you to give up this empire, though there may be some people who in a mood of sudden panic and in a spirit of political apathy actually think that this would be a fine and noble thing to do. Your empire is now like a tyranny: it may have been wrong to take it; it is certainly dangerous to let it go. And the kind of people who talk of doing so and persuade others to adopt their point of view would very soon bring a state to ruin, and would still do so even if they lived by themselves in isolation. For those who are politically apathetic can only survive if they are supported by people who are capable of taking action. They are quite valueless in a city which controls an empire, though they would be safe slaves in a city that was controlled by others.

64   'But you should not be led astray by such citizens as these; nor

should you be angry with me, you who came to the same conclusion as I did about the necessity for making war. Certainly the
enemy have invaded our country and done as one might have
expected they would do, once you refused to give in to them; and
then the plague, something which we did not expect, fell upon us.
In fact out of everything else this has been the only case of something happening which we did not anticipate. And I know that it
is very largely because of this that I have become unpopular, quite
unfairly, unless you are also going to put down to my credit every
piece of unexpected good fortune that comes your way. But it is
right to endure with resignation what the gods send, and to face
one's enemies with courage. This was the old Athenian way: do
not let any act of yours prevent it from still being so. Remember,
too, that the reason why Athens has the greatest name in all the
world is because she has never given in to adversity, but has spent
more life and labour in warfare than any other state, thus winning
the greatest power that has ever existed in history, such a power
that will be remembered for ever by posterity, even if now (since
all things are born to decay) there should come a time when we
were forced to yield: yet still it will be remembered that of all
Hellenic powers we held the widest sway over the Hellenes, that
we stood firm in the greatest wars against their combined forces
and against individual states, that we lived in a city which had been
perfectly equipped in every direction and which was the greatest
in Hellas.

'No doubt all this will be disparaged by people who are politically apathetic; but those who, like us, prefer a life of action will
try to imitate us, and, if they fail to secure what we have secured,
they will envy us. All who have taken it upon themselves to rule
over others have incurred hatred and unpopularity for a time; but
if one has a great aim to pursue, this burden of envy must be
accepted, and it is wise to accept it. Hatred does not last for long;
but the brilliance of the present is the glory of the future stored up
for ever in the memory of man. It is for you to safeguard that
future glory and to do nothing now that is dishonourable. Now,
therefore, is the time to show your energy and to achieve both
these objects. Do not send embassies to Sparta: do not give the
impression that you are bowed down under your present suffer-

ings! To face calamity with a mind as unclouded as may be, and quickly to react against it – that, in a city and in an individual, is real strength.'

65   In this way Pericles attempted to stop the Athenians from being angry with him and to guide their thoughts in a direction away from their immediate sufferings. So far as public policy was concerned, they accepted his arguments, sending no more embassies to Sparta and showing an increased energy in carrying on the war; yet as private individuals they still felt the weight of their misfortunes. The mass of the people had had little enough to start with and had now been deprived of even that; the richer classes had lost their fine estates with their rich and well-equipped houses in the country, and, which was the worst thing of all, they were at war instead of living in peace. In fact, the general ill feeling against Pericles persisted, and was not satisfied until they had condemned him to pay a fine. Not long afterwards, however, as is the way with crowds, they re-elected him to the generalship and put all their affairs into his hands. By that time people felt their own private sufferings rather less acutely and, so far as the general needs of the state were concerned, they regarded Pericles as the best man they had. Indeed, during the whole period of peace-time when Pericles was at the head of affairs the state was wisely led and firmly guarded, and it was under him that Athens was at her greatest. And when the war broke out, here, too, he appears to have accurately estimated what the power of Athens was. He survived the outbreak of war by two years and six months, and after his death his foresight with regard to the war became even more evident. For Pericles had said that Athens would be victorious if she bided her time and took care of her navy, if she avoided trying to add to the empire during the course of the war, and if she did nothing to risk the safety of the city itself. But his successors did the exact opposite, and in other matters which apparently had no connection with the war private ambition and private profit led to policies which were bad both for the Athenians themselves and for their allies. Such policies, when successful, only brought credit and advantage to individuals, and when they failed, the whole war potential of the state was impaired. The reason for this was that Pericles, because of his position, his intelligence, and his known

integrity, could respect the liberty of the people and at the same time hold them in check. It was he who led them, rather than they who led him, and, since he never sought power from any wrong motive, he was under no necessity of flattering them: in fact he was so highly respected that he was able to speak angrily to them and to contradict them. Certainly when he saw that they were going too far in a mood of over-confidence, he would bring back to them a sense of their dangers; and when they were discouraged for no good reason he would restore their confidence. So, in what was nominally a democracy, power was really in the hands of the first citizen. But his successors, who were more on a level with each other and each of whom aimed at occupying the first place, adopted methods of demagogy which resulted in their losing control over the actual conduct of affairs. Such a policy, in a great city with an empire to govern, naturally led to a number of mistakes, amongst which was the Sicilian expedition, though in this case the mistake was not so much an error of judgement with regard to the opposition to be expected as a failure on the part of those who were at home to give proper support to their forces overseas.[28] Because they were so busy with their own personal intrigues for securing the leadership of the people, they allowed this expedition to lose its impetus, and by quarrelling among themselves began to bring confusion into the policy of the state. And yet, after losing most of their fleet and all the other forces in Sicily, with revolutions already breaking out in Athens, they none the less held out for eight years against their original enemies, who were now reinforced by the Sicilians, against their own allies, most of which had revolted, and against Cyrus, son of the King of Persia, who later joined the other side and provided the Peloponnesians with money for their fleet. And in the end it was only because they had destroyed themselves by their own internal strife that finally they were forced to surrender. So overwhelmingly great were the resources which Pericles had in mind at the time when he prophesied an easy victory for Athens over the Peloponnesians alone.

28. This explanation of the failure of the Sicilian expedition is not borne out by the narrative in Books VI-VII.

THE FALL OF POTIDAEA

66 During this same summer the Spartans and their allies made an expedition with 100 ships against the island of Zacynthus, which lies opposite Elis. The inhabitants of Zacynthus were colonists from Achaea in the Peloponnese and were fighting on the side of Athens. On board the ships were 1,000 Spartan hoplites, and the commander of the fleet was Cnemus, a Spartan of the officer class. They landed on the island, and laid waste most of the country; but, as the Zacynthians would not come to terms, they sailed back home again.

67   At the end of the same summer an embassy consisting of Aristeus from Corinth, Aneristus, Nicolaus, and Stratodemus from Sparta, Timagoras from Tegea, and a man from Argos called Pollis, who was acting on his private initiative, was on its way to Asia with the object of persuading the King of Persia to provide money and join the war on the Spartan side. First, however, they came to Sitalces, the son of Teres, in Thrace, wanting, if possible, to induce him to abandon his alliance with Athens and send an army to relieve Potidaea, which was still being besieged by the Athenian forces. They also wanted to have his help in getting across the Hellespont to their destination in Asia, where they were to meet Pharnaces, the son of Pharnabazus, who was going to send them on into the interior to the King. But it happened that there were some Athenian ambassadors with Sitalces – Learchus, the son of Callimachus, and Ameiniades, the son of Philemon. These two suggested to Sitalces' son Sadocus, who had just been made an Athenian citizen, that he should hand the men over to them, and not allow them to cross over to the King of Persia and try to injure the city which Sadocus had chosen for his own. Sadocus agreed, and as they were on their way through Thrace to the ship on which they were going to cross the Hellespont, he had them arrested by some troops whom he had sent with Learchus and Ameiniades with instructions to hand the men over to the two Athenians. They, on receiving the prisoners, brought them to Athens and, as soon as they arrived there, the Athenians, fearing that Aristeus, who even before then appeared to have had the chief hand in all their troubles in Potidaea

and in Thrace, might do them more harm still if he escaped, on that same day, without giving them a trial or allowing them to say what they wished to say in their defence, put them all to death and threw their bodies into a pit. They regarded this action as legitimate retaliation for the way in which the Spartans had been behaving, since they also had killed and thrown into pits all Athenian and allied traders whom they had caught sailing in merchant ships round the Peloponnese. Indeed, at the beginning of the war the Spartans killed as enemies all whom they captured on the sea, whether allies of Athens or neutrals.

68   About the same time, towards the end of the summer, the Ambraciots, with their own forces and also with a large native army which they had raised, marched against Amphilochian Argos and the rest of Amphilochia. The origin of their hostility towards the people of Argos was as follows. After the Trojan War, Amphilochus, the son of Amphiaraus, had returned to his home in Peloponnesian Argos and, not being satisfied with the state of affairs there, had gone to the Ambracian Gulf, and there founded Amphilochian Argos and colonized the rest of Amphilochia. He named the city after his own native land of Argos, and it was the greatest city in Amphilochia, with the most powerful inhabitants. But many generations later the people of Argos were passing through a difficult time, and invited the Ambraciots, who lived on the frontier of Amphilochia, to join their colony. It was from these Ambraciots who became their fellow citizens that they first learned the Hellenic language, which they still speak, the rest of the Amphilochians speaking a language of their own. After a time the Ambraciots drove out the Argives and held the city themselves. The Amphilochians then went over to the Acarnanians, and the Amphilochians and Acarnanians together called in the help of Athens. The Athenians sent them Phormio as general with a fleet of thirty ships, and when he arrived they took Argos by storm and made slaves of the Ambraciots who were there. The Amphilochians and Acarnanians then inhabited the city together. It was after this that the alliance was first formed between the Athenians and the Acarnanians. The hostility felt by the Ambraciots against the Argives began with the enslavement of their own people. Later, when the war broke out, they got together the force that I have

mentioned, consisting of themselves, the Chaonians, and other native tribes in the neighbourhood. They marched on Argos and gained control of the country, but were not able to take the city by assault. They therefore retired and the army dispersed, each contingent returning to its own people.

69   All this happened in the summer. The following winter the Athenians sent twenty ships round the Peloponnese. This fleet was under the command of Phormio, who, basing himself on Naupactus, instituted a blockade to prevent anyone entering or leaving Corinth and the Gulf of Crisa. Six ships, under the command of Melesander, were sent to Caria and Lycia in order to collect tribute from that area and also to prevent Peloponnesian privateers from using it as a base from which to attack the merchant ships sailing from Phaselis and Phoenicia and the Asiatic coast-line. Melesander, after marching inland into Lycia with a force of Athenians from the ships and some allies, was defeated and killed in battle, losing a number of his men.

70   It was in the same winter that the people of Potidaea came to terms with the Athenians, since they were no longer able to hold out against the siege. The Peloponnesian invasions of Attica had failed to make the Athenians withdraw their troops; provisions had given out, and among the many horrors that starvation had brought with it there had actually been cases of cannibalism. So in the end the Potidaeans were forced to make overtures for surrender to the Athenian generals in command, who were Xenophon, the son of Euripides, Hestiodorus, the son of Aristocleides, and Phanomachus, the son of Callimachus. The generals were willing to listen to the proposals, seeing, as they did, how the army was suffering in its exposed position and considering also that Athens had already spent 2,000 talents on the siege. The following terms were agreed upon: the Potidaeans, with their wives and children and auxiliary forces, were to be permitted to leave the town, the men to be allowed to take one garment apiece, the women two: they were also allowed to take with them a fixed sum of money for their journey. So, under the terms of this agreement, they left Potidaea and went to Chalcidice or wherever they could find a place to go. The Athenians, however, blamed the generals for making the agreement without consulting the government at

home, thinking that it was possible to have secured an unconditional surrender. Later they sent out colonists of their own to Potidaea and resettled the place. This all took place in the winter, and so ended the second year of this war recorded by Thucydides.

THE SIEGE OF PLATAEA

71 Next summer the Peloponnesians and their allies, instead of invading Attica, marched against Plataea. The Spartan King Archidamus, the son of Zeuxidamus, was in command. He had encamped in front of Plataea and was about to start laying waste the land when the Plataeans sent representatives to him, who spoke as follows: 'Archidamus and Spartans, there is no justification for this invasion of the land of Plataea. It is, indeed, an action that does no credit either to you or to the men who were your fathers. Remember what was done by the Spartan Pausanias, the son of Cleombrotus. After he had liberated Hellas from the Persians with the help of all the Hellenes who came forward to share the risk in the battle that was fought near our city, he made a sacrifice to Zeus the Liberator in the market-place of Plataea, and calling together all the allies, he gave back to the people of Plataea their land and their city to be held by them as an independent state, guaranteed for ever against unprovoked attack and against foreign domination; and, if our state was threatened, he called upon the allies who were present to come to our help according to their power. This was the promise given to us by your fathers because of the courage and energy which we showed in those times of stress and danger. But you are acting clean contrary to that promise. You have joined forced with the Thebans, who are our bitterest enemies, and are coming with them to make us slaves. We make our appeal, therefore, to the gods who then witnessed the oaths, to the gods of your fathers, and to the gods of our own country, and we tell you not to break the oaths by making an unprovoked attack on the land of Plataea, but to allow us to keep our independence, as Pausanias meant us to do.'

72   At this point in their speech Archidamus interrupted them and said: 'Plataeans, what you say is fair enough, so long as you act up

to what you say. For you may do just as Pausanias wished you to do – that is, you may enjoy your independence and also join the work of liberating those other Hellenes who shared in the dangers of the past with you, who took the oaths together with you, and who are now under Athenian domination. It is to free them and others like them that this army has been raised and this war has broken out. The best thing of all would be for you to take your part in the work of liberation and so to abide by the oaths yourselves. But if this is impossible, then do what we have already asked you to do: remain neutral and live independently; do not join either side; allow both parties to enter your city, but do not allow either party to make use of it in war. And that will satisfy us.'

After hearing this from Archidamus, the Plataean representatives went back to the city and informed the general assembly of what had been said. They then returned to Archidamus with the answer that it was impossible for them to do as he had asked without consulting the Athenians, since their wives and children were in Athens. They said, too, that they were apprehensive about the whole situation with regard to their city. When the Peloponnesian army withdrew, the Athenians might come against them and take control, or else the Thebans might make another attempt at seizing the city by force, since they would have right of entry by treaty according to the proposed terms.

Archidamus attempted to allay their misgivings by saying to them: 'What you must do is to hand over your city and your houses to us Spartans. Show us the boundaries of your land, tell us the number of your fruit trees, and everything else about your property that can be reckoned in numbers. Then go away yourselves wherever you like for the duration of the war. Once the war is over, we will give back to you everything which we received, and until that time comes we will hold it in trust for you, seeing that the land is cultivated and paying you a regular allowance to be sufficient for your needs.'

73   After hearing this the Plataean representatives went back once more to their city and discussed these proposals in the assembly. They then said that they wanted first of all to inform the Athenians of what Archidamus had suggested, and that, if Athens approved, they were willing to accept his suggestion. In the meantime they

asked him for an armistice during which he would not lay waste their land. Archidamus gave them an armistice for the number of days necessary for the journey to Athens and back, and, while it was in operation, did no damage to their country.

The Plataean representatives went to Athens and, after their consultations there, returned to Plataea with the following message: 'Men of Plataea, the Athenians say that in all the time that we have been their allies they have never once abandoned you to an aggressor, nor will they desert you now. Instead they will give you all the help they can, and they solemnly appeal to you in the name of the oaths which your fathers swore not to make any changes in the existing alliance.'

74 The Plataeans heard this message from their representatives and decided not to desert the Athenians, but to endure, if it had to be so, seeing their land laid waste and all the other sufferings that might befall them. They agreed that no more deputations should be sent, but that they should give their reply from the city wall and say that it was not possible for them to do as the Spartans had suggested.

And now King Archidamus, when they had given him their answer, first of all made his appeal to the gods and heroes of the land. 'Gods and heroes,' he said, 'of the land of Plataea, bear witness with me that from the beginning it was in no spirit of aggression, but only because these people had first broken their engagements with us, that we invaded this land in which our fathers offered their prayers to you before they defeated the Persians and which you made a place of good omen for the warfare of the Hellenes; nor, in our actions now, shall we be acting aggressively. We have made a number of reasonable proposals, but these have not been accepted. Grant us your aid, therefore, and see to it that the punishment for what has been done wrong may fall on those who were the first to do evil, and that we may be successful in our aim, which is a just revenge.'

75 After making this appeal to the gods, Archidamus brought his army into action. First, using the trees which they had cut down, they built a palisade round the city to prevent any sorties. They then constructed a mound up against the city wall, and expected that, considering the size of the force engaged on the work, the

capture of Plataea would not take long. They cut down timber from Cithaeron and used it to build a framework, with the logs crossing each other at right angles, on both sides of the mound, in order to keep the material firmly in position. They constructed the mound itself out of wood and stones and earth and anything else that could fill up the space. This work was carried on continuously for seventy days and nights and was done in relays, so that while some were sleeping or taking their food there were always others busy on carrying up the materials. Spartan officers who were appointed to the command of allied contingents stood over them and kept them to their work.

The Plataeans, however, when they saw the mound growing higher and higher, constructed a wooden wall and fixed it on top of their own wall opposite the place where the mound was being built. Inside this wooden framework they built a wall with bricks which they took from the houses near by. The wood had the effect of binding the building together and of preventing it becoming weak as it increased in height. It had also a defensive covering of skins and hides to preserve the woodwork from fire-arrows and to protect the men who were working on the wall. Thus it soon rose to a great height, and the mound opposite kept pace with it. The Plataeans also had the idea of demolishing part of their wall against which the mound was being built and carrying away the
76 loose earth into their city. The Peloponnesians, finding out that they were doing this, filled up the gap by packing clay tightly inside reed wattles, so as to give more solidity to their materials and prevent them being carried away as the earth had been carried away. Outmanoeuvred here, the Plataeans gave up this method, but instead dug a mine from inside their city to a calculated distance underneath the mound, and through this mine again began to carry away the material from which the mound was made. For a long time their besiegers had no idea that this was going on, and in spite of their building the mound failed to rise as it should have done, since the earth was continually being taken away from underneath and the top part settled down into the vacuum.

Even so, however, the Plataeans feared that their small force might not be able to hold out against such great numbers, and they thought out still another measure of defence. They stopped work on the great barricade opposite the mound, and starting from each end of it, at the points where the original lower wall began, they built an inner wall curving back in the shape of a crescent towards the city, so that if the high wall were captured they would still have the protection of this new wall, which would make it necessary for the enemy to construct yet another mound and, as they advanced inside, to have all their trouble over again and in a much more exposed position.

At the same time as they were constructing the mound the Peloponnesians brought up siege engines against the city. One of these was brought to bear on the great barricade facing the mound, and battered down a considerable part of it, causing much alarm among the Plataeans. Others were brought up against various parts of the city wall. Some of these the Plataeans lassoed and then broke; they also suspended great beams by long iron chains fastened to the ends of two poles projecting horizontally from the top of the wall, and whenever an engine was being brought up into position they drew the beam up at an angle to the engine, and let it go with the chains slack, so that it came rushing down and snapped off the nose of the battering ram.

77 After a time, therefore, what with the failure of the siege engines and the building of the counter wall against their mound, the Peloponnesians came to the conclusion that they could not take the city by any of the methods of warfare so far tried, and they began to prepare to build a wall of circumvallation. But first they decided to try the effect of fire and see whether, with the aid of a wind, they could burn the city down, since it was not a very big place. In fact they examined every possible scheme which would enable them to secure the place without going to the expense of a long siege. They brought up bundles of wood and dropped them down from the mound first into the space between it and the wall. Since so many people were taking a hand in the work, this space was soon filled up, and so they went on to heap up the bundles of wood as far inside the city as they could reach from the top. They then set fire to the wood, using sulphur and pitch to make it burn, and produced such a conflagration as had never been seen before, or at any rate greater than any fire produced by human agency; for of course there have been great forest fires on the mountains

which have broken out spontaneously through the branches of trees being rubbed together by the wind. This fire, however, was indeed a very big one, and it very nearly finished the Plataeans off, after they had escaped from all the other attacks made on them. It made a large part of the city quite untenable, and if, as the enemy had hoped, the wind had risen and blown upon the flames, the Plataeans could not have survived. This, however, did not happen, and it is now said also that there was a thunderstorm with a heavy fall of rain which put out the fire, and so saved the situation.

78   After this final failure the Peloponnesians dismissed the greater part of their army, retaining a certain number of troops which were employed on building a wall of circumvallation round the city. The whole circuit was divided up between the various allied states. There were ditches from which they got their bricks on the inside and on the outside of the wall. About the time of the rising of Arcturus the work was finished. They then left behind enough men to guard half the wall, the remaining half being garrisoned by the Boeotians, and withdrew with the rest of their troops, who dispersed to their various cities. The Plataeans had already sent to Athens their wives and children together with the older men and all others who were unfit for military service. Those of them who were left behind to stand the siege amounted to 400 men together with eighty Athenians and 110 women to do the cooking for the garrison. This was the total number at the time of the beginning of the siege, and there were no others inside the walls, either slaves or free men. So began the siege of Plataea.

VICTORIES OF PHORMIO

79 During the same summer and at the same time as the campaign against Plataea, the Athenians, with a citizen army of 2,000 hoplites and 200 cavalry, marched against the Chalcidians in Thrace and the Bottiaeans. This was at the time when the corn was getting ripe. Xenophon, the son of Euripides, with two other generals, was in command.

This force marched up to the city of Spartolus in Bottiaea, destroyed the crops, and had hopes of also receiving the surrender of the city itself through the agency of a pro-Athenian party inside. But others among the citizens who had different views sent to Olynthus, and from Olynthus there arrived hoplites and other troops to defend the town. This force sallied out from Spartolus and was met in battle by the Athenians just outside the city. The Chalcidian hoplites and the auxiliaries who were with them were defeated by the Athenians and retreated into Spartolus; but the Chalcidian cavalry and light troops defeated the cavalry and light troops on the Athenian side. The Chalcidians had a few peltasts from Crusis, and immediately after the engagement some more peltasts from Olynthus came up in support. When the light troops from Spartolus saw this they gained fresh confidence both from the arrival of the reinforcements and from the fact that they had held their own even previously. They therefore launched another attack on the Athenians in which they were supported by the Chalcidian cavalry and by the troops who had just arrived. The Athenians fell back on the two divisions which had been left to guard the baggage. Whenever the Athenians charged, their enemies gave way, and as soon as the Athenians began to retire, they fell upon them again and shot at them with their javelins. The Chalcidian cavalry also kept riding up and charging whenever they saw their chance. Indeed, they were largely responsible for causing a panic among the Athenians, who were routed and then pursued for a considerable distance. Finally they escaped to Potidaea, and afterwards recovered their dead under an armistice. Then they returned to Athens with the remainder of their army. All their generals and 430 men had been killed. The Chalcidians and Bottiaeans put up a trophy, brought in their own dead and dispersed to their various cities.

80   The same summer, not long after this, the Ambraciots and Chaonians persuaded the Spartans to equip a fleet from allied resources and to send an army of 1,000 hoplites to Acarnania. Their object was to conquer the whole of the country and to detach it from the Athenian alliance, and they said that if the Spartans joined them in simultaneous operations by land and sea, the Acarnanians on the coast would be unable to combine for defence, that after gaining possession of Acarnania they could easily subdue Zacynthus and Cephallenia, and that this would make it more difficult for the

Athenians to send their fleets round the Peloponnese; besides this there was a possibility of capturing Naupactus.

The Spartans were won over by these arguments and immediately sent out the hoplites on a few ships under the command of Cnemus, who was still admiral. They gave orders for the fleet to get ready as soon as possible and to sail to Leucas. In all this the Corinthians were particularly energetic in supporting the Ambraciots, who were colonists of theirs. So the ships from Corinth and Sicyon and the other towns in that area made ready for the voyage, and the ships from Leucas, Anactorium, and Ambracia, which arrived there first, waited for the others at Leucas. Meanwhile Cnemus with his 1,000 hoplites crossed over from the Peloponnese without being observed by Phormio, who was in command of the twenty Athenian ships on guard off Naupactus. They then immediately prepared for their march overland. The Hellenic troops with Cnemus consisted of Ambraciots, Leucadians, and Anactorians, in addition to the 1,000 Peloponnesians with whom he arrived. He had also contingents of native troops: there were 1,000 Chaonians, a tribe that is not governed by a king. This force was led by Photius and Nicanor, members of the ruling family who were in office for that year. With the Chaonians there were also some Thesprotians, another tribe that is not ruled by a king. The Molossians and Atintanians were led by Sabylinthus, the guardian of King Tharyps, who was still a minor. The Paravaeans were led by their King Oroedus and with them marched 1,000 Orestians who were subjects of King Antiochus and had been put by him under the command of Oroedus. Perdiccas also, without revealing his intentions to the Athenians, sent 1,000 Macedonians, who arrived too late to take part in the expedition. With this force Cnemus set out on his march, without waiting for the fleet from Corinth. Going through the territory of Amphilochian Argos, they sacked the unfortified village of Limnaea, and arrived in front of Stratus, the biggest town in Acarnania, thinking that, if they captured this place first, the rest of the country would easily fall into their hands.

81   When the Acarnanians saw that they were being invaded by a large army by land and that also they would soon be confronted by an enemy fleet on the sea, they took no combined measures for

defence, but stayed where they were to protect their own particular areas. They sent an appeal for help to Phormio, but he replied that he could not leave Naupactus undefended at the moment when a fleet was just about to sail from Corinth. Meanwhile the Peloponnesians and their allies in three divisions were advancing on Stratus. Their intention was to camp near the city, and if they failed to win it over by negotiation, to make an attack on its fortifications. In their advance the Chaonians and other native troops were in the centre; on their right were the Leucadians and Anactorians and those with them; and on the left was Cnemus with the Peloponnesians and Ambraciots. There were large gaps between the divisions, which would sometimes be out of sight of each other. The Hellenes advanced in good order, keeping a proper look-out, until they pitched camp in a good position. But the Chaonians, who had the greatest reputation for their warlike qualities among the tribes in these parts of the country, felt so sure of themselves that, without waiting to occupy the ground for their camp, they rushed forward with the other native forces, thinking that they would capture the town at one blow and so win the credit for the whole action.

When the Stratians realized that they were still advancing they came to the conclusion that, if they could defeat this isolated division of the army, the Hellenic part of the force would be much less likely to attack them later. They therefore placed parties of men in ambush all round the city, and when the Chaonians drew nearer, they made a concerted attack on them both from the city itself and from the ambushes. This caused a panic among the Chaonians; great numbers of them were killed, and when the other natives saw them giving way, they also broke and fled. Meanwhile neither of the two Hellenic divisions knew that the battle was taking place, because the Chaonians were far in front of them, and it was assumed that they were hurrying on to find a position for a camp. But when the native army came rushing back on them in flight, they took them in behind their lines, brought their two divisions together into one force and stayed where they were for the day. The Stratians did not come to close quarters with them, since their reinforcements from the rest of Acarnania had not yet arrived; but they harassed them from a distance with their slingers and caused them much trouble in this way, since it was impossible to move except under arms. Indeed, it seems that in this form of warfare the Acarnanians are remarkably effective.

82 As soon as it was night, Cnemus hurriedly retreated with his army to the river Anapus, which is about nine miles away from Stratus. Next day he recovered the bodies of the dead under an armistice. The friendly tribe of the Oeniadae were with him, and he retreated through their country before the Acarnanian reinforcements arrived. From there the contingents of his army dispersed to their various homes, and the people of Stratus put up a trophy for their victory over the Chaonians.

83 Meanwhile the fleet from Corinth and from the other allied states on the Crissaean Gulf was supposed to have been acting in support of Cnemus so that the Acarnanians on the coast should not be able to come to the help of their countrymen in the interior. This, however, the fleet was not able to do. About the same time as the battle at Stratus it had been forced to fight with Phormio and the twenty Athenian ships on guard at Naupactus.

Phormio merely kept a watch on the enemy ships as they were coasting up the gulf, since he wanted to attack them in the open sea. As for the Corinthians and their allies, they were by no means contemplating a sea battle, but were equipped more as military transports for the campaign in Acarnania, nor did they imagine that the twenty Athenian ships would venture on a battle with their own force of forty-seven ships. Now, however, when they were sailing along their own coast they saw the Athenians sailing in line with them; and when they tried to make the crossing from Patrae in Achaea to the mainland opposite, on their way to Acarnania, again they saw the Athenians sailing out against them from Chalcis, and the river Euenus. Though they had slipped from their moorings in the night they had still been observed, and so finally they were compelled to fight half-way between the two coasts. The contingents from the various allied states had each its own commander. The Corinthian commanders were Machaon, Isocrates, and Agatharchidas.

The Peloponnesians sailed with their ships in circular formation, the prows facing outwards and the sterns in. The circle was as big as could be without leaving gaps wide enough for the enemy to manoeuvre in, and inside the circle were all the light craft that formed part of the expedition, together with five of the fastest and best-equipped warships which were to be constantly ready to sail outside and come to the relief of any portion of the circumference where the enemy might attack.

84   The Athenian ships, formed in line, sailed round and round them, forcing the circle inwards as they kept sailing in close to the enemy ships and appearing to be on the point of ramming them. Actually they had previously been ordered by Phormio to make no attack until he himself gave the signal. He expected that, so far from keeping their formation, like a force on land, the warships would fall foul of each other, and the smaller craft would add to the confusion: then, too, as he sailed round the Peloponnesians, he was waiting for the wind to blow from the gulf, as it usually did about dawn, and, if the wind rose, he could see that they would be in trouble at once. At the same time he considered that, as his ships were the better sailers, he could attack whenever he liked, and that the best moment for making the attack was when the wind got up. When this did happen, the Peloponnesians were already crowded together and, having to deal both with the wind and with their own small craft, were soon in a state of confusion. Ships fell foul of each other and had to be pushed off with poles; what with the shouting and swearing and the yells from one ship to another, it was impossible to hear what the captains wanted done or the orders given by the boatswains; lacking experience, as they did, they could not clear their oars in the rough sea, and so made the ships more difficult for the steersmen to handle. It was at this moment that Phormio gave the signal. The Athenians attacked, and after first sinking one of the admirals' ships went on to destroy every ship that they came across. In the general confusion the enemy put up no sort of resistance and fled to Patrae and Dyme in Achaea. The Athenians pursued them, capturing twelve ships and making prisoners of most of their crews. They then sailed to Molycrium, put up a trophy on the headland of Rhium, and dedicated a ship to Poseidon. Afterwards they went back to Naupactus. The Peloponnesians with what was left of their fleet sailed immediately along the coast from Dyme and Patrae to the Elean dockyard at Cyllene. Here also, after the battle of Stratus, Cnemus arrived

from Leucas with the ships that should have formed part of the combined fleet.

85   The Spartans now sent out to Cnemus and his fleet an advisory commission consisting of Timocrates, Brasidas, and Lycophron. Their orders were to make ready for another battle at sea and to do better in it and not to be driven off the sea by a few ships. For the Spartans, especially since this was their first taste of naval engagements, found it very difficult to understand what had happened, and so far from thinking that there was anything wrong with their own navy, concluded that the defeat was the result of cowardice, not taking into consideration the contrast between the long experience of the Athenians and the short training which their own crews had received. Consequently it was in a mood of anger that the commissioners were sent out.

When they arrived, they worked in conjunction with Cnemus and sent round to the various states for more ships, and re-equipped the ones they had already so as to make them fit for a naval action. Phormio also sent messengers to Athens with news of the enemy's preparations and of the battle which he had won. He asked the Athenians to send out to him quickly as many ships as possible, since every day that passed he expected to be brought to action. The Athenians sent him twenty ships, but their commander was instructed first of all to sail to Crete. For Nicias, a Cretan from Gortyn who was the Athenian representative there, had persuaded them to sail against Cydonia, a city opposed to Athens, saying that he would win it over to the Athenian side. In fact he was doing all this in the interests of the Polichnitans, who were neighbours of the Cydonians. So he went with the ships to Crete and, supported by the Polichnitans, laid waste the land of the Cydonians. Adverse winds and rough weather there led to the waste of a considerable amount of time.

86   While the Athenians were delayed in Crete, the Peloponnesians at Cyllene, all prepared for battle, sailed along the coast to Panormus in Achaea, where their land army had marched up to give them support. Phormio, too, sailed along the opposite coast to Molycrian Rhium and came to anchor outside the place with the twenty ships with which he had fought the previous battle. This Rhium was friendly to Athens. The other Rhium, in the

Peloponnese, is opposite to it, and there is about three-quarters of a mile of sea between the two, which forms the entry to the Crissaean Gulf. It was at this Rhium, in Achaea, not far from Panormus, where their army was, that the Peloponnesians, with seventy-seven ships, came to anchor when they saw the Athenians also at anchor opposite them.

So for six or seven days they kept their stations opposite each other, training and preparing for the battle. The plan on the one side was not to sail out from the Rhian channel into the open sea, for fear of what had happened to them before: on the other side it was not to sail into the narrow waters, since they thought that a battle in a constricted space was all to the advantage of the enemy. Cnemus and Brasidas and the other Peloponnesian commanders wanted to bring on a battle quickly, before reinforcements arrived from Athens, but they observed that, as a result of the previous defeat, most of their men were downhearted and by no means eager for action. First of all, therefore, they called a meeting of the men and tried to raise their morale by the following appeal:

87   'Peloponnesians, if the result of the last battle has made any of you apprehensive about the battle we are going to fight now, it must be said that there is no good reason for such fears. In the last battle, as you know, we were not properly prepared, and we were on our way not to fight a battle at sea, but a campaign on land. It happened, too, that most of the luck was against us, and it may be also that lack of experience played its part in our failure in our first battle at sea. It was not, therefore, because of any cowardice on our part that we were defeated, nor, merely because this accident has happened, ought we to lose the keen edge of our resolution which, we know, has not been subdued by force and which still has plenty to say for itself. Instead we should remember that accidents may happen to all men, but real courage never alters, and those who have it never use inexperience as an excuse for being anything else but courageous. So far as you are concerned you may lack the enemy's experience, but that is more than made up for by your superior daring. This skill of theirs, which is the thing which you fear most, has to be combined with courage. Then, in the hour of danger, they will remember how to do what they have learnt to do. But if a stout heart is lacking, all the skill in the world will not

avail in the face of peril. Fear drives out all memory of previous instruction, and without the will to resist, skill is useless. So, when you think of their greater experience you must also think of your own greater courage, and when you feel frightened because of the defeat you have suffered, you must remember that at that time you were caught off your guard and unprepared. There are solid advantages on your side – you have the bigger fleet: you are fighting off your own native shores with hoplites ready to support you. And as a rule the side that wins is the side with the numbers and the equipment. There is not one single reason, therefore, why we should lose. Even the mistakes which we made before are now a factor on our side, since we shall be able to learn from them. We expect steersmen and sailors alike to do their duty in a spirit of confidence, no one leaving the post to which he is assigned. We ourselves will certainly be no less efficient than your previous commanders and will prepare for battle in such a way as to leave no one any excuse for playing the coward. Should anyone want to do so, he will be punished as he ought to be, but the brave shall be honoured with the rewards that are due to courage.'

88 In this way the Peloponnesian commanders encouraged their men. Phormio also was alarmed about the morale of his own men. He saw that they were forming into groups among themselves and were obviously frightened by the numbers on the other side. He therefore called them together with the object of putting fresh heart into them and giving them his advice in the present circumstances. He had often spoken to them before, and used to impress on their minds that there was no fleet, however great, that they could not face in battle, and for a long time his sailors had had the proud opinion of themselves that they, as Athenians, would never give way before any numbers of Peloponnesian ships. Now, however, he realized that the sight before their eyes was making them downhearted, and he thought it well to restore confidence. He therefore called the Athenians together and spoke as follows:

89 'I see, my men, that you are alarmed by the enemy's numbers, and I have called this meeting because I do not want you to be frightened when there is no occasion to be so. First of all, the reason why they have equipped this great number of ships and are not meeting us on even terms is that they have been defeated once

already and do not even think themselves that they are a match for us. The thing which gives them most confidence in facing us is that they imagine themselves to have a kind of monopoly in being brave, yet this comforting belief is based simply on their experience in land fighting, owing to which they have won many victories. They think that this experience of theirs will be equally valuable on the sea; but here, if there is anything in their argument, the advantage will be on our side. They are certainly no braver than we are, and as for feeling confident, both they and we have that feeling with regard to the element where we have the greater experience. Then, too, the Spartans who are in command of them are acting for the honour of Sparta, and most of their men are being led into danger much against their will; otherwise they could never have faced the prospect of another naval action after the great defeat they have suffered already. So there is no reason at all for you to fear that they will show any great audacity. It is much more the case that they are frightened of you, and with much better reason, partly because you have beaten them already and partly because they think that you would not be standing up to them now unless you were going to do something altogether worthy of the occasion. When one side is in superior numbers, as our enemy is, it makes its attack relying more on force than on resolution. But if the other side, far weaker in material resources, takes up the challenge, when there is no compulsion to do so, it means that that side has something in mind to fall back upon which is very great indeed. This is what our enemies are reckoning on, and they are more frightened by the unexpectedness of our action than they would be if we were meeting them on reasonably equal terms. Great forces before now have been defeated by small ones because of lack of skill and sometimes because of lack of daring. We are deficient in neither of these qualities.

'Now as for the battle, if I can help it, I shall not fight it in the gulf, nor shall I sail into the gulf. I fully realize that lack of sea room is a disadvantage for a small, experienced, and fast squadron fighting with a lot of badly managed ships. One cannot sail up in the proper way to make an attack by ramming, unless one has a good long view of the enemy ahead, nor can one back away at the right moment if one is hard pressed oneself; it is impossible also to sail through the enemy's line and then wheel back on him – which are the right tactics for the fleet which has the superior seamanship. Instead of all this, one would be compelled to fight a naval action as though it were a battle on land, and under those circumstances the side with the greater number of ships has the advantage. So you can be sure that I shall be watching out for all this as far as I can. As for you, you must stick to your posts in your ships, keep good order, and be on the alert for any word of command. This is especially important as they are at anchor so close to us. And when it comes to action, put your trust in discipline and in silence; in every kind of warfare they count a lot, and particularly in a naval engagement. Meet the enemy, therefore, in a manner worthy of your record in the past. There is a lot at stake for you in this struggle – either to destroy the naval hopes of the Peloponnesians or to bring nearer home to the Athenians their fears for the sea. Let me remind you once more that you have defeated most of this fleet already, and beaten men never have quite the same resolution as they had before when they come up against the same danger for the second time.'

90   So Phormio also encouraged his men. The Peloponnesians, since the Athenians would not sail into the narrow water of the gulf, wanted to lure them into it whether they liked it or not. They therefore put out at dawn, their ships formed up in four lines with the Peloponnesian coast behind them, and began to sail along inside the gulf, their right wing leading, in the same order as they had lain at anchor. In this wing they had placed their twenty best and fastest ships, and their idea was that if Phormio, thinking that they were making for Naupactus, should follow them along in that direction in order to protect the place, these twenty ships should cut the Athenians off and prevent them from sailing through and escaping from the Peloponnesian line when it turned to attack them. As they expected, Phormio was alarmed for the safety of the place, which had been left without a garrison, and as soon as he saw them put out, he hurriedly and much against his will embarked and sailed along his own shore, with the Messenian land forces marching along with him in support.

The Peloponnesians, seeing the Athenians sailing along the coast with their ships in single file and already inside the gulf and close to the land (which was just where they wanted them to be), at one signal suddenly turned and bore down on the Athenians in line, every ship making its best speed, hoping to cut off the whole Athenian fleet. However, the eleven leading ships managed to escape from the Peloponnesian wing and its sudden turning movement and reached open water. The others were caught in the trap; though they tried to escape, they were pushed back on to the shore and put out of action; and those of the Athenians who did not swim ashore were put to death. Some of the ships the Peloponnesians took in tow and dragged off empty; one was taken with the crew aboard; some, which were just being towed away, were rescued by the Messenians, who rushed into the sea in their armour, boarded the ships, and fought back from their decks.

91   Here, then, the Peloponnesians were victorious, and had destroyed the Athenian ships opposed to them. Meanwhile the twenty ships from their right wing were in pursuit of the eleven Athenian ships which had escaped from the turning movement into the open sea. All of these eleven, except for one, got clean away and reached Naupactus, where they formed up by the temple of Apollo with their prows facing the enemy, ready to defend themselves if the Peloponnesians sailed in against them. Soon the Peloponnesians came up, singing a paean of victory as they sailed on together. A considerable way in front of them was a ship from Leucas which was pursuing the one Athenian ship that had been left behind. There happened to be a merchant ship anchored off shore, and the Athenian ship, reaching it first, circled right round it, and then rammed the pursuing boat from Leucas amidships and sank her. It was an unexpected and unlikely action, and it caused a panic among the Peloponnesians, who at the same time, elated by their victory, were sailing up in pursuit in no proper formation. Some of them dropped their oars and lost way in order to let the main body catch up with them – a very dangerous thing to do with the Athenians so close to them, and ready to attack; others, through ignorance of the coast, ran aground in shallow water.

92   Seeing all this happening, the Athenians gained confidence. At one word they gave a shout and fell upon the enemy. The Peloponnesians, owing to the mistakes they had made and the state of disorder in which they were, made only a short resistance, and

then fled in the direction of Panormus, from which they had originally put to sea. The Athenians in close pursuit captured six of the ships nearest to them, and regained their own ships which in the first part of the action had been disabled close to the shore and taken in tow. Some of the crews they killed and took others prisoner. The Spartan Timocrates had been aboard the ship of Leucas which was sunk near the merchant ship, and when his vessel was destroyed he killed himself, and his bódy was washed up in the harbour of Naupactus.

On their return the Athenians put up a trophy at the place from which they had turned on the enemy and won the victory. They recovered the wrecks and the dead bodies on their own shore and gave back to the enemy their own dead under an armistice. The Peloponnesians also put up a trophy for the victory they had won when they disabled the ships in shore, and close to their trophy, at Rhium in Achaea, they made a dedicatory offering of the one ship which they had captured. After this, fearing that reinforcements would arrive from Athens, all, except for the Leucadians, sailed by night into the Crissaean Gulf and to Corinth. Not long after their retreat the Athenian fleet of twenty ships from Crete, which should have been with Phormio before the battle, arrived at Naupactus.

93   So the summer came to an end. But before dispersing the fleet which had retreated to Corinth and the Crissaean Gulf, Cnemus and Brasidas and the other commanders of the Peloponnesians, on the advice of the Megarians, decided at the beginning of winter to make an attempt on Piraeus, the port of Athens, which had been left open and unguarded – naturally enough, considering the great naval superiority of the Athenians. The plan was that each sailor should take his oar, his cushion, and his rowlock thong and go overland from Corinth to the sea on the side of Athens; when they arrived, they were to proceed as quickly as possible to Megara, to launch forty ships which happened to be in the docks at Nisaea, and sail immediately to Piraeus. They knew that there was no fleet on guard at Piraeus; indeed, no one could possibly have expected that the enemy would ever make a surprise attack of this kind; for, it was thought, they would certainly not dare to attack openly in the hope of meeting no opposition, and, even if they had such an idea, it would certainly be discovered first.

This was the Peloponnesian plan, and they immediately put it into practice. They arrived at Nisaea by night and launched the ships. They did not, however, as had been the original intention, sail at once against Piraeus. They were frightened of the danger involved, and also they say that there was something about the direction of the wind which held them back. Instead they sailed to the point of Salamis that looks towards Megara. Here there was a small fort and a squadron of three ships which were there to prevent anything sailing in or out of Megara. They attacked this force, towed off the ships empty, and then, falling upon the place quite unexpectedly, began to lay waste the rest of Salamis.

94   Beacons were lit to warn Athens of an enemy attack, and a panic broke out which was as great as any in the course of the war. For the people in the city thought that the enemy had already sailed into Piraeus, and in Piraeus people thought that they had taken Salamis and were just on the point of sailing into the harbour. And indeed they could easily have done so if they had managed to overcome their apprehensions; certainly the wind would not have stopped them.

At dawn the Athenians mustered in full force at Piraeus, launched their ships, and embarked in a great hurry and with much shouting. With the fleet they sailed to Salamis, and with their land forces they guarded the defences of Piraeus. The Peloponnesians had overrun most of Salamis, but when they realized that the relief force was on its way, they hurriedly sailed back to Nisaea, taking with them their prisoners, their plunder, and the three ships from the guard-post at Budorum. They were also alarmed because of the condition of their ships, which had not been launched for a long time and were letting in water. When they arrived at Megara they went back again to Corinth by land. The Athenians, after failing to find them at Salamis, also returned. After this they took steps to see that Piraeus was better guarded in the future. The entrances to the harbours were closed and other precautions taken.

THRACE AND MACEDONIA

95 About the same time, at the beginning of this winter, Sitalces, the son of Teres, the Odrysian king of Thrace, marched against Perdiccas, the son of Alexander, king of Macedonia, and against the Chalcidians in the Thracian area. Sitalces' aim was to see that a promise made to him was fulfilled and also to fulfil a promise that he had made himself. At the beginning of the war Perdiccas had been in difficulties and had entered into an undertaking with Sitalces on condition that Sitalces reconciled him with the Athenians and did not restore to the throne his brother Philip, who was opposed to him; but Perdiccas had not kept the undertaking which he made. Then, too, Sitalces, at the time when he had allied himself with the Athenians, had agreed to put an end to the Chalcidian war in Thrace. He had two reasons therefore for making this expedition. With him he took Amyntas, the son of Philip, with the intention of making him king of Macedonia, and also some Athenian ambassadors who happened to be visiting him on this business, and Hagnon to act as commander; since the Athenians also were supposed to support him against the Chalcidians with a fleet and as many troops as possible.

96 Starting first with the Odrysians, he called up the Thracian tribes which were subject to him in the area between Mounts Haemus and Rhodope down to the sea; next the Getae on the other side of Haemus and the other tribes which live south of the Danube and more in the direction of the Euxine Sea. Both the Getae and these other tribes are neighbours of the Scythians and are armed in the same way, being all mounted archers. He also summoned a number of the independent Thracian hill tribes who are armed with swords. These are called Dii, and most of them live on Mount Rhodope. Some followed him as mercenaries and some came as volunteers. Then he called up the Agrianians and the Laeaeans and the other Paeonian tribes under his control. These tribes are on the extreme boundaries of his empire, which ends with the Laeaean Paeonians and the river Strymon, which flows from Mount Scombrus through the country of the Agrianians and the Laeaeans; beyond this point live the independent Paeonians.

In the direction of the Triballi, who are also independent, his empire was bounded by the Treres and the Tilataeans, who live to the north of Mount Scombrus and extend westwards as far as the river Oscius. The river rises in the same mountains as the Nestus and the Hebrus. It is a large and uninhabited range of mountains, joined on to Rhodope.

97   The Odrysian empire had a coastline reaching from Abdera to the mouth of the Danube in the Euxine. The voyage along the coast, going by the shortest route and with a following wind all the way, takes a merchant ship four days and four nights; by land a man travelling fast and by the shortest route can get from Abdera to the Danube in eleven days. So much for the length of the coastline. As for its extent into the interior, a man travelling fast would take thirteen days to go from Byzantium to the Laeaeans and the Strymon, which is the part that lies farthest inland. In the reign of Seuthes, who succeeded Sitalces and raised the tribute to its highest, the total amount of tribute coming in from all the native district and from the Hellenic cities was about 400 talents in gold and silver. Then at least an equal amount of gold and silver was contributed in presents, in addtion to woven stuffs, both plain and embroidered, and other materials. These presents were not given only to the king, but also to the chief men and nobles of the Odrysians. Indeed here, and among the other Thracians too, the established custom was just the opposite of what it is in the kingdom of Persia; it was to receive rather than to give, and it was considered more of a disgrace to fail to give a present when one was asked for it than to fail to obtain a present when one asked for it oneself. And such was the power of the Odrysians that this custom was particularly prevalent among them, since it was quite impossible to get anything done unless one first produced a present. So it became a very powerful kingdom. Indeed, in financial resources and general prosperity it was the greatest of all European powers between the Ionian Gulf and the Euxine; though in the strength and numbers of its armed forces it was very definitely inferior to the Scythians, who are beyond comparison bigger than any other European people. In fact if the Scythians were united there is not even in Asia a race that could stand up to them by itself, though of course in governing themselves wisely and in

making an intelligent use of their resources they are below the average level.

98   Sitalces therefore, who was now preparing to march, was King of a great empire. When everything was ready, he set out against Macedonia and proceeded first through his own country and then across the uninhabited mountain range of Cercine which forms the boundary between the Sintians and the Paeonians. He crossed this range by a route which he had made himself on a former occasion by cutting a way through the forests at the time when he was fighting against the Paeonians. Crossing over this mountain from the Odrysian country, they had the Paeonians on the right and the Sintians and Maedians on the left. On the other side of the mountains they came to Doberus in Paeonia, and on the whole march he lost none of his army except through illness. On the contrary, his army was actually augmented, since many of the independent Thracians followed him of their own accord in the hope of plunder; so that his total force is said to have amounted to at least 150,000 men. Most of this force was infantry, only about a third being cavalry. The Odrysians themselves and, next to them, the Getae formed the majority of the cavalry. The most warlike troops among the infantry were the independent swordsmen who came down from Mount Rhodope. The rest of the horde which followed him was formidable chiefly on account of their numbers.

99   This force assembled at Doberus and prepared to descend from the mountains into the kingdom of Perdiccas in Lower Macedonia. In the interior there are Macedonians also – the Lyncestians, the Elimiots, and other tribes – who are allies and dependants of the Macedonian King, but who have separate kings of their own. The part of the country on the sea-coast, known as Macedonia, was first acquired by Alexander, the father of Perdiccas, and by his ancestors, who were originally Temenids from Argos and who became kings in this country after defeating and driving out the Pierians from Pieria who later settled in Phagres and other places under Mount Pangaeus beyond the Strymon (the country between the sea and the lower slopes of Pangaeus is still called the Pierian Gulf), and the Bottiaeans (who are now neighbours of the Chalcidians) from Bottiaea. They also acquired a narrow strip of land in

Paeonia along the river Axius, extending from the mountains to Pella and the sea. Then, by driving out the Edonians, they gained control of the country called Mygdonia, which lies between the Axius and the Strymon. They also drove out the Eordians from the country now called Eordia – most were killed, though a few still live round Physca – and the Almopians from Almopia. These Macedonians from Lower Macedonia also conquered and still hold places that belonged to the other tribes - Anthemus, Crestonia, Bisaltia, and much of upper Macedonia. The whole country is now called Macedonia, and Perdiccas, the son of Alexander, was the king of it at the time of the invasion of Sitalces.

100   Faced with such a large invading army, the Macedonians were unable to stand up to their enemies in battle, and retreated to the various strongholds and fortresses that existed in their country. There were not many of these; the ones that are now in Macedonia were built later by Archelaus, the son of Perdiccas, when he became king. Archelaus also built straight roads through the country, reorganized the cavalry, the arming of the infantry, and equipment in general, so as to put the country in a stronger position for war than it had ever been under all the eight kings who had ruled before him.

Now the Thracian army, moving from Doberus, first of all invaded the country that used to belong to Philip. They took Idomene by assault; Gortynia, Atalanta, and some other places came to terms with them out of loyalty to Philip's son Amyntas, who was with Sitalces. They laid siege to Europus, but failed to capture it.

Next Sitalces advanced into the other part of Macedonia to the left of Pella and Cyrrhus. They did not go beyond this to Bottiaea and Pieria, but laid waste Mygdonia, Crestonia, and Anthemus. The Macedonians never even thought of opposing them with infantry, but they sent for further reinforcements of cavalry from their allies in the interior, and, though in greatly inferior numbers, they made cavalry attacks on the Thracian army when they saw their opportunity. Whenever they did so, being excellent horsemen and armed with breastplates, no one could stand up to them, but they found themselves running into danger by being surrounded by the enormously greater numbers of their enemies, so that in the end they gave up making these attacks, feeling that they were not in sufficient force to risk battle with such superior numbers.

101 Sitalces now entered into negotiations with Perdiccas on the aims of his expedition, and, since the Athenians (who had not believed that he would make the march) had not appeared with their fleet, though they had sent ambassadors to him with presents, he sent off part of his army to attack the Chalcidians and Bottiaeans, forced them to retire behind their fortifications, and laid waste their land.

While Sitalces was in these parts, those who lived to the south – the Thessalians, the Magnetes, and other subjects of the Thessalians, and the Hellenes as far south as Thermopylae – all feared that the army might descend on them, too, and were in a state of readiness for war. The same fears were felt by the Thracians in the north beyond the Strymon, who lived in the plains – the Panaeans, the Odomanti, the Droi, and the Dersaeans, who are all independent tribes. Among the Hellenes, too, who were enemies of Athens, there was much talk of Sitalces, since they feared that he might be induced by the Athenians to fulfil his alliance by marching also against them.

As it happened, he overran Chalcidice, Bottiaea, and Macedonia, laying waste the land; but he was not succeeding in any of the aims for which he had made the invasion, his army was running short of food, and was also suffering from cold; and so he took the advice of his nephew Seuthes, the son of Sparadocus, who was the most important of his commanders, and retreated as quickly as he could. Seuthes had been secretly won over by Perdiccas, who had promised him his daughter in marriage and a large sum of money as well. Sitalces took the advice of Seuthes and quickly returned with his army to his own country after a campaign of thirty days in all, eight of which were spent in Chalcidice. Later Perdiccas gave his daughter Stratonice to Seuthes, as he had promised. So ended the expedition of Sitalces.

102 In the same winter the Athenians in Naupactus, after the dispersal of the Peloponnesian fleet, made an expeditionary campaign under the command of Phormio. Sailing along the coast to Astacus, they landed and marched into the interior of Acarnania with 400 Athenian hoplites from the fleet and 400 Messenians.

They expelled from Stratus, Coronta, and other places various people who were regarded as being unreliable, they restored Cynes, the son of Theolytus, to Coronta, and then went back again to their ships. As for Oeniadae, the only place in Acarnania which had always been anti-Athenian, they decided that it was impossible to march against it in the winter. For the river Achelous, which flows from Mount Pindus through Dolopia and the country of the Agraeans and Amphilochians and the Acarnanian plain, passing by Stratus in the upper part of its course, falls into the sea near Oeniadae and forms lakes all round the city, making it impossible for an army to operate there in the winter because of the flooded ground. Opposite Oeniadae, too, lie most of the islands which are called the Echinades. These islands are actually in the mouths of the Achelous, which is a powerful stream and is constantly silting up the channels, with the result that some of the islands have already become joined to the mainland and, in all probability, the same thing will happen to all the rest before very long. For the current runs swiftly, and is broad and muddy, while the islands lie close together and between them dam up the alluvial deposit, since they are not one behind the other, but are scattered about irregularly, so that they leave no direct channel for the river water to flow into the sea.

The islands are uninhabited and quite small. There is a story about them and Alcmaeon, the son of Amphiaraus. During his wanderings after the murder of his mother the oracle of Apollo is said to have told him to live in this place. The words of the oracle were that he could find no release from the terrors that haunted him until he could discover a place to settle in which, at the time when he killed his mother, the sun had never seen and was not in existence as land; all the rest of the earth was polluted for him. Alcmaeon, as the story goes, was at a loss what to do, but in the end he observed this alluvial deposit of the river Achelous, and came to the conclusion that sufficient land might have formed there to support life since the time that he killed his mother. (He had already been a wanderer for some time.) So he settled in the district near Oeniadae, became the ruler of those parts, and from the name of his son, Acarnan, gave the name to the whole country. This is the story told to us of Alcmaeon.

103   Phormio and his Athenians set sail from Acarnania, arrived at
Naupactus and, at the beginning of spring, sailed back to Athens.
They brought with them the ships that they had captured and all
the free men who had been taken prisoner in their naval actions.
These were exchanged, man for man. So ended this winter and so
ended the third year of this war recorded by Thucydides.

BOOK THREE

REVOLT OF MYTILENE

1 NEXT summer, at the time when the corn was ripe, the Peloponnesians and their allies marched into Attica under the command of the Spartan King Archidamus, the son of Zeuxidamus. They settled down in the country and laid it waste. As on previous occasions, the Athenian cavalry went into action wherever possible and prevented the mass of enemy light troops from leaving the protection of the main body of the army and doing harm in the districts close to the city. The Peloponnesians stayed in Attica for the period for which they had come supplied, and then retired and dispersed to their various cities.

2 Directly after the invasion of the Peloponnesians the island of Lesbos, except for Methymna, revolted from Athens. Even before the war the Lesbians had wanted to revolt, but the Spartans had not been willing to receive them into their alliance; and now they were compelled to revolt before the time that they had planned. They were waiting until they had narrowed the mouths of their harbours and finished the fortifications and the shipbuilding which they had in hand; also for the arrival of various supplies which were due to come from Pontus – archers, corn, and other things that they had sent for. Meanwhile, however, the Tenedians, who were enemies of theirs, the Methymnians, and a certain group of individuals in the city itself, people who represented Athenian interests in Mytilene, informed the Athenians that the Mytilenians were forcibly making the whole of Lesbos into one state under the control of Mytilene, and that the various activities on which they were so busy were planned in cooperation with the Spartans and with the Boeotians, who were their kinsmen, for the purpose of making a revolt; and that unless preventive measures were taken at once, Athens would lose Lesbos.

3 At this time, however, the Athenians were suffering from the

plague and also from the full force of the war which had only just broken out. They thought it would be a very serious thing indeed to have to fight Lesbos as well, with its fleet and with its untapped resources. Thus, rather through a process of wishful thinking, they at first believed that the accusations were untrue. Later, however, when they had sent out representatives and failed to induce the Mytilenians to abandon the idea of the union of Lesbos or to give up their warlike preparations, they became frightened and decided to take action before it was too late. They hurriedly sent out a fleet of forty ships that had been equipped for sailing round the Peloponnese, under the command of Cleippides, the son of Deinias, and two others. It had been reported at Athens that there was a feast held in honour of the Malean Apollo outside the city, and that the whole people of Mytilene took part in this feast; so there was a chance, if they acted quickly, of catching them by surprise. If this plan worked, so much the better; if not, they were to order the people of Mytilene to surrender their ships and to demolish their fortifications, and, if they failed to comply with these demands, to make war on them.

So the fleet set sail. The ten triremes of Mytilene which happened to be serving with the fleet according to the provisions of the alliance were kept back by the Athenians and their crews placed under arrest. Nevertheless news of the expedition reached Mytilene through a man who crossed over from Athens to Euboea, went on foot to Geraestus, found a merchant ship on the point of sailing, and got by sea to Mytilene on the third day after he had left Athens. So the people of Mytilene did not go out to the temple at Malea. Instead they reinforced the unfinished parts of their walls, and their harbours, and stood on guard.

4   Soon afterwards the Athenian fleet sailed in. When the commanders saw what the situation was they said what they had been instructed to say and, as the Mytilenians refused to obey, they made war upon them. The Mytilenians, suddenly forced into a war for which they were unprepared, did make the gesture of sailing out with their fleet to fight a little way in front of their harbour, but were soon chased back again by the Athenian ships, and immediately began to enter into negotiations with the Athenian commanders, wishing, if they could, to have the Athenian fleet recalled

for the time being on any reasonable conditions. The Athenian commanders themselves were doubtful of their ability to deal with the whole of Lesbos, and so they accepted the overtures made to them. An armistice was made, and the Mytilenians sent to Athens a delegation including one of the people who had already informed against them, but had now repented of his action, to try to persuade the Athenians to withdraw their fleet and to make them believe that there was no danger of any revolutions in Mytilene. At the same time they sent ambassadors to Sparta in a trireme which escaped the notice of the Athenian fleet anchored at Malea to the north of the town; for they had little hope that their representatives in Athens would do any good.

The mission to Sparta reached their destination after a difficult voyage across the open sea and started conversations with a view to securing military aid. The mission which had gone to Athens returned without having succeeded in any of its objects, and thus Mytilene and the rest of Lesbos, except for Methymna, went to war with Athens. The Methymnians fought on the Athenian side, as did the Imbrians, the Lemnians and a certain number of the other allies.

The Mytilenians now marched out in full force against the Athenian camp, and in the battle that took place they had rather the better of things, but they lacked confidence in themselves and retired to their city without venturing to camp in the open. Afterwards they kept quiet, not wishing to try their fortune again until they had the support of whatever forces might be coming to them from the Peloponnese. For Meleas, a Laconian, and Hermaeondas, a Theban, now arrived. These two had been sent out to them before the revolt, but had not been able to get to Lesbos before the appearance of the Athenian fleet. Now, after the battle, they managed to steal into the place in a trireme and persuaded the Mytilenians to send another trireme with ambassadors back with them to Sparta. This the Mytilenians did.

6   The Athenians meanwhile were much encouraged by the inaction of the Mytilenians. They summoned forces from their allies, and these forces arrived all the sooner because they saw so little evidence of vigorous action on the part of the Lesbians. They brought their fleet round to a station south of the city and built

two fortified camps, one on each side of the city, blockading both the harbours. They thus deprived the Mytilenians of the use of the sea, though they and the other Lesbians who supported them had control of the land. All that the Athenians held was a small area round their camps; Malea was used only as a port for their ships and a place for their market.

7   While the war in Mytilene was going on as I have described it, the Athenians also sent out, at about the same time of the summer, a fleet of thirty ships round the Peloponnese. This fleet was under the command of Phormio's son Asopius, the Acarnanians having requested that the commander sent out to them should be either a son or a relation of Phormio. Various places on the coast were laid waste by this fleet as it sailed off Laconia. Afterwards Asopius sent most of the ships back to Athens and with twelve ships came himself to Naupactus. He then raised an army from the whole country of Acarnania and marched against Oeniadae. The fleet sailed down the Achelous and the army laid waste the land. Oeniadae, however, showed no signs of giving in, and Asopius, after dismissing his army, sailed himself to Leucas and made a landing at Nericus. On his way back he was killed and a large number of his troops destroyed by the people of those parts who had come out against him, supported by a few soldiers of the garrison. Afterwards the Athenians sailed away, having recovered their dead from the Leucadians under an armistice.

8   Meanwhile the ambassadors from Mytilene who had been sent out in the first ship had been told by the Spartans to come to Olympia, so that the other allies also could hear and discuss what they had to say. They therefore went to Olympia, in the Olympiad at which Dorieus of Rhodes won his second victory, and when, after the festival was over, a meeting of the allies was called, they made the following speech:

9   'Spartans and allies, we know what the established rule among the Hellenes is on this subject. When a state revolts in the middle of a war and deserts its previous allies, those who welcome it into their alliance are just so far pleased with it as they find it useful to them, but otherwise think the worse of it for having betrayed its former friends. And this is a perfectly fair way of looking at things, so long as there is a like-mindedness in policy and feeling, an equality

in power and resources between the state that revolts and the state from which it revolts, and so long as there is no reasonable excuse for making the revolt. These conditions did not apply with regard to us and the Athenians, and no one should think the worse of us for revolting from them in time of danger, after being honoured by them in time of peace.

10   'Justice and honesty are the first subjects with which we shall deal, especially as we are here to ask for your alliance, and we know that there can never be a firm friendship between man and man or a real community between different states unless there is a conviction of honesty on both sides and a certain like-mindedness in other respects; for if people think differently they will act divergently.

'The alliance between us and Athens dates from the end of the Persian war, when you withdrew from the leadership and the Athenians stayed to finish what was left to do. But the object of the alliance was the liberation of the Hellenes from Persia, not the subjugation of the Hellenes to Athens. So long as the Athenians in their leadership respected our independence, we followed them with enthusiasm. But when we saw that they were becoming less and less antagonistic to Persia and more and more interested in enslaving their own allies, then we became frightened. Because of the multiple voting system, the allies were incapable of uniting in self-defence, and so they all became enslaved except for us and for Chios. We, supposed to be independent and nominally free, furnished our own contingents in the allied forces. But with the examples before us of what had already happened, we no longer felt any confidence in Athenian leadership. It seemed very unlikely that, after having brought under their control the states who were fellow members with us, they would refrain from acting towards us, too, in the same way, if ever they felt strong enough to do so.

11   'If we had all still been independent, we could have had more confidence in their not altering the state of affairs. But with most of their allies subjected to them and us being treated as equals, it was natural for them to object to a situation where the majority had already given in and we alone stood out as independent – all the more so since they were becoming stronger and stronger and we were losing whatever support we had before. And in an alliance

the only safe guarantee is an equality of mutual fear; for then the party that wants to break faith is deterred by the thought that the odds will not be on his side.

'In fact the only reason why we were left with our independence was because the Athenians, in building up their empire, thought that they could seize power more easily by having some specious arguments to put forward and by using the methods of policy rather than of brute force. We were useful to them because they could point to us and say that we, who had votes like themselves, could not possibly have joined them unwillingly in their various expeditions and could only be doing so because the people against whom we were being led were in the wrong. By these methods they first led the stronger states against the weaker ones, leaving the strongest to the last in the certainty of finding them, once all the rest had been absorbed, much less formidable to deal with. If, on the other hand, they had started with us, when all the other states still had their strength and had also a centre round which they could stand, they would not have subjugated them so easily. Then also they felt some alarm about our navy, in case it might come together as one force and join you or some other power, and so become a danger to Athens. Another factor in securing our independence was the trouble we took to be on good terms with the Athenian assembly and with their various leading statesmen. Yet, with the examples we had of how they had behaved to others, we never expected to be able to maintain ourselves for long, if this war had not broken out.

12   'How could we feel any genuine friendship or any confidence in our liberty when we were in a situation like this? The terms on which we accepted each other ran counter to the real feelings of both sides. In wartime they did their best to be on good terms with us because they were frightened of us; we, for the same reason, tried to keep on good terms with them in peace-time. In most cases goodwill is the basis of loyalty, but in our case fear was the bond, and it was more through terror than through friendship that we were held together in alliance. And the alliance was certain to be broken at any moment by the first side that felt confident that this would be a safe move to make. So it is wrong to condemn us for breaking away first simply because Athens had not

yet taken action against us, or to say that we ought to have waited until we were quite sure what action they would take. For if we had the same ability as they have for planning action and then putting it off, we should be their equals, and there would be no need for us to be their subjects. As it is, they are always in the position where they can take the initiative in aggression; we should be allowed the initiative in self-defence.

13   'These, Spartans and allies, are the reasons and the causes for our revolt. They are clear enough to convince our hearers that we have not acted improperly, and they constitute sufficient grounds for us to feel alarmed and to look round for what security we can find. Indeed, we wanted to do so long ago, and when it was still peacetime we sent ambassadors to you on the subject; but we could not get your help, since you refused to accept us. Now we have responded immediately to the invitation of the Boeotians and we have decided to make a double break with the past – a break in our relations both with the Hellenes and with the Athenians. As for the Hellenes, we shall no longer join the Athenians in acts of aggression on them, but shall help in the work of liberation; and as for the Athenians, we shall take the initiative in breaking away from them, instead of waiting to be destroyed by them later.

'However our revolt has taken place earlier than we intended and without adequate preparations. This is all the more reason why you should take us into your alliance and send us help quickly, thus revealing yourselves as people capable of helping those who should be helped and at the same time of hurting your enemies. Never has there been such an opportunity. Owing to the plague and the expenses they have incurred, the Athenians are in a state of exhaustion; part of their fleet is sailing round your coasts, and the rest is engaged in blockading us. It is improbable that they have any ships in reserve, and if you invade for the second time this summer with naval and military forces at the same time, they will either be unable to resist your fleet or will have to withdraw their own from your shores and from ours.

'And do not think that you are endangering your own persons for the sake of a country that has nothing to do with you. You may think that Lesbos is a long way away, but you will find that the good it can do you is very close at hand. It is not in Attica, as some people think, that the war will be won or lost, but in the countries from which Attica draws her strength. Her financial power comes from the tribute paid by her allies, and this will be greater still if we are conquered. For there will be no other revolts, our resources will be added to theirs, and we shall be treated more harshly than those who were enslaved before us. But if you give us your whole-hearted support you will gain for yourselves a state which has a large navy (which is the thing you need most); you will be in a much better position for breaking the power of Athens by detaching her allies from her, since the others will be greatly encouraged to come over to you; and you will clear yourselves of the charge that has been made against you of not giving help to those who revolt. Once you come forward in the role of liberators, you will find that your strength in the war is enormously increased.

14   'We ask you, therefore, to respect the hopes set on you by the Hellenes, and to respect Olympian Zeus, in whose temple we stand as suppliants. Come to the help of Mytilene. Be our allies, and do not desert us. It is our own lives that we are risking, but we are doing so in a way by which the general good of all will be the result of our success, and an even more general calamity, if you will not listen to us, will follow upon our failure. Be the men, therefore, that the Hellenes think you and that our fears require you to be.'

15   This was the speech of the Mytilenians. When the Spartans and their allies had heard it, they accepted the proposals made and welcomed the Lesbians into their alliance. They decided on the invasion of Attica and instructed their allies, who were present, to gather at the isthmus as quickly as possible with two-thirds of their total forces. They themselves were the first to arrive there, and they got ready machines for hauling the ships across from Corinth to the sea on the side of Athens, so that they could attack simultaneously by land and sea. In all this they showed great energy, but the other allies were slow in coming in, since they were busy in harvesting their corn and tired of military service.

16   The Athenians were aware that these preparations were being made on the theory that they themselves were weak, and wished to make it clear that the theory was a mistaken one and that they

could easily beat off any attack from the Peloponnesian fleet without recalling their own fleet from Lesbos. They therefore manned 100 ships with their own citizens (excluding the knights and the Pentacosiomedimni) and with their resident aliens, sailed out to the Isthmus, where they made a demonstration of their power and carried out landings just as they pleased on the Peloponnesian coast. The Spartans, finding that matters were not at all what they had expected, came to the conclusion that what the Lesbians had said was untrue; other difficulties faced them in the non-appearance of their allies and the news that the thirty Athenian ships round the Peloponnese were now laying waste the country near Sparta itself. They therefore returned home, but later they got ready a fleet to send to Lesbos. A total of forty ships was ordered from their various allies, and Alcidas was appointed as admiral to sail with the fleet. The Athenians also went back to Athens with their hundred ships when they saw that the Spartans had gone.

17   At the time when this fleet was at sea, Athens seems to have had almost the largest number of ships in action at the same time that she ever had, and beautifully equipped too. Yet the numbers were as great or greater at the beginning of the war. Then a hundred ships were guarding Attica, Euboea, and Salamis; another hundred were sailing round the Peloponnese, and there were other ships at Potidaea and in various other stations, making a grand total of 250 on active service in one summer. It was this, together with the campaign at Potidaea, which was the chief drain on the revenue. For the hoplites in the garrison at Potidaea were paid two drachmae a day (one for the soldier and one for his servant). From the beginning there were 3,000 hoplites, and the number was not reduced till the siege was over. Then, too, there were 1,600 men with Phormio who left before the end of the siege. The crews of the ships were all paid at the same rate. This was the expenditure of money at first, at a time when Athens had the very largest number of ships in service.

18   At the time when the Spartans were at the Isthmus, the Mytilenians, supported by a force of mercenaries, marched by land against Methymne in the belief that they would have the place betrayed to them. They made an assault on the city, but nothing went as they had expected and they withdrew to Antissa, Pyrrha, and

Eresus. They made arrangements for the internal security of these places, strengthened their walls, and then quickly marched home again.

After the Mytilenians had retired, the people of Methymna marched out against Antissa, but they were defeated by the Antissians and their mercenaries, who came outside the walls to fight. Many of the Methymnians were killed and the rest retreated as fast as they could. When the Athenians were informed of this and realized that the Mytilenians were masters of the whole country and that their own soldiers were too few to keep them in check, they sent out at the beginning of the autumn Paches, the son of Epicurus, with 1,000 citizen hoplites under his command. The hoplites rowed the ships themselves, and when they arrived at Mytilene they built a single wall completely surrounding the place, with forts, garrisoned by soldiers, placed at various strong points. Thus Mytilene was now firmly blockaded both from the land and from the sea, and winter was approaching.

19 The Athenians still needed more money for the siege, though they had for the first time raised from their own citizens a contribution of 200 talents. They now sent out twelve ships to collect money from their allies, with Lysicles and four others in command. After sailing to various places and collecting contributions, Lysicles went inland from Myos in Caria across the plain of the Maeander up to the hills at Sandius. There he was set upon by the Carians and by the people of Anaia; he himself and a great part of his army were killed.

20 In the same winter the Plataeans, who were still being besieged by the Peloponnesians and the Boeotians, finding themselves in distress as their provisions ran out, and seeing no hope of help coming to them from Athens or any chance of survival by any other means, made a plan with the Athenians who were besieged with them by which they were to leave the city and do their best to force their way over the enemy's surrounding wall. The originators of the scheme were Theaenetus, the son of Tolmides, a soothsayer, and Eupompides, the son of Daïmachus, who was one of the generals. The original intention was that they should all join in the attempt, but later half of them shrank back from being involved in what seemed to them too risky a venture. There remained

about 220 volunteers who persisted in the idea of breaking out. Their method was as follows: they constructed ladders to reach to the top of the enemy's wall, and they did this by calculating the height of the wall from the number of the layers of bricks at a point which was facing in their direction and had not been plastered. The layers were counted by a lot of people at the same time, and though some were likely to get the figure wrong, the majority would get it right, especially as they counted the layers frequently and were not so far away from the wall that they could not see it well enough for their purpose. Thus, guessing what the thickness of a single brick was, they calculated how long their ladders would have to be.

21   The wall of the Peloponnesians was constructed in the following way. There were in fact two walls, each forming a circle, one directed against Plataea, and one facing outwards to guard against any attack that might be made from Athens. Between the two walls was a space of about sixteen feet, and inside this space were built the huts where the men on guard were quartered. The building was continuous, so that the impression made was that of one thick wall with battlements on either side of it. Every ten battlements there were towers of some size and of the same breadth as the wall, reaching right across from its inner to its outer face, and built so that there was no way past the towers, the only way being through the middle of them. On nights when it was wet and stormy they did not man the battlements, but kept guard from the towers, which were roofed in above and were not far away from each other.

This was the structure of the wall inside which the Plataeans
22 were penned. And now, when everything was ready, they waited for a stormy night with wind and rain and no moon, and then they slipped out of the city, led by the men who had been the originators of the plan. First they crossed the ditch that surrounded the town, and then they came up to the enemy's wall without being detected by the men on guard, who could not see them in the darkness or hear the noise they made as they approached, because it was drowned by the blustering of the wind. They also kept a good distance away from each other, to prevent the risk of their weapons clashing together and giving them away. They were

lightly armed and only wore shoes on the left foot, to stop them slipping in the mud. They reached the battlements at a place half-way between two towers which they knew to be unguarded. The ones who carried the ladders went first and set them in position; next twelve light-armed men, with daggers and breast-plates, climbed up, led by Ammias, the son of Coroebus, who was the first to ascend. His men followed him, and six went to each of the two towers. After them came more light-armed soldiers with spears; their shields were carried by others who came behind them, and they were to give them their shields when they came in contact with the enemy. It was not until most of them had ascended the wall that they were discovered by the sentries in the towers. One of the Plataeans had knocked down a tile from the battlements as he was getting a grip of it, and it made a noise as it fell. The alarm was given immediately, and the troops rushed out to the wall. In the darkness and the storm they had no notion of what the danger was, and at the same moment the Plataeans who were left behind in the city made a sortie and attacked the wall at a point opposite to the place where their comrades were climbing up, so as to distract attention from them as far as possible. So the besieging troops stood still in a state of confusion, no one daring to leave his own sector to reinforce any other point, and unable to guess what was happening. The 300 troops, however, who were specially detailed for service in an emergency, went outside the wall and marched in the direction of the alarm. Fire signals of an enemy attack were made to Thebes; but the Plataeans in the town also displayed a number of fire signals from their own walls, having them all ready made for this very purpose, so as to make the enemy's signals unintelligible, to stop help coming from Thebes, and to prevent the Thebans from having a true idea of what was happening, until their own men who had gone out had escaped and got into safety.

23   Meanwhile the Plataeans were climbing up on to the wall. The first who ascended had captured the two towers and killed the sentries. They then took up their stand in the passages through the towers to prevent any reinforcements coming through against them. They also set up ladders from the wall and sent a number of men up to the tops of the towers; so, by hurling their missiles

both from above and from below, they kept back the enemy from approaching. Meanwhile the main body planted a number of ladders against the outer wall, knocked down the battlements, and kept passing over between the towers. As each man got across he formed up with the others at the edge of the ditch, and from there they shot their arrows and hurled their javelins at all who came up along the wall to prevent their comrades crossing over. When the rest had got across, last of all, and with some difficulty, the men on the towers came down and ran to the ditch, and at that very moment the enemy force of 300 came up, carrying torches. The Plataeans, standing in the darkness at the edge of the ditch, could see them better than they could be seen themselves, and shot their arrows and hurled javelins at the parts of their bodies which were unprotected with armour. The light of the torches made it even more difficult for them to be seen in the darkness, so that even the last of them managed to get across the ditch, though it was a hard business and difficult going. Ice had formed on the surface, not hard enough to walk on, but of the watery kind which comes when the wind is more in the east than in the north, and the snow which fell in the night, with the great wind which was blowing, had raised the level of the water in the ditch so much that they could only just get across with their heads out of the water. Nevertheless it was chiefly because the storm was so violent that they managed to escape at all.

24   The Plataeans then set out from the ditch in one body and took the road to Thebes, with the shrine of the hero Androcrates on their right. They imagined that this road, leading into their enemies' country, would be the very last one that they would be suspected of having taken, and, in fact, when they were on it they saw the Peloponnesians with torches trying to find them on the road to Athens in the direction of Cithaeron and Druos-Kephalae. The Plataeans went for rather more than half a mile on the road to Thebes, and then turned off it and took the road leading to the mountains in the direction of Erythrae and Hysiae. On reaching the mountains they made their way safely to Athens, 212 of them all told. Some of them had turned back to the city before crossing the wall, and one archer had been taken prisoner at the outer ditch.

Finally the Peloponnesians gave up the pursuit and returned to their positions. The Plataeans in the city knew nothing of what had taken place, and were informed by the men who turned back that the whole of the escaping party had been destroyed. So as soon as it was day they sent out a herald to ask for a truce so that they could recover their dead; but they abandoned the idea when they learned the truth. In this way the Plataeans who made the attempt got across the wall and reached safety.

25 At the end of this same winter the Spartan Salaethus was sent from Sparta to Mytilene in a trireme. He went by sea to Pyrrha, and from there went on foot along the bed of a water-course to a place where it was possible to get through the surrounding wall, and so slipped into Mytilene unobserved. There he told the magistrates that Attica was going to be invaded, that the forty ships which were to help them were coming, and that he himself had been sent in advance to tell them the news and to take charge of things generally. The Mytilenians were encouraged by this and became less inclined to try to make terms with Athens. So ended this winter, and so ended the fourth year of this war recorded by Thucydides.

26 Next summer the Peloponnesians sent out to Mytilene the forty-two ships under the command of their admiral Alcidas. They themselves and their allies invaded Attica, so that the Athenians would have trouble on two fronts at once and would find it more difficult to take action against the fleet going to Mytilene. The commander in this invasion was Cleomenes, acting for King Pausanias, the son of Pleistoanax, who was still under age. Cleomenes was the brother of Pleistoanax. The invading forces destroyed everything that had started to grow up again in the districts which they had laid waste previously, and they went on to destroy such property as had been left untouched in earlier invasions. Thus this was the worst invasion of all except the second. The enemy prolonged their stay in Attica and overran most of the country, since they were constantly waiting to hear news of what their fleet, which they thought must have arrived by now, had done in Lesbos. Finally, however, when none of their expectations was realized and their provisions had begun to run out, they retired and dispersed to their various cities.

27 Meanwhile the Mytilenians were forced to come to terms with

the Athenians. Their supplies of food had run out, and the ships from the Peloponnese, so far from putting in an appearance, continued to waste time on the way. The surrender took place under the following circumstances. Salaethus himself had given up hope of the arrival of the ships, and he now issued heavy armour to the people (who previously had been only equipped as light troops), with the intention of leading them out to battle with the Athenians. But as soon as the people found themselves properly armed, they refused any longer to obey the government. They held meetings among themselves and demanded that the authorities should openly produce all the food there was and distribute it among them all; otherwise, they said, they themselves would come to terms with the Athenians and surrender the city to them.

28   The government realized that they were quite incapable of preventing this and also that they would be in danger themselves if an agreement was concluded without them. They therefore joined in coming to terms with Paches and the Athenian army. The terms were as follows: Athens was to have the right to act as she saw fit with regard to the people of Mytilene, and the army was allowed to enter the city; the Mytilenians were to send representatives to Athens to put their case, and until these representatives returned, Paches was to undertake not to imprison or enslave or kill any of the population.

Though these were the terms of the surrender, the party among the Mytilenians who had been most active in the Spartan interest were still terrified – so much so indeed that, when the army entered the city, they felt it necessary to go and take refuge at the altars. Paches raised them up from their suppliant position, promising that he would do them no harm, and put them in custody on Tenedos until he learned what decision the Athenians would come to about them. He also sent triremes to Antissa and occupied the place, and took various other military measures which seemed desirable.

29   Meanwhile the Peloponnesians in the forty ships, who should have hurried to the relief of Mytilene, wasted a lot of time in their voyage round the Peloponnese itself, and then proceeded on their way in a leisurely manner, finally arriving at Delos without being observed by the Athenians at Athens.

From Delos they went on to Icarus and Myconus, and there first heard the news that Mytilene had fallen. Wishing to obtain more precise information, they sailed on to Embatum in Erythraea, arriving there about seven days after the surrender of Mytilene. Here they got the information they required, and began to discuss what they should do in view of what had happened. Teutiaplus, a man from Elis, made a speech giving them the following advice:

30   'Alcidas and fellow commanders from the Peloponnese, I propose that we should sail to Mytilene just as we are and before they know that we are here. In all probability, since they have only just taken the city, we shall find that their precautions have been greatly relaxed; and this will certainly be so by sea, where they have no idea of having to face any possible attack, and where, in fact, our main strength happens to lie. It is likely, too, that their land forces, after their victory, will be dispersed about the houses in the city and not properly organized. So that if we were to attack suddenly and by night, I think that, with the help of those inside the town who are still on our side, we ought to be able to gain control of the place. Let us not be afraid of the danger, but let us remember that this is an example of the unknown factor in warfare, and that the good general is the one who guards against such unknown factors in his own case, but exploits them for attack in the case of the enemy.'

31   Alcidas, however, was unconvinced by this advice. It was then suggested to him by some of the Ionian exiles and by the Lesbians who were in his fleet that, if this risk seemed too great to him, he should seize one of the Ionian cities or Cumae in Aeolia, and use it as a base for organizing revolt in Ionia. This, they claimed, was a distinct possibility, since they would be welcomed everywhere. Their aim would be to cut Athens off from this, the greatest of her sources of revenue, and at the same time to involve her in more expense if she decided to maintain a fleet against them. They said, too, that they thought they could persuade Pissuthnes to come in on their side.

Not even this plan commended itself to Alcidas, whose main idea was, since he had been too late for Mytilene, to get back to the Peloponnese as soon as possible. He therefore put out from Emba-
32 tum and sailed along the coast to the Teian town of Myonnesus.

There he put to death most of the prisoners whom he had taken on the voyage. Later, when he was at anchor at Ephesus, a deputation of Samians from Anaia came to him and told him that it was not the right way to set about the liberation of Hellas by massacring people who had never raised a hand against him, who were not his enemies, but only allies of Athens under compulsion, and that unless he stopped, so far from turning any enemies into friends, he would turn most of his friends into enemies.

Alcidas saw the force of this argument and released all the prisoners from Chios whom he still had and a few others from other places. For when his fleet was sighted the people made no effort to run away; instead they came to meet the ships, under the impression that they must be Athenian, since they never even imagined that, with Athens in control of the sea, a Peloponnesian fleet would come across to Ionia.

33   From Ephesus Alcidas set sail in a hurry and fled. While he was still at anchor off Clarus he had been sighted by the Athenian ships, the *Salaminia* and the *Paralus*,[29] which happened to be sailing from Athens. So, in fear of a pursuit, he set out across the open sea with the firm intention of not putting in to land anywhere at all, if he could help it, until he reached the Peloponnese.

Meanwhile news of his presence had reached Paches and the Athenians from Erythraea – in fact from all directions. For, since the cities of Ionia were not fortified, the inhabitants were greatly afraid that the Peloponnesians, even if they had no intention of remaining, might, as they sailed along, make landings and lay waste the towns. And now the *Paralus* and the *Salaminia* arrived with the news that they had seen the enemy fleet at Clarus. Paches, therefore, immediately set out in pursuit and went after them as far as the island of Patmos. From here he turned back again, since it appeared that Alcidas had got away out of reach. In fact, since he had not managed to overtake the Peloponnesian on the open sea, he thought it a lucky thing that thay had not been discovered anywhere else where they would have been compelled to build a fortified camp, and so have given the Athenians the trouble of organizing a regular blockade by sea and land.

29. These two ships were the élite of the Athenian navy, in service throughout the year for special missions.

34   As he sailed back along the coast he put in, among other places, at Notium, the harbour of Colophon, where the Colophonians had settled after the upper city had been captured, at about the time of the second Peloponnesian invasion of Attica, by Itamenes and his foreign troops who had been called in as a result of the political ambition of individuals. However, the exiles who had settled at Notium again split up into two hostile parties. One of these called in Arcadian and foreign mercenaries from Pissuthnes, quartered them in a part of the town which they cut off from the rest by a wall, and so formed a separate state with the help of the pro-Persian party among the Colophonians from the upper city. The other party at Notium had fled into exile and now called in Paches. Paches invited Hippias, the general of the Arcadian mercenaries inside the fortification, to meet him for a discussion, promising that, if no agreement was reached, he would see that he got back again safe and sound to the fortification. Hippias therefore came out to meet Paches, who put him under arrest, though not into chains. He then made a sudden attack and took the fortification by surprise. He put to death all the Arcadian and foreign troops who were inside, and, later, as he had promised, he brought Hippias back there, and, as soon as he was inside, he had him seized and shot down with arrows. He handed over Notium to the Colophonians, excluding the pro-Persian party among them. Later the Athenians sent out settlers and made a colony of the place under Athenian laws, after having collected together all the Colophonians who could be found in other cities.

35   Paches then returned to Mytilene and reduced Pyrrha and Eresus. He found the Spartan Salaethus in hiding in the city and sent him to Athens, together with the Mytilenians whom he had placed in Tenedos and others whom he considered implicated in the organization of the revolt. He also sent back the greater part of his army. He himself stayed behind with the remainder of his forces and settled matters in Mytilene and the rest of Lesbos as he thought fit.

THE MYTILENIAN DEBATE[30]

36   When Salaethus and the other prisoners reached Athens, the Athenians immediately put Salaethus to death in spite of the fact that he undertook, among other things, to have the Peloponnesians withdrawn from Plataea, which was still being besieged. They then discussed what was to be done with the other prisoners and, in their angry mood, decided to put to death not only those now in their hands but also the entire adult male population of Mytilene, and to make slaves of the women and children. What they held against Mytilene was the fact that it had revolted even though it was not a subject state, like the others, and the bitterness of their feelings was considerably increased by the fact that the Peloponnesian fleet had actually dared to cross over to Ionia to support the revolt. This, it was thought, could never have happened unless the revolt had been long premeditated. So they sent a trireme to Paches to inform him of what had been decided, with orders to put the Mytilenians to death immediately.

Next day, however, there was a sudden change of feeling and people began to think how cruel and how unprecedented such a decision was – to destroy not only the guilty, but the entire population of a state. Observing this, the deputation from Mytilene which was in Athens and the Athenians who were supporting them approached the authorities with a view to having the question debated again. They won their point the more easily because the authorities themselves saw clearly that most of the citizens were wanting someone to give them a chance of reconsidering the matter. So an assembly was called at once. Various opinions were expressed on both sides, and Cleon, the son of Cleaenetus, spoke again. It was he who had been responsible for passing the original motion for putting the Mytilenians to death. He was remarkable among the Athenians for the violence of his character, and at this time he exercised far the greatest influence over the people.[31] He spoke as follows:

30. See the Introduction, pp. 27.

31. This wording is echoed by Thucydides in VI, 35 when he introduces the Syracusan 'demagogue' Athenagoras.

37   'Personally I have had occasion often enough already to observe that a democracy is incapable of governing others, and I am all the more convinced of this when I see how you are now changing your minds about the Mytilenians. Because fear and conspiracy play no part in your daily relations with each other, you imagine that the same thing is true of your allies, and you fail to see that when you allow them to persuade you to make a mistaken decision and when you give way to your own feelings of compassion you are being guilty of a kind of weakness which is dangerous to you and which will not make them love you any more. What you do not realize is that your empire is a tyranny exercised over subjects who do not like it and who are always plotting against you; you will not make them obey you by injuring your own interests in order to do them a favour; your leadership depends on superior strength and not on any goodwill of theirs. And this is the very worst thing – to pass measures and then not to abide by them. We should realize that a city is better off with bad laws, so long as they remain fixed, than with good laws that are constantly being altered, that lack of learning combined with sound common sense is more helpful than the kind of cleverness that gets out of hand, and that as a general rule states are better governed by the man in the street than by intellectuals. These are the sort of people who want to appear wiser than the laws, who want to get their own way in every general discussion, because they feel that they cannot show off their intelligence in matters of greater importance, and who, as a result, very often bring ruin on their country. But the other kind – the people who are not so confident in their own intelligence – are prepared to admit that the laws are wiser than they are and that they lack the ability to pull to pieces a speech made by a good speaker; they are unbiased judges, and not people taking part in some kind of a competition; so things usually go well when they are in control. We statesmen, too, should try to be like them, instead of being carried away by mere cleverness and a desire to show off our intelligence and so giving you, the people, advice which we do not really believe in ourselves.

38   'As for me, I have not altered my opinion, and I am amazed at those who have proposed a reconsideration of the question of Mytilene, thus causing a delay which is all to the advantage of the

guilty party. After a lapse of time the injured party will lose the edge of his anger when he comes to act against those who have wronged him; whereas the best punishment and the one most fitted to the crime is when reprisals follow immediately. I shall be amazed, too, if anyone contradicts me and attempts to prove that the harm done to us by Mytilene is really a good thing for us, or that when we suffer ourselves we are somehow doing harm to our allies. It is obvious that anyone who is going to say this must either have such confidence in his powers as an orator that he will struggle to persuade you that what has been finally settled was, on the contrary, not decided at all, or else he must have been bribed to put together some elaborate speech with which he will try to lead you out of the right track. But in competitions of this sort the prizes go to others and the state takes all the danger for herself. The blame is yours, for stupidly instituting these competitive displays. You have become regular speech-goers, and as for action, you merely listen to accounts of it; if something is to be done in the future you estimate the possibilities by hearing a good speech on the subject, and as for the past you rely not so much on the facts which you have seen with your own eyes as on what you have heard about them in some clever piece of verbal criticism. Any novelty in an argument deceives you at once, but when the argument is tried and proved you become unwilling to follow it; you look with suspicion on what is normal and are the slaves of every paradox that comes your way. The chief wish of each one of you is to be able to make a speech himself, and, if you cannot do that, the next best thing is to compete with those who can make this sort of speech by not looking as though you were at all out of your depth while you listen to the views put forward, by applauding a good point even before it is made, and by being as quick at seeing how an argument is going to be developed as you are slow at understanding what in the end it will lead to. What you are looking for all the time is something that is, I should say, outside the range of ordinary experience, and yet you cannot even think straight about the facts of life that are before you. You are simply victims of your own pleasure in listening, and are more like an audience sitting at the feet of a professional lecturer than a parliament discussing matters of state.

39   'I am trying to stop you behaving like this, and I say that no single city has ever done you the harm that Mytilene has done. Personally I can make allowances for those who revolt because they find your rule intolerable or because they have been forced into it by enemy action. Here, however, we have the case of people living on an island, behind their own fortifications, with nothing to fear from our enemies except an attack by sea against which they were adequately protected by their own force of triremes; they had their own independent government and they were treated by us with the greatest consideration. Now, to act as they acted is not what I should call a revolt (for people only revolt when they have been badly treated); it is a case of calculated aggression, of deliberately taking sides with our bitterest enemies in order to destroy us. And this is far worse than if they had made war against us simply to increase their own power. They learned nothing from the fate of those of their neighbours who had already revolted and been subdued; the prosperity which they enjoyed did not make them hesitate before running into danger; confident in the future, they declared war on us, with hopes that indeed extended beyond their means, though still fell short of their desires. They made up their minds to put might first and right second, choosing the moment when they thought they would win, and then making their unprovoked attack upon us.

"The fact is that when great prosperity comes suddenly and unexpectedly to a state, it usually breeds arrogance; in most cases it is safer for people to enjoy an average amount of success rather than something which is out of all proportion; and it is easier, I should say, to ward off hardship than to maintain happiness. What we should have done long ago with the Mytilenians was to treat them in exactly the same way as all the rest; then they would never have grown so arrogant, for it is a general rule of human nature that people despise those who treat them well and look up to those who make no concessions. Let them now therefore have the punishment which their crime deserves. Do not put the blame on the aristocracy and say that the people were innocent. The fact is that the whole lot of them attacked you together, although the people might have come over to us and, if they had, would now be back again in control of their city. Yet, instead of doing this, they thought it safer to share the dangers, and join in the revolt of the aristocracy.

'Now think of your allies. If you are going to give the same punishment to those who are forced to revolt by your enemies and those who do so of their own accord, can you not see that they will all revolt upon the slightest pretext, when success means freedom and failure brings no very dreadful consequences? Meanwhile we shall have to spend our money and risk our lives against state after state; if our efforts are successful, we shall recover a city that is in ruins, and so lose the future revenue from it, on which our strength is based; and if we fail to subdue it, we shall have more enemies to deal with in addition to those we have already, and we shall spend the time which ought to be used in resisting our present foes in making war on our own allies.

40   'Let there be no hope, therefore, held out to the Mytilenians that we, either as a result of a good speech or a large bribe, are likely to forgive them on the grounds that it is only human to make mistakes. There was nothing involuntary about the harm they did us; they knew what they were about and they planned it all beforehand; and one only forgives actions that were not deliberate. As for me, just as I was at first, so I am now, and I shall continue to impress on you the importance of not altering your previous decisions. To feel pity, to be carried away by the pleasure of hearing a clever argument, to listen to the claims of decency are three things that are entirely against the interests of an imperial power. Do not be guilty of them. As for compassion, it is proper to feel it in the case of people who are like ourselves and who will pity us in their turn, not in the case of those who, so far from having the same feelings towards us, must always and inevitably be our enemies. As for the speech-makers who give such pleasure by their arguments, they should hold their competitions on subjects which are less important, and not on a question where the state may have to pay a heavy penalty for its light pleasure, while the speakers themselves will no doubt be enjoying splendid rewards for their splendid arguments. And a sense of decency is only felt towards those who are going to be our friends in future, not towards those who remain just as they were and as much our enemies as they ever have been.

'Let me sum the whole thing up. I say that, if you follow my advice, you will be doing the right thing as far as Mytilene is concerned and at the same time will be acting in your own interests; if you decide differently, you will not win them over, but you will be passing judgement on yourselves. For if they were justified in revolting, you must be wrong in holding power. If, however, whatever the rights or wrongs of it may be, you propose to hold power all the same, then your interest demands that these too, rightly or wrongly, must be punished. The only alternative is to surrender your empire, so that you can afford to go in for philanthropy. Make up your minds, therefore, to pay them back in their own coin, and do not make it look as though you who escaped their machinations are less quick to react than they who started them. Remember how they would have been likely to have treated you, if they had won, especially as they were the aggressors. Those who do wrong to a neighbour when there is no reason to do so are the ones who persevere to the point of destroying him, since they see the danger involved in allowing their enemy to survive. For he who has suffered for no good reason is a more dangerous enemy, if he escapes, than the one who has both done and suffered injury.

'I urge you, therefore, not to be traitors to your own selves. Place yourselves in imagination at the moment when you first suffered and remember how then you would have given anything to have them in your power. Now pay them back for it, and do not grow soft just at this present moment, forgetting meanwhile the danger that hung over your heads then. Punish them as they deserve, and make an example of them to your other allies, plainly showing that revolt will be punished by death. Once they realize this, you will not have so often to neglect the war with your enemies because you are fighting with your own allies.'

41 So Cleon spoke. After him Diodotus, the son of Eucrates, who in the previous assembly also had vigorously opposed the motion to put the Mytilenians to death, came forward again on this occasion and spoke as follows:

42 'I do not blame those who have proposed a new debate on the subject of Mytilene, and I do not share the view which we have heard expressed, that it is a bad thing to have frequent discussions on matters of importance. Haste and anger are, to my mind, the

two greatest obstacles to wise counsel – haste, that usually goes with folly, anger, that is the mark of primitive and narrow minds. And anyone who maintains that words cannot be a guide to action must be either a fool or one with some personal interest at stake; he is a fool, if he imagines that it is possible to deal with the uncertainties of the future by any other medium, and he is personally interested if his aim is to persuade you into some disgraceful action, and, knowing that he cannot make a good speech in a bad cause, he tries to frighten his opponents and his hearers by some good-sized pieces of misrepresentation. Then still more intolerable are those who go further and accuse a speaker of making a kind of exhibition of himself, because he is paid for it. If it was only ignorance with which he was being charged, a speaker who failed to win his case could retire from the debate and still be thought an honest man, if not a very intelligent one. But when corruption is imputed, he will be suspect if he wins his case, and if he loses it, will be regarded as dishonest and stupid at the same time. This sort of thing does the city no good; her counsellors will be afraid to speak and she will be deprived of their services. Though certainly it would be the best possible thing for the city if these gentlemen whom I have been describing lacked the power to express themselves; we should not then be persuaded into making so many mistakes.

'The good citizen, instead of trying to terrify the opposition, ought to prove his case in fair argument; and a wise state, without giving special honours to its best counsellors, will certainly not deprive them of the honour they already enjoy; and when a man's advice is not taken, he should not even be disgraced, far less penalized. In this way successful speakers will be less likely to pursue further honours by speaking against their own convictions in order to make themselves popular, and unsuccessful speakers, too, 43 will not struggle to win over the people by the same acts of flattery. What we do here, however, is exactly the opposite. Then, too, if a man gives the best possible advice but is under the slightest suspicion of being influenced by his own private profit, we are so embittered by the idea (a wholly unproved one) of this profit of his, that we do not allow the state to receive the certain benefit of his good advice. So a state of affairs has been reached where a good proposal honestly put forward is just as suspect as something thoroughly bad, and the result is that just as the speaker who advocates some monstrous measure has to win over the people by deceiving them, so also a man with good advice to give has to tell lies if he expects to be believed. And because of this refinement in intellectuality, the state is put into a unique position; it is only she to whom no one can ever do a good turn openly and without deception. For if one openly performs a patriotic action, the reward for one's pains is to be thought to have made something oneself on the side. Yet in spite of all this we are discussing matters of the greatest importance, and we who give you our advice ought to be resolved to look rather further into things than you whose attention is occupied only with the surface – especially as we can be held to account for the advice we give, while you are not accountable for the way in which you receive it. For indeed you would take rather more care over your decisions, if the proposer of a motion and those who voted for it were all subject to the same penalties. As it is, on the occasions when some emotional impulse on your part has led you into disaster, you turn upon the one man who made the original proposal and you let yourself off, in spite of the fact that you are many and in spite of the fact that you were just as wrong as he was.

44   'However, I have not come forward to speak about Mytilene in any spirit of contradiction or with any wish to accuse anyone. If we are sensible people, we shall see that the question is not so much whether they are guilty as whether we are making the right decision for ourselves. I might prove that they are the most guilty people in the world, but it does not follow that I shall propose the death penalty, unless that is in your interests; I might argue that they deserve to be forgiven, but should not recommend forgiveness unless that seemed to me the best thing for the state.

'In my view our discussion concerns the future rather than the present. One of Cleon's chief points is that to inflict the death penalty will be useful to us in the future as a means for deterring other cities from revolt; but I, who am just as concerned as he is with the future, am quite convinced that this is not so. And I ask you not to reject what is useful in my speech for the sake of what is specious in his. You may well find his speech attractive, because it fits in better with your present angry feelings about the Mytilenians; but this is not a law-court, where we have to consider what is fit and just; it is a political assembly, and the question is how Mytilene can be most useful to Athens.

45   'Now, in human societies the death penalty has been laid down for many offences less serious than this one. Yet people still take risks when they feel sufficiently confident. No one has ever yet risked committing a crime which he thought he could not carry out successfully. The same is true of states. None has ever yet rebelled in the belief that it had insufficient resources, either in itself or from its allies, to make the attempt. Cities and individuals alike, all are by nature disposed to do wrong, and there is no law that will prevent it, as is shown by the fact that men have tried every kind of punishment, constantly adding to the list, in the attempt to find greater security from criminals. It is likely that in early times the punishments even for the greatest crimes were not as severe as they are now, but the laws were still broken, and in the course of time the death penalty became generally introduced. Yet even with this, the laws are still broken. Either, therefore, we must discover some fear more potent than the fear of death, or we must admit that here certainly we have not got an adequate deterrent. So long as poverty forces men to be bold, so long as the insolence and pride of wealth nourish their ambitions, and in the other accidents of life they are continually dominated by some incurable master passion or another, so long will their impulses continue to drive them into danger. Hope and desire persist throughout and cause the greatest calamities – one leading and the other following, one conceiving the enterprise, and the other suggesting that it will be successful – invisible factors, but more powerful than the terrors that are obvious to our eyes. Then too, the idea that fortune will be on one's side plays as big a part as anything else in creating a mood of over-confidence; for sometimes she does come unexpectedly to one's aid, and so she tempts men to run risks for which they are inadequately prepared. And this is particularly true in the case of whole peoples, because they are playing for the highest stakes – either for their own freedom or for the power to control others – and each individual, when acting as part of a community, has the irrational opinion that his own powers are greater

than in fact they are. In a word it is impossible (and only the most simple-minded will deny this) for human nature, when once seriously set upon a certain course, to be prevented from following that course by the force of law or by any other means of intimidation whatever.

46   'We must not, therefore, come to the wrong conclusions through having too much confidence in the effectiveness of capital punishment, and we must not make the condition of rebels desperate by depriving them of the possibility of repentance and of a chance of atoning as quickly as they can for what they did. Consider this now: at the moment, if a city has revolted and realizes that the revolt cannot succeed, it will come to terms while it is still capable of paying an indemnity and continuing to pay tribute afterwards. But if Cleon's method is adopted, can you not see that every city will not only make much more careful preparations for revolt, but will also hold out against siege to the very end, since to surrender early or late means just the same thing? This is, unquestionably, against our interests – to spend money on a siege because of the impossibility of coming to terms, and, if we capture the place, to take over a city that is in ruins so that we lose the future revenue from it. And it is just on this revenue that our strength in war depends.

'Our business, therefore, is not to injure ourselves by acting like a judge who strictly examines a criminal; instead we should be looking for a method by which, employing moderation in our punishments, we can in future secure for ourselves the full use of those cities which bring us important contributions. And we should recognize that the proper basis of our security is in good administration rather than in the fear of legal penalties. As it is, we do just the opposite: when we subdue a free city, which was held down by force and has, as we might have expected, tried to assert its independence by revolting, we think that we ought to punish it with the utmost severity. But the right way to deal with free people is this – not to inflict tremendous punishments on them after they have revolted, but to take tremendous care of them before this point is reached, to prevent them even contemplating the idea of revolt, and, if we do have to use force with them, to hold as few as possible of them responsible for this.

47   'Consider what a mistake you would be making on this very
point, if you took Cleon's advice. As things are now, in all the
cities the democracy is friendly to you; either it does not join in
with the oligarchies in revolting, or, if it is forced to do so, it
remains all the time hostile to the rebels, so that when you go to
war with them, you have the people on your side. But if you destroy the democratic party at Mytilene, who never took any hand
in the revolt and who, as soon as they got arms, voluntarily gave
the city up to you, you will first of all be guilty of killing those
who have helped you, and, secondly, you will be doing exactly
what the reactionary classes want most. For now, when they start
a revolt, they will have the people on their side from the beginning, because you have already made it clear that the same punishment is laid down both for the guilty and the innocent. In fact,
however, even if they were guilty, you should pretend that they
were not, in order to keep on your side the one element that
is still not opposed to you. It is far more useful to us, I think, in
preserving our empire, that we should voluntarily put up with
injustice than that we should justly put to death the wrong people.
As for Cleon's point – that in this act of vengeance both justice and
self-interest are combined – this is not a case where such a combination is at all possible.

48   'I call upon you, therefore, to accept my proposal as the better
one. Do not be swayed too much by pity or by ordinary decent
feelings. I, no more than Cleon, wish you to be influenced by such
emotions. It is simply on the basis of the argument which you have
heard that I ask you to be guided by me, to try at your leisure the
men whom Paches has considered guilty and sent to Athens,
and to allow the rest to live in their own city. In following this
course you will be acting wisely for the future and will be doing
something which will make your enemies fear you now. For those
who make wise decisions are more formidable to their enemies
than those who rush madly into strong action.'

49   This was the speech of Diodotus. And now, when these two mo-
tions, each so opposed to each, had been put forward, the Athenians, in spite of the recent change of feeling, still held conflicting
opinions, and at the show of hands the votes were nearly equal.
However, the motion of Diodotus was passed.

Immediately another trireme was sent out in all haste, since they feared that, unless it overtook the first trireme, they would find on their arrival that the city had been destroyed. The first trireme had a start of about twenty-four hours. The ambassadors from Mytilene provided wine and barley for the crew and promised great rewards if they arrived in time, and so the men made such speed on the voyage that they kept on rowing while they took their food (which was barley mixed with oil and wine) and rowed continually, taking it in turn to sleep. Luckily they had no wind against them, and as the first ship was not hurrying on its distasteful mission, while they were pressing on with such speed, what happened was that the first ship arrived so little ahead of them that Paches had just had time to read the decree and to prepare to put it into force, when the second ship put in to the harbour and prevented the massacre. So narrow had been the escape of Mytilene.

50   The other Mytilenians whom Paches had sent to Athens as being the ones chiefly responsible for the revolt were, on the motion of Cleon, put to death by the Athenians. There were rather more than 1,000 of them. The Athenians also destroyed the fortifications of Mytilene and took over their navy. Afterwards, instead of imposing a tribute on Lesbos, they divided all the land, except that belonging to the Methymnians, into 3,000 holdings, 300 of which were set apart as sacred for the gods, while the remainder was distributed by lot to Athenian shareholders, who were sent out to Lesbos. The Lesbians agreed with these shareholders to pay a yearly rent of two minae for each holding, and cultivated the land themselves. The Athenians also took over all the towns on the mainland that had been under the control of Mytilene. So for the future the Mytilenians became subjects of Athens. This completes the account of what took place in Lesbos.

THE END OF PLATAEA

51 In the same summer, and after the conquest of Lesbos, the Athenians, under the command of Nicias, the son of Niceratus, made an expedition against the island of Minoa, which lies off Megara. The Megarians had built a tower there and used the island

as an advanced base. Nicias wanted the Athenian blockading force to be based on this island, which was nearer to Megara than the existing stations at Budorum and Salamis; at the same time he wished to prevent the Peloponnesians from sailing out unobserved from there with their triremes, as they had already done, or from sending out raiders; and also to stop any ship entering the port of Megara.

First, with the aid of siege engines used from aboard his ships, he captured two towers projecting into the sea on the side of Nisaea and cleared the entrance into the channel between the island and the coast. He then built a wall at the part by the mainland where it was possible to send troops across by a bridge over the marshes, since the island lay quite close to the mainland. The whole operation took only a few days, and, after he had also built fortifications on the island and left a garrison there, he withdrew with the bulk of his forces.

52   This summer, at about the same time as the above events, the Plataeans, whose provisions had run out and who were no longer able to support the siege, came to terms with the Peloponnesians. The events were as follows. The Peloponnesians had made an attack on the wall and found that the Plataeans were not able to put up any resistance. The Spartan commander, realizing their weakness, had no wish to take the place by storm, because of his instructions from Sparta which had been given with a view to any future peace treaty with Athens under the terms of which each side would have to give back the places that they had conquered in the war: thus Plataea, on the assumption that it had come over voluntarily, would not have to be given back. He sent a herald to ask whether they would voluntarily give up their city to the Spartans and submit themselves to the judgement of Sparta, on the understanding that the guilty would be punished, but no one without a fair trial.

As soon as the herald had delivered his message, the Plataeans, who were now in the last stages of exhaustion, surrendered the city. They were given food by the Peloponnesians for a few days, until the five judges from Sparta arrived. On the arrival of these judges, no formal accusation was drawn up. Instead the Plataeans were called forward and simply asked this one question: 'Have you done anything to help the Spartans and their allies in the present war?' The Plataeans asked permission to speak at greater length, and appointed as their spokesmen Astymachus, the son of Asopolaus, and Lacon, the son of Aieimnestus, who had been in charge of Spartan interests in Plataea. These two came forward and spoke as follows:

53 'Spartans, when we surrendered our city to you, we trusted you and we did not expect to face a trial of this sort, but one more in accordance with usual practice. Nor did we expect to be tried, as we are being tried, by other people. We thought that you yourselves would be our judges and that from you we should be most likely to get fair treatment. As it is, we fear that on both these points we have been deceived. We have reason to suspect that the issue at stake is nothing less than life or death and that you yourselves are not going to act impartially. Our evidence is in the fact that no accusation has been brought forward for us to answer (indeed we had to ask permission to speak at all), and that your short question is so framed that if we answer it truly, we are condemned, and if falsely, detected in our falsehood. Whichever way we look, we are at a loss, and so we are forced to do what seems also to be the safest thing – that is, to speak our minds at all costs. For, situated as we are, words left unspoken might occur to us afterwards and upbraid us with the thought that, if spoken, they might have saved us. Then, too, it is difficult for us to find the power to persuade you. If we were unknown to each other, we could do ourselves good by bringing forward evidence which was new to you; but as it is, we can only tell you things you know already, and what we fear is not so much that you have already decided that our merits will not bear comparison with yours and are making that the basis of your accusation, as that, in order to gratify another state, you are giving us the kind of trial in which the verdict has already been decided in advance. Yet all the same we shall say what we have to say in justification of ourselves, both as regards our quarrel with Thebes and as regards you and the rest of the Hellenes. We shall remind you of our past record and shall try to make you understand our point of view.

54 'In reply to that short question of yours – whether we have done anything to help Sparta and her allies in this war – are you

asking it on the assumption that we are your enemies or that we are your friends? If enemies, then we say that you cannot complain of being injured by us, simply because you have not received help from us; but if you regarded us as your friends, then it is you who have done the wrong by marching against us.

'Our record has been a good one both during the peace and at the time of the Persian War. As for present history, we were not the first to break the peace. As for the past, we were the only state in Boeotia which joined in the common effort for the liberation of Hellas. Though we live inland, we served in the naval battle at Artemisium; in the battle fought on our own territory we stood with you and with Pausanias; and in every other enterprise undertaken by the Hellenes during those years we played a part that was out of all proportion to our strength. And to you Spartans, in particular, at a time when Sparta was in the grip of the greatest panic she has known – after the earthquake, when the helots had revolted and gone to Ithome – we sent a third part of our own citizens to help you. This, we imagine, you have not forgotten.

55   'So much for the course we chose to follow in that very important period of past history. It was only later that we became enemies, and for this you were responsible. When the Thebans were oppressing us, we asked to become your allies, but you rejected us and told us to apply to Athens, because it was nearer and you lived so far away. Nevertheless in this war we never acted against you in an unreasonable manner, nor were we likely to have done so. There was nothing wrong in our refusing your request that we should desert Athens. The Athenians had helped us against Thebes at the time when you were reluctant to help us, and it was no longer honourable for us to forsake them, especially since they had been good friends of ours in the past and it was at our own request that they made us their allies and allowed us to share in some of the privileges of Athenian citizenship. It was natural, therefore, that we should willingly obey their orders. And whether it is you or Athens who give orders to your allies, it is the leaders and not the subordinates who should be held responsible for anything that is done amiss.

56   'As for the Thebans, they have committed frequent acts of aggression against us, and this final act of theirs, which has brought

us to our present plight, is well known to you. It was not only in peace-time, but it was in the period of a religious festival that they seized our city, and in making them suffer for it we acted rightly and in accordance with the general law that one is always justi-fied in resisting an aggressor. It cannot be reasonable that we should now suffer on their account. If you are going to take as your standards of justice your own immediate advantage and their hatred for us, you will stand confessed as people who are more interested in pursuing your own interests than in judging sincerely between right and wrong. Though if the Thebans do seem useful to you now, you must recognize that in the past, at a time when you were in greater danger, we and the other Hellenes were much more useful. Now you are in a position to take the offensive and to make others fear you; but in those days, when the foreign invader threatened us all with slavery, Thebes was on his side. We are entitled, therefore, to set against any errors that we may have com-mitted now the patriotism that we showed then. You will find that our merits greatly outweigh our faults, and that they were shown at a time when it was not an easy thing to find among the Hellenes people to oppose their courage to the might of Xerxes, and when all the greater praise was given to those who, instead of meeting the invasion by acting in the interests of their own safety, chose the path of daring, of danger, and of honour. It was to this class that we belonged, and we were treated with peculiar distinction for the part we played; yet now we are in fear of losing our lives for this very same conduct, for having chosen to do the right thing with regard to Athens rather than the profitable thing with regard to Sparta. Yet the same principles should be made to apply throughout, and it should be recognized that true policy consists not only in safeguarding one's immediate interests, but in seeing to it that a brave ally can feel certain of one's gratitude.

57   'You must consider also that at the moment among most of the Hellenes you are held up as an example of faith and honour. But if you come to an unfair decision in this trial, which cannot escape publicity, since you, the judges, are generally respected and we, the defendants, are not without reputation, beware lest public opinion condemns you, however superior to us you may be, for passing an unworthy sentence on good men and for dedicating in the national

temples spoils taken from the Plataeans, who have done such good
service to Hellas. It will be thought a terrible thing that Sparta
should destroy Plataea, and that the city whose name your fathers
inscribed on the tripod at Delphi for its honours in battle should be
by you, and for the sake of Thebes, wiped off the map of Hellas. Indeed we have fallen low, we who lost our city in the Persian conquest, and now find that you, who used to be our greatest friends,
prefer the Thebans to us. We have been confronted with two of
the greatest ordeals, first of starvation, unless we surrendered the
city, and now of being tried for our lives. So we Plataeans, who
gave our all and more than our all for Hellas, are now rejected by
everyone and left alone with no one to help us. Not one of our old
allies is here to support us, and as for you Spartans, who are our
last hope, we are not sure whether we can trust you.

58   'Yet still, in the name of the gods who witnessed our alliance in
the past and for the sake of our good service to Hellas, we beg you
to relent, and, if you have already been won over by the Thebans,
to change your minds. Ask back from them the gift you may have
promised, so that you will not have to shame yourselves by killing
us. Make us honestly rather than them dishonestly grateful to you,
and do not, as the reward for gratifying others, win for yourselves
a bad name. Our lives may be taken in a short moment, but it will
be long before the infamy of that action is forgotten. So far from
being your enemies, whom it would be natural for you to punish,
we are friends who have been forced into the war against you. To
spare our lives, therefore, would be a righteous judgement: you
should consider, too, that we surrendered to you voluntarily,
stretching out our hands as suppliants, and Hellenic law forbids
killing in these circumstances: then also throughout our history
we have done good to you. Look at the tombs of your fathers who
were killed by the Persians and are buried in our country: every
year we have done honour to them at the public expense, presenting garments and all the proper offerings, bringing to them the
first fruits of everything which at the various seasons our land has
produced; and these offerings were made by us as friends and from
a friendly country, as allies to our old comrades in battle.

'But you, if you come to the wrong decision, will be acting in
just the opposite way. When Pausanias buried them here, he be-

lieved that he was laying their bodies in a friendly soil among people who were friendly too. But if you kill us and make the land of Plataea Theban territory, you will be leaving your fathers and kinsmen in enemy soil, among their murderers, deprived of the honours which they now have. You will also be enslaving the country in which the Hellenes won their freedom, making desolate the temples where they prayed before they conquered the Persians, and at our ancestral sacrifices you will leave empty the places of those who orginally founded them.

59   'You will get no glory, Spartans, from such actions – not for breaking the established laws of Hellas, for sinning against your ancestors, and for killing us, who have done you good service and by whom you have not yourselves been injured, simply for the sake of the hatred felt against us by others. It would be more to your credit to spare our lives, to relent, to look upon us with a wise compassion, thinking not only of the terrible fate with which we are threatened, but also of what manner of men we are over whom this fate impends. Remember, too, how incalculable the future is and how impossible it is to tell who next, however undeservedly, may be exposed to the blows of chance. Thus we, as we have a right to do and as our need impels us, beg you to grant our requests, calling aloud upon the gods of Hellas at whose altars we all worship. We summon up the solemn promises which your fathers made and plead with you not to forget them; and at your fathers' tombs we stand as suppliants, crying out to the dead that they may save us from falling into the power of Thebes – us, who were their dearest friends, from being handed over to the enemies they so greatly hated. We remind them of that day when we fought so gloriously at their side – and now, on this day, we are in danger of suffering the most dreadful of fates.

'And now it is necessary for us to make an end of our speech – necessary, but very difficult for those in our situation, since, when our speech is over, our lives are in the balance. Finally, therefore, we declare that it was not to the Thebans that we surrendered our city. Rather than do that we would have chosen to perish ingloriously by starvation. It was you whom we approached and it was in you that we trusted. And it would be only fair, if our words fail to convince you, to put us back in the condition we were then and let us choose our own way of facing the dangers that would confront us. And at the same time, Spartans, we lay this charge upon you: do not let it be that we your suppliants, men of the city of Plataea which has so ungrudgingly served the cause of Hellas, should be given up out of your hands and out of the trust we reposed in you to the Thebans, our bitterest enemies. Instead be our saviours, and do not, while you liberate the rest of the Hellenes, bring us utterly to destruction.'

60   So the Plataeans spoke. The Thebans, fearing that this speech might have some influence on the Spartans, came forward and said that they also would like to be heard, since the Plataeans had been allowed (unwarrantably, they thought) to speak at length instead of merely answering the question put to them. Permission was granted, and the Thebans spoke as follows:

61   'We should never have proposed making this speech if the Plataeans on their side had given a straight answer to the question asked, and had not turned on us with their accusations, at the same time praising themselves where they were not blamed, and at great length defending themselves against charges which are beside the point and which, in any case, were never made against them. As things are, however, it becomes necessary for us to answer their accusations and to examine their claims, so that neither villainy on our side nor glory on theirs may help them, but that you may hear the truth on both points and so come to your decision.

'Our quarrel goes back to the time when, after we had settled the rest of Boeotia, we founded the city of Plataea together with some other places which we held and from which we had driven out the inhabitants who were of different and mixed nationalities. The Plataeans then refused to abide by the original arrangement and to recognize our supremacy. Proving false to their national traditions, they separated themselves from the rest of Boeotia, and when we used force against them they went over to the Athenians and, with Athenian help, did us much harm, for which they suffered some in return.

62   'Subsequently, during the foreign invasion of Hellas, they say that they were the only state in Boeotia which did not collaborate with the Persians. This is the point which they use most frequently for their own self-glorification and for deriding us. We say that the

only reason why they did not collaborate was because the Athenians did not do so either, and, following up the same principle, we shall find that when the Athenians began to attack the liberties of Hellas, Plataea was the only state in Boeotia which collaborated with Athens.

'Consider, too, what type of government we each had at the time of these events. Our constitution then was not an oligarchy, giving all men equal rights before the law, nor was it a democracy: power was in the hands of a small group of powerful men, and this is the form of government nearest to dictatorship and farthest removed from law and the virtues of moderation. This small group of men hoped to win even greater power for themselves if the Persian invasion was successful, and so they kept the people down by force and brought in the Persians. This was not the action of the city as a whole, since the city was not free to make its own decisions, and it ought not to be reproached for the mistakes it made when it had no regular legal government. Look at what happened after the Persians had withdrawn and Thebes had acquired a legal constitution. You will find that when Athens was encroaching upon the rest of Hellas and attempting to bring our country under their control – most of which, indeed, owing to internal dissension, they already held – we fought and conquered them at Coronea, thus liberating Boeotia; and now, too, we are joining wholeheartedly in the liberation of the other Hellenes, providing not only cavalry but larger forces than any other state among the allies.

63   'So much for the charge that we collaborated with the Persians. We shall now attempt to show that it is you Plataeans, rather than we, who have done wrong to Hellas and who deserve the most exemplary punishment. According to your own account you became allies and citizens of Athens in your own self-defence. If so, then you should merely have called them in against us, and not joined them in their attacks on others. This course was certainly open to you, if you really felt that they were making you do what you did not want to do. You had already, as you are so fond of pointing out, your alliance with Sparta against Persia. This was quite sufficient to keep us from attacking you and – which is the chief point – to allow you to choose your own course without

constraint. No, it was of your own accord, and with no compulsion about it, that you chose to follow the policy of Athens. It
would have been disgraceful, you say, to desert your benefactors.
It was a much more disgraceful and wicked thing utterly to betray
all the Hellenic states, your allies, who were liberating Hellas, than
merely the Athenians, who were enslaving it. Moreover, you did
for them something very different from what they did for you,
and this is something of which you should be ashamed. You, according to your own account, called in Athens because you were
the victims of oppression; you then aided and abetted Athens in
oppressing other people. Yet to pay back a just debt by acting
unjustly is more disgraceful than not to pay at all.

64   'You have made it plain by your actions that if, in the past, you
were the only ones who did not collaborate with Persia, this was
not for the sake of Hellas; it was because Athens did not collaborate
either; and you wanted to be with Athens and against the rest.
And now you claim that the good you did for the sake of others
should be counted in your favour. It is hardly a reasonable suggestion. Athens it was you chose, and with her you must stand or fall.
Nor can you bring forward the alliance that existed in those days
and say that now you are entitled to its protection. You left that
alliance and violated its terms: you did more to help than to hinder
the conquest of Aegina and other fellow members of that alliance:
and you did so of your own accord, while you had the same
constitution as you have to this day, with no one bringing any
force to bear on you, as was the case with us. Finally, just before
your city was blockaded, you were given an offer of immunity if
you remained neutral. This offer you rejected. Who, then, more
than you deserve the hatred of the Hellenes – you who go about to
destroy them while you vaunt your own heroism? As for the good
qualities which you claim once to have possessed, you have shown
us now that they are not part of your real character: your true nature, with its constant aim, now stands revealed. For when Athens
took the wrong road, you went along with her.

'This, then, is what we have to say about our unwilling collaboration with Persia and your willing collaboration with Athens.
65   Now for the final instance where you claim to have suffered from
us, saying that we made an unjustified attack on your city in peace-

time and during a religious festival. We think that here also we shall be found less guilty than you are. Guilty we certainly are, if it was a case of our having initiated an armed attack on your city and laid waste your territory. But how can we be called guilty when what happened was that some of your own citizens, men of substance from the best families, voluntarily called us in, because they wanted to put an end to your foreign alliances and give you back your traditional status as a part of Boeotia? As you say it is the leaders and not the followers who do the wrong. Though, in our opinion, neither they nor we did any wrong at all. They were citizens of Plataea, like yourselves, except that they had more to lose; they opened their own gates to us and took us into their own city not as enemies, but as friends, in order to prevent the bad among you from becoming worse, to give honest men their rights, to bring wisdom into your councils without depriving the city of your persons: far from it, since they were bringing you back into fellowship with your own kindred, and so far from making you the enemies of anyone, they were putting you in a position where all alike would be bound to you by treaty.

66   'And here is a proof that we were not acting as belligerents: without doing anyone any harm, we made a proclamation to the effect that those who wanted a government in accordance with the national traditions of Boeotia were to come over to us. This you did gladly enough at first; you made an agreement with us and stayed quiet, until later you realized how few of us there were. Now, we may appear to have acted somewhat incorrectly in entering your city without being invited by the general mass of your people; but your conduct towards us was of an altogether different order. Instead of avoiding all acts of violence, as we had done, instead of negotiating with us, so that we would leave the city, you broke your agreement and attacked us. Some of us you killed in fight: their fate does not touch us so deeply, since there was at least a certain justice about it. But as for those others, your prisoners, who had stretched out their hands to you for mercy, and whom later you had promised us not to kill – was it not an act of monstrous wickedness to break every law and put them to death? Three crimes you committed, one on top of the other; you broke your agreement, you killed the men later, and you deceitfully

broke the promise you made to us that you would spare them if we did no damage to your property in the country. And now, in spite of all this, you actually declare that it was we who were in the wrong, and that you yourselves should not have to answer for your deeds. Not so, we say – not if these men who are here to judge you reach a right verdict. You will be punished at once for all your crimes.

67 'It is both for your sakes, Spartans, and for our own that we have dealt so fully with these facts. We wanted you to realize that you will be doing right in condemning these men, and we wished to make it appear still more clearly that our own demand for vengeance is a righteous demand. Do not allow your resolution to be weakened by listening to accounts of their good conduct in ancient times – if such indeed it was. A good record ought to be a help to those who are being treated unfairly, but in the case of people who are doing something disgraceful it should merely double their punishment, because in committing crimes they are being false to their own past. And do not let them profit from their wailings and lamentations, their appeals to the tombs of your fathers and to their own friendless state. In reply to this we can point to our own young men, who suffered far more terribly when they were massacred by the Plataeans, and whose fathers either fell at Coronea in the battle that brought Boeotia over to your side, or else are left behind as old men, with their houses desolate, begging you with much more justice to punish these evil-doers. Pity is felt for unmerited suffering; but when people suffer what they deserve, as is the case with the Plataeans, their fate, far from provoking pity, is a matter for satisfaction. As for their present friendless state, they have only themselves to thank for it; they could have had better allies, but they rejected them. Their crime was not provoked by any previous action of ours; it was hate, not justice, that caused their verdict; and for this even now they cannot afford us the satisfaction due. For they will suffer by the process of law, and their position is not, as they make out, that of people stretching out their hands for mercy in battle; it is that of those who have surrendered on condition that they must stand their trial.

'Spartans, it is for you to vindicate the law of Hellas which these men have broken, and to give to us, who have suffered from their crime, the reward due to the energy we have shown in your behalf. Do not allow their speeches to thrust us out of our place in your affections, but make this a demonstration to Hellas that it is deeds, not words, that you will look for. Good deeds do not require long statements; but when evil is done the whole art of oratory is employed as a screen for it. Yet if, as you are doing to-day, those in authority would sum things up in a question addressed to all alike and on that basis come to their decision, then people would be less likely to search for fine phrases to cover up their evil deeds.'

68   So the Thebans spoke, and the Spartan judges decided that their question – whether they had received any help from the Plataeans in the war – was a proper one to ask. Their grounds were that, in accordance with the original treaty made with Pausanias after the Persian War, they had all the time (so they said) counted on Plataean neutrality; later, just before the siege, they had offered them the same conditions of neutrality implied by the treaty, and this offer had not been accepted; the justice of their intentions had, they considered, released them from their obligations under the treaty, and it was at this point that they had suffered injury from Plataea. They therefore brought the Plataeans before them again one by one and asked each of them the same question. 'Have you done anything to help the Spartans and their allies in the war?' As each man replied 'No', he was taken away and put to death, no exceptions being made. Not less than 200 of the Plataeans were killed in this way, together with twenty-five Athenians who had been with them in the siege. The women were made slaves. As for the city, they gave the use of it for one year to some political refugees from Megara and to those of the pro-Spartan party among the Plataeans who still survived. Afterwards they razed it to the ground from its very foundations and built, adjoining the temple of Hera, a large hotel 200 feet in circuit,[32] with rooms upstairs and downstairs. For these building operations they used the roofs and doors of the Plataeans, and out of the other material in the wall – the brass and the iron – they made couches which they dedicated to

32. Temples and cities maintained lodging-houses at shrines that attracted large numbers of visitors.

Hera, for whom they also built a stone temple 100 feet square. The land they confiscated and let it out on ten-year leases to Theban cultivators. It was largely, or entirely, because of Thebes that the Spartans acted so mercilessly towards the Plataeans; they considered that at this stage of the war the Thebans were useful to them. This was the end of Plataea,[33] in the ninety-third year after she became the ally of Athens.

CIVIL WAR IN CORCYRA

69 The forty Peloponnesian ships which had gone to the relief of Lesbos, and which were last described as fleeing across the open sea with the Athenians in pursuit, ran into rough weather off Crete, scattered and made their way to the Peloponnese. Arriving at Cyllene, they found thirteen triremes from Leucas and Ambracia and also Brasidas, the son of Tellis, who had come to act as adviser to Alcidas. After their failure at Lesbos the Spartans wished to reinforce their fleet and sail to Corcyra, where a revolution had broken out. The Athenians at Naupactus had a force of only twelve ships, and so the Spartan plan was to arrive at Corcyra before reinforcements could be sent out from Athens. Brasidas and Alcidas therefore prepared to carry out this plan.

70   The revolution in Corcyra began with the return of the prisoners who had been captured in the naval engagements off Epidamnus. The story was that these prisoners had been released by the Corinthians on the security of 800 talents put down by their official agents in Corinth; in fact they had undertaken to win Corcyra over to the Corinthian side, and they went about their business by approaching the citizens individually with the aim of detaching the city from Athens. And when a ship from Athens and a ship from Corinth arrived with accredited representatives on board, the matter was debated, and the people of Corcyra voted in favour of remaining allies of Athens in accordance with the original agreement, at the same time preserving their friendly relations with the Peloponnese.

The next step of the returned prisoners was to bring to trial

33. Plataea was restored by Sparta in 386 B.C.

Peithias, who had voluntarily offered to look after Athenian interests in Corcyra and who was the leader of the democratic party.
The charge against him was that he was enslaving Corcyra to
Athens. Peithias was acquitted, and retaliated by bringing to trial
five of the richest of his opponents on the charge of having procured vine-props by cutting them on the ground sacred to Zeus
and to Alcinous; the legal penalty was one stater for each stake.
The men were condemned and, because of the amount of money
they would have to pay, they took up their positions in the temples
as suppliants, begging that the damage should be re-assessed.
Peithias, however, who happened to be a member of the Council,
persuaded his colleagues to enforce the legal penalty. Being now
exposed to the full rigour of the law and at the same time learning
that Peithias intended, while he was still a member of the Council,
to persuade the people to make an offensive and defensive alliance
with Athens, the five accused joined up with the rest of their party
and, armed with daggers, suddenly broke in on the Council and
killed Peithias and some sixty others, members of the Council
and private individuals. Some few of those who shared Peithias's
views escaped and took refuge on the Athenian trireme, which was
still in the harbour.

71   After this violent action they called the people of Corcyra to an
assembly and stated that what they had done was all for the best
and would prevent the island being enslaved by Athens. They proposed that for the future they should receive neither side except on
peaceful terms and coming in not more than one ship at a time;
any greater number would be regarded as enemies. No sooner
was the proposal made than they forced it through the Assembly.
They then immediately sent delegates to Athens to give their
own version of what had been done and to try to dissuade the
Corcyraean refugees in Athens from taking any action against
72 them which might lead to a counter-revolution. On their arrival
the Athenians arrested the delegates and all who listened to them
on a charge of sedition and put them in custody in Aegina.

Meanwhile, on the arrival of a Corinthian trireme with delegates from Sparta aboard, the party who held power in Corcyra
attacked the democrats and defeated them in the fighting. When
night came on, the democratic party fell back on the acropolis and

the higher parts of the city. Here they concentrated their forces and built walls, having control also of the Hyllaic harbour. The other side held the town square, round which most of them lived, and the harbour near to it, which faces towards the mainland.

73   Next day there was a little fighting at long range, and each side sent out to the country districts in an attempt to win the support of the slaves by offering them their freedom. The great majority of the slaves joined the side of the democratic party, while their opponents secured the help of 800 mercenaries from the mainland.

74   After a day's interval the fighting broke out again and the democrats, who had the advantage of better positions and superior numbers, were victorious. The women also joined in the fighting with great daring, hurling down tiles from the roof-tops and standing up to the din of battle with a courage beyond their sex. By sunset the oligarchical party were in full retreat and, fearing that the democrats might sweep down upon their arsenal, seize it at the first assault, and put them all to death, they set fire to the houses and the blocks of apartments round the town square, so that there should be no means of approach. They spared neither their own property nor that of others, with the result that a great deal of merchandise was lost in the fire, and, if a wind had risen and blown the flames in the direction of the other buildings, the whole city might well have been destroyed.

The fighting now ceased, and each side posted its sentries and remained quiet for the night. The Corinthian ship stole out of the harbour after the victory of the democrats, and most of the mercenaries got away secretly to the mainland.

75   Next day the Athenian commander Nicostratus, the son of Diitrephes, came up from Naupactus with a force of twelve ships and 500 Messenian hoplites. His aim was to arrange a settlement, and he persuaded the two parties to agree among themselves to bring to trial ten men who had been chiefly responsible (and who immediately went into hiding); the rest were to come to terms with each other and live in peace, and the whole state was to conclude an offensive and defensive alliance with Athens.

Having made this settlement, Nicostratus was on the point of sailing away, but the leaders of the democratic party persuaded him to leave behind five of his ships to act as a check on any movement which their opponents might make, while they themselves would man five of their own ships and send them with him. Nicostratus agreed, and the democratic leaders put down the names of their enemies for service on the ships. Those who were called up, however, fearing that they would be sent off to Athens, seated themselves as suppliants in the temple of the Dioscuri. Nicostratus offered them guarantees and spoke reassuringly to them, but his words had no effect. The democratic party then armed themselves with the pretext that these men could not be sincere in their intentions if they felt doubtful about sailing with Nicostratus. They seized their opponents' arms out of their houses, and would have put to death some of them whom they found there, if they had not been prevented by Nicostratus. The rest of the oligarchical party, seeing what was happening, took up their positions as suppliants in the temple of Hera. There were at least 400 of them. The democrats, fearing that they might do something violent, persuaded them to rise, took them across to the island in front of the temple, and had provisions sent out to them there.

76 At this stage in the revolutions, four or five days after the men had been taken across to the island, the Peloponnesian ships arrived from Cyllene, where they had been stationed since their return from Ionia. There were fifty-three of them, commanded, as before, by Alcidas, though now Brasidas sailed with him as his adviser. This fleet came to anchor in the harbour of Sybota on the mainland, and at daybreak set out for Corcyra.

77 The Corcyraeans were now in a state of the utmost confusion, alarmed both at what was happening inside their city and at the approach of the enemy fleet. They immediately got ready sixty ships and sent them straight out against the enemy, as soon as they were manned, neglecting the advice of the Athenians, which was to let them sail out first and then come out in support of them later with all their ships together. As the Corcyraean ships approached the enemy in this disorganized way, two of them immediately deserted, in other ships the crews were fighting among themselves, and no sort of order was kept in anything. The Peloponnesians observed the confusion in which they were, set

aside twenty of their ships to meet the Corcyraeans, and put all the rest of their fleet against the twelve Athenian ships, among which were the *Salaminia* and the *Paralus*.

78   The Corcyraeans, in their part of the battle, were soon in difficulties, since they were making their attacks inefficiently and in small detachments. The Athenians, afraid of the numbers of the enemy and of the risk of encirclement, did not commit themselves to a general engagement and did not even charge the fleet opposed to them in the centre. Instead they fell upon its wing, where they sank one ship. After this the Peloponnesians formed their ships up in a circle and the Athenians rowed round them, trying to create confusion among them. Seeing this, and fearing a repetition of what had happened at Naupactus, the other Peloponnesians, who had been dealing with the Corcyraeans, came up in support, and then the whole Peloponnesian fleet together bore down on the Athenians, who now began to back water and to retire in front of them. They carried out the manoeuvre in their own good time, wishing to give the Corcyraean ships the fullest opportunity to escape first by keeping the enemy facing them in battle formation. So the fighting went, and it continued until sunset.

79   The Corcyraeans now feared that the enemy would follow up their victory by sailing against the city, or rescuing the men from the island, or by taking some other bold step. So they brought the men back again from the island to the temple of Hera, and put the defences of the city in order. The Peloponnesians, however, in spite of their victory on the sea, did not risk sailing against the town, but sailed back to their original station on the mainland, taking with them the thirteen Corcyraean ships which they had captured. Nor were they any the more disposed to sail against the city on the next day, although the Corcyraeans were thoroughly disorganized and in a state of panic, and although Brasidas is said to have urged Alcidas to do so. Brasidas, however, was overruled, and the Peloponnesians merely made a landing on the headland of Leukimme and laid waste the country.

80   Meanwhile the democratic party in Corcyra were still terrified at the prospect of an attack by the enemy fleet. They entered into negotiations with the suppliants and with others of their party with a view to saving the city, and they persuaded some of them

to go on board the ships. Thus they succeeded in manning thirty ships to meet the expected attack.

The Peloponnesians, however, having spent the time up till midday in laying waste the land, sailed away again, and about nightfall were informed by fire signals that a fleet of sixty Athenian ships was approaching from the direction of Leucas. This fleet, which was under the command of Eurymedon, the son of Thucles, had been sent out by the Athenians when they heard that the revolution had broken out and that Alcidas's fleet was about to

81 sail for Corcyra. Thus the Peloponnesians set off by night, at once and in a hurry, for home, sailing close in to the shore. They hauled their ships across the isthmus of Leucas, so as to avoid being seen rounding the point, and so they got away.

When the Corcyraeans realized that the Athenian fleet was approaching and that their enemies had gone, they brought the Messenians, who had previously been outside the walls, into the city and ordered the fleet which they had manned to sail round into the Hyllaic harbour. While it was doing so, they seized upon all their enemies whom they could find and put them to death. They then dealt with those whom they had persuaded to go on board the ships, killing them as they landed. Next they went to the temple of Hera and persuaded about fifty of the suppliants there to submit to a trial. They then condemned every one of them to death. Seeing what was happening, most of the other suppliants, who had refused to be tried, killed each other there in the temple; some hanged themselves on the trees, and others found various other means of committing suicide. During the seven days that Eurymedon stayed there with his sixty ships, the Corcyraeans continued to massacre those of their own citizens whom they considered to be their enemies. Their victims were accused of conspiring to overthrow the democracy, but in fact men were often killed on grounds of personal hatred or else by their debtors because of the money that they owed. There was death in every shape and form. And, as usually happens in such situations, people went to every extreme and beyond it. There were fathers who killed their sons; men were dragged from the temples or butchered on the very altars; some were actually walled up in the temple of Dionysus and died there.

82   So savage was the progress of this revolution, and it seemed all
the more so because it was one of the first which had broken out.
Later, of course, practically the whole of the Hellenic world was
convulsed, with rival parties in every state – democratic leaders
trying to bring in the Athenians, and oligarchs trying to bring in
the Spartans. In peacetime there would have been no excuse and no
desire for calling them in, but in time of war, when each party
could always count upon an alliance which would do harm to its
opponents and at the same time strengthen its own position, it
became a natural thing for anyone who wanted a change of government to call in help from outside. In the various cities these revolutions were the cause of many calamities, as happens and always
will happen while human nature is what it is, though there may be
different degrees of savagery, and, as different circumstances arise,
the general rules will admit of some variety. In times of peace
and prosperity cities and individuals alike follow higher standards,
because they are not forced into a situation where they have to do
what they do not want to do. But war is a stern teacher; in depriving them of the power of easily satisfying their daily wants, it
brings most people's minds down to the level of their actual circumstances.

So revolutions broke out in city after city, and in places where the
revolutions occurred late the knowledge of what had happened
previously in other places caused still new extravagances of revolutionary zeal, expressed by an elaboration in the methods of seizing
power and by unheard-of atrocities in revenge. To fit in with the
change of events, words, too, had to change their usual meanings.
What used to be described as a thoughtless act of aggression was
now regarded as the courage one would expect to find in a party
member; to think of the future and wait was merely another way
of saying one was a coward; any idea of moderation was just an
attempt to disguise one's unmanly character; ability to understand a question from all sides meant that one was totally unfitted
for action. Fanatical enthusiasm was the mark of a real man, and to
plot against an enemy behind his back was perfectly legitimate self-
defence. Anyone who held violent opinions could always be trusted,
and anyone who objected to them became a suspect. To plot
successfully was a sign of intelligence, but it was still cleverer to

see that a plot was hatching. If one attempted to provide against having to do either, one was disrupting the unity of the party and acting out of fear of the opposition. In short, it was equally praise-worthy to get one's blow in first against someone who was going to do wrong, and to denounce someone who had no intention of doing any wrong at all. Family relations were a weaker tie than party membership, since party members were more ready to go to any extreme for any reason whatever. These parties were not for-med to enjoy the benefits of the established laws, but to acquire power by overthrowing the existing regime; and the members of these parties felt confidence in each other not because of any fellow-ship in a religious communion, but because they were partners in crime. If an opponent made a reasonable speech, the party in power, so far from giving it a generous reception, took every precaution to see that it had no practical effect.

Revenge was more important than self-preservation. And if pacts of mutual security were made, they were entered into by the two parties only in order to meet some temporary difficulty, and remained in force only so long as there was no other weapon available. When the chance came, the one who first seized it boldly, catching his enemy off his guard, enjoyed a revenge that was all the sweeter from having been taken, not openly, but be-cause of a breach of faith. It was safer that way, it was considered, and at the same time a victory won by treachery gave one a title for superior intelligence. And indeed most people are more ready to call villainy cleverness than simple-mindedness honesty. They are proud of the first quality and ashamed of the second.

Love of power, operating through greed and through personal ambition, was the cause of all these evils. To this must be added the violent fanaticism which came into play once the struggle had broken out. Leaders of parties in the cities had programmes which appeared admirable – on one side political equality for the masses, on the other the safe and sound government of the aristocracy – but in professing to serve the public interest they were seeking to win the prizes for themselves. In their struggles for ascendancy nothing was barred; terrible indeed were the actions to which they com-mitted themselves, and in taking revenge they went farther still. Here they were deterred neither by the claims of justice nor by the interests of the state; their one standard was the pleasure of their own party at that particular moment, and so, either by means of condemning their enemies on an illegal vote or by violently usurping power over them, they were always ready to satisfy the hatreds of the hour. Thus neither side had any use for conscientious motives; more interest was shown in those who could produce attractive arguments to justify some disgraceful action. As for the citizens who held moderate views, they were destroyed by both the extreme parties, either for not taking part in the struggle or in envy at the possibility that they might survive.

83   As the result of these revolutions, there was a general deterioration of character throughout the Greek world. The simple way of looking at things, which is so much the mark of a noble nature, was regarded as a ridiculous quality and soon ceased to exist. Society had become divided into two ideologically hostile camps, and each side viewed the other with suspicion. As for ending this state of affairs, no guarantee could be given that would be trusted, no oath sworn that people would fear to break; everyone had come to the conclusion that it was hopeless to expect a permanent settlement and so, instead of being able to feel confident in others, they devoted their energies to providing against being injured themselves. As a rule those who were least remarkable for intelligence showed the greater powers of survival. Such people recognized their own deficiencies and the superior intelligence of their opponents; fearing that they might lose a debate or find themselves out-manoeuvred in intrigue by their quick-witted enemies, they boldly launched straight into action; while their opponents, over-confident in the belief that they would see what was happening in advance, and not thinking it necessary to seize by force what they could secure by policy, were the more easily destroyed because they were off their guard.

84   Certainly it was in Corcyra that there occurred the first examples of the breakdown of law and order. There was the revenge taken in their hour of triumph by those who had in the past been arrogantly oppressed instead of wisely governed; there were the wicked resolutions taken by those who, particularly under the pressure of misfortune, wished to escape from their usual poverty and coveted the property of their neighbours; there were the savage and

pitiless actions into which men were carried not so much for the sake of gain as because they were swept away into an internecine struggle by their ungovernable passions. Then, with the ordinary conventions of civilized life thrown into confusion, human nature, always ready to offend even where laws exist, showed itself proudly in its true colours, as something incapable of controlling passion, insubordinate to the idea of justice, the enemy to anything superior to itself; for, if it had not been for the pernicious power of envy, men would not so have exalted vengeance above innocence and profit above justice. Indeed, it is true that in these acts of revenge on others men take it upon themselves to begin the process of repealing those general laws of humanity which are there to give a hope of salvation to all who are in distress, instead of leaving those laws in existence, remembering that there may come a time when they, too, will be in danger and will need their protection.

85   So, while the people of Corcyra were the first to display in their city the passions of civil war, Eurymedon and the Athenian fleet sailed away. Afterwards the exiled party of the Corcyraeans (about 500 had managed to escape) occupied various fortified posts on the mainland, gained control of the Corcyraean territory across the straits, and used this as a base for making plundering expeditions against their fellow citizens on the island. Thus they did a lot of damage and caused a serious famine in the city. They also sent delegates to Sparta and to Corinth to try to get themselves restored to their position in Corcyra. However, their negotiations were unsuccessful and they then, some time later, got together some ships and some mercenary troops and crossed over to the island with a force of about 600 altogether. There they burned their boats, so that there should be no hope left to them except in a final conquest of the country. They then went up to Mount Istone, built themselves fortifications, and proceeded to make attacks on the party inside the city, keeping control of the country districts.

OPERATIONS IN SICILY AND GREECE

86 At the end of this same summer the Athenians sent out twenty ships to Sicily, where the Syracusans and the people of Leontini

were at war. This fleet was under the command of Laches, the son of Melanopus, and Charoeades, the son of Euphiletus. Apart from Camarina, all the other Dorian cities were in alliance with Syracuse and had also been in alliance with Sparta since the beginning of the war, though they had not taken any active part in it. Leontini had for allies Camarina and the Chalcidian cities. Of the Italian states the Locrians[34] were on the side of Syracuse, and the people of Rhegium supported their kinsmen of Leontini.

The allies of Leontini now sent to Athens, appealing to their ancient alliance and to their Ionian origin, with the request that the Athenians would send them a fleet, since they were being blockaded by the Syracusans on land and from the sea. The Athenians sent the fleet, ostensibly because of their kinship with the Leontinians, though their real aims were to prevent corn being brought in to the Peloponnese from the west and to make a preliminary survey to see whether it would be possible for them to gain control of Sicily. They established themselves at Rhegium in Italy and from there carried on the war in conjunction with their allies.

87   So the summer ended. In the following winter the plague broke out among the Athenians for the second time. In fact it had never entirely stopped, though there had been a considerable decline in its virulence. This second outbreak lasted for no less than a year, and the first outbreak had lasted for two years. Nothing did the Athenians so much harm as this or so reduced their strength for war. In the regular army no less than 4,400 hoplites and 300 cavalry died of it; and among the general mass of the people no one ever discovered how many the deaths were. It was at this time, too, that there occurred the many earthquakes in Athens, Euboea, and Boeotia, particularly in the Boeotian city of Orchomenus.

88   The same winter the Athenians in Sicily and the Rhegians made an expedition with thirty ships against the islands of Aeolus, which could not be attacked during the summer months because of the lack of water there. The islands are inhabited by the Liparaeans, a

34. The Locrians on the mainland of Greece were divided into two divisions, the Opuntian and the Ozolian, whereas the Locrians of the Greek settlement in southern Italy were called Epizephyrian. Whenever Thucydides refers to the latter without the adjective, the convention adopted in this edition is to write 'Locri', not 'Locris'.

colony of Cnidus, and they live in one of the islands, not a very big one, called Lipara. From this centre they go out to culti- vate the other islands: Didyme, Strongyle, and Hiera. The people in those parts believe that in Hiera Hephaestus has his smithy, be- cause at night great flames are seen rising up and in day-time the place is under a cloud of smoke. These islands lie off the coast of the Sicels and the territory of Messina, and they were in alliance with Syracuse. The Athenians laid waste their land and then, since the inhabitants refused to join their side, sailed back to Rhegium. So the winter ended and the fifth year of this war recorded by Thucydides.

89   Next summer the Peloponnesians and their allies, under the command of Agis, the son of Archidamus, the King of Sparta, set out to invade Attica and got as far as the Isthmus. Here, however, there were a number of earthquakes and they turned back again, so that no invasion took place. During this same period when earthquakes were happening so frequently, at Orobiae in Euboea the sea subsided from what was then the shore and afterwards swept up again in a huge wave, which covered part of the city and left some of it still under water when the wave retreated, so that what was once land is now sea. Those of the inhabitants who were unable to escape in time by running up to the high ground were lost in the flood. An inundation of the same kind took place at Atalanta, the island off the coast of Opuntian Locris; here part of the Athenian fortifications were swept away and one out of two ships that were drawn up on the beach was broken to pieces. At Pepare- thus, too, the sea sank back some distance from the shore, but this was not followed by an inundation; there was also an earthquake which destroyed part of the wall, the town hall, and a few other buildings. Events of this kind are caused, in my opinion, by earth- quakes. Where the full force of the earthquake is felt, the sea is drawn away from the shore and then suddenly sweeps back again even more violently, thus causing the inundation. Without an earthquake I do not see how such things could happen.

90   In the same summer various operations were carried out by the different warring parties in Sicily. The Sicilians were fighting among themselves, and the Athenians with their allies also engaged in some expeditions. Here I shall merely refer to what is most

noteworthy: the operations of the Athenian alliance and the measures taken against them by the enemy.

The Athenian general Charoeades had been killed in battle with the Syracusans, and Laches was now in sole command of the fleet. With his allies he set out against Mylae, a place belonging to Messina. There happened to be two battalions of Messinians on garrison duty in Mylae, and these set an ambush for the Athenians when they landed from their ships. However, the Athenians and allies defeated the men in the ambush, inflicting considerable losses. They then made an attack on the fortifications and compelled the people to surrender the acropolis and to join them in marching against Messina. Afterwards, on the approach of the Athenians and their allies, Messina also surrendered and gave the Athenians hostages and all other securities that were required.

91   The same summer the Athenians sent out thirty ships to sail round the Peloponnese under the command of Demosthenes, the son of Alcisthenes, and Procles, the son of Theodorus. They also sent to Melos a force of sixty ships and 2,000 hoplites under the command of Nicias the son of Niceratus. They wished to subdue Melos, which, although it was an island, had refused to submit to Athens or even to join the Athenian alliance. However, though they laid the country waste, the Melians still refused to come to terms; so the fleet left Melos and sailed to Oropus in the Graean territory. Here they put in at night, and the hoplites immediately landed and marched overland to Tanagra in Boeotia, where, in answer to the signals that had been arranged beforehand, they were met by the Athenian army from Athens itself which had marched out in full force under the command of Hipponicus, the son of Callias, and Eurymedon, the son of Thucles. They camped there, spent that day in laying waste the territory of Tanagra, and remained in their positions for the night. Next day they were victorious in a battle against a force which came out against them from Tanagra with the support of a certain number of Thebans. They captured some arms, put up a trophy, and then retreated, the main army going back to Athens and the others to their ships. Nicias with his sixty ships then sailed along the coast, laying waste parts of Locris that were on the sea, and afterwards returned home.

92   It was about this time that the Spartans founded their colony of

Heraclea in Trachis. They did so for the following reasons. The nation of the Malians is made up of three tribes, the Paralians, the Hiereans, and the Trachinians. The Trachinians had suffered badly in a war with their neighbours, the Oetaeans, and at first were on the point of putting themselves under the protection of Athens. However, they were doubtful whether Athens could provide them with sufficient security, and so they sent to Sparta, appointing Tisamenus to be their spokesman. The people of Doris, the mother country of Sparta, who had also suffered from the Oetaeans, joined the Trachinians in their mission to Sparta and made the same requests. After hearing the ambassadors, the Spartans decided to send out the colony, since they wished to help both the Trachinians and the Dorians. Also it seemed to them that the new city would be well placed for the war against Athens since it could be used as a naval base directed against Euboea, with the advantage of a very short crossing, and it would also be useful as a position lying on the route to Thrace. There was every reason, therefore, why they should be enthusiastic about founding the place.

First of all they consulted the god at Delphi, and, when they had received a favourable reply, they sent out settlers from Sparta itself and from other cities in the Spartan area; they also called for volunteers from other parts of Hellas, with the exception of the Ionians, the Achaeans, and some other peoples. The founders of the city and leaders of the expedition were three Spartans: Leon, Alcidas, and Damagon. So they established and fortified anew the city now called Heraclea, which is about four and a half miles from Thermopylae and rather over two miles from the sea. They began to construct docks, and, to make their position secure, built a wall on the side towards Thermopylae near the pass itself.

93   The foundation of this city at first caused considerable apprehension in Athens, since it appeared to be aimed at Euboea, the crossing being such a short one to the Euboean town of Cenaeum. Afterwards, however, things turned out quite differently, and the new settlement did no harm at all to Athens. The reason for this was that the Thessalians, who were the dominant power in the area and whose territory was threatened by the new foundation, were frightened of having a powerful state on their frontiers, and

so were constantly doing damage and making war on the new settlers until they wore them down to a state of insignificance. This was in spite of the fact that they were originally very numerous, since people came in confidently to a settlement under Spartan management, in the belief that the city would be safe. Nevertheless, it was in fact the governors sent out from Sparta itself who were very largely responsible for the decline of the city and the drop in its population; their harsh and often unjust administration had the effect of frightening away the majority of the colonists, so that it was all the easier for their neighbours to get the upper hand over them.

94   In the same summer, about the time that the Athenians were in Melos, the other Athenian fleet of thirty ships, which was sailing round the Peloponnese, after having first ambushed and destroyed some garrison troops at the Leucadian town of Ellomenus, proceeded to attack Leucas itself. Their army had been considerably reinforced by the Acarnanians, who, with the exception of Oeniadae, joined them in full force, by the Zacynthians, by the Cephallenians, and by fifteen ships from Corcyra. Under the pressure of superior numbers the people of Leucas had to remain quiet, while they saw their land laid waste both outside the isthmus and in the part inside where the city itself and the temple of Apollo stand. The Acarnanians urged the Athenian commander Demosthenes to blockade the city by building a wall to cut it off; it would be quite easy, they thought, to starve it into surrender, and this would mean getting rid of a place that had always been hostile to them.

However, Demosthenes at the same time was being persuaded by the Messenians that, with the large force now at his disposal, it would be a good idea to attack Aetolia. The Aetolians constituted a threat to Naupactus; also, if he conquered them, it would be easy to win over to the Athenian side all the other continental tribes in that area. It was true that the Aetolians were a large and warlike nation, but they lived in unfortified villages scattered widely apart; they were only lightly armed, and, so the Messenians said, could be quite easily subdued before they could mobilize a united army for their defence. The Messenians urged Demosthenes first to attack the Apodotians, then the Ophionians, and finally the

Eurytanians, who are the largest tribe in Aetolia, and, so it is said, speak a language which is almost unintelligible and eat their meat raw. Once these tribes were conquered, there would be no difficulty about winning over the rest.

95   Demosthenes agreed to this plan, partly in order to please the Messenians, but particularly because he thought that, if the Aetolians were added to his continental allies, he would be able, without using any Athenian man-power, to invade Boeotia by land; the route would be through Ozolian Locris to Cytinium in Doris, keeping Parnassus on the right until he descended into Phocis. The Phocians, he thought, would, since they had always been friendly to Athens, willingly join him in the invasion; if not, they could be forced to do so; and, once in Phocis, he was already on the frontiers of Boeotia.

He therefore, against the will of the Acarnanians, set out from Leucas with his whole force and sailed along the coast to Sollium. Here he told the other Acarnanians of his plan, but they gave it an unfavourable reception because he had not agreed to blockade Leucas. So he himself, with the rest of his army, the Cephallenians, Messenians, Zacynthians, and 300 Athenian citizens who were serving as marines on their own ships, started on his campaign against Aetolia. The fifteen ships from Corcyra had now returned home.

He made his base at Oeneon in Locris, since the Ozolian Locrians were allies of Athens, and it had been arranged that they, with all their available forces, should march into the interior and join him there. As they were neighbours of the Aetolians, and were armed in the same way, it was thought that their assistance would be extremely useful because of their knowledge both of the country and of the local methods of warfare.

96   Demosthenes camped for the night with his army in the precinct of Nemean Zeus, where the poet Hesiod is said to have been killed by the local inhabitants, having been told by an oracle that he was destined to suffer this fate at Nemea, and at dawn set out to invade Aetolia. On the first day of his march he took Potidania, on the second day Crocylium, and on the third Tichium. Here he halted and sent back the booty to Eupalium in Locris. His plan was to go on subduing the country as far as the Ophionians

and, if they refused to submit, to return to Naupactus and there make a second expedition against them.

The invasion, however, did not take the Aetolians by surprise. They had known about it from the time when the plans were first made, and now, when the army had marched into their country, they came up in great force, with contingents from the whole area, including even the most distant Ophionian tribes, the Bomians, and the Callians, whose country extends towards the Malian Gulf.

97 The Messenians, however, continued to give Demosthenes the same advice as before. They assured him that the conquest of Aetolia was a simple matter, and urged him to push on as fast as possible, capturing the villages one by one as he came to them, and not to allow the whole people time to oppose him with a united army. Led on by this advice, and trusting in his own luck, since so far nothing had gone wrong, Demosthenes did not wait for the Locrian reinforcements who were due to arrive and who would have made up his main deficiency, which was in light-armed javelin-throwers. Instead he marched againt Aegitium and took the place by assault. The inhabitants escaped and took up positions on the hills above the town, which stood on high ground about nine miles from the sea.

At this point the Aetolians, who had come up with their main army as far as Aegitium, made an attack on the Athenians and their allies. They came running down from the hills on all sides, hurling their javelins, falling back whenever the Athenian army advanced, and coming on again as soon as it retired. So for some time the fighting went on in this way, with alternate advances and retreats, in both of which the Athenians had the worst of it.

98 Nevertheless they managed to hold out so long as the archers still had arrows and were able to use them, since the light-armed Aetolians fell back before the volleys. But once the captain of the archers was killed, his men scattered; the soldiers had become tired out with having constantly to make the same wearisome manoeuvres; the Aetolians pressed hard upon them with their volleys of javelins, so that finally they turned and fled. Many were killed after rushing down into dried-up water-courses from which there was no road up or in other parts of the battlefield where they lost their way; for Chromon, their Messenian guide, had fallen in the fighting. Thus

great numbers were killed on the spot immediately after the rout,
overtaken by the fast-moving and light-armed Aetolians with their
javelins. The main body, however, took the wrong road and
rushed into the forest, where there were no paths by which they
could escape and which was set on fire by the enemy so that it
burned all round them. Everything, in fact, which could happen
in a flight happened to the Athenian army, and men perished by
every form of death. The survivors with great difficulty escaped to
the sea and to Oeneon in Locris, the place from which they had
started. Great numbers of the allies were killed, together with
about 120 hoplites from Athens itself. These Athenians, so many
of them and all in the prime of life, were certainly the best men
from the city itself who perished in this war. Demosthenes' colleague, Procles, was also killed.

After recovering their dead from the Aetolians under an armistice, the army returned to Naupactus, embarked on their ships
and went back to Athens. Demosthenes stayed behind either at
Naupactus or in the area, since he was afraid to face the Athenians
after what had happened.

99   At about the same time the Athenians in Sicily sailed to Locri[35]
and made a landing there, defeated the Locrians who came against
them, and captured a fort on the river Halex.

100   In the same summer the Aetolians, even before the Athenian
expedition against them, had sent representatives to Corinth and
to Sparta asking for an army to be sent out to them to be used
against Naupactus, which was calling in the Athenians. The Aetolian representatives were Tolophus, an Ophionian, Boriades, an
Eurytanian, and Tisander, an Apodotian. Their request was
granted, and about the beginning of autumn the Spartans sent
out 3,000 hoplites from their allies, 500 of whom came from the
newly founded colony of Heraclea in Trachis. The Spartan Eurylochus was in command, and he was accompanied by two other
Spartans, Macarius and Menedaïus.

101   The army assembled at Delphi, and from there Eurylochus sent
heralds to the Ozolian Locrians, since the route to Naupactus ran
through their country, and at the same time he wanted to detach
them from their alliance with Athens. He got most support in

35. See III, 86 and footnote 34 there.

Locris from the people of Amphissa, who were frightened of making enemies of the Phocians. These were the first to give hostages,
and they persuaded the others to do so also out of fear of the invading army; first, their neighbours the Myonians, who held the
most difficult passes into Locris, and then the Iphians, Messapians,
Tritaeans, Chalaeans, Tolophonians, Hessians, and Oeanthians. All
of these joined in the expedition. The Olpaeans produced hostages,
but did not join the army. The Hyaeans only gave hostages after
the capture of Polis, one of their villages.

102   When everything was ready and the hostages had been put for
safe keeping in Cytinium in Doris, Eurylochus set out with his
army against Naupactus, going through the country of the
Locrians. On the march he captured two of their towns, Oeneon
and Eupalium, which had refused to join him. By the time he
reached the territory of Naupactus, he had been reinforced by the
arrival of the Aetolian army, and together they laid waste the
land and captured the outer portion of the city which was unprotected by the wall. They also attacked and took Molycrium, a
Corinthian colony subject to Athens.

Meanwhile the Athenian Demosthenes, who had remained in
the area after the disaster in Aetolia, had heard of the approach of
the army and feared for the safety of Naupactus. He went and persuaded the Acarnanians (though with considerable difficulty, because of his retreat from Leucas) to send a force to relieve the town.
They sent with him on board his ships 1,000 hoplites, who entered Naupactus and made the place secure. Before their arrival
there had been reason to fear that, because of the large area of wall
to be defended and the small numbers of troops available for
defence, the city would not have been able to hold out.

When Eurylochus and his allies found that the army had got
inside Naupactus, they realized that it was no longer possible to
capture the city by assault, and withdrew their forces. But instead
of going back to the Peloponnese they went into the country that
used to be called Aeolis and is now called Calydon and Pleuron –
also to other places in that area, and to Proschium in Aetolia. This
was because the Ambraciots had come and urged them to join in
making a combined attack on Amphilochian Argos and the rest
of Amphilochia and Acarnania, saying that, once these countries

were subdued, all the rest of the mainland would come over to the Spartan side. Eurylochus agreed to these proposals. He dismissed his Aetolian troops, and with the rest of his army stayed quietly in these parts, until the time should come for the Ambraciots to mobilize and for him to come up and join them before Argos. So the summer ended.

END OF SIXTH YEAR OF WAR

103 The following winter the Athenians in Sicily, with their Hellenic allies and those of the Sicels who had joined them (these had previously been allies of Syracuse, but had been harshly governed by the Syracusans and had now revolted), marched against the Sicel town of Inessa, the acropolis of which was garrisoned by Syracusans. They made an assault on the place, but were unable to take it, and so withdrew. On the retreat the Athenian allies were in the rear and the Syracusans from the citadel came out and attacked them, routing a large part of their army and killing a considerable number of them. After this Laches and the Athenians made some landings from their fleet in Locri and defeated at the river Caïcinus a force of about 300 Locrians who came up with Proxenus, the son of Capaton, to oppose them. They captured some arms and then withdrew.

104 In the same winter the Athenians, no doubt because of some oracle, carried out ceremonies of purification on Delos. In former times the tyrant Pisistratus also had purified the island, though not the whole of it–only as much of it as could be seen from the temple. On the present occasion, however, the whole island was purified in the following way. All the tombs of those who had died in Delos were dug up, and it was proclaimed that in future no deaths or births were to be allowed in the island; those who were about to die or to give birth were to be carried across to Rhenea,[36] which is so close to Delos that when Polycrates, the tyrant of Samos, and ruler over so many other islands, in the period of his naval supremacy, conquered Rhenea, he dedicated it to the Delian Apollo by binding it to Delos with a chain.

36. See 1, 8 and footnote 5 there.

After the purification the Athenians celebrated for the first time the five-yearly festival of the Delian games. There had been also in the distant past a great gathering of the Ionians and neighbouring islanders at Delos. They used to come there to the festival with their wives and children, just as the Ionians now go to the festival at Ephesus, and they used to hold contests there in athletics, poetry, and music, each city producing its own chorus. That this was so is made perfectly clear by the following lines of Homer, from his hymn to Apollo[37]:

Chiefly, O Phoebus, your heart found delight in the island of Delos.
There, with their long robes trailing, Ionians gather together,
Treading your sacred road, with their wives and their children about them,
There they give you pleasure with boxing and dancing, and singing,
Calling aloud on your name, as they set in order the contests.

And in the following lines, from the same hymn, he makes it clear that there were also contests in music and poetry and that the Ionians went there to take part in them. After celebrating the Delian dance of the woman, he ends his praise of them with these verses, in which also he refers to himself:

Maidens, I say farewell to you all, and I pray that the favour
Light on you of Apollo and Artemis. Then in the future
Think of me, and whenever some other man among mortals
Weary with travel comes to this place and questions you, saying
'Tell me, maidens, the name of the man who is sweetest of singers.
Tell me the name of the one in whom you have chiefly delighted,'
Then, in your gentle way, you must all together make answer
'Blind is the singer. He lives in the rock-bound island of Chios.'

We thus have the evidence of Homer that in ancient times also there was a great gathering and festival at Delos. Later the islanders and the Athenians still sent choruses and sacred offerings, but the contests and most of the other ceremonies were discontinued, probably because of the difficulties of the times, and remained out of use until this occasion when the Athenians celebrated the games, including in them horseracing, which was a new event.

37. See the Introduction, p. 17–18.

105   The same winter the Ambraciots, as they had promised Eurylochus at the time when they persuaded him to remain with his
army, marched out against Amphilochian Argos with a force of
3,000 hoplites. They invaded the territory of Argos and occupied
Olpae, a stronghold on a ridge near the sea, which in earlier times
had been fortified by the Acarnanians and used as a general law
court for their people. It is about two and three-quarter miles
from the city of Argos on the coast.

Meanwhile the Acarnanians with one division of their army
went to the relief of Argos; with the other division they camped
at the place in Amphilochia called Crenae, or 'the Springs', to
watch for the Peloponnesians with Eurylochus and see that they
did not slip through and join up with the Ambraciots. They also
sent to Demosthenes, who had led the expedition into Aetolia,
and asked him to command them. They sent too for the twenty
Athenian ships which were cruising off the Peloponnese under the
command of Aristotle, the son of Timocrates, and Hierophon, the
son of Antimnestus.

The Ambraciots at Olpae also sent a messenger to their city
asking their fellow-countrymen to march out in full force to their
support, since they feared that Eurylochus's army would not be
able to force its way through the Acarnanians, and that then they
themselves would either have to fight in isolation or, if they wanted
to retreat, would find that a dangerous thing to do.

106   Meanwhile as soon as the Peloponnesians with Eurylochus heard
that the Ambraciots at Olpae had arrived, they immediately left
Proschium and came up to their support. After crossing the
Achelous, they marched through Acarnania, which they found
empty of its inhabitants, who had all gone to the relief of Argos.
On their right was the city of the Stratians with its garrison, and
on their left the rest of Acarnania. Marching through the land of
the Stratians, they went on through Phytia, skirted Medeon, and
proceeded through Limnaea. At this point they left Acarnania
behind them and entered the country of the Agraeans, who were
on friendly terms with them. Coming to Mount Thyamus, which
is in Agraean territory, they made their way across and descended
into the territory of Argos when it was already dark. They then
took a route between the city of Argos and the Acarnanians, who

were watching for them at Crenae, got through unobserved, and joined up with the Ambraciots in Olpae.

107   The two armies were now united, and at dawn they took up a position at the place called Metropolis and camped there. Soon afterwards the Athenians in the twenty ships, who were coming to the relief of Argos, sailed into the Ambracian Gulf. With them was Demosthenes with 200 Messenian hoplites and sixty Athenian archers. The fleet lay off shore opposite the hill at Olpae. Meanwhile the Acarnanians and those few of the Amphilochians who had not been forcibly kept back by the Ambraciots had already entered Argos and were preparing to give battle to the enemy. They chose Demosthenes as commander-in-chief of the whole allied army, to act in cooperation with their own generals, and Demosthenes led them out and encamped near Olpae in a place where a large ravine separated the two armies.

For five days neither side made a move, but on the sixth day they both drew up in order of battle. The Peloponnesian army was the larger of the two and it outflanked the army of Demosthenes, who, fearing encirclement, placed about 400 hoplites and light troops in an ambush in a hidden pathway that was overgrown with bushes. These troops were to come up from the ambush at the moment that battle was joined and to take the enemy's projecting wing from the rear.

When the preparations on both sides were completed, they moved forward to battle. Demosthenes, with the Messenians and a few Athenians, was on the right, and the centre and left were made up of the various divisions of the Acarnanians and the Amphilochian javelin-throwers who were present. On the other side the line was formed of mixed detachments of Peloponnesians and Ambraciots, except in the case of the Mantineans, who were all together on the left, though not on the extreme left wing, which was held by Eurylochus and his own troops facing Demos-

108   thenes and the Messenians. When the two armies got to grips, the Peloponnesians on the left outflanked the enemy and were beginning to encircle their right wing, when the Acarnanians from the ambush set upon them from the rear and broke them at the first attack so completely that no one stood his ground to put up any resistance. Indeed, the panic into which they were thrown

spread to most of the rest of the army; for when the others saw the defeat of Eurylochus's men, who were the best troops they had, they themselves became even more terrified. Most of the honours in this action went to the Messenians with Demosthenes, who were in this part of the field. Meanwhile the Ambraciots, the best soldiers of all the tribes in these parts, and those on the right wing defeated the forces opposed to them and pursued them to Argos. On their return from the pursuit, however, they saw that the main body had been defeated, they were set upon by the rest of the Acarnanians, and it was only with great difficulty that they managed to get back to Olpae. Many of them were killed, since in trying to break through they kept no order and showed no discipline – all, that is, except the Mantineans, who kept in a compact body and preserved better order than any other part of the army during the retreat.

109   The battle lasted until the evening. Next day Menedaïus, who, after the death of Eurylochus and of Macarius, had taken over the command, found himself at a loss what to do after the great defeat that he had suffered. If he stayed there, he did not see how he could stand a siege, cut off as he was by land and by the Athenian fleet on the sea, and if he retreated there seemed little prospect of getting away safely. He therefore approached Demosthenes and the Acarnanian generals, not only to recover the dead but also asking for a truce under which he would be able to retreat. They gave him back the dead, put up a trophy themselves, and took up their own dead, which numbered about 300; as for the question of allowing them to retreat under a truce, they publicly refused to come to terms on this point with the whole army, but Demosthenes and his Acarnanian colleagues made a secret agreement allowing the Mantineans and Menedaïus and the other leaders and most important people among the Peloponnesians to get away at once. Demosthenes' aim was in part to weaken the army of the Ambraciots and their mercenary followers, but chiefly he wanted to bring the Spartans and the Peloponnesians into discredit with the Hellenes in these parts, as people who put their own safety first and let down their allies.

The enemy therefore brought in their dead and buried them quickly, as best they could, and those to whom the permission

110 had been given began to make secret plans how to get away. Meanwhile news came to Demosthenes and the Acarnanians that the Ambraciots from the city were marching out through Amphilochia in full force, as they had been asked to do by the first messenger from Olpae. Their intention was to join their fellow countrymen in Olpae, and they knew nothing about what had happened. Demosthenes immediately sent out part of his force to make road-blocks and to occupy strong points in the line of the enemy's advance, and at the same time prepared to march out against them with the rest of his army.

111   Meanwhile the Mantineans and the others included in the agreement, on the pretence of collecting vegetables and firewood, went out of camp and made off in groups of two or three, all the time collecting the things which they were supposed to have gone out to get. When they were already some distance from Olpae they began to move on faster. But the Ambraciots and others who had gone out with them in regular detachments also began to hurry when they saw them moving away, and ran after them to catch them up. The Acarnanians at first thought that the whole lot of them were getting away, contrary to the agreement; they pursued the Peloponnesians and, believing that they were being betrayed, threw a few javelins at some of the Peloponnesian generals who tried to hold them back by telling them that they were retreating under a truce. Afterwards, however, they let the Mantineans and the Peloponnesians go, and began to kill the Ambraciots. And here a good deal of confusion arose through the difficulty of telling who was Ambraciot and who was Peloponnesian. About 200 of them were killed; the rest fled across the frontier into Agraea and found shelter there with Salynthius, the King of the Agraeans, who was their friend.

112   Meanwhile the Ambraciots from the city arrived at Idomene. This is the name given to two high hills, the bigger of which had been seized during the night by the advance party which Demosthenes had sent out from his army. They had not been observed by the Ambraciots and had got up on to the hill before them, but the Ambraciots were the first to get to the smaller hill, and they made their camp on it.

Demosthenes with the rest of the army, after having had their evening meal, set out as soon as night began to fall. He himself, with half of the army, marched towards the pass, and the other half went through the mountains of Amphilochia. Just before dawn he fell upon the Ambraciots while they were still sleeping. They had no knowledge of what had happened and were in fact inclined to believe that Demosthenes' men were their own countrymen; for Demosthenes had purposely put the Messenians in front with instructions to speak to them in the Doric dialect, so as to disarm the suspicion of the sentries who in any case would not be able to recognize them by sight, as it was still dark.

So, as soon as he fell upon their army, he routed it. Most of them were killed where they were. The rest fled into the mountains, but the roads had already been occupied, the Amphilochians knew their own country, and had the advantage of being lightly armed against their heavily armed opponents, who, ignorant of the country and with no idea where to turn, rushed into the ravines or into the places where ambushes had already been set for them, and so were cut down. In their frantic efforts to escape, some of them actually turned to the sea, which was not far off. There they saw the Athenian ships sailing up the coast just at the same time as the action on land, and such was their panic at the moment that they swam towards them, thinking it better for them to die, if die they must, at the hands of those on board the ships than at the hands of barbarous and hated Amphilochians. After such disasters it was only very few out of the great army of the Ambraciots who got back safely to their city.

The Acarnanians, after stripping the bodies of the dead, put up a 113 trophy and returned to Argos. Next day a herald came to them from the Ambraciots who had fled from Olpae to the country of the Agraeans. He had come to ask permission to take up the dead who had been killed after the first battle when they had gone out with the Mantineans, although not included in the agreement by which the Mantineans were covered. When the herald saw the arms that had been taken from the Ambraciots who had come from the city, he was amazed at the number of them, since he did not know what had happened and imagined that the arms were those from the Ambraciot army to which he belonged himself. Someone, under the mistaken idea that the herald had come from the troops at Idomene, asked him what he was so surprised about and inquired how many had been killed. 'About two hundred,' said the herald.

'Not if we are to judge by the arms here,' said the other man, taking him up. 'Why, they come to more than a thousand.'

'Then,' said the herald, 'they cannot be the arms of those who were fighting with us.'

'They certainly are,' said the other – 'that is, if you were fighting at Idomene yesterday.'

'But there was no fighting at all yesterday,' said the herald. 'It was the day before, in the retreat.'

'However that may be,' the other man said, 'we were certainly fighting with these men yesterday. It was a relief force coming from the city of the Ambraciots.'

On hearing this, the herald realized that the reinforcements coming from the city had been destroyed. He cried out loud, and, overwhelmed by the extent of the disaster, went away at once without doing what he came to do and without asking any more for the recovery of the bodies.

In fact, this was, in all the war, certainly the greatest disaster that fell upon any single Hellenic city in an equal number of days. I have not recorded the numbers of the killed, because the number said to have been destroyed is incredible, considering the size of the city. However, I do know that if the Acarnanians and Amphilochians had been willing to follow the advice of Demosthenes and the Athenians and to seize Ambracia, they could have done so without striking a blow. As it was they feared that if the Athenians occupied the place, they would be even more dangerous neighbours to them than those they had now.

114   Afterwards they divided up the spoils, giving a third to the Athenians and distributing the rest among their own cities. The Athenian share was captured on the voyage home. What is now to be seen dedicated in the Attic temples is the 300 sets of armour which were specially set aside for Demosthenes and which he brought back with him by sea. Incidentally, after the disaster in Aetolia, it was now, with this achievement to his credit, a much safer thing for him to return home.

The Athenians in the twenty ships also returned to Naupactus.

After the departure of Demosthenes and the Athenians, the Acarnanians and Amphilochians granted a truce to the Ambraciots and Peloponnesians who had taken refuge with Salynthius and the Agraeans. These had now left Salynthius and gone to Oeniadae, and were allowed to retreat from there unmolested. For the future the Acarnanians and Amphilochians made a treaty for 100 years with the Ambraciots. The terms were that the two parties were to give mutual aid to each other in defending their own territories, but the Ambraciots were not to be required to join the Acarnanians in any campaign against the Peloponnesians, nor were the Acarnanians to be required to join the Ambraciots against the Athenians. The Ambraciots were to give back the hostages and the towns they held which belonged to the Amphilochians, and were not to give support to Anactorium, which was at war with the Acarnanians. On these terms hostilities were brought to an end. Afterwards the Corinthians sent a garrison of their own citizens to Ambracia, a force of 300 hoplites under the command of Xenoclides, the son of Euthycles. This force arrived after a difficult journey across the continent. This completes the account of what happened in Ambracia.

115   In the same winter the Athenians in Sicily made a landing in the territory of Himera, being supported in this operation by the Sicels, who invaded the frontier districts from the interior. They also sailed to the islands of Aeolus. On their return to Rhegium they found the Athenian general Pythodorus, the son of Isolochus, who had been sent out to take over the command of the fleet from Laches. The allies in Sicily had sailed to Athens and persuaded the Athenians to send out more ships to support them. The Syracusans, they pointed out, were already in control of their land and, though they were being kept off the sea by a small fleet, they were beginning to equip a fleet of their own so as to put an end to this state of affairs. The Athenians therefore manned forty ships to send out to them, thinking that in this way the war in Sicily would be over all the sooner, and at the same time regarding this as a useful naval exercise. So they sent out one of the generals, Pythodorus, with a few ships, and prepared to send out the main body later under Sophocles, the son of Sostratides, and Eurymedon, son of Thucles. Pythodorus meanwhile took over the command of the

fleet from Laches, and at the end of the winter sailed against the Locrian fort which had previously been captured by Laches. He returned again after having been defeated in battle by the Locrians.

116   At the very beginning of spring, as had happened on former occasions, a stream of lava came down from Etna and destroyed some of the land of the Catanians, who live on the slopes of Etna, which is the biggest mountain in Sicily. It is said that this was the first eruption for fifty years, and that, since Sicily was colonized by the Hellenes, there have been three eruptions in all.

These were the events of this winter, and with it ended the sixth year of this war recorded by Thucydides.

BOOK FOUR

ATHENIAN SUCCESS AT PYLOS

1 NEXT summer, at the time when the corn was beginning to ripen, ten Syracusan and ten Locrian ships sailed to Messina in Sicily and took over the place on the invitation of the inhabitants. Thus Messina revolted from Athens. The move had been engineered by the Syracusans mainly because they saw that the place afforded a base against Sicily and they feared that in the future the Athenians might use it as such and come to attack them with a larger force. The Locrians were chiefly activated by their hatred of the people of Rhegium, whom they now wished to crush by making war on them from both sides of the strait, and, at the same time as the naval expedition, they invaded the territory of Rhegium with all their forces in order to prevent it sending help to Messina. In this operation they were helped also by some exiles from Rhegium who were with them and invited them to intervene. Party struggles had been going on in Rhegium for some time, and it was now impossible for them to resist the Locrians, who were, for this reason, all the more ready to attack them. After laying waste the country, the Locrian land forces withdrew, while their ships remained to guard Messina. At the same time other ships were being manned in order to take up their station at Messina and to carry on the war from there.

2 About the same time of the spring, before the corn was fully ripe, the Peloponnesians and their allies invaded Attica under the command of the Spartan King Agis, the son of Archidamus. They settled down in the country and laid waste the land.

Meanwhile the Athenians sent out to Sicily the forty ships which they had been equipping, with the other two generals, Eurymedon and Sophocles. The third general, Pythodorus, had already arrived in Sicily. Eurymedon and Sophocles were also instructed, as they sailed up the coast, to do what they could for the Corcyraeans in the city who were suffering from the raids made on them by the exiled party in the mountains. Sixty Peloponnesian ships had also sailed to support the exiles and, since there was a serious famine in the city, their view was that it would be easy to gain control of affairs there. Demosthenes, since his return from Acarnania, held no official position, but the Athenians allowed him, at his own request, to make what use he liked of this fleet of theirs on its way round the Peloponnese.

3   When they were off the coast of Laconia, they heard that the Peloponnesian ships had already arrived at Corcyra. Eurymedon and Sophocles were for hurrying on to Corcyra, but Demosthenes wanted them first to put in at Pylos to carry out his plan, and then to sail on from there. The others objected, but a storm happened to get up, and so the ships were forced to go to Pylos. Demosthenes immediately proposed fortifying the place – this being, in fact, the reason why he had joined the expedition. He pointed out to them that there was plenty of timber and stone available, that the place was in a naturally strong position, and, together with most of the country round, uninhabited. Pylos is about forty-five miles from Sparta in what used to be the country of the Messenians. The Spartans call the place 'Coryphasium'. The others, however, told him that if he wanted to waste Athenian money he could find plenty of other desolate headlands round the Peloponnese to occupy, apart from this one. To Demosthenes, on the other hand, this one seemed to have great advantages: it had a harbour close by, and the Messenians, whose country this used to be and who spoke the same dialect as the Spartans, were capable, he thought, of doing a lot of damage if they had this place as a base, and would also be a very reliable garrison for it.

4   Demosthenes then put his plan up for consideration to the company commanders, but he failed to convince either the generals or the army of its merits. So he remained there doing nothing during the period of bad weather, until the soldiers themselves, who were tired of having nothing to do, suddenly had the idea of forming themselves into gangs and building fortifications for the place. So they set to work and kept on with it. They had no iron tools for shaping the stones, but they picked them out by hand, carried them along, and arranged them so that they would fit in with each

other. Where mortar was required, they carried it on their backs (since they had no hods), stooping down, so as to carry as much of it as possible, and clasping their hands behind them to prevent it slipping off. In fact they did everything they could to hurry on with the work and to finish the more vulnerable parts before the Spartans could come up to attack it. For most of the place was itself a natural stronghold and did not require any fortifying.

5   The Spartans meanwhile had a festival which they were celebrating, and they did not take the news of the occupation of Pylos seriously, being sure that, once they marched out against it, either the Athenians would withdraw or else they would easily storm the position. The fact that their main army was still in front of Athens also played a part in keeping them back.

The Athenians spent six days in fortifying the place on the side facing the land and in the other most necessary parts. They then left Demosthenes behind with five ships as a garrison, and hurried on their way to Corcyra and Sicily with the main body of the fleet.

6   When the Peloponnesians in Attica heard of the capture of Pylos, they immediately withdrew and returned home. The Spartans and Agis, their King, considered that here was a threat to their vital interests; also the invasion had taken place early, while the corn was still green, so that there was a general shortage of provisions; then, too, the weather had been much more rainy and stormy than might have been expected at this time of the year, and this had caused hardship in the army. There were various reasons, therefore, for the early withdrawal and for this invasion being a very short one. They only stayed fifteen days in Attica.

7   About the same time the Athenian general Simonides captured Eion in the Thracian area, a colony of Mende, but hostile to Athens. Simonides had collected a force consisting of a few Athenians from the garrisons and a number of allies from the neighbourhood. Eion was handed over to him by treachery, but immediately afterwards the Chalcidians and Bottiaeans came up, and Simonides was forced out of the town with considerable losses.

8   When the Peloponnesians returned from Attica, the Spartans themselves and the troops from the subordinate towns nearest to

Sparta immediately marched to the relief of Pylos. The other Lacedaemonians followed more slowly, since they had only just come home from the other campaign. Orders were issued all round the Peloponnese for troops to proceed as quickly as possible to Pylos, and they also sent for their sixty ships in Corcyra. These ships were dragged across the isthmus of Leucas, thus escaping the notice of the Athenian fleet at Zacynthus, and reached Pylos, where the land forces had already arrived. However, while the Peloponnesian fleet was still on its way there, Demosthenes had anticipated them and had secretly sent out two ships to inform Eurymedon and the Athenian fleet at Zacynthus that Pylos was in danger and to urge them to come to his help. The fleet followed his instructions and sailed to Pylos as fast as possible.

Meanwhile the Spartans made ready to attack the fortification both from the land and from the sea, expecting to capture it easily, since it had been built in a hurry and had only a few men to defend it. However, they expected that the Athenian fleet from Zacynthus would come to its support, and so they intended, if they should fail to take the place before them, to block up the entrances to the harbour, so that the Athenians would not be able to enter it and take up their positions there. For the island of Sphacteria lies close in to the shore, stretching across the harbour and making it a safe place with narrow entrances – room for two ships abreast on the side nearest Pylos and the Athenian fortifications, and for eight or nine on the other side nearest the mainland. Sphacteria was covered in woods and, being uninhabited, there were no paths on it. It is about a mile and a half long. The Spartan plan was to block up the harbour entrances with lines of ships placed close together with their prows facing the sea; and, since they feared that the enemy might occupy the island and make use of it against them, they carried some hoplites across to it and placed others on the mainland. So, according to the Spartan plan, the Athenians would have enemies to face both on the island and on the mainland; they would not be able to land on either, and, since there were no harbours on the coast of Pylos itself towards the open sea – only, in fact, the harbour behind Sphacteria – the Athenian fleet would have no base for operations in relief of their men in Pylos. Thus the Spartans would not have to run the risk of a battle at sea and, in all probability, would capture the place by siege, since it was unprovisioned and had been seized on the spur of the moment. Having decided on this plan, they sent the hoplites across to the island, choosing the men by lot from each division of their army. Various parties had been across, done their spell of duty, and been relieved: the last of these forces to cross, and the one that was caught there, numbered 420 hoplites, with helots to attend on them. This force was commanded by Epitadas, the son of Molobrus.

9   Meanwhile Demosthenes made his own preparations to meet the Spartan attack which he could see was coming to him from the land and sea at once. He dragged up under the fortification the triremes that remained out of the ones that had been left him and protected them with a stockade. The sailors who had been serving on them he armed with shields – all of poor quality and most of them made of osiers, since it was impossible to procure arms in this deserted spot. Even these arms, in fact, had been obtained from a thirty-oared privateer and from a pinnace belonging to some Messenians who happened to put in an appearance. These Messenians also supplied a force of about forty hoplites, which Desmothenes used with the rest. He posted most of his men, fully armed or not, in the best-fortified and strongest sector, which faced the land, with instructions to meet any attack that might be made by the land forces. He himself picked out of the whole army a force of sixty hoplites and a few archers, and with these went outside the wall down to the sea at the point where he thought the enemy were most likely to attempt a landing. It was difficult and rocky ground, facing the open sea, but it was here that the Athenian wall was weakest, and this fact, Demosthenes thought, would encourage them to try to force their way through. For the Athenians had never imagined that they would be confronted with superior naval forces, and had consequently not fortified this sector properly, so if the enemy could once force a landing, he would have it in his power to capture the position. Here, therefore, Demosthenes went right down to the sea, and drew up his hoplites in order to stop the enemy, if possible, from landing. To encourage them, he spoke to them as follows:

10 'Soldiers, all of us together are in this, and I do not want any of

you in our present awkward position to try to show off his intelligence by making a precise calculation of the dangers which surround us; instead we must simply make straight at the enemy, and not pause to discuss the matter, confident in our hearts that these dangers, too, can be surmounted. For when we are forced into a position like this one, calculations are beside the point: what we have to do is to stake everything on a quick decision. And in fact I consider that the odds are on our side, so long as we are determined to hold our ground and do not throw away our very real advantages through being frightened by the enemy's numbers. One thing in our favour is the fact that this is a difficult place for a landing, but this is an advantage to us only if we stand firm. Once we give way, the going, however difficult it is, will become easy for them, since there will be no one to resist them. And even if we do manage afterwards to push them back, we shall find the enemy harder to deal with because of his difficulties in the retreat. They will be easiest to repel while they are still on board their ships, since, once they land, they will already be on even terms with us. As for their numbers, there is no need to be too frightened. However many of them there are, they can only engage with small detachments at a time, because of their inability to bring the ships close in shore. Then, too, it is not the case of our having to fight against an army with superior numbers on land, where conditions are equal; on the contrary, they are operating from their ships, and on the sea quite a number of circumstances have to combine favourably, if action is to be effective. So I consider that the enemy's difficulties make up for our lack of numbers, and at the same time I call upon you, as Athenians who know from experience all about landing from ships on foreign shores and how impossible it is to force a landing if the defenders stand firm and do not give way through fear of the surf or the frightening appearance of the ships as they sail in – remembering this, stand firm now yourselves, meet the enemy right down at the water's edge, and preserve this position and our own lives.'

11   After these heartening words from Demosthenes, the Athenians felt more confident and marched down to meet the enemy, taking up their positions along the edge of the sea. And now the Spartans came into action and made their assault on the fortification both

with their land forces and with their ships. There were forty-three of these, and the admiral Thrasymelidas, the son of Cratesicles, a regular Spartan officer, sailed with them in person. He made his attack exactly where Demosthenes was expecting it.

The Athenians now had to defend themselves on both sides, from the land and from the sea. The enemy came up in detachments of a few ships at a time, since there was no room to bring greater numbers inshore, and, while some rested, others kept up the attack, showing the greatest enthusiasm, and cheering each other on in their efforts to force back the defenders and capture the fortification. It was Brasidas who distinguished himself more than anyone else. He was in command of a trireme, and when he saw that, because of the difficult nature of the ground, the captains and steersmen, even at points where it did seem possible to land, were hanging back for fear of damaging their ships, he shouted out to them, asking them what was the point in sparing ships' timbers and meanwhile tolerating the existence of an enemy fortress in their own country, telling them to break up their ships so long as they forced a landing, and appealing to the allies, in return for all the benefits they had received from Sparta, to sacrifice their ships now for her sake, to run them aground, to make a landing some way or other, and to overwhelm the place and its defenders.

12   So Brasidas spurred on the others. At the same time he compelled his own steersman to run the ship ashore and took his stand on the gangway. As he was trying to land, the Athenians fell upon him and, after receiving many wounds, he fainted and fell down into the bows of the ship. His shield slipped from his arm into the sea and later, when it was thrown up on the shore, was picked up by the Athenians and used for the trophy which they erected for their success in this attack.

As for the others, they were resolute enough, but still could not force a landing because of the difficulty of the ground and because the Athenians stood firm and did not yield an inch. It was indeed a strange alteration in the ordinary run of things for Athenians to be fighting a battle on land – and Spartan land too – against Spartans attacking from the sea, and for Spartans to be trying to make a naval landing on their own shores, now hostile to them, against Athenian opposition. For at this time Sparta chiefly prided herself on being a land power with an unrivalled army and Athens on being a sea power with the greatest navy in existence.

13   So for this day and part of the next the attacks continued. By then the Spartans had given up the attempt, and on the third day they sent some of their ships to Asine to fetch timber for making siege engines, since they hoped by the use of these to assault successfully the part of the wall near the harbour, where, though the fortifications were higher, the landing was easier. At this point the Athenian fleet from Zacynthus arrived. It now consisted of fifty ships, since it had been reinforced by some of the ships on patrol at Naupactus, and by four others from Chios.

When they saw that the mainland and the island were both thick with hoplites and that the enemy ships were in harbour and showing no signs of sailing out, the Athenians, finding nowhere where they could anchor, sailed off for the time being to the uninhabited island of Prote, which is not far away. Here they passed the night, and on the next day set out prepared for battle. Their intention was to fight in the open sea, if the enemy would sail out to meet them: if he would not, they would sail in themselves and attack him in the harbour. The Spartans, on their side, did not put out to sea, nor had they blocked the entrances to the harbour, as they had meant to do. They stayed quietly on shore and occupied themselves in manning their ships and preparing, in the event of the Athenians sailing in, to fight inside the harbour, which is by no means a small one.

14   Seeing this, the Athenians sailed in to attack by both entrances. The main body of the enemy's fleet was already at sea and in line, and the Athenians fell upon it and put it to flight. They pursued it as far as they could in the limited space, disabled a number of ships and captured five, one of them complete with its crew. They then began to ram the ships which had fled back to the shore and to put out of action others that were still getting their crews aboard, before they could put to sea. Others they took in tow with their own ships and dragged off empty, since the crews had fled.

At this sight the Spartans were overwhelmed with horror, since it meant that their own men were now cut off on the island. They rushed into the battle and, going into the sea in their armour, seized hold of the ships and tried to drag them back again, everyone throwing himself into the action as though everything depended on himself alone. There was shouting and confusion everywhere, and here, too, in this battle of the ships a reversal in the usual methods of the two sides. For the Spartans, in their desperate excitement, were actually fighting a sea battle on land, and the victorious Athenians, in their anxiety to take the fullest possible advantage of their success, were fighting an infantry battle from their ships.

After a bitter struggle, with many wounded on both sides, the action was broken off, the Spartans having rescued the empty ships except for the ones that had been captured first. Both sides returned to their camps; the Athenians put up a trophy, gave back the dead, secured the wrecks, and immediately began to cruise round the island; their enemies there were cut off, and so they guarded it closely. The Peloponnesians on the mainland, who had now come up in full force, stayed in their positions before Pylos.

15 When the news of what had happened at Pylos reached Sparta, such a serious view of it was taken that it was decided that members of the government should go down to the camp and make up their minds on the spot what ought to be done about it. There they found that it was impossible to relieve their men on the island and, since they did not want to risk being starved out or else forced to surrender by superior numbers, they decided to conclude an armistice at Pylos with the Athenian generals, if they would agree to it, and also to send ambassadors to Athens with a view to ending the war and so getting back their own men as quickly as possible.

16 The generals accepted their proposals and an armistice was arranged on the following terms:

That the Spartans should bring to Pylos and deliver over to the Athenians all their ships which had taken part in the battle, together with all other warships in Laconia, and that they should make no attack on the fortification either by land or by sea.

That the Athenians should allow the Spartans on the mainland to send to their men on the island a specified quantity of corn, already kneaded. The ration was to be two quarts of barley meal, one pint of wine, and a portion of meat for each man, and half the same quantities for each servant.

That these rations should be sent in under Athenian supervision, and no voyages were to be made to the island except with permission.

That the Athenians should continue to keep watch on the island just as before, but they were not to land on it and not to attack the Peloponnesian army either by land or by sea.

That on the slightest infringement of these terms by either side, the armistice should at once be considered at an end. That the armistice should remain in force until the return of the Spartan representatives from Athens.

That the Athenians should take these representatives to Athens in a trireme and bring them back again.

That on their return the armistice should be ended, and that the Athenians should restore the ships in the same condition as they had received them.

These were the terms of the armistice. The ships, about sixty in all, were handed over, and the Spartan representatives were sent on their way. When they arrived at Athens, they made the following speech:

17   'Athenians, the Spartans have sent us here to deal with the question of our men on the island and to try to come to an arrangement with you which will do you good and bring to us, in our present plight, as much honour as can be expected in the circumstances. If we speak at some length, you must not regard this as being contrary to our tradition. It is certainly our way not to use many words when few are enough; but on occasions where words are required to point out something important which needs to be done, then we use them more freely. And do not listen to what we have to say in a hostile spirit or imagine that we think you ignorant and are trying to lecture you. You may be sure that we respect your intelligence and are simply reminding you of how wise decisions are arrived at.

'You are now in a position where you can turn your present good fortune to good use, keeping what you hold and gaining honour and reputation besides. Thus you will avoid the mistake so often made by those who meet with some extraordinary piece of good luck and then go on pressing forward in the hope of more still, because of the very unexpectedness of their first success. But those who have had most experience of changes both for the better and the worse are rightly the least inclined to believe that good luck will last. Certainly both your city and ours have had experience enough to learn this lesson.

18 'Look, for example, at what has happened to us now. We, with the greatest reputation of any state in Hellas, have come here to you in order to ask for what previously we thought it was in our power to give. And this has not been caused by any decline in our power or by the kind of arrogance that proceeds from acquiring new power. Our resources are the same as ever; we simply miscalculated them, and this is a mistake that may be made by everyone. It is not reasonable, therefore, for you to think that because of your present strength and your recent acquisitions, fortune also will always be on your side. True wisdom is shown by those who make careful use of their advantages in the knowledge that things will change (and so too they will show more intelligence than others when things are going wrong with them); as for war, they will know that its course is governed by the total chances in operation and can never be restricted to the conditions that one or other of the two sides would like to see permanently fixed. Such people, by avoiding the over-confidence which may spring from a success in war, are less likely than anyone to make mistakes and are most anxious, if they can, to come to terms during the period of their own good fortune.

'This, Athenians, is what you have the opportunity to do now with us, and so to avoid what may happen later, if you fail to agree with us and afterwards, as is quite possible, suffer a defeat. For then it would be thought that even your present successes were merely due to luck, whereas now you are in a position to leave behind you a safe and sure reputation both for strength and for wisdom.

19 'Sparta calls upon you to make a treaty and to end the war. She offers you peace, alliance, friendly and neighbourly relations. In return she asks for the men on the island, thinking it better for both sides that the affair should not proceed to the bitter end – whether, by some stroke of luck, the men should manage to force an escape, or else be subdued by your blockade and fall still further into your power. In our view, where great hatreds exist, no lasting settlement can be made in a spirit of revenge, when one side gets the better of things in war and forces its opponent to swear to

carry out the terms of an unequal treaty; what will make the
settlement lasting is when the party that has it in his power to act
like this takes instead a more reasonable point of view, overcomes
his adversary in generosity, and makes peace on more moderate
terms than his enemy expected. In such a case, so far from wanting
to get his own back for the violence that has been done to him, the
enemy is already under an obligation to pay back good for good,
and so is the more ready, from a sense of honour, to abide by the
terms that have been made. And men are more inclined to act in
this way towards their greatest enemies than towards people with
whom they have only minor differences. Then, too, when others
are willing to make concessions it is natural for one to give way
gladly oneself, just as it is natural, if one meets with an attitude of
arrogance, to face things out to the end, even against one's better
judgement.

20   'As for Sparta and Athens, if ever there was a good time for
making peace it is now, before some irremediable event overtakes
us, something which would force us into an unending hatred of
you, personal as well as political, and would deprive you of the
hope of what we are offering you at this moment. Now is the
time for us to be reconciled, while the final issue is still undecided,
while you have won glory and can have our friendship as well,
and we, before any shameful thing has taken place, can, in our
present distress, accept a reasonable settlement. Let us choose for
ourselves peace instead of war, and give to the rest of the Hellenes
a respite from their sufferings. For this they will think that it is
you rather than we whom they have to thank. As for the war in
which they are engaged, they are not certain who began it; but
peace now depends chiefly upon you, and if peace is made, it is to
you that their gratitude will go. By accepting our proposals you
can have the firm friendship of Sparta, a friendship which is not
extorted from her but which is offered to you freely and which
you will oblige her by accepting. Think also of the advantages
which can reasonably be expected to follow. For if we, Athens and
Sparta, stand together, you can be sure that the rest of Hellas, in
its inferior position, will show us every possible mark of honour.'

21   So the Spartan delegates spoke. Their assumption was that
Athens had wanted to make peace even earlier, had only been

prevented from doing so by Spartan opposition, and would now gladly embrace the opportunity offered and return the men. The Athenians, however, aimed at winning still more, and, as for making peace, they considered that while they had the men on the island they could do so whenever they liked. The man who, more than others, encouraged them in this attitude was Cleon, the son of Cleaenetus, a popular figure of the time who had the greatest influence with the masses. He persuaded them that the right reply to make was this: that, first, the men should surrender themselves and their arms and be brought to Athens; then, Sparta must give back Nisaea, Pegae, Troezen, and Achaea, all of which places had not been conquered in war but had been given up by Athens by the terms of the previous peace treaty which had been made at a time of difficulty when Athens was in much greater need of peace than she was at the moment. If this was done, Sparta should recover her men and a truce should be made for as long a period as the two parties should decide.

22   To this answer the Spartan delegates made no reply, but they asked for a committee to be appointed with whom they could discuss each point separately and so in a calm atmosphere try to find a basis for agreement. This was enough to bring Cleon down upon them in full force. He said that he had always known that there was nothing upright in their intentions, and now the fact was proved by their unwillingness to say a word to the whole people and their preference for dealing with a small committee. No, if their intentions were sincere, then let them speak out in front of everyone.

The Spartans, however, saw that it was impossible for them to speak in front of the people. They saw that even if they did decide to make concessions in their present difficult position, they might well speak and still not get what they wanted, and find that what they had said would give them a bad name with their allies, and that, in any case, the Athenians were not likely to accept their proposals in a reasonable spirit. So they left Athens without having achieved anything.

23   Their return meant the end of the armistice at Pylos, and the Spartans asked for their ships back again, as had been agreed. But the Athenians alleged that the treaty had been broken by a Spartan

attack on the wall. They also brought forward some other complaints which seemed hardly worth mentioning and refused to give the ships back, taking their stand on the precise wording of the agreement where it was laid down that the least infringement of the terms would mean that the armistice was at an end. The allegations were denied by the Spartans who, after making a formal protest against the injustice of the Athenian action with regard to the ships, went back and prepared to renew the fighting.

So at Pylos war was waged vigorously by both sides. The Athenians always had two ships on patrol by day, sailing round the island in opposite directions, and at night the whole fleet was anchored all round it except, when the weather was stormy, on the side facing the open sea. Twenty more ships had arrived from Athens to help in the blockade, so that there were now seventy altogether. Meanwhile the Peloponnesians were in camp on the mainland and kept up their attacks on the wall, on the look-out for any opportunity which might present itself for saving their men on the island.

FINAL VICTORY AT PYLOS

24 Meanwhile the Syracusans and their allies in Sicily had finished equipping the rest of their fleet and brought it up to join the ships that were guarding Messina. From there they carried on the war, the main instigators in all this being the Locrians, because of their hatred of Rhegium, whose territory they had invaded in full force. The Syracusans also wanted to try their fortunes in a naval engagement, since they saw that at the moment the Athenians only had a few ships and had been informed that the main fleet which was supposed to join them in Sicily was engaged in the blockade of Sphacteria. If they could establish their naval superiority they thought that they could easily gain control of Rhegium by blockading it from the land and from the sea; and this would at once put them in a very strong position. For the headland of Rhegium in Italy is so close to Messina in Sicily that it would be impossible for the Athenians to operate there with their fleet and control the strait. This is the stretch of sea between Rhegium and Messina at

the point where Sicily is nearest to the continent. It is the Charybdis of the legends through which Odysseus is supposed to have sailed. Indeed it has quite naturally got the name for being a dangerous place because of the narrowness of the channel and the strength of the currents that pour into it from the two great seas on either side, the Tyrrhenian and the Sicilian.

25   As it happened, the Syracusans and their allies were compelled to fight an action in these narrow waters, and late in the day, in an attempt to secure the passage through of one of their own boats. With rather more than thirty ships they put out against sixteen Athenian and eight Rhegian ships. In the engagement they were defeated by the Athenians and lost one ship; they then hurriedly retired, each ship shifting for itself, to their bases at Messina and Rhegium, and night put an end to any further fighting. After this the Locrians withdrew from the territory of Rhegium. The Syracusan and allied ships united and came to anchor at Cape Pelorus in the territory of Messina, having their ground forces with them in support. The Athenians and Rhegians sailed up to them here and, seeing that their ships were not manned, made an attack on them, but themselves lost one ship which was caught by a grappling iron, though the crew escaped by swimming. Afterwards the Syracusans manned their ships and were having them towed close to the shore in the direction of Messina when the Athenians made another attack. But the Syracusans turned suddenly away from shore and got in their attack first, sinking one ship. So they brought their ships into the harbour at Messina, having had rather the better of things altogether in the voyage along the coast and in the earlier engagement.

The Athenians then sailed to Camarina, on the news that the city was going to be betrayed to the Syracusans by Archias and his party. In their absence the Messinians went out in full force with their army and their fleet against the Chalcidian colony of Naxos, which is on their frontiers. On the first day they drove the Naxians inside their walls and laid waste the country. Next day they sailed round with their fleet by way of the river Acesines and laid waste the land in that area, while their army moved forward in the direction of the city. Meanwhile, however, considerable numbers of the Sicels had come down from the mountains to help fight against the Messinians. At the sight of them the Naxians took fresh heart and also encouraged themselves with the belief that the Leontinians and their other Hellenic allies were on their way to help them. So they made a sudden sortie from the town and fell upon the Messinians, routing their army and killing more than a thousand of them. Those who survived had the greatest difficulty on their way back, since the natives kept up their attacks on the roads and killed great numbers of them. The fleet put in to Messina, and afterwards the various contingents returned to their own ports.

Immediately after this the Leontinians and their allies, with the Athenians, took advantage of Messina's losses and attacked the place. The Athenians in their ships made for the harbour, while the army moved forward against the city. However, a sortie was made by the Messinians and some Locrians with Demoteles, who had been left behind to garrison the city after the disaster. These troops made a sudden attack and routed most of the army of the Leontinians, killing great numbers of them. The Athenians, seeing this, landed from their ships and came up in support. Falling upon the Messinians when they were in a disorganized state, they chased them back again into the city. Then, after putting up a trophy, they returned to Rhegium. After this the Hellenes in Sicily continued to make war on each other by land, but the Athenians took no part in it.

26   Meanwhile at Pylos the Athenians were still besieging the Spartans on the island, and the Peloponnesian army remained in its positions on the mainland. Lack of food and water made the blockade a difficult operation for the Athenians. There was no spring except one on the acropolis of Pylos, and that was only a small one. Most of them had to scrape about in the shingle on the beach for such water as they could find to drink. Then there was the lack of room, which made it necessary for them to camp close together, and there was no port for the ships, so that some had to take it in turn to have their meals ashore while the rest were anchored out at sea. But it was the unexpectedly long time taken over the operation which caused the greatest discouragement, since they had imagined that a few days would be enough to subdue these men besieged on a desert island and with only brack-

ish water to drink. The fact was that the Spartans had called for volunteers to bring into the island ground corn, wine, cheese, and any other form of food useful in a siege. Large rewards in money were offered and their freedom was promised to any helots who succeeded in bringing the food in. There were many ready to take the risk of doing so, and particularly the helots, who put to sea from various parts of the Peloponnese and brought their boats in by night to the side of the island facing the open sea. Especially they watched out for the chance of having a wind behind them to carry them in. It was easier to escape the notice of the triremes on guard when the wind blew from the sea, since it then became impossible for them to anchor all round the island, while the helots had had their boats valued and ran them ashore without minding whether they were damaged or not so long as they got there, and the hoplites were always ready waiting for them at the landing-places. However, all who made the attempt in calm weather were intercepted. Divers also swam in under water from the harbour, dragging behind them by a cord skins containing poppyseed mixed with honey and pounded linseed. At first these managed to escape notice, but later a look-out was kept for them. So the two sides employed every scheme they could think of, one for importing provisions, the other to detect and prevent it.

27   At Athens, meanwhile, when people heard the news of the army's hardships and of how food was being carried in to the men on the island, they were at a loss what to do and feared that the advent of winter might put a stop to the blockade. They saw that it would then be impossible to send convoys with supplies round the Peloponnese; there was nothing at Pylos itself – indeed not even in summer could they supply the place adequately; nor could the ships maintain the blockade in a district where there were no harbours. It seemed that either the men would escape because the siege would have to be abandoned, or else they would wait for a period of bad weather and sail away on the boats that brought them their food. Most of all the Athenians were alarmed by the attitude of Sparta, since it was thought that the reason the Spartans had ceased to offer negotiations was that they felt confident in the strength of their own position. Now, therefore, they regretted not having accepted the proposed truce.

As for Cleon, he realized that he was becoming unpopular because of the part he had played in preventing the agreement, and he declared that those who brought news from Pylos were not telling the truth. The messengers then suggested that, if the Athenians did not believe them, they should send out inspectors to see for themselves, and Cleon himself was chosen together with Theagenes for this post. He now realized that he would be compelled either to come back with the same report as that of the men whom he had just been attacking or else, if he said the opposite, be shown up as a liar; but he saw that the general feeling among the Athenians was not averse from sending out another expeditionary force, and so he told them that they ought not to be sending out inspectors and wasting time and letting their opportunities slip away from them; instead, if they believed in the truth of what had been reported, they should sail out against the men. He then pointed at Nicias, the son of Niceratus, who was then general and whom he hated. Putting the blame on him, he said that, if only the generals were real men, it would be easy to take out a force and capture the Spartans on the island; certainly he himself would have done so, if he had been in command.

28　　At this there was a certain amount of murmuring among the Athenians against Cleon for not being willing to sail now, if the whole thing seemed to him so easy, and Nicias, noticing this and at the same time finding himself attacked by Cleon, told him that, so far as the generals were concerned, he could take out whatever force he liked and see what he could do himself. Cleon's first impression was that this offer was only made as a debating point, and so he was ready enough to accept it; but when he realized that the command was being handed over to him quite genuinely, he began to back out of it, saying that it was Nicias, not he, who was general. He was now indeed thoroughly scared, since he never imagined that Nicias would have gone so far as to give up his post to him. Nicias, however, repeated his offer and called the Athenians to witness that he was standing down from the command in Pylos. The Athenians behaved in the way that crowds usually do. The more that Cleon tried to get out of sailing to Pylos, and the more that he tried to take back what he had said, the more they encouraged Nicias to hand over his command and they shouted at Cleon, telling him that he ought to sail. The result was that Cleon, finding that there was no longer any possibility of going back on what he had said, undertook to go on the voyage. He came forward and said that he was not frightened of the Spartans and would sail without taking a single man from Athens, only the Lemnians and Imbrians who were in the city and the peltasts who had come from Aenus to offer their help and 400 archers who were available from other quarters. With this force, together with the troops now at Pylos, he claimed that within twenty days he would either bring the Spartans back to Athens alive or would kill them on the spot. This irresponsible claim caused a certain amount of laughter, though the more intelligent members of his audience were not displeased with it, since they calculated that they would enjoy an advantage either way; either they would get rid of Cleon for the future – which was what they rather expected – or, if they were wrong about this, they would have the Spartans in their power.

29   Cleon therefore made his arrangements in the assembly and, when the Athenians had voted that he should command the expedition, he chose to have Demosthenes, one of the generals at Pylos, associated with him in the command. He then prepared to put to sea as soon as possible. He chose Demosthenes as his colleague because he heard that he was already planning to make a landing on the island. The soldiers were suffering great hardships because of the awkwardness of their position and, finding themselves more the besieged than the besiegers, were eager to fight things out. And Demosthenes himself had gained confidence from the fact that there had been a fire on the island. Previously he had been apprehensive because most of the island was wooded and, since it had never been inhabited, there were no tracks: all this he thought was to the advantage of the enemy, for if he landed with a large army they could make damaging attacks on him from positions beyond the reach of his observation; he could have no clear idea of the enemy's forces or of any mistakes they might make, because they would be covered by the woods, whereas every mistake made by his own army would be seen by the enemy, who could thus attack him unexpectedly at any point they chose, since the initiative would be in their hands. If, on the other hand,

he should force them to fight at close quarters in the wooded areas, he considered that a small force which knew the country would be worth more than a large force which did not. His own army, in spite of its size, might get cut to pieces without knowing what was happening, since the lack of visibility would prevent one detach-
30 ment from helping the other as it should. These calculations of his were largely based on the Aetolian disaster, which had been, to some extent, caused by the forests.

It happened, however, that one of the soldiers who, because of the lack of space, were forced to put in to the extreme points of the island and have their meals there with patrols set to prevent them being surprised, accidentally set fire to a part of the wood. The wind then got up, and nearly the whole of the wood was unintentionally burnt down. It was this that enabled Demosthenes to see that there were more Spartans on the island than he thought. He had imagined previously that the rations brought in were for a smaller number. But he also saw that the island was now easier to land on, and he began to make preparations for the attempt, thinking that now was the time for the Athenians to make a really serious effort to achieve their object. So he sent for troops from the allies in the neighbourhood and went ahead with all his other arrangements.

Cleon had already sent a messenger to say that he was coming, and he now arrived at Pylos with the troops for which he had asked. After conferring together, the two generals first of all sent a herald to the camp on the mainland to ask if they were willing to avoid bringing matters to a head: if so, they should instruct the men on the island to surrender themselves and their arms to the Athenians with the guarantee that they should suffer only a mild form of imprisonment until the time that a general settlement should be reached. This offer was refused.

31   The generals then waited for one day, and on the day following embarked all their hoplites on a few ships, put to sea while it was still dark, and landed just before dawn on both sides of the island – from the open sea and from the harbour – about 800 of them al-together. They then ran forward against the first post on the island. The enemy's dispositions were as follows: in this first guard post there were about thirty hoplites; the centre and the most level

part, where the water was, was held by the main body under their commander Epitadas; and a small detachment guarded the very end of the island opposite Pylos, where steep cliffs went down into the sea and where from the land also there were great difficulties in making an attack on it, since there was also an old fort there, made of stones roughly fitted together, and they thought that this would be useful to them if they were hard pressed and forced to retreat.

32   This being the Spartan disposition of forces, the Athenians over-ran the first guard post and immediately destroyed the men there, who were still asleep or trying to arm themselves. The landing had taken them by surprise, since they thought that the ships were only sailing as usual to their stations for the night. At dawn the rest of the army landed. This consisted of the crews of rather more than seventy ships (except for the lowest rank of rowers), armed as best they could be, 800 archers, at least 800 peltasts, the Messinian contingents, and all the other troops at Pylos except those who were actually guarding the fortification. Under the direction of Demosthenes this force was divided into companies of roughly 200 men – sometimes more and sometimes less – who occupied the highest points of ground, with the object of causing the enemy the greatest possible embarrassment; for he would be surrounded on all sides and have no single point against which to counter-attack; instead he would always be exposed to great numbers in every direction, and if he attacked those in front he would be shot at from the rear, if he attacked those on one flank, he would be shot at by those on the other. Wherever he went, he would have enemies behind him, lightly armed and the hardest of all to deal with, since with their arrows, javelins, stones, and slings they were effective at long range and it was impossible to come to close quarters with them; for in running away they had the advant-age in speed, and as soon as the pursuit was relaxed back they came again. This was the original plan made by Demosthenes for the landing, and it was this plan which was now put into operation.

33   Meanwhile the troops under Epitadas, who constituted the main body of the enemy force on the island, as soon as they saw that their first post had been overwhelmed and that an army was coming to

attack them, fell in and moved forward against the Athenian hoplites with the intention of coming to close quarters. The hoplites were facing them, and the light troops were on their flanks and at their rear. They were unable, however, to engage with the hoplites or to reap the advantages of their own specialized training. They themselves were held up by the weapons shot at them from both flanks by the light troops, and the Athenian hoplites, instead of moving forward to meet them, remained in their positions. Though they drove back the light troops at any point where they ran in and approached too closely, they still fought back even in retreat, since they had no heavy equipment and could easily outdistance their pursuers over ground where, since the place had been uninhabited up till then, the going was rough and difficult and where the Spartans in their heavy armour could not press their pursuit.

34   This fighting at long range continued for some time. In the end the Spartans were no longer able to counter-attack as quickly as before at the points where their line was threatened, and the light troops gained confidence from finding that their enemy was reacting more slowly to their attacks; they could see that they had many times the numbers of troops that the Spartans had and they had now become accustomed to the idea that these Spartans were not quite so terrible as they had thought, since their first experience of them had not been so dreadful as they had imagined it would be at the time when they had landed. Then they had been obsessed with the idea that they were actually going to attack Spartans, but now they began to despise their enemy, shouting as they charged down upon him in a mass and letting fly with stones and arrows and javelins and every weapon that came to hand. The Spartans were not used to this kind of fighting, and they were thrown into consternation by the shouting which accompanied the attacks; great clouds of dust rose from the ashes where the wood had been recently burned, and what with the arrows and stones loosed from so many hands and flying through the dust-cloud, it became impossible to see in front of one. Things now began to go hard with the Spartans; their felt helmets could not keep out the arrows; when they were hit with spears the broken shafts stuck in their armour, and they themselves, unable to see

what was in front of them, had no means of fighting back; words
of command were inaudible, being drowned by the shouting of
the enemy; danger was on every side, and they could see no possible way either of defending themselves or of escaping.

35   Finally, after many of them had been wounded, penned in as
they were and unable to move freely, they closed their ranks and
fell back on the fort at the end of the island, which was not far off
and was garrisoned by their own men. And now, seeing them give
way, the light troops shouted all the louder and bore down upon
them with even greater confidence. Those whom they managed
to intercept on their retreat were killed, but the majority of the
Spartans reached the shelter of the fort and, joining up with their
garrison there, took up positions along the whole extent of the
fortification so as to defend it at every point where it might be
attacked. The Athenians followed them up and, since the strength
of the position made it impossible for them to surround the place
in an encircling movement, they attacked it from in front and tried
to storm it. For a long time, indeed for most of the day, both sides
held out, tired as they were with the fighting and the thirst and the
sun, the Athenians trying to dislodge the enemy from the high
ground and the Spartans struggling to maintain their position.
But it was now easier for the Spartans to defend themselves than
it had been, since there were no forces encircling them on the
flanks.

36   It seemed that the struggle might continue indefinitely. But the
commander of the Messinians approached Cleon and Demosthenes
and told them that all this effort was getting them nowhere; if,
however, they were prepared to let him have some of the archers
and the light troops, he would go round to the enemy's rear by a
route which he could find and then he felt confident that the assault
could be pressed home. They gave him what he asked for, and he
set out from a point which was out of sight, so that the Spartans
would not observe him. Then, picking his way as best he could
along the steep cliffs of the island, and going by a route which the
Spartans had left unguarded, since they had trusted in the natural
strength of the position, he managed with the greatest difficulty to
get round behind them without being observed and suddenly
appeared on the high ground in their rear, striking panic into the

Spartans by the unexpectedness of the thing and giving still greater confidence to the Athenians by the sight of what they had been waiting for.

The Spartans were now exposed to attack on both sides. Indeed, to compare small things with great, they were in the same situation as in the battle of Thermopylae, where the Spartan army was destroyed by the Persians getting round behind them by the path. So these Spartans were now caught between two fires and were no longer able to stand their ground. What with the superior numbers of their enemy and their own exhaustion from lack of food, they fell back, and now the Athenians were masters of the approaches.

37   At this point Cleon and Demosthenes stopped the fighting and kept their men back. They realized that any further retreat on the part of the Spartans would mean that they would be destroyed by their army, and they wanted to bring them to Athens alive, if by chance their spirit could be broken and, yielding to the weight of the dangers that surrounded them, they would listen to an appeal to lay down their arms. Accordingly they made a proclamation through a herald, asking if they would surrender themselves and their arms to the Athenians to be dealt with at their discretion.

38   When the Spartans heard the words of the herald, most of them lowered their shields and waved their hands to show that they accepted the offer. The fighting now came to an end, and a meeting took place between Cleon and Demosthenes and the Spartan commander Styphon, the son of Pharax. Of their previous commanders, the first, Epitadas, had been killed, and the second in command, Hippagretas, though still alive, was lying among the dead bodies and was thought to be dead himself. Styphon had been chosen, according to the Spartan practice, to take over the command in the third place, if anything happened to the two senior officers. Now Styphon and his advisers said that they wished to send a herald to the Spartans on the mainland to ask what they should do. The Athenians refused to let any of them go, but themselves invited heralds to come from the mainland, and, after questions and answers had been exchanged two or three times, the last man to sail across to them from the Spartans on the mainland brought the following message: 'The Spartans order

you to make your own decision about yourselves, so long as you do nothing dishonourable.' They, after discussing the matter among themselves, surrendered themselves and their arms. For that day and the following night the Athenians kept them under guard, and on the next day, after putting up a trophy on the island, they got ready to sail, distributing the prisoners among the captains of triremes to be guarded by them. The Spartans on the mainland sent a herald over and took back the bodies of their dead. The numbers of those killed and captured alive on the island were as follows. Altogether 440 hoplites had crossed over, and of these 292 were taken alive to Athens, the rest having been killed. About 120 of the prisoners were of the Spartan officer class. The Athenian losses were light, since there had been nothing in the nature of a pitched battle.

39   The total time taken over the siege, from the naval battle until the battle on the island, was seventy-two days. For about twenty days, during which the delegates who were making proposals of peace were absent, rations were allowed in, and for the rest of the time their food was smuggled in to them. Supplies of corn and other food were found on the island, since their commander Epitadas had issued smaller rations than were available from his stocks. The Athenians and the Peloponnesians now each withdrew their main forces from Pylos and went home. Cleon had kept his promise, however mad he may have been to have made it. For, just as he had undertaken to do, he brought the men back within twenty days.

40   This event caused much more surprise among the Hellenes than anything else that happened in the war. The general impression had been that Spartans would never surrender their arms whether because of hunger or any other form of compulsion; instead they would keep them to the last and die fighting as best they could. It was hard to believe that those who had surrendered were the same sort of people as those who had fallen. Indeed, there was an occasion afterwards when an Athenian ally in order to insult one of the prisoners from the island asked him whether it was the ones who had fallen who were the real Spartans. The reply was that 'spindles (by which he meant arrows) would be worth a great deal if they could pick out brave men from cowards', a remark which was

intended to show that the ones who died were simply the ones who came in the way of the stones and the arrows.

41   When the prisoners had been brought to Athens, the Athenians decided to keep them in prison until a settlement was arrived at, but that, if the Peloponnesians invaded Attica before then, they would take the men out and kill them. Pylos was firmly garrisoned, and the Messenians from Naupactus sent some of their best troops back there to what was in fact their old country, since Pylos was in what used to be Messenia. These troops carried out raids into Laconia and, helped by the fact that they spoke the same dialect as the inhabitants, did a lot of damage. The Spartans had had no previous experience of this type of guerilla warfare and, as the helots began to desert, they feared the spread of revolution in their country and became exceedingly uneasy about it. Though they did not want to reveal this to the Athenians, they still sent representatives to Athens and tried to get back Pylos and the prisoners. The Athenians, however, were aiming at gaining still more and, though frequent representations were made to them, they sent every Spartan representative back empty-handed. This completes the account of what happened at Pylos.

FURTHER ATHENIAN SUCCESSES

42 The same summer, just after the events related above, the Athenians made an expedition against the territory of Corinth. The force consisted of eighty ships, 2,000 Athenian hoplites, and 200 cavalry on board horse transports. These were supported by allied contingents from Miletus, Andros, and Carystus. Nicias, the son of Niceratus, with two colleagues, was in command.

This force set sail, and at dawn put in to land between Chersonese and Rheitus at the beach in the country overlooked by the Solygian hill. In ancient times the Dorians established themselves on this hill and made war on the Corinthians in the city, who were Aeolians; and there is now a village on the hill called Solygia. This beach where the fleet put in is about a mile and a half from the village, seven miles from Corinth, and two and a quarter from the Isthmus.

The Corinthians had already had information from Argos that the Athenian expeditionary force was directed against them, and some time previously had brought up all their troops to the Isthmus. The exceptions were those who lived beyond the Isthmus and 500 men who were away on garrison duty in Ambracia and Leucadia. All the rest were there in full force watching for the Athenian landing.

The Athenians, however, sailed in by night and escaped observation. The Corinthians were informed of the fact by beacons and came up quickly to resist them, leaving half of their army at

43 Cenchriae, in case the Athenians should march against Crommyon. Battus, one of the two generals who were present in the battle, took a company with him and went to occupy the village of Solygia, which was unfortified. The other general, Lycophron, attacked the enemy with the rest. First the Corinthians attacked the Athenian right wing, which had just landed in front of Chersonese, and then they joined battle with the rest of the army. It was hard hand-to-hand fighting throughout. The right wing of the Athenians with the Carystians, who were placed at the extreme end of the line, stood up to the Corinthians and, though with difficulty, pushed them back. The Corinthians then retired to a stone wall on the rising ground behind them, hurled down the stones on the Athenians, and, after singing the paean, charged them again. The Athenians met the attack, and once again the fighting was hand to hand. Now another Corinthian company came up to reinforce their left wing and beat back the Athenian right, driving it down to the sea; and then once again the Athenians and Carystians drove them back from the ships. Meanwhile the rest of the forces on both sides were fighting stubbornly, especially the Corinthian right wing, where Lycophron was meeting the attack of the Athenian left; for they expected that the Athenians would try to break through to the village of Solygia.

44 So for a long time both sides stood firm and yielded no ground. The Athenians had the advantage of their cavalry in the battle (the Corinthians having no cavalry at all), and finally the Corinthians were routed, and retreated to the hill, where they halted and stayed still without making any attempt to come down again. Most of their fatal casualties, including Lycophron their general,

took place in this rout of their right wing. So far as the rest of their army was concerned, it was forced back in the manner described, but there was no question of a general flight or of a very determined pursuit, so that they fell back to the higher ground and there took up their positions.

The Athenians, finding that the enemy was no longer offering battle, took up their dead, stripped the bodies of the enemy dead, and immediately put up a trophy. Meanwhile the half of the Corinthian army stationed at Cenchriae to guard against the Athenians sailing against Crommyon could not get a clear view of the battle because of Mount Oneion, but they saw the dust rising and, realizing what was happening, came to the relief at once. So also did the older men from the city of Corinth when they found out what the situation was.

The Athenians, seeing all these forces moving up against them, thought that they were reinforcements coming from the neighbouring Peloponnesian states, and quickly retreated to their ships, taking with them the spoils of battle and their own dead except for two, whose bodies they could not find and which were left on the field. Going on board the ships, they crossed over to the islands lying off the coast and from there sent a herald back and recovered under a truce the bodies which they had left behind. Two hundred and twelve Corinthians lost their lives in the battle, as against rather less than fifty Athenians.

45   The Athenians then set out from the islands and on the same day sailed to Crommyon in the territory of Corinth, about thirteen miles from the city. Here they came to anchor, laid waste the land, and spent the night on shore. Next day they first sailed along the coast to the territory of Epidaurus and made a landing there; then they proceeded to Methana, which is between Epidaurus and Troezen, and cut the peninsula off from the mainland by building a wall across the isthmus. They left behind a garrison which afterwards carried out raids on the territories of Troezen, Haliae, and Epidaurus. When the fortification of this place was completed, the fleet sailed back to Athens.

46   About the same time as the events related above Eurymedon and Sophocles, after leaving Pylos with the Athenian fleet for Sicily, arrived at Corcyra and marched with the party in the city

against the party which had established itself on Mount Istone after the revolution, gained control of the country districts and did much damage to the party in the city. They attacked their strong-hold and took it. The defenders, however, escaped in one body to some high ground. There they accepted the following terms: that they were to surrender their mercenary troops, and that they themselves were to give up their arms and abide by the judgement of the people of Athens. The generals brought them across under truce to the island of Ptychia to be kept under arrest there until they could be sent to Athens, on the understanding that if any of them were caught trying to escape, the treaty would cease to be effective in the case of all of them.

At this point the leaders of the popular party at Corcyra, fearing that when the prisoners got to Athens the Athenians might not put them to death, adopted the following scheme. They secretly sent in to the island people who were on friendly terms with a few of the prisoners and got to work on them, pointing out that they were only speaking for their own good, that it would be much wiser for them to run away as quickly as possible, and that they themselves would provide them with a boat; all this because the

47 Athenian generals were on the point of handing them over to the popular party in Corcyra. These methods of persuasion were successful. The escape was so organized that they were caught in the act of sailing out, the treaty thereupon became void, and all the prisoners were given up to the people of Corcyra. Much of the responsibility for this must rest with the Athenian generals. They made it obvious that, they themselves being on the way to Sicily, they did not want others to have the credit of taking the prisoners to Athens, and this attitude of theirs encouraged the conspirators to act boldly and made their arguments more con-vincing.

When they had the prisoners in their hands the Corcyraeans shut them up in a large building, and afterwards took them out in batches of twenty at a time and made them pass between two lines of hoplites drawn up to form a lane along which the prisoners went bound together, and were beaten and stabbed by those between whom they passed when anyone saw a personal enemy among them. Men with whips went along with them to hurry on their

48 way those who were going forward too slowly. About sixty men
were taken out in this way and killed before the others in the
building realized it, since they thought that they were only being
moved from one prison to another. Finally, however, someone
told them, and they became aware of what was happening and
called out for the Athenians to kill them themselves, if they wished
to do so. They refused any longer to go out of the building and
said that they would do their utmost to prevent anyone coming
into it. The Corcyraeans themselves had no idea of forcing their
way in by the door; instead they got up on to the top of the building, demolished the roof, and hurled down tiles and shot arrows
at the people below, who protected themselves as well as they
could, though in fact most of them now began to take their own
lives by driving into their throats the arrows that were shot at
them or by hanging themselves with cords taken from some beds
that happened to be there, or with strips made out of their own
clothing. Night fell on the scene and for a great part of the night
they were still doing themselves to death by all manner of means
and still being killed by the arrows of those on the roof. When it
was day the Corcyraeans piled them up and bundled them on to
wagons and took them outside the city. The women who had been
captured in the stronghold were sold as slaves.

In this way the Corcyraeans in the mountains were destroyed by
the popular party. It had been a great revolutionary struggle, but,
so far as the period of this war is concerned, it was now over,
since of the two parties one had practically ceased to exist. The
Athenians meanwhile sailed away to Sicily, their original destination, and carried on the war with their allies there.

49   At the end of the summer the Athenians in Naupactus supported
by the Acarnanians made an expedition against Anactorium, the
Corinthian city that lies at the entrance to the Ambracian Gulf.
They took the city by treachery, and the Acarnanians then sent
out settlers themselves from all parts of their country and occupied
the place. So the summer ended.

50   In the following winter Aristides, the son of Archippus, one of
the commanders of the Athenian ships which were sent out to
collect money from the allies, captured at Eion, on the Strymon, a
Persian called Artaphernes, who was on his way to Sparta from

the King of Persia. He was taken to Athens, and there the Athenians had his dispatches translated from the Assyrian characters and read them. A number of subjects were mentioned, but the main point for the Spartans was this – that the King did not understand what they wanted, since the many ambassadors who had come to him all said different things: if, therefore, they had any definite proposals to make, they were to send him some delegates with this Persian. Afterwards the Athenians sent Artaphernes back in a trireme to Ephesus and sent some ambassadors with him. There, however, they heard that Artaxerxes, the son of Xerxes, had just died (his death took place just about this time), and they returned home.

51   The same winter the people of Chios also demolished their new fortifications as the result of pressure from the Athenians, who suspected them of contemplating a revolt. They did, however, secure from the Athenians the most reliable guarantees possible that Athens had no intention of altering the existing state of affairs in Chios. So ended the winter, and with it the seventh year of this war recorded by Thucydides.

52   At the very beginning of the following summer there was a partial eclipse of the sun at the time of the new moon, and at the beginning of the same month there was an earthquake. Now the exiled party from Mytilene and the rest of Lesbos, setting out, most of them, from the mainland, and supported by mercenaries hired from the Peloponnese and others engaged locally, captured Rhoeteum and then gave it back again without having done any damage for a ransom of 2,000 Phocacan staters. Afterwards they marched against Antandrus and took the city as the result of treachery. Their plan was to liberate the other cities also which are known as the Actaean cities and which used to be possessions of Mytilene, but now were held by Athens, and they attached particular importance to Antandrus. Once they established themselves there it would be easy for them to build ships, since there was timber on the spot, and Ida was so close; other supplies would also be available, and, with this base in their hands, they could easily make raids on Lesbos, which was not far away, and subdue the Aeolian towns on the mainland. This was the plan which they intended to put into operation.

53   In the same summer the Athenians made an expedition against
Cythera with a force of sixty ships, 2,000 hoplites, a small number
of cavalry, and some allied contingents from Miletus and other
places. The commanders were Nicias, the son of Niceratus, Nicostratus, the son of Diitrephes, and Autocles, the son of Tolmaeus.
Cythera is an island lying off Laconia opposite Malea. The population is Spartan, though they belong to the semi-independent class.
Every year a Commissioner for Cythera was sent out there from
Sparta, and they also used to send out regularly a garrison of
hoplites. In fact they took great care of the place, since it was the
port for merchant ships from Egypt and Libya and also served as a
protection to Laconia from attack by pirates from the sea – which
is its one vulnerable point, since the whole of Laconia juts out
into the Sicilian and the Cretan seas.

54   Here the Athenian expeditionary force put in to land. With ten
ships and 2,000 hoplites from Miletus they captured the city of
Scandea, on the sea; with the rest of their force they made a landing on the part of the island that faces Malea and moved forward
against the city of Cythera, where they found all the inhabitants
drawn up ready to meet them. Battle was joined, and for some
time the people of Cythera stood firm, but finally they were
routed and took refuge in the upper city. Afterwards they came to
terms with Nicias and the other commanders, agreeing to submit
themselves to the discretion of Athens so long as their lives were
guaranteed. Negotiations had been going on previously between
Nicias and some of the people of Cythera, and it was because of
this that the surrender was arranged so quickly and on terms so
advantageous, both for the present time and for the future, to the
Cytherians. Otherwise the Athenians would have expelled the
population of the island, since they were of Spartan blood and their
island lay so close to Laconia.

     After the surrender the Athenians occupied the town of Scandea
on the harbour and put a garrison into Cythera itself. They then
sailed to Asine, Helus, and most of the places on the coast, making
landings and spending the night on shore whenever it was convenient to do so. So for about seven days they went on laying the
country waste.

55   As for the Spartans, who saw Athens in possession of Cythera

and who expected that there would be other landings of the same
sort on their territory, there was no one point where they met the
Athenians in full force. Instead they sent all over the country
garrisons of hoplites, the size of each one depending on the needs
of the particular area, and in general they stayed very much on the
defensive. What they feared was that there might be a revolution
against the government after the great and unexpected disaster at
Sphacteria, with Pylos and Cythera now in enemy hands, and
committed as they were on every side to a form of warfare where
mobility was what counted and where attacks were difficult to
guard against. Thus they raised a force of 400 cavalry and a force
of archers – something quite at variance with their normal way of
doing things – and in fact they now became more than ever
irresolute in their military conduct; they were faced with something outside the scope of their existing organization, namely a
war fought on the seas and fought against Athenians – people who
thought that every moment when they were not attacking was so
much sacrificed from their expectation of achievement. Then, too,
they were very greatly disheartened by the many unpredictable
blows of fortune which had fallen upon them in such a short time,
and they were constantly afraid that some other disaster might
overtake them like the one at Sphacteria. For this reason they
lacked confidence when they went into battle; they had had no
previous experience of misfortune, and so their morale collapsed
and they thought that whatever step they took would prove to be
a mistake.

56   So now when the Athenians laid waste the Spartan coasts they
rarely met with any resistance. When a landing was made in the
area of any particular garrison, the defenders were in the mood
which I have described and considered that they were in insufficient
numbers for action. There was one garrison which did make a
stand in the neighbourhood of Cotyrta and Aphrodisia, and when
it charged it caused a panic among the scattered crowd of light
armed troops; but on being confronted with the hoplites it fell
back again, losing a few men and leaving some arms on the field.
The Athenians put up a trophy for this action before sailing away
to Cythera.

From Cythera they sailed round the coast to Epidaurus Limera, and after laying waste part of the country they came to Thyrea which is part of the Cynurian country on the frontier between Laconia and the territory of Argos. It was a Spartan possession, but the Spartans had given it over as a home for the exiled people of Aegina because of the help they had given to Sparta at the time of the earthquake and the revolt of the helots, and because they had always been on the side of Sparta in spite of the fact that they were subjects of Athens.

57   While the Athenians were still on their way, the Aeginetans abandoned the fortifications on the coast which they were in the process of constructing, and retreated to the upper city where they lived and which is rather more than a mile from the sea. One of the Spartan garrisons in the area, which had been helping them with their fortifications, refused the request of the Aeginetans to come inside the city wall with them, since they thought it would be dangerous for them to be shut up inside. Instead they retired to higher ground and there, considering the odds too great for them, they stayed without making a move. Meanwhile the Athenians landed, moved forward at once with their whole army and captured Thyrea. They burnt the city and looted the property inside. They took back with them to Athens all the Aeginetans who were not killed in the fighting, together with their Spartan commander, Tantalus, the son of Patrocles, who had been wounded and taken prisoner. They also took with them a few people from Cythera whom for security reasons they thought should be removed. These the Athenians decided should be placed on the islands; the rest of the inhabitants of Cythera were to keep their own land and pay a tribute of four talents; all the Aeginetans who had been taken prisoner were, because of the inveterate hatred between the two peoples, to be put to death; and Tantalus was to be imprisoned with the other Spartans from Sphacteria.

PEACE IN SICILY

58 The same summer in Sicily an armistice was arranged first between the people of Camerina and Gela. Afterwards representatives from all the other Sicilian states met together at Gela and discussed

the possibilities of making a general settlement. A number of different points of view were expressed as the various delegates came forward with their complaints and their claims in respect of matters in which they considered they were being unfairly treated. Finally Hermocrates, the son of Hermon, a Syracusan, whose speech was in fact the most influential of all, spoke to the conference as follows:

59   'Men of Sicily, in what I am going to say I shall not be speaking as a representative of a city of minor importance or of one which has suffered particularly heavily through the war; what I want to do is to put clearly before you all the policy which I consider to be the best one for Sicily as a whole. That war is an evil is something which we all know, and it would be pointless to go on cataloguing all the disadvantages involved in it. No one is forced into war by ignorance, nor, if he thinks he will gain from it, is he kept out of it by fear. The fact is that one side thinks that the profits to be won outweigh the risks to be incurred, and the other side is ready to face danger rather than accept an immediate loss. If, however, on these very points both sides happen to be choosing the wrong moment for action, then there is something to be gained from attempts at mediation. And this, if we could only be convinced of it, is just what we need most at the present time.

'When we went to war in the first place we all, no doubt, had the idea of furthering our own private interests, and we have the same idea now that we are attempting, by a process of claims and counterclaims, to arrange a settlement. And if things do not work out so that everyone goes away with what he considers his due,

60 then no doubt we shall go to war again. Yet, if we are sensible, we should realize that this conference is not simply concerned with the private interests of each state; we have also to consider whether we can still preserve the existence of Sicily as a whole. It is now, as I see it, being threatened by Athens, and we ought to regard the Athenians as much more forcible arguments for peace than any words that can be spoken by me. They are the greatest power in Hellas, and here they are among us with a few ships, watching for us to make mistakes, and, though by nature we must be their enemies, they are, under the cover of a legal alliance, trying to arrange matters to suit themselves. Now if we fight among

ourselves and call in the help of the Athenians, who are only too
willing to join in whether they are called for or not; if we then
proceed to use our own resources in weakening ourselves, thus
doing the preliminary work for their future empire, the likely
thing to happen is that, when they see us exhausted, they will
come here one day with larger forces and will attempt to bring all
of us under their control.

61   'Yet, if we are sensible, our aim in calling in allies and running
additional risks should be to win for ourselves something that does
not belong to us rather than to ruin what we have already. We
should realize that internal strife is the main reason for the decline
of cities, and will be so for Sicily too, if we, the inhabitants, who
are all threatened together, still stand apart from each other, city
against city. Having grasped this point, we should make friends,
man with man and city with city, and should set out on a united
effort to save Sicily as a whole. No one should have the idea that,
while the Dorians among us are enemies to the Athenians, the
Chalcidians are quite safe because of their Ionian blood. Athenian
intervention has nothing to do with the races into which we are
divided; they are not attacking us because they hate one or the
other; what they want is the good things of Sicily which are the
common property of us all. They made this quite clear recently by
the way in which they received the invitation of the Chalcidians.
The Chalcidians had never once sent any help to Athens according
to their treaty with her; but Athens went out of her way zealously
to provide even more than the treaty bound her to do. Now it is
perfectly understandable that the Athenians should have these
ambitions and should be making their plans accordingly. I am not
blaming those who are resolved to rule, only those who show an
even greater readiness to submit. For men in general it is always
just as natural to take control when there is no resistance as to
stand out against aggression. And we are making a great mistake
if, knowing all this, we fail to take our precautions, or if we have
come here on the assumption that we have anything more important to do than to join forces in dealing with the danger that
threatens us all. We could quickly be rid of it, if we would agree
among ourselves, since the Athenians are not attacking us from
bases in their own country, but only from bases in the country of

those states here who have called them in. So instead of war following upon war, our differences are quietly settled in peace; and as for those who were called in from outside, they came here with what looked like a good excuse for their evil ends, but they will now have a really good reason to go away without having attained them.

62   'These, so far as the Athenians are concerned, are the great advantages to be found in adopting a wise policy. But apart from this, since it is admitted by everyone that peace is the greatest of blessings, ought we not therefore to make peace among ourselves? Suppose that one of you enjoys an advantage now or another one labours under some handicap, do you not think that in both cases, for preserving the advantage and for remedying the handicap, peace is better than war? Has not peace its honours and its glories, less attended by danger than those to be won in war? And are there not all those other advantages in peace, to describe which countless words would be required – as would be required also to enumerate the miseries of war?

'These are the points to consider; and so, instead of making light of my advice, you should make use of it, each one for his own preservation. And if there is anyone here who is convinced that either by violence or because of the justice of his cause he can attain some object of his own, let him not take too much to heart the disappointment of his ambition. He must realize that many before now have set out to punish aggression, and many others also have been confident that their power would secure them some advantage. Of these, the former, so far from being revenged, have often been destroyed, and with the latter it has often happened that, instead of gaining anything for themselves, they have had to give up what they had already. If an injury has been done, it does not necessarily follow that an attempt to redress it will be successful; nor can strength be relied upon simply because it is confident in itself. That imponderable element of the future is the thing which counts in the long run, and, just as we are most frequently deceived by it, so too it can be of the greatest possible use to us; for, if we all fear it alike, we shall think twice before we attack each other.

63   'We have now two reasons for being afraid: there is this

unspecified fear of an inscrutable future and there is the actual presence of the Athenians to terrify us. If therefore every one of us
does not get exactly everything that he thought he would get, we
should recognize that there are good grounds here to prevent this
happening. Let us instead dismiss from our territory the enemy
who is threatening us, and for ourselves, if we cannot make a peace
that will last for ever, let us at least come to terms for as long a
period as possible and put off our private quarrels to another time.
In a word, let us realize that by following my advice we shall each
keep the freedom of our own cities, and in these cities will be able
to act in the true spirit of independent men, returning good for
good and evil for evil; whereas if we take the opposite course we
shall be under the power of others, and then there will no longer
be any question of our being able to do harm to an opponent; the
very best that can happen to us is that we shall be forced to become
friends with our greatest enemies and enemies to those with whom
we should be friends.

64   'As for me, I am, as I said at the beginning, the representative of
a great city, more likely to be interested in aggression than in self-
defence. Yet, when I consider the dangers of the future, I am
prepared to give way to others. I do not think it right to do such
injuries to my enemies that I ruin myself, nor, out of a mad love
of aggression, to imagine that I can command fortune, which is
out of my control, in the same way as I can be the master of my
own designs. Instead I am prepared to make all reasonable concessions. And I call upon the rest of you to follow my example –
give way to each other rather than be forced to do so by our
enemies. There is nothing to be ashamed of in making concessions
to one's own people, a Dorian to a Dorian or a Chalcidian to
another of his own race, and, taken all together, we are all of us
neighbours, living together in the same country, in the midst of
the sea, all called by the same name of Sicilians. There will be
occasions, no doubt, when we shall go to war again and also when
we shall meet together among ourselves and make peace again.
But when we are faced with a foreign invasion, we shall always, if
we are wise, unite to resist it, since here the injury of any one state
endangers all the rest of us. And we shall never again in future call
in allies from outside or arbitrators. By acting in this way we shall

be conferring immediately two benefits on Sicily – release from the̅ Athenians and the cessation of civil war; and for the future we shall have a country that is free in itself and not so much in danger from abroad.'

65   This was the speech of Hermocrates. The Sicilians took his advice and agreed among themselves to end the war, each state keeping what it had already, except that the people of Camarina were to have Morgantina on payment of a fixed sum of money to Syracuse. Those who were allies of the Athenians summoned the Athenians commanders and told them that they were going to make peace and that the treaty would apply also to the Athenians. Peace was then made, with the approval of the Athenian commanders, and afterwards the Athenian fleet sailed away from Sicily. However, when they arrived home the Athenians in Athens banished two of the generals, Pythodurus and Sophocles, and fined the third, Eurymedon, on the grounds that they had been bribed to leave Sicily when it was in their power to have taken control of the island. Such was the effect on the Athenians of their present good fortune that they thought that nothing could go wrong with them; that the possible and the difficult were alike attainable, whether the forces employed were large or wholly inadequate. It was their surprising success in most directions which caused this state of mind and suggested to them that their strength was equal with their hopes.

FIGHTING AT MEGARA

66 The following events also took place in the same summer. The Megarians in the city of Megara were suffering badly from the war with Athens, since the Athenians invaded their country twice every year in full force. They were also hard pressed by their own exiles at Pegae who had been driven out in a revolution by the democratic party and were now causing trouble by acts of brigandage. They therefore began to talk among themselves to the effect that it would be a good thing to recall the exiles and not allow the city to be weakened by having to fight two enemies at once. The friends of the exiled party, seeing how the general talk

was going, came forward more openly themselves and kept insisting on the merits of the proposal. As for the leaders of the democratic party, they realized that, because of all the sufferings they had undergone, the mass of the people would be incapable of standing firm in their support, and so in terror they entered into negotiations with the Athenian generals, Hippocrates, the son of Ariphron, and Demosthenes, the son of Alcisthenes, with a view to surrendering the city to them. They considered that they would be safer this way than if the party whom they had exiled was brought back.

The arrangement made was that the Athenians should first occupy the long walls (nearly a mile long, from the city to the harbour of Nisaea), to prevent the Peloponnesians coming up in support from Nisaea, which had been entirely garrisoned by their troops, in order to make sure of the loyalty of Megara. Afterwards they would try to secure the surrender of the upper town, and, once the first move had been carried out, the Megarians would be more likely to agree to this.

67   When the two sides had made their plans about what was to be said and done, the Athenians sailed by night to Minoa, the island off Megara, and with 600 hoplites under the command of Hippocrates established themselves in a quarry not far off, from which stones used to be taken for the walls. Demosthenes, the other general, with a force consisting of Plataeans and Athenian home guards, placed himself in ambush near the temple of Enyalius, which was even nearer. No one that night knew anything of what was going on, except those who were supposed to know.

Just before dawn the party in Megara who were to betray the city began to carry out the plan. So as to secure the opening of the gates, they had been in the habit for some time past, with the permission of the officer on guard, of taking out by night a sculling boat which they carried on a cart along the ditch to the sea, pretending that they were going on a raid. Before daybreak they used to bring the boat back on the cart through the gates and take it inside the walls – the idea being, so they said, to bewilder the Athenian blockading force at Minoa, since at dawn there would be no boat visible at all in the harbour.

So now, when the cart was at the gates and the gates were

opened in the usual way to let the boat in, the Athenians (with whom all this had been planned) saw what was happening and came out of their ambush, running as fast as they could, so as to get there before the gates were shut again and while the cart was still in the entrance to stop them being shut. At the same time the Megarians on the Athenian side began to kill the guards at the gate. The first to run inside were Demosthenes and his Plataeans and home guards at the place where the trophy now stands. By now the Peloponnesians who were nearest the scene of action had realized what was happening and were coming to the rescue, but they were engaged and defeated by the Plataeans, who secured the gates and kept them open for the entry of the Athenian hoplites.

68   Then, as the Athenians troops came pouring in, each man made for the wall. At first some of the Peloponnesian garrison stood firm and fought back, and a few of them were killed. Most of them, however, ran away, terrified by this enemy attack by night and at finding the Megarian traitors also fighting against them, and imagining that the whole people of Megara had gone over to the other side. It also happened that the Athenian herald on his own initiative shouted out a proclamation saying that any Megarian who wished to do so was to come over and join the Athenians. When the Peloponnesians heard this, their resistance collapsed. They felt sure now that they were being attacked by the combined forces of Athens and Megara, and they took refuge in Nisaea.

By dawn the walls had already been captured and the Megarians in the city were in a state of great confusion. The people who had been in contact with the Athenians, supported by the rest of the democratic party, who knew what the idea was, said that what they must do was to open the gates and march out to battle. Once the gates were opened it had been agreed that the Athenians were to rush in, and that the pro-Athenian party, to avoid the risk of being hurt, were to be marked out from the rest by putting on a lot of olive oil. By now it was all the safer for them to open the gates, because the 4,000 Athenian hoplites from Eleusis with 600 cavalry had arrived according to the arrangements made, after having marched all night.

The pro-Athenian party had put the oil on themselves and were already at their positions by the gates when one of them who was in the plot revealed it to the opposite party, who then all joined together and came up saying that there must be no going out of the city; indeed, they had never risked doing so before, when they were stronger than now; and that it was wrong to put the city into such an obviously dangerous position. And they went on to say that if their advice was not taken, then the fighting would start there and then. They gave no sign that they knew what the plot was, but merely insisted that their advice was the best, and at the same time they stayed close to the gates and watched them, so that the conspirators had no chance of doing what they meant to do.

69   The Athenian generals realized that something had gone wrong with the plan and that it was no longer possible to capture the city by assault. They therefore started immediately to blockade Nisaea, thinking that, if they could take the place before help arrived, Megara also would soon surrender. Iron, stone-masons, and everything else required were quickly brought up from Athens. They started from the wall which they held and from there walled off the place from Megara by building fortifications that extended down to the sea at each side of Nisaea. Each detachment of the army had its own sector of the wall or ditch to complete; stones and bricks from the suburbs were used, and they cut down fruit trees and other wood for the building of palisades where necessary. There were also some of the houses in the suburbs, which, when they had been strengthened with battlements, came naturally into the system of fortification.

So for the whole of this day the work went on. Next day by the afternoon, when the wall was very nearly finished, the garrison in Nisaea grew frightened. They were without food (since they used to get their provisions daily from the upper city), they had no expectations that the Peloponnesians would come up quickly to help them, and they assumed that the Megarians were against them. So they surrendered to the Athenians on the condition that they should each be ransomed, after giving up their arms, for a fixed sum of money; their Spartan commander and any other Spartans there might be in the place were to be dealt with as the Athenians thought fit. On these terms the surrender was arranged and the garrison came out. The Athenians then demolished the long walls at the point where they joined the city of Megara, took possession of Nisaea, and made preparations for their next move.

70   Now at this time the Spartan officer Brasidas, the son of Tellis, happened to be in the neighbourhood of Sicyon and Corinth getting ready an army for Thrace. As soon as he heard of the capture of the walls he became alarmed about the Peloponnesian garrison in Nisaea and feared that Megara itself might be captured. He therefore sent to the Boeotians, instructing them to come quickly with their army and meet him at Tripodiscus, a village in the Megarid below Mount Geraneia. At the same time he set out himself with 2,700 Corinthian hoplites, 400 Phliasians, 600 Sicyonians, and all the troops of his own command that had already been enrolled, expecting to find that Nisaea had not yet been captured. When he found that it had been (he had marched out to Tripodiscus by night), he took 300 picked men from his army and, before his presence could be detected, marched up to the city of Megara without being observed by the Athenians, who were down by the sea. His idea was to say that he would attempt to recapture Nisaea and, if possible, he would actually make the attempt; but most important of all was to get into Megara and hold it. He therefore asked the Megarians to let him and his men inside the town and told them that he had hopes of recovering Nisaea.

71   But the two parties in Megara were both apprehensive. One party feared that he might restore the exiles and drive them out; the other party that the democrats, just because of this fear of theirs, might attack them and so, with fighting going on inside and the Athenians on the watch so close outside, the city would be lost. They therefore refused to let Brasidas in, both sides preferring to remain quiet and see what the future would bring. They all expected that there would be a battle between the Athenians and the relieving army, and each side thought it safer for themselves not to join the party of their friends until that party had been victorious in battle.

Brasidas, after failing to get his own way, went back to the rest 72 of his army. At dawn the Boeotians joined him. Even before Brasidas sent to them they had intended to come to the help of Megara, thinking that the danger in which it stood affected them too, and they had already mustered in full force at Plataea. When

the messenger from Brasidas arrived they became all the more
eager to help and sent him 2,200 hoplites and 600 cavalry, returning home with the greater part of their forces. The whole army
was now together, and amounted to at least 6,000 hoplites.

The Athenian hoplites were round Nisaea and along the sea-
shore, drawn up in formation; but the light troops were dispersed
over the plain. These light troops were driven back to the sea by
the Boeotian cavalry, whose attack came as a complete surprise
to them, since previously no help had ever come to Megara from
anywhere. The Athenian cavalry then rode out against the Boeotians, and engaged them. In this cavalry battle, which lasted for a
considerable time, both sides claim to have won. The leader of the
Boeotian cavalry and a few others who had pushed forward as far
as Nisaea itself were certainly killed by the Athenians and stripped
of their armour; and the Athenians, with these dead bodies in their
hands, gave them back under a truce and put up a trophy. But
with regard to the battle as a whole, it ended without either side
having won a decisive victory, and the Boeotians went back to
their own army, while the Athenians went back to Nisaea.

73   After this Brasidas and his army moved nearer to the sea and to
the city of Megara. They took up a position on suitable ground
and stayed there in battle formation, expecting that the Athenians
would attack them and knowing that the people of Megara were
waiting to see which side would win. This plan seemed to them a
good one from every point of view; there was no need for them
to make the first move or go out of their way to risk the danger of
battle, since they were making it perfectly clear that they were
prepared to defend themselves, and so might fairly be able to
claim a victory without having to exert themselves; and at the
same time this suited their interests with regard to Megara. For if
they had failed to appear, there would have been no chance for
them at all. They would certainly have been regarded as defeated
and would have lost the city at once. As it was, it was quite
possible that the Athenians might not be inclined to join battle and
they might attain their object without having to do any fighting
at all. And this, in fact, was what happened. The Athenians formed
up outside the long walls and, since no attack was made on them,
they also remained in their positions. According to the calculations

of their generals they would be running an undue risk in starting a battle against superior numbers. They had already gained most of their objects; now, if they won the battle, they would capture Megara, but if they lost, the strength of the best divisions in their hoplite army would be seriously impaired. The enemy, on the other hand, had a force consisting of contingents from various states, each one of which was only risking a portion of its entire army, and consequently they might be expected to show greater daring. So for some time they stood still and neither side made a move. The Athenians then went back to Nisaea, and afterwards the Peloponnesians also retired to their original positions. At this the friends of the exiled party in Megara gained confidence and, on the supposition that Brasidas had been victorious and the Athenians were no longer willing to give battle, opened the gates to Brasidas and the commanders from the various states, welcomed them into the city and entered into negotiations with them, the pro-Athenian party being now too terrified to stir.

74   After this Brasidas allowed his allied contingents to disperse to their various cities, and himself returned to Corinth, where he went on with preparations he had started already for the expeditionary force for Thrace. The Athenians also returned home, and those of the Megarians in the city who were most implicated in the plot with the Athenians, knowing that they had been discovered, immediately slipped away. The others joined in discussions with the friends of the exiles and recalled the exiled party from Pegae, after solemn oaths had been sworn that they would merely give the city the best council they could and there would be no recriminations for the past.

However, as soon as the exiles got into power they held a review of the hoplites, the various bodies of troops being stationed in different parts of the city. They then picked out about a hundred men, personal enemies and also those who appeared to have been the chief collaborators with the Athenians. The people were then forced to give their verdict openly on these men, and they were condemned and put to death. A strict oligarchy was then established in the city. It was a change of government made after a revolution by a very few people, and yet it lasted for a very long time.

BRASIDAS IN THRACE

75 In the same summer the Mytilenians were going to carry out their plan of fortifying Antandros, but Demodocus and Aristides, the commanders of the Athenian ships sent out to collect tribute, heard when they were at the Hellespont (the third commander, Lamachus, with ten ships had sailed into the Pontus) that the place was being fortified and feared that it might become just as much a danger as Anaia was to Samos. This was where the exiled party from Samos had established themselves and from which they helped the Peloponnesians by sending them pilots for their fleet, at the same time creating a state of disturbance in the city of Samos and welcoming all exiles from there.

76   They therefore collected forces from the allies and set sail. They defeated in battle those who came out from Antandros to oppose them and retook the place. Not long afterwards Lamachus, who had sailed into the Pontus, lost his ships while at anchor in the river Calex, in the territory of Heraclea, as a result of a sudden flow of water caused by floods in the upper country. He himself with his army went on foot through the Bithynian Thracians who live in Asia beyond the straits and reached Chalcedon, the Megarian colony at the mouth of the Pontus.

The same summer, directly after the return from the Megarid, the Athenian general Demosthenes arrived at Naupactus with forty ships. There had been some people in the cities of Boeotia who had been intriguing with him and with Hippocrates with a view to overthrowing the regime and introducing a democracy, as at Athens. Ptoeodorus, an exile from Thebes, had taken the chief part in these negotiations, and the plans made were as follows. The town of Siphae, which is on the sea in Thespian territory in the Gulf of Crisa, was to be betrayed to Athens by one party. Another party, from Orchomenus, were to hand over Chaeronea (which belongs to what used to be called Minyan, but is now called Boeotian Orchomenus), and the exiled party from Orchomenus were particularly active in the plot and hired troops from the Peloponnese. Some Phocians also took part in it. Chaeronea is on the frontier of Boeotia, close to the city of Phanotis in Phocis.

Meanwhile the plan was for the Athenians to seize Delium, the temple of Apollo in the territory of Tanagra looking towards Euboea. All this was to be done at the same time on a fixed day, so that the Boeotians, instead of being able to march out against the Athenians in full force at Delium, would have to deal with local troubles, each in their own area. If everything went well and Delium could be fortified, it was expected that, even though there might not be an immediate revolution in the cities of Boeotia, nevertheless the existing state of affairs could not last for long once these places were occupied, and the whole land exposed to raiding parties, and an easy refuge open to all who were against the government. Things, in fact, would in the end go as the conspirators wished, since the Athenians would be there to support the rebels, and the government would be unable to produce a united force to oppose them.

77　This was the plan as arranged. Hippocrates himself, with an army from Athens, was to march into Boeotia when the time came. Meanwhile he sent Demosthenes out first with the forty ships to Naupactus, so that he could raise an army in that area from the Acarnanians and other allies and then set sail to receive the surrender of Siphae. A day was fixed between them on which both operations were to be carried out simultaneously. When Demosthenes arrived he found that Oeniadae had been compelled by the combined forces of the Acarnanians to join the Athenian alliance. He himself called up all the allied forces in the area and marched against Salynthius and the Agraeans. After compelling them also to join in with Athens, he made his preparations so that he could arrive at Siphae on the day that had been arranged.

78　About the same time of the summer Brasidas was on his way to the Thracian area with 1,700 hoplites. When he reached Heraclea in Trachis he sent on a messenger to his friends in Pharsalus, asking them to escort him and his army on their way. As a result the following people came to him at Melitia in Achaea – Panaerus, Dorus, Hippolochidas, Torylaus, and Strophacus, who was the official representative of the Chalcidians. Brasidas then set out, conducted also by some other Thessalians, including Niconidas from Larissa, who was a friend of Perdiccas.

It was never an easy thing to go through Thessaly unescorted, and of course with an army it was harder still. Indeed, to go through a neighbour's country without permission was something which among all Hellenic states alike provoked suspicion. Then, too, the people of Thessaly had always been on good terms with Athens. So that, if the local form of government had been demo-cratic instead of being in the hands of a powerful class, Brasidas would never have been able to go forward. Even as it was he was met on his march at the river Enipeus by some people of the other party who were for preventing him from going further and who asserted that he was acting illegally in travelling there without the consent of the whole people. To this the reply given by those who were escorting him was that they would certainly not lead him through the country against the will of the inhabitants; it was merely that he had arrived unexpectedly and they, who were friends of his, were going with him. Brasidas himself said that he came as a friend to the land of Thessaly and to its people; it was against the Athenians, with whom he was at war, not against the Thessalians that his army was directed; he knew of no quarrel between Thessaly and Sparta to prevent either party going through the other's territory; now, if they refused him permission, he would certainly go no further (nor, indeed, could he); nevertheless he did not think it right that they should stop him.

When they heard this, the Thessalians went away, and Brasidas, on the advice of those who were escorting him, pushed on at full speed without halting, before any larger force should gather to prevent him. He thus got the whole way to Pharsalus on the day that he left Melitia, and camped on the river Apidanus. From there he went to Phacius, and from Phacius to Perrhaebia. At this point the Thessalians who had escorted him went back again, and the Perrhaebians, who are subjects of Thessaly, brought him to Dium, a Macedonian town under Mount Olympus on the Thessalian frontier, which is in the kingdom of Perdiccas.

79   In this way Brasidas got through Thessaly without any opposi-tion before any force could be assembled to stop him, and reached Perdiccas and Chalcidice. For it was Perdiccas and the Thracian towns in revolt from Athens who, alarmed at the Athenian suc-cesses, had managed to get the army to march from the Pelopon-nese. The Chalcidians thought that the next Athenian attack

would be against them (and at the same time the neighbouring cities who had not revolted also sent secret invitations to the Peloponnese); Perdiccas, though not openly at war with Athens, was also frightened because of his past differences with the Athenians, and in particular wanted to subdue Arrhabaeus, the King of the Lyncestians.

80 The fact that at the time Sparta was doing so badly made it easier for them to get this army from the Peloponnese. For now that the Athenians were making their attacks on the Peloponnese, and particularly on the actual territory of Sparta, the Spartans thought that the best way of diverting these attacks would be to give Athens, too, the same kind of trouble by sending an army to her allies, particularly as these allies were prepared to supply the army and were asking for it in order to be able to revolt. The Spartans were also glad to have a good excuse for sending some of their helots out of the country, since in the present state of affairs, with Pylos in enemy hands, they feared a revolution. In fact they were so frightened of their unyielding character and of their numbers that they had had recourse to the following plan. (Spartan policy with regard to the helots had always been based almost entirely on the idea of security.) They made a proclamation to the effect that the helots should choose out of their own number those who claimed to have done the best service to Sparta on the battlefield, implying that they would be given their freedom. This was, however, a test conducted in the belief that the ones who showed most spirit and came forward first to claim their freedom would be the ones most likely to turn against Sparta. So about 2,000 were selected, who put garlands on their heads and went round the temples under the impression that they were being made free men. Soon afterwards, however, the Spartans did away with them, and no one ever knew exactly how each one of them was killed.

Now, on this present occasion, the Spartans were glad to send out 700 as hoplites to serve with Brasidas. The rest of his army 81 were mercenaries whom he had raised from the Peloponnese. Brasidas himself was sent out by the Spartans largely because it was his own wish, though the Chalcidians also were eager to have him, a man who in Sparta itself had a great reputation for energy in every direction and who on his foreign service had shown himself to be so valuable to his country. And on this occasion it was his upright and moderate conduct towards the cities which caused most of them to revolt and enabled him to take others by treachery, so that when Sparta wanted to make peace (as she did in the end) she was in the position of having places to offer in exchange for those held by Athens, and in the meantime the Peloponnese was relieved of much of the burden of the war. Then, too, in the later period of the war, after the Sicilian expedition, the chief factor in creating a pro-Spartan feeling among the allies of Athens was the gallantry of Brasidas and the wisdom which he showed at this time – qualities which some knew from experience of them and others assumed because they had been told of them. He was the first to be sent out in this way, and by the excellent reputation which he won for himself on all sides he left behind a rooted conviction that the rest also were like him.

82   Now, as soon as the Athenians heard of his arrival in Thrace they declared war on Perdiccas, since they regarded him as being responsible for the expedition, and they kept a closer watch on 83 their allies in that area. Perdiccas, with Brasidas's army added to his own forces, immediately marched against Arrhabaeus, the son of Bromerus, King of the Lyncestian Macedonians, whose country bordered upon his own and whom, since he had a quarrel with him, he wished to subdue. But when he arrived with his army and Brasidas with it at the pass into Lyncus, Brasidas said that, before making war, he wished first to go and negotiate with Arrhabaeus, and see if he could make him join the Spartan alliance. Arrhabaeus had in fact already made overtures himself, saying that he was prepared to accept Brasidas as an arbitrator, and the Chalcidian representatives who were present had also advised him that in order to ensure having the full support of Perdiccas for their own affairs it was as well not to make his path too smooth for him at the outset. Then, too, the envoys whom Perdiccas had sent to Sparta had given the impression, while they were there, that he would bring into the Spartan alliance a great number of the places on his borders; and, on the basis of this, Brasidas thought himself entitled to consider the wider implications in dealing with Arrhabaeus. Perdiccas, on the other hand, replied that he had not brought

Brasidas there to act as an arbitrator in the differences that existed
between him and Arrhabaeus; his function was simply to destroy
those enemies whom he, Perdiccas, pointed out; and that while he
was maintaining half of Brasidas's army, it would be wrong for
Brasidas to enter into negotiations with Arrhabaeus. Brasidas,
however, would not accept this view. Against the wishes of Perdiccas he negotiated with Arrhabaeus and was persuaded by him
to lead his army away without invading his country. After this
Perdiccas, considering that he was being badly treated, paid only a
third of the expenses for the army, instead of a half.

84   In the same summer and directly afterwards Brasidas with the
Chalcidians marched against Acanthus, the colony of Andros, just
before the time of the vintage. On the question of receiving him
there were two distinct parties – on the one side those who had
joined the Chalcidians in inviting him, and on the other the
general mass of the people. However, because of their fears for
their fruit which was still outside the walls, the people were persuaded by Brasidas to allow him to come in by himself, and to
listen to what he had to say before they reached a final decision.
Thus Brasidas was allowed to enter and came before the assembly.
He was not at all a bad speaker either, for a Spartan. His speech to
them was as follows:

85   'Acanthians, the Spartans have sent out me and my army in
order to make good the cause which we proclaimed at the beginning of the war – namely that we were going to war with Athens
in order to liberate Hellas. If we have come late, it is because the
war at home has taken an unexpected course. What we hoped to
do was to bring Athens to the dust by our own unaided efforts and
without your having to risk anything. Now you must not blame
us for our delay, since, as soon as we got the chance, we have come,
and with your help we shall do our best to make the Athenians
give in. But I am amazed to find that instead of welcoming me
gladly you have shut your gates against me. We Spartans thought
that we were coming to allies who wanted us, who were imagining us with them even before we actually arrived; and so we
accepted all the risks of a march lasting for many days through
foreign country and put all our energy into the venture. It will be
a bad thing indeed if it turns out that you have different ideas and

are going to resist your own liberation and that of the other Hellenes. It is not only a case of you yourselves being against me:
others, too, to whom I go will be less likely to join me, since they
will think it very strange that you, to whom I came first – you,
with your important city and well known as you are for your
intelligence – have failed to welcome me. It will be impossible for
me to make people believe in my purpose; they will think either
that there is something unreal about the liberation which I offer,
or else that I have come here weak and powerless to defend you
against the Athenians, if they attack. Yet it was this same army of
mine which the Athenians, though in superior numbers, would
not venture to attack when I went to the relief of Nisaea, and it is
86 not likely that they will send across the sea against you an army as
big as the one they had there. As for me, I have not come here to
do harm to the Hellenes: my mission is to liberate them, and I can
point to the most solemn oaths sworn by my home government
guaranteeing the independence of all allies whom I bring over to
their side. And there is no question of our wanting to gain your
alliance by forcible or by treacherous means; it is just the opposite:
it is we who want to join you and help you to escape from your
bondage to Athens. It seems to me that I have given you very
adequate proofs of my intentions, and I see no reason why I personally should be mistrusted or thought to be incapable of protecting you. It is you who should, in my opinion, pluck up
courage and declare for me.

'Some of you may fear certain individuals and may be reluctant
to help me, in case I should put the city into the hands of some
group or other: such apprehensions are completely unjustified. I
have not come here to take sides in your internal affairs, and I do
not think that I should be giving you real freedom if I were to take
no notice of your own constitutions and were to enslave either the
many to the few or the few to the many. That would be even
worse than being governed by foreigners, and we Spartans would
earn no gratitude that way for our pains. Instead of honour and
glory, we should find reproach. We should show that we ourselves had fallen a prey to those very vices of which we accuse the
Athenians and because of which we are fighting this long war;
only these vices would be more hateful in us than in people who

never started by proclaiming their virtue. For it is more disgraceful, at least for those who have a name to lose, to gain one's ends by deceit which pretends to be morality than by open violence. Straightforward aggression has a certain justification in the strength that is given us by fortune; but the other form of attack comes 87 simply from the treacherous devices of an evil mind. To us these principles are of the utmost importance, and we are extremely careful to abide by them; and, in addition to the oaths which we have sworn, you could have no more reliable guarantee than is to be found in comparing our words with the actual facts, and so coming to the necessary conclusion that it is in our interest to act as we say we shall.

'If, now that I have made my position plain, you are going to say that you are unable to help, but have friendly feelings and so ought not to be made to suffer for rejecting me; that you regard liberty as a risky thing to have, that it is right to offer it only to those capable of receiving it and not to force it on anyone against his will, then I shall call upon the gods and heroes of your country to witness that I came here to help you and could not make you understand it. I shall lay waste your land and try to bring you over by force. And, once this point has been reached, I shall not consider that I am doing anything wrong. I shall consider that I have two good reasons on my side which force me to take this action: first, I must prevent Sparta from suffering from the money which you, our friends, will go on paying to the Athenians, if you refuse to join us; secondly, I must not allow the Hellenes to be hindered by you from throwing off their chains. Otherwise we should have no right at all to act as we are doing. We Spartans are only justified in liberating people against their own will, because we are acting for the good of one and all alike. We have no imperialistic ambitions; our whole effort is to put an end to imperialism, and we should be doing wrong to the majority, if we were to put up with your opposition to the independence which we are offering to all.

'Think of what I have said and make a wise decision. Make it your aim to be the first beginners of liberty in Hellas and ensure for yourselves an everlasting glory. Avoid the losses which might fall upon you as individuals, and win for your whole city the best and fairest of names.'

88   This was the speech of Brasidas. The people of Acanthus, after much had been said on both sides, voted by ballot, and the majority, partly because they were swayed by Brasidas's oratory, partly because they were frightened about their fruit, decided to revolt from Athens. They received the army inside the city, though first they made Brasidas pledge his own word for the oaths sworn by the Spartan government when they sent him out, guaranteeing the independence of all the allies whom he should win over. Soon afterwards Stagirus, a colony of Andros, also joined in the revolt from Athens. All this took place in the summer.

ATHENIAN DEFEAT AT DELIUM

89 It was at the beginning of the following winter that the places in Boeotia were supposed to be handed over to the Athenian generals Hippocrates and Demosthenes. Demosthenes was to be at Siphae with his fleet and Hippocrates was to go to Delium. However, a mistake was made about the dates on which they were each to set out. Demosthenes sailed to Siphae first with a force of Acarnanians and many other allies from those parts on board his ships, but failed to achieve anything. The plot had been betrayed by a Phocian from Phanotis called Nicomachus, who gave information to the Spartans, who in turn informed the Boeotians. Relief forces came up from the whole of Boeotia; Hippocrates was not yet there to make his diversion; and so Siphae and Chaeronea were firmly occupied in advance, and those who were in the plot, once they discovered that the mistake had been made, took no further action in the cities.

90   It was after this, and when the Boeotians had already returned from Siphae, that Hippocrates arrived at Delium with an army raised from the whole citizen body of Athens together with the resident aliens and foreigners in the city. Here he encamped with his army and began to fortify Delium in the following way. A ditch was dug all round the temple and its precincts; the earth thrown up from the digging was made to form a rampart in which stakes were fixed; vine wood was cut from the temple grounds and thrown in, together with stones and bricks from the houses

near by which they demolished. So they did everything they could to raise the level of the fortifications. Wooden towers were put up where necessary and where the temple buildings were inadequate for defence. (There was a point where the old colonnade had collapsed.) They began working on the third day after leaving Athens and continued during the fourth day and on the fifth day until dinner-time. Then, since most of the work was finished, the army moved away from Delium about a mile and a quarter on the return journey. Most of the light troops went straight on from here, but the hoplites halted for a rest. Hippocrates was still at Delium busy with his organization of the garrison and with making the proper arrangements for finishing the remainder of the fortifications.

91   During these five days the Boeotians were bringing up their forces to Tanagra. When the contingents had come in from all the cities and they found that the Athenians had already set out on their homeward journey, ten out of the eleven Commanders of Boeotia were opposed to the idea of giving battle, since the Athenians were no longer in Boeotia, but round about the frontier at Oropus when they halted. But Pagondas, the son of Aeolidas, one of the two Commanders of the Boeotians from Thebes (the other one was Arianthides, the son of Lysimachidas) and who was at this time in supreme command of the whole force, wanted to bring on a battle, thinking that the risk was worth taking. He had the men up in front of him by companies, so that they should not all leave their arms at the same time, and urged them to attack the Athenians and go out against them boldly. His address was as follows:

92   'Men of Boeotia, it ought never to have entered into the head of any one of us, your generals, that we should avoid battle with the Athenians simply because we no longer find them in our own country. They came here across the frontier, they have built a fortified post here, and their intention is to lay waste our land. They are therefore, I should imagine, still our enemies in the place from which they set out to do us harm; indeed they are our enemies wherever we may manage to catch them. And if at the present moment any of you think that it is safer to leave them alone, you should get rid of that idea. When one is being attacked and has to

think about the safety of one's own country, one cannot go in for calculations about what is prudent. That is more the thing to be done by those whose own country is secure and who, in the desire to make further conquests, are deliberately attacking someone else. And it is your tradition to fight a foreign army of invasion, whether it is in your country or anywhere near it. Much more should we do so in the case of Athenians, who also share the same frontier with us. In all relations with one's neighbours freedom is the result of being able to hold one's own, and as for these neighbours, who, not content with those close to them, are trying to spread their domination far and wide, with them we must simply fight it out to the last. We have, just across the water, the example of Euboea, and we know also how most of the rest of Hellas feels about Athens. And we should realize that, while others fight battles with their neighbours for one frontier or another, in our case, if we are conquered, there will be no more frontier disputes, because there will be only one frontier for the whole country. They will just come in and take what we have by force. In fact the Athenians are the most dangerous of all people to have living next door to one.

'Then, too, when people attack their neighbours in a spirit of great confidence in their own strength – as is the case with the Athenians now – they usually march all the more boldly against an enemy who makes no move against them and only defends himself on his own ground, but when they find someone who comes out to meet them outside his own frontiers and who will, if the occasion arises, take the initiative in attack, they are not so ready to come to grips. We have experience of this ourselves in dealing with these Athenians. By our victory over them at Coronea, in the days when, because of our internal quarrels, they were occupying Boeotia, we made our country secure right up to the present day. This is what we should remember, and the older ones among us must live up to what they did in the past, while the younger men, sons of those who did such great deeds at that time, must make it their endeavour not to disgrace that gallant reputation which is theirs by inheritance. We can be confident that we shall have on our side the god whose temple they have unlawfully fortified and now hold, confident too in the favourable appearance of the victims which we have sacrificed. Let us then go forward against them and show them that they must get what they want by attacking people who will not defend themselves, but as for us, we make it a point of honour always to fight for the freedom of our country and never unjustly to enslave the country of others, and from us they will not get away without having to fight for it.'

93   With these words of encouragement Pagondas persuaded the Boeotians to attack the Athenians. He quickly got his army on the move and led them forward, since it was already late in the day. When he was near the Athenian army, he halted in a position where, because of a hill in between, neither side could see the other, and there he put his troops into formation and prepared for battle.

Hippocrates was at Delium, but when he received the news that the Boeotians were advancing he sent orders to his army to form up into line, and not long afterwards was with them himself. He had left about 300 cavalry at Delium to guard the place if it was attacked and also to look out for their opportunity to intervene in the battle against the Boeotians.

The Boeotians detached some troops specially to deal with this force, and, when their preparations were complete, appeared over the crest of the hill and halted in the order in which they intended to fight. They had 7,000 hoplites, more than 10,000 light troops, 1,000 cavalry, and 500 peltasts. On the right were the troops from Thebes and its surroundings; in the centre were the Haliartians, the Coronaeans, the Copaeans, and others living round the lake; on the left were the Thespians, the Tanagraeans, and the Orcho-menians; the cavalry and the light troops were posted at each wing. The Thebans were drawn up twenty-five shields deep, the others in varying formations. So much for the Boeotian army and its order of battle.

94   On the Athenian side the hoplites were drawn up eight deep along the whole front, the numbers being equal to those of the enemy, and the cavalry were posted on each wing. There were no properly armed light troops present on this occasion, nor did Athens possess any. The ones who had joined in the invasion had been in much greater numbers than those on the Boeotian side, but most of them had merely followed the army inadequately armed, as part of the general expedition of foreigners and citizens

from Athens, and, since they started first on their way home, only a very few were still present.

Now that the armies were drawn up and on the point of joining battle, the general Hippocrates went along the Athenian ranks and encouraged them by speaking to them as follows:

95   'Athenians, this will only be a short speech, but a short speech is as good as a long one when it is addressed to brave men. I do not wish to rouse your emotions so much as to remind you of the facts. I do not want any of you to think that because we are in the country of foreigners this danger into which we are throwing ourselves does not concern us. We shall fight in their country, but we shall be fighting for our own. If we are victorious, the Peloponnesians, without the support of the Boeotian cavalry, will never again invade our land, and in one battle you will both gain this country and do much to free your own. Go forward, then, to meet them in the spirit of citizens of a city which we are all proud to call the first in Hellas, and like sons of the fathers who defeated these people before at Oenophyta with Myronides and so became the masters of Boeotia.'

96   Hippocrates, making this speech of encouragement, had got halfway along the line, but was prevented from going farther; for now the Boeotians, after Pagondas also had hurriedly addressed them, sang the paean and began to move forward down the hill. The Athenians advanced against them and the armies met together at a run. No contact was made between the extreme wings of either army, since both were alike held up by water-courses in the way. But everywhere else the fighting was stubborn, with shield pressing against shield. The Boeotian left, as far as the centre, was defeated by the Athenians, who did much damage here, particularly among the Thespians. For when the troops supporting them had given way, the Thespians were surrounded in a narrow space and cut down in close fighting. Some of the Athenians too were killed here by their own men who were confused by the encircling movement and mistook their identity.

In this part of the field, then, the Boeotians had the worst of it and fled back to the troops who were still fighting. But on the right, where the Thebans were, they got the better of the Athenians, pushing them back step by step at first and keeping up their pressure. It also happened that Pagondas, seeing that his left wing was in difficulties, had sent two squadrons of cavalry round the hill out of sight of the Athenians. When they suddenly came into view they caused a panic in the Athenian wing that had been victorious, since the soldiers imagined that this was another army bearing down on them. And now, what with this panic on one wing and with the Thebans pushing on and breaking through on the other, the whole Athenian army took to flight. Some fled towards Delium and the sea, others to Oropus, others to Mount Parnes or in any direction which seemed to offer hope of safety. The Boeotians followed them up and cut them down – particularly the Boeotian cavalry and the Locrians, who had come up just after the rout began. The pursuit, however, was cut short by the coming on of night, and so the bulk of the fugitives escaped more easily than they would have done otherwise. Next day the troops at Oropus and Delium returned home by sea, leaving a garrison at Delium,

97 which, in spite of everything, they still held. The Boeotians put up a trophy, collected their own dead, stripped the bodies of the Athenian dead, and set a guard over them. They then went back to Tanagra and made their plans for an assault on Delium.

Meanwhile a herald from the Athenians on his way to ask for the Athenian dead was met by a Boeotian herald, who turned him back, telling him that nothing was to be gained until he, the Boeotian, had completed his own mission. The Boeotian herald then came before the Athenians and delivered his message from the Boeotians, which was as follows: 'that the Athenians had done wrong and transgressed against Hellenic law. It was a rule established everywhere that an invader of another country should keep his hands off the temples that were in that country. The Athenians, however, had fortified Delium and were living in it. They were doing all the things there that men do in unconsecrated ground; they were drawing and using in the ordinary way the water which Boeotians never were allowed to touch except for the washing of hands before sacrifices. It was therefore for the god as well as for themselves that the Boeotians, in the name of the divinities of the place and of Apollo, warned the Athenians first of all to leave the temple and then take back what was their own.'

98 After this speech from the herald, the Athenians sent their own

herald to the Boeotians and declared that they had done nothing wrong with regard to the temple, nor would they do any harm to it in the future, if they could help it; it was not with any such intentions that they had occupied the temple in the first place, but only to use it in self-defence against the Boeotians, who were the real aggressors; under Hellenic law whoever was in control of a piece of country, whether large or small, invariably also took possession of the temples in that country, with the duty to maintain, as far as possible, the usual religious ceremonies; the Boeotians themselves and most other people who had driven out the original inhabitants of a place and occupied it themselves now regarded as their own the temples which, when they had first occupied them, were the property of others; the same would hold good of the Athenians if they had conquered more of Boeotia; as it was, the part that they occupied they considered as belonging to them, and did not propose to leave it of their own accord; as for disturbing the water, that was a case of necessity and not done because of any lack of proper religious feeling; they had been forced to use it in order to defend themselves against the Boeotians who had first invaded Attica; and it was reasonable to suppose that even the god would look indulgently on any action done under the stress of war and danger; certainly the altars of the gods were the refuge of those who had committed involuntary crimes, and it was proper to describe as real offenders against the law not those whose circumstances compelled them to take some rather violent step, but those who did evil when they were under no necessity of so acting; as for the dead bodies, the Boeotian attitude was a great deal more irreligious than the Athenian, for the Boeotians wanted to exchange the dead for the temple and the Athenians refused to give up the temple in order to receive back what was theirs by right; they demanded, therefore, that the condition that they should withdraw from Boeotia should be dropped; where they stood was Boeotian soil no longer; it was ground conquered by Athenian arms; let the Boeotians therefore follow the established custom and allow them to recover their dead under a truce.

99　To this the Boeotians replied that if the Athenians were in Boeotia they must leave that country before taking up their dead; if, on the other hand, they were in their own country, they could do as they wanted. The Boeotian view was that although the country round Oropus, where in fact the bodies were (since the battle had been fought on the frontier), was subject to Athens, the Athenians could not go and get the bodies without Boeotian permission. They saw no reason to grant a truce which was to operate on Athenian territory, and they considered that they were making a perfectly fair reply to the Athenians by using the formula 'first evacuate Boeotia, and then take what you are asking for'. The Athenian herald listened to what they said and returned without having achieved his object.

100   The Boeotians had immediately sent for javelin-throwers and slingers from the Malian Gulf. They were also reinforced by 2,000 Corinthian hoplites, who arrived after the battle, by the Peloponnesian garrison which had left Nisaea and by some Megarians. With this force they marched on Delium and made an assault on the fortifications. Various methods of attack were employed, and in the end they took the place by means of an engine constructed in the following manner. They took a great beam, sawed it in two parts, both of which they completely hollowed out, and then fitted the two parts closely together again, as in the joints of a pipe. A cauldron was then attached with chains to one end of the beam, and an iron tube, curving down into the cauldron, was inserted through the hollow part of the beam. Much of the surface of the beam itself was plated with iron. They brought up this machine from some distance on carts to the part of the wall that had been principally constructed of vines and other wood. When it was close to the wall, they inserted into their end of the beam large bellows and blew through them. The blast, confined inside the tube, went straight into the cauldron which was filled with lighted coals, sulphur, and pitch. A great flame was produced which set fire to the wall and made it impossible for the defenders to stay at their posts. They abandoned their positions and fled; and so the fortification was captured. Of the garrison some were killed and 200 were taken prisoner; most of the rest got to their ships and returned home.

101   Delium was recaptured on the seventeenth day after the battle, and soon afterwards the Athenian herald, knowing nothing of what had taken place, came back again to ask for the dead. Now

the Boeotians gave them to him without replying as they had done previously. Nearly 500 Boeotians fell in the battle, and nearly 1,000 Athenians, among whom was Hippocrates, the general; also a great number of light troops and baggage carriers.

Not long after this battle Demosthenes, not having met with any success in his voyage to Siphae and in the plans for the betrayal of that place, took the army which he had on board his ships (the Acarnanians, and Agraeans, and the 400 Athenian hoplites) and made a landing in the territory of Sicyon. Before all his ships had come to shore the people of Sicyon came up in force, routed the troops who had landed and drove them back to their ships, killing some and making prisoners of others. They then put up a trophy and gave back the dead bodies under an armistice.

About the same time as the battle of Delium occurred the death of Sitalces, the King of the Odrysians, who had marched against the Triballi and been defeated by them in battle. Seuthes, the son of Sparadocus, his nephew, succeeded to the kingdom of the Odrysians and of the rest of Thrace which had formed part of the dominion of Sitalces.

BRASIDAS CAPTURES AMPHIPOLIS

102 The same winter Brasidas with his allies from Thrace marched against Amphipolis, the Athenian colony on the river Strymon. There had been previous attempts to found a colony at the place where the city now stands – first by Aristagoras of Miletus, at the time when he was in flight from King Darius. He, however, was driven out by the Edonians. Thirty-two years after this the Athenians sent out there 10,000 settlers from their own citizens and volunteers from other places. This expedition was destroyed by the Thracians at Drabescus. Twenty-nine years afterwards the Athenians made another attempt, sending out Hagnon, the son of Nicias, as leader of the colony. They drove out the Edonians and established themselves at this place, which used to be called Nine Ways. The base from which they started their operations was Eion, their seaport and trading post at the mouth of the river, three miles from the present city, which was called Amphipolis by

Hagnon, because it was surrounded on two sides by the river Strymon, and he built it in such a way that it was a conspicuous sight both from the sea and from the side facing the mainland where he built a long wall across the loop of the river.

103   It was against this town that Brasidas now marched. He started from Arnae in Chalcidice, and by the evening arrived at Aulon and Bromiscus, where Lake Bolbe runs into the sea. After stopping for a meal, he pushed on during the night. The weather was stormy and there was snow in the air. He therefore made all the speed he could, as he wished to get to Amphipolis before anyone knew of his coming, except for the party who were to betray the place. Those who were plotting with him were some settlers from Argilus, a colony of Andros, who lived in Amphipolis and who were supported by others too who had been won over either by Perdiccas or by the Chalcidians. But the prime movers were the people of Argilus itself, who lived close by, had always been viewed with suspicion by the Athenians, and had their own designs on Amphipolis. The arrival of Brasidas in Thrace was their great opportunity, and for some time they had been intriguing with their fellow countrymen inside the city with a view to having the place betrayed. They now received Brasidas into Argilus and revolted from Athens. The same night before dawn they brought his army to the bridge over the river. The town itself is some distance from the crossing of the river and the walls did not reach down to it as they do now. The bridge was only lightly guarded, and Brasidas easily forced his way through and crossed the bridge, partly because there was treachery among the guard, partly because of the stormy weather and the unexpectedness of his attack. Thus at one stroke he gained possession of everything belonging to the

104   people of Amphipolis in the whole area outside the walls. His crossing of the bridge had been a complete surprise to the people in the city; some of those outside had been taken prisoner, others had fled inside the walls; and all this produced a great state of disturbance inside Amphipolis, particularly as the citizens themselves were mistrustful of each other. It is even said that Brasidas would probably have taken the city there and then, if he had marched straight on and not allowed his army to turn aside for plunder.

As it was, after he had overrun the country outside the walls, and when he found that his expectations from those inside the city were not being realized, he camped there with his army and made no further move for the present. In fact the party which was opposed to those who wanted to betray the town was in the majority and had succeeded in preventing the gates being opened immediately. They and Eucles, the general from Athens who was there to defend the place, sent to the other general in Thrace, Thucydides, the son of Olorus, the author of this history, who was then at the island of Thasos, a colony of the Parians, about half a day's sail from Amphipolis, asking him to come to their relief. As soon as he heard the news, he set sail at once with the seven ships that he had with him. His first aim, certainly, was to reach Amphipolis in time to prevent its surrender, and, if he failed in that object, at any rate to secure Eion before Brasidas could get there.

105   Brasidas meanwhile was alarmed at the prospect of the naval relief force coming from Thasos, and had also heard that Thucydides possessed the right of working the gold-mines in that part of Thrace and because of this had great influence with the inhabitants of the mainland. He therefore did his best to gain the town as quickly as possible, fearing that, once Thucydides had arrived, the people of Amphipolis would be confident that he could secure their safety by bringing up allied forces both from the sea and from the interior, and that thus the chance of getting them to surrender would be gone. He therefore put forward very moderate terms, making a proclamation to the effect that all who wished to do so, whether Amphipolitans or Athenians, could remain in the city with possession of their property and full political rights guaranteed to them; and those who did not wish to remain could take their property away with them and leave within five days.

106   This proclamation produced a considerable swing of opinion among the mass of the people, especially so because the Athenian element in the city was a small one, the majority being of mixed nationalities. Large numbers too of those who had been taken prisoner outside had relatives inside the city. Compared with what they had feared, they regarded the proclamation as a very fair offer; the Athenians were glad at having the opportunity to leave, since they considered that they had more to fear than the rest and at the same time did not expect that relief would come to them

quickly; while the general mass of the people found that they were being relieved unexpectedly from danger and also suffering no deprivation of their political rights. Seeing this change of feeling among the people, who would no longer listen to the Athenian general on the spot, those who were working with Brasidas now came forward openly to advocate his proposals; and so an agreement was reached and Brasidas was received into the city on the terms of his proclamation. In this way the city was surrendered, and late on the same day Thucydides with his ships sailed into Eion. As for Amphipolis, Brasidas had just taken it, and he was within a night of taking Eion too. If the ships had not arrived so quickly to relieve it, it would have been in his hands by dawn.

107   After this Thucydides organized the defence of Eion to keep it safe from any immediate attack by Brasidas and to secure it for the future. He received into it all those who, according to the terms of the treaty, had decided to move down from Amphipolis. Brasidas, with a number of boats, suddenly sailed down the river to Eion, to see if he could seize the headland running out from the wall, and so command the entrance. This attack was supported by land forces as well, but both attacks were beaten off and he went back to Amphipolis to arrange matters there. The Edonian city of Myrcinus came over to him, after the Edonian King Pittacus had been killed by the sons of Goaxis and by his own wife Brauro, and also, not long afterwards, the Thasian colonies Galepsus and Oesime. Perdiccas also arrived directly after the capture and worked in cooperation with Brasidas.

108   The capture of Amphipolis caused great alarm at Athens. The place was not only useful because it supplied timber for shipbuilding and brought in revenue; there was also the fact that, although the Spartans, provided that they got an escort from the Thessalians, could reach the allies of Athens up to the line of the Strymon, they could not go any further so long as they did not control the bridge, since there was a great lake formed by the river above the town and in the direction of Eion they were exposed to the blockade of Athenian triremes. Now, however, these difficulties appeared to have been removed. The Athenians also feared that their allies would revolt, since Brasidas was behaving with

great moderation and was constantly declaring wherever he went that his mission was the liberation of Hellas. The cities subject to Athens, when they heard of the capture of Amphipolis, of the terms being offered, and of the considerate behaviour of Brasidas himself, eagerly embraced the idea of a change, made overtures to him, begging him to march on into their territory, and vied with each other in being the first to revolt. Indeed, they fancied that this was a perfectly safe thing to do, though, as was proved later on, the power of Athens was as great as had been their mistake in underestimating it. As it was, their judgement was based more on wishful thinking than on a sound calculation of probabilities; for the usual thing among men is that when they want something they will, without any reflection, leave that to hope, while they will employ the full force of reason in rejecting what they find unpalatable. Then too there was the fact that the Athenians had just been defeated in Boeotia, and there was the untrue, but attractive, statement of Brasidas that at Nisaea the Athenians had not dared to engage even the army that he had there himself. All this produced a feeling of confidence and a belief that no steps would be taken by Athens to secure her interests. But what most of all made them ready to undertake all kinds of risks was the pleasurable excitement of the moment, and the fact that it looked for the first time as though they were going to find the Spartans acting with real energy.

All this did not escape the notice of the Athenians, who, so far as was possible at such short notice and in winter, sent garrisons to the various cities. Brasidas sent messengers to Sparta asking for another army to be sent out to him, and meanwhile began to arrange for the building of triremes on the Strymon. The Spartans, however, did nothing for him, partly becuase their leading men were jealous of him, partly because what they really wanted was to recover the prisoners made on the island and to end the war.

109   In the same winter the Megarians recaptured their Long Walls, which the Athenians had held, and razed them to the ground.

Brasidas, after the capture of Amphipolis, marched with his allies against the place called Acte. This is the jutting out headland, with the King of Persia's canal on the landward side, and with the

high mountain of Athos at the end facing the Aegean sea. The
cities in Acte are Sane, a colony of Andros, which is just by the
canal on the sea facing towards Euboea, and also Thyssus, Cleone,
Acrothoi, Olophyxus, and Dium – all these latter towns being
inhabited by mixed foreign races, speaking both Greek and their
own dialects. There is also a small Chalcidian element, but the
majority are Pelasgian, of the Tyrrhenian race that once lived in
Lemnos and Athens, together with Bisaltians, Crestonians, and
Edonians. The cities are all small ones. Most of them came over to
Brasidas, but Sane and Dium held out against him, and he stayed
in their territory with his army, laying waste their land.

110   When he found that they would not give in, he marched at once
against Torone in Chalcidice, which was occupied by the Athenians. A few people there had invited him to come and were prepared to betray the place to him. He arrived in the darkness just
before dawn and halted with his army near the temple of the
Dioscuri, rather more than a quarter of a mile from the city. The
Athenian garrison and most of the people in Torone knew nothing
of his being there, but those who had been intriguing with him
knew that he was coming (a few of them had gone out secretly to
meet him) and were keeping a look-out for his arrival. As soon as
they knew that he had arrived, they received into the town seven
light-armed men with daggers. Twenty men had originally been
detailed for this operation, but only these seven, commanded by
Lysistratus, an Olynthian, had the courage to enter. They got past
the fortifications facing the sea without being noticed, climbed up
the hill on which the city stands, killed the garrison guarding the
higher post, and broke open the postern gate on the side of
Canastraeum.

111   Meanwhile Brasidas with the rest of his army moved forward a
little and then halted. He sent 100 peltasts out in front, so that,
when any gate was opened and when the agreed signals were
made, they should rush in first. As the time went on and they
could not understand the delay, they gradually got close up to the
city. Their allies inside Torone had been arranging matters with
the party that had already entered. When they had broken down
the postern gate and set open the gates into the market square by
cutting through the bar, they first brought some troops round and

let them in by the postern, so that by making a sudden attack from the rear and from both sides they might cause panic among the citizens who knew nothing of what was going on. They then raised the fire-signal, as had been arranged, and took in the rest of the peltasts by the gates facing the market-place.

112   As soon as Brasidas saw the signal, he ordered his troops to rise to their feet and went forward at the double. They were all shouting out together, and so caused the utmost consternation among the people in the city. Some rushed straight in by the gates, others climbed up over some square pieces of timber which were placed against the wall and were used for hauling up stones for the re-building of a part of the wall that had fallen down. Brasidas himself with the main body went straight forward up the hill to the higher part of the city, since he wanted to make quite sure of occupying the whole city from top to bottom. The rest of his force scattered throughout the town in all directions.

113   So the city was captured while most of the people of Torone were still in a state of confusion, not yet aware of what was happening. The conspirators, however, and others of their way of thinking joined up at once with the invading army. As for the Athenians, there were about fifty hoplites sleeping in the market-place. When they realized what had happened, a few of them were killed fighting; but the rest escaped, some by land, some to the two ships that were on patrol there, and took refuge in Lecythus, a fortified post which they had taken over and held. It is at the ex-tremity of the city, jutting out into the sea, and cut off by a narrow isthmus. Here also the pro-Athenian element among the people of Torone took refuge with them.

114   It was now day, and Brasidas, having the city firmly in his hands, made a proclamation to the citizens of Torone who had taken refuge with the Athenians, inviting all who wished to do so to return to their own property and guaranteeing them their civil rights with no reprisals. He also sent a herald to the Athenians asking them to evacuate Lecythus, since it was Chalcidian territory, and saying that they could leave under an armistice, taking all their belongings with them. The Athenians refused to leave the place, but asked for a truce for one day in order to take up their dead. Brasidas gave a truce for two days and spent these days in fortify-

ing the houses nearby, while the Athenians also strengthened their own positions.

Meanwhile he called a meeting of the people of Torone and made much the same speech as he had made at Acanthus. He said that it would not be fair to think the worse of those who had worked with him for the capture of the city, or to regard them as traitors; they had not aimed at enslaving the city, nor had they taken bribes for what they did, but had acted entirely for the good of Torone and for its freedom. Nor would it be right for those who had not taken a hand in the work to imagine that they would not share equally in its results; he had not come to do harm either to cities or to individuals. This, in fact, was why he had made the proclamation to those who had taken refuge with the Athenians; he thought no worse of them for being friendly with the Athenians; only when they got to know the Spartans, they would be just as friendly with them, indeed much more so, since Spartans acted more justly than Athenians; it was simply from lack of experience that they were now afraid of Sparta. He then urged them all to make up their minds to be loyal allies, and to recognize that from now on they would be held responsible for anything done amiss. As for the past, they could not be held to have done wrong to Sparta; it was rather they themselves who had been wronged by the superior power of others, and, if they had opposed him in any way, he was ready to overlook it.

115   After this speech to confirm their morale, as soon as the truce was over he made his attack on Lecythus. The Athenian defences consisted of a badly constructed wall and some houses with parapets. For one day they beat off the attack. On the next day the enemy were bringing up against them an engine from which they meant to throw down fire on the wooden part of the fortifications; their troops were already drawing up close to the point where it seemed to them that the engine would be most effective and where the fortifications could most easily be stormed. To meet this threat the Athenians had erected a wooden tower on top of a house, and into this they carried a number of great jars and casks of water and large stones; a number of men also went up into the tower. But the weight was too heavy for the house to bear, and it suddenly collapsed with a loud crash. This caused more vexation than alarm

among the Athenians who were close to the scene of action and saw what had happened, but those who were farther off, and particularly those who were some distance away, thought that the fortifications had already been stormed at this point, and at once 116 fled to the sea and their ships. Brasidas saw them leaving the parapet and realized what was happening. He charged forward with his army and took the place immediately, killing all those whom he found inside.

In this way the Athenians evacuated the position, and crossed over in their warships and transports to Pallene.

Brasidas, when he was on the point of making the assault, had proclaimed that he would give thirty silver minae to the man who first scaled the wall. Now, there is a temple of Athene in Lecythus, and Brasidas, considering that the capture was due to divine help rather than human means, gave the thirty minae to the goddess for her temple, dismantled the fortifications at Lecythus, cleared the ground, and consecrated it all to the goddess. The rest of the winter he spent in re-organizing the places which he had already won and in making plans for future conquests. So the winter ended and with it the eighth year of the war.

ARMISTICE BETWEEN ATHENS AND SPARTA

117 In the spring before the next summer the Spartans and the Athenians made an armistice for one year. The Athenians calculated that in this way Brasidas would not be able to win over any more of their dependencies before they had had time to take measures for their security; they might then, if it suited them, extend the agreement. The Spartans correctly estimated these Athenian apprehensions and thought that, once Athens had had a respite from hardship and toil, she would be all the more ready to come to a general agreement by giving back the prisoners and making peace for a longer period. They were particularly anxious to get back the men while the successes of Brasidas still continued. And they thought that they were in the position to claim that, if Brasidas won more victories and made up all the ground lost to the Athenians, even though they might be deprived of the men captured at

Sphacteria, they would still be able to fight it out on equal terms with a good prospect of final victory. Sparta and her allies therefore made an armistice on the following terms:

118   'With regard to the temple and oracle of the Pythian Apollo we agree that all who wish should have the right to consult the oracle without fraud and without fear, according to the established laws of each man's country. This has been agreed by the Spartans and by the allies present, and they undertake to send heralds to the Boeotians and Phocians and to do their best to persuade them to subscribe to the agreement.

'With regard to the treasure belonging to the god we agree to take measures to find out those who have been guilty in respect of this treasure, both we and you proceeding with justice and equity according to our own laws; and that all others who wish to do so, may do the same, each according to the law of his country. On the above points the Spartans and their allies are agreed.

'On the following points also the Spartans and the other allies are agreed, if the Athenians are prepared to make a treaty. It is proposed that each side should remain in its own territory, holding what it now holds: the troops in Coryphasium are to remain within Buphras and Tomeus: the troops in Cythera are to enter into no communication with the Peloponnesian League, neither we with them, or they with us: the troops in Nisaea and Minoa are not to cross the road leading from the gates of the temple of Nisus to the temple of Poseidon and from there straight on to the bridge at Minoa: the Megarians and the allies are also bound not to cross this road: the Athenians are to retain the island which they have taken, but there is to be no communication between it and the allies or the allies and it: in the territory of Troezen each side is to keep what it now holds, according to the agreement made with the Athenians.

'With regard to travel by sea, in respect of their own coastline and that of their allies, the Spartans and their allies may travel in any ship rowed by oars and not exceeding a tonnage of 500 talents. They may not travel in ships of war. That all heralds and embassies, with their appropriate staffs, who are dealing with the ending of the war and the settlement of claims are to be guaranteed a safe conduct, going and coming, to Peloponnese or to Athens, by land and by sea.

'That during the truce neither side is to receive deserters, whether free men or slaves.

'That claims made by us against you and by you against us are to be settled in accordance with the laws of our countries, and points in dispute are to be submitted to arbitration, without recourse to war.

'The above articles have been agreed upon by the Spartans and their allies. But if you have any better or fairer proposals to make, we invite you to come to Sparta and inform us of them. Neither Sparta nor her allies will reject any just suggestion that you make. But if you send delegates, let them come with full powers, as you have asked us to do. The armistice is to last for one year.

'Approved by the people.

'The tribe of Acamantis held the prytany. Phaenippus was secretary, Niciades chairman. Laches proposed the motion, in the name of the good fortune of the Athenians, that an armistice should be made on the terms offered by Sparta and her allies and approved by the people; that the armistice should last for one year, beginning on that very day, the fourteenth of the month of Elaphebolion; that during the period of the armistice ambassadors and heralds should go between the two countries to discuss means for reaching a permanent peace settlement; that the generals and prytanes should call an assembly of the people, so that the Athenians should first be able to discuss the terms on which an embassy to negotiate a final settlement should be admitted; that the embassy now present should at once pledge itself before the people to abide by the terms of this truce for one year.'

19   These were the terms agreed upon by Athens and Sparta with their respective allies. The agreement was made on the twelfth of the Spartan month Gerastius. Those who took part in the agreement and poured the libations were the Spartans Taurus, the son of Echetimides, Athenaeus, the son of Pericleidas, and Philocharidas, the son of Eryxidaïdas; the Corinthians Aeneas, the son of Ocytus, and Euphamidas, the son of Aristonymus; the Sicyonians Damotimus, the son of Naucrates, and Onasimus, the son of Megacles; the Megarians Nicasus, the son of Cecalus, and Menecrates, the

son of Amphidorus; the Epidaurian Amphias, the son of Eupaïdas; and the Athenian generals Nicostratus, the son of Diitrephes, Nicias, the son of Niceratus, and Autocles, the son of Tolmaeus.

This was the armistice agreed upon, and during the whole time that it was in force conferences were taking place with a view to making a more general settlement.

120   In the days when these negotiations were going on Scione, a city in Pallene, revolted from Athens and went over to Brasidas. The Scionaeans say that they come from Pellene in the Peloponnese and that originally, while on the voyage back from Troy, they were driven ashore at this place by the storm in which the Achaeans were caught, and so settled there. As soon as the revolt happened, Brasidas sailed across by night to Scione. One of his own triremes went in front, and he himself followed some way behind in a small boat, his idea being that, if he fell in with a boat bigger than his own small craft, the trireme would be there to protect him, and if another trireme of equal strength were to appear, it would in all probability leave the small boat alone and attack the larger one, thus making it possible for him to get through safely.

After he had crossed over, he called a meeting of the people of Scione, and made a speech much like those he had made at Acanthus and Torone. He added that they deserved the very greatest praise because, although Pellene inside the isthmus was cut off by the Athenian occupation of Potidaea and although they were thus practically in the position of islanders, they had nevertheless come forward of their own accord to claim their freedom, instead of timorously standing by until some pressure from outside was brought to bear on them in the direction of what was so obviously their own good. This was a sign that on other occasions, too, where great qualities were required they would show the same courage and resolution; and, if he could settle matters as he intended, he would consider the people of Scione as in very truth the most loyal friends of Sparta and he would do them honour in every way.

121   The people of Scione were greatly heartened by such language; there was a general feeling of confidence, even among those who previously had been opposed to what was being done; they

resolved to throw themselves into the war, and welcomed Brasidas with every mark of honour. He was publicly crowned with a gold crown as the liberator of Hellas, and private individuals used to come up to him and deck him with garlands, as though he were a famous athlete. He himself crossed back again, leaving with them a small garrison for the time being, and not long afterwards sent a larger force over, since his intention was to attempt Mende and Potidaea with the help of the people of Scione. He thought that, Scione being in the position of an island, the Athenians would certainly send out a force against it, and he wanted to be a move ahead of them. Negotiations too were actually going on between himself and the other cities with a view to having them betrayed.

122   Just when he was on the point of making his attempt on these places a trireme arrived with the commissioners who were carrying round the news of the armistice, Aristonymus representing Athens, and Athenaeus representing Sparta. The army then returned to Torone and the commissioners informed Brasidas of the terms of the agreement. All the Spartan allies in Thrace accepted what had been arranged and Aristonymus declared himself satisfied except in the case of Scione, which he refused to include in the armistice since he found, on reckoning up the days, that the revolt had occurred after the armistice had been agreed upon. Brasidas strongly objected, claiming that it had actually taken place before, and refused to give the city up. Aristonymus reported the situation to Athens, and the people wanted immediately to send a force out against Scione. The Spartans then sent an embassy to say that this would amount to a breach of the truce; trusting in the word of Brasidas, they claimed the city for themselves, but were ready to submit the matter to arbitration. The Athenians, however, were not at all inclined to risk the result of arbitration; instead they were eager to send out an expeditionary force at once, since they were furious at the idea that now even islanders dared to revolt from them, and to trust in Spartan land power, which, in fact, would do them no good. Also the true facts about the revolt supported the Athenian argument rather than the Spartan one. The revolt of Scione took place two days after the armistice. So, on the motion of Cleon, a decree was passed immediately to recapture Scione and to put its inhabitants to death. As they now had nothing else

on their hands, the Athenians prepared to carry this decree into effect.

123   Meanwhile Mende, a city in Pallene, and a colony of the Eretrians, revolted from Athens. Brasidas received the people of Mende as allies and considered himself justified in so doing, although they had quite obviously come over to him at a time when the armistice was in force, because he also had some complaints to make about some Athenian infringements of the truce. The people of Mende were therefore all the more ready to take the risk when they saw that Brasidas was determined to support them and when they drew the appropriate conclusions from the fact that he would not give up Scione. It was also the case that those in Mende who were working with Brasidas were few in number; they had made their decision, as already related, and they were not now going to give up, for now they feared that their conspiracy would come to light, and so they forced their fellow citizens into a course that was against the better judgement of the majority. The news of this made the Athenians still more infuriated and they made their preparations to attack both cities. Brasidas expected the attack and sent away the women and children from Scione and Mende for safe-keeping to Olynthus in Chalcidice. He also sent over to them a force of 500 Peloponnesian hoplites and 300 Chalcidian peltasts, all under the command of Polydamidas. Those left behind in Scione and Mende made their combined preparations to meet an Athenian attack which was expected to come quickly.

END OF NINTH YEAR OF WAR

124 Meanwhile Brasidas and Perdiccas made a second expedition together into Lyncus against Arrhabaeus. Perdiccas's army consisted of the forces of his Macedonian subjects together with a force of hoplites from the Hellenes living in Macedonia; Brasidas had with him the remainder of his Peloponnesian army and also Chalcidians, Acanthians, and contingents from his other allies in such force as was available. There were altogether about 3,000 Hellenic hoplites; the total cavalry force of Macedonians and Chalcidians came

to nearly 1,000, and there was also a great crowd of native troops. After entering the country of Arrhabaeus they found the Lyncestians camped there ready to meet them and took up a position opposite. The infantry on both sides were on rising ground and there was a plain between the two armies. First the cavalry of both sides rode down into the plain and began the battle. Then the Lyncestian hoplites came down from their hill to join their cavalry and to offer battle; Brasidas and Perdiccas now led their men forward to meet them; battle was joined and the Lyncestians were defeated with heavy loss. The survivors escaped to higher ground and there remained without making a move.

After the battle the victorious army put up a trophy, and then stayed where they were for two or three days, waiting for the Illyrian mercenaries who were supposed to be joining Perdiccas. Perdiccas then wanted to move forward against the villages of Arrhabaeus and was reluctant to stay still any longer. Brasidas, however, was worried about Mende, fearing for its fate if the Athenians sailed up before he could get back; at the same time he was disinclined to move forward without the support of the Illyrians and instead favoured a retreat.

125   While this point was being disputed, news arrived that the Illyrians had betrayed Perdiccas and had now joined forces with Arrhabaeus. The Illyrians are a race of fighters, and the fear of them now made both parties agree on the advisability of a retreat; but, owing to the quarrel, no definite arrangements had been made as to when it should begin. When night came on the Macedonians and the whole crowd of native troops suddenly took fright in one of those irrational panics that are apt to occur in very large armies; convinced that forces many times the size of the one that had actually arrived were moving forward and were practically upon them, they broke into sudden flight and made off in the direction of home. Perdiccas at first did not realize what was happening, but when he did find out, he was compelled to set out without seeing Brasidas, since the armies were encamped some distance away from each other. At dawn Brasidas discovered that the Macedonians had gone and saw that the Illyrians with Arrhabaeus were on the point of attacking him. He formed his hoplites into a square, with the light troops in the centre, and took his own

measures for a retreat. The youngest soldiers were detailed to charge out against the enemy at any point where an attack was made, and Brasidas himself with 300 picked men brought up the rear. With these troops he intended to face about during the retreat and beat back the enemy forces who pressed most closely on them. Now, before the enemy came near, he used the short time he had in making the following speech to encourage his men:

126   'Peloponnesians, I should not be giving you advice as I do now, but only saying a few words of encouragement, if it were not for the fact that I imagine that you are down-hearted because of your isolated position in face of an attack by a barbarian army which is in great force. As it is, what with the desertion of our friends and the numbers of our enemies, there are a few things of which I want to remind you and there is some advice I want to offer in an attempt to satisfy you on the most important points.

'The reason why you are expected to be brave in war is not because you have allies with you on every occasion, but because of the courage which is your birthright. It is not your way to be frightened of numbers on the other side, you who come from states where it is not the many who rule the few, but rather the other way about, and where to fight and to conquer has been the one and only basis of national power. As for barbarians, it is inexperience which makes you frightened of them now; yet from the battle which you have already fought with the Macedonians among them, from the estimate I have formed of them myself, and from what I have heard from others you can be sure that they are not going to prove very terrible. When an enemy makes a show of strength, but is in fact weak, a true knowledge of the situation will give confidence to the other side; but when one side has advantages that can really be relied upon, the less their opponents know about them the more boldly they will attack. These opponents of ours now may look to inexperienced eyes as though they were going to be dangerous. Their numbers seem to be terrific; their shouts and yells are insupportable; the way they wave their arms about in the air looks pretty threatening. But it is not quite the same thing when they come up against troops who stand their ground against all this. As they fight in no sort of order, they have no sense of shame about giving up a position under pressure. To run forwards and to run backwards are equally honourable in their eyes, and so their courage can never really be tested, since, when every man is fighting on his own, there is always a good excuse for everyone saving his own skin. In fact, rather than meet you in close fighting, they think it safer to make you frightened and to run no risks themselves. Otherwise they would join battle, instead of simply making a noise. You should therefore be able to see clearly enough that everything about them which you thought frightening amounts in real fact to very little, alarming as it may be to the eye and to the ear. Stand firm, then, when they charge, and, when the time comes, retreat again in a disciplined and orderly manner. You will get into safety all the quicker like this, and you will know in the future that mobs of this kind, once their first attack is met firmly, only show off their courage by making threats of what they are going to do, meanwhile keeping well out of the way themselves; whereas, if one gives way to them, they are quick enough to press home their advantage and show how brave they are when there is no danger involved.'

127   After making this speech Brasidas began to lead his army off, and the natives, seeing what was happening, came on, shouting loudly and making a great din, thinking that he was running away from them and that they would catch him up and destroy him. But they found that wherever they attacked troops ran out from the ranks to meet them, and Brasidas himself with his picked men stood firm against their main force. To their surprise, there was no giving in to their first assault, and afterwards each charge they made was met with the same resistance, and, as soon as they gave up their attacks, the retreat continued. Thus the majority of the native army gave up attacking the Hellenes with Brasidas in the open country. Leaving a part of their force behind to follow up and harass his march, the rest ran ahead after the Macedonians who were in flight, killing all whom they overtook, and so reached and occupied, before Brasidas could get there, the narrow pass between two hills that leads into the country of Arrhabaeus, knowing that this was the only route by which he could retreat. Here, just as he got to the most difficult part of the road, they came at him from all sides with the object of trapping him.

128   When Brasidas saw what they were doing, he ordered his 300 to

run forward, everyone as fast as he could and without preserving their formation, to the hill which he thought was the easiest one of the two to take, and to try to dislodge the natives who had already occupied it, before any more of them had got there in the general encircling movement. The 300 attacked and got the better of the natives on the hill, and now the main force of the Hellenes could move forward to it more easily. Once they saw their men driven off the high ground here, the natives became terrified and no longer pressed their pursuit, thinking that the Greeks had already got to the frontier and escaped. Brasidas, now that he had got on to the high ground, went forward in greater safety and on the same day reached Arnisa, the first place he came to in the Kingdom of Perdiccas. His troops were furious with the Macedonians for having left them in the lurch by their retreat and, taking things into their own hands, they unyoked and slaughtered any cattle that they came upon on the road and appropriated for themselves all the equipment which, as was natural in a panic-stricken retreat by night, had been abandoned. It was because of this that Perdiccas began to regard Brasidas as an enemy and to feel towards the Peloponnesians a hatred that scarcely fitted in with his anti-Athenian policy. He now departed from the necessary implications of this and set to work to get rid of the Peloponnesians as soon as possible by coming to an arrangement with Athens.

129   When Brasidas got back to Torone from Macedonia, he found that the Athenians were already in possession of Mende. He decided that it was now impossible for him to cross over into Pallene and re-establish the position there, so he stayed where he was and kept a good watch on Torone. It was about the same time as the campaign in Lyncus that the Athenians, having completed the preparations referred to already, sailed out against Mende and Scione with a force of fifty ships, ten of which were from Chios, 1,000 citizen hoplites, 600 archers, 1,000 Thracian mercenaries, and some peltasts from their allies in the area. This force was under the command of Nicias, the son of Niceratus, and Nicostratus, the son of Diitrephes. Setting out with the fleet from Potidaea, they came to land opposite the temple of Poseidon and advanced against Mende. The people of Mende were reinforced by 300 troops from Scione and by the Peloponnesians who were there to help them.

Altogether there were 700 hoplites with Polydamidas in command, and this army was camped outside the city in a strong position on a hill. Nicias made an attempt to reach them by a path running up the hill, taking with him 120 light troops from Methone, sixty picked men from the Athenian hoplites, and the whole force of archers. However, after suffering some casualties he found himself unable to force the position. Nicostratus meanwhile, with all the rest of the army, approached the hill from a different direction farther off. It was a very difficult ascent and his troops were thrown into great confusion; indeed, the whole Athenian army came very close to being defeated. So for that day, since the people of Mende and their allies showed no signs of giving in, the Athenians retired and encamped. At nightfall the Mendaeans went back inside their city.

130 Next day the Athenians sailed round to the side near Scione, captured the suburbs, and spent the whole day in laying waste the country. No one came out to oppose them, and in fact there was now a division of opinion inside the city. At night the 300 troops from Scione went home. On the following day Nicias with half the army advanced to the frontier between Mende and Scione and laid waste the land. Nicostratus with the other half took up a position in front of the city near the northern gates on the road to Potidaea. It was at this point inside the walls that the arms of the Mendaeans and their Peloponnesian allies were piled, and now Polydamidas began to form his men up for battle, encouraging the Mendaeans to make a sortie. But the Mendaeans were now split into two factions, and someone from the democratic party answered Polydamidas back and said that they would not go out and that they did not want a war. For this reply Polydamidas dragged the man forward by the arm and began to knock him about. This infuriated the people, who immediately seized hold of their weapons and set upon the Peloponnesians and those of the opposite party who were collaborating with the Peloponnesians. They routed them at the first attack, partly because the fighting had broken out so suddenly, partly through fear of the gates being opened to the Athenians, since it was thought that this attack was the result of some previous arrangement made with them. Those who were not killed on the spot took refuge in the acropolis, which

they had held from the beginning. And now the whole Athenian army (for by this time Nicias had returned and was close to the city) burst into Mende. The gates had been opened without any terms having been offered or accepted, and the Athenians sacked the town as though they had captured it by assault. Indeed, the generals found it difficult to restrain their troops from massacring the inhabitants. Afterwards they told the people of Mende that they might continue to govern themselves as before and should put on trial those whom they regarded as responsible for the revolt. They cut off the party in the acropolis by building walls down to the sea on both sides of it and setting guards along the walls.

Now that they held Mende, the Athenians turned next to Scione.
131 Here the people of Scione and the Peloponnesians marched out against them and took up a strong position on a hill in front of the city. Without capturing this hill, there was no chance of the enemy being able to build blockading walls. The Athenians made a strong frontal assault on the hill, defeated and drove down the troops who were holding it, and then, after making their camp and putting up a trophy, prepared to build their lines of circum-vallation. Not long after, when they were already busy on this work, the troops besieged in the acropolis of Mende forced their way through the guard on the sea-shore and reached Scione in the darkness. Most of them managed to slip through the besieging army and got into the city.

132 While Scione was being invested, Perdiccas sent a herald to the Athenian generals and made peace with Athens. This was because of the hatred he felt for Brasidas in connection with the retreat from Lyncus, directly after which he had begun to negotiate with the Athenians. The Spartan Ischagoras was just then on the point of marching with an army to join Brasidas, and Perdiccas, partly because Nicias urged him, now that peace had been made, to give some proof to the Athenians that he could be relied upon, partly because he himself no longer wanted Peloponnesians in his coun-try, got to work with his friends in Thessaly (where he was always on good terms with the leading men), and so put such obstacles in the way of the Spartan expeditionary force that they did not even approach the Thessalians. Ischagoras himself, however, with

Ameinias and Aristeus did succeed in reaching Brasidas. They had been sent out by the Spartans to inspect the state of affairs, and they brought with them from Sparta (contrary to the usual practice of their government) some quite young men to be appointed as governors of the cities, so that this task should not have to be entrusted to the people available on the spot. Brasidas put Clearidas, the son of Cleonymus, in charge of Amphipolis, and Pasitelidas, the son of Hegesander, in charge of Torone.

133   The same summer the Thebans demolished the walls of the Thespians, bringing forward against them the charge of being pro-Athenian. They had always wanted to do this, and now they had an easy opportunity, since the flower of the Thespian youth had fallen in the battle with the Athenians.

Also in the same summer the temple of Hera at Argos was burnt down through the negligence of the priestess Chrysis, who put a lighted torch near the garlands and then fell asleep, with the result that they all caught fire and blazed up before she was aware of it. Chrysis herself immediately fled by night to Phlius out of fear of the Argives. They, according to the regular procedure, appointed another priestess named Phaeinis. At the time of her flight Chrysis had been priestess for eight years of this war and half the ninth.

Towards the end of the summer the blockading walls round Scione were completed, and the Athenians, leaving behind a garrison to man the walls, returned with the rest of their army.

34   In the following winter there was no military action between Athens and Sparta because of the armistice. But the Mantineans and Tegeans, with their allies on each side, fought a battle at Laodocium in the territory of Orestheum. In this battle the victory remained undecided, since each side routed one wing of the opposing army and both sides put up trophies and sent offerings of the spoil to Delphi. There were heavy losses in both armies and night put an end to the fighting when the issue was still in doubt. The Tegeans, however, spent the night on the field and put up their trophy at once, while the Mantineans retreated to Bucolion and put up theirs afterwards.

135   At the end of the same winter, in fact almost at the beginning of spring, Brasidas moved again and tried to seize Potidaea. He

reached the place by night and had planted a ladder against the wall before he was discovered. The ladder was planted just in those few moments when the guard on duty was passing on the bell and before he had time to return to his post. However, the alarm was given immediately afterwards, before his men were in position, and Brasidas quickly led his army back again, without waiting till it was day. So the winter ended and so ended the ninth year of this war recorded by Thucydides.

BOOK FIVE

BATTLE OF AMPHIPOLIS

1 NEXT summer the year's truce, lasting up to the Pythian games, came to an end. During the armistice the Athenians expelled the Delians from Delos, thinking that, because of some crime committed in the past, they had been in a state of pollution when they were consecrated and that it was this which they had omitted to attend to at the time of the previous ceremony of purification, when, as I have already described, they removed the tombs of the dead and considered that in this way the purification had been properly carried out. As for the Delians, Pharnaces gave them the town of Atramyttium in Asia, and here they settled just as they arrived from Delos.

2 Cleon got his way with the Athenians and, after the armistice, sailed out against the towns in the Thracian area. He had with him 1,200 hoplites and 300 cavalry from Athens, a still larger force from the allies, and thirty ships. First he put in to Scione, which was still being besieged, and increased his forces by taking some of the hoplites from the army there. He then sailed into the port of Cophos in the territory of Torone and not far from the city. He was informed by deserters that Brasidas was not in Torone and that those inside the place were not strong enough to meet him in battle. He therefore set out with the army from Cophos towards the city, sending ten ships round to sail into the harbour. First he came to the fortifications which Brasidas had put up in front of the city with the idea of including the suburbs in the circuit, and where he had pulled down part of the old wall, so making the whole into 3 one city. Here the Spartan commander Pasitelidas and the garrison which he had at his disposal came up and tried to beat back the Athenian attack. However, they were hard put to it themselves, and at the same time the Athenian ships that had been sent round were sailing into the harbour; Pasitelidas was afraid that the ships

might reach the city and find it undefended and that, with the
fortifications also taken, he would be trapped; so he abandoned
the fortification and took his troops back at the double into the city.
However, before he got there the Athenians from the ships had
taken Torone, and their army on land followed straight on after
him and forced its way in over the part of the old wall which
had been demolished. Some of the Peloponnesians and people of
Torone were killed on the spot in the fighting, others, including
Pasitelidas the commander, were taken prisoners. Meanwhile
Brasidas was coming to the relief of Torone, but while he was on
his way he heard that the place was captured and went back again.
He had been about four miles short of arriving in time. Cleon and
the Athenians put up two trophies, one by the harbour and one by
the fortifications; they made slaves of the wives and children of
the Toronaeans; the men of Torone, the Peloponnesians, and any
Chalcidians who were there they sent back to Athens. All these
returned home later, the Peloponnesians when peace was made and
the others in an exchange of prisoners with the Olynthians.

At about this same time the Boeotians captured, as a result of
treachery, the fortress of Panactum on the Athenian frontier.

Cleon, meanwhile, after posting a garrison in Torone, set out on
the voyage round Athos on his way to Amphipolis.

4   About the same time Phaeax, the son of Erasistratus, with two
colleagues set sail in two ships as ambassador from Athens to Italy
and Sicily. The reason for this was as follows: when the Athenians
had withdrawn from Sicily after the general agreement, the people
of Leontini had enrolled a number of new citizens and the democratic party there was planning a redistribution of the land. The
governing classes, realizing this, called in the help of the Syracusans
and drove the democrats out. The democrats were scattered over
the country, while the richer classes made an arrangement with
the Syracusans by which they abandoned and dismantled their
city and came to live in Syracuse with Syracusan citizenship. Later
some of them became dissatisfied, left Syracuse, and took over a
district of the city of Leontini called Phocaeae, also Briccinniae,
a fortified post in the territory of Leontini. Most of the democrats
who had been exiled previously came to join them and proceeded
to carry on the war from these fortified places. On hearing of this,

the Athenians sent Phaeax out with the idea of persuading their
allies on the spot and, if possible, the other Sicilians to make a combined military effort against Syracuse in view of her lust for power,
and so to save the democrats of Leontini. Phaeax reached Sicily and
won over the people of Camarina and of Agrigentum, but at
Gela matters went against him, and he did not go on to the other
states, since he realized that he would not be successful with them.
Instead he returned through the country of the Sicels to Catana,
went to Bricciniae where he encouraged the garrison, and then
5 sailed back to Athens. On his way out to Sicily and on the way
back he also entered into negotiations with some of the cities in
Italy with a view to securing friendly relations with Athens; he
met too some Locrian settlers who had been exiled from Messina.
They had been sent out as colonists at a time after the general
Sicilian settlement when there was party strife in Messina. One
side had called in the Locrians and for a period Messina came under
Locrian control. They were on their way back to Locri when he
met them, and he did no harm to them, since he had already come
to an agreement with the Locrians about a treaty with the Athenians. The Locrians were the only ones amongst the allies who did
not make peace with Athens at the time of the Sicilian agreement.
Nor would they have done so at this time if they had not been in
difficulties because of the war against the Hipponians and the Med-
maeans, who lived on their frontiers and were colonists of theirs.
After this Phaeax returned in due course to Athens.

6   Cleon, it will be remembered, was sailing round the coast from
Torone to Amphipolis. He based himself on Eion, and after making
an unsuccessful attack on the Andrian colony of Stagirus, took by
storm Galepsus, the colony of Thasos. He then sent representatives
to Perdiccas, urging him to bring his army up in support according to the terms of the alliance; he also sent envoys into Thrace,
to Polles the King of the Odomantians, who was to bring as many
Thracian mercenaries as possible. He himself, while waiting for
their arrival, stayed quiet in Eion.

Brasidas on his side was informed of all this and took up a
defensive position on Cerdylium. This is a place belonging to the
Argilians, on high ground across the river, not far from Amphipolis, with good views in all directions, so that no move made by

Cleon and his army could escape notice. This, in fact, was what Brasidas expected – that Cleon would be contemptuous of the numbers opposed to him and would move up against Amphipolis with the troops that he had with him. At the same time he made his own preparations; he engaged 1,500 Thracian mercenaries and called up the whole Edonian army of cavalry and peltasts. He had also 1,000 Myrcinian and Chalcidian peltasts in addition to those in Amphipolis. His total force of hoplites came to about 2,000, and he had 300 Hellenic cavalry. Brasidas kept 1,500 of these with him in his position on Cerdylium; the rest were posted in Amphipolis with Clearidas.

7   For some time Cleon made no move, but finally he was forced to do what Brasidas had expected. Inactivity made the soldiers discontented, and their thoughts began to turn to the comparison between the daring and skill of Brasidas and the incompetence and weakness of their own commander, whom, they remembered, they had been unwilling enough to follow even when they left home. Cleon was aware of this grumbling and, not wanting the army to get depressed by being constantly in the same position, he broke up his camp and moved forward. He was in the same confident frame of mind that he had been in at Pylos, where his success had convinced him of his intelligence. So now he had no idea that anyone would come out to fight him; he was just going up, he said, to examine the position, and the reason that he was waiting for reinforcements was not so as to have a margin of safety in case he was compelled to fight, but so as to be able to surround the city entirely and then take it by assault. So he went forward and posted his army on a strong hill in front of Amphipolis. He himself examined the marshes of the river Strymon and how the land lay on the Thracian side of the city. He thought he could retire whenever he wished without fighting, since no one was to be seen on the walls and no one came out of the gates, which were all shut. In fact it seemed to have been a mistake not to have brought siege engines with him, as then he might have taken the city in its defenceless state.

8   As soon as Brasidas saw the Athenian army on the march, he came down from Cerdylium and entered Amphipolis. He did not come out of the town and draw up his army to face the Athenians

because he lacked confidence in his own forces and thought them inferior, not in numbers (they were about equal), but in quality, since the Athenians on this expedition were first-rate troops and with them were the best of the Lemnians and the Imbrians. Brasidas therefore prepared to attack in a less obvious manner. He thought that if he revealed to the enemy the numbers of his own troops and their rough-and-ready equipment, he would be less likely to win a victory than if he kept them out of sight, thus preventing his opponents from feeling a justifiable contempt for them. He therefore picked out 150 hoplites and, leaving the rest under the command of Clearidas, decided to make a sudden attack before the Athenians withdrew. He thought that, once their reinforcements arrived, he would never get another opportunity like this of catching them alone. So he called the whole army together and made the following speech, partly to encourage them and partly to explain his plan:

9   'Peloponnesians, there is no need for me to do more than just mention the facts that we come from a country where courage has always preserved freedom and that you are Dorians about to fight with Ionians, whom you are in the habit of beating. What I shall do is to explain to you the idea behind my plan of action, so that no one need feel disheartened by thinking we shall be at a disadvantage if we attack with a part rather than with the whole of our army. It is, according to my calculations, because they despise us and because they have no idea that anyone will come out to fight them that the enemy have come up to the position in which they are and are now looking carelessly about them in no sort of order. But success goes to the man who sees more clearly when the enemy is making mistakes like this and who, making the most of his own forces, does not attack on obvious and recognized lines, but in the way that best suits the actual situation. And it is by these unorthodox methods that one wins the greatest glory; they completely deceive the enemy, and are of the greatest possible service to one's own side. So at this juncture, while they are still confident and unready, while they are thinking, so far as I can see, more of slipping away than of standing their ground, in this moment when their spirits are relaxed, and before they have time to pull themselves together, I propose to charge out at the double with my own

troops against the enemy's centre, taking them, if possible, by surprise. You, Clearidas, afterwards, when you see that I am already in action and (as is probable) creating a panic among them, are to take your own troops, including the Amphipolitans and the other allies, and to open the gates suddenly, charge out, and get among the enemy as quickly as you can. This is the way in which we are most likely to make them frightened; for when a second force appears later on the scene it causes more terror among the enemy than the force with which he is actually fighting at the time. You, Clearidas, must show the qualities that one expects of a Spartan officer, and you allies must follow him boldly. Remember that what makes a good soldier is his readiness to fight, his sense of honour, and his discipline, and that this day, if you show yourselves men, will win you your freedom and the title of allies of Sparta; the alternative is slavery to Athens; here the best you could hope for would be not to be carried off to the slavemarket or put to death; otherwise your servitude would be harsher than what you have known in the past, and you would also hinder the liberation of the rest of the Hellenes. No, there must be no giving in on your side, seeing how much there is at stake. As for me, I shall show that I do not only give advice to other people, but am also able to practise what I preach.'

10   After this speech Brasidas made his own preparations for the attack, and posted the rest of the troops with Clearidas at the Thracian Gates, ready to charge out, as had been agreed.

The Athenians meanwhile had seen Brasidas coming down from Cerdylium, and had seen him in the city, into which they could look from outside, sacrificing near the temple of Athene and making various dispositions. Cleon at this time had gone farther forward to reconnoitre the ground, and it was now announced to him that the whole enemy army could be seen inside the city and that the feet of numbers of men and horses were visible under the gates, giving the impression that they were going to come out and attack. On hearing this, Cleon hurried to the spot. He saw what the position was and, since he did not wish to risk a general battle until his reinforcements arrived, and imagined that he would have time to withdraw, he gave orders for the retreat to be sounded. His instructions were for the army to fall back in the direction of Eion, and for the left wing to lead the way – which was, in fact, the only possible method of retiring. Then, thinking that he had plenty of time in hand, he personally began to lead away the right wing, making it wheel round, and so exposing its unarmed side to the enemy. It was at this point that Brasidas, seeing that his opportunity had come and that the Athenian army was on the move, said to his own troops and to the others: 'These people will never stand up to us. That is clear enough from all the jostling about of spears and heads. When soldiers get into that state they can hardly ever face an attack. Let me have the gates opened for me, as I ordered, and let us set on them as fast as we can. We are sure to win.'

He then came out by the gate in the palisade and by the first gate in the long wall, which was then in existence. He went forward at the double straight along the road where, as one goes past the steepest part of the town, the trophy now stands, and he fell upon the Athenians, who were at the same time terrified by their own disorganized state and thrown off their balance by the audacity of his action. Here he routed the Athenian centre, and now Clearidas, following his instructions, charged out from the Thracian gates and bore down upon them too. The result was panic among the Athenians, attacked, as they were, suddenly, unexpectedly, and from two sides. Their left wing in the direction of Eion, which had already got some distance on its way, immediately broke and fled. Once this wing had given way, Brasidas turned against the right wing. Here he was wounded, but the Athenians did not realize that he had fallen, since he was lifted up by those about him and carried off the field.

The Athenian right put up more of a resistance. Cleon himself had no intention of standing his ground; he immediately took to flight and was overtaken and killed by a Myrcinian peltast. But his hoplites formed up in close order on a hill, where they beat back two or three attacks made on them by Clearidas, and only gave way in the end when they were surrounded by the Myrcinian and Chalcidian cavalry and the peltasts, whose weapons thrown from a distance made them break their ranks. So now the whole Athenian army was in flight. Many had been killed in the battle or by the Chalcidian cavalry and the peltasts; the survivors escaped with difficulty by various tracks over the mountains and so got to Eion.

Those who had lifted up Brasidas and brought him safely out of the battle, took him into the city while the life was still in him. He heard the news that his army had been victorious, and soon afterwards he died. The rest of the army came back from the pursuit with Clearidas, stripped the dead bodies, and put up a trophy.

11   Afterwards all the allied troops paraded for the funeral of Brasidas, which took place at the public expense in front of what is now the market-place. The people of Amphipolis made an enclosure round his tomb, and for the future they sacrificed to him as to a hero and honoured him by holding games and making annual offerings to him. They gave him the official title of founder of their colony, and they demolished all the buildings of Hagnon, destroying everything that could possibly remind them of the fact that Hagnon had founded the place. It was Brasidas, they considered, who had been their preserver, and at the same time, because of their fear of Athens, they were exceedingly anxious to have the Spartan alliance. As for Hagnon, being at war with Athens, they could no longer honour him with the same profit as before, or with the same goodwill.

They also gave back their dead to the Athenians. About 600 of the Athenians had fallen, and only seven on the other side. This was the result of there having been no set battle, but only the unforseen panic-ridden affair that I have described. After taking up their dead the Athenians sailed back home, and Clearidas with his army remained to deal with the affairs of Amphipolis.

12   About the same time, towards the end of summer, the Spartans Ramphias, Autocharidas, and Epicydidas were bringing out reinforcements consisting of 900 hoplites to the towns in the Thracian area. When they arrived at Heraclea in Trachis they recognized various matters there which seemed to them to require attention, and it was while they were spending their time on this that the battle of Amphipolis was fought. And so the summer came to an end.

PEACE OF NICIAS

13 At the very beginning of winter, Ramphias and his force advanced
to Pierium in Thessaly. The Thessalians, however, were unwilling
to let them go farther; Brasidas, for whom they were bringing re-
reinforcements, was dead; so they turned back home, thinking that
the time for action had passed now that the Athenians had been
defeated and had gone away, and that they themselves were not
capable of carrying out the plans which Brasidas had had in mind.
But their main reason for returning was that they knew at the
time when they set out that Spartan opinion was, in fact, in favour
of peace.

14 Indeed, what now took place was that, after the battle at Amphipolis and the withdrawal of Ramphias from Thessaly, neither side
went on with the war. Instead they began to think how to make
peace. The Athenians had suffered a serious blow at Delium and
another one soon afterwards at Amphipolis; they no longer possessed the same confidence in their strength which had induced
them to reject previous offers of peace, in the belief that their good
fortune at that time would carry them through to final victory.
The were also apprehensive about the allies, fearing that they
might be encouraged by these defeats to revolt on a more serious
scale, and they regretted that they had not seized upon the excellent
opportunity of making peace after Pylos. The Spartans on their
side had found that the war had gone very differently from what
they had imagined when they believed that they could destroy the
power of Athens in a few years simply by laying waste her land.
The disaster suffered on the island had been something which had
never been known before in Sparta; her territory was being raided
from Pylos and from Cythera; the helots were deserting, and
there was always the fear that even those who remained loyal
might gain confidence from the others and take advantage of the
situation to make a revolution, as they had done in the past. It
happened, too, that the thirty years' truce between Sparta and
Argos was on the point of expiring; the Argives refused to renew
it unless Cynuria was given back to them, and it seemed impossible
to fight Athens and Argos at once. They also suspected that some

of the states in the Peloponnese had the intention of going over to Argos, as indeed they did.

15   Both sides, therefore, had cogent reasons for making peace, the Spartans, perhaps, most of all, since they were extremely anxious to get back the men who had been captured on the island. Among these men were Spartans of the officer class, important people themselves and related to members of the government. Sparta had begun to negotiate directly after their capture, but the Athenians were then doing so well that they would not listen to any reasonable proposals. After the defeat at Delium, however, the Spartans, realizing that Athens would now be more inclined to come to terms, immediately concluded the armistice for one year, in which it was provided that meetings should take place to see whether

16 this period could be extended. Now Athens had suffered another defeat at Amphipolis, and Cleon and Brasidas were dead – the two people who on each side had been most opposed to peace, Brasidas because of the success and honour which had come to him through war, Cleon because he thought that in a time of peace and quiet people would be more likely to notice his evil doings and less likely to believe his slander of others. This was the moment, then, when even greater efforts to secure peace were made by the two statesmen who had the best claims to influence in each city, the Spartan King Pleistoanax, the son of Pausanias, and Nicias, the son of Niceratus, who had done better in his military commands than anyone else of his time. So now, while still untouched by misfortune and still held in honour, Nicias wished to rest upon his laurels, to find an immediate release from toil and trouble both for himself and for his fellow citizens, and to leave behind him the name of one whose service to the state had been successful from start to finish. He thought that these ends were to be achieved by avoiding all risks and by trusting oneself as little as possible to fortune, and that risks could be avoided only in peace. As for Pleistoanax, he was being attacked by his enemies in connection with his restoration; whenever anything went wrong, they invariably brought his name forward in an attempt to convince the Spartans that what had happened was due to this illegal restoration of his. The charge made against him was that he and his brother Aristocles had bribed the priestess at Delphi to give oracles to the Spartan delegations

which had come on various official visits, commanding them to
bring home from abroad the seed of the demigod son of Zeus, or
else they would have to plough with a ploughshare of silver. He
was exiled because he was supposed to have been bribed to retreat
from Attica, and, because of his fear of the Spartans, he had built
half of his house inside the grounds of the temple of Zeus. So in the
end, according to his accusers, he had induced the Spartans in the
nineteenth year of his exile to Lycaeum to bring him back with
the same dances and sacrifices as they had used originally in the
institution of their kings at the time of the foundation of Sparta.

17 He was naturally distressed by these accusations and he thought
that in peacetime disasters would not occur; also that, once the
Spartans got back their prisoners, his enemies would have no bases
from which to attack him, whereas during a state of war those in
the highest position must necessarily get blamed for every misfortune that took place. He was therefore extremely anxious to
come to terms with Athens.

Discussions went on throughout this winter, and as spring
drew near there were threats from Sparta of another invasion;
orders were sent round to the cities to prepare for building permanent fortifications in Attica – all this in order to make the
Athenians more inclined to accept the terms offered. During the
discussions various claims were put forward by each side, and in the
end it was agreed that peace should be made on the basis of each
party's giving back what it had acquired during the war, except
that Athens was to retain Nisaea. (When Athens had put in a claim
for Plataea, the Thebans had replied that they had not taken the
place by force, but held it as the result of an agreement reached
freely, and with no element of treachery, with the citizens. The
Athenians pointed out that the same held good of their occupation
of Nisaea.) Once this point was reached the Spartans called a meeting
of their allies, all of whom voted in favour of peace except for the
Boeotians, the Corinthians, the Eleans, and the Megarians, who
were opposed to what was being done. The treaty was then concluded and peace was made between Athens and Sparta, each side
swearing to the following provisions:

18 'The Athenians, the Spartans and their allies made a treaty and
swore to it, city by city, as follows:

'With regard to the Panhellenic temples, everyone who wishes, according to the customs of his country, to sacrifice in them, to travel to them, to consult the oracles, or to attend the games shall be guaranteed security in doing so, both by sea and by land.[38] At Delphi the consecrated ground and the temple of Apollo and the Delphians themselves shall be governed by their own laws, taxed by their own state, and judged by their own judges, both the people and the territory, according to the custom of the place.

'The treaty is to be in force between the Athenians, with their allies, and the Spartans, with their allies, for fifty years without fraud or damage by land or sea.

'It shall not be lawful to take up arms with intent to do injury either for the Spartans and their allies against the Athenians and their allies, or for the Athenians and their allies against the Spartans and their allies, in any way or by any means whatever. If any dispute should arise between them, they are to deal with it by law and by oath, as may be agreed between them.

'The Spartans and their allies are to give back Amphipolis to the Athenians. In the case of all cities given back by the Spartans to the Athenians, the inhabitants shall have the right to go where they please taking their property with them.

'These cities are to pay the tribute fixed by Aristides and are to be independent. So long as they pay the tribute, it shall not be lawful for the Athenians or their allies to take up arms against these cities, once the treaty has been made. The cities referred to are Argilus, Stagirus, Acanthus, Scolus, Olynthus, and Spartolus. These cities are to be allied neither to Sparta nor to Athens. If, however, the Athenians persuade the cities to do so, it shall be lawful for the Athenians to make them their allies, provided that the cities themselves are willing.

'The Mecybernaeans, the Sanaeans, and Singaeans shall inhabit their own cities, as shall the Olynthians and Acanthians. The Spartans and their allies shall give back Panactum to the Athenians. The Athenians shall give back Coryphasium, Cythera, Methana, Ptelium, and Atalanta to the Spartans; also all Spartans

38. Compare the wording (with its specific reference to Delphi) in the opening clause of the armistice agreement (IV, 118).

who are in prison in Athens or in any other prison in the Athenian dominions.

'The Athenians shall let go the Peloponnesians besieged in Scione and all others in Scione who are allies of Sparta, and those whom Brasidas sent in there, and any other allies of Sparta who are in prison in Athens or in any other prison in the Athenian dominions. The Spartans and their allies shall in the same way give back all Athenians or allies of Athens whom they have in their hands. With regard to Scione, Torone, Sermyle, and any other cities in Athenian hands, the Athenians may act as they think fit.

'The Athenians shall take an oath to the Spartans and their allies, city by city. The oath taken shall be the most binding one that exists in each city, and seventeen representatives on each side are to swear it. The words of the oath shall be these: "I shall abide by the terms of this treaty honestly and sincerely." In the same way the Spartans and their allies shall take an oath to the Athenians. This oath is to be renewed annually by both sides. Pillars are to be set up at Olympia, Pythia, the Isthmus, in the Acropolis at Athens, and in the temple at Amyclae in Lacedaemon.

'If any point connected with any subject at all has been overlooked, alterations may be made, without any breach of oath, by mutual agreement and on due consideration by the two parties, the Athenians and the Spartans.

19   'The treaty comes into effect from the 27th day of the month of Artemisium at Sparta, Pleistolas holding the office of ephor; and at Athens from the 25th day of the month of Elaphebolium, in the archonship of Alcaeus.

'Those who took the oath and poured the libations were as follows: For the Spartans, Pleistoanax, Agis, Pleistolas, Damagetus, Chionis, Metagenes, Acanthus, Daithus, Ischagoras, Philocharidas, Zeuxidas, Antiphus, Tellis, Alcinadas, Empedias, Menas, and Laphilus. For the Athenians, Lampon, Isthmonicus, Nicias, Laches, Euthydemus, Procles, Pythodorus, Hagnon, Myrtilus, Thrasycles, Theagenes, Aristocrates, Iolcius, Timocrates, Leon, Lamachus, and Demosthenes.'

20   This treaty was made at the very end of the winter and the

beginning of spring, directly after the City festival of Dionysus, just ten years, with the difference of a few days, after the first invasion of Attica and the beginning of this war. It is better to calculate on the time basis which I have used rather than to trust to any reckoning based on the names of magistrates in the various states or of those who have held some honoured position and so are used to date events in the past. By this method there can be no accuracy, since a particular event may have taken place at the beginning or the middle or at any time during their periods of office. But by reckoning in summers and winters, as I have done here, it will be found that, each of these being equivalent to half a year, there were ten summers and ten winters in this first war.

21 It fell by lot to the Spartans to begin the process of restoring what they held, and they immediately released all their prisoners of war. They also sent as their representatives to the Thracian area Ischagoras, Menas, and Philocharidas to instruct Clearidas to hand over Amphipolis to the Athenians and to order their other allies to accept the terms of the treaty as applied to each one of them. As, however, these terms were not to their liking, they refused to do so. Nor would Clearidas, who wanted to keep on good terms with the Chalcidians, give up Amphipolis. He claimed that it was impossible to do so against their will, and, taking with him representatives from the place, he set out quickly himself for Sparta in order to defend himself against any accusations of disobedience which might be made by Ischagoras and his commission, and also to find out if it was still possible for the treaty to be altered. When he found that Sparta was tied to the agreement he returned immediately with instructions to surrender the place, if possible, and in any case to bring out all the Peloponnesians who were in it.

22 The allies also happened to have their representatives present at this time in Sparta, and the Spartans urged those of them who had not accepted the treaty to do so now. The allies, however, stuck to the same formula which they had used when they had first rejected the plan, and said that unless a fairer treaty could be produced, they would not accept it. The Spartans, finding that their allies would not listen to them, dismissed their representatives and proceeded to form an alliance with Athens. After the deputation

of Ampelidas and Lichas, Argos had refused to renew her treaty with Sparta, and now the Spartan view was that if an alliance between Sparta and Athens could be concluded, Argos, without Athenian aid, would no longer be a menace and the rest of the Peloponnese also, which might, if it had been possible, have joined Athens would now remain quiet. Discussions took place with Athenian representatives on the spot, agreement was reached and oaths were exchanged ratifying an alliance on the following terms:

23 'Sparta and Athens shall be allies for fifty years, under the conditions to be set out. In case of any enemy invasion of Spartan territory or hostile action against the Spartans themselves, the Athenians are to come to the aid of Sparta in the most effective way possible, according to their resources. But if by this time the enemy has laid waste the country and gone away, then that city shall be held to be in a state of war with both Sparta and Athens and shall be punished by them both. Peace shall be made by Sparta and Athens jointly and simultaneously. These provisions are to be carried out honestly, promptly, and sincerely.

'In case of any invasion of Athenian territory or hostile action against the Athenians themselves, the Spartans are to come to the aid of Athens in the most effective way possible, according to their resources. But if by this time the enemy has laid waste the country and gone away, then that city shall be held to be in a state of war with both Sparta and Athens and shall be punished by them both. Peace shall be made by Sparta and Athens jointly and simultaneously. These provisions are to be carried out honestly, promptly, and sincerely.

'In case of a rising of the slaves, the Athenians are to come to the aid of Sparta with all their strength, according to their resources.

'This treaty shall be sworn to by the same people on either side who took the oath for the previous treaty. The oath shall be renewed every year by the Spartans going to Athens for the Dionysia and by the Athenians going to Sparta for the Hyacinthia. Each party shall set up a pillar, the one at Sparta to be near the statue of Apollo at Amyclae, the one at Athens near the statue of Athene on the Acropolis.

'If the Spartans and the Athenians should wish to add or take away anything from the terms of this alliance, they may do it jointly together without any breach of oath.

24   'Those who took the oath for the Spartans were Pleistoanax, Agis, Pleistolas, Damagetus, Chionis, Metagenes, Acanthus, Daithus, Ischagoras, Philocharidas, Zeuxidas, Antiphus, Alcinadas, Tellis, Empedius, Menas, and Laphilus; and for the Athenians, Lampon, Isthmonicus, Laches, Nicias, Euthydemus, Procles, Pythodorus, Hagnon, Myrtilus, Thrasycles, Theagenes, Aristocrates, Iolcius, Timocrates, Leon, Lamachus, and Demosthenes.'

This alliance was made soon after the peace treaty. The Athenians gave back to the Spartans the men captured on the island, and the summer of the eleventh year began. This completes the account of the first war, which went on without intermission for the ten years before this date.

NEGOTIATIONS WITH ARGOS

25 After the peace treaty and the alliance between Sparta and Athens, made after the ten years' war, when Pleistolas was ephor in Sparta and Alcaeus archon in Athens, there was peace so far as those who had accepted the terms were concerned. But Corinth and various other cities in the Peloponnese were trying to upset the agreement, and Sparta found herself immediately in fresh trouble with her allies. Then, too, as time went on the Spartans also lost the confidence of the Athenians because they failed to carry out some of the terms of the treaty. It is true that for six years and ten months they refrained from invading each other's territory; abroad, however, the truce was never properly in force, and each side did the other a great deal of harm, until finally they were forced to break the treaty made after the ten years, and once more declare war openly upon each other.

26   The history of this period also has been written by the same Thucydides, an Athenian, keeping to the order of events as they happened by summers and winters, down to the time when the Spartans and their allies put an end to the empire of Athens and occupied the Long Walls and Piraeus. By then the war had lasted

altogether twenty-seven years. And it would certainly be an error of judgement to consider the interval of the agreement as anything else except a period of war. One has only to look at the facts to see that it is hardly possible to use the word 'peace' of a situation in which neither side gave back or received what had been promised; and apart from this there were breaches of the treaty on both sides in connection with the Mantinean and Epidaurian wars, and in other respects, too; the allies in the Thracian area continued hostile as before; and the Boeotians were in a state of truce which had to be renewed every ten days. So, if one puts together the first ten years' war, the uneasy truce which followed it, and the subsequent war, one will find, reckoning by summers and winters, that my estimate of the number of years is correct within a few days – also that, for those who put their faith in oracles, here is one solitary instance of their having been proved accurate. I myself remember that all the time from the beginning to the end of the war it was being put about by many people that the war would last for thrice nine years. I lived through the whole of it, being of an age to understand what was happening, and I put my mind to the subject so as to get an accurate view of it. It happened, too, that I was banished from my country for twenty years after my command at Amphipolis; I saw what was being done on both sides, particularly on the Peloponnesian side, because of my exile, and this leisure gave me rather exceptional facilities for looking into things. I shall now, therefore, go on to describe the disputes that took place after the ten years' war, the breach of the treaty, and the warfare which came afterwards.

27   When the fifty years' truce and, later, the alliance had been concluded, the embassies from the Peloponnese, which had been summoned to discuss these matters, returned from Sparta. All went back to their own cities except for the Corinthians, who first went to Argos and entered into negotiations with some of the members of the Government there, saying that Sparta, so far from doing good to the Peloponnese, was seeking to enslave it by making this treaty and this alliance with Athens, once her bitterest enemy; the time had now come for Argos to consider how the Peloponnese could be preserved; their suggestion was that a decree should be passed inviting any Hellenic state that chose, provided that such

a state were independent and would deal with other states on a basis of legality and equality, to enter into a defensive alliance with Argos; for this purpose it would be better to appoint a few people with special powers rather than to negotiate through the popular assembly, so that secrecy could be preserved in the cases of those whose applications for alliance were not accepted. They said that many would want to join through hatred of the Spartans. After making these suggestions the Corinthians returned home.

28   The people in Argos with whom they had been in touch referred the proposal to the Government and to the people, and the Argives passed the decree and chose twelve men who were empowered to negotiate alliances with any Hellenic state that wished to do so, except for Sparta and Athens, neither of which was to be admitted unless the matter was first put before the people of Argos. The chief reason why the Argives adopted this policy was because they saw that war between them and Sparta was bound to come, now that their treaty was on the point of expiring, and also they hoped to gain the leadership of the Peloponnese. For this was the time when the reputation of Sparta had sunk very low indeed and she was despised for the losses she had suffered; whereas Argos was very well off in every direction, having taken no part in the Attic war, indeed having profited greatly from her position of neutrality.

The Argives therefore were prepared to receive into their alliance
29 any Hellenic state that wished to join. The first to come over to them were the Mantineans and their allies, through fear of Sparta. During the war with Athens the Mantineans had conquered and brought under their power a large part of Arcadia, and they thought that now Sparta had the time to deal with other matters, she would not allow them to keep what they had won. They were therefore glad to be able to turn to Argos, which was, they thought, a great city, the traditional enemy of Sparta, and a democracy like their own city. Once Mantinea had left the Spartan alliance there was great agitation among the other states in the Peloponnese and discussion as to whether it would not be better for them to do the same thing; they accounted for Mantinea's change of front by supposing her to have especial sources of information, and at the same time they were angry with Sparta, in particular because of

the part of the treaty with Athens where it was laid down that no breach of oath would be involved if the Spartans and Athenians together wished to add or take away anything from the terms. It was this clause which was chiefly responsible for creating the disturbance throughout the Peloponnese and making the states suspect that Sparta was planning to enslave them with the aid of Athens. The right thing, they thought, was that alterations in the treaty should be made only with the consent of all the allies. There was consequently a general feeling of alarm, and state after state began to move in the direction of forming an alliance with Argos.

30   The Spartans realized that this agitation was going on in the Peloponnese, also that Corinth had started it and was intending herself to join the Argive alliance. They therefore sent ambassadors to Corinth in the hope of preventing this from happening. The ambassadors protested against the way Corinth had initiated the whole scheme and said that, if Corinth were to desert Sparta and join Argos, she would be guilty of breaking her oath; she was already in the wrong in refusing to accept the treaty with Athens, when it was expressly laid down that a majority vote of the allies should be binding on all, unless the gods or heroes prevented it in any way. The Corinthians had with them at the time representatives of those allies who had also refused to accept the treaty with Athens; in fact they had been specially summoned previously. In front of these allies the Corinthians replied to the Spartans. They did not openly state the points where they considered themselves to have been badly treated – such as not getting back Sollium or Anactorium from Athens, and other cases where they thought their claims had not been met; instead they used the pretext that they could not betray their allies in Thrace, to whom, they said, they had sworn a separate oath at the time when Potidaea first revolted, and had given other guarantees later; they were not, therefore, breaking their oath to the allies by not accepting the treaty with Athens; they had given guarantees in the name of the gods to these others in Thrace, and to betray them would amount to perjury; 'unless the gods or heroes prevent it' was the phrase used, and it seemed to them that here was a case of the gods preventing it.

This was the Corinthian statement with regard to their former oaths. With regard to the Argive alliance, they said that they would discuss the question with their friends and do what they decided was the right thing. The Spartan ambassadors then returned home.

There were ambassadors from Argos also in Corinth at the time, and they urged the Corinthians to enter into alliance with them without delay. The Corinthians, however, instructed them to be present at their next meeting.

31   Just after this an embassy from the Eleans arrived and, after first making an alliance with Corinth, went on, according to their instructions, to Argos, and became allies of the Argives. This was because of a quarrel between Elis and Sparta in connection with Lepreum. Some time previously Lepreum had been at war with some of the Arcadians and had gained the alliance of Elis by promising them half their land. At the end of the war the Eleans left all the land to the people of Lepreum to be cultivated by them, and fixed a rent of one talent to be paid to Olympian Zeus. This rent was paid up to the time of the war with Athens; then the Lepreans, using the war as an excuse, ceased paying and, when the Eleans brought pressure to bear on them, appealed to Sparta. The case was now referred to Sparta, but the Eleans, thinking it unlikely that they would get their due, refused to accept Spartan arbitration and laid waste the land of Lepreum. This did not prevent the Spartans from deciding that Lepreum was an independent state and that Elis was the aggressor; and, on the grounds that Elis had failed to abide by the terms of arbitration, they put a garrison of hoplites into Lepreum. To the Eleans this meant that Sparta had received the allegiance of a state which had revolted from them; they brought forward the agreement in which it was stated that the allies should keep at the end of the Attic war everything which they possessed at the beginning of it, and, claiming that they had been treated unfairly, went over to the Argives, and made the alliance with them, as described above.

Immediately after them the Corinthians and the Chalcidians of Thrace joined the Argive alliance. The Boeotians and Megarians pursued a common policy and made no move. They did not suffer from Spartan interference, and they thought that the democratic government at Argos would be less congenial to their own aristocratic governments than was the constitution of Sparta.

32   About the same time in this summer the Athenians reduced
Scione. They put to death the men of military age, made slaves of
the women and children, and gave the land to the Plataeans to live
in. They also brought the Delians back again to Delos – a move
suggested both by Athenian misfortunes in battle and by an oracle
from the god in Delphi.

At the same time war broke out between the Phocians and the
Locrians.

Corinth and Argos were now in alliance, and their representatives went to Tegea to try to get her to revolt from Sparta. They
realized the importance of Tegea and thought that, if she would
come over to them, the whole of the Peloponnese would be on
their side. The Tegeans, however, said that they would do nothing
against Sparta, and the Corinthians, who up to this moment had
been acting with great energy, now became much less forward in
the matter, fearing that now none of the other states would come
over to them. Still they approached the Boeotians with the request
that they would become allies of Corinth and Argos and pursue a
joint policy with them; they also asked the Boeotians to accompany
them to Athens and to obtain for them, too, a ten days' truce like
the one arranged between the Athenians and Boeotians soon after
the fifty years' treaty; in case of the Athenians refusing to do this,
they urged the Boeotians to denounce the armistice and not make
any truce in future without Corinthian participation. These were
the Corinthian requests, and, so far as the alliance with Argos was
concerned, the Boeotians said that they must wait; they did, however, accompany the Corinthians to Athens, but failed to secure a
ten days' truce for them. Instead the Athenians replied that Corinth
had her treaty already, if she was an ally of Sparta. Nevertheless
the Boeotians would not denounce their own ten days' truce, in
spite of all appeals made to them by Corinth and accusations that
they had promised to do so. As for Corinth, her armistice with
Athens lacked the ratification of oaths.

33   The same summer the Spartans in full force marched into
Arcadia against the Parrhasians under the command of Pleistoanax,
the son of Pausanias, King of Sparta. The Parrhasians were subjects of Mantinea, and one of their political parties had asked for
Spartan help; at the same time the Spartans wanted, if possible, to

destroy the fortress of Cypsela, which the Mantineans had built and garrisoned in Parrhasian territory and which commanded the district of Sciritis in Laconia. The Spartans laid waste the land of the Parrhasians, and the Mantineans, leaving their city in the hands of an Argive garrison, used their own forces to defend the territory of their allies. They were, however, unable to save the fortress at Cypsela or the Parrhasian cities, and so they returned home. The Spartans made the Parrhasians independent, demolished the fortress, and then went back to Sparta.

34　　The same summer the soldiers who had gone out to Thrace with Brasidas returned to Sparta. They had been brought home by Clearidas after the treaty. The Spartans decreed that the helots who had fought with Brasidas should be given their freedom and allowed to live wherever they liked, and not long afterwards they settled them with the already freed helots at Lepreum, on the frontier between Laconia and Elis, Sparta being already on bad terms with Elis. As for those Spartans who had been captured on the island and who had surrendered their arms, it was feared that they might think they were going to be at a great disadvantage because of what had happened to them and that, if they retained their rights, they might start a revolution. They were therefore deprived of the rights of citizenship, though some of them were already in important positions. The deprivation meant that they were debarred from holding any command, and not allowed to buy or to sell. After a period of time, however, their rights were

35　restored to them. The same summer the Dians took Thyssus, a town on Acte in Athos, which was allied to Athens.

All through this summer there was free intercourse between the Athenians and the Peloponnesians, but from the moment the treaty was agreed upon there was suspicion on both sides because of the failure of each to give back the places that should have been given back. It had fallen by lot to Sparta to begin by restoring Amphipolis and the other towns; this she had not done, nor had she got the treaty accepted by her Thracian allies, or by the Boeotians, or by the Corinthians. The Spartans were always saying that, if her allies still refused to accept the treaty, they would join with the Athenians in compelling them to do so; dates were suggested after the expiry of which those who still refused to come in were to be declared enemies of both parties, but nothing was ever committed to writing. The result was that, when the Athenians saw that none of these promises was being actually fulfilled, they suspected Sparta of bad faith; not only did they refuse her request to have Pylos restored to her, but they regretted having given up the prisoners taken on the island and they held on to the other places, waiting until Sparta fulfilled her part of the agreement. The Spartans, on the other hand, claimed that they had done the best they could; they had given up all the Athenian prisoners in their hands, they had withdrawn their soldiers from Thrace and done everything else that it was in their power to do; as for Amphipolis, they said that they did not have sufficient control over the place to be able to hand it over, but they would try to bring the Boeotians and Corinthians into the treaty, to get Panactum back, and to see that all Athenian prisoners in Boeotia were sent home. Meanwhile they claimed that Pylos should be given back, or at least that the Messenians and helots should be withdrawn, just as Sparta had withdrawn her own troops from Thrace, and that the Athenians should, if they wished, garrison the place themselves. After a number of conferences and long discussions during this summer, the Spartans managed to persuade the Athenians to withdraw from Pylos the Messenians, and the rest of the helots and deserters from Laconia. These were settled by the Athenians at Cranii in Cephallenia. So for this summer there was a state of peace and mutual intercourse between Athens and Sparta.

36   Next winter, however, there were different ephors at Sparta from the ones who had been in office at the time the treaty was made, and some of them were actually opposed to the treaty. Embassies arrived from the Spartan League; representatives from Athens, Boeotia, and Corinth were also there, and, after a lot of discussion with each other, came to no agreement at all. They were then setting off home when Cleobulus and Xenares, the ephors who were particularly anxious to put an end to the peace, approached the Boeotians and Corinthians privately. They advised them to follow a common policy whenever possible, and suggested that the Boeotians should first become allies of Argos and then try to bring themselves and Argos into alliance with Sparta. In this way, they pointed out, Boeotia would be least likely to be forced

into accepting the treaty with Athens; for Sparta would prefer the friendship and alliance of Argos even if that meant the hostility of Athens and the breaking up of the treaty; the Boeotians no doubt knew that Sparta had always wanted the friendship of Argos on fair and honourable terms, since, in her view, this would make it much easier to carry on the war outside the Peloponnese. Meanwhile they asked the Boeotians to hand over Panactum to them so that they might, if possible, exchange it for Pylos, and so be in a better position for making war on Athens.

37   The Boeotians and Corinthians set off home with these messages for their governments from Xenares and Cleobulus and their other friends in Sparta. On their way back they were met by two men who held important positions in the government of Argos and who had been waiting for them on the road. These two men suggested that the Boeotians also should become allies of Argos, like the Corinthians, the Eleans, and the Mantineans, and said that, if this could be brought about, it was their belief that the alliance, acting as one body, would be in a position to make war or peace just as it wished whether with Sparta or with any other power. The Boeotian ambassadors were delighted with this proposal, for they found themselves being asked to do just what their friends in Sparta had suggested; and the two Argives, when they discovered that their proposition was welcome, went away, after having undertaken to send ambassadors to the Boeotians. On their return the Boeotians reported to their government both what they had heard in Sparta and from the Argives whom they had met on the road. The government was pleased with the news and entered into the plan all the more willingly because of the coincidence that their friends in Sparta were asking for the very thing that Argos herself wanted. Not long afterwards representatives from Argos arrived with the proposals as already outlined, and the Boeotian government, after indicating its approval, sent them home with the promise that they would send representatives of their own to Argos to negotiate the alliance.

38   In the meantime the commanders of Boeotia, the Corinthians, the Megarians, and the ambassadors from Thrace decided first of all to exchange oaths among themselves to come to each other's help on any occasion when it was required and not to make war

or peace separately; after this, it was proposed, the Boeotians and Megarians, who were acting in concert, should ally themselves with Argos. But before the oaths were exchanged the Commanders of the Boeotians communicated these proposals to the four Councils of Boeotia, who form the supreme authority of the state. Their recommendation was that oaths should be exchanged with all cities who were willing to join a defensive alliance with Boeotia, but the members of the Councils refused to agree to this, since they were afraid of acting in opposition to Sparta by entering into a league with Corinth, which had revolted from the Spartan confederacy. For the commanders of Boeotia had not informed the Councils of what had taken place in Sparta, and of how they had been advised by the ephors Cleobulus and Xenares and their other friends first of all to become allies of Argos and Corinth and then afterwards to join with Sparta; their view was that, even if they said nothing about all this, the Councils would still vote in accordance with the decisions and the advice of the Commanders of Boeotia. Now, with this check to the whole affair, the Corinthians and the ambassadors from Thrace went away without having achieved anything, and the Commanders of Boeotia, who had intended previously to try to make the alliance with Argos, if they could get their way on the first point, now gave up the idea of bringing the question of Argos before the Councils, and did not send representatives to Argos as they had promised. In fact the whole plan suffered from neglect and procrastination.

39   In this same winter the Olynthians assaulted Mecyberna, a town garrisoned by Athenians, and took the place.

All this time discussions had been going on between the Athenians and Spartans with regard to the restoration of places which each side still held, and now the Spartans, in the hope that if Athens got back Panactum from the Boeotians, they themselves would recover Pylos, sent an embassy to Boeotia with the request that Panactum and the Athenian prisoners should be put into Spartan hands, so that they might be exchanged for Pylos. The Boeotians, however, said that they would do so only on condition that Sparta made a separate alliance with them as she had done with Athens. The Spartans realized that this would involve a breach of faith with Athens, since it was laid down in the treaty that neither side should make peace or war without the other; on the other hand, they wanted to have Panactum to offer in exchange for Pylos, and at the same time there was strong pressure in favour of the deal with Boeotia from the party which wanted to put an end to the peace. So at the very end of winter, or beginning of spring, they made the alliance with the Boeotians, who immediately began to dismantle the fortifications of Panactum. This ended the eleventh year of the war.

ALLIANCE BETWEEN ATHENS AND ARGOS

40 By the beginning of the following summer the Argives had begun to fear that they were going to be isolated and that the whole alliance would go over to Sparta. The ambassadors promised by the Boeotians had not appeared; they saw that Panactum was being dismantled and heard of the separate alliance between Boeotia and Sparta. They believed, too, that Sparta had persuaded the Boeotians to destroy Panactum and to join the pact with Athens, and that Athens was aware of all this, so that now they could not even count upon an alliance with Athens, whereas previously they had been confident that, with Athens and Sparta at variance, supposing their treaty with Sparta came to an end, they could always fall back on the Athenian alliance. Thus the Argives found themselves in an awkward position and feared that the result of their refusal up to now to renew the treaty with Sparta and of their ambition to become the leaders of the Peloponnese might be that they would have to fight Sparta, Tegea, Boeotia, and Athens all at once. They therefore sent off representatives to Sparta as fast as they could, choosing for this post Eustrophus and Aeson, who seemed most likely to be acceptable to the Spartans, in the conviction that their best course under existing circumstances was to make a treaty with Sparta on whatever terms were available and be left in peace and quiet.

41   Arrived in Sparta, the Argive representatives discussed with the Spartans the conditions for a treaty. First of all they insisted that the question of the Cynurian land should be settled by arbitration, the arbitrator to be either a city or an individual. There have been

constant disputes about this district which is on the frontier between the two states. It includes the towns of Thyrea and Anthene and is occupied by the Spartans. The Spartans refused even to discuss this point, but said that, if Argos would agree, they were prepared to accept the same terms as in the previous treaty. Nevertheless the Argive representatives managed in the end to get the Spartans to agree to the following arrangement: for the present there should be a peace treaty for fifty years, but each side should have the right, provided that there was no plague or war in Sparta or in Argos, to issue a challenge to the other and decide the question of the disputed land by battle – as had once been done in the past, when both sides claimed that they had won – no to be pursuit allowed across the frontiers of Argos or of Sparta. This idea seemed at first to the Spartans simply a piece of foolishness, but they wanted friendly relations with Argos at almost any price, and so they accepted the Argive proposals and had them drawn up in writing. Before, however, they should be considered binding, they asked the Argive representatives to return to Argos and submit the proposals to the people; then, if they were approved by the people they were to come to Sparta for the feast of the Hyacinthia and take the oaths. The representatives accordingly set out for home.

42   Meanwhile, during these negotiations of the Argives, the Spartan representatives Andromedes, Phaedimus, and Antimenidas were supposed to receive from the Boeotians Panactum and the prisoners, and to restore them to Athens. As for Panactum, they found the Boeotians had acted on their own account and had dismantled the fortress on the pretext that at some time in the distant past, when there had been a dispute about the place, oaths had been exchanged between the two peoples that neither should build there, though both should have rights of pasture. As for the Athenian prisoners of war held by the Boeotians, Andromedes and his colleagues took charge of them and brought them back to Athens. Here they restored the prisoners and informed the Athenians of the demolition of Panactum. This they regarded as being equivalent to handing the place back, since it could now no longer be used by any power hostile to Athens; however, when they expressed this view, Athenian opinion was outraged. The Athenians considered that

Sparta had shown bad faith both in regard to the demolition of Panactum, which should have been restored to them intact, and also because, as they now found out, Sparta had made a separate alliance with the Boeotians, in spite of all the previous undertakings that Sparta and Athens would combine forces in order to compel those states to accept the treaty which had hitherto refused to do so. The Athenians could think of other points, too, where the agreement had not been kept; they considered that they had been cheated, and they gave a rough answer to the Spartan representatives before they sent them away.

43   Now that relations between Athens and Sparta had taken this turn for the worse, the party in Athens also which wanted to put an end to the peace began to make itself felt immediately. The leader of this group was Alcibiades, the son of Clinias, a man who was still young in years (or would have been thought so in any other city in Hellas), but who had reached a position of importance owing to the respect in which his family was held. He was genuinely convinced that the best thing for Athens was an alliance with Argos – though it is true also that considerations of his own dignity affected his opposition to the peace with Sparta. He did not like the the fact that the Spartans had negotiated the treaty through Nicias and Laches, paying no attention to him because of his youth; nor had they treated him with the respect he thought due to the fact that in the past his family had looked after Spartan interests in Athens – a post which his grandfather had given up, but which he himself wanted to take on again, as he had shown by his attentions to the prisoners captured on the island. He considered therefore that in every direction he was receiving less than his due, and from the first he had opposed the peace, saying that the Spartans could not be relied upon, and that their only object in making the treaty was to be able in this way first to crush Argos and afterwards to isolate Athens and attack her. Now, with relations strained as they were, he at once sent a personal message to the Argives, urging them to come as quickly as possible to Athens with the Mantineans and the Eleans and to make proposals for an alliance; this, he said, was the right moment for doing so, and he would do everything he could to help.

44   This message was received by the Argives, who now realized

that the Athenians, so far from having had a hand in the alliance with Boeotia, were in reality on extremely bad terms with Sparta. The Argives therefore sent no instructions to their representatives who had gone to Sparta with the idea of negotiating a treaty, and instead began to look towards Athens, thinking that, if war broke out, they would have in her an ally whose friendship was of long standing, who was a sister democracy, and whose naval power was great. So they immediately sent representatives to Athens to negotiate an alliance; with them also came representatives from Elis and Mantinea.

A deputation also hurried to Athens from Sparta. It consisted of people who were supposed to be on good terms with the Athenians – Philocharidas, Leon, and Endius – and it came because the Spartans were afraid that Athens, in her present angry mood, might ally herself with Argos; also to ask for Pylos in exchange for Panactum and to defend the Spartan action with regard to the alliance with Boeotia by claiming that it was not an alliance 45 directed against Athens. The Spartan delegates spoke in front of the Council on these points and made it clear that they had come with full powers to reach an agreement on all other matters in dispute. This speech of theirs made Alcibiades afraid that, if they repeated it in front of the Assembly, they might win the people over to their side and that the Argive alliance might be rejected. He therefore used the following expedient against them. By pledging his word to the Spartans he persuaded them that, if they made no mention of their full powers in the assembly, he would give Pylos back to them, saying that he himself would get the Athenians to agree to this, just as it was now he who was opposing the idea; he would also arrange for the other points to be settled. His plan was to drive a wedge between the Spartans and Nicias, and also he intended by attacking them in the assembly for having no sincerity in their intentions and for never saying the same thing twice to bring about the alliance with Argos, Elis, and Mantinea. And so indeed it happened. When they came forward in front of the people and, in reply to a question, said just the opposite to what they had said in the Council – namely that they had not come with full powers – the Athenians lost all patience with them, and listened instead to Alcibiades, who now attacked the Spartans even more bitterly than before. They were in fact prepared to bring in the Argives and those who had come with them immediately and to make them their allies. However, before anything was finally settled there was an earthquake and this assembly was adjourned.

46   In the assembly held on the following day Nicias, in spite of the fact that the Spartans had been tricked and he himself had been equally deceived by their failure to admit that they had come with full powers, nevertheless still insisted that it was better to be friends with Sparta. His proposal was that the negotiations with Argos should be postponed and that they should send again to Sparta to find out what her intentions were. To have the war put off, he said, would increase the prestige of Athens and injure that of Sparta; everything was going well for Athens, and i t was therefore the best policy to safeguard this success as long as possible, while for Sparta, in her present difficulties, it would be a positive god-send to risk her hand as soon as she could. In this way he persuaded the Athenians to send a deputation, in which he was included himself, to tell the Spartans that, if they really meant well, they should give back Panactum intact, give back Amphipolis, and renounce their alliance with the Boeotians unless they subscribed to the peace treaty (this being in accordance with the provision that neither side was to have the right to conclude separate agreements). The ambassadors were also instructed to say that the Athenians, too, if they wanted to act illegally, might already have made an alliance with the Argives, who were in fact in Athens for this very purpose. Other instructions also with regard to other complaints were given to Nicias and his colleagues, who were then sent to Sparta.

When they arrived they said what they had come to say, and pointed out finally that unless Sparta would give up her alliance with the Boeotians (so long as the Boeotians remained outside the peace settlement), Athens on her side would enter into alliance with Argos and the friends of Argos. The Spartans refused to give up the Boeotian alliance – this under the influence of the party of Xenares the ephor and of those who thought along the same lines. They did, however, renew the oaths at the request of Nicias, who was frightened at the prospect of returning home with nothing accomplished and of then being attacked – as indeed he was, since he was regarded as being responsible for the treaty with the Spartans.

On his return the Athenians heard that nothing had been gained from Sparta. This and the thought that they were being treated unjustly infuriated them. The Argives and their allies were still at Athens, and Alcibiades introduced them before the ssembly. A treaty and alliance with them were concluded on the following terms:

47 'The Athenians, the Argives, the Mantineans, and the Eleans, for themselves and for the allies under their control, made a treaty for a hundred years, to be without fraud or damage, by land and by sea.

'It shall not be lawful to take up arms with intent to do injury either for the Argives, Eleans, Mantineans, and their allies against the Athenians and the allies under Athenian control, or for the Athenians and their allies against the Argives, Eleans, Mantineans, and their allies, in any way or by any means whatever.

'The Athenians, the Argives, the Mantineans, and the Eleans shall be allies for a hundred years on the following terms:

'In case of an enemy invasion of Athenian territory, the Argives, Mantineans, and Eleans are to go to the help of Athens as the Athenians may require them to do so, in the most effective way possible, according to their resources. But if, by this time, the enemy has laid waste the country and gone away, then that city shall be held to be in a state of war with the Argives, the Mantineans, the Eleans, and the Athenians and shall be punished by all of these. Peace shall not be made with that city by any of these states separately, but only with the approval of them all.

'In the same way, the Athenians are to go to the help of Argos, Mantinea, and Elis in case of any enemy invasion of Argive, Mantinean, or Elean territory, as these states may require them to do so, in the most effective way possible, according to their resources. But if by this time the enemy has laid waste the country and gone away, then that city shall be held to be in a state of war with the Athenians, the Argives, the Mantineans, and the Eleans and shall be punished by all of them. Peace shall not be made with that city by any of these states separately, but only with the approval of them all.

'No army marching on any hostile mission shall be permitted to pass through the territories of the allied powers themselves or of the allies under their control, nor shall any force be allowed to pass by sea, unless all the states – Athens, Argos, Mantinea, and Elis – vote in favour of allowing such passage. With regard to the troops sent out to the help of another city, the city which sends them shall be responsible for feeding them for thirty days from their arrival in the city which has asked for them and shall also supply them on their return journey. But if their services are required for a longer period, the city that sent for them shall be responsible for their supplies at the rate of three Aeginetan obols a day for a hoplite, archer, or light infantryman, and an Aeginetan drachma for a cavalryman.[39] The city which sends for the troops shall have the command of them while the war is in its own territory. But in the case of the cities deciding upon a joint expedition, the command shall be divided equally among all the cities.

'The treaty shall be sworn to by the Athenians for themselves and their allies, and it shall be sworn to city by city by the Argives, Mantineans, Eleans, and their allies. Each shall swear by the oath which is most binding in his own country, and it shall be taken over full-grown sacrificial victims. The words of the oath shall be these:

'"I will stand by this alliance and its articles, justly, innocently, and sincerely, and will not transgress the same in any way or by any means whatever."

'The oath shall be taken at Athens by the Council and the city magistrates, and shall be administered by the Prytanes; at Argos by the Council, the Eighty, and the Artynae, and shall be administered by the Eighty; at Mantinea by the Demiurgi, the Council, and the other magistrates, and shall be administered by the Theori and Polemarchs; at Elis by the Demiurgi, the magistrates, and the Six Hundred, and shall be administered by the Demiurgi and the Thesmophylaces. The oaths shall be renewed by the Athenians going to Elis, Mantinea, and Argos thirty days before the Olympic Games; by the Argives, Eleans, and

39. See Appendix 2.

Mantineans going to Athens ten days before the great Panathen-
aeic festival.

'The articles of the treaty, the oaths, and the alliance shall be in-
scribed on a stone pillar by the Athenians in the Acropolis, by the
Argives in the market-place in the temple of Apollo, by the
Mantineans in the temple of Zeus in the market-place; and at
Olympia a brazen pillar shall be erected jointly by them at the
Olympic Games now at hand.

'Should these cities decide on the advisability of making any
addition to the above articles, whatever they shall all agree upon
after consultation together shall be regarded as binding.'

48   So the treaty and alliance were concluded, yet the treaty between
Athens and Sparta was not, because of this, denounced by either
party. Corinth, though an ally of Argos, did not come into the
new treaty; nor indeed had she joined in the offensive and defensive alliance concluded previously between the Eleans, Argives, and
Mantineans. At that time she had stated that she was satisfied with
the first alliance, which was purely defensive and bound the con-
tracting parties to come to each other's aid, but not to join in
making war on anyone. So the Corinthians took up a position
independent from that of their allies and again began to look in the
direction of Sparta.

49   This summer were celebrated the Olympic Games, in which the
Arcadian Androsthenes won the wrestling and boxing for the first
time. The Spartans were refused access to the temple by the Eleans
and so prevented from sacrificing or competing in the games. This
was because the Spartans had not paid the fine which had been
imposed upon them by the Eleans according to the Olympic law.
The Elean case was that the Spartans had made an attack on Fort
Phyrcus and had sent hoplites of theirs into Lepreum during the
period of the Olympic truce. The fine imposed was 2,000 minae,
two minae for each hoplite, as is laid down in the law. The Spartans on their side sent a delegation to protest against this award.
They claimed that the truce had still not been proclaimed in
Sparta at the time when they sent out the hoplites. The Eleans
replied that the truce was already in force at Elis (it is among the
Eleans themselves that the truce is first proclaimed), that they were

thus living on a peace-time basis, expecting no attack, and had been taken unawares by this act of Spartan aggression. The Spartan answer to this was that there was no point in proclaiming the truce at Sparta, if at that time the Eleans had really believed Sparta to have done wrong; but in fact they had proclaimed it, thus showing that they did not believe this at all, and that after the proclamation there had been no further attacks on Elean territory. The Eleans still stuck to their point, that nothing would convince them that Sparta had not committed an act of aggression; they were prepared, however, if Sparta gave them back Lepreum, to make no claim to their own share of the money and to pay themselves on behalf of Sparta what was due to the god.

50   This proposal was unacceptable to Sparta, and the Eleans then made another. The Spartans need not give back Lepreum, if they were averse from doing so, but they should go up to the altar of Olympian Zeus, since they were so anxious to have access to the temple, and there swear an oath in front of the Hellenes, guaranteeing to pay the fine at a future date.

When this proposal also was turned down, the Spartans were refused access to the temple, and sacrificed at home. All the other Hellenes took part in the games, except the people of Lepreum. The Eleans, however, were still afraid that the Spartans might use force in order to take part in the sacrifices, and they kept their young men under arms to guard against such action. In this they were supported by 1,000 Argives and 1,000 Mantineans, also by some Athenian cavalry, who were waiting for the festival at Harpina. However, there was great alarm at the assembly at the prospect of the Spartans appearing with an army, especially after Lichas, the son of Arcesilaus, a Spartan, had been given a beating by the umpires on the course. The reason for this was as follows. The chariot and pair belonging to Lichas had won the race, but, as he had no right to enter for the event, it was announced that the victor was the Boeotian people. Lichas had then come out on to the course and crowned the charioteer in order to show that the chariot was his own. As a result of this incident, people were more afraid than ever, and there was a general expectation that something was likely to happen. The Spartans, however, made no move and allowed the festival to pass off quietly.

After the Olympic Games the Argives and their allies went to Corinth to ask the Corinthians to join them. A delegation from Sparta was there also. Long discussions took place, but in the end nothing came of them, as there was an earthquake, and they all returned to their cities. So the summer ended.

51   Next winter there was a battle between the people of Heraclea in Trachis and the Aenianians, Dolopians, Malians, and some of the Thessalians. These are all tribes in the neighbourhood of Heraclea, and were all hostile to it, since it was their territory in particular which was threatened by this fortified post. Ever since the city had been founded they had opposed it and done it all the harm they could, and now in this battle they defeated the people of Heraclea, many of whom were killed, including the Spartan commander, Xenares, the son of Cnidis. So the winter ended and with it the twelfth year of the war.

CAMPAIGNS IN THE PELOPONNESE

52 At the very beginning of the following summer the Boeotians took over the city of Heraclea, which was in a bad enough state after the battle, and expelled the Spartan Agesippidas for incompetence in governing the place. Their reason for taking over the town was fear of the Athenians occupying it while Sparta was involved in her difficulties in the Peloponnese. Nevertheless this action of the Boeotians caused offence at Sparta.

In the same summer Alcibiades, the son of Clinias, who was now one of the generals at Athens, with the backing of the Argives and the allies, went into the Peloponnese, taking with him a few Athenian hoplites and archers and picking up on his way contingents from the allies there. With this army he marched through the Peloponnese, made various arrangements in connection with the alliance, and persuaded the people of Patrae to extend their walls down to the sea. He also intended to build a fortified post himself near the Achaean Rhium, but was prevented from doing this by forces brought up from Corinth and Sicyon and other places likely to suffer if his plan were carried out.

53   The same summer war broke out between Epidaurus and Argos.

The pretext was that the Epidaurians did not send an offering for their grazing land which they were supposed to send to Apollo Pythaeus, the Argives being chiefly responsible for the temple. But quite apart from this ground of complaint, Alcibiades and the Argives had decided, if possible, to gain control of Epidaurus, partly in order to keep Corinth quiet and partly so that Athenian reinforcements from Aegina would have a shorter passage than the voyage round Scyllaeum. The Argives therefore prepared to invade Epidaurus by themselves to enforce the payment of the offering.

54 At about the same time the Spartans in full force, under the command of their King, Agis, the son of Archidamus, marched out to Leuctra on their frontier opposite Mount Lycaeum. No one, not even the cities which had sent contingents, knew what was the aim of this expedition. However, the sacrifices for crossing the frontier did not appear favourable, and the Spartans returned home themselves and sent round instructions to their allies to be ready to march out after the next month, which was the month of Carneus and is a sacred period for the Dorians.

Once the Spartans had retreated, the Argives marched out on the fourth day from the end of the month before Carneus. For the whole time that their expedition lasted they called each day the fourth from the end of the month, and they proceeded to invade and lay waste Epidaurus. When the Epidaurians summoned their allies to help them, some made the excuse that it was the sacred month, and others, thought they advanced as far as the frontier, made no further move.

55 While the Argives were in Epidaurus, representatives of the cities, on the invitation of the Athenians, met together at Mantinea. In the discussion that took place, the Corinthian Euphamidas said that there was a discrepancy between what they were saying and what they were actually doing; while they were sitting there talking about peace, the Epidaurians and their allies and the Argives stood facing each other on the battle-field; first of all, therefore, representatives from each side should go and separate the two armies, and then would be the time to talk again about peace. This suggestion was adopted, and they went and secured the retirement of the Argives from Epidaurus. Afterwards they met together

again, but came no nearer to reaching agreement than they had before, and the Argives once more invaded Epidaurus and laid the country waste. The Spartans did march out as far as Caryae, but on this occasion, too, the frontier sacrifices were unfavourable, and so they went back again. The Argives laid waste about a third of the territory of Epidaurus and then returned home. A thousand Athenian hoplites under the command of Alcibiades had come to support them, but when he found that the Spartan expedition had come to an end and that his men were no longer needed, Alcibiades withdrew. And so this summer passed.

56   Next winter the Spartans eluded the Athenian blockade and sent in by sea to Epidaurus a garrison of 300 men under the command of Agesippidas. The Argives then went to the Athenians and complained of their having allowed this movement to take place by sea in contravention of the terms of the treaty, where it was laid down that neither party should allow an enemy to go through its territory. They stated that they would consider themselves to have been unfairly treated unless the Athenians would now put into Pylos a force of Messenians and helots to operate against the Spartans. Alcibiades persuaded the Athenians to inscribe on the Laconian pillar at the end of the main inscription the words 'The Spartans have not kept their oaths', and to send the helots of Cranii to Pylos to raid the country. Apart from this they took no further action.

During this winter fighting continued between the Argives and the Epidaurians. No pitched battle was fought, but there were ambushes and raids, in which there were a certain number of casualties now on one side, now on the other. At the end of the winter, when it was nearly spring, the Argives took scaling-ladders and went to Epidaurus, hoping to find it undefended because of the war and to capture it by force; but they returned without having met with any success. So the winter ended and the thirteenth year of the war.

57   In the middle of the next summer, the Spartans, seeing that their allies, the Epidaurians, were hard put to it and that in the rest of the Peloponnese some states were in revolt and others turning against Sparta, decided that the mischief would spread still further unless they took the initiative at once. They therefore marched

against Argos with their whole army, including the helots. The Spartan King Agis, the son of Archidamus, was in command; the Tegeans and other Spartan allies in Arcadia marched with them. The allies from the rest of the Peloponnese and from outside it assembled at Phlius. From Boeotia came 5,000 hoplites, 5,000 light troops, 500 cavalry, and 500 dismounted troops trained to operate with the cavalry. Two thousand hoplites came from Corinth. The rest brought their different contingents, though the Phliasians, in whose country the army was based, brought their entire force.

58   The preparations being made by the Spartans had been known to the Argives from the first. They waited until the Spartans were moving towards Phlius to join the rest of their allies, and then they, too, marched out. They were reinforced by the Mantineans with their allies and by 3,000 hoplites from Elis. Moving forward, they made contact with the Spartans at Methydrium in Arcadia. Each side took up positions on a hill, and the Argives, finding the Spartans isolated from the rest of their allies, prepared to give battle. Agis, however, broke camp in the night without being observed and went on to Phlius, where he joined the other allies. At dawn the Argives saw what had happened and marched first to Argos and then to the Nemean road, which was the route by which they expected that the Spartans and their allies would come down from the mountains. Agis, however, did not take the road they expected. He gave marching orders to the Spartans, Arcadians, and Epidaurians, and, going by another difficult road, made his way down into the plain of Argos. The Corinthians, Pellenians, and Phliasians marched by another steep road. The Boeotians, Megarians, and Sicyonians were ordered to come down by the Nemean road, where the Argives were posted, so that, if the Argives went down to the plain to oppose Agis and his troops, they might fall upon them from the rear with the cavalry. After making these arrangements, Agis made his way into the plain and began to lay waste Saminthus and other places.

59   Realizing what had happened, the Argives left Nemea and came to meet him. It was now day. On their route they came in contact with the army of the Phliasians and the Corinthians, and killed a few of the Phliasians, losing a slightly greater number of their own men at the hands of the Corinthians. Meanwhile the Boeotians,

Megarians, and Sicyonians were marching on Nemea, according to their instructions. Here they found that the Argives were no longer holding their positions; instead they had gone down into the plain, where they saw their property being destroyed, and were now forming up in order of battle, with the Spartans also forming up against them. In fact the Argives were hemmed in on all sides. On the plain they were cut off from their city by the Spartans and the troops with them; on the hills above them were the Corinthians, Phliasians, and Pellenians; and in the direction of Nemea were the Boeotians, Sicyonians, and Megarians. They had no cavalry, since the Athenians, alone of their allies, had not yet arrived.

The greater part of the army of the Argives and their allies, so far from realizing how dangerous their position was, thought that they were going to fight on very favourable conditions, with the Spartans cut off in their own country close to their city. However, there were two men among the Argives (Thrasylus, who was one of the five generals, and Alciphron, who represented Spartan interests at Argos) who thought differently. Just as the armies were on the point of meeting, these two went forward, held a conference with Agis, and urged him not to bring on a battle, saying that the Argives were prepared to submit to fair and equal arbitration any complaints that Sparta had to make against them, and to make a treaty and live in peace for the future. In saying this 50 they spoke entirely for themselves, with no authority from the mass of the army. Agis, too, in accepting their proposals, acted on his own responsibility, and did not even discuss the question with the majority. He took into his confidence only one man among the high officers who were serving with him, and made a truce for four months, in the course of which time the Argives were expected to carry out what they had promised. He then immediately led his army off, giving no explanation to any of his other allies.

The Spartans and their allies followed the leadership of Agis, as they were bound to do by law, but they blamed him bitterly among themselves. There had been, they thought, a most excellent opportunity for joining battle, with the enemy surrounded on every side by infantry and cavalry, and now they were going away without having done anything worthy of the great strength they had. This was indeed the finest Hellenic army that had ever been brought together, and it was seen at its best while it was still all in one united force at Nemea. The Spartans were there with their whole army – the Arcadians, Boeotians, Corinthians, Sicyonians, Pellenians, Phliasians, and Megarians, all with picked troops; in fact a force that looked as though it could hold its own not only against the Argive League but against another such League in addition. As it was, the army retreated, putting the blame, as we have seen, on Agis, and the various contingents returned to their own states.

The Argives on their side were even more bitter in their protests against those who had made the truce without consulting the people. They, too, thought that they could never have had a better opportunity and that the Spartans had been allowed to escape; for the battle would have been fought under the walls of their city, and they would have had many brave allies on their side. On their return they began to stone Thrasylus in the Charadrus – the place where they try all cases arising out of a campaign before they enter the city. Thrasylus escaped with his life by taking refuge at the altar; his property, however, was confiscated.

61   After this, reinforcements arrived from Athens, 1,000 hoplites and 300 cavalry under the command of Laches and Nicostratus. In spite of everything, the Argives still shrank from breaking their truce with Sparta, and so they asked the Athenians to go away, and refused to grant their request to be allowed to speak in front of the assembly. The Mantineans and Eleans, however, who were still at Argos, supported the Athenian claim and finally compelled the Argives to accede to it. Alcibiades, who was there as ambassador, spoke for the Athenians in front of the Argives and their allies. He said that the treaty had not been lawfully made without the consent of the rest of the alliance, and that they should now, since the Athenians had arrived at such a favourable moment, get on with the war. The allies were won over by these arguments and immediately marched against Orchomenus in Arcadia, all except the Argives, who, in spite of having agreed with the rest, stayed behind at first, though later they also joined the expedition.

The whole allied force now took up its positions before Orchomenus, besieging the place and making assaults upon it. One of their chief reasons for wanting to have Orchomenus was that inside the city there were hostages from Arcadia, put there by the Spartans. The people of Orchomenus were alarmed by the weakness of their own fortifications and by the size of the enemy army; there was no sign of any help coming to them, and they were afraid that, before it did, they would be destroyed. They therefore surrendered on condition that they should join the alliance, give hostages of their own to the Mantineans, and give up also the hostages left there by the Spartans.

62   Now that they had taken Orchomenus, the allies discussed which of the other places to attack next. The Eleans were in favour of going against Lepreum, the Mantineans were for Tegea, and in this were supported by the Argives and the Athenians. Angry at the fact that they had not voted for the attack on Lepreum, the Eleans returned home. The other allies made their preparations at Mantinea for marching against Tegea. Inside Tegea itself there was a party who were arranging to surrender the place to them.

BATTLE OF MANTINEA

63 The Spartans, returned from Argos after making the four months' truce, were extremely indignant with Agis for not having conquered Argos when he had had such an opportunity as, they thought, had never occurred before; since it was by no means easy to bring together so many allied troops of such a high quality. But when news arrived of the capture of Orchomenus they were still more infuriated and, carried away by passion in a manner quite unlike themselves, were in favour of pulling down the house of Agis immediately and fining him 10,000 drachmae. Agis, however, begged them not to do so, and promised that when he had taken the field again he would atone for his faults by some noble action; if not, they could do with him what they liked. They therefore gave up the idea of fining him and of demolishing his house, and for the time being made a law which had never existed in Sparta previously, to the effect that ten Spartans of the officer class

should be chosen to act with him as advisers, and that without their authority he should not be empowered to lead an army out of the city.

64   Meanwhile news came to them from their friends in Tegea, who said that, unless they came quickly, Tegea would go over from them to Argos and her allies; in fact, it was already on the point of doing so. Now at last the Spartans moved quickly and came to the help of Tegea with their entire force both of citizens and helots in greater numbers than on any other occasion. They advanced to Orestheum in Maenalia and ordered the Arcadians who were in alliance with them to mobilize and follow in their tracks to Tegea. They themselves went as far as Orestheum with their whole army, and from there sent back a sixth part of the Spartans, consisting of the oldest and youngest troops, to guard their homes. They arrived at Tegea with the rest of their forces, and were soon joined there by their Arcadian allies. They also sent to Corinth and to the Boeotians, Phocians, and Locrians, telling them to bring up their forces as quickly as possible to Mantinea. This meant giving them short enough notice, and at the same time it was not easy for them to cut across the enemy-occupied country which lay between them and Mantinea unless they waited for each other and united all their forces together; nevertheless they made all the haste they could.

Meanwhile the Spartans, joined by the Arcadian allies who were there, invaded the territory of Mantinea, made their camp near the
65   temple of Heracles, and began to lay the country waste. When the Argives and their allies saw them, they took up a strong position, very difficult to approach, and there formed up in order of battle. The Spartans immediately advanced against them, and came up as close as a stone's throw or a javelin's cast. At this point one of the older men in the army, seeing that they were advancing against such a strong position, shouted out to Agis that he was trying to cure one evil with another, meaning by this that he was wanting to make up for the retreat from Argos, for which he had been blamed, by now courting danger at the wrong time. Agis, whether because of what the old soldier had shouted out or because he himself had suddenly changed his mind, quickly led his army back again before it had come to actual fighting. Going into the territory

of Tegea, he began to divert the water from there into the territory of Mantinea. This water is a constant cause of fighting between the Tegeans and the Mantineans because of the harm it does to the country into which it flows, and Agis planned to make the enemy, when they saw what was happening, come down from the hill to stop him diverting the water, and so fight a battle on the level ground. He therefore stayed where he was for that day, and spent the time in altering the course of the water.

The Argives and their allies were astonished at the fact that the enemy, after advancing so close to them, had then suddenly retreated. At first they did not know what to make of it, but afterwards, as the retreat proceeded and the enemy disappeared from sight, while they themselves stood still and made no effort to pursue, they once more began to blame their generals, who had, they thought, allowed the Spartans to escape on the previous occasion, when they were trapped in front of Argos, and now these same Spartans were running away again with no one pursuing them, getting away, in fact, in their own good time, while the Argive army was being betrayed. The generals were bewildered for the moment, but afterwards led the army down from the hill and went forward into the plain, where they camped with the intention of advancing on the enemy.

66   Next day the Argives and their allies formed up in the order in which they meant to fight if they made contact with the enemy, and the Spartans, coming back after their operations with the water to their old camp near the temple of Heracles, found themselves faced with an opposing army quite close to them, which had now all moved forward from the hill and was already in battle order. It was a moment when the Spartans were more startled than they could ever remember having been before. They had only the shortest possible time for getting ready, and each man took up his position with the utmost speed and alacrity, Agis, their King, giving the necessary orders, according to the law. When a King is leading the army, all instructions are given by him personally. He gives the word to the divisional commanders and it is passed on from them to the regimental commanders, from them to the company commanders, from them to the platoon commanders, and

from them to the platoons. So, too, if an order has to be passed along the line, it is done in the same way and quickly becomes effective, as nearly the whole Spartan army, except for a small part, consists of officers serving under other officers, and the responsibility for seeing that an order is carried out falls on a great many people.

67   On the left wing were the Sciritae, who, in a Spartan army, always have the privilege of occupying this position as a separate force. Next to them were the soldiers of Brasidas from Thrace and the helots who had been freed because of good conduct in the field. Then came the Spartans themselves, regiment after regiment. Next were the Arcadians from Heraea, and then the Maenalians. On the right wing were the Tegeans, with a few Spartans at the very end. The cavalry was posted at both wings.

This was the Spartan order of battle. On the other side the right wing was held by the Mantineans, since the action was taking place in their country; next to them were the allies from Arcadia, and then the thousand picked troops from Argos who had been given by the State a long course of military training at the public expense; next to them were the rest of the Argives, and then their allies, the Cleonaeans and Orneans; finally the Athenians were on the extreme left and had their own cavalry with them.

68   The arrangement and composition of the two armies were as above. The Spartan army looked the bigger, but it would be impossible for me to give the exact numbers either of the whole armies or of the various divisions on each side. The secrecy with which their affairs are conducted meant that no one knew the numbers of the Spartans, and for the rest it was impossible to rely on the estimates given, since it is human nature to boast about the size of one's own forces. The following method of calculation, however, makes it possible to estimate the numbers of Spartans engaged on this occasion. Not counting the Sciritae, who were 600 in all, there were seven regiments fighting in the battle. In each regiment there were four companies, and in each company four platoons. Four men fought in the front rank of each platoon; in depth the arrangement was not the same throughout, but depended on the decision of the commanders of the regiments; on the whole, though, they were drawn up eight deep. The first

rank, along the whole line, not counting the Sciritae, consisted of 448 men.

69　　The armies were now on the point of joining battle, and the generals on each side spoke to the troops under their command to encourage them. The Mantineans were told that they were to fight for their country, that it was a question of power or of slavery, of keeping the power which they had won or of relapsing again into the slavery of the past. The Argives were told that the battle was for their old position of supremacy, for the equal share in the Peloponnese which they had once had, to prevent them being deprived of this for ever, and at the same time to requite the many wrongs that had been done to them by an enemy and a neighbour. The Athenians were told of the glory they would win if, fighting at the side of so many brave allies, they showed themselves second to none, that to defeat the Spartans in the Peloponnese would make their own power greater and more secure, and that no one would ever again come to invade the territory of Athens. This was the type of encouragement given to the Argives and their allies. The Spartans on their side spoke their words of encouragement to each other man to man, singing their war songs, and calling on their comrades, as brave men, to remember what each knew so well, realizing that the long discipline of action is a more effective safeguard than hurried speeches, however well they may be delivered.

70　　After this the two armies met, the Argives and their allies advancing with great violence and fury, while the Spartans came on slowly and to the music of many flute-players in their ranks. This custom of theirs has nothing to do with religion; it is designed to make them keep in step and move forward steadily without breaking their ranks, as large armies often do when they are just about to join battle.

71　　While they were still approaching each other, King Agis decided to take the following measures. It is true of all armies that, when they are moving into action, the right wing tends to get unduly extended and each side overlaps the enemy's left with its own right. This is because fear makes every man want to do his best to find protection for his unarmed side in the shield of the man next to him on the right, thinking that the more closely the shields are locked together, the safer he will be. The fault comes originally from the man on the extreme right of the front line, who is always trying to keep his own unarmed side away from the enemy, and his fear spreads to the others who follow his example. So on this occasion the Mantineans on their wing stretched a long way beyond the Sciritae, and the Spartans and Tegeans stretched even farther beyond the Athenians, since their army was the bigger. Agis feared that his left would be encircled, and came to the conclusion that the Mantineans were outflanking it by too much. He therefore ordered the Sciritae and the troops who had served under Brasidas to move across to the left, so as to make their line level with that of the Mantineans, and he told the generals Hipponoidas and Aristocles to march into the gap thus formed and fill it up with two regiments taken from the right wing. He considered that this manoeuvre would strengthen the line opposing the Mantineans while still leaving him with a numerical superiority on his right.

72 What happened, however, was that, since the orders were given at such short notice and when the armies were actually on the move, Aristocles and Hipponoidas refused to go where they were told to go – because of this they were later found guilty of cowardice and banished from Sparta – and the enemy closed in before the Sciritae had had time to fill up the gap themselves (for Agis had ordered them to join up again with the main body as soon as he found that the two regiments had not moved into position). Certainly, so far as skill in manoeuvring goes, the Spartans had had the worst of it in every respect, but certainly they now showed that in courage they had no equals. Once the fighting began, the Mantinean right broke through the Spartan Sciritae and the troops who had been under Brasidas. Then the Mantineans, with their allies and the thousand picked troops of Argos, swept into the gap in the Spartan line that had still not been filled up. Here they surrounded the Spartans, killed many of them, and drove them right back as far as their wagons, where they killed some of the older men who were on guard there. So in this part of the field the Spartans were defeated. But with the rest of their army, and especially the centre, where King Agis was himself with the 300 troops called 'the knights', they fell upon the older men of the Argives and what are called 'the five companies', and upon the Cleonaeans, the

Orneans, and the Athenians stationed next to them, and put them all to flight; most of them, in fact, did not even stand up to the first shock, but gave way immediately when the Spartans charged, some being actually trampled underfoot in their anxiety to get away before the enemy reached them.

73 Now that the army of the Argives and their allies had given way at this point, contact was lost between them and their two wings, and at the same moment the Spartans and Tegeans on the right were sweeping round the Athenians with the troops outflanking them. The Athenians thus found themselves threatened from every direction; on one side they were being surrounded and on the other they were already defeated. In fact, they would have suffered more heavily than any other part of the army if they had not had their cavalry with them to help them. It also happened that, when Agis saw his left wing in difficulties (the one opposed to the Mantineans and the 1,000 Argives), he ordered the whole of the rest of his army to go to the relief of the part that was being defeated. While this movement was going on and the Spartan army was marching past and away from them, the Athenians with the defeated part of the Argives had plenty of time to escape. Meanwhile the Mantineans and their allies and the picked troops of the Argives ceased to press forward against the enemy. Seeing that their own side had been defeated and that the Spartans were bearing down on them, they took to flight. Many of the Mantineans were killed, but most of the picked Argive troops got away safely. They were not, however, pressed hard or for a long time on the flight and during the retreat. The Spartans will fight for a long time, stubbornly holding their ground until the moment they have put their enemy to flight; but once this moment comes they do not follow him up a great way or for long.

74 So the battle went, as nearly as possible as I have described it. It was certainly the greatest battle that had taken place for a very long time among Hellenic states, and it was fought by the most renowned cities in Hellas. The Spartans took up a position in front of the enemy dead and at once put up a trophy and stripped the bodies of those who had fallen. Taking up their own dead, they brought them back to Tegea and buried them there. The enemy dead they gave back under an armistice. Of the Argives, Orneans,

and Cleonaeans 700 were killed, of the Mantineans 200, and of the Athenians and Aeginetans 200, including both generals. On the Spartan side the allies suffered so little as to be hardly worth mentioning; as for the losses among the Spartans themselves, it was difficult to find out the truth; they were said, however, to have had about 300 killed.

75   When it was clear that there was going to be a battle, Pleistoanax, the other King, had come up with reinforcements consisting of the oldest and youngest troops. He reached Tegea and then, after hearing the news of the victory, went back again. The Spartans also sent messengers to turn back their allies from Corinth and from beyond the Isthmus. They then returned home themselves, dismissed their allies and, since it was the date of the Carnean holidays, proceeded to celebrate the festival. So by this one action they did away with all the reproaches that had been levelled against them by the Hellenes at this time, whether for cowardice, because of the disaster in the island, or for incompetence and lack of resolution on other occasions. It was now thought that, though they might have been cast down by fortune, they were still in their own selves the same as they always had been.

On the day before this battle the Epidaurians took advantage of the fact that the territory of Argos was left undefended, and invaded it in full force, killing many of the guards who had been left behind when the main Argive army had marched away.

After the battle 3,000 hoplites from Elis arrived as reinforcements to the Mantineans and also 1,000 Athenians, in addition to the force already there. All these allies immediately marched on Epidaurus, while the Spartans were celebrating the Carnean festival, and, sharing the work out among themselves, began to build a wall round the city. Though the others gave it up, the Athenians quickly completed the part assigned to them, which was round Cape Heraeum. They all left detachments to form a garrison for this fortification and then dispersed to their various cities. So the summer ended.

76   At the very beginning of the following winter, when the Carnean festival was over, the Spartans marched out and, arriving at Tegea, sent on to Argos proposals for a settlement. Even before

this time there had been a pro-Spartan party who wanted to over-throw the democracy in Argos, and now, after the battle, this party was in a much better position to persuade the people to accept the proposals. They wanted first to make peace with Sparta, to follow this up by making an alliance, and then finally to launch their attack on the democratic party. It was Lichas, the son of of Arcesilaus, who arrived from Sparta, where he had the official post of looking after the interests of Argive citizens. He now brought two proposals to Argos, one to be effective in war, if they wished to go on fighting, and one for peace, if they preferred peace. Alcibiades happened to be in Argos, and there were prolonged discussions; however, the pro-Spartan party, who could now show their hand more openly, persuaded the Argives to accept the proposal for a settlement, which was as follows:

77   'The Assembly of Sparta is prepared to make an agreement with the Argives on the following terms:

'The Argives shall give back to the Orchomenians their children and to the Maenalians their men, and shall give back to the Spartans the men they hold in Mantinea.

'The Argives shall evacuate Epidaurus and demolish the fortification there. If the Athenians refuse to leave Epidaurus, they shall be considered enemies of the Argives and of the Spartans and of the allies of Sparta and of the allies of Argos.

'If the Spartans have any children in their power, they shall give them back each to his own city.

'With regard to the offering due to the god, the Argives, if they wish, shall impose an oath on the Epidaurians; if not, they shall swear it themselves.

'All the cities in the Peloponnese, both great and small, shall be independent according to their national traditions. If any power from outside the Peloponnese invades Peloponnesian territory with hostile intent, the parties to this agreement shall unite to repel the invasion in such a way as shall be decided upon as most just and fair to the Peloponnesians.

'The allies of Sparta outside the Peloponnese shall be included in the treaty on the same terms as the Spartans, and the allies of Argos shall be included in the treaty on the same terms as the Argives, all being left in possession of what belongs to them. This treaty shall be submitted to the allies for their agreement. If the allies have any objections to raise, they shall refer the treaty to their home governments.'

78   This was the proposal which the Argives accepted first, and the Spartan army then left Tegea and went home. There was now regular communication between the two states, and not long afterwards the same party as before succeeded in getting the Argives to give up their alliance with Mantinea, Athens, and Elis and to make a treaty of peace and alliance with Sparta. It was concluded on the following terms:

79   'The Spartans and Argives agree to a treaty of peace and alliance for fifty years on the following terms:

'All disputes shall be settled by fair and impartial arbitration, in accordance with the customs of each state.

'The other cities in the Peloponnese shall have the right to join this treaty and alliance, as free and independent states, in full possession of what belongs to them, and with all disputes to be settled by fair and impartial arbitration in accordance with the customs of each state. The allies of Sparta outside the Peloponnese shall be included in the treaty on the same terms as the Spartans themselves, and the allies of Argos shall be included in the treaty on the same terms as the Argives themselves, all being left in possession of what belongs to them.

'If it should be necessary to send out a combined expeditionary force in any direction, the Spartans and Argives shall consult together and decide the question in the way most fair to the allies.

'If any of the cities inside or outside the Peloponnese is involved in a dispute concerning frontiers or any other matter, the dispute shall be settled. But if one of the allied cities comes into conflict with another allied city, they shall refer the dispute to another city regarded as impartial by both parties. Disputes between private individuals shall be settled in accordance with the laws of the states concerned.'

80   So this treaty and alliance came into force, and both sides gave back to each other whatever they had gained in war or in other ways.

They now followed a concerted policy and passed a decree not to receive any herald or delegation from the Athenians unless they abandoned their fortified posts in the Peloponnese and left the country; also not to make peace or war with any other power except jointly. This policy was pursued with energy. Both powers sent ambassadors to Thrace and to Perdiccas and persuaded him to take the oath of alliance with them. Though he did not break with Athens immediately, he had every intention of doing so, because he saw that this was what Argos had done, and his own family had come originally from Argos. They also renewed their old oaths with the Chalcidians and took new ones.

Apart from this, the Argives sent ambassadors to the Athenians, telling them to evacuate the fortification at Epidaurus. The Athenians saw that their own men were outnumbered by the rest of the garrison, and sent out Demosthenes to take charge of the withdrawal. When he arrived he organized an athletic contest outside the walls and, using this as a blind, as soon as the rest of the garrison had gone out, he shut the gates behind them. Later the Athenians renewed their treaty with Epidaurus and gave back the fortification themselves.

81   After the Argives had left the alliance, the Mantineans, though at first they took an independent stand, found that they were not strong enough to act without Argos, and in the end they also came to an agreement with Sparta and gave up control of the cities.

The Spartans and Argives now made a combined expedition with 1,000 men each. First the Spartan force went by itself to Sicyon and reorganized the government there on more oligarchical lines; afterwards the two forces united and suppressed the democracy at Argos, replacing it with an oligarchical government favourable to Sparta. This happened towards the end of the winter, just before spring. So the fourteenth year of the war ended.

82   In the following summer the people of Dium, in Athos, revolted from the Athenians and joined the Chalcidian League. The Spartans also took various measures in Achaea, making matters easier for them there than they had been previously.

Meanwhile the democrats at Argos had formed into a party again and regained their confidence. They waited till the very day that the Gymnopaedic festival was to be celebrated at Sparta, and then made their attack on the oligarchs. In the fighting that broke out in the city the democrats were victorious; they killed some of their enemies and exiled others. The Spartans had so far not appeared in response to previous appeals from their friends in Argos, but now they put off the Gymnopaedia and marched to their help. At Tegea, however, they heard that the oligarchs had been defeated and, in spite of the appeals of those who had escaped, refused to advance farther; instead they went back home and celebrated the Gymnopaedic festival. Afterwards ambassadors arrived both from the Argives in the city and from the exiled party. The allies were also present and, after much had been said on both sides, the Spartans reached the conclusion that the party in the city had done wrong, and decided to march against Argos. But time went by, and the expedition was constantly being put off. Meanwhile the democrats in Argos, out of fear of the Spartans, began to turn again towards the Athenian alliance, thinking that in this lay their greatest hopes of safety, and they built long walls down to the coast, so that with Athenian help they would be able, if they were blockaded by land, to import what they needed by sea. There were other cities in the Peloponnese, too, who knew about the building of the walls. The whole of the Argive people, men, women, and slaves, joined in the work of building, and carpenters and masons came to help them from Athens. So the summer ended.

83   In the following winter the Spartans, hearing of the building of the walls, marched against Argos with all their allies except the Corinthians. There was also a certain element inside Argos itself which was collaborating with them. King Agis, the son of Archidamus, led the expedition. The help which they had expected to get from their party inside the city failed to materialize. But they captured and demolished the walls that were being built, and took the Argive town of Hysia, putting to death all the free men who fell into their hands. They then went back and returned to their various cities. Afterwards the Argives also marched out into Phlius and laid the country waste before they returned again. This was because Phliasia was sheltering the exiles from Argos, most of whom had settled there.

In the same winter the Athenians blockaded Macedonia. Their

complaints against Perdiccas were that he had sworn alliance with Argos and Sparta, and that he had failed in his duty as an ally of Athens at the time when the Athenians had prepared an expedition against the Chalcidians in Thrace and against Amphipolis, under the command of Nicias, the son of Niceratus; this expedition had had to be broken up chiefly because Perdiccas had not played his part. He was therefore declared an enemy.

So this winter ended, and so ended the fifteenth year of the war.

THE MELIAN DIALOGUE[40]

84 Next summer Alcibiades sailed to Argos with twenty ships and seized 300 Argive citizens who were still suspected of being pro-Spartan. These were put by the Athenians into the nearby islands under Athenian control.

The Athenians also made an expedition against the island of Melos. They had thirty of their own ships, six from Chios, and two from Lesbos; 1,200 hoplites, 300 archers, and twenty mounted archers, all from Athens; and about 1,500 hoplites from the allies and the islanders.

The Melians are a colony from Sparta. They had refused to join the Athenian empire like the other islanders, and at first had remained neutral without helping either side; but afterwards, when the Athenians had brought force to bear on them by laying waste their land, they had become open enemies of Athens.

Now the generals Cleomedes, the son of Lycomedes, and Tisias, the son of Tisimachus, encamped with the above force in Melian territory and, before doing any harm to the land, first of all sent representatives to negotiate. The Melians did not invite these representatives to speak before the people, but asked them to make the statement for which they had come in front of the governing body and the few. The Athenian representatives then spoke as follows:

85 'So we are not to speak before the people, no doubt in case the mass of the people should hear once and for all and without

40. See Appendix 3.

interruption an argument from us which is both persuasive and incontrovertible, and should so be led astray. This, we realize, is your motive in bringing us here to speak before the few. Now suppose that you who sit here should make assurance doubly sure. Suppose that you, too, should refrain from dealing with every point in detail in a set speech, and should instead interrupt us whenever we say something controversial and deal with that before going on to the next point? Tell us first whether you approve of this suggestion of ours.'

86 The Council of the Melians replied as follows:

'No one can object to each of us putting forward our own views in a calm atmosphere. That is perfectly reasonable. What is scarcely consistent with such a proposal is the present threat, indeed the certainty, of your making war on us. We see that you have come prepared to judge the argument yourselves, and that the likely end of it all will be either war, if we prove that we are in the right, and so refuse to surrender, or else slavery.'

87 *Athenians:* If you are going to spend the time in enumerating your suspicions about the future, or if you have met here for any other reason except to look the facts in the face and on the basis of these facts to consider how you can save your city from destruction, there is no point in our going on with this discussion. If, however, you will do as we suggest, then we will speak on.

88 *Melians:* It is natural and understandable that people who are placed as we are should have recourse to all kinds of arguments and different points of view. However, you are right in saying that we are met together here to discuss the safety of our country and, if you will have it so, the discussion shall proceed on the lines that you have laid down.

89 *Athenians:* Then we on our side will use no fine phrases saying, for example, that we have a right to our empire because we defeated the Persians, or that we have come against you now because of the injuries you have done us – a great mass of words that nobody would believe. And we ask you on your side not to imagine that you will influence us by saying that you, though a colony of Sparta, have not joined Sparta in the war, or that you have never done us any harm. Instead we recommend that you should try to get what it is possible for you to get, taking into consideration

what we both really do think; since you know as well as we do
that, when these matters are discussed by practical people the
standard of justice depends on the equality of power to compel
and that in fact the strong do what they have the power to do and
the weak accept what they have to accept.

90　*Melians:* Then in our view (since you force us to leave justice
out of account and to confine ourselves to self-interest) – in our
view it is at any rate useful that you should not destroy a principle
that is to the general good of all men – namely, that in the case of
all who fall into danger there should be such a thing as fair play
and just dealing, and that such people should be allowed to use
and to profit by arguments that fall short of a mathematical
accuracy. And this is a principle which affects you as much as
anybody, since your own fall would be visited by the most
terrible vengeance and would be an example to the world.

91　*Athenians:* As for us, even assuming that our empire does come
to an end, we are not despondent about what would happen next.
One is not so much frightened of being conquered by a power
which rules over others, as Sparta does (not that we are concerned
with Sparta now), as of what would happen if a ruling power is
attacked and defeated by its own subjects. So far as this point is
concerned, you can leave it to us to face the risks involved. What
we shall do now is to show you that it is for the good of our own
empire that we are here and that it is for the preservation of your
city that we shall say what we are going to say. We do not want
any trouble in bringing you into our empire, and we want you to
be spared for the good both of yourselves and of ourselves.

92　*Melians:* And how could it be just as good for us to be the slaves
as for you to be the masters?

93　*Athenians:* You, by giving in, would save yourselves from disaster; we, by not destroying you, would be able to profit from
you.

94　*Melians:* So you would not agree to our being neutral, friends
instead of enemies, but allies of neither side?

95　*Athenians:* No, because it is not so much your hostility that
injures us; it is rather the case that, if we were on friendly terms
with you, our subjects would regard that as a sign of weakness in
us, whereas your hatred is evidence of our power.

96   *Melians:* Is that your subjects' idea of fair play – that no distinction should be made between people who are quite unconnected with you and people who are mostly your own colonists or else rebels whom you have conquered?

97   *Athenians:* So far as right and wrong are concerned they think that there is no difference between the two, that those who still preserve their independence do so because they are strong, and that if we fail to attack them it is because we are afraid. So that by conquering you we shall increase not only the size but the security of our empire. We rule the sea and you are islanders, and weaker islanders too than the others; it is therefore particularly important that you should not escape.

98   *Melians:* But do you think there is no security for you in what we suggest? For here again, since you will not let us mention justice, but tell us to give in to your interests, we, too, must tell you what our interests are and, if yours and ours happen to coincide, we must try to persuade you of the fact. Is it not certain that you will make enemies of all states who are at present neutral, when they see what is happening here and naturally conclude that in course of time you will attack them too? Does not this mean that you are strengthening the enemies you have already and are forcing others to become your enemies even against their intentions and their inclinations?

99   *Athenians:* As a matter of fact we are not so much frightened of states on the continent. They have their liberty, and this means that it will be a long time before they begin to take precautions against us. We are more concerned about islanders like yourselves, who are still unsubdued, or subjects who have already become embittered by the constraint which our empire imposes on them. These are the people who are most likely to act in a reckless manner and to bring themselves and us, too, into the most obvious danger.

100   *Melians:* Then surely, if such hazards are taken by you to keep your empire and by your subjects to escape from it, we who are still free would show ourselves great cowards and weaklings if we failed to face everything that comes rather than submit to slavery.

101   *Athenians:* No, not if you are sensible. This is no fair fight, with honour on one side and shame on the other. It is rather a question

of saving your lives and not resisting those who are far too strong for you.

102   *Melians:* Yet we know that in war fortune sometimes makes the odds more level than could be expected from the difference in numbers of the two sides. And if we surrender, then all our hope is lost at once, whereas, so long as we remain in action, there is still a hope that we may yet stand upright.

103   *Athenians:* Hope, that comforter in danger! If one already has solid advantages to fall back upon, one can indulge in hope. It may do harm, but will not destroy one. But hope is by nature an expensive commodity, and those who are risking their all on one cast find out what it means only when they are already ruined; it never fails them in the period when such a knowledge would enable them to take precautions. Do not let this happen to you, you who are weak and whose fate depends on a single movement of the scale. And do not be like those people who, as so commonly happens, miss the chance of saving themselves in a human and practical way, and, when every clear and distinct hope has left them in their adversity, turn to what is blind and vague, to prophecies and oracles and such things which by encouraging hope lead men to ruin.

104   *Melians:* It is difficult, and you may be sure that we know it, for us to oppose your power and fortune, unless the terms be equal. Nevertheless we trust that the gods will give us fortune as good as yours, because we are standing for what is right against what is wrong; and as for what we lack in power, we trust that it will be made up for by our alliance with the Spartans, who are bound, if for no other reason, then for honour's sake, and because we are their kinsmen, to come to our help. Our confidence, therefore, is not so entirely irrational as you think.

105   *Athenians:* So far as the favour of the gods is concerned, we think we have as much right to that as you have. Our aims and our actions are perfectly consistent with the beliefs men hold about the gods and with the principles which govern their own conduct. Our opinion of the gods and our knowledge of men lead us to conclude that it is a general and necessary law of nature to rule whatever one can. This is not a law that we made ourselves, nor were we the first to act upon it when it was made. We found it already

in existence, and we shall leave it to exist for ever among those who come after us. We are merely acting in accordance with it, and we know that you or anybody else with the same power as ours would be acting in precisely the same way. And therefore, so far as the gods are concerned, we see no good reason why we should fear to be at a disadvantage. But with regard to your views about Sparta and your confidence that she, out of a sense of honour, will come to your aid, we must say that we congratulate you on your simplicity but do not envy you your folly. In matters that concern themselves or their own constitution the Spartans are quite remarkably good; as for their relations with others, that is a long story, but it can be expressed shortly and clearly by saying that of all people we know the Spartans are most conspicuous for believing that what they like doing is honourable and what suits their interests is just. And this kind of attitude is not going to be of much help to you in your absurd quest for safety at the moment.

106   *Melians:* But this is the very point where we can feel most sure. Their own self-interest will make them refuse to betray their own colonists, the Melians, for that would mean losing the confidence of their friends among the Hellenes and doing good to their enemies.

107   *Athenians:* You seem to forget that if one follows one's self-interest one wants to be safe, whereas the path of justice and honour involves one in danger. And, where danger is concerned, the Spartans are not, as a rule, very venturesome.

108   *Melians:* But we think that they would even endanger themselves for our sake and count the risk more worth taking than in the case of others, because we are so close to the Peloponnese that they could operate more easily, and because they can depend on us more than on others, since we are of the same race and share the same feelings.

109   *Athenians:* Goodwill shown by the party that is asking for help does not mean security for the prospective ally. What is looked for is a positive preponderance of power in action. And the Spartans pay attention to this point even more than others do. Certainly they distrust their own native resources so much that when they attack a neighbour they bring a great army of allies with them.

It is hardly likely therefore that, while we are in control of the sea, they will cross over to an island.

110   *Melians:* But they still might send others. The Cretan sea is a wide one, and it is harder for those who control it to intercept others than for those who want to slip through to do so safely. And even if they were to fail in this, they would turn against your own land and against those of your allies left unvisited by Brasidas. So, instead of troubling about a country which has nothing to do with you, you will find trouble nearer home, among your allies, and in your own country.

111   *Athenians:* It is a possibility, something that has in fact happened before. It may happen in your case, but you are well aware that the Athenians have never yet relinquished a single siege operation through fear of others. But we are somewhat shocked to find that, though you announced your intention of discussing how you could preserve yourselves, in all this talk you have said absolutely nothing which could justify a man in thinking that he could be preserved. Your chief points are concerned with what you hope may happen in the future, while your actual resources are too scanty to give you a chance of survival against the forces that are opposed to you at this moment. You will therefore be showing an extraordinary lack of common sense if, after you have asked us to retire from this meeting, you still fail to reach a conclusion wiser than anything you have mentioned so far. Do not be led astray by a false sense of honour – a thing which often brings men to ruin when they are faced with an obvious danger that somehow affects their pride. For in many cases men have still been able to see the dangers ahead of them, but this thing called dishonour, this word, by its own force of seduction, has drawn them into a state where they have surrendered to an idea, while in fact they have fallen voluntarily into irrevocable disaster, in dishonour that is all the more dishonourable because it has come to them from their own folly rather than their misfortune. You, if you take the right view, will be careful to avoid this. You will see that there is nothing disgraceful in giving way to the greatest city in Hellas when she is offering you such reasonable terms – alliance on a tribute-paying basis and liberty to enjoy your own property. And, when you are allowed to choose between war and safety, you will not be so

insensitively arrogant as to make the wrong choice. This is the safe rule – to stand up to one's equals, to behave with deference towards one's superiors, and to treat one's inferiors with moderation. Think it over again, then, when we have withdrawn from the meeting, and let this be a point that constantly recurs to your minds – that you are discussing the fate of your country, that you have only one country, and that its future for good or ill depends on this one single decision which you are going to make.

112   The Athenians then withdrew from the discussion. The Melians, left to themselves, reached a conclusion which was much the same as they had indicated in their previous replies. Their answer was as follows:

'Our decision, Athenians, is just the same as it was at first. We are not prepared to give up in a short moment the liberty which our city has enjoyed from its foundation for 700 years. We put our trust in the fortune that the gods will send and which has saved us up to now, and in the help of men – that is, of the Spartans; and so we shall try to save ourselves. But we invite you to allow us to be friends of yours and enemies to neither side, to make a treaty which shall be agreeable to both you and us, and so to leave our country.'

113   The Melians made this reply, and the Athenians, just as they were breaking off the discussion, said:

'Well, at any rate, judging from this decision of yours, you seem to us quite unique in your ability to consider the future as something more certain than what is before your eyes, and to see uncertainties as realities, simply because you would like them to be so. As you have staked most on and trusted most in Spartans, luck, and hopes, so in all these you will find yourselves most completely deluded.'

114   The Athenian representatives then went back to the army, and the Athenian generals, finding that the Melians would not submit, immediately commenced hostilities and built a wall completely round the city of Melos, dividing the work out among the various states. Later they left behind a garrison of some of their own and some allied troops to blockade the place by land and sea, and with the greater part of their army returned home. The force left behind stayed on and continued with the siege.

115   About the same time the Argives invaded Phliasia and were ambushed by the Phliasians and the exiles from Argos, losing about
eighty men.

Then, too, the Athenians at Pylos captured a great quantity of
plunder from Spartan territory. Not even after this did the Spartans renounce the treaty and make war, but they issued a proclamation saying that any of their people who wished to do so were
free to make raids on the Athenians. The Corinthians also made
some attacks on the Athenians because of private quarrels of their
own, but the rest of the Peloponnesians stayed quiet.

Meanwhile the Melians made a night attack and captured the
part of the Athenian lines opposite the market-place. They killed
some of the troops, and then, after bringing in corn and everything
else useful that they could lay their hands on, retired again and
made no further move, while the Athenians took measures to
make their blockade more efficient in future. So the summer came
to an end.

116   In the following winter the Spartans planned to invade the
territory of Argos, but when the sacrifices for crossing the frontier
turned out unfavourably, they gave up the expedition. The fact
that they had intended to invade made the Argives suspect certain
people in their city, some of whom they arrested, though others
succeeded in escaping.

About this same time the Melians again captured another part
of the Athenian lines where there were only a few of the garrison
on guard. As a result of this, another force came out afterwards
from Athens under the command of Philocrates, the son of De-
meas. Siege operations were now carried on vigorously and, as
there was also some treachery from inside, the Melians surrendered
unconditionally to the Athenians, who put to death all the men of
military age whom they took, and sold the women and children
as slaves. Melos itself they took over for themselves, sending out
later a colony of 500 men.[41]

41. That there were Melian survivors, who were restored by Lysander
at the end of the war, is stated by Xenophon (*Hellenica*, II, 2, 9).

BOOK SIX

1 In the same winter the Athenians resolved to sail again against Sicily with larger forces than those which Laches and Eurymedon had commanded, and, if possible, to conquer it. They were for the most part ignorant of the size of the island and of the numbers of its inhabitants, both Hellenic and native, and they did not realize that they were taking on a war of almost the same magnitude as their war against the Peloponnesians.

The voyage round Sicily takes rather under eight days in a merchant ship, yet, in spite of the size of the island, it is separated from **2** the mainland only by two miles of sea. The settlement of the place in ancient times and the peoples who inhabited it are as follows: It is said that the earliest inhabitants of any part of the country were the Cyclopes and Laestrygonians. I cannot say what kind of people these were or where they came from or where they went in the end. On these points we must be content with what the poets have said and what anyone else may happen to know. The next settlers after them seem to have been the Sicanians, though according to the Sicanians themselves they were there first and were the original inhabitants of the country. The truth is, however, that they were Iberians who were driven out by the Ligurians from the district of the river Sicanus in Iberia. The island, which used to be called Trinacria, was in their time called Sicania after them, and they still live up to the present time in the western part of Sicily.

After the fall of Troy, some of the Trojans escaped from the Achaeans and came in ships to Sicily, where they settled next to the Sicanians and were all called by the name of Elymi. Their cities were Eryx and Egesta, and there also came to live in these settlements some of the Phocians who had been carried by storms on their way from Troy first to Libya and afterwards to Sicily.

The Sicels crossed over into Sicily from Italy, where they had lived previously and from which they were driven by the Opicans. According to tradition, which seems a quite likely one, they made the crossing on rafts, after having waited for a wind to blow from the mainland, though they probably sailed in by other means also. Even now there are still Sicels in Italy, and it was from the name of a King of the Sicels called Italus that Italy got its name. Coming with a large army, they defeated the Sicanians in battle and drove them into the south and west of the island, which they now caused to be called Sicily instead of Sicania. They occupied and continued to enjoy the best parts of the country for about 300 years, from the time they crossed over until the arrival of the Hellenes in Sicily. Even now they still hold the centre and north of the island.

There were also Phoenicians living all round Sicily. The Phoenicians occupied the headlands and small islands off the coast and used them as posts for trading with the Sicels. But when the Hellenes began to come in by sea in great numbers, the Phoenicians abandoned most of their settlements and concentrated on the towns of Motya, Soloeis, and Panormus where they lived together in the neighbourhood of the Elymi, partly because they relied on their alliance with the Elymi, partly because from here the voyage from Sicily to Carthage is shortest.

So much for the non-Hellenic peoples of Sicily, who were 3 settled as I have described. The first of the Hellenes to arrive were Chalcidians from Euboea with Thucles, their founder. They founded Naxos and built the altar of Apollo Archegetes, which now stands outside the city and is where visitors to the games first sacrifice when they are sailing from Sicily. Syracuse was founded in the following year by Archias, one of the Heraclids from Corinth. First he drove out the Sicels from 'the island' where the inner city now is – though it is no longer surrounded by water. Later the outer city also was taken inside the walls and the place became very populous.

In the fifth year after the foundation of Syracuse, Thucles and the Chalcidians set out from Naxos, fought with and drove out the Sicels, and founded Leontini. They then founded Catana, though the settlers of Catana themselves chose Euarchus to be their founder.

4   About the same time Lamis arrived in Sicily with colonists from Megara. He founded a place called Trotilus on the river Pantacyas, and later went from there, and for a short time joined up with the Chalcidians in Leontini. After being driven out by them, he founded Thapsus, and then died. His followers were forced to leave Thapsus and founded the place called Hyblaean Megara. Hyblon, a King of the Sicels, gave them the territory and invited them in. Here they lived for 245 years, after which they were driven out from the city and its territory by Gelon, the tyrant of Syracuse. Before this happened, however, 100 years after they had settled there, they sent out Pamillus and founded Selinus. Pamillus had come from their mother city Megara to join with them in making the new foundation.

Gela was founded by Antiphemus from Rhodes and by Entimus from Crete, who joined in leading out a colony there in the forty-fifth year after the foundation of Syracuse. The city took its name from the river Gelas; the part where the acropolis is now and which was first fortified is called Lindii. They adopted a constitution of the Dorian type.

One hundred and eight years (to the best of one's reckoning) after the foundation of their own city, the people of Gela founded Acragas, giving the city its name from the river Acragas, and making Aristonous and Pystilus the founders; the constitution was the same as that of Gela.

Zancle was originally founded by pirates who came from Cumae, the Chalcidian city in Opicia, but later a large number of people came from Chalcis and the rest of Euboea and joined in settling the place. The founders were Perieres from Cumae and Crataemenes from Chalcis. It was first called Zancle, which was the name given to it by the Sicels because the place is shaped like a sickle and their word for this is 'zanclon'. Later, however, the first settlers were driven out by some Samians and other Ionians who put in to Sicily on their flight from the Persians, and not long after this Anaxilas, the tyrant of Rhegium, drove out the Samians, colonized the city with people of mixed races, and renamed it Messina after his own home country.

5   Himera was founded from Zancle by Euclides, Simus, and Sacon. The majority of those who formed the colony were Chalcidians,

though they were joined by some exiles from Syracuse called the Myletidae, who had been defeated in a party struggle there. The dialect was a mixture of Chalcidian and Doric; the constitution was largely Chalcidian.

Acrae and Casmenae were founded by the Syracusans; Acrae seventy years after Syracuse, Casmenae nearly twenty years after Acrae.

Camerina was first founded by the Syracusans 135 years (to the best of one's reckoning) after the foundation of Syracuse. Its founders were Daxon and Menecolus. But the people of Camerina were driven out of their city by the Syracusans, who made war on them because they revolted, and some time later Hippocrates, the tyrant of Gela, took over their land in exchange for some Syracusan prisoners of war and resettled the city of Camarina, acting as founder himself. Once again the inhabitants were driven out, this time by Gelon, and the city was settled for the third time by the people of Gela.

6   These were the peoples, Greek and foreign, which inhabited Sicily, and it was an island of this size that the Athenians were now so eager to attack. In fact they aimed at conquering the whole of it, though they wanted at the same time to make it look as though they were sending help to their own kinsmen and to their newly acquired allies there. They were particularly encouraged by a delegation from Egesta in Athens at the time, who were most eager to secure Athenian intervention. The Egestaeans had gone to war with their neighbours the Selinuntines because of marriage rights and a piece of disputed territory. The Selinuntines had called in the Syracusans as allies, and were now pressing Egesta hard both by land and sea. So the Egestaeans reminded the Athenians of the alliance made in the time of Laches, during the war in which Leontini was concerned, and begged them to send a fleet and to come to their help. They put forward a number of arguments, but the main one was that if Syracuse, after driving out the people of Leontini, were allowed to escape scot-free, and to go on destroying the remaining allies of Athens until she acquired complete control of Sicily, the danger would then have to be faced that at some time or other the Syracusans, who were Dorians themselves, would come with a large force to the aid of their Dorian kinsmen

and would join the Peloponnesians, who had originally sent them out as colonists, in the work of utterly destroying the power of Athens. It would be a wise thing, therefore, for Athens to make use of the allies she still had and to put a check on Syracuse, especially as Egesta would supply sufficient money to finance the war.

The Athenians heard these arguments frequently repeated in their assemblies by the Egestaeans and their supporters, and voted in favour of first sending delegates to Egesta in order to see whether the money which they said was in the treasury and the temples really did exist, and at the same time to find out what the position was with regard to the war with the Selinuntines. And so

7 the Athenian delegation was sent off to Sicily.

In the same winter the Spartans and their allies (except the Corinthians) marched into the territory of Argos, laid waste a small amount of land and carried off some wagon-loads of corn. They settled the exiles from Argos at Orneae and left them a few troops from the main army. Then, after arranging a truce for a certain time between Orneae and Argos, according to which neither side was to do harm to the other's territory, they returned home with their army. Soon afterwards there arrived an Athenian force of thirty ships and 600 hoplites, and the Argives with their whole army marched out with the Athenians and besieged the people in Orneae for one day; in the night the garrison succeeded in escaping, since the besiegers camped at some distance from the town. When the Argives discovered this on the next day, they razed Orneae to the ground and then returned home, as did the Athenians also with their ships.

The Athenians also sent by sea to Methone on the frontiers of Macedonia a cavalry force of their own and the Macedonian exiles who were in Athens. These were employed in raids on the territory of Perdiccas. The Spartans sent to the Chalcidians in Thrace, whose truce with Athens could be terminated on ten days' notice, and urged them to join the war on the side of Perdiccas, but they refused to do so. So the winter came to an end and the sixteenth year of this war recorded by Thucydides.

LAUNCHING OF THE SICILIAN EXPEDITION

8 At the beginning of spring next year the Athenian delegation came back from Sicily. They were accompanied by the Egestaeans, who brought sixty talents of uncoined silver – a month's pay for sixty ships, which was the number they were going to ask the Athenians to send them.

The Athenians held an assembly and listened to what the Egestaeans and their own delegation had to say. The report was encouraging, but untrue, particularly on the question of the money which was said to be available in large quantities in the treasury and in the temples. So they voted in favour of sending sixty ships to Sicily and appointed as commanders with full powers Alcibiades, the son of Clinias, Nicias, the son of Niceratus, and Lamachus, the son of Xenophanes, who were instructed to help the Egestaeans against the Selinuntines, to reestablish Leontini also, if things went well with them in the war, and in general to make the kind of provisions for Sicily which might seem to them most in accordance with Athenian interests.

Five days later another assembly was held to discuss the quickest means of getting the ships ready to sail and to vote any additional supplies that the generals might need for the expedition. Nicias had not wanted to be chosen for the command; his view was that the city was making a mistake and, on a slight pretext which looked reasonable, was in fact aiming at conquering the whole of Sicily – a very considerable undertaking indeed. He therefore came forward to speak in the hope of making the Athenians change their minds. The advice he gave was as follows:

9 'It is true that this assembly was called to deal with the preparations to be made for sailing to Sicily. Yet I still think that this is a question that requires further thought – is it really a good thing for us to send the ships at all? I think that we ought not to give such hasty consideration to so important a matter and on the credit of foreigners get drawn into a war which does not concern us. So far as I am concerned personally, I gain honour by it and I am less frightened than most people about my own safety – not that I think that a man is any the worse citizen for taking reasonable care

of his own safety and his own property; such men are, in fact, particularly anxious, for their own sakes, that the city should prosper. However, just as in the past I have never spoken against my convictions in order to gain honour, so I shall not do it now, but shall tell you what I think is for the best. I know that no speech of mine could be powerful enough to alter your characters, and it would be useless to advise you to safeguard what you have and not to risk what is yours already for doubtful prospects in the future. I shall therefore confine myself to showing you that this is the wrong time for such adventures and that the objects of your ambition are not to be gained easily.

10   'What I say is this: in going to Sicily you are leaving many enemies behind you, and you apparently want to make new ones there and have them also on your hands. Possibly you think that the peace treaty which you have made gives you security; and, so long as you make no move, no doubt this treaty will continue to exist in name (for it has become a nominal thing, thanks to the intrigues of certain people here and in Sparta); it will certainly not stop our enemies from attacking us immediately, if in any part of the world any considerable forces of our own should suffer a defeat. In the first place, they only made the peace because of their misfortunes; it was forced on them, and in the matter of prestige we had the advantage. Then also in the treaty itself there are a number of points still not settled. There are some states, too, and important ones as well, who have not yet accepted the peace terms even as they stand. Some of these are openly at war with us, others, because Sparta has not yet made a move, are still holding back, but our truces with them are renewable every ten days, and it is extremely likely that, once they find us with our forces divided (which is just what we are in such a hurry to do), they will be only too eager to make war on us together with the Sicilians, whom they would rather have had as allies in the past than almost any other people. All these are points to be considered; we have not yet come safely into harbour, and this is no time for running risks or for grasping at a new empire before we have secured the one we have already. For the fact is that the Chalcidians in Thrace have been in revolt from us for many years and are still unsubdued; and in other areas, too, we get only a grudging obedience from our subjects. And

now we rush to the help of Egesta, of all places – an ally of ours, we say, which has been wronged; meanwhile doing nothing about putting right our own wrongs which we have suffered all this time from the rebels.

11   'Yet these rebels, once crushed, could be kept down; whereas even if we did conquer the Sicilians, there are so many of them and they live so far off that it would be very difficult to govern them. It is senseless to go against people who, even if conquered, could not be controlled, while failure would leave us much worse off than we were before we made the attempt. My opinion is, too, that Sicily, as it is at present, is not a danger to us, and that it would be even less of a danger if it came under the control of Syracuse (the possibility with which the Egestaeans are always trying to frighten you). As things are now it is possible that some Sicilians might come against us independently because of their affection for Sparta; but, supposing them to be all under the control of Syracuse, it is hardly likely that one empire would attack another, because if they were to join the Peloponnesians in destroying our empire, they would probably find that their own empire would be destroyed by the same people and for the same reasons. The best way for us to make ourselves feared by the Hellenes in Sicily is not to go there at all; and the next best thing is to make a demonstration of our power and then, after a short time, go away again. We all know that what is most admired is what is farthest off and least liable to have its reputation put to the test; and if anything went wrong with us, they would immediately look down on us and join our enemies here in attacking us. This is, in fact, Athenians, your own experience with regard to Sparta and her allies. Your successes against them, coming so unexpectedly compared with what you feared at first, have now made you despise them and set your hearts on the conquest of Sicily. But one's enemy's misfortunes are insufficient grounds for self-satisfaction; one can only feel real confidence when one has mastered his designs. And we ought to realize that, as a result of the disgrace they have suffered, the Spartans have only one thought, and that is how they can even now regain their own reputation by over-throwing us – as is natural when one considers that military honour is the be-all and the end-all of their existence. So, if we

keep our senses, we shall see that what we are fighting for has nothing to do with these Egestaeans in Sicily, who do not even speak our own language: our real problem is to defend ourselves vigorously against the oligarchical machinations of Sparta.

12   'We should also remember that it is only recently that we have had a little respite from a great plague and from the war, and so are beginning to make good our losses in men and money. The right thing is that we should spend our new gains at home and on ourselves instead of on these exiles who are begging for assistance and whose interest it is to tell lies and make us believe them, who have nothing to contribute themselves except speeches, who leave all the danger to others and, if they are successful, will not be properly grateful, while if they fail in any way they will involve their friends in their own ruin.

'No doubt there is someone sitting here who is delighted at having been chosen for the command and who, entirely for his own selfish reasons, will urge you to make the expedition – and all the more so because he is still too young for his post. He wants to be admired for the horses he keeps, and because these things are expensive, he hopes to make some profit out of his appointment. Beware of him, too, and do not give him the chance of endangering the state in order to live a brilliant life of his own. Remember that with such people maladministration of public affairs goes with personal extravagance; remember, too, that this is an important matter, and not the sort of thing that can be decided upon and acted upon by a young man in a hurry.

13   'It is with real alarm that I see this same young man's party sitting at his side in this assembly all called in to support him, and I, on my side, call for the support of the older men among you. If any one of you is sitting next to one of his supporters, do not allow yourself to be brow-beaten or be frightened of being called a coward if you do not vote for war. Do not, like them, indulge in hopeless passions for what is not there. Remember that success comes from foresight and not much is ever gained simply by wishing for it. Our country is now on the verge of the greatest danger she has ever known. Think of her, hold up your hands against this proposal, and vote in favour of leaving the Sicilians alone to enjoy their own country and manage their own affairs

within the boundaries (perfectly satisfactory to us) which now divide us from them – the Ionian sea, for the voyage along the coast, and the Sicilian sea, for the direct voyage. And let the Egestaeans, in particular, be told that, just as they started their war with the Selinuntines without consulting Athens, so they must themselves be responsible for making peace; and in the future we are not making allies, as we have done in the past, of the kind of people who have to be helped by us in their misfortunes, but who can do nothing for us when we need help from them.

14   'And I call upon you, the president of the assembly, as you know it is your business to care for the city's interests and as you wish to show yourself a good citizen, to put this question to the vote and allow the Athenians to debate the matter once again. And if you shrink from putting the matter to the vote again, you must remember that you cannot be blamed for a violation of the law when there are so many witnesses here on your side. Consider, too, that in this way you will be acting as the physician for your misguided city, and that the duty of those who hold office is simply this, to do all the good they can to their country, or in any case never to do any harm that can be avoided.'

15   After this speech of Nicias most of the Athenians who came forward to speak were in favour of making the expedition and not going back on the decision which had already been passed, though a few spoke on the other side. The most ardent supporter of the expedition was Alcibiades, the son of Clinias. He wanted to oppose Nicias, with whom he had never seen eye to eye in politics and who had just now made a personal attack on him in his speech. Stronger motives still were his desire to hold the command and his hopes that it would be through him that Sicily and Carthage would be conquered – successes which would at the same time bring him personally both wealth and honour. For he was very much in the public eye, and his enthusiasm for horse-breeding and other extravagances went beyond what his fortune could supply. This, in fact, later on had much to do with the downfall of the city of Athens. For most people became frightened at a quality in him which was beyond the normal and showed itself both in the lawlessness of his private life and habits and in the spirit in which he acted on all occasions. They thought that he was aiming at

becoming a dictator, and so they turned against him. Although in a public capacity his conduct of the war was excellent, his way of life made him objectionable to everyone as a person; thus they entrusted their affairs to other hands, and before long ruined the city.

On this occasion Alcibiades came forward and gave the following advice to the Athenians:

16   'Athenians, since Nicias has made this attack on me, I must begin by saying that I have a better right than others to hold the command and that I think I am quite worthy of the position. As for all the talk there is against me, it is about things which bring honour to my ancestors and myself, and to our country profit as well. There was a time when the Hellenes imagined that our city had been ruined by the war, but they came to consider it even greater than it really is, because of the splendid show I made as its representative at the Olympic games, when I entered seven chariots for the chariot race (more than any private individual has entered before) and took the first, second, and fourth places, and saw that everything else was arranged in a style worthy of my victory. It is customary for such things to bring honour, and the fact that they are done at all must also give an impression of power. Again, though it is quite natural for my fellow citizens to envy me for the magnificence with which I have done things in Athens, such as providing choruses and so on, yet to the outside world this also is evidence of our strength. Indeed, this is a very useful kind of folly, when a man spends his own money not only to benefit himself but his city as well. And it is perfectly fair for a man who has a high opinion of himself not to be put on a level with everyone else; certainly when one is badly off one does not find people coming to share in one's misfortunes. And just as no one takes much notice of us if we are failures, so on the same principle one has to put up with it if one is looked down upon by the successful: one cannot demand equal treatment oneself unless one is prepared to treat everyone else as an equal. What I know is that people like this – all, in fact, whose brilliance in any direction has made them prominent – are unpopular in their life-times, especially with their equals and also with others with whom they come into contact; but with posterity you will find people claiming relationship with them, even where none exists, and you will find their countries

boasting of them, not as though they were strangers or disreputable characters, but as fellow-countrymen and doers of great deeds. This is what I aim at myself, and because of this my private life comes in for criticism; but the point is whether you have anyone who deals with public affairs better than I do. Remember that I brought about a coalition of the greatest powers of the Peloponnese, without putting you to any considerable danger or expense, and made the Spartans risk their all on the issue of one day's fighting at Mantinea, and though they were victorious in the battle, they have not even yet quite recovered their confidence.

17   'So, in my youth and with this folly of mine which is supposed to be so prodigious, I found the right arguments for dealing with the power of the Peloponnesians, and the energy which I displayed made them trust me and follow my advice. Do not therefore be afraid of me now because I am young, but while I still have the vigour of my youth and Nicias the reputation for being lucky, make the best use you can of what each of us has to offer. Do not change your minds about the expedition to Sicily on the grounds that we shall have a great power to deal with there. The Sicilian cities have swollen populations made out of all sorts of mixtures, and there are constant changes and rearrangements in the citizen bodies. The result is that they lack the feeling that they are fighting for their own fatherland; no one has adequate armour for his own person, or a proper establishment on the land. What each man spends his time on is in trying to get from the public whatever he thinks he can get either by clever speeches or by open sedition – always with the intention of going off to live in another country, if things go badly with him. Such a crowd as this is scarcely likely either to pay attention to one consistent policy or to join together in concerted action. The chances are that they will make separate agreements with us as soon as we come forward with attractive suggestions, especially if they are, as we understand is the case, in a state of violent party strife. As for their hoplites, they have not got so many as they boast of; it is the same with them as with the rest of the Hellenes; the numbers never came up to the estimate made by each state of its own power; in fact the falsification was a very big one, and even in this present war Hellas has barely succeeded in arming herself adequately.

'The position in Sicily, then, is, so far as my information goes, as I have said; indeed, it is even easier than that, since we shall also have a number of non-Hellenic peoples who, through hatred of the Syracusans, will join us in our attack on them. And as for the position at home, if you look at it in the right way you will see that there is nothing here to hinder us. They talk about the enemies we shall leave behind us if we sail, but our fathers left behind them these same enemies when they had the Persians on their hands as well, and so founded the empire, relying solely on their superiority in sea-power. The Peloponnesians have never had so little hope of success against us as they have now. True enough that, if they really had the confidence, they have the strength to invade us by land, but they could do this whether we sailed to Sicily or not. They can do us no harm at all with their fleet, since we shall be leaving behind us a fleet of our own quite capable of dealing with theirs.

18   'There seems to be, therefore, no reasonable argument to induce us to hold back ourselves or to justify any excuse to our allies in Sicily for not helping them. We have sworn to help them, and it is our duty to help them, without raising the objection that we have had no help from them ourselves. The reason why we made them our allies was not that we wanted them to send us reinforcements here, but in order that they should be a thorn in the flesh for our enemies in Sicily, and so prevent them from coming here to attack us. This is the way we won our empire, and this is the way all empires have been won – by coming vigorously to the help of all who ask for it, irrespective of whether they are Hellenes or not. Certainly if everyone were to remain inactive or go in for racial distinctions when it is a question of giving assistance, we should add very little to our empire and should be more likely to risk losing it altogether. One does not only defend oneself against a superior power when one is attacked; one takes measures in advance to prevent the attack materializing. And it is not possible for us to calculate, like housekeepers, exactly how much empire we want to have. The fact is that we have reached a stage where we are forced to plan new conquests and forced to hold on to what we have got, because there is a danger that we ourselves may fall under the power of others unless others are in our power. And you

cannot look upon this idea of a quiet life in quite the same way as others do – not, that is, unless you are going to change your whole way of living and make it like theirs is.

'In the assurance therefore that, in going abroad, we shall increase our power at home, let us set out on this voyage. It will have a depressing effect on the arrogance of the Peloponnesians when they see that we despise the quiet life we are living now and have taken on the expedition to Sicily. At the same time we shall either, as is quite likely, become the rulers of all Hellas by using what we gain in Sicily, or, in any case, we shall do harm to the Syracusans, and so do good to ourselves and our allies. Our security is guaranteed by our navy, so that we can either stay there, if things go well, or come back again; for we shall have naval superiority over all the Sicilians put together.

'Do not be put off by Nicias's arguments for non-intervention and his distinctions between the young and the old. Let us instead keep to the old system of our fathers who joined together in counsel, young and old alike, and raised our state to the position it now holds. So now in the same way make it your endeavour to raise this city to even greater heights, realizing that neither youth nor age can do anything one without the other, but that the greatest strength is developed when one has a combination where all sorts are represented – the inferior types, the ordinary types, and the profoundly calculating types, all together. Remember, too, that the city, like everything else, will wear out of its own accord if it remains at rest, and its skill in everything will grow out of date; but in conflict it will constantly be gaining new experience and growing more used to defend itself not by speeches, but in action. In general, my view is that a city which is active by nature will soon ruin itself if it changes its nature and becomes idle, and that the way that men find their greatest security is in accepting the character and the institutions which they actually have, even if they are not perfect, and in living as nearly as possible in accordance with them.'

19   This was the speech of Alcibiades. After listening to him, and to the Egestaeans and to some exiles from Leontini who came forward as suppliants, reminding them of their oaths and begging for help, the Athenians became much more eager than before to make

the expedition. Nicias realized that there was no longer any hope of diverting them from their course by using the arguments that he had used already, but thought that there was a possibility of making them change their minds if he were to make an exaggerated estimate of the forces required. He therefore came forward again and spoke as follows:

20   'I see, Athenians, that you are quite determined on the expedition, and I hope it may turn out as we all wish. I shall now tell you what my opinion is as things stand at present. We are going to set out against cities which are, according to my information, of considerable strength, not subjects of one another and not wanting the kind of change by which they would be glad to escape from some oppressive government and accept a new government on easier terms; very unlikely, in fact, to give up their freedom in order to be ruled by us. The numbers also of the Hellenic cities are very large for one island. Apart from Naxos and Catana, which I expect will join us because of their racial connection with Leontini, there are seven other cities equipped with military and naval forces very much along the same lines as our own, particularly Selinus and Syracuse, our main objectives. They have great numbers of hoplites and archers and javelin-throwers, great numbers of triremes, and plenty of men to form the crews. They have money, not only in the hands of private people, but also in the temples of Selinus, and Syracuse also receives the payment of first-fruits from some of the native peoples. But the greatest advantage they have over us is in the number of their horses and in the fact that they grow their own corn and do not have to import any.

21   'To deal with a power of this kind we shall need something more than a fleet with an inconsiderable army. We must have in addition a large army of infantry to sail with us, if we want our actions to come up to what we have in mind, and are not to be restricted in our movements by the numbers of their cavalry; especially if the cities are frightened of us and combine among themselves, leaving us with no friends except the Egestaeans to provide us with cavalry with which to meet them. It would be disgraceful if we were forced to retire or to send back later for reinforcements owing to insufficient foresight to begin with. We must start, then, with a force that is large enough for its task, and

we must realize that we are going to sail a long way from our own country on an expedition very different from any of those which you may have undertaken against any of your subjects in this part of the world, when you have had your alliance to fall back on and when supplies have been easy to obtain from friendly territory. Instead of this, we are cutting ourselves off from home and going to an entirely different country, from which during the four winter months it is difficult even for a messenger to get to Athens.

22   'I think, therefore, that we ought to take a large army of hoplites from Athens and from our allies – from the subject states, and also any whom we can persuade or hire to come with us from the Peloponnese. We must have large forces of archers and of slingers, so as to hold our own against the enemy cavalry. And we must have a very decided superiority at sea, so as to make it easier for us to bring in our supplies. We must take our own corn from here (wheat, that is to say, and parched barley), and a proportion of bakers from the mills must be requisitioned and paid for their services, so that, in case we are ever weather-bound, the expedition may have its supplies; for not every city will be able to receive a force as large as ours will be. In other respects, too, we must equip ourselves to the best of our ability in order to avoid having to depend on other people, and in particular we must take with us as much money as possible from here, since you may be sure that so far as the money at Egesta is concerned, and which is supposed to be all ready for us, it is more likely to be there in theory than in fact.

23   'So we must leave Athens with a force that is not only a match for their forces, except in the numbers of hoplites available for a pitched battle, but actually much superior to them in every direction; and even so we shall find it hard enough to conquer the enemy and come off safely ourselves. We must act on the assumption that we are going off to found a city among foreigners and among enemies, and that those who do this have either to become masters of the country on the very first day they land in it, or be prepared to recognize that, if they fail to do so, they will find hostility on every side. Fearing this and knowing that we shall have need of much good counsel and more good fortune (a hard thing to be sure of, since we are but men), I wish to leave as little

as possible to fortune before I sail, and to set out with an army that, according to all reasonable probability, should be secure. This I believe to be the best way to guarantee the general interests of the city and the safety of those of us who are going to serve in the campaign. If anyone thinks differently, I invite him to take the command instead of me.'

24   In making this speech Nicias thought that either the Athenians would be put off by the scale of the armament required, or, if he was forced to make the expedition, he would in this way sail as safely as possible.

The Athenians, however, far from losing their appetite for the voyage because of the difficulties in preparing for it, became more enthusiastic about it then ever, and just the opposite of what Nicias had imagined took place. His advice was regarded as excellent, and it was now thought that the expedition was an absolutely safe thing. There was a passion for the enterprise which affected everyone alike. The older men thought that they would either conquer the places against which they were sailing or, in any case, with such a large force, could come to no harm; the young had a longing for the sights and experiences of distant places, and were confident that they would return safely; the general masses and the average soldier himself saw the prospect of getting pay for the time being and of adding to the empire so as to secure permanent paid employment in future. The result of this excessive enthusiasm of the majority was that the few who actually were opposed to the expedition were afraid of being thought unpatriotic if they voted against it, and therefore kept quiet.

25   Finally one of the Athenians came forward and addressed Nicias personally, telling him that there was no need to make excuses or to delay matters any further; instead let him now say in front of everyone what forces the Athenians were to vote for him. Nicias spoke reluctantly, and said that he would go further into this with his colleagues in a quieter atmosphere, but, so far as he could see at present, they ought to sail with at least 100 triremes; transports would come from the Athenian shipping in whatever number was decided upon, and others should be sent for from the allies; the total force of hoplites, Athenian and allied, should be not less than 5,000 and, if possible, more; the rest of the force should be in

proportion – archers from Athens and from Crete, slingers – all
this and anything else that seemed necessary should be got ready
and taken with them.

26   When the Athenians heard this, they immediately voted that
the generals should have full powers with regard to the numbers
of the army and to the expedition in general, to act as they thought
best. After this the preparations began; instructions were sent to
the allies, lists of those to be called up were made in Athens. It was
all the easier to provide for everything as the city had just recovered from the plague and the years of continuous war, and as
a number of the young had grown to manhood, and capital had
accumulated as a result of the truce.

27   While these preparations were going on it was found that in one
night nearly all the stone Hermae in the city of Athens had had
their faces disfigured by being cut about. These are a national institution, the well-known square-cut figures, of which there are
great numbers both in the porches of private houses and in the
temples. No one knew who had done this, but large rewards were
offered by the state in order to find out who the criminals were,
and there was also a decree passed guaranteeing immunity to anyone, citizen, alien, or slave, who knew of any other sacrilegious
act that had taken place and would come forward with information
about it. The whole affair, indeed, was taken very seriously, as it
was regarded as an omen for the expedition, and at the same time
as evidence of a revolutionary conspiracy to overthrow the democracy.

28   Information was in fact forthcoming from some resident aliens
and some personal servants. They had nothing to say about the
Hermae, but told of some other cases which had happened previously when statues had been defaced by young men who were
enjoying themselves after having had too much to drink, and also
of mock celebrations of the mysteries held in private houses. One
of those accused was Alcibiades, and this fact was taken up by
those who disliked him most because he stood in the way of their
keeping a firm hold themselves of the leadership of the people, and
who thought that, if they could drive him out, they would step
into the first place. They therefore exaggerated the whole thing
and made all the noise they could about it, saying that the affair of

the mysteries and the defacement of the Hermae were all part of a plot to overthrow the democracy, and that in all this Alcibiades had had a hand; evidence for which they found in the unconventional and undemocratic character of his life in general.

29   Alcibiades denied the charges made against him on the spot and was prepared to stand his trial before sailing on the expedition, the preparations for which had now been completed, and to be examined as to whether he had done any of the things with which he was accused; he should suffer the penalty, if found guilty, and, if acquitted, should take up his command. He begged them not to listen to attacks made on him in his absence, but, if he was really guilty, to put him to death there and then, and he pointed out how unwise it would be to send him out in command of such a large army with such serious accusations still hanging over his head. His enemies, however, were afraid that, if the case was brought on at once, he would have the goodwill of the army and that the people would be lenient to him because of the popularity he had won by getting the Argives and some of the Mantineans to join in the expedition. They therefore did all they could to put things off and prevent the trial taking place, and produced some more speakers who said that Alcibiades ought to sail now, and not hold up the departure of the army, but that he should be tried on his return within a fixed number of days. Their plan was to bring some more serious accusation against him (which they could do all the more easily when he was away) and then to send for him and bring him back to stand his trial. It was decided, therefore, that Alcibiades should sail.

30   After this, when it was already midsummer, they put to sea for Sicily. Most of the allies, with the ships carrying corn and the smaller craft and the rest of the equipment, had previously received instructions to assemble at Corcyra, so as to cross the Ionian sea from there in one body to the promontory of Iapygia. But the Athenians themselves and any of their allies who were in Athens at the time went down to Piraeus at dawn on the day appointed and manned the ships for putting out to sea. The rest of the people, in fact almost the entire population of Athens, citizens and foreigners, went down to Piraeus with them. Those who were natives of the country all had people to see off on their way, whether

friends or relatives or sons, and they came full of hope and full of lamentation at the same time, thinking of the conquests that might be made and thinking, too, of those whom they might never see again, considering the long voyage on which they were going 31 from their own country. At this moment when they were really on the point of parting from each other with all the risks ahead, the danger of the situation came more home to them than it had at the time when they voted for the expedition. Nevertheless they were heartened with the strength they had and with the sight of the quantities of every kind of armament displayed before their eyes. As for the foreigners and the rest of the crowd, they came merely to see the show and to admire the incredible ambition of the thing.

Certainly this expedition that first set sail was by a long way the most costly and the finest-looking force of Hellenic troops that up to that time had ever come from a single city. In numbers of ships and hoplites it was no greater than the force which Pericles took to Epidaurus and the same force which went against Potidaea with Hagnon, which consisted of 4,000 Athenian hoplites, 300 cavalry, and 100 triremes, with the addition of fifty more ships from Lesbos and Chios and many allied troops as well. That force, however, went only on a short voyage and was only equipped in the ordinary way, whereas this expedition was planned with a view to its being away for a long time and was equipped for both kinds of fighting, whichever should be required, both with warships and with ground troops. The fleet was in a high state of efficiency and had cost a lot of money to both the captains and the State. Every sailor received a drachma a day from the Treasury, which also provided empty ships (sixty fighting ships and forty for the transport of hoplites) all manned with the best crews available. The captains, too, offered extra pay, in addition to that provided by the State to the *thranitae* and the rest of the crews, and they went to great expense on figure-heads and general fittings, every one of them being as anxious as possible that his own ship should stand out from the rest for its fine looks and for its speed. As for the land forces, they had been chosen from the best men who were liable for calling-up, and there had been much rivalry and much pains spent by everyone on his armour and personal equipment. It therefore happened that there was not only all this competition among the Athenians themselves, each with regard to his own particular piece of responsibility, but to the rest of Hellas it looked more like a demonstration of the power and greatness of Athens than an expeditionary force setting out against the enemy. It would have been found that a grand total of many talents of money were being taken out of the city, if one reckoned up the sums spent by the State and the private expenses of those who were serving – a total which would include what the State had already spent and what was being sent out in the hands of the generals, what individuals had spent on personal equipment, what the captains had spent and were still to spend on their ships; and, in addition to all this, there would have to be included the money for private expenses which everyone was likely to have taken with him over and above his pay from the State on an expedition which was to last for a long time, and also what the soldiers or traders took with them for purposes of exchange. And what made this expedition so famous was not only its astonishing daring and the brilliant show that it made, but also its great preponderance of strength over those against whom it set out, and the fact that this voyage, the longest ever made by an expedition from Athens, was being undertaken with hopes for the future which, when compared with the present position, were of the most far-reaching kind.

32   When the ships were manned and everything had been taken aboard which they meant to take with them on the voyage, silence was commanded by the sound of the trumpet, and the customary prayers made before putting to sea were offered up, not by each ship separately, but by them all together following the words of a herald. The whole army had wine poured out into bowls, and officers and men made their libations from cups of gold and of silver. The crowds on the shore also, the citizens and others who wished well to the expedition, joined together in the prayers. Then, when the hymn had been sung and the libations finished, they put out to sea, first sailing out in column, and then racing each other as far as Aegina. So they made good speed on their way to Corcyra, where the other force of their allies was assembling.

THE DEBATE AT SYRACUSE

At Syracuse news of the expedition arrived from many quarters, but for a long time none of it was believed. In fact there was an assembly held in which speeches such as those which follow were made, some by speakers who believed in the story of the Athenian expedition and some by those who took the opposite view. Among the speakers was Hermocrates, the son of Hermon. He considered that he knew what the real facts were, and he came forward and gave the following advice:

33   'You may well think that I, like others, am saying something incredible when I tell you the truth about this invasion, and I know that when one makes a statement or produces news that seems incredible, one not only fails to convince one's hearers, but is thought to be a fool into the bargain. However, I shall not be frightened of this, and I shall not remain quiet when my city is in danger and when I am quite sure in myself that I know what I am talking about rather better than others do. The fact, surprising as it seems to you, is that the Athenians have set out against you with a very large force, both military and naval. Ostensibly this is be-cause they are allies of Egesta and they wish to restore Leontini, but in reality it is because they want Sicily, and particularly this city of ours, since they think that, once they have conquered Syracuse, they will easily get hold of the rest of the island.

'Make up your minds, then, that they will soon be here, and now consider how you can best meet them with the resources available. Do not despise the invasion, or you will be caught off your guard; do not disbelieve in it, or you will be neglecting everything that matters. And those who do believe in the news need not be frightened of the daring and power of the Athenians. They will not be able to do us any more harm than we can do them, and the fact that they are coming with so large a force is far from being a disadvantage to us. Indeed, it is much better that way, when one considers the rest of the Sicilians, who will be terrified, and therefore all the more willing to become our allies. And if in the end we defeat them or force them to go back without having attained their objects (for I am certainly under no apprehension that they will get what they expect to get), that will be a very glorious action indeed for us, and one which, in my opinion, is by no means unlikely. There have certainly not been many great expeditions, either Hellenic or foreign, which have been successful when sent far from home. They cannot come in greater numbers than the inhabitants of the country and their neighbours, all of whom will unite together through fear; and if things go wrong with them because of lack of supplies in a foreign country, even though they themselves are chiefly responsible for their failure, they nevertheless leave the honours of war to those against whom their plots were made. This was just what happened to these very Athenians, who, after the defeat of the Persians, which was very much a matter of accident, won a great name simply because it was against Athens that the Persians set out. It is not unlikely that the same sort of thing will happen in our case, too.

34   'Let us therefore make our preparations here in a spirit of confidence. We must send to the Sicels, in some cases to make sure that we can depend on them, in others to attempt to make treaties of friendship and alliance with them. We must send representatives to the rest of Sicily to point out that the danger threatens all alike, and we must also send to Italy so as to gain alliances there for ourselves or else to see that they do not receive the Athenians. I think, too, that it would be advisable to send to Carthage also. They would be far from being surprised; in fact, they are constantly under the apprehension that one day the Athenians will come and attack their city. Thus they would very possibly think that, if they let our cause go by default, they would be in trouble themselves, and they might be willing to come to our help in one way or another, secretly if not openly. Certainly, if they were willing, they could help us more than any other power in existence, since they have the greatest quantities of gold and silver, which is what supports both war and everything else. Let us also send to Sparta and to Corinth urging them to send help to us here quickly and at the same time to go forward with the war in Hellas. What I think is the best thing of all for us to do at this moment is something which you, with your stay-at-home habits, are not in the least likely to see the point of; nevertheless I shall say what it is. If all the Sicilians together, or at least as many of us as possible,

would be prepared to launch every available ship and, taking two months' supplies with us, would meet the Athenians at Tarentum and the promontory of Iapygia and make it clear to them that before there is any question of fighting for Sicily they will have to fight for their passage across the Ionian sea, this would have the most powerful effect on their minds, and would force them to reflect that while we are there on guard with a base in friendly country (since Tarentum will receive us), they have a great stretch of open sea to cross with the whole of their expeditionary force, and that because of the length of the voyage it will be difficult for this force to keep its order, but easy for us to attack it as it comes up slowly and in detachments. And if they, on their side, were to bring into action against us the whole body of their fast-sailing ships, having first lightened them of their burdens, we could either, assuming them to have been rowing for a long time, attack them when they were tired out, or, if we preferred it, we could always fall back on Tarentum; while they, on the other hand, would be short of rations, having crossed the sea simply in order to fight a battle, and would find themselves in difficulties lying off this deserted part of the country. They would either have to stay where they were, and be blockaded, or else try to sail on along the coast, which would mean leaving behind the rest of their forces and facing the discouraging prospect of not knowing for certain whether the cities would receive them. I certainly think myself that they would be held back by these considerations and would not put to sea from Corcyra at all. Time would be spent in deliberations, and in sending out scouts to discover our numbers and our position, and they would find the season gone and winter upon them; or else they would be so taken aback by this surprise move of ours that they would give up the expedition entirely, especially as, according to my information, their most experienced general has no wish to be in command and would be glad of an excuse to return, if one could be seen in any serious action on our part. Reports of our numbers would, I am quite sure, be exaggerated, and it is in accordance with what they hear that men make up or alter their minds. Then, too, the people who attack first, or at any rate make it clear to the aggressors that they are going to defend themselves, are the ones who are most feared, because it is then thought that they are ready to take up the challenge. This is just what would happen now to the Athenians. They are attacking us on the assumption that we are not going to defend ourselves, and they have a right to hold such a poor view of us, because we failed to help the Spartans to destroy them. But if they were to see us acting with a daring that they do not anticipate, they would be more frightened by the very unexpectedness of the thing than they would be by the power which we really have. It is this daring action, therefore, which I am most anxious that you should take; but if you will not, then I urge you to make every other preparation for war as quickly as possible. Let everyone remember that while contempt for an enemy's attack can best be shown by the valiance with which one meets it, the most useful thing for us now is to act as though in the midst of danger and to realize that the safest steps we can take are those taken under the influence of fear. The Athenians are coming: the Athenians are, I am sure of it, already on their voyage: the Athenians are very nearly here.'

35   This was the speech of Hermocrates. As for the people of Syracuse, there were a number of conflicting opinions among them. Some thought that there was no possibility of the Athenians coming and no truth in what Hermocrates had said; others were of the opinion that, even if they did come, they could do no harm that would not be paid back to them in full measure; others dismissed the idea altogether and turned the whole thing into a joke. Only a very few believed Hermocrates and felt apprehensive about the future. The leader of the democratic party was Athenagoras, a man who at that time had very great influence with the people.[42] He now came forward and spoke as follows:

36   'Only cowards or people with no sense of patriotism are not anxious for the Athenians to be as mad as they are made out to be, and for them to come here and fall into our power. But as for those who spread such reports and try to scare you with them, I am not surprised at their audacity, but I am surprised at their lack of intelligence, if they imagine that their motives are not perfectly obvious. They have reasons of their own to be frightened, and they want to put the whole city into a state of alarm, so that in the general panic they may disguise their own. So now all these reports

42. For the parallel with Cleon, see III, 36 and footnote 31 there.

mean is this: they have not arisen in the natural way, but have been made up on purpose by certain people who are always starting these agitations. You, if you are sensible, will not take such reports as a basis for calculating probabilities, but instead will consider what a clever and a widely experienced people, as, in my view, the Athenians are, would be likely to do. It is not likely that they would leave the Peloponnesians behind them and, with the war in Hellas still not satisfactorily settled, would go out of their way to take on a new war on just as big a scale. In fact I personally am of opinion that they are pleased enough to find that it is not a case of us going to attack them, considering the numbers and the strength of our cities.

37   'But if they really did come, as they are said to be coming, then I think that Sicily is in a better position than the Peloponnese for going through with the war, because Sicily is better equipped in every way; and I think that this city of ours is by itself much stronger than their supposed army of invasion, even if it were twice as big as it is said to be. I know certainly that they will not have any horses with them, nor will they get any here, except for a few from the Egestaeans; nor will they have a force of hoplites equal to ours, coming, as they will have to do, by sea. In fact it will be a hard enough job for them just to get their ships all this way here, however little they carry. And then there is all the rest of their necessary equipment, and it has to be a lot, considering the size of this city of ours. Indeed, I am so sure of what I say that I think that, even if they brought with them here another city as big as Syracuse and planted it down on our borders and made war from it upon us – even then they would have very little chance of survival; and how much less of a chance will they have with the whole of Sicily united, as it will be, against them, with their own base a mere fortification thrown up by a naval expedition, living in tents, and only provided with the barest necessities, unable to move in any direction because of our cavalry? Taking everything into account, I doubt whether they will be able to effect and consolidate a landing at all; so very much superior, I think, are our forces to theirs.

38   'But, as I tell you, the Athenians know all this, and I am quite sure that they are occupied in safeguarding their own possessions.

What is happening is that there are certain people here in Syracuse who are making up stories which are neither true nor likely to become true. This is not the first time that I have noticed these people; in fact I am constantly aware of them; if foiled in action, they resort to stories of this kind or even more villainous fabrications, and their aim is to make you, the mass of the people, frightened, and so gain control of the government themselves. And I am really afraid that their continual efforts may one day be actually successful. We ourselves are too feeble: we do not forestall them before they act; we do not follow them up with vigour once we have detected them. It is because of this that our city rarely enjoys a period of tranquillity, and is involved in continual party strife and struggles more within herself than against the enemy; and there have been cases, too, of dictatorships and of powerful groups seizing the Government illegally. I shall make it my endeavour, if you will only support me, to see to it that nothing like this is ever allowed to happen in our days. And my methods will be to bring you, the masses, over to my way of thought, and then to come down heavily on those who are engaged in these plots, not merely when they are caught in the act (it is not so easy to catch them like that), but also for all those things which they would like to do, but cannot. When dealing with an enemy it is not only his actions but his intentions that have to be watched, since if one does not act first, one will suffer first. And as for those who want an oligarchy, I shall show them up, when necessary, and I shall keep my eye on them, and I shall even be a teacher to them; for so, I think, I shall be most likely to turn them from their wicked path.

'And now here is a question that I have often asked myself: what is it that you young men really want? Is it to hold office immediately? But that is against the law, and the law was not made to keep able people out; it was made simply because you are unfit for office. Is it that you do not want to live on the same terms as everyone else? But members of the same State ought, in justice, to enjoy the same rights. There are people who will say that democracy is neither an intelligent nor a fair system, and that those who have the money are also the best rulers. But I say, first, that what is meant by the *demos*, or people, is the whole State, whereas ar oligarchy is only a section of the State; and I say next that though

the rich are the best people for looking after money, the best counsellors are the intelligent, and that it is the many who are best at
listening to the different arguments and judging between them.
And all alike, whether taken all together or as separate classes, have
equal rights in a democracy. An oligarchy, on the other hand,
certainly gives the many their share of dangers, but when it comes
to the good things of life not only claims the largest share, but goes
off with the whole lot. And this is what the rich men and the
young men among you are aiming at; but in a great city these
things are beyond your reach. What fools you are! In fact the
stupidest of all the Hellenes I know, if you do not realize that your
aims are evil, and the biggest criminals if you do realize this and
40 still have the face to proceed with them. But there is still time for
you, if not to repent, at any rate to become instructed and to pro-
mote the interests of your country that are shared by all your
countrymen. Remember that by so doing the good citizens among
you will get not only a fair, but more than a fair share, whereas if
you have other ends in view you run the risk of being deprived of
everything. Give up spreading these rumours and understand that
we know what the idea is and we are not going to put up with it.
Even if the Athenians are on their way, this city of ours will deal
with them in a manner worthy of herself; and we have our
generals who will attend to all this. And if, as I think myself, there
is no truth at all in these reports, the city is not going to be thrown
into a panic by the rumours you spread and cast itself into a voluntary slavery by choosing you to be its rulers. The city is capable of
looking into things by itself, and it will judge the words you speak
as though they were positive actions; it will not be robbed by
hearsay of the liberty it now enjoys, but will try to preserve that
liberty by taking practical steps to prevent any such thing happening.'

41   This was the speech of Athenagoras. One of the generals then
stood up and refused to allow any other speakers to come forward.
He spoke himself on the situation as follows: 'It is not a wise thing
either for speakers to make these attacks on each other, or for the
hearers to give countenance to them. Instead we should be giving
our attention to the reports which have reached us and seeing how
we can all of us – the State as a whole and each individual in it –

best deal with the invaders. Even if there is no need, there is no harm in having the State furnished with horses and arms and everything that is glorious in war. We shall undertake the responsibility for this and see to the details. Nor is there any harm in sending to the cities to find out what their feelings are and in doing anything else that may be thought useful. We have seen to some of these matters already, and anything that we find out shall be brought to your notice.'

After this speech from the general, the Syracusans dissolved the assembly.

THE ATHENIANS ARRIVE IN SICILY

42 The Athenians and all their allies with them were now in Corcyra. First the generals held a final review of the whole force and arranged the order in which they were to anchor and encamp. They divided the fleet into three parts and allotted one part to each general. This was so that they should not have to sail all together, which would mean difficulties with regard to water and harbourage and supplies whenever they landed, and also so that they could preserve their order better and be easier to handle, with each division having its own commander. They then sent on three ships to Italy and Sicily in order to find out which cities would receive them. These ships were instructed to turn back and meet them on their way, so that they might know what the conditions were before they put in to land.

43   After this the Athenians with this great armament put to sea from Corcyra and began to make the crossing to Sicily. They had 134 triremes in all and two fifty-oared ships from Rhodes. A hundred of these triremes were from Athens – sixty for fighting and forty for use as transports – and the rest of the fleet came from Chios and the other allies. There were 5,100 hoplites in all. These included 1,500 Athenian citizens drawn from the regular calling-up lists and 700 from the lowest property class (called thetes), who served as marines, the rest being allied troops, some of whom were subjects of Athens, though there were also 500 Argives and 250 Mantineans and other mercenary troops. There were altogether

480 archers, eighty of whom were Cretans, 700 slingers from
Rhodes, 120 exiles from Megara, serving as light troops, and one
horse transport carrying thirty horses.

44   This was the strength of the first expeditionary force that went
over to the war. Its supplies were carried by thirty merchant ships
which were laden with corn and had aboard them the bakers,
masons, and carpenters together with all the tools for building
fortifications. A hundred smaller craft, requisitioned like the merchant ships, sailed with them, and there were many others also,
both merchant ships and smaller boats, which followed the expedition voluntarily in order to do trade. These now all left
Corcyra and crossed over the Ionian gulf together.

The whole force reached land at the promontory of Iapygia and
Tarentum and various other points, according to the course they
were steering. They then sailed down the Italian coast, finding that
the cities would not provide them with a market or even allow
them inside their walls, but would only give them water and
liberty to anchor, and, in the case of Tarentum and Locri, not even
this. So they arrived at Rhegium, the extreme point of Italy. Here
they were all united again and, since they were not admitted inside
the city, they made a camp outside in the ground sacred to Artemis,
where a market also was provided for them, drew their ships up
on shore, and made no further move for the time being. Negotiations were opened with the people of Rhegium, the Athenians
urging them because of their Chalcidian origin to come to the help
of Leontini, which was also a Chalcidian city. They replied, however, that they would not join either side, but would wait for a
general decision from all the Greeks in Italy and would then act
in accordance with it. The Athenians then turned their attention
to the state of affairs in Sicily and considered what was the best
course to take. Meanwhile they waited for the ships which they
had sent ahead to return from Egesta, as they wanted to know
whether the sums of money mentioned in Athens by the messengers really existed.

45   News was now reaching the Syracusans from all sides and definite information came from their own intelligence officers that
the fleet was at Rhegium. They therefore set to work with all their
energies to meet the situation and no longer failed to believe in its

existence. Garrisons were put into some of the cities of the Sicels, ambassadors were sent to others; troops were dispatched to the fortified posts in the country; in the city the horses and arms were checked to see that everything was in order, and all other measures were taken on the assumption that they would soon, indeed at any moment, be at war.

46   Meanwhile the three ships that had been sent ahead came from Egesta to the Athenians at Rhegium. The news they brought was that the promised sums of money did not exist and that only thirty talents were available. The generals were at once discouraged, both because this first hope of theirs had come to nothing and also because of the refusal of the people of Rhegium to join forces with them, being, as they were, the first people whom they had attempted to win over and the likeliest ones, too, considering that they were of the same race as the people of Leontini and had always been on good terms with Athens. Nicias indeed was not surprised by the news from Egesta, but the other two generals had not expected it at all. At the time when the first ambassadors from Athens had come to look into the question of the money, the Egestaeans had deceived them by the following plan. They took the Athenians to the temple of Aphrodite at Eryx and showed them the treasure laid up there in offerings – bowls, goblets, censers, and much else, which, being silver, looked imposing to the eye though the value in money was comparatively small. They also entertained the ships' crews in their private houses, and did this by collecting together all the cups of gold and silver in Egesta itself, borrowing others from the neighbouring cities, Phoenician or Hellenic, and then letting each host produce them at the banquets as though they were his own property. All used pretty much the same articles and everywhere there was a great abundance of them, so that the Athenians from the ships were astonished at it and, when they got back to Athens, told everyone of the vast quantities of valuable objects which they had seen. Deceived themselves, they had at that time succeeded in converting the rest, and now, when the news got round that the money in Egesta did not exist, they were much blamed by the soldiers.

The generals consulted on what steps to take under the circum-
47 stances. Nicias's view was that they should sail with the whole

force to Selinus, which was the main objective of the expedition, and, if the Egestaeans provided money for the whole army, then they should reconsider matters. If they did not, they should require them to provide supplies for the sixty ships which they had asked for, and should stay and see that either by force or by agreement a settlement was reached between Egesta and Selinus. They should then sail along the coast past the other cities, making a demonstration of the power of Athens and, after showing how ready she was to come to the help of her friends and allies, should sail back home again, unless they should happen to find some quick and unexpected way of doing good to the people of Leontini or of winning over any of the other cities to their side. They should not, he considered, put the state in danger by wasting her own resources.

48 Alcibiades said that, after having sailed out in such force, they ought not to disgrace themselves by going home with nothing to show for it. They should send heralds to all the cities except Selinus and Syracuse; they should approach the Sicels, encouraging some of them to revolt from Syracuse and trying to win the friendship of others, so that they would be able to get corn and troops from them. The first step should be to gain the support of Messina, which lay directly in their way and was the gate of Sicily and would also serve as an excellent harbour and base for the army. After having won over the cities, they would know who was going to support them in the war, and then would be the time to attack Syracuse and Selinus, unless Selinus came to terms with Egesta and Syracuse allowed them to restore Leontini.

49 Lamachus said that they ought to sail straight to Syracuse and fight their battle under the city walls as quickly as possible, while the enemy were still not ready for them and were most frightened of them. It is at the beginning, he said, that every army inspires most fear; but if time is allowed to pass before it shows itself, men's spirits revive and, when they actually do see it, they are less impressed than they would have been. So a sudden attack now, while the enemy were still terrified at the thought of it, would give Athens the best chance of victory and would most seriously affect the morale of the Syracusans, who would be confronted with the sight of numbers which would never appear greater than at the present moment, who would be apprehensive of all the

sufferings in store for them, and most of all terrified at having to risk battle immediately. It was likely, too, that, through not believing that the Athenians were coming, many of the Syracusans would be cut off outside the city in the country districts; thus, while they were still trying to bring their property inside the walls, the army, if it won a victory and established itself in front of the city, would not go short of money. So, too, the rest of the Sicilians would at once be less inclined to ally themselves with Syracuse and would be more likely to come over to the Athenians without waiting to see which side was going to win. He recommended Megara for their naval station. It was a place to which the fleet could retire and which could be used as a base for a blockade. It was uninhabited and not far from Syracuse either by land or sea.

50 These were the views expressed by Lamachus. However, he ended by giving his support to the plan of Alcibiades. After this Alcibiades sailed across to Messina in his own ship and attempted to negotiate an alliance. In this he was unsuccessful, the reply being that they would not receive the Athenians inside their city, though they would provide them with a market outside. Alcibiades then sailed back to Rhegium.

Immediately afterwards the generals manned sixty ships out of the whole force, took provisions aboard, and sailed along the coast to Naxos, leaving the rest of the army behind at Rhegium with one general in command. The Naxians received them inside their city, and they then sailed on to Catana. Here the people refused to receive them, since there was a pro-Syracusan party in the city, and they went on to the river Terias, where they camped for the night. Next day they sailed to Syracuse, with all their ships in single file, except for ten which they sent on in front with instructions to sail into the great harbour and see whether the Syracusans had a fleet launched, and to make a proclamation from their ships as they sailed up that the Athenians had come to restore the people of Leontini to their own land in accordance with their alliance and in virtue of their kinship with them; that any Leontinians, therefore, who were in Syracuse should leave the city without fear and come and join the Athenians, who were their friends and benefactors. When they had made the proclamation, they made a reconnaissance of the city and the harbours and the general lie of the land to see where they would have to make their base for carrying on the war. They then sailed back again to Catana.

51 Here an assembly was held and, though the people of Catana would not allow the army inside their city, they invited the generals to come in and to say what they had to say. While Alcibiades was speaking and the citizens were all intent upon the assembly, the soldiers managed to get into the city without being noticed. They came in by breaking down a badly built gate in the walls, and they proceeded to stroll about in the market-place. As soon as the pro-Syracusan party in Catana saw the army inside, they became terrified and slipped away (there were not very many of them), and the rest voted in favour of an alliance with the Athenians and invited them to bring over the remainder of their forces from Rhegium. After this the Athenians sailed across to Rhegium, put to sea again for Catana with their whole force now united and, on their arrival, began to build their camp.

52 News then reached them from Camarina that if they went there the city would come over to their side, and also that the Syracusans were manning a fleet. They therefore sailed first with the whole force along the coast to Syracuse. Here they found no signs of a fleet being manned, and went on along the coast to Camarina, where they put in to the beach and sent a herald to the city. The people of Camarina, however, would not receive them, saying that they were bound by oath only to receive the Athenians if they came in one single ship, unless they themselves asked for more to be sent. Meeting with no success here, the Athenians sailed away again. They landed and made a raid on Syracusan territory, but lost a few stragglers from their light troops when the Syracusan cavalry came up. And so they returned to Catana.

THE STORY OF HARMODIUS AND ARISTOGITON

53 At Catana they found the *Salaminia* arrived from Athens for Alcibiades with orders that he should sail home to answer the charges made against him by the state, and for some other people also in the army against whom information had been laid with regard to the sacrilegious treatment of the mysteries and also, in

some cases, with regard to the Hermae. For, after the expedition had set sail, the Athenians had been just as anxious as before to investigate the facts about the mysteries and about the Hermae. Instead of checking up on the characters of their informers, they had regarded everything they were told as grounds for suspicion, and on the evidence of complete rogues had arrested and imprisoned some of the best citizens, thinking it better to get to the bottom of things in this way rather than to let any accused person, however good his reputation might be, escape interrogation because of the bad character of the informer. The people had heard stories of the dictatorship of Pisistratus and his sons, and knew how oppressive it had been in its later stages; they knew also that it was not because of themselves and Harmodius that it had come to an end, but because of the Spartans. They were consequently always in a state of fear and apt to look at everything suspiciously.

54   In fact the bold action undertaken by Aristogiton and Harmodius was due to a love affair. I shall deal with this in some detail, and show that the Athenians themselves are no better than other people at producing accurate information about their own dictators and the facts of their own history. Pisistratus was an old man when he died, still holding the dictatorship. After him it was not Hipparchus, as most people think, but Hippias, the eldest, who took over power. Harmodius was then a most beautiful young man in the flower of his youth, and was loved and possessed by Aristogiton, a citizen who belonged to the middle class. Harmodius was approached, though without success, by Hipparchus, the son of Pisistratus, and he told Aristogiton of this, who, being in love as he was, was greatly upset and was afraid that Hipparchus, with all his power, might take Harmodius by force. He therefore began at once, so far as he could in his position, to plot to overthrow the dictatorship. Meanwhile Hipparchus made another attempt, equally unsuccessful, to seduce Harmodius. Afterwards he had no intention of using force, but planned to insult him somehow in a way which would not reveal his real motives for doing so. Indeed, he exercised his authority in a manner that was easy for people to bear and ruled without making himself hated. These particular dictators, in fact, showed for a very long time both high principles and intelligence in their policy. The taxes they imposed

on the Athenians were only a twentieth of their incomes, yet they greatly improved the appearance of their city, carried through their wars successfully, and made all the proper religious sacrifices. In all other respects the city was still governed by the laws which had existed previously, except that they took care to see that there was always one of their own family in office. Among those of them who held the yearly office of archon in Athens was the son of the dictator Hippias, who was called Pisistratus after his grandfather. It was he who, in his year of office, dedicated the altar of the twelve gods, which is in the market-place, and the altar of Apollo in the Pythium. Later the altar in the market-place was extended to a greater length by the Athenian people and the inscription was obliterated. But one can still read in faded letters the inscription on the altar in the Pythium, which is as follows:

Hippias' son, Pisistratus, set up this record of office,
Here on the holy ground sacred to Pythian Apollo.

55   As for the fact that Hippias was the eldest son and the one who held power, this is something which I assert confidently on the basis of more accurate information than others possess. It can be seen also that this is true from the following point. Of all the legitimate brothers it is only in the case of Hippias that there is any record of children being born, as is shown both by the altar and by the pillar set up on the Athenian acropolis to commemorate the crimes of the dictators. On this pillar no child of Thessalus or of Hipparchus is mentioned, but there are five children of Hippias borne to him by Myrrhine, the daughter of Callias, the son of Hyperechides. Now, it is likely that the eldest brother would be the first to marry. And on the same pillar his name comes next after the name of his father, which is again the natural thing, since he was the next oldest to him and he held the dictatorship. Certainly I cannot believe that Hippias could ever have seized power so easily and so much at a moment's notice, if Hipparchus had been dictator at the time of his death, and Hippias himself had tried to establish his power on the very same day. The fact is that he had been long used to making the citizens fear him and his bodyguard obey him, and so he took control of the situation without being seriously challenged, showing none of the hesitation

that would be shown by a younger brother who lacked a long previous experience of holding power. As for Hipparchus, he became famous because of his unfortunate fate, and then also got the credit with posterity for having been the dictator.

56   To return to Harmodius; Hipparchus, after having been refused by him, proceeded to insult him as he had planned. He and his brother first invited a sister of Harmodius to come and carry a basket in a procession, and then, when she came, told her to go back again, saying that she had never been invited at all, as she was not fit to be in the procession. Harmodius was greatly upset by this, and for his sake Aristogiton also became all the more incensed. They had now arranged everything with those who were going to join them in their attempt, and only waited for the great feast of the Panathenaea, which was the only day on which the citizens, who were taking part in the procession, could gather together in arms without exciting suspicion. Aristogiton and Harmodius were to begin, and the others were to come to their support immediately against the bodyguard. There were not many conspirators, for reasons of security, and also it was hoped that those who were not actually in the plot would, once they saw even a few people ready to take the risk, join in on the spur of the moment and, since they had arms in their hands, come forward to regain their own liberty.

57   When the day of the festival came, Hippias with his bodyguard was outside the city in the Ceramicus organizing the order of march for the procession. Harmodius and Aristogiton had their daggers ready and were preparing to take action when they saw one of their fellow-conspirators talking in a friendly manner with Hippias (who, in fact, never made it difficult for anyone to approach him). They then became frightened, thinking that the plot had been betrayed and that they were on the very point of being arrested. First, however, they wished, if possible, to have their revenge on the man who had done them the injury and been the cause of their running all those risks, and so they rushed inside the gates just as they were, came upon Hipparchus by the Leocorium, and immediately fell upon him without a thought for their safety, but acting entirely under the impulse of rage caused, in the one case, by love and in the other by wounded pride. So they struck him down and killed him. Aristogiton, as the crowd ran up,

escaped the bodyguard for the time being, but was arrested later and died no easy death. Harmodius was killed on the spot.

58 When the news was brought to Hippias in the Ceramicus, instead of going to the place where the murder had been committed, he immediately approached the armed men in the procession before they, who were some distance away, realized what had happened. He put on, to meet the situation, an expression of face which gave nothing away, pointed to a certain piece of ground, and told the men to go there without their arms. They, thinking that he had something to say to them, did as they were told, and Hippias then ordered his bodyguard to take the arms away, and began at once to pick out the men whom he thought guilty and all who were found carrying daggers – shields and spears being the arms that were customarily carried in a procession.

59 In this way the conspiracy of Harmodius and Aristogiton originated in the wounded feeling of a lover, and their reckless action resulted from a momentary failure of nerve. But after this the dictatorship became more oppressive to the Athenians. Hippias was now more frightened himself, and he put to death many of the citizens. At the same time he began to look abroad to find a possible place of refuge for himself in case of revolution. At least there is no doubt that after this he, though an Athenian, gave his daughter Archedice to a Lampsacene, Aeantides, the son of the dictator of Lampsacus, Hippocles, and this was because he knew that they had great influence with the Persian King Darius. The tomb of Archedice is in Lampsacus, and it bears the following inscription:

> Daughter of him who was greatest in Hellas of that generation
> Archedice lies here. Hippias was her father.
> Daughter she was and wife and sister and mother of rulers,
> Yet in her own heart never harboured a feeling of pride.

Hippias held the dictatorship at Athens for three more years, and in the fourth year was deposed by the Spartans and the exiled Alcmaeonids. He was then given a safe conduct to Sigeum and went on to Aeantides at Lampsacus, and from there to the Court of King Darius. Twenty years later in his old age he set out from there with the Persians on the expedition to Marathon.

RECALL OF ALCIBIADES

60 These events had impressed themselves on the people of Athens and, recalling everything that they had heard about them, they were now in an angry and suspicious mood with regard to those who had been accused in connection with the mysteries; everything that had happened was, they thought, part of a plot aiming at setting up an oligarchy or a dictatorship. With public opinion inflamed as it was, there were already a number of worthy citizens in prison and there was no sign of things getting any easier; in fact every day showed an increase in savagery and led to more arrests being made. At this point one of the prisoners who was thought to be most guilty was persuaded by a fellow-prisoner to come forward with information which may have been either true or false. Both opinions are held, though in fact no one, either then or later, was able to say for certain who did the deed. The one prisoner, however, succeeded in persuading the other that it was better for him, even if he had not done it, to make himself safe by getting a promise of impunity and to put an end to the present state of suspicion in the city; for he would be in a safer position if he made a confession with impunity than if he denied the charges and was brought to trial. The prisoner in question therefore came forward with information incriminating himself and others with regard to the Hermae. The Athenian people were delighted at having now, as they imagined, discovered the truth, after having been previously in a terrible state at the idea that the conspirators against the democracy might never be found out. They at once released the informer himself, and with him all whom he had not accused. Those against whom he had given evidence were brought to trial and all who were secured were put to death. The death sentence was passed on all who managed to escape and a price was set on their heads. In all this it was impossible to say whether those who suffered deserved their punishment or not, but it was quite clear that the rest of the city, as things were, benefited greatly.

61   As for Alcibiades, the same enemies of his who attacked him even before he set sail now renewed their attacks, and the Athenians

took a serious view of the matter. Now that they thought they had discovered the truth about the Hermae, they were all the more inclined to believe that the sacrilege with regard to the mysteries, in which he was implicated, had been done by him as part and parcel of the same plot against the democracy. It also happened that just at the time when all this agitation was going on, a small force of Spartans had marched up as far as the Isthmus on some business which concerned them and the Boeotians. This, of course, was put down to the intrigues of Alcibiades, and it was thought that the Spartans were there, not because of the Boeotians, but by arrangement with him, and that, if the Athenians had not forestalled them by arresting the people against whom the information had been laid, the city would have been betrayed. They actually slept for one night under arms in the temple of Theseus inside the city. Also at about the same time the friends of Alcibiades in Argos were suspected of a plot against the democracy there, and because of this the Athenians handed over to the Argive people to be put to death all the Argive hostages whom they had in preventive custody in the islands.

Alcibiades therefore was surrounded by suspicions on all sides, and the Athenians, wishing to try him and put him to death, sent, as we have seen, the *Salaminia* to Sicily to fetch him and the others against whom information had been laid. The instructions were to order him to return and defend himself in the courts, but not to arrest him. This was because they were anxious to avoid causing a disturbance which would affect both their own troops and the enemy in Sicily, and especially because they wanted to retain the services of the Mantineans and Argives, who, they thought, had been persuaded to join the expedition by the influence of Alcibiades.

So he and the other accused persons left Sicily in his own ship and sailed with the *Salaminia* as though on the way back to Athens. But when they reached Thurii they parted company with her, and left their ship and went into hiding, since they were afraid to go back and stand a trial with all the prejudice against them that there was. The crew of the *Salaminia* spent some time in looking for Alcibiades and his companions, but in the end, since they were nowhere to be found, set sail and went away. Not long afterwards

Alcibiades, now in exile, crossed on a boat from Thurii to the Peloponnese, and the Athenians passed sentence of death by default on him and on those with him.

ATHENIAN VICTORY BEFORE SYRACUSE

62 After this the Athenian generals that remained in Sicily divided the whole force into two parts, took one each by lot, and sailed with the whole for Selinus and Egesta. Their aims were to discover whether the Egestaeans would produce the money and to examine the state of affairs in Selinus and find out about the points in dispute between her and Egesta. They sailed along the coast of Sicily on the side facing the Tyrrhenian sea, with the land on their left, and put in at Himera, which is the only Hellenic city in these parts. Here the citizens would not receive them and they sailed on again. On their way they captured Hyccara, a small fortified place on the coast which belonged to the Sicanians, but was at war with Egesta. They made slaves of the inhabitants and gave the place itself to the Egestaeans, whose cavalry had joined them. The army then went back again by land through the country of the Sicels and arrived at Catana, while the fleet with the slaves on board sailed along the coast. Nicias had sailed directly to Egesta along the coast from Hyccara and, after receiving thirty talents and doing some other business there, rejoined the rest of the expedition. The slaves were disposed of and raised a price of 120 talents. They also sailed round to their allies among the Sicels and urged them to send an army. And with half of their own forces they went against the enemy city of Hybla in the territory of Gela, but failed to capture it. So the summer came to an end.

63 At the very beginning of the following winter the Athenians were in active preparation for their attack on Syracuse, and the Syracusans on their side were getting ready to move against the Athenians. For after the Athenians had failed to make an immediate attack, as they had at first feared and expected they would do, the Syracusans gained confidence with every day that went by. And now, when they found that their enemies were sailing far away from them on the other side of Sicily, and that they had gone

to attack Hybla and failed to take the place by assault, they thought all the worse of them and (just as large numbers are apt to do when they feel confident) kept urging their generals to lead them forward to Catana, since the Athenians would not come against them. Syracusan cavalry on reconnaissance was constantly riding up to the Athenian army and, among other insulting remarks used, asked them whether they had not really come to settle down in someone else's land rather than to resettle the people of Leontini in their own.

64   The Athenian generals saw what the position was and planned to bring the Syracusans out in full force as far as possible from their city, while they themselves meanwhile would sail along the coast by night in their ships and occupy a suitable position for a camp at their leisure. They realized that this would not be so easy to do either if they made a landing from their ships in the face of troops ready to meet them, or if they were seen marching overland, since in this case their own light troops and camp-followers would have to suffer a great deal from the Syracusan cavalry, which was very numerous, while they themselves had no cavalry at all; whereas if they followed the proposed plan, they would occupy a position where the cavalry could do them no harm worth speaking of. (Some Syracusan exiles who were with them had told them of the piece of ground near the Olympieium, which was the place they did occupy in the end.)

The generals therefore thought out the following scheme for carrying out their plan. They sent to Syracuse a man whom they could trust and whom the Syracusan generals thought was on their own side. He was a man from Catana, and said that he had come from certain people in that town whose names were known to the Syracusan generals, who knew, too, that these were among the remainder of the pro-Syracusan party in Catana. He told them that the Athenians were in the habit of sleeping at night inside the city at some distance from the places where their arms were kept; if, therefore, the Syracusans would fix a day and come at dawn with their entire force to attack the Athenian expedition, their supporters in Catana would close the gates on the troops inside the city and would set fire to the ships, and then the Syracusans could attack the stockade and would easily overpower the men inside it.

He said that there were many people in Catana who would join in the operation, that they were ready for immediate action, and that he himself had come from them.

65   The Syracusan generals, confident as they were in any case, and having already decided, even without this information, to make an attack on Catana, showed a remarkable lack of precaution and believed what they were told. They immediately fixed a day on which they would appear and sent the man back to Catana. Their allies from Selinus and from some other places were already with them, and they now issued instructions for the whole Syracusan army to march out. When everything was ready and the time fixed for their arrival had almost come, they set out for Catana and camped for the night by the river Symaethus, in the territory of Leontini. As soon as the Athenians heard that they were on their way, they took their entire army, including any Sicels and others who had joined them, put them all aboard their ships and boats, and sailed by night to Syracuse. When day came the Athenians were landing opposite the Olympieium to occupy the ground for their camp, and the Syracusan cavalry, who had ridden up first to Catana and found that the whole expedition had put to sea, had turned back and reported the news to the infantry. They then all turned round and went back to defend their city.

66   Meanwhile, as the Syracusans had a long march in front of them, the Athenians had plenty of time to place their forces in an excellent position where they could begin a general engagement whenever they liked, and where the Syracusan cavalry would have the least chance of doing them damage either during a battle or before it, since on one side there were walls, houses, trees, and a marsh in the way, and on the other side there were steep cliffs. They also felled the trees in the neighbourhood, carried them down to the sea, and built a stockade alongside their ships. At Dascon, which was the point most vulnerable to enemy attack, they hurriedly constructed a fort with stones which they picked up and with timber. They also broke down the bridge over the Anapus. No one came out of the city to interrupt them in these preparations, and the first to appear were the Syracusan cavalry, who were followed later by all the infantry together. At first they marched up close to the Athenian army, then, when the Athenians did not

move out against them, turned back, crossed the road to Helorus, and camped there for the night.

67   Next day the Athenians and their allies prepared for battle. The order was as follows: on the right wing were the Argives and Mantineans, the Athenians were in the centre, and the rest of the line was filled by the other allies. Half of the army was drawn up in advance, eight deep; the other half was in a hollow square, also eight deep, covering the tents, and had orders to be ready to move up to the support of any part of the front line which they saw to be in difficulties. The non-combatants were placed inside this square.

The Syracusans drew up the whole of their line of hoplites sixteen deep. This line included the entire army of Syracuse, together with the allies who had come to support them. Most of these were from Selinus; the next important force was the cavalry from Gela, amounting to 200, and there were about twenty cavalry and fifty archers from Camarina. The cavalry, at least 1,200 strong, was drawn up on the right, and next to them were the javelin-throwers. As the Athenians were going to attack first, Nicias went along the lines encouraging the whole army and the various nationalities in it with the following words:

68   'There is no need for me to make a long speech of encouragement since we are all going into the same battle together. And in my opinion this army of ours itself gives better grounds for confidence than a good speech backed up by a weak force. For where we have Argives, Mantineans, Athenians, and the best of the islanders all together in a great combined force of excellent troops, how can we help feeling confident of victory? Especially when what we have to confront is a mass levy, not picked troops like ourselves, and a levy of Sicilians, too, who may look down on us but will not stand up to us, since they are more rash than experienced as soldiers. Remember this, too: we are far from home, and there is no friendly territory anywhere near, unless you fight for it and gain it. In fact I am telling you just the opposite of what I am sure the enemy are saying to encourage themselves. They are saying that the struggle in front of them is for their own country; I say that the struggle in front of us is for a country which is not ours, and that unless we win, we shall not find it easy to get away, since their cavalry will be upon us in great force. Remember then,

all of you, what is due to yourselves, and go forward against the enemy boldly and in the knowledge that our present necessity and the straits we should be in if we lost are more terrible than the forces opposed to us.'

69   After these words of encouragement Nicias at once led the army forward. The Syracusans were not at this moment expecting to go into action so soon, and some had actually gone away to the city which was not far off. These now came running up as fast as they could and, though late arrivals, took their places with the others as soon as they reached the main body. Indeed, neither in this battle nor in the others did the Syracusans show any lack of enthusiasm or daring; within the limits of their military experience they were not inferior in courage, and it was only when their lack of experience let them down that they reluctantly gave up their resolution, too. So now, though they had not expected that the Athenians would attack first, and though they were forced to fight in a hurry, they took up their arms at once and went forward into action.

First the stone-throwers, slingers, and archers on both sides engaged each other in front of the main lines of battle, with now one party and now another having the advantage, as is normal with these light troops. Then soothsayers brought forward the usual victims for sacrifice and trumpeters sounded the charge to the hoplites. So they went into action, the Syracusans to fight for their country and each man of them for his life on that day and his liberty thereafter; while on the other side the Athenians fought to conquer a country that was not their own and to save their own country from suffering by their defeat; the Argives and independent allies to help the Athenians in conquering what they had come to conquer and, as the reward of victory, to see again the country they had left behind; as for the allies who were subjects, they were spurred on chiefly by the desire to save their lives at the present time, which they could scarcely hope to do unless they were victorious; there was also the secondary consideration that, if they helped Athens in adding to her empire, they might themselves be governed less oppressively.

70   The armies now came to close quarters, and for some time no ground was yielded on either side. Meanwhile there were some claps of thunder and flashes of lightning with heavy rain, all of

which added to the fears of the Syracusans, who were fighting their first battle and had very little familiarity with war, while in the more experienced ranks of their enemies these events were regarded merely as what might be expected at this time of the year, and what really caused apprehension was the fact that the Syracusans were resisting so long without giving in. It was the Argives who first forced the Syracusan left wing back, and then the Athenians broke through the troops in front of them. The Syracusan army was now cut in two and took to flight. The Athenians did not pursue them far. They were prevented from doing so by the numbers of still undefeated Syracusan cavalry who charged and drove back any of the hoplites whom they saw pressing the pursuit in advance of the rest. Nevertheless they followed up the enemy as far as it was safe to do so in compact bodies, and then returned to their own lines and put up a trophy.

The Syracusans rallied together again at the road to Helorus, formed up as well as they could under the circumstances, and even sent a garrison of their own citizens to the Olympieium, since they were afraid that the Athenians might make off with some of the treasure there. The rest of them went back again to the city. The Athenians did not go to the temple; they collected their dead, put them on a pyre, and camped there for the night. Next day they gave the Syracusans back their dead under an armistice. About 260 of the Syracusans and allies had been killed. They then collected the bones of their own dead, of whom there were about fifty, Athenians and allies, and, taking with them the arms which they had stripped from the enemy, sailed back to Catana. They did this because it was now winter and they thought that they were not yet in a position to carry on the war from their base before Syracuse. First, cavalry would have to be sent for from Athens and collected from their allies in Sicily if they were not to be completely outclassed in this respect; money also must be procured in Sicily and sent to them from Athens; some of the cities, which they hoped would now after the battle be more likely to listen to them, must be won over to their side, and corn and all other things necessary must be provided with a view to making the attack on Syracuse in the spring. So, with these plans in mind, the Athenians sailed back to Naxos and Catana for the winter.

THE DEBATE AT CAMARINA

After they had buried their dead the Syracusans held an assembly at which Hermocrates, the son of Hermon, came forward to speak. He was in every way a remarkably intelligent man, and in the war had not only shown the qualities that come from experience but also won a name for his personal courage. He now raised their spirits and refused to allow them to become despondent because of what had happened. It was not a case, he said, of their spirit having been subdued; what had done the harm was their lack of discipline. Even then they had not been so much outclassed as might have been expected, especially if one considered that they were themselves, as it were, amateurs in the art of war and had been fighting against the most experienced troops in Hellas. What had done great harm, too, was the number of the generals (there were fifteen of them) and the fact that there were too many people giving orders, while the men in the ranks were disorganized and indisciplined. If, however, they had a small number of really experienced generals and spent the winter in organizing the hoplite forces, providing arms for those who had not got them, so that there should be as many as possible in the army, and instituting compulsory military training, then, he said, they would have every reason to expect victory over the enemy; they had the courage already, and the discipline would come as the result of training. There would be, in fact, an automatic improvement in both respects, as discipline would be learnt in the school of danger and courage would rise to greater heights of heroism when supported by the confidence that comes from experience. As for choosing the generals, they should be few in number and they should have unrestricted power; the people should swear an oath to them guaranteeing that they would be allowed to carry out their responsibilities exactly as they thought fit. This would give additional security with regard to matters that should be kept secret, and would allow the whole defence programme to be carried through smoothly without the need for giving continual explanations for what was being done.

73   The Syracusans listened to him and voted in favour of

everything which he had recommended. They elected just three generals – Hermocrates himself, Heraclides, the son of Lysimachus, and Sicanus, the son of Execestes. They sent representatives to Corinth and to Sparta in order to secure the aid of an allied force and to try to persuade the Spartans for their sake to declare war on Athens and carry it on vigorously, so that the Athenians would either have to withdraw from Sicily or would be handicapped in sending more troops out to their army already there.

74   The Athenian forces in Catana sailed at once to Messina in the hope that the place was going to be betrayed to them, but the plan came to nothing. This was because Alcibiades, when he laid down his command after his recall and realized that he was going to be exiled, had given information about the plot, in which he was concerned himself, to the pro-Syracusan party in Messina. They had put the leading conspirators to death even before the Athenians arrived, and now in the general disturbance the same party rose up in arms, and so succeeded in keeping the Athenians out. For about thirteen days the Athenians stayed there; then, since they were exposed to the weather and short of supplies and meeting with no success, they went back to Naxos, where they built sheds for the storage of equipment, surrounded their camp with a palisade, and so passed the winter. They sent a trireme to Athens for money and for cavalry to be with them in the spring.

75   During the winter the Syracusans built a wall on to their city taking in the ground of Apollo Temenites and running all along the part that looks towards Epipolae, so that, in case of a defeat, they could not be so easily shut in by a blockading wall as when the area was smaller. They also built one fort at Megara and another at the Olympieium, and stuck stakes into the sea at all the possible landing-places. Then, when they knew that the Athenians were spending the winter at Naxos, they marched out to Catana in full force, laid the land waste, burned the tents and camp of the Athenians, and so returned home. They heard, too, that, on the strength of the alliance made in the time of Laches, the Athenians were sending representatives to Camarina to see whether they could gain her support, and they therefore sent representatives of their own there to oppose the move. They suspected that the people of Camarina had not been very willing to send them what

they did send for the first battle, and that after they saw that the Athenians had been successful in the battle they might in future refuse to give them any more help, and instead join the Athenians on the basis of their former friendship with them. Hermocrates was one of those who came from Syracuse to Camarina, and on the Athenian side there were Euphemus and others. An assembly of the Camarinaeans was held, and Hermocrates, wishing to make his attack on the Athenians first, spoke as follows:

76   'Camarinaeans, we did not come on this mission because we were afraid that the forces which the Athenians have could frighten you; it was more the words that they were going to speak which made us fear that they might convince you before you had had an opportunity of hearing what we have to say on our side. The reasons they put forward for being here in Sicily are known to you, but we all have a suspicion of what their real intentions are. In my opinon what they want to do is not so much to give Leontini back what was hers as to take away from us what is ours. Certainly it is scarcely logical for them to be destroying cities in Hellas and restoring cities in Sicily, to be showing all this care for the Leontinians, who are Chalcidians, because of their racial connection with them and meanwhile to be holding down in subjection the actual inhabitants of Chalcis in Euboea, whose colonists the Leontinians are. The fact is that just as they won an empire in Hellas, so they are trying to win another one here, and by exactly the same methods. The alliance of Ionians and others racially connected with Athens voluntarily accepted Athenian leadership in the war to get their own back from Persia; but the Athenians deprived them all of their independence, accusing some of failure to fulfil their military obligations, some of fighting among themselves, bringing forward, in fact, any plausible excuse to fit each particular case. So, in making this stand against Persia, Athens was not fighting for the freedom of Hellas, nor were the Hellenes fighting for their own; what Athens wanted was to substitute her own empire for that of Persia, and the other Hellenes were simply fighting to get themselves a new master whose intelligence was not less but who made a much more evil use of it than did the old.

77   'However, there is plenty of scope for attacking the record of a city like Athens, and we have not come here now to tell you the

story of her misdoings; you know them already. What is more to
the point is to blame ourselves. We have in front of us the example
of the Hellenes in the mother country who have been enslaved
through not supporting each other; we now find the Athenians
employing the same sophistries against us – restoration of their
kinsmen of Leontini, military aid to their allies of Egesta – yet we
are not prepared to unite and resolutely make it clear to them that
what they have to deal with here is not Ionians, Hellespontians,
and islanders who may change masters, but are always slaves either
to the Persians or to someone else, but free Dorians from the independent Peloponnese living in Sicily. Are we waiting until we
are taken over separately, city by city, though we are well aware
that this is the only chance they have of conquering us and we see
that this is just the method they are adopting – sometimes trying
to create dissension among us by their arguments, sometimes
stirring up wars among us by holding out hopes of an alliance
with them – doing, in fact, all the harm they can by using the
most flattering language possible on every particular occasion?
And when fellow Sicilians who live at a distance from us are
destroyed first, do we imagine that the danger will not come to
each of us in our turn or that misfortunes will be confined to those
who suffer before our turn is reached?

78   'Some of you may have the idea that it is Syracuse, not Camarina, which is the enemy of Athens, and may object to running
risks for my country. Anyone who thinks like this must remember
that if he fights in my country he will be fighting just as much for
his own country as for mine, and will be all the safer in having
me as his ally and not having to fight alone, as he would have to
do if I were destroyed first. Let him remember, too, that what
Athens is aiming at is not so much to punish the hostility of Syracuse as to secure the friendship of Camarina by using us Syracusans
as a pretext. And if anyone envies us or even fears us (and superior
powers are both envied and feared), and because of this wants
Syracuse to be weakened in order to make us less arrogant, but
still to survive for the sake of his own security, then he is wanting
something which is not humanly possible. One cannot regulate
fortune to fit in with what one has decided one wants to happen.
And if his calculations went wrong, he would soon have miseries

of his own to bewail, and would very probably be wishing that he could once again be envying my prosperity. Yet that will be impossible if he abandons us now and refuses to take his share in the dangers which, whatever may be said, do in fact threaten him just as much as us. It may be said that he would be fighting to preserve our power, but in reality it would be for his own survival. One would have thought that you Camarinaeans would have been the most likely people of all to have foreseen this, considering that you are on our boundaries and are next on the danger list. One would have expected that instead of giving us the half-hearted support which you are giving, it would rather have been the case that you would have come to us of your own accord and, just as you would have asked for our help if the Athenians had attacked Camarina first, so now you would be openly urging us not to make any concessions to the enemy. As it happens, however, no such vigorous action has yet been taken either by you or by the rest.

79   'It may be that out of cowardice you will attempt to do the right thing both by us and by the invaders, and will say that you have an alliance with the Athenians. But this alliance was made by you not against your friends, but against any enemies that might attack you, and as for the Athenians, you were only bound to help them when they were the victims of aggression, not when, as now, they are the aggressors against your neighbours. Even the people of Rhegium, in spite of being Chalcidians, refuse to help restore their fellow Chalcidians of Leontini. It would be strange if they were to show such an illogical degree of common sense in seeing the real meaning of the apparently fair claims made upon them, while you, with logic as your pretext, should prefer to assist those who are by nature hostile to you, and should turn against your own kinsfolk, helping their bitterest enemies to destroy them. This is certainly not doing the right thing. Instead of this, you should be helping us, and you ought not to be afraid of their fleet and army; there is nothing there to be frightened of so long as we all stand together, but only if we fail to do this and drift apart – which is just what they are trying to bring about. You saw that even when they came against us by ourselves and defeated us in battle they failed to achieve their objects and had to retire at once.

80   'There is therefore no reason for despondency so long as we

stick together, and every reason for us to join wholeheartedly in the alliance, especially as help is coming to us from the Peloponnesians, who in military affairs are better than the Athenians in every way. And no one ought to think that it is either fair to us or safe for you to adopt the cautious policy of saying that you are allies of both sides and therefore will help neither one nor the other. It may look legally fair, but in fact it is not. If the defeat of the conquered and the victory of the conquerors comes from your not joining in the struggle, then the positive result of your inaction has been that you have failed to help one side to safety and allowed the other to proceed unchecked on a course of evil. Surely the honourable thing to do is this – to come to the side of the victims of aggression, who are also of the same blood as you are, and so to defend the common interests of Sicily and prevent your Athenian friends from doing wrong.

'This, finally, is what we Syracusans say: there is no point in our going into careful explanations either with you or with the rest about things which you know just as well as we do; we entreat you, however, and, if our appeal fails, we most solemnly protest that, while the Ionians, our perpetual foes, are plotting against us, you, our fellow Dorians, are betraying us. If the Athenians conquer us, they will owe that achievement to your decision, but will receive the credit for it themselves, and will take as the prize of victory the very people who helped them to win it. If, on the other hand, the victory goes to us, you will scarcely escape paying the penalty for having been the cause of our danger. Think carefully, therefore, and now make your choice: you may either run no risks and become slaves at once, or else, standing together with us, you may save yourselves, and so both avoid the disgrace of being dominated by the Athenians and escape the lasting hatred which otherwise we should feel for you.'

81   After this speech of Hermocrates, Euphemus, the Athenian representative, spoke as follows:

82   'The reason we came here was to renew the former alliance, but now, after this attack from the Syracusan, I am forced to speak about our empire and the good reasons we have for holding it. As a matter of fact the Syracusan representative himself put forward the best piece of evidence on this point when he said that the

Ionians are always the enemies of the Dorians. That is quite true. Now, we are Ionians and the Peloponnesians are Dorians; they are more numerous than we are and they live close to us. We therefore looked about for the best means of preserving our independence, and after the Persian war, by which time we had built our navy, we broke free from the Spartan empire and from Spartan leadership. They had no more right to give us orders than we had to give orders to them, except that at the time they were stronger. We ourselves were appointed to the leadership of those who had previously been under the King of Persia, and we continue to manage their affairs. Our view is that in this way we are least likely to fall under the domination of the Peloponnesians, since we have the power to defend ourselves, nor, if one considers the real facts of the situation, do we think that we have done anything wrong in subjugating the Ionians and the islanders, who, according to the Syracusans, are our oppressed kinsmen. The fact is that these kinsmen joined the Persians in attacking their mother country – namely, Athens – and, unlike us, when we abandoned our city, did not have the courage to revolt, which would have meant losing their property. Instead of this they chose to be slaves themselves and wanted to make us slaves too.

83   'We therefore deserve the empire which we have, partly because we supplied to the cause of Hellas the largest fleet and a courage that never looked back, while these subjects of ours harmed us by being just as ready to act in the service of Persia, partly because we wanted to have the strength to hold our own in relation to the Peloponnesians. We are not making any dramatic statements such as that we have a right to rule because single-handed we overthrew the foreign invader, or that the risks we took were for the liberty of these subjects of ours any more than for the liberty of everyone, ourselves included; no one can be blamed for looking after his own safety in his own way. So now it is for our own security that we are in Sicily, and we see that here your interests are the same as ours. This we can prove from what the Syracusans are saying against us and from the suspicions of us which you yourselves, in your rather over-anxious mood, no doubt entertain; because we know that when people are frightened and suspicious they enjoy for the moment an argument that fits in with their feelings, but in

the end, when it comes to the point, they act in accordance with their interests.

'We have told you that it is because of fear that we hold our empire in Hellas, and it is also because of fear that we have come here to settle matters for our own security, together with our friends; not to enslave anybody, but rather to prevent anybody from being enslaved.

84 'No one must imagine that the interest which we take in you has nothing to do with ourselves. You have only to reflect that so long as you are safe and strong enough to hold your own against Syracuse, the Syracusans will not find it so easy to do us harm by sending a force to help the Peloponnesians. Therefore what you do concerns us very much indeed. On the same principle it is perfectly reasonable for us to restore their independence to the people of Leontini and, so far from making them our subjects like their kinsmen in Euboea, to see that they are as powerful as possible, so that they may help us by being a source of irritation to Syracuse, planted on her frontiers and based on their own territory. In Hellas we are strong enough in ourselves to deal with our enemies, and when the Syracusan representative says that it is illogical for us to enslave Chalcidians in Hellas and liberate them in Sicily, he should remember that it is to our interest that in Hellas they should be unarmed and should merely contribute money, but here in Sicily we should like to see both the people of Leontini and all our 85 other friends as independent as possible. When a man or a city exercises absolute power the logical course is the course of self-interest, and ties of blood exist only when they can be relied upon; one must choose one's friends and enemies according to the circumstances on each particular occasion. And here in Sicily what suits our interest is not to weaken our friends, but to use the strength they have to render our enemies powerless. This is something which you must not doubt. In Hellas our leadership of our allies is adapted to make each ally most useful to us. The Chians and Methymnians provide ships and are independent: most of the others have rather harsher terms and pay regular contributions of money; while some allies, although they are islanders and easy for us to take over, enjoy complete freedom, because they are in convenient positions round the Peloponnese. It is reasonable to

suppose, therefore, that here, too, in our Sicilian policy, we should be guided by our own interests and, as we say, by our fear of Syracuse. The aim of the Syracusans is to rule over you, and their policy is to make you unite on the basis of your suspicions of us and then to take over the empire of Sicily themselves either by force or, when we have retired without achieving anything, because there will be no one to dispute it with them. This is bound to happen if you do unite with them, since so great a combined force would no longer be easy for us to deal with, and, once we had disappeared from the scene, they would be quite strong enough to take their measures against you.

86   'Anyone who does not agree with this will find that the facts are against him. When you asked for our help originally, what you held in front of us was the fear that, if we allowed you to fall into the power of Syracuse, we ourselves would be in danger. It is hardly fair for you now to mistrust the very same argument which you thought was the one to convince us then, or to be suspicious of us because we have come against Syracuse with a force rather larger than you expected. The people you ought to distrust are the Syracusans. We for our part cannot stay here without your support, and even if we were so base as to deprive you of your independence we could not keep you under our control because of the length of the voyage and the difficulty of garrisoning large cities armed on the lines of continental powers. The Syracusans, on the other hand, are your close neighbours; they are not living in a camp, but in a city bigger than the force we have with us; they are constantly intriguing against you, and whenever they get a chance of carrying out their plans they take it, as they have shown in the case of Leontini among others. And now they have the face to ask you for your help against the very people who have been preventing their designs and have up to now kept Sicily independent. They must have a poor idea of your intelligence! We on our side invite you to a much more real safety when we urge you not to betray the safety which we get from you and you get from us and to reflect that for Syracuse, even without allies, the way is always open because of their numbers to attack you, whereas you will not often get the chance of defending yourselves with such forces on your side as we are offering. And if, because

of your suspicions, we have to return with nothing accomplished, or even defeated, the time will come when you will wish to see just a fraction of these forces, but the time will have passed when their presence will be able to do you any good.

87 'But we trust that neither you, Camarinaeans, nor the others will be swayed by the calumnies of the Syracusans. We have told you the whole truth about what we are suspected of, and we will now summarize the argument to remind you of it and, we hope, to convince you. We say that in Hellas we rule in order not to be ruled; in Sicily we come as liberators in order not to be harmed by the Sicilians; we are forced to intervene in many directions simply because we have to be on our guard in many directions; now, as previously, we have come as allies to those of you here who are being oppressed; our help was asked for, and we have not arrived uninvited. And it is not for you to constitute yourselves judges of our behaviour or to act like schoolmasters and try to make us change our ways. That is not an easy thing to do now. Instead you ought to grasp and make full use of everything in our interventionism and our general character which fits in with your interests, and you should reflect that these characteristics of ours, so far from doing harm to all alike, are to the majority of the Hellenes a positive blessing. It is something which has its effect on all men everywhere, even in places where we are not established, because the possibility of our intervention is always something to be considered both by those who fear aggression and those who are actually planning an aggressive move; the former can hope for our help, the latter must reflect that, if we do intervene, their enterprise is likely to be a dangerous one; so in both cases we make ourselves felt: the potential aggressor is forced, even against his will, to behave reasonably, and those who might have been his victims are saved without having to exert themselves. Do not reject this security which all who ask can have and which is now available to you. Do as the others do: join with us and, instead of always having to be on your guard against the Syracusans, transform the situation at last and threaten them as they have threatened you.'

88 This was the speech of Euphemus. The state of feeling among the people of Camarina was as follows. They were well disposed

to the Athenians, except in so far as they thought they might enslave Sicily, and they were always opposed to their neighbours the Syracusans. They feared Syracuse, however, just because of this proximity quite as much as they feared Athens, and it was through fear that the Syracusans might win even without them that they had sent them originally the small force of cavalry. So for the future they thought it best to give their practical support, though as little of it as possible, to Syracuse; but for the moment, in order to avoid giving the impression that they had treated Athens with disrespect (particularly as the Athenians had won the battle), they decided to give the same answer to each side. So, after their discussion had proceeded along these lines, they replied that since a state of war existed between two parties, both of which were their allies, they thought that the only way at present of keeping the oaths they had sworn was not to help either side. The representatives of Syracuse and of Athens then went away.

ALCIBIADES IN SPARTA

While the Syracusans went on with their own preparations for war, the Athenians encamped at Naxos attempted to win over to their side as many of the Sicels as possible. Those of them who lived more in the coastal plains and were subjects of Syracuse generally refused to cooperate; but the Sicels of the interior, whose settlements had always been independent, immediately, with few exceptions, joined the Athenians. They brought down corn to the coast for the army, and some produced money as well. The Athenians marched against those who refused to join them and forced some to do so; in other cases they were prevented by garrisons or reinforcements sent out by the Syracusans.

The Athenian winter quarters were moved from Naxos to Catana, where the camp burned by the Syracusans was rebuilt and where they spent the remainder of the winter. A trireme was sent on a mission of goodwill to Carthage to see if any help could be gained from them, and they also sent to Etruria, where some of the cities had offered of their own accord to join them in the war. Messengers, too, were dispatched to the Sicels and to Egesta with instructions to ask for as many horses as possible to be sent, and all the time they were getting ready the bricks and iron and everything else necessary for building siege works, with the intention of opening the campaign at the beginning of spring.

Meanwhile the Syracusan representatives who had been sent out to Corinth and Sparta called in on their way up the coast at the Greek cities in Italy and tried to persuade them to resist the Athenian action, which was aimed, they said, just as much against Italy as against Sicily. When they reached Corinth discussions were held, and they asked for Corinthian aid on the grounds of their racial connection with that city. The Corinthians immediately voted in favour of giving them ungrudgingly all the help they could themselves, and at the same time sent representatives to accompany them to Sparta and to join them in trying to persuade the Spartans to do their part by making war more openly on Athens in Hellas and by sending a force to Sicily.

Alcibiades and those who were exiled with him were also in Sparta when the representatives arrived from Corinth. He had crossed immediately from Thurii in a merchant ship and gone first to Cyllene in Elis and then, on the invitation of the Spartans themselves, to Sparta. He had secured a guarantee for his safety, since he had reason to fear the Spartans because of his share in the events at Mantinea. So now it happened that in the Spartan assembly the Corinthians, the Syracusans, and Alcibiades were all making the same requests and urging the same arguments. The ephors and other magistrates, though they were prepared to send representatives to Syracuse to prevent the Syracusans coming to terms with Athens, were not very willing to send any military assistance. Alcibiades then came forward, roused up Spartan opinion, and incited them to action by the following speech:

89   'The first thing I must do is to deal with the prejudice which you feel against me, so that you may listen to matters of common interest without being biased by any suspicion of me personally. My ancestors used to hold the position of official representatives for Sparta in Athens; because of some misunderstanding they gave up this position, but I myself took it up again and put my services at your disposal, particularly with regard to the losses which you sustained at Pylos. I remained anxious to help you throughout,

but when you made peace with Athens you negotiated through my personal enemies, thus putting them in a stronger position and discrediting me. You have therefore no right to blame me for the injuries you suffered when I turned to Mantinea and to Argos and opposed you in various other ways. And if in those days when you were actually suffering any of you were unreasonably angry with me, the time has now come for you to look at the matter in its true light and to change your views. Or if anyone thought the worse of me because I was rather on the side of the people, here again he should see that this was no good reason for being against me. My family has always been opposed to dictators; democracy is the name given to any force that opposes absolute power; and so we have continued to act as the leaders of the common people. Besides, since democracy was the form of government in Athens, it was necessary in most respects to conform to the conditions that prevailed. However in the face of the prevailing political indiscipline, we tried to be more reasonable. There have been people in the past, just as there are now, who used to try to lead the masses into evil ways. It is people of this sort who have banished me. But we were leaders of the State as a whole, and our principles were that we should all join together in preserving the form of government which had been handed down to us under which the city was most great and most free. As for democracy, those of us with any sense at all knew what that meant, and I just as much as any. Indeed, I am well equipped to make an attack on it; but nothing new can be said of a system which is generally recognized as absurd. As for changing the system, that appeared to us as unsafe while you were engaged in war with us.

90 'So much for the things which have created prejudice against me. I now want you to listen to what I have to say on the subject which you are to discuss – a subject on which I am perhaps peculiarly well qualified to speak. We sailed to Sicily to conquer first, if possible, the Sicilians, and after them the Hellenes in Italy; next we intended to attack the Carthaginian empire and Carthage herself. Finally, if all or most of these plans were successful, we were going to make our assault on the Peloponnese, bringing with us all the additional Hellenic forces which we should have acquired in the west and hiring as mercenaries great numbers of native

troops – Iberians and others who are now recognized as being the best fighting material to be found in those parts. In addition to our existing fleet we should have built many more triremes, since Italy is rich in timber, and with all of them we should have blockaded the coast of the Peloponnese, while at the same time our army would be operating on land against your cities, taking some by assault and others by siege. In this way we hoped that the war would easily be brought to a successful conclusion and after that we should be the masters of the entire Hellenic world. As for money and provisions, there could be no fear of them running short, since sufficient supplies were to be provided by our new conquests in the west without touching our revenues here in Hellas.

91 'You have now heard from the man who knows most about it what were in fact the objects of the present expedition; and the generals who are left will, if they can, continue just the same to carry out these plans. What you must now realize is that, unless you help her, Sicily will be lost. The Sicilians lack the experience which Athens has, but might even now survive if they all united together. The Syracusans by themselves, however, whose total force has already been defeated in one battle and who are at the same time blockaded by sea, will not be able to hold out against the Athenian forces now in Sicily. And if Syracuse falls, all Sicily falls with it, and Italy soon afterwards. It would not then be long before you were confronted with the dangers which I have just told you threatened you from the west. So do not imagine that it is only the question of Sicily that is under discussion; it will be the question of the Peloponnese unless you quickly take the following measures: you must send out to Sicily a force of troops that are able to row the ships themselves and to take the field as hoplites as soon as they land; and – what I consider even more useful than the troops – you must send out as commander a regular Spartan officer to organize the troops that are there already and to force into the service those who are shirking their duty. This is the way to put fresh heart into your friends and make the waverers less frightened of joining in. Then, too, the war in Hellas must be carried on more openly. This will have the effect of stiffening Syracusan resistance, when they see that you are taking an interest in them, and will make it harder for the Athenians to reinforce their army in Sicily.

And you must fortify Decelea in Attica; it is the thing of which the Athenians have always been most frightened, and they think that of all the adversities of the war this is the only one that they have not experienced. The surest way of harming an enemy is to find out certainly what form of attack he is most frightened of and then to employ it against him. He is likely to know himself more accurately than anyone else where his danger lies, and that is why he is frightened. As for what you will gain and what you will force Athens to lose if you fortify Decelea, I shall merely summarize the most important points, omitting many others. Most of the property in the area will come into your hands, some by capture, some without your having to move a finger. Athens will immediately be deprived of her revenues from the silver mines at Laurium and from what she gets at present from the land and from the law-courts. Most important of all, she will lose her tribute from the allies, since they will pay it in much less regularly and will cease to be overawed by Athens herself once they see that you are

92 now really making war seriously. How quickly and how energetically these things are done depends on you, Spartans; I am perfectly confident that they can be done, and I do not think that I am likely to be wrong.

'I claim also that none of you should think the worse of me if, in spite of my previous reputation for loving my country, I now join in vigorously with her bitterest enemies in attacking her; nor should you suspect my argument on the grounds that it derives simply from the strong feelings of an exile. I am an exile because of the villainy of the men who drove me out, not out of any wish, if you listen to me, to help you. And the worst enemies of Athens are not those who, like you, have only harmed her in war, but those who have forced her friends to turn against her. The Athens I love is not the one which is wronging me now, but that one in which I used to have secure enjoyment of my rights as a citizen. The country that I am attacking does not seem to me to be mine any longer; it is rather that I am trying to recover a country that has ceased to be mine. And the man who really loves his country is not the one who refuses to attack it when he has been unjustly driven from it, but the man whose desire for it is so strong that he will shrink from nothing in his efforts to get back there again.

And so, Spartans, I think that you should not hesitate to make use of my services in every kind of danger or hardship. You should remember the argument that everyone uses and realize that just as I did you much harm when I was your enemy, so I can be of considerable service to you as a friend: of Athens I have certain knowledge, whereas with regard to Sparta I had to proceed by guesswork. My advice to you is to recognize that it is your basic interests which are now being discussed: you must not shrink from undertaking the campaigns in Sicily and in Attica; the presence of only a fraction of your forces in Sicily will ensure great results, and you will destroy both the present power and the future prospects of Athens. After that you yourselves will live in safety and be the leaders of the whole of Hellas, which will follow you voluntarily, not because of force, but from goodwill.'

93   This was the speech of Alcibiades. The Spartans even before this had intended to march against Athens, but were still hesitating and examining the risks involved. Now, however, after hearing all the points raised by Alcibiades, who, they considered, knew the facts better than anyone, they were all the more confirmed in their intentions. The result was that they had now definitely set their minds on fortifying Decelea and on sending help immediately to the Sicilians. They appointed Gylippus, the son of Cleandridas, to be commander for the Syracusans and instructed him to consult with the Syracusans and Corinthians, and so find the best and quickest way under present circumstances of getting reinforcements into Sicily. Gylippus asked the Corinthians to send him two ships to Asine at once, to equip the other ships that they intended to send, and to have them ready to sail when the time came. After having agreed on these points, the various deputations left Sparta.

Meanwhile the Athenian trireme from Sicily, which had been sent by the generals for money and cavalry, arrived at Athens. After hearing what was required, the Athenians voted to send the money for the expedition and the cavalry. So the winter ended and the seventeenth year of this war recorded by Thucydides.

MORE ATHENIAN SUCCESSES AT SYRACUSE

94 Next year, at the very beginning of spring, the Athenians in Sicily put to sea from Catana and sailed along the coast to Megara in Sicily. The Megarians, as I have already said, were driven out by the Syracusans in the time of Gelon's dictatorship, and the Syracusans still held their land. Here they landed and laid waste the country, and after making an unsuccessful attack on a Syracusan fort, went on along the coast with both army and ships to the river Terias. Here they moved into the plain and laid it waste, burning the corn; they met a small force of Syracusans and killed some of them; then, after putting up a trophy, they went back again to their ships. Next they sailed back to Catana for revictualling and went on with their whole force against Centoripa, a town of the Sicels. After receiving the surrender of this town, they went back again, first burning the corn of the people of Inessa and Hybla. On their return to Catana they found that the cavalry force had arrived from Athens. There were 250 cavalrymen, with their equipment, but without horses, the idea being that the horses could be procured in Sicily. There were thirty mounted archers, and 300 talents of silver.

95 The same spring the Spartans marched against Argos and got as far as Cleonae. Here an earthquake occurred, and they went back again. After this the Argives invaded the border territory of Thyrea and plundered a great deal of Spartan property, which was sold for no less than twenty-five talents.

Not much later in the same summer the people of Thespiae attempted to overthrow their Government, but were unsuccessful. Help arrived from Thebes, and some of the revolutionaries were captured and some took refuge in Athens.

96 The same summer the Syracusans heard that the Athenians had got their cavalry and were on the point of attacking them. They thought that, unless the Athenians could control Epipolae – the precipitous piece of ground lying directly above the city – they would find it difficult, even if victorious in battle, to build a wall to cut the city off. They therefore decided to guard the approaches to Epipolae to prevent the enemy making their way up unobserved

by this route, which was, indeed, the only practicable one, since the rest of the ground is high and slopes down to the city so that it is all within sight from inside. It is called 'Epipolae' (or 'the Heights') by the Syracusans because it lies above the level of the rest. The Syracusans therefore went out at dawn in full force to the meadows along the river Anapus and held a review of their hoplites. Their new generals, Hermocrates and the others, had just taken over their commands. They first set aside from the hoplites a specially picked force of 600 men, under the command of Diomilus, an exile from Andros, who were to guard Epipolae and to stand by ready for action immediately wherever else they might be required.

97   Meanwhile the Athenians, on this very same morning, were putting their own troops in order. They had left Catana and put into land with their whole force opposite the place called Leon, rather more than half a mile from Epipolae. The army had been landed and the fleet had come to anchor at Thapsus, which is a peninsula with a narrow isthmus jutting out into the sea and not far from the city of Syracuse either by land or water. The Athenian naval forces built a stockade across the isthmus and stayed quiet at Thapsus. The army went straight for Epipolae at the double and made the ascent by way of Euryelus before the Syracusans realized what was happening or could bring forces up from the meadows where the review was being held. Diomilus with his 600, and all the rest as fast as they could, came up to the relief, but they had nearly three miles to go from the meadow before making contact with the enemy. The Syracusan attack was therefore made in a more or less disorganized way and, defeated in battle on Epipolae, they retired to the city. About 300 of them were killed, including Diomilus. Afterwards the Athenians put up a trophy and gave the Syracusans back their dead under an armistice. Next day they marched down to the city itself, but as no one came out to meet them, they went back again and built a fort at Labdalum, on the edge of the cliffs of Epipolae and looking towards Megara, so as to have a place to store their equipment and money whenever they went out either to give battle or to work on the wall which they proposed to build.

98   Soon after this 300 cavalry came to them from Egesta and about

100 from the Sicels, the Naxians, and others. They already had the 250 Athenian cavalrymen, for whom they had got horses, some purchased, some sent to them from Egesta and Catana. Altogether, therefore, they now had a cavalry force of 650.

After leaving a garrison in Labdalum, the Athenians moved on to Syca, where they settled down and quickly constructed the fort called the Circle. The speed with which they carried out these building operations dismayed the Syracusans, who determined to come out and give battle and put a stop to them. Indeed, the two armies were already facing each other, when the Syracusan generals saw that their own army was in bad order and could not easily be brought into line. They therefore led their men back into the city, except for some cavalry detachments, who stayed behind and succeeded in preventing the Athenians from carrying stones or going far from the protection of their main body of troops. One division of Athenian hoplites, however, with the whole cavalry force, charged the Syracusan cavalry and routed them. They killed a certain number of them and then put up a trophy for the cavalry action.

99   Next day part of the Athenian forces went on with the building of the wall north of the Circle, and part collected stones and wood, which they put down at intervals in the direction of Trogilus on the shortest line for their blockading wall, which was to extend from the great harbour to the sea at the other side. The Syracusans, on the advice of their generals, and particularly of Hermocrates, gave up the idea of risking any more regular battles with the Athenians and decided instead to start building a counter-wall out in the direction where the Athenians intended to build their own wall. If they could get it finished in time it would have the effect of cutting the Athenian lines, and if, while it was being built, the Athenians were to attack, they would only use a part of their forces to meet such an attack, since they would have already built stockades behind which they would be protected, whereas the Athenians would have to suspend their building operations and use their whole force in dealing with them. They therefore came out and began to build a wall out from their city below the Athenian Circle and at right angles to the Athenian wall. They cut down the olive trees in the temple grounds and used them for

building wooden towers. The Athenian fleet had not yet sailed round from Thapsus into the great harbour, and so the Syracusans still controlled the coast, while the Athenians brought their provisions by land from Thapsus.

100   The time came when the Syracusans thought that their stockades and the building of their counter-wall were well enough advanced. The Athenians had not come out to interrupt them in their work, since they were afraid of dividing their forces and so fighting at a disadvantage, and at the same time they wanted to hurry on with their own wall of encirclement. So the Syracusans left one division of troops to guard the wall that they had constructed and went back into the city.

The Athenians destroyed the pipes which carried the drinking-water underground into Syracuse. Then they waited for the time when those of the Syracusans who were not on duty were in their tents at mid-day or, in some cases, had even gone away into the city, and when those actually manning the stockades were off their guard. Three hundred picked Athenian hoplites and some specially selected light troops, who were given heavy armour, were instructed to go out suddenly at the double against the counter-wall; the rest of the army was divided into two: one part under one of the generals went towards the city, in case of reinforcements coming out from there; the other part with the other general went to the stockade by the postern gate. The 300 made their attack and took the stockade. The garrison abandoned it and fled inside the wall round the precinct of Apollo Temenites, closely followed by their pursuers, who burst inside, but were forced out again by the Syracusans, and in this action some Argives and a few Athenians lost their lives. The whole army then fell back, destroyed the counter-wall, pulled up the stockade, carried off the stakes for themselves, and put up a trophy.

101   Next day the Athenians from the Circle began to build fortifications on the cliff above the marsh which on this side of Epipolae looks towards the great harbour, and which was on the shortest line for their wall, which was to run down over the more level ground and over the marsh to the harbour.

The Syracusans now came out and began building another stockade out from their city through the middle of the marsh, with a ditch alongside, so as to make it impossible for the Athenians to carry their wall down to the sea. The Athenians, once they had finished their fortifications on the cliff, again attacked the Syracusan stockade and ditch. The fleet was ordered to sail round from Thapsus into the great harbour of Syracuse, and at dawn the army came down from Epipolae into the plain and made their way over the marsh by laying down doors and planks over the parts where the mud was thickest and the ground firmest. By daybreak they had captured the ditch and the whole of the stockade except for a small section which they captured later. Fighting now broke out, and the Athenians were victorious. The right wing of the Syracusans fled to the city and the left to the river. Wishing to cut them off from crossing, the 300 picked Athenian troops hurried towards the bridge at the double. The Syracusans, most of whose cavalry was also in this part of the field, rallied under the influence of fear and went against the 300 Athenians, routed them, and drove on into the Athenian right wing, the first detachment of which was also thrown into confusion by their attack. Lamachus, seeing this, came up in support from the Athenian left, bringing with him the Argives and a few archers. After crossing over a ditch, he and a few others who had gone with him were left isolated there, and he and five or six of his men were killed. The Syracusans immediately and hurriedly snatched them up and took them to a place of safety beyond the river before they could be recovered; then, as the rest of the Athenian army was approaching, they fell back themselves.

102   Meanwhile those of them who had originally fled to the city saw what was going on, recovered confidence themselves, and came out and formed up against the Athenians on their front; they also sent a part of their force against the Circle on Epipolae, thinking that they would find it undefended and would capture it. They did in fact capture and destroy the Athenian outwork of 1,000 feet, but the Circle was saved by Nicias, who happened because of ill-health to have been left behind there. Nicias ordered the servants to set fire to the mechanical appliances and the timber which was thrown down in front of the wall, realizing that lack of troops made it impossible to save the position in any other way. His calculation was correct: the fire prevented the Syracusans

from coming any further, and they went back again. Help was already coming up to the Circle from the Athenians down below, who were driving back the troops opposed to them there, and at the same time the Athenian fleet from Thapsus, as it had been instructed, was sailing into the great harbour. When they saw this, the Syracusans on the high ground fell back hurriedly and, with the whole of the rest of their army, went back inside the city, thinking that with their existing forces they no longer had a chance of preventing the Athenians from building their wall down to the sea.

103   After this the Athenians put up a trophy, gave the Syracusans back their dead under an armistice, and received the bodies of Lamachus and those who had died with him. They now had their entire force, naval and military, all together, and, beginning from Epipolae and the cliffs, they built a double wall down to the sea, shutting the Syracusans in. Supplies for the army were now being brought in from all parts of Italy; many of the Sicels, too, who had previously been waiting to see how things went, now allied themselves with the Athenians, who were also reinforced by three fifty-oared ships from Etruria. Everything, in fact, was going as they hoped. The Syracusans, with no kind of help coming to them from the Peloponnese, no longer thought that they could win the war, and were beginning to discuss terms of surrender among themselves and with Nicias, who was now, after the death of Lamachus, in sole command. Nothing was definitely settled, but, as might have been expected considering their difficulties and the fact that they were now more closely besieged than ever, a number of overtures were made to Nicias, and there was still more of the same kind of discussion inside the city. Their present misfortunes also led to a suspicious attitude among themselves, and, thinking that the harm had come from the bad luck or the treachery of the generals under whom they had suffered these defeats, they deposed the generals they had and replaced them by others – Heraclides, Eucles, and Tellias.

104   Meanwhile the Spartan Gylippus and the ships from Corinth were off Leucas, all anxious to come to the help of Sicily as quickly as possible. The news that reached them, however, was alarming, and all supported the untrue story that Syracuse was now entirely

cut off by the blockading walls. Gylippus therefore gave up all hope of Sicily, but, as he wanted to preserve Italy, he and the Corinthian Pythen, with two Spartan and two Corinthian ships, hurriedly crossed the Ionian gulf to Tarentum. The Corinthians were to man, in addition to their own ten ships, two Leucadian and two Ambraciot ships and were then to follow after him. From Tarentum Gylippus sent an embassy to Thurii and renewed the rights of citizenship which his father had had there. He failed, however, to gain the support of Thurii and put to sea again and sailed along the Italian coast. Opposite the Terinean Gulf he was caught and driven out to sea by the wind, which blows very violently in these parts when it sets from the north. After an extremely stormy passage he got back again to Tarentum, where he dragged up on shore and refitted the ships which had suffered most from the storm. Nicias heard of his coming but, like the Thurians, despised the small number of his ships and, thinking that they could only be operating as privateers, took no precautions against them for the moment.

105 About the same time in this summer the Spartans and their allies invaded Argos and laid waste most of the country. The Athenians came to the help of Argos with thirty ships. This constituted a most obvious breach of their treaty with Sparta. Previously they had given armed assistance to the Argives and Mantineans by means of raids from Pylos and at other points in the Peloponnese rather than by making landings in Laconia, and though there had been frequent requests from the Argives that they would send some troops and merely land in Laconia with them and then, after doing a little damage, go away again, they had always refused to do so. Now, however, under the command of Pythodorus, Laespodias, and Demaratus, they made landings at Epidaurus Limera, Prasiae, and various other places, and laid waste the land, consequently giving Sparta a better reason for saying that she was acting in self-defence against Athens. After this, when the Athenian fleet had left Argos and the Spartans had also gone home, the Argives invaded Phliasia, laid some of the land waste, killed some of the people, and then returned.

BOOK SEVEN

GYLIPPUS ARRIVES IN SYRACUSE

1 WHEN their ships had been refitted, Gylippus and Pythen sailed along the coast from Tarentum to Epizephyrian Locri. They now received more reliable news to the effect that Syracuse was not yet entirely blockaded, and that it was still possible for an army to get into the city by way of Epipolae. They then discussed whether to leave Sicily on their right and run the risk of sailing in by sea, or whether they should leave the coast on their left and go first to Himera, and, taking a force from Himera and any other troops they could get to join them, go into Syracuse by land. They decided on sailing to Himera, particularly as the four Athenian ships, which Nicias had in the end sent out when he heard they were at Locri, had not yet arrived at Rhegium.

So, before these ships arrived, they crossed the strait and, after putting in at Rhegium and Messina, came to Himera. Here they persuaded the people of Himera to join them in the war, to follow them with their own forces to Syracuse, and to provide arms for those of the crews of their ships who were not armed already. The ships themselves were dragged up on land at Himera. They sent messengers to the people of Selinus, asking them to meet them with their entire force at an appointed place. The Geloans also promised to send a small force, as did some of the Sicels, who were now much more willing to come over to their side after the recent death of Archonidas, who had been King over some of the Sicels in those parts, had exercised considerable power, and had been a friend of Athens. They were also influenced by the fact that Gylippus had come from Sparta, apparently full of confidence. Gylippus now took with him about 700 of his sailors and marines, who had been armed, 1,000 hoplites and light troops, and 100 cavalry from Himera, some light troops and cavalry from Selinus, a few Geloans, and about 1,000 Sicels altogether. With this force he set out for Syracuse.

2   Meanwhile the Corinthian fleet from Leucas were coming up as fast as they could, and one of the Corinthian commanders – Gongylus by name – though he started last in a single ship, was the first to reach Syracuse, arriving just before Gylippus. He found that the Syracusans were on the point of holding an assembly to discuss how they could put an end to the war. He succeeded in preventing this, and put fresh heart into the Syracusans by telling them that there were more ships still to come and that Gylippus, the son of Cleandridas, had been specially sent out by the Spartans to be their commander-in-chief. Syracusan confidence was restored, and they marched out at once in full force to meet Gylippus, finding that he was already quite near.

Gylippus himself first captured a Sicel fort on his way called Ietae, then put his army in order of battle and advanced to Epipolae. He made his way up by the route which the Athenians had used first, by Euryelus, and then, with the Syracusans, moved forward against the Athenian fortifications. He had arrived in the nick of time. The Athenians had already completed a double wall of nearly a mile down to the great harbour, except for a small section by the sea, which they were still building, and in the section from the Circle to Trogilus and the sea at the other side stones for building were already laid down for most of the distance, and some parts were either half or completely finished. Syracuse had thus been in very great danger indeed.

3   The sudden appearance of Gylippus and the Syracusans bearing down on them caused some confusion among the Athenians at first, but they formed up ready to meet them. Gylippus halted at a short distance away and sent forward a herald to say that, if they would leave Sicily in five days, taking their property with them, he was prepared to make peace. The Athenians treated the proposal with contempt and sent the herald back without a reply. Both sides then prepared for battle. Gylippus, however, saw that the Syracusans were in a disorganized state and could not easily be brought into line, and so he withdrew his army to a place where the ground was more open. Nicias, instead of leading the Athenians forward against him, remained in a defensive position by the wall, and

when Gylippus saw that they were not going to attack, he led off his army to the high ground of Temenitis and there spent the night.

Next day he led out the greater part of his forces and drew them up opposite the Athenian walls in order to prevent the Athenians from sending help to any other quarter. He then sent a detachment against the fort at Labdalum and captured it, putting to death all who were found inside. The place was not visible from the Athenian lines. On the same day an Athenian ship moored off the harbour was captured by the Syracusans.

4   After this the Syracusans and their allies began to build a single wall which started from the city and was to go at an angle up across Epipolae, so that, unless the Athenians could put a stop to it, they would have no further possibility of investing the city. The Athenians had already gone up to the higher ground after having completed their wall down to the sea. There was a section of their fortifications which was weak, and Gylippus came out with his army by night and attacked it. The Athenians, however, happened to be spending the night outside the fortifications, and, realizing what was happening, advanced to meet him. Gylippus then quickly withdrew his own force, and the Athenians built this section of the wall higher and guarded it themselves, leaving the rest of the fortifications to be guarded by their allies, each with their own section to look after.

Nicias also decided to fortify the place called Plemmyrium, which is a headland directly opposite the city which juts out into the sea and makes the entrance to the great harbour a narrow one. He thought that if this place were fortified, it would be easier to bring in supplies, since their blockading fleet would be nearer the enemy, at the mouth of the harbour; also it would be no longer necessary, as it was at present, to sail out against the enemy from the far corner of the great harbour, if their fleet showed any signs of activity. Nicias was already beginning to pay more attention to the war by sea, considering that now, after the arrival of Gylippus, their prospects on land were less hopeful than they had been. He therefore brought the fleet and a body of troops across to Plemmyrium and built three forts there. Most of the equipment was stored in them, and the larger merchant vessels and the fighting ships now made this their station. It was from this time that the crews began to experience considerable hardship, and this move was the chief reason for the deterioration. The water they used was in short supply and was not available near at hand, and when the sailors went out to collect fuel, casualties were always occurring because of the Syracusan cavalry which controlled the land. Because of the occupation of Plemmyrium, the Syracusans had stationed one-third of their cavalry at the village of Olympieium, to prevent the Athenians coming out and plundering the country.

Nicias now learned that the rest of the Corinthian fleet was approaching, and sent twenty ships to intercept them, with orders to lie in wait for them round Locri and Rhegium and the approach to Sicily.

5   All this time Gylippus was going on with the wall across Epipolae, making use of the stones which the Athenians had put down in a line for their own work. At the same time he always led out his army of Syracusans and allies and drew them up in front of the fortification, and the Athenians drew up their army opposite him. Finally, when he thought the moment favourable, he took the initiative and attacked. The battle was fought at close quarters between the two lines of fortifications, where no use could be made of the Syracusan cavalry. The Syracusans and their allies were defeated and took up their dead under an armistice, and the Athenians put up a trophy. Gylippus then called together his army and told them that the fault had not been theirs, but his own; he had brought their lines too far inside the fortified area, and had thus deprived them of the help of their cavalry and javelin-throwers; now he proposed to lead them to the attack a second time; they must remember, he said, that so far as material resources went they would be at no disadvantage, and as for morale, it would be an intolerable thing if Peloponnesians and Dorians could not feel certain of defeating and driving out of the country these Ionians and islanders and rabble of all sorts.

6   After this, when he thought the right time had come, he once more led his men into action. Nicias and the Athenians held the view that, even if the enemy showed no disposition to offer battle, they themselves would have to try to stop the building of the

cross wall. This wall already almost reached the extreme end of the Athenian fortifications, and, once it was pushed past them, it would amount to much the same thing whether they fought and conquered continually or whether they never fought at all. The Athenians therefore advanced to meet the Syracusans. This time when Gylippus joined battle he had led his hoplites out rather farther from the fortifications than on the previous occasion. His cavalry and javelin-throwers were posted on the Athenian flank in the open ground beyond the ends of the two walls. In the battle the cavalry charged and routed the Athenian left wing, which was opposed to them, with the result that the rest of the army also was beaten by the Syracusans and driven back headlong behind its fortifications. Next night the Syracusans achieved their object with their cross wall and carried it past the end of the Athenian fortifications. It was now no longer possible to stop them, and the Athenians, even if they were victorious in battle, had been deprived for the future of all chance of investing the city.

7   After this the other twelve ships – Corinthian, Ambraciot, and Leucadian – under the command of the Corinthian Erasinides, sailed into the harbour. They had not been observed by the Athenian ships who were on the look-out for them, and their crews now helped the Syracusans in building the rest of the cross wall. Gylippus went away into the other parts of Sicily to recruit troops. He intended to raise both land and naval forces and at the same time to win over those cities which so far had either not shown much willingness to help or had kept out of the war altogether. A delegation of Syracusans and Corinthians was also sent to Sparta and Corinth to ask for troops to be sent over somehow or other, either in merchant ships or in transports, or in whatever seemed the likeliest way, since the Athenians on their side were also sending for fresh troops. Meanwhile the Syracusans manned a fleet and began to train the crews with a view to challenging the enemy on the sea also, and in every other respect they now showed themselves full of confidence.

8   Nicias was aware of the position and, seeing that every day which passed brought new strength to the enemy and increased his own difficulties, he sent a personal message to Athens. He had already in the past sent in frequent reports of the various actions

as they had taken place, but now he sent a dispatch of particular urgency, since he felt that the position was a very dangerous one and that unless the home Government acted with great speed and either recalled the expedition or sent out very considerable reinforcements, it could not possibly survive. He was afraid, however, that the messengers might not report the facts as they really were, either through lack of ability in speaking, or bad memory or a desire to say something which would please the general mass of opinion. He therefore wrote a letter, thinking that in this way the Athenians would know what his views were without having them distorted in the course of transmission, and would so have the truth of the matter in front of them to discuss. With this letter and with other verbal instructions the messengers went away, and Nicias turned his attention to the army. His policy now was to stand more upon the defensive and to avoid all unnecessary risks.

9   At the end of the same summer the Athenian general Euetion, acting in cooperation with Perdiccas, marched against Amphipolis with a large force of Thracians. He failed to capture the place, but brought his triremes round into the Strymon and, basing himself on Himeraeum, blockaded the city from the river. And so the summer ended.

LETTER OF NICIAS

10   In the following winter the messengers from Nicias arrived in Athens. They said what they had been told to say verbally, answered questions arising from this, and delivered Nicias's letter. The clerk of the city came forward and read it to the Athenians. It was as follows:

11   'Athenians, you know what has been done by us in the past from many other letters. It is now essential that you should know what our situation is at present and should come to a decision about it. In battle we had, on most occasions, proved ourselves superior to the Syracusans, against whom we were sent out, and we had built the fortifications which we now occupy, when Gylippus arrived from Sparta with an army raised from the Peloponnese and from some of the cities in Sicily. He was defeated by us in the first battle,

but in the battle next day we were overpowered by the numbers of his cavalry and javelin-throwers, and had to retreat behind our fortifications. Now, owing to the superior numbers of the enemy, we are forced to remain inactive and have had to give up the building of the blockading wall. In fact we cannot make use of our total force, since a large part of our hoplites must be employed in the defence of our own lines. The enemy meanwhile have built a single wall and carried it past the end of our fortifications, so that there is now no longer any possibility of our being able to blockade the city, unless a strong force could be found to attack and capture this wall of theirs. The position therefore is that we, who thought we were the besiegers, have become in fact the besieged, at least on land, since we cannot go far into the country because of their cavalry.

12   'They have also sent representatives to the Peloponnese to ask for more troops, and Gylippus has set out on a mission to the cities in Sicily. He intends to persuade the cities that have so far been neutral to join the war on his side, and to get, if he can, from the others still more infantry and also material for the navy. Their plan is, so far as I can see, to attack our fortifications with their infantry and at the same time to engage us also by sea with their fleet. And none of you must think it strange that I use the words "also by sea". The fact is, as the Syracusans know well, that our fleet was originally in first-class condition; the timbers were sound and the crews were in good shape. Now, however, the ships have been at sea so long that the timbers have rotted, and the crews are not what they were. We cannot drag our ships on shore to dry and clean them, because the enemy has as many or more ships than we have, and keeps us in the constant expectation of having to face an attack. We can see them at their manoeuvres, and the initiative is in their hands. Moreover, it is easier for them

13 to dry their ships, since they are not maintaining a blockade. As for us, we could hardly do so even if we had a great numerical superiority in ships and were not forced, as we are at present, to use all of them for the blockade. For the slightest falling-off in the efficiency of the watch we keep would mean the loss of our supplies, which even now are difficult enough to bring in past Syracuse.

'Our crews have deteriorated, and continue to do so for the following reasons. The sailors have to go out a long way for fuel, for plunder, and for water, and frequent casualties occur because of the enemy cavalry. With the enemy now on equal terms with us, our slaves are beginning to desert. As for the foreigners in our service, those who were conscripted are going back to their cities as quickly as they can; those who were originally delighted with the idea of high pay and thought they were going to make money rather than do any fighting now find that, contrary to their ex-pectations, the enemy is not only holding out against us but is actually opposing us on the sea, and are either slipping away as deserters or making off in one way or another – which is not difficult, considering the size of Sicily. There are some who have actually bought Hyccaric slaves and then persuaded the captains of ships to take these slaves aboard instead of themselves, thus ruining the efficiency of the fleet.

14 'You do not need to be told that a crew is only at its best for a short time, and it is only a small number of the sailors who can get the ship on her way and then continue rowing as they ought to do. But the greatest of all my troubles is that since you are by nature so difficult to control, I, the general, am unable to put a stop to all this, nor can we get replacements for the crews from anywhere else. The enemy have a number of sources for fresh man-power, but we on our side have only the men we brought here with us, and are compelled to use these not only for keeping the ships in service, but for replacing our losses as well. For the cities now allied with us, Naxos and Catana, cannot produce the men. The enemy need only one thing more: if the places in Italy from which we get our supplies see the state we are in and, finding that you are not reinforcing us, go over to the other side, hunger will force us to submit, and Syracuse will win the war without having to strike a blow.

'I might certainly have sent you a different account from this, and one that would have given you more pleasure, but I could not have told you anything more useful, if what you require is to have a clear idea of the position here before you reach your decisions. Besides, I know the Athenian character from experience: you like to be told pleasant news, but if things do not turn out in the way you have been led to expect, then you blame your informants afterwards. I therefore thought it safer to let you know the truth.

15   'So far as the original objects of the expedition are concerned, you can have no right to find fault with the conduct either of your soldiers or your generals. Now, however, the whole of Sicily is united against us; a fresh army is expected from the Peloponnese, while our troops on the spot are not sufficient to deal even with the opposition we have at present. The time therefore has come for you to decide either to recall us, or else to send out another force, both naval and military, as big as the first, with large sums of money, and also someone to relieve me of the command, as a disease of the kidneys has made me unfit for service. I think I can claim some consideration from you, since, in the time when I had my health, I did you much good service in the various commands which I have held. Whatever you intend to do must be done at the very beginning of spring, and must not be put off, as the enemy will soon be receiving his reinforcements from Sicily and, though the troops from the Peloponnese will take rather longer to arrive, you will find that, unless you give your attention to the matter, the Sicilian contingents will get here before we are ready for them, and the Peloponnesians, as they did before, will slip through unobserved.'

16   These were the contents of Nicias's letter. The Athenians, after they had heard it, refused to relieve him of his command, but appointed two of the officers in Sicily, Menander and Euthydemus, to share it with him, so that he should not have to bear the whole weight of responsibility by himself in his sickness. These two officers were appointed temporarily, until the arrival of the other two generals who had been chosen in Athens as Nicias's colleagues. The Athenians voted in favour of sending out another military and naval force, drawn partly from the citizens on the lists for calling-up and partly from the allies. Demosthenes, the son of Alcisthenes, and Eurymedon, the son of Thucles, were the generals chosen to share the command with Nicias. Eurymedon was sent out to Sicily at once, about the time of the winter solstice, with ten ships and 120 talents of silver. He was to tell the troops there that help was coming to them and that their interests would
17 be looked after. Demosthenes stayed behind to organize the

expedition. He intended to set sail at the beginning of spring, and busied himself in sending to the allies for troops and in raising money and ships and hoplites from Attica.

The Athenians also sent twenty ships round the Peloponnese to see that no one crossed over to Sicily from Corinth or from the Peloponnese in general. Since their representatives had returned with the better news from Sicily, the Corinthians had become much more confident. They realized that even the fleet which they had sent before had proved far from useless, and they were now preparing to send out a force of hoplites to Sicily in merchant ships, and the Spartans were doing the same thing with troops drawn from the rest of the Peloponnese. The Corinthians also manned twenty-five ships with the intention of offering battle to the blockading squadron at Naupactus – a plan which would also have the advantage of making it harder for the Athenians at Naupactus to prevent the sailing of their merchant ships, since they would have to give their attention to the Corinthian triremes facing them in line of battle.

18   The Spartans also prepared to invade Attica, as they had already decided to do and as they had been asked to do by the Syracusans and Corinthians, who, when they heard that Athens was sending reinforcements to Sicily, hoped that this would be stopped by an invasion. Alcibiades, too, was constantly urging them to fortify Decelea and to carry on the war with vigour. But what chiefly encouraged the Spartans to act with energy was their belief that Athens, with two wars on her hands – one against them and one against the Sicilians – would be now easier to crush. There was also the fact that the Spartans considered that Athens had been the first to break the peace treaty. In the first war they thought that the fault had been more on their side, partly because the Thebans had entered Plataea in peace time and partly because, in spite of the provision in the previous treaty that there should be no recourse to arms if arbitration were offered, they themselves had not accepted the Athenian offer of arbitration. They therefore thought that there was some justice in the misfortunes they had suffered and took to heart the disaster of Pylos and their other defeats. But now, in addition to the constant raids from Pylos, the Athenians had come out with thirty ships from Argos and laid waste part of

Epidaurus and Prasiae and other places; also whenever any dispute arose on doubtful points in the treaty, it was Sparta who had offered to submit to arbitration and Athens who had refused the offer. It was now Athens therefore, the Spartans thought, who was in the wrong through having committed exactly the same fault as theirs had been before, and they went into the war with enthusiasm. This winter they sent round to their allies for supplies of iron and got ready all the other materials for building fortifications. At the same time they organized a force of their own and conscripted other forces from the rest of the Peloponnese to be sent out in merchant ships to the help of their allies in Sicily. So the winter ended, and the eighteenth year of this war recorded by Thucydides.

FORTIFICATION OF DECELEA

19 At the very beginning of the next spring, earlier than ever before, the Spartans and their allies invaded Attica under the command of their King Agis, the son of Archidamus. First they laid waste the country in the plain and then proceeded to fortify Decelea, dividing the work out among the various cities. Decelea is about thirteen or fourteen miles from the city of Athens and roughly the same distance, or rather further, from Boeotia. The fort was built to threaten and control the plain and the richest parts of the country, and it was visible from Athens itself.

While the Peloponnesians and their allies in Attica were building the fort, their countrymen at home sent off, at about the same time, the hoplites to Sicily in the merchant ships. The Spartans sent picked men from among the helots and freedmen, 600 hoplites in all, under the command of Eccritus, a regular Spartan officer. The Boeotians sent 300 hoplites under the command of Xenon and Nicon, both from Thebes, and of Hegesander from Thespiae. These, starting out from Taenarum in Laconia, were among the first to put out to sea; but soon after they had set out, the Corinthians sent out a force of 500 hoplites, partly of Corinthian citizens and partly of Arcadian mercenaries. Alexarchus, a Corinthian, was put in command of this army. The Sicyonians, too, sent out, at

the same time as the Corinthians, 200 hoplites under the command
of Sargeus, a Sicyonian. Meanwhile the twenty-five Corinthian
ships which had been manned during the winter lay at anchor
opposite the twenty Athenian ships at Naupactus, until they were
satisfied that their hoplites in the merchant vessels had got clear
away from the Peloponnese. It was for this reason that they had
been manned originally, so that the Athenians would have to give
their attention to the triremes and leave the merchant ships alone.

20   The Athenians themselves meanwhile, at the very beginning of
spring and while Decelea was being fortified, sent thirty ships
round the Peloponnese under the command of Charicles, the son
of Apollodorus, who was instructed to go to Argos and ask them
for hoplites for his fleet according to the terms of the alliance. They
also sent Demosthenes out to Sicily, as they had already decided to
do, with a fleet of sixty ships from Athens and five from Chios,
1,200 Athenian hoplites from the regular calling-up lists, and as
many of the islanders as could be brought into the service from
their respective islands. From the other subject allies they took
whatever they could supply that would be useful for the war.
Demosthenes was instructed first of all to sail round the Peloponnese with Charicles and join him in attacking the coasts of Laconia.
He therefore sailed to Aegina and then waited for the rest of his
own force to arrive and for Charicles to pick up the troops from
Argos.

21   In Sicily, at about the same time in this spring, Gylippus came to
Syracuse with as large a force as he had been able to raise from the
various cities which he had persuaded to help. He called the Syracusans together and told them that they ought now to man as
many ships as possible and try their fortune in a battle at sea, saying
that the effect of this on the war in general would be, he expected,
something well worth all the risks involved. Here he was strongly
supported by Hermocrates, who joined him in persuading the
Syracusans not to be downhearted at the prospect of facing the
Athenians on the sea; Athenian naval experience, he said, was not
something born in the Athenians, nor would it last for ever; in
fact the Athenians were more landsmen than the Syracusans and
had only taken to the sea when forced to do so by the Persians.
And, he said, what daring people, like the Athenians, find most

awkward is to be confronted with equal daring on the other side; Athens, sometimes without any real superiority in strength, was in the habit of terrorizing her neighbours by the very audacity of her attacks; the same method might now be used by Syracuse against Athens. The idea of Syracusans daring so unexpectedly to stand up to the Athenian navy would, he was quite sure, have such a disturbing effect on the enemy that it would amply make up for anything they might lose owing to Athenian skill and their own inexperience. He therefore urged them to see what they could do with their fleet and not to hang back.

22   So the Syracusans, on the advice of Gylippus and Hermocrates and others, resolved to fight at sea and began to man their ships. When the fleet was ready for action, Gylippus led out the whole of his infantry forces by night. He himself proposed to attack the forts on Plemmyrium by land. Meanwhile, as had been previously arranged, the thirty-five Syracusan triremes from the great harbour were sailing up against the enemy and the other forty-five from the smaller harbour, where their dockyards were, sailed round to join those inside and at the same time to threaten Plemmyrium, so that the Athenians would be confused by having to face an attack from both directions.

The Athenians on their side quickly manned sixty ships. With twenty-five of them they fought the thirty-five Syracusan ships in the great harbour, and with the rest they set out to meet the ships that were sailing round from the dockyards. They went into action immediately in front of the mouth of the great harbour, one side trying to force a way in, the other trying to keep them out, and for a long time neither side gave way.

23   Meanwhile the Athenians in Plemmyrium had gone down to the sea and were giving their whole attention to the naval battle. They were thus taken off their guard by Gylippus, who made a sudden attack on the forts in the early morning. First he captured the biggest one, and afterwards the other two also, the garrisons of which did not wait for him, when they saw the biggest fort taken so easily. Those who had been in the fort that was captured first and who managed to make their escape to a merchant ship and to various small craft had considerable difficulty in getting to the camp, as they were chased by a fast sailing trireme sent after

them by the Syracusans, who at this time were having the better
of things in the naval engagement in the great harbour. But by
the time the two other forts were captured, the Syracusans were
already losing the battle, and so the men who escaped from the
forts got along the shore more easily. What happened was that the
Syracusan ships fighting off the mouth of the harbour had forced
the Athenian ships back and had then sailed inside; but as they
kept no sort of order and fell into confusion among themselves
they presented the victory to the Athenians, who routed them
first and then the other ships which up to then had been having the
upper hand in the great harbour. They sank eleven of the Syracusan ships and killed most of the men on board except for the crews
of three ships, who were made prisoners. Three ships of their own
had been lost. They dragged ashore the wrecks of the Syracusan
ships, put up a trophy on the small island in front of Plemmyrium
and then returned to their camp.

24   The Syracusans had not fared well in the naval engagement, but
they held the forts in Plemmyrium and for these they put up three
trophies. They dismantled one of the two forts last captured, but
restored and garrisoned the other two. In the capture of the forts
many men had been killed or taken prisoner, and a great deal of
property altogether had fallen into the enemy's hands. The Athenians had used the forts as a general depot and there had been inside
them much property and corn belonging to the merchants, much
also belonging to the captains; in fact the masts and other equipment for forty triremes were captured there, apart from three
triremes which had been drawn up on shore. This capture of
Plemmyrium was indeed the greatest and the principal cause of the
deterioration of the Athenian army. Convoys with supplies were
no longer safe even at the entrance to the harbour, since the Syracusans had ships waiting to intercept them, and it was now necessary to fight if supplies were to be brought in at all. In other
respects, too, this event had produced a feeling of bewilderment
in the army and a decline in morale.

25   After this the Syracusans sent out twelve ships under the com-
mand of Agatharchus, a Syracusan. One of these went to the
Peloponnese with representatives aboard who were to say that in
Syracuse hopes were running high and to urge the Peloponnesians

to an even more vigorous war effort in Hellas. The eleven other ships sailed to Italy, since they had information that boats laden with various stores were on their way to the Athenians. These boats they intercepted and destroyed most of them. They also went to the territory of Caulonia and burned up a quantity of timber for ship-building which lay there ready for the Athenians. After this they came to Locri, and, while they were at anchor there, one of the merchant ships from the Peloponnese arrived with some Thespian hoplites on board. The Syracusans took these hoplites aboard their own ships and set off home, sailing along the coast. The Athenians with twenty ships were on the look-out for them at Megara and captured one of their ships with its crew, but failed to overtake the others, all of which escaped and reached Syracuse.

There was also some fighting at long range in the harbour around the stakes which the Syracusans had driven in to the sea-bed in front of their old dockyards so that their ships could lie at anchor behind this barrier and the Athenians would not be able to row up and ram them. The Athenians now brought up a ship of 10,000 talents burden, fitted with wooden towers and screens along the sides. In the small boats they rowed up to the stakes, fastened ropes round them, and dragged them up with windlasses, or broke them off short, or dived under the water and sawed through them. The Syracusans shot at them from the dockyards, and the Athenians in the big ship replied. Finally the Athenians pulled up most of the stakes. The most difficult part of the stockade to deal with was the part that was out of sight; for some of the stakes that had been driven in did not project above the surface of the water, so that it was dangerous to sail up in case one ran one's ship on them as on a hidden reef. However, these also were dealt with by divers who were paid to go down and saw them through. Nevertheless the Syracusans succeeded in driving in other stakes to replace them. There were also a number of other expedients resorted to by both sides, as might be expected with the two armies facing each other at such close quarters; skirmishes were constantly going on and all kinds of stratagems were tried.

The Syracusans also sent delegations of Corinthians, Ambraciots, and Spartans to the various cities with news of the capture of Plemmyrium and to explain that in the naval engagement their defeat had been due to their own disorder rather than to the enemy's superior strength; they were also to make it clear that the situation in general was regarded as very hopeful and to ask for reinforcements, both naval and military, against the enemy, since the Athenians also were expected to arrive with a fresh army, and if they could not destroy the army on the spot before the new one arrived, the war would be over.

26   While all this was going on in Sicily, Demosthenes had got together the relief force which he was to take out there. Setting out from Aegina, he sailed to the Peloponnese and joined Charicles and the thirty Athenian ships. They then took the Argive hoplites on board, and sailed to Laconia. First they laid waste part of Epidaurus Limera, and then landed in Laconia opposite Cythera, where the temple of Apollo stands. They laid waste part of the country and fortified a sort of isthmus so that the Helots might have a place to which they could desert, and so that raiding parties, as at Pylos, might have a base from which to operate. When he had helped Charicles to occupy this place, Demosthenes at once sailed on to Corcyra, in order to pick up allied forces from that area and then to cross over to Sicily as quickly as possible. Charicles stayed until he had completed the fortification. Then, leaving a garrison to hold it, he himself went back home with the thirty ships, and the Argives also.

27   In this same summer there arrived in Athens 1,300 peltasts from the Dii, one of the Thracian tribes who are armed with short swords. They were meant to have sailed to Sicily with Demosthenes, and, as they had arrived too late for this, the Athenians resolved to send them back to Thrace, where they came from, since it seemed too expensive – each man was paid a drachma a day – to retain their services for dealing with the attacks made on them from Decelea.

The position was that, ever since Decelea had been first fortified by the whole of the invading army during the summer and had then been used as a hostile post against the country, with garrisons from the various cities relieving each other at fixed intervals, Athens had suffered a great deal. Indeed, the occupation of Decelea, resulting, as it did, in so much devastation of property and loss of manpower, was one of the chief reasons for the decline of Athenian power. The previous invasions had not lasted for long and had not prevented the Athenians from enjoying the use of their land for the rest of the time; now, however, the enemy were on top of them throughout the year; sometimes there were extra troops sent in to invade the country; sometimes it was only the normal garrison overrunning the land and making raids to secure supplies; and the Spartan King Agis was there in person, treating the whole operation as a major campaign. The Athenians therefore suffered great losses. They were deprived of the whole of their country; more than 20,000 slaves, the majority of whom were skilled workmen, deserted, and all the sheep and farm animals were lost. As the cavalry rode out to Decelea every day to make attacks on the enemy or to patrol the country, the horses were lamed on the rough ground and by the continuous hard work to which they 28 were put, or else were wounded by the enemy. Then the supplies of food from Euboea, which previously had been brought in by the quicker route overland from Oropus through Decelea, now, at great expense, had to go by sea round Sunium. Every single thing that the city needed had to be imported, so that instead of a city it became a fortress. By day detachments took it in turn to mount guard on the battlements, by night all except the cavalry were on duty, some at the various armed posts and others on the walls. So, summer and winter, there was no end to their hardships. What wore them down more than anything else was the fact that they had two wars on their hands at once, and indeed they had got themselves into such a state of obstinate resolution that no one would have believed it possible if he had been told of it before it actually happened. For it was incredible that, besieged by the Peloponnesians who were based on a fortress in Attica, they should not only not leave Sicily, but actually stay on and lay siege in just the same way to Syracuse, a city which was in itself as big as Athens, and should give the Hellenic world such an astonishing demonstration of their power and of their daring; how astonishing can be seen from the fact that at the beginning of the war some thought that, if the Peloponnesians invaded Attica, Athens might survive for a year, and while others put the figure at two or three years, no one imagined she could last for more than that; yet now,

in the seventeenth year after the first invasion, having suffered
every kind of hardship already in the war, here were the Athenians
going out to Sicily and taking upon themselves another war on
the same scale as that which they had been waging all this time
with the Peloponnesians.

For all these reasons – the great damage done by the occupation
of Decelea and the other heavy expenses which fell upon them –
the Athenians were becoming embarrassed financially, and it was
about this time that they imposed upon their subjects a tax of five
per cent on all imports and exports by sea, thinking that this would
bring in more money. Expenditure was not the same as it had
been, but had grown bigger as the war grew bigger, while revenue
was declining.

29   In their present financial difficulties, the Athenians had no wish
to incur additional expense, and therefore sent back at once the
Thracians who had arrived too late to serve with Demosthenes.
Diitrephes was appointed to command them on their return
journey and, as they were to sail through the Euripus, he was instructed to use them in doing whatever damage he could to the
enemy on their voyage along the coast. He first landed them at
Tanagra and carried off some plunder in a quick raid; then he
sailed across the Euripus in the evening from Chalcis in Euboea,
landed in Boeotia, and led them against Mycalessus. He spent the
night unobserved near the temple of Hermes, which is nearly two
miles from Mycalessus, and at daybreak assaulted the city, which is
not a big one, and captured it. The inhabitants were caught off
their guard, since they never expected that anyone would come so
far from the sea to attack them. Their wall, too, was weak and in
some places had collapsed, while in others it had not been built at
all high, and the gates were open, since they had no fear of being
attacked. The Thracians burst into Mycalessus, sacked the houses
and temples, and butchered the inhabitants, sparing neither the
young nor the old, but methodically killing everyone they met,
women and children alike, and even the farm animals and every
living thing they saw. For the Thracian race, like all the most
bloodthirsty barbarians, are always particularly bloodthirsty
when everything is going their own way. So now there
was confusion on all sides and death in every shape and form.

Among other things, they broke into a boys' school, the largest in the place, into which the children had just entered, and killed every one of them. Thus disaster fell upon the entire city, a disaster more complete than any, more sudden and more horrible.

30 The Thebans meanwhile heard the news and came to the rescue. They caught up with the Thracians before they had gone far, took away their booty, struck terror into them, and drove them down to the Euripus and the sea, where the boats that had brought them were lying at anchor. Most of those who were killed were killed while embarking, since they did not know how to swim, and the crews, when they saw what was happening on shore, anchored their ships out of range of the arrows. In the rest of the retreat the Thracians did very creditably against the Theban cavalry, which attacked them first, and put up a good defence by adopting the tactics of their country, that is to say by charging out in detachments and then falling back again. In this part of the action only a few of them were killed, but a considerable number who had stayed behind to plunder were destroyed in the town itself. Altogether the Thracians lost 250 out of 1,300 men. Of the Thebans and others who were in the relief force about twenty cavalrymen and hoplites were killed, including Scirphondas, who was one of the Commanders of Boeotia. Mycalessus lost a considerable part of its population. It was a small city, but in the disaster just described its people suffered calamities as pitiable as any which took place during the war.

ATHENIAN DEFEAT IN THE GREAT HARBOUR

31 Demosthenes, as we have seen, had gone on towards Corcyra after the building of the fortification in Laconia. He found anchored at Pheia, in Elis, a merchant ship in which the Corinthian hoplites intended to sail across to Sicily. This ship he destroyed, but the men escaped, and secured another ship later in which they sailed. After this he came to Zacynthus and Cephallenia, took some hoplites aboard, and sent for others from the Messenians at Naupactus. He then went across to the Acarnanian mainland opposite, to Alyzia and to Anactorium, which was held by the Athenians.

While he was in this area he was met by Eurymedon, who was sailing back from Sicily, where, as already mentioned, he had been sent during the winter with the money for the army. Eurymedon told him, among other things, that he had heard while actually on his voyage that the Syracusans had captured Plemmyrium. They were also joined here by Conon, the commander at Naupactus, who told them that the twenty-five Corinthian ships stationed opposite him showed no signs of abandoning their hostile attitude and were, in fact, intending to bring on a naval battle. He asked them therefore to send him some ships, since his own eighteen were not sufficient to deal with the enemy's twenty-five. So Demosthenes and Eurymedon sent off with Conon ten of the fastest ships which they had to join the squadron at Naupactus. They themselves made their arrangements for collecting their whole force together; Eurymedon, who had turned back with Demosthenes and now shared with him the command to which he had been appointed, sailed to Corcyra, ordered them to man fifteen ships, and enlisted hoplites, while Demosthenes raised slingers and javelin-throwers from the Acarnanian area.

32   Meanwhile the representatives from Syracuse who, as already related, had gone to the various cities after the capture of Plemmyrium had met with a good response and were now on the point of bringing back with them the troops that they had raised. Nicias, however, was informed of their intentions, and sent to Centoripa and Alicyae and to other Sicels who were his allies and who controlled the route, asking them not to let the reinforcements through, but to join up together and bar their way, since there was no other route that they could even attempt to take, because the Agrigentines would not allow them to go through their territory. So, when the troops from the Sicilian cities were on the march, the Sicels did as the Athenians had asked them, organized an ambush with three bodies of their own troops, and fell upon the enemy suddenly and when they were off their guard. They killed about 800, including all the representatives except one. This was the one from Corinth, and he led the survivors, about 1,500 in all, to Syracuse.

33   About the same time the Camarinaeans also arrived with reinforcements for Syracuse – 500 hoplites, 300 javelin-throwers, and

300 archers. The Geloans, too, sent crews for five ships, 400 javelin-throwers, and 200 cavalry. Now indeed practically the whole of Sicily, except for Agrigentum, which was neutral, joined together and, instead of just watching how things would go, as they had been doing, came in with Syracuse against the Athenians.

After the disaster in the Sicel country the Syracusans gave up the idea of an immediate attack on the Athenians. Meanwhile Demosthenes and Eurymedon, now that their forces from Corcyra and from the mainland were ready, crossed the Ionian gulf with the whole of their expedition to the headland of Iapygia. Setting out from here, they put in at the Iapygian islands called the Choirades, and took on board 150 Iapygian javelin-throwers of the Messapian tribe. Then, after they had renewed an old friendship with the local ruler, Artas, who had provided the javelin-throwers, they went on and reached Metapontum in Italy. Here they persuaded the people, in accordance with their alliance, to send with them 300 javelin-throwers and two triremes, and with this addition to their force they sailed along the coast to Thurii, where they found that there had just been a revolution and that the anti-Athenian party had been exiled. As they wanted to bring their whole force together here for review and to see whether anything had been left behind, and at the same time were anxious to persuade the Thurians to join them in the expedition as willingly as possible and to take advantage of the present situation by forming an offensive and defensive alliance with Athens, they stayed on at Thurii and occupied themselves with making these arrangements.

34   About this same time the Peloponnesians in the twenty-five ships that were stationed opposite the Athenian squadron at Naupactus in order to protect the convoys of merchant ships for Sicily had made themselves ready for battle and had manned some additional ships so as to make their numbers very little less than those of the Athenians. They were anchored off Erineus in Achaea in the territory of Rhypae, and, as the place where they were anchored was crescent-shaped, the infantry from Corinth and the other allies in the area came up in support and was drawn up along the projecting headlands at each side of the bay, while the ships held the space between and blocked the way in. Polyanthes, a Corinthian, was in command of the fleet.

The Athenians sailed out against them from Naupactus with thirty-three ships under the command of Diphilus. At first the Corinthians made no move, then, when they thought the time had come, they raised the signal and went forward into battle against the Athenians. For a long time there was no giving way on either side. The Corinthians lost three ships, and the Athenians, though none of theirs was sunk outright, had seven ships put out of action through being rammed head on and having their fore-ships stove in by the Corinthian triremes, which had been built out wider at each side of the prow for this very purpose. There was thus little to choose in the battle between the two sides, either of which might claim the victory, although it was the Athenians who became masters of the wrecks, since the wind drove them out to sea and the Corinthians showed no disposition to come out again and fight for them. So the action was broken off, and there was no pursuit, nor were any men captured on either side. This was because the Corinthians and Peloponnesians were fighting close to the land and so could easily make their escape, while on the Athenian side no ship was sunk. The Athenians sailed back to Naupactus, and the Corinthians immediately put up a trophy, claiming the victory on the grounds that they had put out of action the greater number of ships, and considering that they had not lost the battle for just the same reason that the Athenians did not claim to have won it. For the Corinthians counted it a victory if they were not thoroughly defeated, and the Athenians considered that they had lost if they did not win easily. However, when the Peloponnesians had sailed away and their infantry forces had been disbanded, the Athenians also put up a trophy in Achaea claiming the victory. The trophy was put up rather over two miles from Erineus, where the Corinthians had been at anchor. So ended the naval action.

35 The Thurians had now been put in a state to join the force of Demosthenes and Eurymedon with 700 hoplites and 300 javelin-throwers, and the two generals ordered the fleet to sail along the coast to the territory of Croton, while they themselves first reviewed the whole army by the river Sybaris and then led it through the territory of Thurii. When they reached the river Hylias, the people of Croton sent messengers to them to say that they would

not allow the army to march through their country. The Athenians therefore went down the river and camped on the shore at the mouth of the Hylias, where they were met by the fleet. Next day they embarked and sailed along the coast, putting in at all the cities except Locri, until they reached Petra in the territory of Rhegium.

36   The Syracusans, meanwhile, had heard of their approach and were anxious to make another attack both on sea and with their other forces on land, which had been specially brought together in order to go into action before the Athenian reinforcements arrived. In the equipment of their fleet they made various changes, which, on the basis of their experience in the previous naval battle, were calculated to give them some advantages; in particular, they cut down the length of the prows to make them more solid, put extra material into the sides by the cat-heads, and from the cat-heads themselves they built in stays of timber which went through to the ships' sides, a distance of about nine feet, and projected outwards to about the same distance. They were thus following the same method as the Corinthians, who had strengthened their ships at the prows before fighting with the Athenians at Naupactus. The Syracusans thought that in this way they would have an advantage over the Athenian ships, which, instead of being constructed like theirs, were light in the prow, because the usual Athenian tactics were not to meet the enemy head on, but to row round and ram him amidships; and the fact that the battle would be in the great harbour, where there would be many ships in a small space, was in their favour, since, charging prow to prow and striking with stout solid rams against hollow and weak ones, they would stave in the enemy's foreships, while, in that narrow space, the Athenians would not be able to use their skill in manoeuvre on which their confidence was based; there could be no sailing round in circles and no breaking through the line and wheeling back again, as the Syracusans would do their best to prevent them breaking through the line, and lack of space would prevent them trying the encircling manoeuvre. In fact this system of charging prow to prow, which previously had been regarded as a sign of lack of skill in the steersman, was now going to be the chief method employed by the Syracusans, since it would give

them the greatest advantages. For, if the Athenians were pushed back, they could only back water in the direction of the shore, and then only for a short way and towards one limited portion of the shore – that is, the part in front of their own camp. The rest of the harbour would be controlled by the Syracusans, and, if the Athenians were pressed back, they would be crowded all together in the same small space, and would fall foul of each other and get into a state of confusion. In fact it was just this which did most harm to the Athenians in all the naval battles – not having, as the Syracusans had, the whole area of the harbour at their disposal for backing water. As for sailing round into the open water, that would be impossible, since it was the Syracusans who were in the position of sailing in from the open sea or backing water towards it, and such an operation would be made all the more difficult for the Athenians because Plemmyrium was in hostile hands and the mouth of the harbour was not a large one.

37   After making these plans to fit in with the existing state of their skill and strength, the Syracusans, who were now also more confident than before as a result of the previous naval battle, proceeded to attack the Athenians by land and sea at once. Gylippus led out the troops from the city rather before the rest, and brought them up to the Athenian wall at the part where it faced the city. Meanwhile the troops from the Olympieium, which included the hoplites there, the cavalry, and the Syracusan light forces, moved up to the wall from the other side. Immediately after this the ships of the Syracusans and their allies sailed out to attack. The Athenians thought at first that the enemy was only going to attack by land, and when they saw the ships also suddenly bearing down on them, there was a certain amount of disturbance; some were taking up their positions on or in front of the walls; some had hurried out to meet the advancing forces, great numbers of cavalry and javelin-throwers, coming from the Olympieium and the country outside; others were manning the ships and also taking up position along the beach to support them. Once they were manned, they put out against the enemy with seventy-five ships. The Syracusans had about eighty.

38   Much of the day was spent in making attacks and retiring again and trying out each other's strength. Neither side was able to

accomplish anything worth speaking of, though the Syracusans sank one or two of the Athenian ships. The action was then broken off, and at the same time the land forces withdrew from the walls.

On the following day the Syracusans made no move and gave no indications of what they were going to do next. Nicias, however, seeing that there had been nothing to choose between the two sides in the naval battle and expecting that the enemy would make another attack, made the captains refit all damaged ships and had a line of merchant vessels anchored outside of the stockade which had been fixed in the sea in front of their ships to serve as an enclosed harbour. The merchant vessels were placed at intervals of about 200 feet, so that it would be possible for any ship that was in difficulties to retreat safely and sail out again in its own time. The whole of the day until nightfall was spent by the Athenians in making these arrangements.

39   Next day, earlier than before but with the same plan of campaign, the Syracusans went into action against the Athenians by land and sea. For a great part of the day the two fleets held out against each other, attacking and counter-attacking just as they had done before; but finally Ariston, the son of Pyrrhicus, a Corinthian and the best steersman in the Syracusan fleet, persuaded their naval commanders to send to the appropriate officials in the city and order them to move the market down to the sea as quickly as possible and to compel all who had provisions to sell to bring them down and sell them there, so that they could get the sailors ashore at once, have their meal close by the ships and then, after a short interval, make another attack this very day on the Athenians when they were not expecting it.

40   The commanders took this advice; a messenger was sent and the market was got ready. The Syracusans suddenly backed water, went back again towards the city, and immediately disembarked and had their meal on the spot. The Athenians, on their side, were under the impression that the Syracusans had backed away towards their city because they thought they were beaten, and so they disembarked in a leisurely way, and began to attend to their various jobs, including the getting ready of their meal, in the belief that they would certainly not have to fight again on that day. Suddenly, however, the Syracusans manned their ships and

sailed out to attack for the second time. The Athenians, in great confusion and most of them still not having eaten, got aboard in no sort of order and with considerable difficulty managed to put out against the enemy. For some time both sides watched each other and made no attack; finally, however, the Athenians decided that, instead of allowing themselves to get tired out by going on waiting, it would be better to go into action at once, and so, cheering each other on, they charged the enemy and began fighting. The Syracusans met their attack prow to prow, as they had intended, and with the specially constructed beaks of their ships stove in the Athenian bows to a considerable distance; the javelin-throwers on the decks also did a lot of damage to the Athenians, but much more harm still was done by the Syracusans who went about in small boats, slipped in under the oars of the Athenian ships and sailing close in to the sides hurled their weapons in upon the sailors.

41 In the end, fighting hard in this way, the Syracusans were victorious and the Athenians turned and fled between the merchant ships to their own anchorage. The Syracusan ships pressed the pursuit as far as the merchant ships; they were prevented from going further by the beams armed with 'dolphins' which were suspended from the merchant ships to guard the passages in between them. Two of the Syracusan ships in the first flush of victory went too near and were destroyed, one of them being captured with its crew. Seven Athenian ships were sunk and many were disabled; as for the crews, the Syracusans took most of them prisoner and killed others. They then retired and put up trophies for both of the naval actions. They now felt fully confident of having a decided naval superiority and thought also that they were quite capable of dealing with the enemy forces on land.

ATHENIAN DEFEAT AT EPIPOLAE

42 And now, just when the Syracusans were getting ready to make a second attack by land and sea, Demosthenes and Eurymedon arrived with the reinforcements from Athens – about seventy-three ships, including the foreign vessels, about 5,000 hoplites from

Athens and her allies, a great force of javelin-throwers both from Hellas and from outside, and slingers and archers and everything else that could be required. It was a moment when the Syracusans and their allies felt real dismay; there seemed to be no term set for their deliverance from danger, when they saw that, in spite of the fortification of Decelea, another army almost as big as the first one had come out against them and that in every direction the power of Athens was showing itself so great. As for the first Athenian force, it had had a bad time, but now its confidence began to return.

Demosthenes saw how things were and considered that it was impossible for him to let matters drift and find himself in the same position as Nicias had been in. For Nicias had appeared formidable enough when he first arrived, but when, instead of attacking Syracuse at once, he spent the winter in Catana, he brought himself into contempt and allowed Gylippus to steal a march on him by bringing in an army from the Peloponnese, which the Syracusans would never even have sent for if Nicias had attacked at once, since they thought that they could deal with him by themselves, and by the time they realized their inferiority they would have been completely blockaded by the walls, so that even if they did send for help then, it could not have done them so much good. Bearing all this in mind and realizing that he, too, was most formidable now on the very first day of his arrival, Demosthenes wished to make full use immediately of the terror which his army inspired at this moment. He saw that the Syracusan counter-wall, by which they had prevented the Athenians from blockading them, was only a single one, and that if one could gain control of the way up to Epipolae and then of the camp there, this wall could easily be captured, since no one would even stay there to resist: he therefore set out energetically to put this plan into operation. It was, he thought, the quickest way of ending the war, for he would either be successful and take Syracuse, or else would withdraw the expedition and not allow the Athenians serving in it to have their lives uselessly thrown away or the resources of their whole country squandered.

First of all, therefore, the Athenians went out and devastated the land of the Syracusans round the river Anapus. They now enjoyed

the superiority which they had had at first both with their army
and their fleet, for neither on land nor sea did the Syracusans come
out to oppose them, except with the cavalry and javelin-throwers
from the Olympieium. Next Demosthenes decided to use siege
engines for making a first attempt on the counter-wall. However,
when he brought the engines up they were set on fire by the
enemy who were defending the wall, and all attacks made at
various points by the rest of the army were driven back. He therefore thought it best not to wait any longer and, after having obtained the consent of Nicias and his fellow commanders, began to
put into operation his original plan for making the attack on
Epipolae.

By day it seemed impossible to approach and make the ascent
unobserved, so he ordered provision for five days, took with him
all the masons and carpenters, supplies of arrows, and everything
else that would be required, if they were successful, for the work
of fortification, and set out for Epipolae about midnight with
Eurymedon and Menander and the whole army, Nicias being left
behind in the Athenian fortifications.

They came up to Epipolae by way of Euryelus (the same route
as that by which the first army had ascended originally) and, unobserved by the enemy sentries, reached the fort which the Syracusans had there, captured it, and killed some of the garrison.
Most of them, however, escaped at once to the camps, of which
there were three on Epipolae, defended by outworks, one of the
Syracusans, one of the other Sicilians, and one of the allies; they
brought the news of the attack to these camps and also told it to
the 600 Syracusans who had been the defenders of this part of
Epipolae on the first occasion and who now came out at once to
meet the attack. Falling in with Demosthenes and the Athenians,
they were routed by them, though they fought bravely. The
Athenians immediately pressed on forward so as not to lose their
present impetus before they had reached their objectives. Others
from the very beginning of the action were occupying the Syracusan counter-wall, the garrison of which put up no resistance, and
were tearing down the battlements. Now the Syracusans, the
Syracusan allies, and Gylippus and his troops came up from the
outworks and joined the battle; but the daring of this attack by

43

night was something which they had not expected; their charge lacked resolution and they were at first forced back on the retreat. The Athenians went on forward, but were now beginning to lose cohesion. They thought the victory was theirs, and wanted as quickly as possible to cut right through the rest of the enemy army that had not yet been brought into action, so that there should be no relaxation of their attack and no chance for the enemy to rally against them again. The Boeotians were the first to stand up to them. They charged the Athenians, routed them, and put them to flight.

44   From this moment the Athenians fell into great disorder and did not know where to turn. Indeed, it was difficult to find out from either side exactly how things happened. In daylight those who take part in an action have a clearer idea of it, though even then they cannot see everything, and in fact no one knows much more than what is going on around himself. But in a battle by night (and this was the only one that took place between great armies in this war) how could anyone be sure of what happened exactly? There was a bright moon, but visibility was only what might be expected by moonlight; they could see the outline of figures in front of them, but could not be sure whether these belonged to their own side or not. And there were great numbers of hoplites on both sides moving about in a small area. Some of the Athenians were already defeated, others had not been defeated at all and were coming up fresh to the attack. Then a large part of the rest of their army had only just made the ascent or was still on the way up, so that they did not know in which direction to march. After the rout that had taken place, everything in front of them was now in disorder, and the noise made it difficult to tell who was who. The Syracusans and their allies were cheering each other on in their victory with loud shouts (this being the only possible means of communication in the darkness) and at the same time were meeting all attacks. The Athenians were trying to find each other and taking all who came towards them to be enemies, even though they might be people on their own side now escaping back again. By constantly asking for the watchword, which was the only way they had of recognizing each other, they caused much confusion among themselves, by all asking for it at once, and at the same

time revealed it to the enemy. It was less easy for them to discover the watchword of the Syracusans, who, being victorious and in a compact body, did not have the same difficulties in recognizing each other. The result was that when the Athenians met a detachment of the enemy which was weaker than they were, it escaped them through knowing their watchword, while, if they themselves failed to give the answer, they were killed. But it was the singing of the paean which did them as much, or even more harm than anything, because of the uncertainty caused by having much the same paean sung on both sides. Thus when the Argives and Corcyraeans and other Dorian elements in the army started singing their paean they produced as much panic among the Athenians as the enemy did. So, once the original confusion had taken place, many parts of the army ended by falling upon each other, friend against friend and citizen against citizen, not only causing panic among themselves, but actually fighting hand to hand, and only being parted with difficulty. The way down again from Epipolae was only a narrow one, and in the pursuit many men lost their lives by throwing themselves down from the cliffs. As for those who got down safely from the heights to the plain, most of them, and particularly the soldiers of the first expedition, who had a better knowledge of the ground, escaped to the camp, but there were a number of those who had recently arrived who lost their way and wandered about the country. When day came these were rounded up and killed by the Syracusan cavalry.

45 Next day the Syracusans put up two trophies, one at the approach to Epipolae and one at the place where the Boeotians had first made their stand. The Athenians took back their dead under an armistice. Many had been killed, both Athenians and allies, though the quantity of arms captured was out of proportion to the numbers of the dead, since those who had been forced to jump down from the cliffs had abandoned their shields, and, while some were killed, others of them escaped.

46 After this the Syracusans, because of such an unexpected piece of good fortune, recovered all the confidence which they had had before. They sent out Sicanus with fifteen ships to Acragas, which was in a state of revolution, to see whether he could bring the city over to their side. Gylippus went off again by land into the other

parts of Sicily to raise still another army, with the assurance that there was now a good prospect of actually forcing the Athenian lines, after the way that the battle at Epipolae had gone.

47   Meanwhile the Athenian generals discussed the situation in the light of the defeat which they had suffered and the general weakness which they observed in their army. They recognized that their efforts had been unsuccessful and they saw that the soldiers hated the idea of staying on. Many of them were ill, partly because this was the season of the year when there is most sickness, partly because the camp was situated in marshy and unhealthy ground; also the whole future looked desperate. Demosthenes therefore thought that they ought not to stay any longer and, in accordance with his original idea in making the venture at Epipolae, now that it had failed he voted for going away and not wasting time over it, while it was still possible to cross the sea and while they could claim a naval superiority at least with regard to the newly arrived ships. It was better for Athens, he said, for them to fight against those who were building fortifications in Attica than against the Syracusans, who could no longer be conquered easily; also it was unreasonable to stay on in front of the city spending large sums of money with nothing to show for it.

48   This was the view taken by Demosthenes. Nicias was quite prepared to agree that their affairs were in a bad way, but did not want the fact of their weakness to be proclaimed or to have it reported to the enemy that the Athenians in full council were openly voting in favour of the withdrawal; for they would then find it much harder to do so secretly, when they did decide upon the step. Then, too, from his own private sources of information he still had some grounds for hoping that, if they persevered with the siege, the enemy's position would become worse than their own. They would wear the Syracusans out, he hoped, through shortage of money, especially as now with the ships at their disposal they had a greater command of the sea. There was also a party in Syracuse who wanted to betray the place to the Athenians, and this party was always sending to Nicias and urging him not to give up the siege. Nicias was aware of all this and, though in fact he held back because he still could not make up his mind what course to take and was still considering the question, in the speech

which he delivered openly on this occasion he refused to lead the army away. He was sure, he said, that the Athenians would not approve of the withdrawal, unless it had been voted for at Athens. They themselves could see the facts as they were and reach a decision about them without having to depend on the reports of hostile critics; but this was not the case with the voters at Athens, whose judgements would be swayed by any clever speech designed to create prejudice. He said, too, that many, in fact most of the soldiers in Sicily who were now crying out so loudly about their desperate position, would, as soon as they got to Athens, entirely change their tune and would say that the generals had been bribed to betray them and return. For his own part, therefore, knowing the Athenian character as he did, rather than be put to death on a disgraceful charge and by an unjust verdict of the Athenians, he preferred to take his chance and, if it must be, to meet his own death himself at the hands of the enemy. And, he said, in spite of everything, the Syracusans were in a worse position than they were. Because of their payments to their mercenaries, their expenditure on fortresses in the open country, and then the maintenance, which had now lasted for a year, of a large fleet, they were already short of money and would soon not know where to turn. They had spent 2,000 talents already, and had run up large debts in addition; and if, through failing to produce the pay, they were to lose even a small portion of their present force, they would at once be in a bad way, since they depended more on mercenaries than on men who, like the Athenians, were bound to serve. He therefore said that they ought to stay where they were and go on with the siege, and not go away defeated because of money, in which they were far superior.

49   Nicias stuck to this point of his because he had accurate information of the state of affairs in Syracuse. He knew that they were short of money and that there was a considerable party there which favoured the Athenians and which kept sending to him and urging him not to give up the siege. Besides which, on the sea at least he felt more confidence in victory than before.

Demosthenes, on the other hand, was entirely opposed to the idea of going on with the siege. If, he said, they could not lead the army away without a vote from Athens, and if they had to stay in

Sicily, then they should move to Thapsus or to Catana. From either of these places the army would be able to overrun a considerable extent of country, could supply itself by laying waste enemy territory, and would so do the enemy harm; while the fleet would be able to fight in the open sea, and instead of being in a confined space, which was all to the advantage of their opponents, they would have plenty of room, and so be able to make use of their skill, and not be forced, whenever they charged or retired, to carry out these manoeuvres in a cramped and circumscribed place. Altogether, he said that he could not approve in any way of their staying where they were; instead they should move at once, and without any delay at all. In this view Eurymedon supported him. Nicias, however, continued to oppose the idea, and in the whole business a kind of lack of resolution began to appear; there was procrastination, and at the same time a feeling that Nicias, in sticking so firmly to his point, might have some special sources of information. So the Athenians delayed and went on staying where they were.

50   Gylippus and Sicanus now returned to Syracuse. Sicanus had not been successful with regard to Acragas, as the pro-Syracusan party there had been driven out while he was still at Gela. Gylippus, however, came with another large army raised in Sicily and also with the hoplites who had been sent out in the spring from the Peloponnese in the merchant ships and who had come to Selinus from Libya. Bad weather had carried them to Libya. The people of Cyrene had given them two triremes with pilots, and on their voyage along the coast they had given help to the Euesperitae who were being besieged by the Libyans. After defeating the Libyans, they had gone along the coast to the Carthaginian trading settlement of Neapolis, from which there is the most direct crossing to Sicily – a voyage of only two days and a night. From here they crossed over and arrived at Selinus.

As soon as they arrived, the Syracusans prepared to make another attack on the Athenians both by land and sea. The Athenian generals, seeing that the enemy was now reinforced with another army and that their own position, so far from improving, was getting worse every day in every respect, and in particular was becoming increasingly difficult because of the sickness among the men, now regretted that they had not moved earlier, and, as not even Nicias was now so much against it, except that he opposed the idea of an open vote, they gave orders as secretly as possible for everyone to be prepared to sail out from the camp when the signal was given. When everything was ready and they were on the point of sailing, there was an eclipse of the moon, which was at the full. Most of the Athenians took this event so seriously that they now urged the generals to wait, and Nicias, who was rather over-inclined to divination and such things, said that, until they had waited for the thrice nine days recommended by the sooth-sayers, he would not even join in any further discussion on how the move could be made. So the Athenians, delayed by the eclipse, stayed on afterwards.

51   The Syracusans in their turn heard of this and became much more determined than ever not to relax their pressure on the Athenians, who now seemed to have admitted themselves that they no longer possessed superiority either on land or sea, since otherwise they would not have made the plan for sailing away. At the same time they did not want them to settle in some other part of Sicily where they would be more difficult to fight against; instead, their aim was to force the Athenians to fight at sea as quickly as possible, in a position where the advantages were on the side of Syracuse. So they manned their ships and put the crews into training for what seemed to them the right number of days. When the time came, on the first day they made an assault on the Athenian walls. A small force of hoplites and cavalry came out to meet them from some of the gates in the fortifications, and the Syracusans cut off some of the hoplites, routed them, and drove them back. In the narrow entrance the Athenians lost seventy horses and a few hoplites.

52   For that day the Syracusan army withdrew, but on the next they sailed out with seventy-six ships and at the same time advanced towards the walls with their ground forces. The Athenians put out against them with eighty-six ships and, coming to close quarters, went into action. Eurymedon, who was in command of the Athenian right wing, sailed out from the main body more in the direction of the land with the idea of encircling the enemy, but the Syracusans and their allies first defeated the Athenian centre, and

then caught Eurymedon in the part of the harbour where there is a narrow bay. Eurymedon was killed and the ships with him were destroyed. They then drove back the whole Athenian fleet and forced the ships ashore.

53   When Gylippus saw that the enemy fleet was defeated and then driven ashore beyond the shelter of their stockade and camp, he took part of his army and came along by the breakwater to give support, with the intention of destroying the crews as they landed and of making it easier for the Syracusans to tow off the ships, this part of the shore being in their hands. On the Athenian side the Etruscans were watching this point, and when they saw Gylippus's men advancing in disorder, they went out against them, charged and routed their vanguard, and drove it into the marsh of Lysimeleia. Soon, however, the Syracusans and their allies appeared in greater force, and the Athenians, fearing for their ships, came out to meet them and, after a successful engagement, drove them back. They killed a few of their hoplites, and rescued most of the ships, bringing them back into the shelter of their camp. Eighteen, however, were captured by the Syracusans and their allies, and all the men aboard them killed. In an attempt to set fire to the rest of them, the Syracusans filled an old merchant ship with faggots and pieces of pinewood, set it alight, and, since the wind was blowing towards the Athenians, let it drift down on them. The Athenians, fearing for their ships, took counter-measures to extinguish the fire, and after putting out the flames and preventing the ship coming near to them, escaped from this danger.

54   Afterwards the Syracusans put up a trophy for the naval action and for the action by the wall where they had cut off the hoplites and captured the horses. The Athenians put up a trophy for the fighting where the Etruscans had driven the enemy infantry into the marsh and where they themselves had won the victory with the rest of their army.

55   This was indeed a great victory for the Syracusans, and it had been won at sea, where until now they had been afraid of the naval reinforcements which had come with Demosthenes. The Athenians were now utterly disheartened; they could scarcely believe that this had happened, and they wished all the more that the expedition had never been made. These were the only cities they

had come up against which were of the same type as their own, democracies like themselves, and places of considerable size, equipped with naval and cavalry forces. They had been unable to make use of a fifth column or to offer the prospect of a change in the form of government as a means for gaining power over them; nor had they been able to exploit a great superiority in material force; instead most of their efforts had been unsuccessful; even before this they had not known what to do, and now, after this wholly unexpected defeat at sea, they were at their wits' end.

56   The Syracusans now began to sail about the harbour without fear of attack and planned to block up the mouth, so that the Athenians would no longer be able to slip away from them and escape, even if they wanted to. For them it was no longer a question simply of saving themselves; what they wanted to do now was to prevent the enemy from saving himself. They thought, quite correctly, that they were now the stronger, and realized that, if they could beat the Athenians and their allies on land and sea, it would be an achievement that would make them famous throughout Hellas. The other Hellenes would be immediately liberated or else freed from their fears, since it would be impossible for Athens, with her remaining strength, to stand up to the war that would then be waged against her; the credit for all this would go to the Syracusans, and greatly would they be honoured for it both in the present and in future generations. There were other reasons, too, which made this struggle a glorious one: they would be conquering not only the Athenians but their many allies as well; nor did the Syracusans stand alone; their own allies were there too, and it was in the company of Corinthians and Spartans that they were taking the lead, having put their city forward into the post of danger, and having been the chief architects and initiators of victory on the sea.

No doubt the sum total of the forces enrolled in this war under Athens and Sparta was greater, but otherwise there had certainly never been so many peoples gathered together in front of a single 57 city. The following were the states on the two sides, for and against Sicily, who came and fought at Syracuse to help either in the conquest or the defence of the island. They stood together not because of any moral principle or racial connection; it was rather because of the various circumstances of interest or of compulsion in each particular case. The Athenians themselves, being Ionians, came of their own free will against the Dorian Syracusans, and with them came their colonists, who still spoke the same dialect and had the same laws as the Athenians – the Lemnians, Imbrians, Aeginetans (that is, the people who were then occupying Aegina), and also the Hestiaeans who lived at Hestiaea in Euboea. Of the rest of the forces in the expedition some came as subjects of the Athenians, others as independent allies, others as mercenaries. In the class of tribute-paying subjects were the Euboean peoples from Eretria, Chalcis, Styria, and Carystus, the peoples from the islands of Ceos, Andros, and Tenos, and from Ionia the peoples of Miletus, Samos, and Chios. Of these last, the people of Chios were not in the tribute-paying class, but provided ships instead and came as independent allies. These were all, generally speaking, Ionians and, except for the Carystians who are Dryopes, descended from the Athenians. They were subjects, certainly, and served under compulsion, but still they were Ionians fighting against Dorians. There were also people of the Aeolian race – the Methymnians, subjects who provided ships instead of paying tribute, and the Tenedians and Aenians, who were in the tribute-paying class. These Aeolian peoples fought under compulsion against their fellow-Aeolians and founders, the Boeotians who were with the Syracusans. Only the Plataeans, though Boeotians themselves, fought against the other Boeotians for the good reason that they were their enemies. The peoples of Rhodes and Cythera were both Dorian; the Cythereans were colonists from Sparta and fought on the side of the Athenians against the Spartans with Gylippus; and the Rhodians, who were Argives by race, were forced to make war on the Dorian Syracusans and on their own colonists, the Geloans, who were serving with the Syracusans. As for the islanders round the Peloponnese, the Cephallenians and Zacynthians joined the expedition as independent powers, though in fact, with Athens in command of the seas, their position as islanders left them little freedom of choice. The Corcyraeans were not only Dorians, but actually Corinthians, and were openly joining in against Corinthians and Syracusans, though they were colonists of Corinth and racially connected with Syracuse. They could claim that they were obliged to take this course, but in fact they were acting of their own free will, because of their hatred of Corinth. The Messenians, as they are now called, from Naupactus and from Pylos, which at this time was occupied by the Athenians, were also brought into the war. There were also a few exiles from Megara, who now found themselves in the position of fighting against fellow-Megarians from Selinus.

The rest of the expedition served more on a voluntary basis. It was not so much because of the alliance as because of hatred for Sparta, and the prospect of making quick personal profits for themselves, that the Dorian Argives fought against other Dorians at the side of the Ionian Athenians. The Mantineans and other mercenaries from Arcadia were in the habit of marching against any enemy who was pointed out to them as such at the time, and the fact that they were serving for pay now made them regard the Arcadians in the Corinthian service as just as much their enemies as anyone else. The Cretans, too, and the Aetolians were hired troops, and so it came about that the Cretans who had joined the Rhodians in the foundation of Gela, so far from fighting on the same side as their own colony, were voluntarily and for pay fighting against it. There were Acarnanians also in the service, some of whom had come for pay, but most out of friendship for Demosthenes and goodwill towards their Athenian allies. All these lived on the Hellenic side of the Ionian Gulf. Of the Greek cities in Italy there were the Thurians and the Metapontines, who had joined the expedition because they were forced into it by the revolutionary situation in which they were caught up. Of the Greek cities in Sicily there were the people of Naxos and of Catana; and of those who did not speak Greek there were the Egestaeans, who had called for Athenian intervention, and most of the Sicels; while from outside Sicily there were some Etruscans fighting because of their hatred for Syracuse, and some Iapygian mercenaries. All these peoples served on the Athenian side.

58   On the other side the following states came to the help of Syracuse. There were the people of the neighbouring city of Camarina, the people of Gela, who live next to them, and then, leaving out Acragas which took no part in the war, the people of Selinus,

living at the end of the island. All these are situated in the part of Sicily that faces Libya. The people of Himera came from the part facing the Tyrrhenian sea and are the only Hellenes in that area; they were also the only people who came at all from there to the help of Syracuse. The above were the Hellenic peoples of Sicily who were allied with Syracuse; all of them Dorians and all independent; of the non-Hellenic races there were only those of the Sicels who did not go over to the Athenians. Of the Hellenes outside Sicily there were the Spartans, who provided a regular Spartan officer as commander, and an army of freedmen and helots; the Corinthians, who alone came with both ground forces and a fleet; the Leucadians and Ambraciots, who came because of their racial connection with Corinth; mercenaries from Arcadia engaged by the Corinthians; some conscripted troops from Sicyon; and, from outside the Peloponnese, the Boeotians. But, in comparison with these contingents from abroad, the Sicilians, living as they did in great cities, supplied on their own account a greater quantity of every kind of armament. There were great numbers of hoplites, ships, and horses, and an almost unlimited supply of man-power for other uses. And again, one might say that Syracuse herself produced more than all the rest put together, both because of the size of the city and because it was the Syracusans who were in the greatest danger.

59   Such were the forces brought in to help either side. At this time they were all present on both sides, and neither received any more help later.

SYRACUSAN VICTORY AT SEA

The Syracusans and their allies now had every reason to think that it would be a fine thing for them if they could follow up their naval victory by capturing the whole of this huge Athenian force and not letting it escape either by sea or by land. They therefore started at once to block up the mouth of the great harbour, which is nearly a mile wide, with a line of triremes broadside on and merchant ships and other craft at anchor; they also made all their other preparations in case the Athenians should venture upon another battle at sea. In fact there was no respect in which they did not contemplate action on a great scale.

60   When the Athenians saw the harbour being closed and realized what the enemy's plan was, they called a council of war. The generals and senior officers assembled and discussed the difficulties of their position, one of the greatest of which was that they no longer had a stock of provisions (supposing that they were going to sail away, they had sent to Catana, telling them not to send provisions in), and were not likely to get any in the future unless they could gain naval superiority. They therefore decided to abandon the upper walls, to build a cross wall close to the ships enclosing the smallest possible space that would be sufficient to accommodate the stores and the sick, and, leaving a detachment there as a garrison, to use the rest of the army for manning every single ship, sea-worthy or not, putting everyone on board, and so fight it out at sea; then, if they were victorious, they would go to Catana, and if not, they would burn their ships, and march away by land in battle order for the nearest friendly place, Hellenic or foreign, which they could reach.

After deciding upon this plan, they carried it out at once. They came down from the upper walls and manned every ship they had, making everyone go on board who was of an age to be of any use at all. Altogether they manned about 110 ships and put on board them large numbers of archers and javelin-throwers from the Acarnanian and other foreign contingents, doing, in fact, everything they could do within the limits imposed on them by necessity and by the nature of their plan. And when nearly everything was ready, Nicias, seeing that the soldiers were out of heart because of having been defeated so thoroughly and so unexpectedly at sea, and that, because of the shortage of provisions, they wanted to fight it out as soon as possible, called them all together and first gave them some words of encouragement, speaking to them as follows:

61   'Soldiers of the Athenians and of the allies, the struggle in front of us involves us all, and each one of us, just as much as the enemy, will be fighting for his life and for his country, since, if we win this battle with our ships, each man can see again his own native city, wherever it may be. But we must not be downhearted or behave

like people with no experience, who, if they lose the first battles, are frightened ever afterwards and think that things will always turn out in the same way. On the contrary, you Athenians here, who have already had experience of many wars, and you allies of ours who have constantly fought at our side, must remember that there is an unpredictable element in warfare and, in the hope that we, too, may have fortune with us, you must be prepared to go into battle again and fight worthily of this great army of yours which you can see with your own eyes.

62   'This time we have discussed with the steersmen and, within the limits of our means, have provided everything that we considered would be of help to us against the massed formation of enemy ships which must be expected in this narrow harbour and against the forces which they have on deck – the two things that did us damage before. We shall have large numbers of archers and javelin-throwers on board and a mass of men which, if we were fighting a naval action in the open sea, we should never have used, since the over-weighting of the ships would deprive us of the advantages of our superior skill; but here, forced as we are to fight a land battle on the sea, all this will prove useful. We have also discovered what has to be done on our side in altering the construction of our ships, and, to deal with the extra thickness of the enemy's prows, which did us most harm of all, we shall have grappling-irons which, so long as our soldiers on deck do their part of the work properly, will prevent an enemy ship from backing away again, once it has charged. For the fact is that we have been forced into fighting a land battle from our ships, and the best thing for us seems to be neither to back water ourselves nor to allow the enemy to do so, especially as all the shore, except for the part occupied by our troops, is hostile ground.

63   'Remember this, and fight it out to the limit of your strength. Do not be driven back on to the shore, but, when ship meets ship, make it your resolve not to break the action off until you have cleared the enemy's decks of their hoplites. I am saying this not so much to the sailors as to the hoplites, since this is more the job of the men on deck, and we still have even now the advantage in most ways with our infantry. As for the sailors, I advise them, in fact I beg and entreat them, not to be too much cast down by past

events. Think of the pleasure it is and how much worth preserving that all this time you, though not really Athenians, have, through knowledge of our language and imitation of our way of life, been considered as Athenians and been admired for it throughout Hellas, that you have had your proper share in all the advantages of our empire, while in the respect shown to you by our subjects and in freedom from ill treatment you have had even more than your share. So, since with you alone we freely share our empire, it is only right that you should not betray it now. You must look down on Corinthians, whom you have beaten so often, and on Sicilians, none of whom even thought of standing up to us when our navy was at its best, and you must drive them back and show that even in sickness and disaster your skill is worth more than the force and the fortune of any one else.

64   'As for the Athenians among you, I must once again remind you of this also: you have no more ships like these left in your dock-yards, and no reserve of men fit to fight as hoplites; and, if this action should end in anything else except victory for you, our enemies here will at once sail against Athens, and those of us who are left at Athens will be incapable of resisting a combination of the forces they have against them there now and a new invasion force from here. So, while you will find yourselves at once at the mercy of the Syracusans (and you know well how you intended to treat them when you attacked them first), your countrymen at home will be at the mercy of the Spartans. Since, therefore, the fate of both you and them rests upon this one battle, now, if ever, is the time to stand out firm and to remember, each and all, that those of you who are going to go aboard the ships are the army and navy of the Athenians, the whole state that remains, and the great name of Athens. In this cause if any man has skill or courage greater than another, now, if ever, when he can help himself and save us all, is the time for him to show it.'

65   After making this speech Nicias at once ordered the ships to be manned. Gylippus and the Syracusans, seeing the actual prepara-tions going on, were quite capable of realizing that the Athenians were going to fight at sea, and they had also been told of their in-tention to use grappling-irons. In addition to all their other measures, they specially provided against this by stretching hides

over the prows and much of the upper part of their ships, so that when the grappling-irons were thrown they would slip off again without getting a good grip. When everything was ready, Gylippus and the generals encouraged their men by speaking to them as follows:

66   'Syracusans and allies, we think that most of you are aware of the honour which we have won already and of the honour which remains to be won in the coming battle. Otherwise you would not have gone after it so bravely. But if there is anyone who does not realize this as fully as he should, we will explain it to him. The Athenians came to this country first of all to enslave Sicily and then, if successful in that, to enslave the Peloponnese and the rest of Hellas. They already possessed the greatest empire that ever has been possessed by Hellenes, past or present. You were the first people to stand up to their navy, which gave them everything, and in the battles fought on sea you have already defeated them before now, and there is good reason to suppose you will do so again on this occasion. When people think that they are especially good at something and find that it is just here that they are frustrated, the whole view that they take of themselves alters and they become less confident than they would have been if they had never believed in their superiority in the first place: the unexpectedness of their failure to make good their pretensions produces a tendency to give in even when this is unjustified by the actual strength which they have available. This, in all probability, is now

67 happening to the Athenians. With us, however, the spirit which we had originally, and which enabled us to go out and seek danger while we were still inexperienced, is now the firmer, and added to that is the conviction that, after having beaten the champions, we are the champions ourselves. So each man's hope is doubled; and in going into action it is generally the case that where hopes are highest hearts are stoutest.

'As for the attempts they are making to copy our own equipment, they are known to us from our own methods of fighting, and we shall be provided against all of them. And when one thinks of all the hoplites they will have on deck, contrary to their usual methods, and all the javelin-throwers – landsmen nearly all of them on board ships, Acarnanians and the rest, who will not even

find out how they are to throw their weapons from a sitting position – it is difficult to see how they can help impairing the efficiency
of the ships and all getting into a state of confusion among themselves as they move in a way that is not what they are used to.
Certainly – if any of you is frightened by the fact that he is going
into action against superior numbers – the mere numbers of their
ships will be of no help to them. In a small space great numbers of
ships will be the slower at carrying out the manoeuvres required,
and will be particularly vulnerable to the methods of attack which
we have adopted. But for the real truth of the situation you must
hear what we ourselves believe to be information based on reliable
reports. The fact is that their sufferings have been so overwhelming that they have been forced by the hopelessness of their present
position into a state of desperation where, trusting in luck more
than in good management, they will take their chance, as best they
may, and either force their way out and sail away or else, after the
attempt, make their retreat by land, since they know that things
could not be worse for them than they are at present.

68   'And so against these men, our greatest enemies, disorganized as
they are and betrayed by their own fortune, let us go into battle
with anger in our hearts; let us be convinced that in dealing with
an adversary it is most just and lawful to claim the right to slake
the fury of the soul in retaliation on the aggressor, and also that we
shall have that greatest of all pleasures, which consists, according
to the proverb, in taking vengeance on an enemy. That they are
not only enemies but the most deadly enemies of all is known to
each one of you, since it was to enslave our country that they came
here and, if they had been successful, they would have inflicted
upon our men the bitterest of pains, have heaped upon our children and wives the greatest of outrages, and given to the whole city
the most shameful of names. There is no excuse, therefore, for any
softening of the heart or any feeling that it would be a good thing
for us if they went away without bringing us into any further
danger. They will do that in any case, even if they win. But we
fight for something that is worth fighting for, if our wishes are, as
we can expect, fulfilled, if we inflict the proper punishment on
these men and hand down to the whole of Sicily the liberty which
she used to enjoy, but now more firmly established than before.

Of all risks that can be run these are the rarest, when failure brings no great loss and success confers no little gain.'

69 After making this speech to encourage their own soldiers, the Syracusan generals and Gylippus immediately began to man their ships, seeing that the Athenians were doing the same thing. And Nicias, half-distraught by the present position, realizing how much was at stake and how imminent already the hazard, and thinking, as men do think in moments of great crisis, that when everything has been done there is still something that needs doing, when everything has been said there is still something left unsaid, again called to him personally all the captains of triremes, man by man, addressing each by his father's name and his own name and the name of his tribe. He entreated those who had an established and brilliant reputation not to betray that reputation now, and those whose ancestors were famous men not to deface the great deeds of their forbears; he reminded them of their country, the freest in the world, and of how all who lived there had liberty to live their own lives in their own way; and he said other things too – the things that men can be expected to say when they are actually on the edge of the event and do not bother to avoid giving the impression of using conventional language; instead they bring forward the kind of appeals that can generally be used on all occasions: wives, children, gods of the native land; yet still they cry out these names aloud, since, in the terror of the moment, they believe that they will help.

So these words of encouragement seemed to Nicias himself still to fall short of their mark and to be no more than barely adequate to the occasion. After speaking to them, he went back and led the infantry to the sea, posting them along the shore in as long a line as he could, so that they might help as much as possible in giving confidence to the men aboard the ships. And now the commanders of the fleet, Demosthenes, Menander, and Euthydemus, put out from their own camp and sailed straight for the barrier across the mouth of the harbour and the opening that had been left in it, to try to force their way out.

70 The Syracusans and their allies had put out already with about the same number of ships as before. Part of their fleet guarded the way out, and others were all round the rest of the harbour, in order

to charge the Athenians from all directions at once. At the same time their infantry was there ready for action at all points along the shore where ships might put in. The commanders of the Syracusan fleet were Sicanus and Agatharchus, each of whom led one wing of the whole force, and Pythen and the Corinthians were in the centre.

When the Athenians on their side came up to the barrier with the impetus of their first charge, they overpowered the ships stationed in front of it and tried to break down the obstructions. After this the Syracusans and their allies bore down on them from all sides, and soon the fighting was not only in front of the barrier but all over the harbour. And hard fighting it was – more so than in any of the previous battles. There was no hanging back among the rowers on either side in bringing their ships into action whenever they were ordered, and among the steersmen there were great battles of skill and great rivalry between each other. And when ship met ship, the soldiers on board did their best to see that what was done on deck was up to the standard shown elsewhere; every one, in fact, each in his own job, strove to appear the best. Many ships crowded in upon each other in a small area (indeed, never before had so many ships fought together in so narrow a space. There were almost 200 of them on the two sides); consequently there were not many attacks made with the ram amidships, since there was no backing water and no chance of breaking through the turning about; collisions were much more frequent, ship crashing into ship in their efforts to escape from or to attack some other vessel. All the time that one ship was bearing down upon another, javelins, arrows, and stones were shot or hurled on to it without cessation by the men on the decks; and once the ships met, the soldiers fought hand to hand, each trying to board the enemy. Because of the narrowness of the space, it often happened that a ship was ramming and being rammed at the same time, and that two, or sometimes more, ships found themselves jammed against one, so that the steersmen had to think of defence on one side and attack on the other and, instead of being able to give their attention to one point at a time, had to deal with many different things in all directions; and the great din of all these ships crashing together was not only frightening in itself, but also made it impossible to hear the orders given by the boatswains. And indeed, in the ordinary course of duty and in the present excitement of battle, plenty of instructions were given and plenty of shouting was done by the boatswains on either side. To the Athenians they cried out, urging them to force the passage and now, if ever, to seize resolutely upon the chance of a safe return to their country; and to the Syracusans and their allies the cry was that it would be a glorious thing to prevent the enemy from escaping and for each man to bring honour to his own country by winning the victory. Then, too, the generals on each side, if they saw anyone at all backing away without good reason, would shout out to the captain by name and ask, in the case of Athenians, whether they were retreating because they thought they would feel more at home on land where their enemies were supreme than on the sea, which, with so much labour, they had made their own, and, in the case of the Syracusans, whether they were running from an enemy who was himself in flight, since they knew well enough that the Athenians, for their part, were longing to get away as best they could.

71   While the issue of the battle at sea still hung in the balance, great was the stress and great the conflict of soul among the two armies on the shore, the Syracusans being all on edge to win an even greater glory than before, and the invaders fearing lest they might find themselves even worse off than they were already. For the Athenians everything depended upon their navy; their fears for the future were like nothing they had ever experienced; and, as the battle swung this way and that, so, inevitably, did their impressions alter as they watched it from the shore. The sight was close in front of them and, as they were not all at once looking in the same direction, some saw that at one point their own side was winning, and took courage at the sight and began to call upon the gods not to deprive them of their salvation, while others, looking towards a point where their men were being defeated, cried out aloud in lamentation, and were more broken in spirit by the sight of what was being done than were the men actually engaged in the fighting. Others were looking at some part of the battle where there was nothing to choose between the two sides, and, as the fight went on and on with no decision reached, their bodies,

swaying this way and that, showed the trepidation with which their minds were filled, and wretched indeed was their state, constantly on the verge of safety, constantly on the brink of destruction. So, while the result of the battle was still in doubt, one could hear sounds of all kinds coming at the same time from this one Athenian army – lamentations and cheering, cries of 'We are winning' and of 'We are losing', and all the other different exclamations bound to be made by a great army in its great danger. Much the same were the feelings of the men on board the ships, till finally, after the battle had lasted for a long time, the Syracusans and their allies broke the Athenian resistance, followed them up with great shouting and cheering, and chased them back, clearly and decisively, to the land. And now the whole fleet, apart from the ships which were captured afloat, ran on shore, some going one way, some another, and the men fled from their ships towards the camp. As for the army on land, the period of uncertainty was over, now one impulse overpowered them all as they cried aloud and groaned in pain for what had happened, some going down to give help to the ships, some to guard what was left of their wall, while others (and these were now in the majority) began to think of themselves and how they could get away safe. Indeed, the panic of this moment was something greater than anything they had ever known. They were now in much the same state as that into which they had forced their enemies at Pylos; then, when the Spartans lost their ships they lost at the same time the men who had crossed over to the island, and now the Athenians had no hope of getting away safely by land, unless some miracle happened.

DESTRUCTION OF THE ATHENIAN EXPEDITION

72 After this hard-fought fight, in which many men and many ships had been lost on both sides, the victorious Syracusans and their allies took up the wrecks and the dead bodies, sailed back to their city, and put up a trophy. But the Athenians were so oppressed by the present weight of their misfortune that they never even thought of asking for permission to take up their dead or the

wreckage. Instead they wanted to retreat at once and on that very night. Demosthenes, however, went to Nicias and proposed that they should once again man the ships that they had left and do their best to force their way out at dawn. He pointed out that they still had more ships left fit for service than the enemy; for the Athenians had about sixty ships left, and their opponents had less than fifty. Nicias agreed with this proposal, but when they wanted to man the ships, the sailors would not go on board, being so demoralized by their defeat that they no longer regarded victory as a possibility.

73   The Athenians, therefore, were now all resolved to retreat by land. Hermocrates, the Syracusan, suspected that this was their plan, and thought that it would be a dangerous thing for Syracuse if so large an army were to get away by land and settle in some part of Sicily from which it could wage war against them again. He therefore approached the authorities and pointed out that they ought not to allow the Athenians to escape by night, saying that, in his personal opinion, the Syracusans and their allies should go out of the city at once in full force and build road-blocks and occupy and garrison the passes. The authorities saw the force of his argument as clearly as he did himself, and thought that his plan should be carried out; however, they did not think that it would be at all easy to get their own people to obey orders, considering that they were just beginning to celebrate the occasion and were relaxing after their great victory at sea, and were also holding a festival (there happened to be a sacrifice to Heracles on that day); most of them, in fact, in their great joy in their victory, had started drinking at the festival, so that it looked as though about the last thing they could be persuaded to do at this particular moment would be to take up their arms and march out to battle. Taking all this into consideration, the magistrates decided that the idea was impossible to carry out in practice, and Hermocrates, failing to get any further with them, proceeded to put the following plan of his own into operation. What he feared was that in the night the Athenians might have the start of them and so get over the most difficult part of the route unopposed; therefore as soon as it began to grow dark he sent down to their camp some friends of his own with a cavalry detachment. These men rode up to within earshot

and called out to some of the soldiers, pretending that they were friendly to the Athenians (for there were, in fact, some people who brought news to Nicias about what was happening inside the city), and asking them to tell Nicias not to lead the army away during the night, since the Syracusans were guarding the roads; instead he should retreat, in his own time and after making the proper preparations, by day. After saying this, they went away, and those
74 who had heard them passed on the message to the Athenian generals, who, on the strength of what they were told, put off the retreat for the night, in the belief that the information was genuine.

And now, since even after all this they failed to start immediately, they decided to wait for the next day too, so that the soldiers could pack their most essential luggage as best they could; then, leaving everything else behind, they were to set off, taking with them only what was absolutely necessary for each man's personal needs. Meanwhile the Syracusans and Gylippus set out first with their land forces, built road-blocks in the country on the routes which the Athenians were likely to take, posted guards at the fords of the streams and rivers, and arranged themselves so as to be able to meet and to stop the retreating army at the points which they chose. And with their ships they sailed up to the Athenian ships and dragged them from the beach. Some had been burned by the Athenians themselves, according to their original plan; as for the others, the Syracusans towed them away as they liked, just as each one was driven ashore, and brought them, with no opposition from anyone, to their city.

75 Afterwards, when Nicias and Demosthenes thought that the preparations were complete, came the time for the army to move, two days after the naval battle. It was a terrible scene, and more than one element in their situation contributed to their dismay. Not only were they retreating after having lost all their ships, and instead of their high hopes now found themselves and the whole state of Athens in danger, but in the actual leaving of the camp there were sad sights for every eye, sad thoughts for every mind to feel. The dead were unburied, and when any man recognized one of his friends lying among them, he was filled with grief and fear; and the living who, whether sick or wounded, were being left behind caused more pain than did the dead to those who were

left alive, and were more pitiable than the lost. Their prayers and their lamentations made the rest feel impotent and helpless, as they begged to be taken with them and cried out aloud to every single friend or relative whom they could see; as they hung about the necks of those who had shared tents with them and were now going, following after them as far as they could, and, when their bodily strength failed them, reiterated their cries to heaven and their lamentations as they were left behind. So the whole army was filled with tears and in such distress of mind that they found it difficult to go away even from this land of their enemies when sufferings too great for tears had befallen them already and more still, they feared, awaited them in the dark future ahead. There was also a profound sense of shame and deep feelings of self-reproach. Indeed, they were like nothing so much as the fleeing population of a city that has surrendered to its besiegers, and no small city at that, since in the whole crowd of them marching to-gether there were not less than 40,000 men. Each of them carried with him whatever he could that would be useful, and, contrary to the usual practice, the hoplites and cavalry carried their own provisions themselves while under arms, some because they had no servants, some because they did not trust the servants they had; many of these had deserted in the past, and most of the rest were doing so now. Yet even so they did not carry a sufficient amount, since there was no longer any food in the camp. And then there was the degradation of it all and the fact that all without exception were afflicted, so that, although there may be some lightening of a burden when it is shared with many others, this still did not make the burden seem any easier to bear at the time, especially when they remembered the splendour and the pride of their setting out and saw how mean and abject was the conclusion. No Hellenic army had ever suffered such a reverse. They had come to enslave others, and now they were going away frightened of being en-slaved themselves; and instead of the prayers and paeans with which they had sailed out, the words to be heard now were directly contrary and boded evil as they started on their way back, sailors travelling on land, trusting in hoplites rather than in ships. Nevertheless, when they considered the greatness of the danger that still hung over them, all this seemed able to be borne.

76   Nicias, seeing the discouragement of the army with its hopes so
totally eclipsed, went along the ranks and then did the best he
could to encourage and to comfort them, and, as he went from
one line to another, he raised his voice louder and louder in his
eagerness to be of help and in his wish that the good that his
words might do should reach as far as possible:

77   'Athenians and allies, even now we must still hope on. You have
been saved from worse straits than these before now. And you
must not reproach yourselves too much for the disasters of the
past or for your present undeserved sufferings. I myself am
physically no stronger than any one among you (in fact you see
what my illness has done to me), nor, I think, can anyone be
considered to have been more blessed by fortune than I have been
in my private life and in other respects; but I am now plunged
into the same perils as the meanest man here. Yet throughout my
life I have worshipped the gods as I ought, and my conduct towards men has been just and without reproach. Because of this I
still have a strong hope for the future, and these disasters do not
terrify me as they well might do. Perhaps they may even come
to an end. Our enemies have had good fortune enough, and, if
any of the gods was angry with us at our setting out, by this time
we have been sufficiently punished. Other men before us have
attacked their neighbours, and, after doing what men will do, have
suffered no more than what men can bear. So it is now reasonable
for us to hope that the gods will be kinder to us, since by now we
deserve their pity rather than their jealousy. And then look at
yourselves; see how many first-rate hoplites you have marching
together in your ranks, and do not be too much alarmed. Reflect
that you yourselves, wherever you settle down, are a city already
and that there is no other city in Sicily that could easily meet your
attack or drive you out from any place where you establish yourselves. As for the march, you must see to its safety and its good
order yourselves, and let this one thought be in the mind of every
man among you – that on whatever spot of ground he is forced to
fight, there, if he wins it, he will find a country and a fortress. We
shall hurry forward, marching by night as well as by day, since
our supplies are short, and once we can reach some friendly place in
the country of the Sicels, whom, because of their fear of Syracuse,

we can still rely upon, then you can consider yourselves safe. We have already sent instructions to them to meet us and to bring supplies of food with them. In a word, soldiers, you must make up your minds that to be brave now is a matter of necessity, since no place exists near at hand where a coward can take refuge, and that, if you escape the enemy now, you will all see again the homes for which you long, and the Athenians among you will build up again the great power of Athens, fallen though it is. It is men who make the city, and not walls or ships with no men inside them.'

78   While he was speaking to the troops, Nicias was going along the ranks, and wherever he saw that they were not in close formation or were out of order, he brought them together and set them in their correct positions. Demosthenes did the same for the troops under his command and spoke to them in much the same terms. The army marched in a hollow square, the troops of Nicias being in front and those of Demosthenes at the rear; the hoplites were at the outside, and the baggage-carriers and general mass of the army were in the middle.

When they reached the crossing of the river Anapus they found a body of Syracusan and allied troops drawn up there to guard it. These they routed and, gaining control of the ford, pushed on farther, with the Syracusan cavalry attacking them on the flanks and the light troops harassing them with their missiles. The Athenians advanced about four and a half miles that day, and halted for the night on a hill. Next day they were on the march early, went forward about two miles, and descended to some level ground, where they camped, with the intention of procuring food from the houses, since the place was inhabited, and of carrying water with them from there, as for many furlongs in front of them, in the direction which they intended to take, the supply of water was not plentiful. Meanwhile the Syracusans went on and fortified the pass that lay ahead of them. It was a place where there was a steep hill with a rocky ravine at each side of it, and it was called the Acraean cliff.

Next day the Athenians went forward, and the cavalry and javelin-throwers of the Syracusans and their allies came up in great numbers from both sides, hampering their march with volleys of javelins and with cavalry charges on their flanks. After fighting for a long time, the Athenians finally went back again to the same camp as before. They no longer had the same supplies of provisions, since it was now impossible to leave the camp because of the enemy cavalry.

79 Early in the morning they set forward again and forced their way up to the hill which had been fortified. Here they found in front of them the enemy's infantry ready to defend the fortification and drawn up many shields deep, since the place was a narrow one. The Athenians charged and assaulted the wall: missiles rained down on them from the hill, which rose steeply, so that it was all the easier for those on it to be sure of hitting their target; and, finding it impossible to break through, they retreated and rested. At the same time there were some claps of thunder with some rain, as often happens when it gets near autumn, and this made the Athenians still more discouraged, for they saw in all these events omens of their own destruction. While they were resting, Gylippus and the Syracusans sent part of their army to build fortifications in the rear of the Athenians on the route by which they had come forward; but the Athenians sent back some of their own men to counter this move and succeeded in preventing it. Afterwards they fell back more in the direction of the plain and there spent the night.

Next day they went on again, and the Syracusans came all round them and attacked them from every side and wounded many of them, giving way whenever the Athenians charged, and resuming their attacks as soon as they retired. In particular they attacked the rearguard, hoping that, if they could rout some detachments separately, this would cause a panic throughout the whole army. For a long time the Athenians held out, fighting in this way; finally, after having advanced a little over half a mile, they halted in the plain to rest, and the Syracusans left them and went back to their own camp.

80 During the night Nicias and Demosthenes, seeing the wretched state in which their army was, now in want of every kind of necessity and with numbers of men disabled in the numerous attacks of the enemy, decided to light as many fires as possible and to lead their forces away. Instead of going by the route which they had intended to take, they were now to go towards the sea, in the

opposite direction to the part guarded by the Syracusans. This new route, instead of leading towards Catana, would take the army to the other side of Sicily, towards Camarina, Gela and the other Hellenic and non-Hellenic cities in that area. They therefore lit a number of fires and marched away in the night. What happened to them was something which happens in all armies, and most of all in the biggest ones. Fears and alarms are apt to break out, especially when troops are marching by night, through enemy country and with the enemy himself not far away. So the Athenian army fell into confusion. The division under Nicias, as it was leading the way, kept together and got a long distance ahead of the rest, while the troops under Demosthenes – rather more than half of the whole army – lost contact with each other and marched in some disorder. Nevertheless, they reached the sea at dawn and, taking the Helorine road, marched on with the intention of getting to the river Cacyparis and following its course up into the interior, where they hoped to join forces with the Sicels whom they had sent for. When they reached the river they found that here also was a detachment of Syracusans who were building a wall and a stockade to block the crossing place. They forced their way through these troops, crossed the river, and, following the advice of their guides, marched on again to another river called the Erineus.

81   Meanwhile, when it was day and the Syracusans and their allies found that the Athenians had gone, most of them accused Gylippus of having deliberately let them escape, and, since there was no difficulty in finding the route which they had taken, they quickly hurried after them, and caught up with them about the time of the midday meal. The troops they came up with were those under Demosthenes, who were behind the rest and were marching more slowly and in worse order, because of the confusion which, as already mentioned, had taken place during the night. The Syracusans went into action and attacked them at once and, surrounding them with their cavalry all the more easily because they were separated from the rest, hemmed them in on one spot. Nicias's troops were five or six miles ahead of them, as Nicias was leading his men on faster, in the belief that, as things were, their safety lay not in standing their ground and fighting, unless they had to, but

in retreating as fast as possible and only fighting when they were forced to do so. Demosthenes, however, had been on the whole in more continual difficulties, since the rear-guard was always attacked first by the enemy; and now, when he realized that the enemy were in pursuit, instead of pushing on, he formed his men up in battle order, and the loss of time involved in this operation led to his being surrounded. He and the Athenians with him were now in a state of great confusion. They were penned into a place which had a wall all round it, with a road on both sides and great numbers of olive trees, and they were under a rain of missiles from every direction. This method of attack was naturally adopted by the Syracusans in preference to hand-to-hand fighting, since to venture themselves against men who had been driven desperate would now be more in the interests of the Athenians than in their own; and at the same time they began to spare themselves a little, so as not to throw away their lives before the moment of victory which was now a certainty; besides, they thought that by these methods they would in any case break down the resistance of the Athenians and make them prisoners.

82   As it was, after attacking the Athenians and allies all day long and from every side with their missiles, they saw that they were now worn out with their wounds and with all the other sufferings they had endured. Gylippus and the Syracusans and their allies then made a proclamation first to the islanders, offering their liberty to any who would come over to them; and a few cities did so.[43] Afterwards terms of surrender were agreed upon for all the troops serving under Demosthenes: they were to lay down their arms on the condition that no one was to be put to death either summarily, or by imprisonment, or by lack of the necessities of life. They then surrendered, 6,000 of them in all, and gave up all the money in their possession, which they threw into the hollows of shields, filling four of them. They were then immediately taken to the city. On the same day Nicias with his men reached the river Erineus. He crossed the river and halted his army on some high ground.

83   Next day the Syracusans caught up with him, told him that the troops under Demosthenes had surrendered, and invited him to do

43. See Appendix 1.

so also. Nicias did not believe it, and a truce was arranged so that he could send a horseman to go and see. When the messenger had gone and returned with the news that they had surrendered, Nicias sent a herald to Gylippus and the Syracusans, saying that he was prepared to make an agreement with them in the name of the Athenians that, in return for letting his army go, they would pay back to Syracuse all the money that she had spent on the war; until the money should be paid he would give them Athenian citizens as hostages, one man for each talent. The Syracusans and Gylippus would not accept these proposals. They attacked and surrounded this army as they had the other, raining missiles on them from all sides until the evening. These men, too, were wretchedly off in their want of food and other necessities. Nevertheless, they intended to wait until the dead of night and then to go on with their march. As they were taking up their arms, the Syracusans realized what they were doing and raised their paean. The Athenians, finding that they were discovered, laid down their arms again, except for about 300 men, who forced their way through the guards and went on through the night as best they could.

84   When day came Nicias led his army on, and the Syracusans and their allies pressed them hard in the same way as before, showering missiles and hurling javelins in upon them from every side. The Athenians hurried on towards the river Assinarus, partly because they were under pressure from the attacks made upon them from every side by the numbers of cavalry and the masses of other troops, and thought that things would not be so bad if they got to the river, partly because they were exhausted and were longing for water to drink. Once they reached the river, they rushed down into it, and now all discipline was at an end. Every man wanted to be the first to get across, and, as the enemy persisted in his attacks, the crossing now became a difficult matter. Forced to crowd in close together, they fell upon each other and trampled each other underfoot; some were killed immediately by their own spears, others got entangled among themselves and among the baggage and were swept away by the river. Syracusan troops were stationed on the opposite bank, which was a steep one. They hurled down their weapons from above on the Athenians, most of whom,

in a disordered mass, were greedily drinking in the deep river-bed. And the Peloponnesians came down and slaughtered them, especially those who were in the river. The water immediately became foul, but nevertheless they went on drinking it, all muddy as it was and stained with blood; indeed, most of them were fighting among themselves to have it.

85   Finally, when the many dead were by now heaped upon each other in the bed of the stream, when part of the army had been destroyed there in the river, and the few who managed to get away had been cut down by the cavalry, Nicias surrendered himself to Gylippus, whom he trusted more than he did the Syracusans, telling him and the Spartans to do what they liked with him personally, but to stop the slaughter of his soldiers. After this Gylippus gave orders to take prisoners, and all the rest, apart from a large number who were hidden by the soldiers who had captured them, were brought in alive. They also sent in pursuit of the 300 who had broken through the guards during the night, and captured them as well. The number of prisoners taken over in a body by the state was not very large; great numbers, however, had been appropriated by their captors; in fact the whole of Sicily was full of them, there having been no fixed agreement for the surrender, as in the case of the troops of Demosthenes. Then a considerable part of the army had been killed outright, since this had been a very great slaughter – greater than any that took place in this war. Large numbers, too, had fallen in the constant attacks made on them during the march. Nevertheless, there were many who escaped, some at the time, and others, after having been enslaved, ran away afterwards. These found refuge in Catana.

86   The Syracusans and their allies now brought their forces together into one, took up the spoils and as many of the prisoners as they could, and went back to their city. They put the Athenian and allied prisoners whom they had taken into the stone quarries, thinking that this was the safest way of keeping them. Nicias and Demosthenes they put to death, against the will of Gylippus, who thought that it would be a fine thing indeed for him if, on top of everything else, he could bring the enemy generals back to Sparta. It so happened that one of them, Demosthenes, was Sparta's greatest enemy because of the campaign at Pylos and in the island,

while the other, for the same reasons, was Sparta's best friend. For Nicias had done his utmost to secure the release of the Spartans captured on the island by persuading the Athenians to make peace. Because of this the Spartans were well-disposed towards him, and it was in this that Nicias himself had chiefly trusted when he surrendered himself to Gylippus. But some of the Syracusans who had been in contact with him were afraid, so it was said, that this fact might lead to his being examined under torture, and so bringing trouble on them at the very moment of their success. Others, particularly the Corinthians, feared that, since he was rich, he might escape by means of bribery and do them still more harm in the future. So they persuaded their allies to agree and put him to death. For these reasons or reasons very like them he was killed, a man who, of all the Hellenes in my time, least deserved to come to so miserable an end, since the whole of his life had been devoted to the study and the practice of virtue.

87   Those who were in the stone quarries were treated badly by the Syracusans at first. There were many of them, and they were crowded together in a narrow pit, where, since there was no roof over their heads, they suffered first from the heat of the sun and the closeness of the air; and then, in contrast, came on the cold autumnal nights, and the change in temperature brought disease among them. Lack of space made it necessary for them to do everything on the same spot; and besides there were the bodies all heaped together on top of one another of those who had died from their wounds or from the change of temperature or other such causes, so that the smell was insupportable. At the same time they suffered from hunger and from thirst. During eight months the daily allowance for each man was half a pint of water and a pint of corn. In fact they suffered everything which one could imagine might be suffered by men imprisoned in such a place. For about ten weeks they lived like this all together; then, with the exception of the Athenians and any Greeks from Italy or Sicily who had joined the expedition, the rest were sold as slaves. It is hard to give the exact figure, but the whole number of prisoners must have been at least 7,000.

This was the greatest Hellenic action that took place during this war, and, in my opinion, the greatest action that we know of in

Hellenic history – to the victors the most brilliant of successes, to the vanquished the most calamitous of defeats; for they were utterly and entirely defeated; their sufferings were on an enormous scale; their losses were, as they say, total; army, navy, everything was destroyed, and, out of many, only few returned. So ended the events in Sicily.

BOOK EIGHT[44]

ALARM AT ATHENS

1 WHEN the news reached Athens, for a long time people would not believe it, even though they were given precise information from the very soldiers who had been present at the event and had escaped; still they thought that this total destruction was something that could not possibly be true. And when they did recognize the facts, they turned against the public speakers who had been in favour of the expedition, as though they themselves had not voted for it, and also became angry with the prophets and soothsayers and all who at the time had, by various methods of divination, encouraged them to believe that they would conquer Sicily. They were feeling the stress in every department and on every front, and now, after this last blow, great indeed was the fear that beset them and the consternation. Not only was the state as a whole and the mind of every man in it weighed down by the thought of the loss of so many hoplites, cavalry, and men of military age who, they saw, could not be replaced; they saw, too, that the numbers of ships in the docks were inadequate, as was the money in the treasury, and that there were no crews for the ships. So at the moment they had little hope of being able to survive; they thought that their enemies in Sicily, after their great victory, would set sail immediately with their fleet for Piraeus, that their enemies at home would now most certainly redouble their efforts and attack them with all their might by land and sea, and that their own allies would revolt and join in the attack. Nevertheless, with their limited resources, it was decided that they must not give in; they would equip a fleet, getting the timber from wherever they could; they would raise money, and see that their allies, particularly Euboea, remained loyal; and in Athens itself they would take measures of economy and reform, appointing a body of older

44. See Appendix 4.

men to give their advice on the situation, whenever the occasion arose. In fact, like all democracies, now that they were terrified, they were ready to put everything in order. Their decisions were carried out at once, and so the summer came to an end.

2   Next winter the whole of Hellas, after the great disaster in Sicily, turned immediately against Athens. Those who had not been allied with either side thought that, even though they were not asked, they ought not to keep out of the war any longer and should go against the Athenians of their own accord, since the Athenians, in the view of each state, would have gone against them, if they had been successful in Sicily, and at the same time they thought that the war would soon be over and that they would gain credit from taking part in it. And those who were allies of Sparta were all the more eager than before to be freed quickly from all the sufferings they had endured so long. In particular the subjects of Athens were all ready to revolt; indeed they were more ready than able, since they were incapable of taking a dispassionate view of things, and would not admit the possibility that Athens might survive the coming summer. In Sparta all this produced a mood of confidence, and what was even more encouraging was the probability that in the spring they would be joined by their allies from Sicily in great force and now with the additional advantage of the navy which they had had to build. And so, with good reasons for confidence in every direction, the Spartans determined to throw themselves into the war without any reservations, calculating that, when once it was successfully over, they would be free for the future from the kind of danger which might have beset them if Athens had added the resources of Sicily to her own, and that, when the power of Athens had been destroyed, they themselves would be left secure in the leadership of all Hellas.

3   Their king, Agis, therefore set out immediately this winter with a force from Decelea and raised money from the allies for the building of a fleet. Turning towards the Malian Gulf, on the strength of the old quarrel he carried off from the Oetaeans most of their property that could be carried off and made them pay a sum of money. He then compelled the Achaeans of Phthiotis and other subjects of the Thessalians in that area to give him hostages and money, doing this against the will and in spite of the protests

of the Thessalians themselves. He sent the hostages to be kept at Corinth and tried to bring their compatriots into the Spartan League. The Spartans also sent in their requisitions to the cities for the building of 100 ships. Twenty-five were to be built by themselves and twenty-five by the Boeotians; the Phocians and Locrians were to build fifteen between them; fifteen were to come from the Corinthians; ten from the Arcadians, Pellenians, and Sicyonians together; and ten from the Megarians, Troezenians, Epidaurians, and Hermionians together. All other preparations were made also for opening the campaign at the very beginning of spring.

4   The Athenians, too, were busy with the measures which they had planned. In this same winter they procured timber and began ship-building; they fortified Sunium, so as to give security to their cornships in rounding the point; they evacuated the fortified post in Laconia, which they had built on their voyage to Sicily; wherever else they thought that money was being spent unnecessarily, they economized by cutting down expenses; and in particular they kept a close watch on their allies, to guard against revolt.

5   While both sides were in this way as actively engaged in preparing for war as they had been at the beginning, the Euboeans were the first to send representatives to Agis, during this winter, to discuss making a revolt from Athens. Agis welcomed their proposals and summoned from Sparta Alcamenes, the son of Sthenalaïdas, and Melanthus to take command in Euboea. These officers arrived with a force of about 300 freed helots, and Agis began to make arrangements for their crossing over. Meanwhile, however, some Lesbians arrived who also wished to revolt, and, as their claims were supported by the Boeotians, Agis was persuaded to leave Euboea alone for the time being. Instead he proceeded to organize the revolt in Lesbos, giving them Alcamenes, who was to have sailed to Euboea, as governor. The Boeotians promised ten ships and Agis another ten. All this was done without consultation with the government in Sparta, since all the time that Agis was at Decelea with his own army he had the power to send troops wherever he wished, to raise fresh forces, and to levy money. Indeed, it would be true to say that during this period the allies paid much more attention to him than to the government in

Sparta, since he had his army with him and could make himself felt immediately wherever he went.

BEGINNING OF PERSIAN INTERVENTION

While he was dealing with the Lesbians, the Chians and the Erythraeans, who were also ready to revolt, applied not to Agis but to Sparta. With them came also a representative from Tissaphernes: the governor appointed by King Darius, the son of Artaxerxes, over the coastal area. Tissaphernes also supported the idea of Spartan intervention and promised to maintain their army. He had recently been asked by the King to produce the tribute from his province, for which he was in arrears, since he had not been able to raise it from the Hellenic cities because of the Athenians. He thought, therefore, that by damaging the Athenians he would be more likely to get the tribute and would also bring Sparta into alliance with the King, and so, as the King had commanded him, either take alive or put to death Amorges, the bastard son of Pissuthnes, who was leading a revolt in Caria.[45]

6   Thus the Chians and Tissaphernes were acting together for the same object. And about the same time there arrived at Sparta, Calligeitus, the son of Laophon, a Megarian, and Timagoras, the son of Athenagoras, a Cyzicene, both exiles from their own cities, living at the Court of Pharnabazus, the son of Pharnaces. They had been sent by Pharnabazus to try to get a fleet to operate in the Hellespont, so that he might do himself just what Tissaphernes wanted to do – that is to say, procure the tribute by getting the cities in his province to revolt from the Athenians, and gain the credit for bringing the Spartans into alliance with the King.

Each of the two parties – that of Pharnabazus and that of Tissaphernes – was trying to make its own separate arrangements, and so there was much canvassing in Sparta about whether a fleet and army should be sent first to Ionia and Chios or to the Hellespont. The Spartans, however, were very much on the side of the Chians and of Tissaphernes, who were also supported by Alcibiades who was a family friend of Endius, one of the ephors, and on very good terms with him. It was because of this family connection

45. See Appendix 4.

that his house had adopted its Laconic name; 'Alcibiades', in fact, was used as a surname by Endius. Nevertheless the Spartans first sent Phrynis, one of the perioeci, to Chios to find out whether they had as many ships as they said and whether the city was in other respects as strong as it had been made out to be. Phrynis came back with the news that all this was just as they had been told, and they then immediately made an alliance with the Chians and the Erythraeans and voted to send them forty ships, assuming there to be already sixty ships available on the spot, according to what the Chians had said. Their first intention was to send ten of these ships themselves, with their admiral Melanchridas. Later, however, there was an earthquake, and instead of Melanchridas they sent Chalcideus, and instead of the ten ships they only equipped five in Laconia. So the winter ended and the nineteenth year of this war recorded by Thucydides.

7   At the very beginning of the next summer the Chians were asking urgently for the ships to be sent, and were afraid that the Athenians might get to know of what had been arranged; for, of course, the negotiations had been carried on secretly. The Spartans therefore sent three of their own citizens of the officer class to Corinth, so as to have the ships dragged as quickly as possible across the Isthmus from the sea on the other side to the sea on the side of Athens and to order the whole fleet, including the ships which Agis had equipped for Lesbos, to sail for Chios. The total number of ships there from the allied states was thirty-nine.

8   Calligeitus and Timagoras, who were acting for Pharnabazus, took no part in the expedition to Chios, and did not contribute the money (twenty-five talents) which they had brought with them to pay for sending a force out; their intention was to sail later with another expedition on their own. Agis, however, when he saw that the Spartans were set upon going to Chios first, fell in with their views himself. The allies assembled for discussion at Corinth, and it was decided that they should first sail to Chios under the command of Chalcideus, who was equipping the five ships in Laconia, then to Lesbos under Alcamenes, the commander already chosen by Agis, and finally should go on to the Hellespont, where Clearchus, the son of Ramphias, was to be given the command. To begin with, only half the ships were to be brought across the

Isthmus, and these were to set sail at once, so that the Athenians would have their attention divided between these outgoing ships and the other ones that were to be brought across later. This voyage was being made quite openly, in contempt of the weakness of the Athenians, since they had so far shown no sign of having any considerable fleet. So the allies did as they had decided, and immediately brought twenty-one ships across the Isthmus.

9   They were now anxious to start the voyage, but it was the date of the Isthmian festival, and the Corinthians were reluctant to sail with them until they had celebrated it. Agis was quite prepared to make the expedition his own personal responsibility, so that the Corinthians would not be in the position of breaking the Isthmian truce, but the Corinthians would not agree to this and matters were held up. During this time the Athenians began to realize what was happening in Chios and sent Aristocrates, one of their generals, there and confronted the Chians with the evidence. When they denied it, the Athenians ordered them to show their good faith by sending ships to join their fleet, and the Chians sent seven. The reason why these ships were sent was because the general mass of the people at Chios knew nothing of the negotiations, and the oligarchical party were not yet ready to have the people against them until they had something solid to depend upon, and, because of the delay that had taken place, they were no longer expecting the Peloponnesians to arrive.

10   Meanwhile the Isthmian games were held. The Athenians had been officially invited to attend, and did so. They now got a much clearer idea of the whole situation with regard to Chios, and on their return to Athens they immediately took steps to see that the fleet should not leave Cenchriae without their knowledge. After the festival the enemy set sail for Chios with twenty-one ships under the command of Alcamenes. The Athenians sailed up to them at first with an equal number of ships and tried to draw them on into the open sea. The Peloponnesians, however, turned back without following them far, and the Athenians also retired, since they did not regard the seven Chian ships in their number as reliable. Later they manned some other ships, making a total of thirty-seven in all, and, keeping up with the enemy fleet as it went along the coast, drove it into Spiraeum, an uninhabited harbour

in Corinthian territory nearly on the frontiers of Epidaurus. The Peloponnesians lost one ship in the open water, but got the rest together and brought them to anchor. The Athenians then attacked from the sea with their fleet, and also made a landing on the coast. This produced a state of great panic and disorder. The Athenians forced ashore and disabled most of the enemy ships and killed Alcamenes, the commander, with only small loss to themselves.

11   When this action was over, the Athenians left enough ships to blockade the enemy fleet, and with the rest of their own anchored at the small island nearby and made a camp there. They sent to Athens for reinforcements, since the Peloponnesians also had been reinforced: the Corinthians had come to help save the ships on the day after the battle, and the other people in the neighbourhood came soon afterwards. Seeing how difficult it was to maintain a garrison in this desolate place, the Peloponnesians were at a loss what to do and thought first of burning the ships; in the end, however, they decided to haul them ashore and settle down to guard them with their army until they should have the luck to find some good chance of getting away. Agis also, when he heard the news, sent them a regular Spartan officer called Thermon. The Spartans had had the first news of the sailing of the fleet from the Isthmus, since Alcamenes had been instructed by the ephors to send off a horseman as soon as this took place, and their intention was to send out immediately their own five ships under the command of Chalcideus, accompanied by Alcibiades. But now, when they were all set for this operation, the news came of the fleet having taken refuge in Spiraeum, and the Spartans were so discouraged by the fact that their first venture in the Ionian war had turned out a failure, that they gave up the idea of sending the ships from their country and were more inclined to recall some of those that had already set out.

12   Alcibiades saw this, and again used his influence with Endius and the other ephors. He urged them not to shrink from making the voyage and pointed out that they would get to Chios before the Chians heard of the disaster that had happened to the fleet. Once he was on Ionian soil, he said, he would easily persuade the cities to revolt by informing them of the weakness of Athens and of the active policy of Sparta; and they would regard his evidence as

being particularly reliable. To Endius in private he pointed out that it would be a fine thing for him to be the means of organizing the revolt in Ionia and of securing for Sparta the alliance of the King of Persia, instead of letting the credit for this go to Agis. Alcibiades himself was not on good terms with Agis. So he persuaded Endius and the other ephors and, setting out with the five ships and with the Spartan Chalcideus, made the voyage as fast as possible.

13   About this time the sixteen Peloponnesian ships from Sicily, which had been through the war there with Gylippus, were on their way home. Off Leucadia they were caught and given a rough time of it by the twenty-seven Athenian ships under Hippocles, the son of Menippus, who was there to intercept the ships from Sicily. After losing one ship, the rest escaped from the Athenians and sailed in to Corinth.

14   Chalcideus and Alcibiades, in order to keep their movements secret, arrested and took with them all whom they met with on their voyage. They first put in at Corycus, on the mainland, where they let their prisoners go and arranged a meeting between themselves and some of the Chians who were in the plot. The Chians urged them to sail up to the city without giving notice of their arrival, and this was what they did, appearing suddenly before Chios. While the democratic party were in a state of bewilderment and panic, the oligarchs had arranged matters so that the Council should be sitting at the time. Speeches were made by Chalcideus and Alcibiades, who said that many more ships were on their way, but made no mention of the blockade of the fleet in Spiraeum. The Chians, followed by the Erythraeans, then revolted from Athens. After this they sailed to Clazomenae with three ships and brought this city also into the revolt. The Clazomenaeans at once crossed over to the mainland and fortified Polichna, so as to have, if it became necessary, a place to retreat into from the island where they lived. In fact all those who had joined the revolt were now busy in building fortifications and making ready for war.

15 The news of Chios quickly reached Athens. The Athenians considered that they were now very definitely and seriously in danger, and that the rest of their allies, after the greatest city among

them had changed sides, would not be content to remain inactive. So great was their alarm at this moment that they immediately cancelled the penalties attaching to anyone who either made or put to the vote a proposal for using the 1,000 talents which all through the war they had been so eager to avoid laying their hands upon.[46] They now voted in favour of using this money and of manning a large number of ships. They were to send out at once, under the command of Strombichides, the son of Diotimus, the eight ships from the blockading force at Spiraeum which had left the force to go in pursuit of the ships with Chalcideus and, having failed to make contact with them, had returned: these were to be reinforced soon afterwards by twelve more ships, under Thrasicles, also from the blockading squadron. The seven Chian ships taking part with them in the blockade at Spiraeum were recalled; the slaves on board were given their liberty and the free men were imprisoned. They quickly manned and sent off ten fresh ships to blockade the Peloponnesians in replacement of all those that had been withdrawn, and they planned to man thirty others. In fact great energy was shown and everything done for the relief of Chios was done on a big scale.

16   Meanwhile Strombichides came to Samos with his eight ships, and, taking one Samian ship with him, sailed to Teos and warned the inhabitants against making any hostile move. Chalcideus was also sailing to Teos from Chios with twenty-three ships and with the army of the Clazomenaeans and Erythraeans marching along the coast in support. Strombichides heard of this in time, sailed out again from Teos, and when he was out at sea and saw how many the ships from Chios were, fled towards Samos with the enemy in pursuit. At first the people of Teos would not allow the army inside their city, but they did so after the Athenians had taken to flight. The troops took no action at the moment, as they were waiting for Chalcideus to come back from the pursuit; but, as he took time over this, they started on their own to demolish the fortifications which the Athenians had built on the side of the city of Teos facing the mainland. They were joined in this work by a small number of native troops who came up under the command of Stages, an officer of Tissaphernes.

46. See II, 24.

17   Chalcideus and Alcibiades had driven Strombichides into Samos. Then, after arming the crews of the ships from the Peloponnese and leaving them at Chios, they recruited rowers from Chios to take their places and, manning twenty other ships as well, set sail for Miletus to start a revolt there. Alcibiades, who was on good terms with the leading people in Miletus, wanted to bring the city over before the ships from the Peloponnese arrived and so, by organizing revolt in as many cities as possible with the aid of the Chian forces and of Chalcideus, gain all the credit for the Chians and himself and Chalcideus and, as he had promised, for Endius, who had sent the expedition out. So for most of their voyage they escaped observation and started the revolt in Miletus, arriving there a little before Strombichides and Thrasicles, who had just come from Athens with twelve ships and who had joined in the pursuit. The Athenians sailed up close on their heels with nineteen ships and, as the people of Miletus would not receive them, took up their position at Lade, the island off Miletus. Directly after the revolt of Miletus the first alliance between the King of Persia and the Spartans was concluded by Tissaphernes and Chalcideus.[47] It was as follows:

18   'The Spartans and their allies made a treaty of alliance with the King and Tissaphernes on the following terms:

'All the territory and all the cities held now by the King or held in the past by the King's ancestors shall be the King's. As for the money and everything else which has been coming in to the Athenians from their cities, the King and the Spartans and their allies shall co-operate in preventing the Athenians from receiving the money or anything else.

'The war with the Athenians shall be carried on jointly by the King and the Spartans and their allies. It shall not be permitted to bring the war with the Athenians to an end unless both parties are agreed, the King on his side, and the Spartans and their allies on their side. Any people who revolt from the King shall be regarded as enemies by the Spartans and their allies; and any people who revolt from the Spartans and their allies shall, in the same way, be regarded as enemies to the King.'

47. See Appendix 4.

19   This was the treaty of alliance. Directly afterwards the Chians manned ten more ships and sailed to Anaia, wishing to get news of those in Miletus, and at the same time to organize revolt in the cities. However, they received a message from Chalcideus telling them to sail back again and saying that Amorges was coming up with an army by land. So they sailed to the temple of Zeus and came in sight of sixteen ships sailing up under the command of Diomedon, who had started from Athens even later than Thrasicles. When they saw them, the Chians took to flight, one of their ships making for Ephesus and the rest for Teos. The Athenians captured four ships empty, the crews having managed to get to land. The rest took refuge in the city of Teos. The Athenians then sailed away to Samos, and the Chians, acting in conjunction with their land forces, put to sea with their remaining ships and brought first Lebedus and then Erae into the revolt. After this both fleet and army returned home.

20   At about this same time the twenty Peloponnesian ships in Spiraeum which, as will be remembered, had been chased in there and were being blockaded by an equal number of Athenian ships suddenly broke out, defeated the Athenians, capturing four of their ships, and sailed back to Cenchriae, where they got ready again for the voyage to Chios and Ionia. Here they were joined by Astyochus as admiral, who came to them from Sparta and was now given the supreme command at sea.

After the land forces had withdrawn from Teos, Tissaphernes came there himself with an army. He pulled down whatever was left of the fortifications at Teos and then went away. Not long after his departure Diomedon arrived with ten Athenian ships and made an agreement with the Teians by which they should receive the Athenians as they had received the enemy. He then sailed along the coast to Erae and, after failing to take the place by assault, sailed back again.

21   At about this time also there took place the rising of the people against the ruling classes in Samos. This was done in co-operation with some Athenians who were there with three ships. The people of Samos put to death about 200 in all of the most prominent people in the governing class, exiled 400 more, and took their land and houses for themselves. After this the Athenians passed a

decree giving them their independence, regarding them as being now quite reliable, and they took over the government of the city for the future. The landowners were entirely excluded from the government and no intermarriage was any longer permitted between them and the people.

22   After this, in the same summer the Chians, who continued to show the same energy in action as at first, who were in force enough even without the Peloponnesians to bring the cities into the revolt, and who had the additional reason of wanting to have as many as possible to share their own danger, set out on their own with thirteen ships for Lesbos. The instructions from Sparta had been to go next to Lesbos, and from there to the Hellespont. At the same time the army, composed of the Peloponnesians who were there and the allies from that area, moved along the coast towards Clazomenae and Cumae. The army was under the command of Eualas, a regular Spartan officer. The fleet, commanded by Diniadas, a Spartan not of the regular officer class, sailed first to Methymna and brought it into the revolt. They left four ships there, and went on with the rest and brought in Mitylene also.

23   Now the Spartan admiral Astyochus set out according to plan with four ships from Cenchriae and arrived at Chios. Three days after his arrival the Athenian fleet of twenty-five ships, under the command of Diomedon and Leon, who had come from Athens later with a reinforcement of ten ships, sailed to Lesbos. On the same day, late in the evening. Astyochus put to sea and, taking one Chian ship with him, sailed to Lesbos to give what help he could. He reached Pyrrha, and on the next day went on from there to Eresus, where he was informed that Mytilene had been taken by the Athenians with no trouble at all. Sailing up, as they had done, unexpectedly, they had put in to the harbour, defeated the Chian ships, made a landing, and, driving back all opposition, had seized the city. Astyochus received this news from the Eresians and from the Chian ships which had been left with Eubulus at Methymna and had taken to flight after the capture of Mytilene. One of these ships was captured by the Athenians, but three of them fell in with Astyochus, who, instead of going on to Mytilene as he had intended, organized the revolt of Eresus and armed the people there. He then sent the hoplites from his own ships by land along the

coast to Antissa and Methymna, under the command of Eteonicus, while he himself sailed along with them in his own ships and the three Chian ships, hoping that when the Methymnians saw them they would gain confidence and continue in a state of revolt. Since, however, everything in Lesbos went against him, he took his own troops on board and sailed back to Chios. The troops also which were on the ships and were to have gone to the Hellespont were sent back to their various cities. After this six of the allied Peloponnesian ships at Cenchriae came out and joined them at Chios. The Athenians, after restoring the situation in Lesbos, sailed from there to Polichna on the mainland, which was being fortified by the Clazomenaeans. They captured the place and took the people back to their city on the island, except for those who had been responsible for the revolt, who withdrew to Daphnus. So Clazomenae became Athenian again.

24   In the same summer the Athenians who were at Lade, blockading Miletus with twenty ships, made a landing in Milesian territory at Panormus and killed the Spartan general Chalcideus, who had come out to meet them with a few men. Three days later they crossed over and put up a trophy, but the Milesians pulled it down again, as it had not been set up while the Athenians were masters of the field.

Now also Leon and Diomedon with the Athenian fleet from Lesbos were carrying on the war from their ships against the Chians. Their bases for these operations were the islands off Chios, called the Oenussae, the fortresses of Sidussa and Pteleum, which they held in the territory of Erthrae, and Lesbos itself. They had with them hoplites who had been called up from the regular lists and been compelled to serve as marines. Landings were made at Cardamyle and at Bolissus, and the Athenians defeated in battle the Chians who came against them, inflicting heavy casualties and laying waste the country in that area. They defeated them again in another battle at Phanae and in a third battle at Leuconium. After this the Chians no longer came out to fight, and the Athenians ravaged the country, which was extremely well stocked and had had no damage done to it ever since the time of the Persian wars. Indeed, after the Spartans, the Chians are the only people I know of who have kept their heads in prosperity and who, as their city increased in power, increased also their own measures for its security. One may think that this revolt was an example of over-confidence, but they never ventured upon it until they had many good allies ready to share the risk with them and until they saw that, after the disaster in Sicily, not even the Athenians themselves were any longer pretending that their affairs were not in a really desperate state. And if, incalculable as is the life of man, they made a mistake, there were many others who thought, like them, that Athens was on the point of collapse, and who came also to realize their error. Now, cut off from the sea and ravaged by land, there were some among them who aimed at bringing the city over to the Athenians. The authorities were aware of this, but took no action themselves. Instead they brought in the admiral Astyochus from Erythrae with four ships which were with him, and consid-ered how they could put a stop to the conspiracy with the least possible disturbance, either by taking hostages or by some other method.

25   While this was the state of affairs at Chios, there came out from Athens at the end of this same summer a force of 1,000 Athenian hoplites, 1,500 Argives (500 of which were light troops, but had been given heavy armour by the Athenians) and 1,000 allied hop-lites. This force sailed in forty-eight ships, some of which were transports, and was commanded by Phrynichus, Onomacles, and Scironides. They first sailed into Samos and then crossed over to Miletus and made their camp there. The Milesians came out with 800 hoplites of their own, the Peloponnesians who had come with Chalcideus and some mercenary troops in the pay of Tissaphernes, who was present himself with his cavalry, and joined battle with the Athenians and their allies. The Argives, on the wing which they held, rushed forward in advance of the rest in the confident belief that they had only Ionians to deal with, who would not stand up to them. Advancing in some disorder, they were defeated by the Milesians and lost nearly 300 men. On the other hand, the Athen-ians first defeated the Peloponnesians, then drove back the native troops and the general mass of the army, without making con-tact with the Milesians, who, after they had routed the Argives, saw the rest of their army defeated and fell back inside their city. So the Athenians, with no further opposition, halted under the

very walls of Miletus. In this battle the Ionians on both sides defeated the Dorians. The Athenians conquered the Peloponnesians who were opposed to them; and the Milesians conquered the Argives. After putting up a trophy, the Athenians prepared to build a blockading wall round the place, which stands on an isthmus. They believed that if they could gain Miletus the other places would come over to them without any difficulty.

26   Meanwhile, however, when it was already late in the evening, they received the news that the fifty-five ships from the Peloponnese and from Sicily might be expected at any moment. Twenty-two of these ships, twenty from Syracuse and two from Selinus, had come from the Sicilians, who had been urged on principally by the Syracusan Hermocrates to take their share in finishing off what was left of the power of Athens. The ships which were being equipped in the Peloponnese were also ready by this time, and both fleets had been given to the Spartan Therimenes to take to the admiral Astyochus. They now put in first to Leros, the island before Miletus; then, hearing that the Athenians were in front of the town, they sailed on from there into the Gulf of Iasus in order to find out what the position at Miletus was. They got the news of the battle from Alcibiades, who had come on horseback to Teichiussa in Milesian territory, which was the place on the gulf where they had put in for the night. Alcibiades had been present at the battle himself, fighting with the Milesians and Tissaphernes, and his advice to them was to come to the help of Miletus as quickly as possible and prevent it being walled in, unless they wanted to lose Ionia and the whole campaign. They decided therefore to go to the relief of Miletus as soon as it was dawn.

27   Phrynichus, the Athenian commander, had received accurate information from Leros about the enemy fleet and, though his colleagues were in favour of staying where they were and fighting a decisive battle at sea, he said that he personally would not do so and he would, to the best of his ability, prevent them or anyone else from doing so either. He added that whenever afterwards they might have an opportunity to fight, knowing exactly what the numbers of the enemy were and what they had to put against him, with all their preparations made fully and in their own time, he would never risk battle against reason through fear of being told

it was disgraceful not to do so. There was nothing disgraceful in the idea of an Athenian fleet withdrawing on the right occasion; what would be much more disgraceful in every way would be to to be defeated, and for Athens to fall not only into disgrace but into extreme danger. After the disasters that had happened to her she was scarcely in the position, unless it were absolutely necessary, to take the offensive at all, even with a really strong force; certainly there could be no justification for her to run into danger of her own choice and when there was no question of compulsion. He told them to take on board as quickly as possible the wounded and the troops and the equipment they had brought with them, to leave behind everything that they had taken from the enemy's country, so as to lighten the ships, to sail to Samos, and, when once all their ships were brought together there, to use that as a base for offensive action at the right time. These were his views, and on these views he acted. The intelligence of his decision was recognized even more afterwards than at the time, and it was not on this occasion alone that Phrynichus showed intelligence, but in every other position of trust which he occupied. So, on that very evening the Athenians moved their forces from Miletus without reaping the fruit of their victory, and the Argives, furious at having been defeated, hurriedly set sail from Samos and went home.

28   At dawn the Peloponnesians put out from Teichiussa and came into Miletus after the Athenians had gone. They stayed there for one day, and on the next took with them the Chian ships which had originally been driven back into the harbour with Chalcideus and sailed away to pick up the equipment which they had unloaded at Teichiussa. When they arrived there, Tissaphernes came up with his army and persuaded them to sail to Iasus, which was held by his enemy Amorges. So they made a sudden attack on Iasus and took it, the inhabitants never imagining that the ships were not Athenian. In this action the Syracusans particularly distinguished themselves. Amorges, the bastard son of Pissuthnes, who was in revolt from the King, was captured alive by the Peloponnesians and handed over to Tissaphernes for him to take to the King, if he wanted to, according to his instructions. Iasus was sacked, and the army took a great deal out of it, since the place was wealthy from of old. They took over the mercenary troops who had been serving with Amorges and included them in their own forces, without doing them any harm, since most of them came from the Peloponnese; they handed over the town to Tissaphernes together with all the prisoners, both free men and slaves, at the agreed price of one Doric stater a head, and then they returned to Miletus. Pedaritus, the son of Leon, had been sent out from Sparta to take the command at Chios, and they arranged for him to go by land as far as Erythrae, taking with him the mercenaries who had been with Amorges. At Miletus they made Philip governor there. And so the summer came to an end.

29   Next winter when Tissaphernes had seen to the garrisoning of Iasus he went on to Miletus, and, as he had promised at Sparta, gave a month's pay to all the ships at the rate of an Attic drachma a day for each man. He proposed paying only three obols for the future, until he had consulted the King, but would, he said, pay the full drachma if that was the King's wish. Hermocrates, the Syracusan commander, protested against this; no stand was made about the pay by Therimenes, who was not an admiral, and was merely sailing with the fleet to hand it over to Astyochus. An agreement was reached by which an extra sum equal to five ships' pay was to be given, in addition to the three obols a day for each man. For fifty-five ships Tissaphernes was paying thirty talents a month, and to the rest, above that number, the payment was in the same proportion.

30   The same winter the Athenians at Samos, who had now been joined by thirty-five more ships from home under Charminus and Strombichides and Euctemon, brought together all their ships from Chios and elsewhere with a view to drawing lots among the commanders and dividing the force into a naval expedition to blockade Miletus and a combined naval and military expedition to operate against Chios. This plan was carried out. Strombichides, Onomacles, and Euctemon sailed against Chios, which fell to their lot, with thirty ships, taking with them in transports some of the 1,000 hoplites who had been at Miletus; the other commanders, with seventy-four ships, stayed at Samos in control of the sea and used their naval power against Miletus.

31   Astyochus, it will be remembered, was at Chios collecting hostages because of the conspiracy. He stopped doing this when he

heard that the ships with Therimenes had arrived and that matters
with regard to the alliance were going better, and put out to sea
with ten Peloponnesian and ten Chian ships. After making an
unsuccessful attack on Pteleum, he sailed along the coast to Clazomenae and ordered the pro-Athenian party there to move inland
to Daphnus and to join forces with the Peloponnesians. Tamos
also, the King of Persia's officer in Ionia, issued orders to the same
effect and at the same time. As the people of Clazomenae refused
to obey, he made an attack on their city, which was unwalled, and
then, after the attack had failed, sailed away. Strong winds drove
him himself into Phocaea and Cumae, and the rest of his ships put
in at the islands near Clazomenae – Marthussa, Pele, and Drymus-
sa. They stayed there eight days because of the winds, plundering
and using up the property of the Clazomenaeans that had been
stored there; then, putting what was left on board their ships,
they sailed away to Phocaea and Cumae to join Astyochus.

32   While he was there representatives from the Lesbians arrived,
wanting to start another revolt. Their arguments convinced
Astyochus, but the Corinthians and the other allies, because of their
previous failure, showed no enthusiasm for the idea. So he put to
sea and sailed for Chios. The ships ran into a storm, but all arrived
there finally from different directions. After this Pedaritus, who,
as mentioned above, was coming along the coast by land from
Miletus, reached Erythrae and from there crossed over with his
army to Chios. He also had under his command in Chios about
500 men with their arms who had been left there from the five
ships by Chalcideus. When some Lesbians came and expressed their
readiness to revolt, Astyochus put the matter up to Pedaritus and
the Chians and said that they ought to provide naval support and
bring about the revolt of Lesbos, and so either gain more allies for
themselves or at any rate, even if they failed, do harm to the Athenians. They would not agree, however, and Pedaritus refused to let
him have the Chian ships.

33   Astyochus then took five of the Corinthian ships, one from
Megara, one from Hermione, and the ships from Sparta with
which he had arrived, and sailed for Miletus to take up his command as admiral. He told the Chians in no uncertain terms that if
they ever wanted his help, he would most certainly not give them

any. He anchored off Corycus in the territory of Erythrae and
spent the night there. The Athenians from Samos who were sailing with their army against Chios were also there at anchor at
the other side of a hill which separated the two forces, so that
neither saw the other. At night, however, a letter arrived from
Pedaritus to say that some Erythraean prisoners had arrived from
Samos, who had been tried on the understanding that they would
betray Erythrae to the Athenians. Astyochus therefore sailed
back at once to Erythrae, and so just escaped falling in with the
Athenians. Pedaritus also sailed across to meet him. They held an
inquiry into the supposed case of treachery, and after discovering
that the whole thing was a story made up by the men so as to get
themselves released from Samos, they dropped the charge against
them and sailed away, Pedaritus going to Chios and Astyochus
resuming his voyage to Miletus.

34   Meanwhile the Athenian force that was sailing round from
Corycus met with three Chian warships off Arginus and went after
them as soon as they were sighted. A great storm came on, and the
Chian ships managed to get to safety in the harbour, but the three
Athenian ships which were farthest in front were wrecked and
driven ashore near the city of Chios, the crews being either killed
or captured. The other ships got to safety in the harbour under
Mount Mimas called Phoenicus. From here they went on later
and put into Lesbos, where they prepared for the building of
the fortifications.

35   In the same winter the Spartan Hippocrates sailed from the
Peloponnese with ten Thurian ships commanded by Dorieus, the
son of Diagoras, and two other commanders, one Spartan ship and
one Syracusan ship. He arrived at Cnidus, where a revolt had
already been organized by Tissaphernes. When it was known at
Miletus that they had arrived, they were instructed to employ
half their fleet in guarding Cnidus and to keep the rest at sea off
Triopium, a headland of Cnidus and sacred to Apollo, and seize all
the merchant ships putting in there on the voyage from Egypt.
Hearing of this, the Athenians sailed out from Samos and captured the six ships keeping a look-out at Triopium, though the
crews escaped. Afterwards they sailed into Cnidus, made an assault
on the city, which was unwalled, and nearly took it. Next day they

made another attack, but this time did less damage, as the inhabitants had put up better defences during the night and had been joined by the crews who had escaped from the ships at Triopium. So the Athenians withdrew and, after laying waste the country of the Cnidians, sailed back to Samos.

36 It was about this time that Astyochus came to the fleet at Miletus. The Peloponnesians still had plenty of everything in their camp. Pay was adequate, and the soldiers still had left the large sums of money looted from Iasus. The Milesians, too, showed themselves ready and willing to support the war. The Peloponnesians, however, were still not satisfied with the first agreement with Tissaphernes, made by Chalcideus. They thought that Tissaphernes was getting more from it than they were, and, while Therimenes was still there, they made another agreement, which was as follows:[48]

37 'An agreement made between the Spartans and the allies with King Darius and the sons of the King and with Tissaphernes for a treaty of friendship on the following terms:

'Neither the Spartans nor the allies of the Spartans shall make war against or do any damage to the country or the cities which now belong to King Darius or did belong to his father or to his ancestors.

'No tribute shall be taken from these cities either by the Spartans or by the allies of the Spartans.

'Neither King Darius nor any of the subjects of the King shall make war against or do any damage to the Spartans or to the allies. If the Spartans or their allies should need help from the King, or if the King should need help from the Spartans or their allies, it shall be right and proper to take whatever steps are decided upon between the two parties. Both parties shall make war jointly against the Athenians and their allies; and if peace is made, both parties shall make peace jointly.

'All troops that are in the King's country, by the King's request, shall have their expenses paid by the King.

'If any of the states who have made this agreement with the

48. See Appendix 4.

King shall attack the King's country, the others shall take all practicable measures to stop them and to defend the King. If anyone
in the King's country or in the countries under the King's control
shall attack the country of the Spartans or their allies, the King
shall take all practicable measures to stop this and to defend the
Spartans and their allies.'

38   After this agreement Therimenes handed over the fleet to Astyochus. He sailed away himself in a small boat and was lost at sea.

The Athenians had now crossed with their forces from Lesbos to
Chios and, being in control both of the land and the sea, began to
fortify Delphinium, a position which could be easily defended from
the land, and which also had harbours and was not far from the
city of Chios. As for the Chians, they were disheartened by the
result of many battles before this, and were also far from being
united among themselves. Now that the party of Tydeus, the son
of Ion, had been put to death by Pedaritus on a charge of being
pro-Athenian, the rest of the city was held down forcibly by an
oligarchy, and the people were suspicious of one another and
apathetic. Consequently they did not think that either they themselves or the mercenaries of Pedaritus were capable of standing up
to the Athenians. However, they sent to Miletus and asked Astyochus to help them. This he refused to do, and Pedaritus sent to
Sparta to complain of his conduct.

39   While this was the Athenian position at Chios, their ships from
Samos were constantly sailing out against the enemy fleet in
Miletus. However, as the enemy would not come out to meet
them, they went back again to Samos, and took no further action.

In the same winter the twenty-seven ships which had been
equipped by the Spartans for Pharnabazus after the negotiations
carried out by the Megarian Calligeitus and the Cyzicene
Timagoras put to sea from the Peloponnese and set sail for
Ionia at about the time of the solstice. They were commanded
by Antisthenes, a Spartan of the officer class. With him the Spartans also sent out eleven other regular officers to act as advisers to
Astyochus. One of these was Lichas, the son of Arcesilaus. Their
instructions were that, on reaching Miletus, they should be
jointly responsible for managing affairs in general in the most

efficient way; that, if they thought it wise, they were to send out a fleet consisting of the ships they had with them or of a greater or smaller number of ships to the Hellespont to Pharnabazus; and, if the eleven agreed, they were to dismiss Astyochus from his naval command and appoint Antisthenes in place of him. This was because Astyochus was considered suspect as a result of the letters sent by Pedaritus. They sailed from Malea across the open sea and, putting in at Melos, met with ten Athenian ships, three of which they captured empty and burned. After this, since they were afraid that the Athenian ships which had escaped from Melos would give the news (as, in fact, they did) of their approach to the Athenians in Samos, they sailed to Crete, and so, having taken the precaution of making their voyage longer, put in at Caunus in Asia. Here they considered themselves safe, and from here they sent a message to the fleet at Miletus asking for a convoy along the coast.

40   During this time the Chians and Pedaritus still went on sending messengers to Astyochus, in spite of his reluctance to move. They begged him to come with his whole fleet to help them, besieged as they were, and not to allow the greatest of the allied cities in Ionia to be cut off from the sea and to be ravaged and laid waste by land. There were many slaves in Chios – more, in fact, than in any other city except Sparta; they were also, because of their number, punished particularly severely when they did wrong; and now, when it appeared that the Athenian army was firmly established behind fortifications, most of them immediately deserted and went over to the Athenians, and, because of their knowledge of the country, it was these who did the most harm. The Chians therefore said that Astyochus must help them, while there was still some possibility of stopping the Athenians, while Delphinium was still in process of being fortified and the fortifications were not yet complete, and while the enemy were still engaged in constructing a higher wall to cover their camp and their fleet. Although Astyochus, after the threats he had made, had not intended to help them, he now prepared to do so, since he saw that the allies also were anxious that this should be done.

41   Meantime news came from Caunus of the arrival of the twenty-seven ships and the commissioners from Sparta. To provide a convoy for such a fleet, so as to give his own side greater control of the

the sea, and to bring in safely the Spartans who had come to inquire into his conduct seemed to Astyochus matters which must
be put before everything else, and so he at once abandoned the
idea of going to Chios and set sail for Caunus. On his voyage along
the coast he landed at the Meropid Cos. The city was unfortified
and had collapsed in an earthquake which was certainly the greatest one that can be remembered. He sacked the city, the inhabitants
of which had fled to the mountains, over-ran the country, and
made off with everything in it except for the free men, whom he
let go. From Cos he came to Cnidus by night, but was forced by
the advice of the Cnidians to go straight on just as he was, without
disembarking the sailors, against the twenty Athenian ships under
the command of Charminus, one of the commanders at Samos,
who was on the watch for the approach of those same twenty-
seven ships from the Peloponnese which Astyochus was going to
join. The Athenians at Samos had heard from Melos that they were
coming, and Charminus was on the look-out for them off Syme,
Chalce, Rhodes, and Lycia, having heard already that they were at
Caunus.

42   Astyochus therefore sailed to Syme just as he was, before his
arrival was known of, in the hope of catching these ships somewhere in the open sea. As the result of rain and bad visibility, his
ships lost contact with each other and got into disorder in the darkness. When it was dawn his fleet was scattered, and what was now
visible to the Athenians was only his left wing, while the rest of his
ships were still coming up, each on its own, round the island.
Charminus and the Athenians with less than their whole force of
twenty ships quickly put out against the enemy, in the belief that
the ships they saw were the ones from Caunus for which they
were on the look-out. Going into action, they immediately sank
three ships, disabled some others, and were generally having the
better of things in the engagement until they were surprised by
the appearance of the main body of the enemy fleet and found
themselves surrounded on all sides. They then took to flight and,
after losing six ships, escaped with the rest to the island of Teut-
lussa, and from there to Halicarnassus. After this the Peloponnesians put in to Cnidus, where they were joined by the twenty-
seven ships from Caunus. They then sailed out with their whole

fleet, put up a trophy at Syme, and came back again to their anchorage at Cnidus.

43   The Athenians came out with all their ships from Samos when they heard of the naval engagement and sailed to Syme. They did not offer battle to the fleet in Cnidus, nor did that fleet offer battle to them. They then picked up the naval equipment left at Syme and, touching at Lorymi on the mainland, sailed back to Samos.

All the Peloponnesian ships were now together at Cnidus. Necessary repairs were carried out and discussions were opened between the eleven Spartan commissioners and Tissaphernes, who was there to meet them, on any points in the previous arrangements which they found unsatisfactory and on the question of future policy in carrying on the war most efficiently and most profitably both for them and for him. Lichas in particular took a serious view of the existing situation and said that neither of the treaties could be regarded as valid, neither that of Chalcideus nor that of Therimenes; it was monstrous if the King were now going to lay claim to all the country controlled by himself or his ancestors in the past; that would involve putting back into slavery all the islands, Thessaly, Locris, and everything up to Boeotia, and would mean that Sparta was offering to the Hellenes not liberation but Persian domination. He therefore proposed that another and a better treaty should be made; the existing ones were entirely unacceptable and they did not want to receive his pay on such conditions. At this Tissaphernes was furious and went away in a rage without having settled anything.

44   Appeals for intervention had come to the Peloponnesians from some of the leading people in Rhodes, and they now decided to sail there, hoping to bring over to their side an island which had considerable importance both because of its large seafaring population and because of its land forces; also they thought that they would be able to pay the expenses of their fleet from the resources of their own alliance, without asking for money from Tissaphernes. So they set sail from Cnidus at once in this same winter and put in first at Camirus in Rhodian territory with ninety-four ships. The mass of the inhabitants, who knew nothing of the negotiations, were terrified and ran away, especially as the city was unfortified. Later, however, the Spartans got them into an assembly together

with the people of the two cities of Lindus and Ialysus and persuaded the Rhodians to revolt from Athens. So Rhodes went over to the Peloponnesians.

About this time the Athenians, who had heard what was happening, sailed with their fleet from Samos to Rhodes with the intention of getting there before the Peloponnesians. They came into sight out at sea, but as they had arrived a little too late, they sailed away for the time being to Chalce, and from there to Samos. Later they carried on the war against Rhodes by making attacks from their bases in Chalce and in Cos. The Peloponnesians raised a sum of thirty-two talents from the Rhodians. Otherwise they remained inactive for eighty days and dragged their ships up on shore.

THE OLIGARCHIC COUP

45 At this time, and even earlier, before they moved to Rhodes, the following intrigues were going on. After the death of Chalcideus and the battle at Miletus, Alcibiades became suspect to the Peloponnesians, and a letter was sent by them from Sparta to Astyochus with orders to put him to death. He was a personal enemy of Agis and was generally considered unreliable. In his alarm Alcibiades first sought refuge with Tissaphernes and then used his influence with him to do all the harm he possibly could to the cause of the Peloponnesians. He became his adviser in everything, and it was he who cut down the rate of pay so that, instead of an Attic drachma, only three obols a day were offered, and even that not regularly. He told Tissaphernes to say to the Peloponnesians that the Athenians had had longer experience than they had in running a navy and only gave their own men three obols a day, not so much because they could not afford more, as in order to prevent their sailors getting out of hand through having too much and either impairing their fitness by spending money on the kind of things which lead to bad health or deserting their ships, as they might do, if they were not leaving behind arrears of pay as a security for their proper conduct. He also advised him to bribe the captains of triremes and the commanders from the various

states so as to secure their agreement, except for the Syracusans. And Hermocrates was the only one of them who opposed him on behalf of the whole allied force. As for the cities which came to ask for money, he sent them about their business and, refusing their requests himself in the name of Tissaphernes, said that, so far as the Chians were concerned, they were the richest people in Hellas and it was sheer effrontery on their part, when in any case they were being preserved by forces from outside, to suggest that other people should risk both their lives and their money in liberating them; as for the other cities, he said that before they had revolted they had had to pay money to Athens, and they were quite in the wrong if they were now unwilling to contribute as much or even more for their own defence. He pointed out, too, that at the moment Tissaphernes was carrying on the war at his private expense and that it was therefore reasonable for him to be economical, but as soon as money was sent down to him from the King he would give them their pay in full and would give all reasonable assistance to the cities.

46   To Tissaphernes Alcibiades also gave the advice not to be in too much of a hurry to end the war and not to consent to bring in the Phoenician fleet which he was equipping or to take more Hellenes into his pay; the result of this would be to give the control of both land and sea to one Power, whereas it was better to have the two parties each in possession of its own separate sphere of influence, so that if the King had trouble with one of them, he would always be able to call in the other against it. If, on the other hand, one State were to gain control of both the land and the sea, the King would be at a loss where to find allies to help to undermine its supremacy, unless he was prepared in the end to come forward himself and, at the cost of great expense and great danger, fight it out to the finish. It was more economical to let the Hellenes wear each other out among themselves while the King incurred only a fraction of the expense and none of the risk. Alcibiades said also that he would find that the Athenians were the better people with whom to share power: they were not so ambitious to acquire an empire on land, and both their policy and their actions in the war fitted in best with the King's interests, since an alliance with the Athenians would be on the basis of conquering the sea

for Athens and conquering for the King those Hellenes who lived
in the King's territory, whereas the Spartans, on the other hand,
had come as liberators and it was hardly likely that, after liberating
Hellenes from their fellow Hellenes, they would not also free them
from subjugation to foreigners, unless the King could get rid of
them first. Alcibiades therefore recommended him first to
wear both sides out and then, after weakening the power of Athens
as much as possible, to get the Peloponnesians out of the country
at once. Tissaphernes on the whole agreed with this policy, or
appears to have done so, judging from his actions. He took Alcibiades into his confidence on the strength of his having given such
good advice on these subjects; he was niggardly about providing
the pay for the Peloponnesians and he opposed the idea of their
fighting a battle at sea; instead he pretended that the Phoenician
ships were coming and that they could then fight with all the
advantages on their side. Thus he did them a lot of harm and
caused a decline in the morale and efficiency of their navy, which
had been very great. Altogether, in a manner too obvious to be
mistaken, he showed an unreadiness to help them in the war.

47   Alcibiades, when he was with Tissaphernes and the King, gave
them this advice not only because he thought it was the best he
could offer, but also because he was looking out for a way to be
recalled to his own country. He knew that, if he did not destroy
it, a time would come when he might persuade the Athenians to
call him back from exile, and he thought that his best chance of
persuading them would be if it appeared that he was on friendly
terms with Tissaphernes. And this, in fact, was what did happen.
When the Athenian forces at Samos realized that he had great
influence with Tissaphernes, they took action largely of their own
accord, but also because of the messages sent by Alcibiades to the
leading men among them, in which he asked them to make his
views known to the best people in the army and to say that, if
there were an oligarchy instead of that corrupt democracy which
had exiled him, he was ready to return to his country and take his
part with his countrymen, and make Tissaphernes their friend.
Thus the captains of the Athenian ships in Samos and the leading
men in the army set themselves to the task of overthrowing the
democracy.

48   The agitation began in the forces at Samos, and from there spread later to Athens. Various people crossed over from Samos and discussed matters with Alcibiades, who held out hopes that he could secure the friendship first of Tissaphernes and afterwards of the King, so long as there was no democracy, the abolition of which would give the King more confidence in them. The members of the most powerful class of Athenians, who were also suffering most from the war, now began to entertain great hopes on their own account of seizing power for themselves and of coming out victorious in the war. When they came back to Samos they got hold of the right people and formed their own party from them, and said openly to the main body of the forces that the King would be their friend and would provide them with money if Alcibiades were recalled and the democracy abolished. The general opinion of the camp may have been upset for the moment by these intrigues, but it calmed down owing to the agreeable prospect of getting pay from the King.

After they had made their views clear to the troops in general, those who were working for an oligarchy held meetings among themselves and with most of their party and reconsidered what Alcibiades had to offer. The general opinion was that they could have confidence in his plans and that they could easily be carried out; but Phrynichus, who was still general, entirely disagreed with this. He believed, quite correctly, that oligarchy and democracy were all one to Alcibiades and that what he was really after was to get recalled by his friends and come back to Athens as a result of a change in the existing constitution; whereas for the Athenians themselves the one thing to be guarded against was just this – internal revolution. And so far as the King was concerned, now that the Peloponnesians were in control of important cities in his empire and were a match for Athens on the sea, it was not a likely or an easy thing for him to involve himself in difficulties by joining in with the Athenians, whom he did not trust, when he had the opportunity of making friends with the Peloponnesians, from whom he had never suffered any harm. As for the states in the Athenian alliance, who, no doubt, were promised oligarchical governments simply because Athens herself was no longer to be a democracy, Phrynichus said that he was perfectly sure that this prospect would not have the effect either of winning over the cities now in revolt or of making the others any more reliable; they were more interested in being free under whatever kind of government they happened to have than in being slaves, whether under an oligarchy or a democracy; besides, they saw no reason to suppose that they would be any better off under the so-called upper classes than under the democracy, considering that when the democracy had committed crimes it had been at the instigation, under the guidance, and, usually, for the profit of these upper classes themselves. With these classes in control, people could be put to death by violence and without a trial, whereas the democracy offered security to the ordinary man and kept the upper classes in their place. He was quite sure, he said, that this was what the cities had learned from their own experience, and this was what they thought. For his own part, therefore, he was entirely opposed to the ideas of Alcibiades and the intrigues now going on.

49   However, the members of the party who were present at the meeting did not alter their ideas. They adopted the programme put before them and prepared to send Pisander and others as their representatives to Athens, where they were to negotiate for the recall of Alcibiades and for getting rid of the democracy, and so make Tissaphernes the friend of the Athenians.

50   Phrynichus now saw that a proposal would be made to recall Alcibiades and that the Athenians would agree to do so. Considering the way he had opposed this in his speech, he was afraid that if Alcibiades did get back he would make him suffer for having tried to prevent it. He therefore adopted the following scheme. He sent a secret message to Astyochus, the Spartan admiral, who at that time was still in the neighbourhood of Miletus, and told him that Alcibiades was betraying the Spartan interest by making Tissaphernes the friend of the Athenians. His letter also contained a clear account of all other matters, and there was a plea that his own action, in plotting against a personal enemy even at the cost of his country's interests, should be understood. Astyochus, however, never thought of taking action against Alcibiades, who, in fact, no longer came within his reach as he had done. Instead he went up from the coast to see him and Tissaphernes at Magnesia, told them the contents of the letter from Samos, and turned informer

himself. It was said, indeed, that in order to make money for himself he had sold his services to Tissaphernes, offering to share his information both on this subject and on all others; and this was why he dealt so weakly with the question of the pay not being produced in full.

Alcibiades at once sent a letter to the authorities in Samos accusing Phrynichus for what he had done and asking that he should be put to death. Phrynichus was now thoroughly disturbed, and found himself in very great danger indeed as a result of the information laid against him. He wrote again to Astyochus, protesting against his failure to keep secret the contents of his first letter, and said that he was now prepared to give them the chance of destroying the whole Athenian force in Samos; he wrote down detailed instructions as to how he should act, Samos being unfortified, and declared that, since his life was in danger for their sakes, no one could now blame him for doing this or anything else to escape being destroyed by his greatest enemies.

This information also was passed on by Astyochus to Alcibiades. 51 Phrynicus, however, was told in time that Astyochus was betraying his confidence and that a letter on the subject could be expected any moment from Alcibiades. He therefore got in first with the news and informed the army that, Samos being unfortified as it was and the whole fleet not being at anchor in the harbour, the enemy was going to make an attack on the camp; he said that he was quite sure of this and that they ought to fortify Samos as quickly as possible and generally be on the alert. As he was in command himself, he had the power to see that all this was done. The Athenians set to work at the fortifications and so, as a result of all this, Samos, which would have been fortified in any case, was fortified all the sooner. Not long afterwards the letter arrived from Alcibiades saying that the army was betrayed by Phrynichus and that the enemy were going to attack. However, people did not think that Alcibiades' evidence could be trusted; instead it was assumed that he knew what the enemy's plans were and, out of personal ill-feeling, had tried to fasten on Phrynichus the charge of being concerned in them too. His message, therefore, so far from doing Phrynichus any harm, merely confirmed what he had said already.

52   After this Alcibiades went on with his attempts to persuade Tissaphernes to become the friend of the Athenians. Tissaphernes himself was afraid of the Peloponnesians because they had more ships on the spot than the Athenians; on the other hand, he was still willing to be won over, if he could see his way to it, particularly now that he was aware of the disagreement expressed by the Peloponnesians at Cnidus about the treaty of Therimenes. The quarrel about this had taken place already, since at this time the Peloponnesians were in Rhodes. On this subject the argument used earlier by Alcibiades, about the Peloponnesians liberating all the cities, had been proved right by the statement made by Lichas to the effect that it was intolerable for any agreement to stand under which the King was to rule over all the states that ever had been ruled over in the past by himself or by his fathers. Alcibiades, therefore, with so much to gain or lose by his efforts, was constantly in touch with Tissaphernes, and did everything he could to bring him round.

53   And now Pisander and the other representatives of the Athenians sent out from Samos reached Athens and spoke in front of the people, giving them a general idea of their programme and pointing out in particular that if they recalled Alcibiades and if they changed the democratic constitution, it would be possible for them to have the King as their ally and to win the war against the Peloponnesians. Much opposition was expressed with regard to altering the democracy; there was a great outcry from the enemies of Alcibiades at the idea of his being brought back from exile in a manner which involved breaking the law; and the priestly families of the Eumolpidae and the Ceryces lodged their protests on behalf of the mysteries – which had been the reason for his banishment – and in the name of the gods prohibited his return. Pisander then came forward in the face of a great deal of violent opposition and, taking separately each one of those who had spoken against his proposals, asked him the following question: 'Now that the Peloponnesians have as many ships as we have ready to fight us at sea, now that they have more cities as their allies, and now that the King and Tissaphernes are supplying them with money, while ours is all gone, have you any hope that Athens can survive unless someone can persuade the King to change sides and come over to

us?' When they replied that they had not, he then spoke straight out and said to them: 'Well, then, that is impossible unless we have a more integrated form of government, with the power in fewer hands, so that the King may trust us. At the moment what we have to think about is our survival, not the form of our constitution. (We can always change that later, if we do not like it.) And we must bring Alcibiades back, because he is the only person now living who can arrange this for us.'

54 The idea of an oligarchy was very badly received by the people at first, but when Pisander had made it perfectly clear that there was no other way out, their fears (and also the fact that they expected to be able to change the constitution again later) made them give in. They voted that Pisander and ten others should sail out and make whatever arrangements seemed best to them with Tissaphernes and Alcibiades. At the same time, since Pisander had also raised objections against Phrynichus, the people relieved him and his colleague Scironides of their commands, and sent out Diomedon and Leon to take their places in command of the fleet. Pisander had discredited Phrynichus by claiming that he had betrayed Iasus and Amorges;[49] he did so because he thought that Phrynichus was not the right person for the deal now being made with Alcibiades. Pisander also made contact with the clubs that already existed in Athens for mutual support in lawsuits and in elections. He urged them to unite and to follow a common policy for getting rid of the democracy. Then, after making all other arrangements required by the situation so that there should be no further delay, he and the ten others set out on their voyage to Tissaphernes.

55 In the same winter Leon and Diomedon, who had by now joined the Athenian fleet, made an attack on Rhodes. They found that the Peloponnesian ships were drawn up on shore, but they made a landing and, after defeating in battle the Rhodians who came out to oppose them, retired to Chalce, which they now used as an operational base in preference to Cos, as it was easier there for them to see if the Peloponnesian fleet made any movement.

Xenophantidas, a Laconian, now came to Rhodes from Pedaritus in Chios, and told them that the Athenian fortifications were now completed and that, unless they came to the rescue with their whole

49. See Appendix 4.

fleet, the fate of Chios was sealed. The Peloponnesians decided to do so; but in the meantime Pedaritus himself with his own force of mercenaries and with the whole army of the Chians made an attack on the fortification protecting the Athenian ships, took a section of it, and gained possession of some of the ships that were hauled up on land. The Athenians counter-attacked, first of all routed the Chians, and then defeated the rest of the army attached to Pedaritus. Pedaritus himself was killed, as were many of the Chians, and a great quantity of arms was captured.

56　　After this the Chians were even more closely blockaded than before by land and sea, and the famine there was great.

And now the Athenian representatives with Pisander arrived at the court of Tissaphernes and entered into discussions with a view to reaching the agreement they had come to make. Alcibiades, however, did not quite know where he stood with Tissaphernes, who was more frightened of the Peloponnesians than of the Athenians and who still followed Alcibiades' own advice and wanted to wear both sides out. He therefore got out of the difficulty by the following scheme, so as to make an agreement impossible because of the extravagant demands made of the Athenians by Tissaphernes. In my opinion Tissaphernes had the same end in view, though in his case it was because of fear, whereas Alcibiades, once he saw that Tissaphernes would not make an agreement anyway, wanted the Athenians to think, not that he was incapable of winning him over, but that it was they who were not offering enough, when Tissaphernes had already been won over and was willing to join them. Speaking for Tissaphernes, who was present, Alcibiades made such exaggerated demands that it was the Athenians who were left with the responsibility for the breakdown of the talks, even though for a long time they had agreed to everything that was asked of them. He first claimed for Tissaphernes the whole of Ionia; then the islands off the coast and various other concessions. To all this the Athenians raised no objections, and finally, at the third session, fearing that they would really find out how little power he had, he put in the claim that the King should be allowed to build ships and sail along his own coast wherever and with as large a fleet as he pleased. Here was a point where the Athenians could yield no further ground. They saw no good purpose in going on with the discussions and, considering that they had been deceived by Alcibiades, went away in an embittered frame of mind and returned to Samos.

57   Directly afterwards, in the same winter, Tissaphernes went along the coast to Caunus. He wanted to get the Peloponnesians back again to Miletus and, after making another treaty with them on the best terms he could arrange, to supply them with pay, so as not to find himself in a state of open hostility with them. He was afraid that, if many of their ships were left short of pay, they would either be forced to fight the Athenians and would be defeated, or else that there would be no crews for the ships and the Athenians would get what they wanted without any help from him. He was still alarmed at the prospect of the Peloponnesians laying waste the mainland in order to find supplies. After calculating and weighing up all this on the basis of his policy of keeping the two Hellenic forces in balance against each other, he sent for the Peloponnesians, gave them their pay, and made a third treaty with them, which was as follows[50]:

58   'In the thirteenth year of the reign of Darius, in the ephorate of Alexippidas at Sparta, a treaty was made in the plain of the Maeander by the Spartans and their allies with Tissaphernes, Hieramenes, and the sons of Pharnaces concerning the interests of the King and the interests of the Spartans and their allies.

'The country of the King in Asia shall be the King's, and the King shall take what measures he pleases with regard to his own country. The Spartans and their allies shall not go against the King's country with any hostile intent; nor shall the King go against the country of the Spartans and their allies with any hostile interest. If any of the Spartans or their allies makes an attack on the King's country, the Spartans and their allies are to prevent it; and if any one from the King's country makes an attack on the country of the Spartans or of their allies, the King is to prevent it.

'Tissaphernes shall provide pay, as under the existing agreement, for the ships now present, until the arrival of the King's ships. After the arrival of the King's ships, the Spartans and their allies may, if they wish, make themselves responsible for the

50. See Appendix 4.

payment of their own ships; but, if they prefer to receive their pay from Tissaphernes, Tissaphernes is to provide it, and at the end of the war the Spartans and their allies are to repay to him the money which they shall have received.

'After the arrival of the King's ships, the fleet of the Spartans and their allies and the King's fleet shall act together in carrying on the war in the way that seems best to Tissaphernes and to the Spartans and their allies. If they wish to make peace with the Athenians, the two parties shall each have their say in making the peace.'

59   This was the treaty; and after it Tissaphernes made preparations for bringing up the Phoenician fleet, in accordance with the terms of the treaty, and for carrying out his other promises, and aimed at making it appear that he was at any rate starting to do what he had said he would do.

60   When this winter had almost ended the Boeotians captured Oropus, which was held by an Athenian garrison, as the result of treachery. Those who collaborated with the Boeotians were some people from Eretria and from Oropus also who were planning for the revolt of Euboea. Oropus being directly opposite Eretria, it was bound, so long as it was in Athenian hands, to constitute a great threat both to Eretria and the rest of Euboea. Now that they controlled Oropus, the Eretrians went to Rhodes and asked the Peloponnesians to intervene in Euboea. The Peloponnesians, however, were more inclined to go to the relief of Chios in its distress, and they put out from Rhodes with their whole fleet and sailed there. Round Triopium they came in sight of the Athenian fleet sailing out at sea from Chalce. Neither of the fleets attacked the other, and the Athenians went back to Samos and the Peloponnesians to Miletus. They now realized that it was impossible to relieve Chios without fighting a battle at sea.

So this winter ended, and the twentieth year of this war recorded by Thucydides.

61   At the very beginning of the next summer Dercyllidas, a Spartan of the officer class, was sent out with a small force by land to the Hellespont in order to bring about the revolt of Abydos, which is a colony of Miletus. At the same time the Chians, while Astyochus

could find no means of coming to their help, were forced by the pressure of the siege to fight a battle at sea. While Astyochus was still at Rhodes they had obtained from Miletus to act as their commander after the death of Pedaritus a regular Spartan officer called Leon, who had made the voyage out in company with Antisthenes. He now came with twelve ships which had been on guard at Miletus – five Thurian, four Syracusan, one from Anaia, one from Miletus, and one belonging to Leon himself. The Chians then marched out in full force and took up a strong position; at the same time they put out with thirty-six of their ships and went into action against the Athenian fleet of thirty-two. After a hard fight at sea, in which the Chians and their allies had rather the better of things, they retired, since it was now late, to their city.

62 It was directly after this that Dercyllidas completed his march up the coast from Miletus. Abydos in the Hellespont revolted and joined him and Pharnabazus; Lampsacus followed suit two days later. When Strombichides heard of this he hurriedly set out from Chios to relieve the places, taking with him twenty-four Athenian ships, including some transports carrying hoplites. The people of Lampsacus marched out against him, but he defeated them in battle, and took Lampsacus, which was unfortified, without any further trouble. The slaves and property he took as booty and then, after resettling the free men in their homes, went on to Abydos. Here the people would not come over to him, and he failed to take the place by assault; so he sailed across to the opposite coast to Sestos, the city in the Chersonese once occupied by the Persians, and made this his base for the defence of the whole Hellespont.

63 During this time the Chians had greater control of the sea, and Astyochus and the Peloponnesians at Miletus gained confidence when they heard of the naval action and of the departure of Strombichides with his ships. Astyochus sailed along the coast to Chios with two ships, collected the fleet from there, and then with his whole fleet all together bore down on Samos. As the Athenians were suspicious of each other, they did not put out against him, and he sailed back again to Miletus.

This attitude among the Athenians is explained by the fact that it was about this time, or even earlier, that the democracy in

Athens had been brought to an end. After Pisander and the other delegates had returned to Samos from Tissaphernes they still further strengthened their control over the army itself, and made approaches to the most important people in Samos with a view to getting them to join in setting up an oligarchy, in spite of the fact that the Samians had just had an anti-oligarchical revolution. At the same time the Athenians in Samos discussed matters among themselves and decided that, as for Alcibiades, they would leave him alone, since he did not want to join them (nor did he seem the proper person to come into an oligarchy anyway); meanwhile they would take matters into their own hands, since they were compromised already, and see how they could keep their movement going; at the same time they would continue to hold out against the enemy in the war, and would willingly contribute money and anything else required from their private estates, since the hardships now to be incurred were not so much for the sake of other people as for themselves.

64　　After encouraging each other by such arguments, they immediately sent off Pisander and half the delegates to Athens to take action there, and instructed them to set up oligarchies in all the subject states at which they called on the way. The other half were sent in different directions to the other subject cities. Diitrephes also, who was in the vicinity of Chios and had been appointed to take command in the Thracian area, was sent out to take up his appointment. When he reached Thasos he put an end to the democracy there. Within two months after he left, the Thasians began to fortify their city, considering that they had no longer anything to gain from an aristocratic government which attached them to Athens, when every day they expected to gain their freedom from Sparta. There were already some of them who had been exiled by the Athenians and were now with the Peloponnesians and, in collaboration with their friends inside the city, doing their utmost to have a fleet sent and to bring about the revolt of the island. These people saw things going exactly as they wished: their city was being set straight without involving them in any risks, and the democracy, which would have opposed them, had been suppressed. So with regard to Thasos the measures taken by the Athenian oligarchical party had the opposite effect to that intended, and, in my opinion, the same thing happened in a number of other subject states. As soon as the cities had got governments where the power was more concentrated and where there was no fear of having once's practices denounced, they went straight on to complete freedom, and were not in the least attracted by the unreality of what the Athenians offered as 'reform'.

65   On their voyage Pisander and the others abolished the democracies in the cities, as had been decided. From some places they also took hoplites to add to their forces, and so came to Athens. Here they found that most of the work had already been done by members of their party. Some of the younger men had formed a group among themselves and had murdered without being detected a certain Androcles, who was one of the chief leaders of the popular party and had also been largely responsible for the banishing of Alcibiades. They had, therefore, two reasons for assassinating him – because he was a demagogue and because they imagined they would be doing something to please Alcibiades, who, they thought, was coming back from exile and bringing with him the friendship of Tissaphernes. There were also some other people whom they regarded as undesirable and did away with secretly. In public they put forward a programme demanding that no one should draw pay except members of the armed forces, and that the number of those with a share in the government should be limited to 5,000, and that these should be the people best qualified to serve the State either in their own proper persons or financially.

66   This was merely a piece of propaganda designed for the general public, since it was the revolutionaries themselves who were going to take over power in the city.

Nevertheless the Assembly and the Council chosen by lot still continued to hold meetings. However, they took no decisions that were not approved by the party of the revolution; in fact all the speakers came from this party, and what they were going to say had been considered by the party beforehand. People were afraid when they saw their numbers, and no one now dared to speak in opposition to them. If anyone did venture to do so, some appropriate method was soon found for having him killed, and no one tried to investigate such crimes or take action against those suspected of them. Instead the people kept quiet, and were in such a state of terror that they thought themselves lucky enough to be left unmolested even if they had said nothing at all. They imagined that the revolutionary party was much bigger than it really was, and they lost all confidence in themselves, being unable to find out the facts because of the size of the city and because they had insufficient knowledge of each other. For the same reason it was impossible for anyone who felt himself ill-treated to complain of it to someone else so as to take measures in his own defence; he would either have had to speak to someone he did not know or to someone he knew but could not rely upon. Throughout the democratic party people approached each other suspiciously, everyone thinking that the next man had something to do with what was going on. And there were in fact among the revolutionaries some people whom no one could ever have imagined would have joined in an oligarchy. It was these who were mainly responsible for making the general mass of people so mistrustful of each other and who were of the greatest help in keeping the minority safe, since they made mutual suspicion an established thing in the popular assemblies.

67   This was the state of affairs when Pisander and the others arrived. They immediately did what was left to do. First they called a general assembly and proposed that a committee of ten should be chosen and given full powers; these men should draw up their proposals and on a fixed day should put before the people their ideas for the best possible government. Next, when the day came, they held the assembly in a narrow space at Colonus, about a mile out of the city, on ground sacred to Poseidon. Here the committee brought forward one proposal and one only, which was that any Athenian should be allowed to make whatever suggestions he liked with impunity; heavy penalties were laid down for anyone who should bring a case against such a speaker for violating the laws or who should damage him in any other way. Now was the time for plain speaking, and it was at once proposed that the holding of office and drawing of salaries under the present constitution should now end; that five men should be elected as presidents; that these should choose 100 men, and each of the 100 should choose three men; that this body of 400 should enter

the Council chamber with full powers to govern as they thought best, and should convene the 5,000 whenever they chose.[51]

68   It was Pisander who proposed this resolution and who in general showed himself most openly in favour of doing away with the democracy. But the man who had planned the whole thing so as to bring it to this point, and who had given most thought to it, was Antiphon, one of the ablest Athenians of his times. He had a most powerful intellect and was well able to express his thoughts in words; he never came forward to speak in front of the assembly unless he could help it, or competed in any other form of public life, since the people in general mistrusted him because of his reputation for cleverness; on the other hand, when other people were engaged in lawsuits or had points to make before the assembly, he was the man to give the best and most helpful advice to those who asked him for it. And after the restoration of the democracy and the setting up of courts where the acts of the Four Hundred (later reversed by the people) came in for very rough treatment, Antiphon was himself on trial for his life, charged with having helped to set up this very government, and his speech in his own defence seems to have been the best one ever made up to my time. Phrynichus also showed himself most remarkably enthusiastic for the oligarchy. He was afraid of Alcibiades, and conscious that he knew about his intrigues with Astyochus at Samos; and he thought that it was unlikely that Alcibiades would ever be recalled by an oligarchy. Once he had joined the movement, Phrynichus proved much the stoutest-hearted of them all in facing danger. Theramenes, the son of Hagnon, was also one of the leaders of the party that put down the democracy – an able speaker and a man with ideas. It was not surprising, therefore, that an undertaking carried out by so many intelligent men should have succeeded, in spite of its difficulties; for it was no easy matter about 100 years after the expulsion of the tyrants to deprive the Athenian people of its liberty – a people not only unused to subjection itself, but, for more than half of this time, accustomed to exercise power over others.

69   The assembly, after ratifying the proposals, with no word spoken in opposition, was dissolved. Next they brought the Four

51. See Appendix 4.

Hundred into the Council chamber in the following way. Because of the enemy at Decelea all Athenians were constantly either on the walls or standing by near their arms at the various posts. On the day in question, therefore, they let those who were not in the secret go home as usual, and gave instructions to the members of their own party to wait about quietly, not actually by the arms, but at a little distance away, and, if there was any opposition shown to what was being done, to seize the arms and suppress it. There were also some Andrians and Tenians, 300 Carystians, and some of the colonists from Aegina, who had been sent out there to live by the Athenians. All these had come specially for this purpose with their own arms, and had been given the same instructions as the others. When they were all in their positions, the Four Hundred appeared, each carrying a dagger concealed on his person and accompanied by the 120 'Hellenic youths' whom they made use of when there was any rough work to be done. Coming in upon the members of the Council chosen by lot who were sitting in the Council chamber, they told them to take their pay and go. They had brought with them themselves all the pay due to them for the rest of their term of office and gave it to them as they went out.

70   When the Council had made way for them like this, with no objection raised, and the rest of the citizens kept quiet and took no kind of action, the Four Hundred took their places in the Council chamber, and for the moment occupied themselves with choosing by lot officers from among themselves to deal with the Council business and in making the prayers and sacrifices to the gods that are made on entering office. Afterwards, however, they made great changes in what had been the democratic system of government, though they took no steps to recall the exiles, because of Alcibiades; but in other respects they ruled the city with a strong hand.

Some men, though not many, whom they thought it conven-ient to be done away with, were put to death; others were im-prisoned or sent into exile. They also made overtures to Agis, the King of Sparta, who was at Decelea, saying that they were willing to come to terms and that it would be reasonable for him to agree to do so, since he would be dealing with them rather than with the untrustworthy democracy.

71   But Agis did not believe that the situation in Athens was settled
or that the people would give up their ancient liberty so quickly.
He thought that, if they were to see a large Spartan army, there
would be disturbances; in fact he was far from convinced that they
were not even now in a state of unrest. He therefore gave an
unconciliatory reply to the messengers from the Four Hundred
and, after sending to Sparta for a large additional force, he came
down himself soon afterwards with the garrison from Decelea
and advanced right up to the walls of Athens, hoping that disturbances would make them more likely to submit to terms dictated
by Sparta, or else that, in the general confusion which would
probably take place inside and outside the city, they might even
surrender without a fight. He felt confident of capturing the Long
Walls, because they would not be adequately defended. However,
instead of there being any signs of trouble inside the city when he
drew near, the Athenians sent out their cavalry and detachments of
hoplites, light troops, and archers, shot down some of his troops
who had advanced too close to them, and carried off the arms and
the dead bodies. Agis now realized what the position was and led
his army back again. He himself stayed with his own troops in
their position at Decelea; the reinforcements, after remaining for
a few days in Attica, were sent home again. After this the Four
Hundred still continued to make overtures to Agis, and he was
now more inclined to receive them. On his advice they sent
representatives to Sparta to negotiate a settlement, and were
anxious to bring the war to an end.

72   They also sent ten men to Samos to secure the goodwill of the
army. They were to explain that the oligarchy had not been
established to do any harm to the city or the citizens, but in order
to preserve the state as a whole, and that it was not only 400 but
5,000 who shared in the government; although, because of their
expeditions and other employments which took them abroad, as
many as 5,000 Athenians had never yet assembled, however important the subject under discussion. They were also told what was
the right line to take on other points, and were then sent out
directly after the new government was installed, since the Four
Hundred feared (and their fears were justified by the event) that
the men serving in the navy would not be willing to keep in their

own place under the oligarchical system, and that the trouble might start there, and end in the new government itself being thrown out.

73   In fact there was already at Samos a swing of opinion against the idea of an oligarchy. The following events had taken place just about the time when the Four Hundred were organizing their conspiracy. The Samians, who, as already mentioned, had risen against the dominant classes and who constituted the democracy, had changed round again and been won over by Pisander, when he came there, and by the Athenians at Samos who were in the conspiracy. About 300 of them had joined the conspiracy; they now regarded the rest of the population as being 'the democracy' and intended to attack them. They also put to death an Athenian called Hyperbolus, a wretched character, who had been ostracized, not because anyone was afraid of his power or prestige, but because he was a thoroughly bad lot and a disgrace to the city. In doing away with him they were acting in cooperation with Charminus, one of the generals, and with some of the Athenians who supported them. Thus they demonstrated their reliability to the Athenians, with whom they carried out some other actions of the same kind, and were now all ready for an attack on their own democracy. The Samian democrats, however, realized what was going to happen, and gave information about it to Leon and Diomedon, two of the generals who, because of the respect in which they were held by the Athenian people, gave only a reluctant support to the idea of an oligarchy. They also told Thrasybulus, who was captain of a trireme, and Thrasylus, who was serving as a hoplite, and others who had always given the impression of being most opposed to the conspirators. They begged them not to let the Samians be destroyed and Samos, through which alone they had been able to keep their empire together, be alienated from Athens. When they heard this, those to whom the appeal was made approached the soldiers individually and urged them to put a stop to what was going on. They gave particular attention to the crew of the *Paralus*, each man of which was a free-born Athenian citizen, and all of whom had always been thoroughly opposed to the idea of an oligarchy, even when there was no question of such a thing existing. Leon and Diomedon also detached some ships to protect

the Samians, in case they sailed anywhere else themselves. The result was that when the 300 made their attack on the people, all these, and particularly the crew of the *Paralus*, came to the rescue; the Samian democrats were victorious; some thirty of the 300 were put to death, and three others, who had been mainly responsible for the revolt, were exiled. They took no reprisals on the rest, giving all their full rights to live together in future under a democratic constitution.

74   The *Paralus*, with Chaereas, the son of Archestratus, on board – an Athenian who had shown great energy in the change over to democracy – was at once sent out by the Samians and by the army to Athens to give the news of what had happened, they themselves not yet having been informed that the Four Hundred were in power. When they sailed into harbour, the Four Hundred immediately arrested two or three of the crew of the *Paralus*, took over the ship itself, and put the rest of the men on board another ship, a troop-carrier which was to be on patrol round Euboea. Chaereas, as soon as he saw what the position was, managed to slip away, and got back again to Samos, where he gave the soldiers a very exaggerated account of the terror in Athens. He told them that flogging was in general use as a punishment, that no one could say a word against the government, that outrages were being committed against the wives and children of the soldiers themselves, and that the Four Hundred were planning to seize and imprison the relatives of all those in service at Samos who were not of their own way of thought, and to have them put to death unless the army at Samos submitted to them. And he added much else that was untrue.

75   After hearing this, the soldiers' first impulse was to turn on the chief promoters of the oligarchy and anyone else, too, who had had anything to do with it, and to do them to death. Finally, however, they gave up this idea and listened to the more moderate party who pointed out the danger of losing everything, with the enemy fleet close at hand and ready to fight. After this Thrasybulus, the son of Lycus, and Thrasylus, who had been the two most active people in bringing about the change in opinion, now wanted to make it quite plain that democracy was to be the rule in Samos. They made all the soldiers, and especially those of the

oligarchical party, swear the most binding oaths to the effect that they would abide by the democratic constitution, that they would avoid dissension, that they would carry on with energy the war against the Peloponnesians, and that they would be the enemies of the Four Hundred and hold no relations with them. All the Samians of military age joined them in swearing the same oath; the army co-operated with the Samians in all affairs and was ready to share with them the outcome of the risks which were being run, considering that there was no way to safety either for the Samians or themselves, but only certain destruction, if they were subdued either by the Four Hundred or by the enemy at Miletus.[52]

76   This period, then, was one of sharp conflict, with the army trying to force a democracy on the city, and the Four Hundred an oligarchy upon the army. The army immediately held an assembly, at which they dismissed from office the existing generals and any of the captains of triremes whom they suspected and chose new captains and generals instead of them, including Thrasybulus and Thrasylus, who were in command already. Speakers stood up and made encouraging speeches, saying, among other things, that there was no need to despair because the city had revolted from them: it was a case of the minority parting company with the majority, who were also better equipped in every way; they had the entire fleet and they could force the other cities to pay them money just as if they had their base in Athens, since in holding Samos they were holding a city which, so far from being weak, had actually, at the time of the war with Athens, come very close to depriving the Athenians of their control of the sea; and as far as the enemy were concerned they had the same base for operations as before. With the navy in their possession, they were better placed for securing supplies than were the people in Athens. Even previously it was only because they were holding this advance post at Samos that the Athenians at home had been able to control the sea routes into Piraeus; and the position now was that if the people at home refused to give them back the constitution, it would be easier for the army at Samos to deprive Athens of the use of the sea than for

52. The Samians remained loyal allies of Athens to the end, and in 405 B.C., after the defeat at Aegospotami, the Athenians voted citizenship to all Samians: Meiggs–Lewis, *Greek Historical Inscriptions*, no. 94.

the Athenians to deny its use to the army in Samos. Then, with regard to winning victory over the enemy, Athens was of little or no use to them; it was no loss to lose people who no longer had any money to send them (in fact the soldiers had to shift for themselves) and were also incapable of giving them good advice – which is the thing that justifies the control of armies by the State. In fact this was where the home government, by doing away with the institutions of the country, had put themselves in the wrong, whereas the army were abiding by these institutions and would try to force the people at home to do so too. So, if it was a question of having good advisers, here again the army had the advantage over the city. Then there was Alcibiades: they had only to guarantee him his security and his recall from exile, and he would be happy to bring them the alliance of the King. And the main thing was, that even if they failed in everything, with so large a navy there were still many places where they could retire and where they would find both cities and land.

77   So they spoke at the assembly, and so they encouraged each other; nor were they any less active in preparing for the war. The delegates sent out to Samos by the Four Hundred heard what the position was when they were at Delos and remained there without making any further move.

78   There were also disturbances at about this time in the Peloponnesian fleet at Miletus, where the men openly complained that all their prospects were being ruined by Astyochus and Tissaphernes. Astyochus had refused to fight a naval battle earlier on, at the time when they were still at the peak of their efficiency and when the Athenian fleet was small, nor would he fight now, when the Athenians were supposed to be in a state of civil war among themselves and had not yet concentrated all their ships in one place. Instead they were kept waiting about for this Phoenician fleet from Tissaphernes, which existed only in theory, and the chances were that they would be worn out in the process. As for Tissaphernes, apart from his failure to produce these ships, he was ruining their navy by not paying the men regularly and not paying them in full. Therefore, they said, there must be no more delay. A decisive naval engagement must be fought. The Syracusans were particularly insistent on this.

79   The allies and Astyochus were aware of this agitation, and had held a meeting and decided to fight a decisive battle. So, when they received the news of the disturbances at Samos, they put to sea with their entire fleet of 112 ships, and set sail for Mycale, ordering the Milesians to proceed there by land. The Athenians with the eighty-two ships from Samos were at anchor at Glauce in Mycale; at this point it is only a short distance from Samos to the mainland, looking towards Mycale. When they saw the Peloponnesian ships approaching, they retired to Samos, since they did not think they were numerically strong enough to risk everything on a battle. They were also expecting Strombichides to come to reinforce them from the Hellespont with the ships that had gone from Chios to Abydos. For they had heard in advance from Miletus that the enemy intended to fight and had sent a messenger to Strombichides. The Athenians therefore withdrew to Samos, and the Peloponnesians put into Mycale and camped there with the infantry from Miletus and from the other districts nearby. Next day they were intending to sail out against Samos when they got the news that Strombichides with the ships from the Hellespont had arrived, and they at once sailed back again to Miletus. Now that the Athenians had been reinforced, they also sailed out with 108 ships against Miletus, wishing to fight a decisive battle: but as no one put out against them, they sailed back again to Samos.

80   In the same summer directly after this the Peloponnesians, since they were not inclined to put out against the Athenians with their whole fleet because they did not regard themselves as a match for them, and being in difficulties about finding the money for so many ships, especially as Tissaphernes was not paying them properly, sent off Clearchus, the son of Ramphias, with forty ships to Pharnabazus, in accordance with the original instructions from the Peloponnese. Pharnabazus was asking for this fleet and was prepared to pay for it; and at the same time offers to start a revolt had been made to them from Byzantium. So these Peloponnesian ships put out into the open sea in order to escape the notice of the Athenians on their voyage. After running into a storm, most of them, with Clearchus, got into Delos and later came back to Miletus. Clearchus then set out again and came to the Hellespont by land, where he took over his command. Meanwhile ten of his

ships, under the command of the Megarian Helixus, had got through safely to the Hellespont and brought about the revolt of Byzantium. After this the Athenians at Samos heard of what had happened and sent out naval reinforcements to keep a watch on the Hellespont; and there was a naval action, which did not last long, off Byzantium between eight ships on each side.

81 Now the leading men at Samos, and particularly Thrasybulus, who, ever since he had organized the change in the government, had stuck to the policy of having Alcibiades recalled, finally got this point of view accepted by the mass of the soldiers in an assembly. They voted that he should be recalled and should be guaranteed security, and Thrasybulus sailed to Tissaphernes and brought Alcibiades back to Samos, believing that their only hope of safety was in his detaching Tissaphernes from the Peloponnesians and bringing him over to their side. An assembly was held, and Alcibiades, after complaining about and lamenting over his own hard fate in having been exiled, dealt at length with the general political situation and made his audience full of hope for the future. He gave a very exaggerated idea of the strength of his own influence with Tissaphernes, his objects being to make the oligarchy at home frightened of him and so bring about the dissolution of the political clubs, to gain the more credit for himself with the army at Samos, and to give them the greater confidence, and also to disappoint the enemy of their present hopes by making relations between them and Tissaphernes as bad as possible. So Alcibiades, taking great credit to himself for it all, made the following promises. He said that Tissaphernes had given him a positive assurance that, so long as he could trust the Athenians, he would never let them go short of supplies while he had anything left of his own, not even if he ended up by having to sell his own bed; that he would bring the Phoenician fleet now at Aspendus to the Athenians instead of to the Peloponnesians; but that he could only feel sure of the Athenians if Alcibiades were brought back safe from exile to become his security for them.

82 After hearing all this and much more as well, the army immediately elected Alcibiades general to serve with the previous ones and put everything into his hands. There was now not a man who for anything in the world would have parted with his present

hopes of coming through safely and of taking vengeance on the Four Hundred; in fact such was the contempt which they now felt for their enemies on the spot, as a result of what had been said, that they were actually ready to sail against Piraeus. Alcibiades, however, was altogether against the idea of sailing to Piraeus and leaving their more immediate enemies behind, though many people were strongly in favour of it. He said that first, since he was now elected general, he would sail over to Tissaphernes and arrange with him about the conduct of the war. And he went away directly after this assembly had broken up, so as to give the impression that there was complete confidence between them, and also wishing to increase his own value in the eyes of Tissaphernes and impress him with the fact that he had now been elected general, and was thus able either to do him good or to do him harm. The fact was, then, that Alcibiades was using the Athenians to frighten Tissaphernes, and Tissaphernes to frighten the Athenians.

83   The Peloponnesians at Miletus got to know of the recall of Alcibiades and, though they had been mistrustful enough of Tissaphernes before, now became much more embittered against him than ever. What had occurred was that, when the Athenians had sailed up to Miletus and the Peloponnesians had declined to go out against them and fight, Tissaphernes, already unpopular because of Alcibiades, had made himself even more so by becoming still more lax in providing pay. The soldiers therefore got together in groups, as they had done before, and brought in with them other influential people, not only from the army. They began to reckon up their grievances: they had never yet received their full pay; what they had got was short of the full amount, and even then was not paid regularly; so, unless they either fought a decisive naval action or else moved to some place where they could be sure of supplies, the men would leave the ships; the person responsible for all this was Astyochus, who, for his own private profit, fell in with everything that Tissaphernes suggested.

84   One of the results of these discussions of their grievances was a disturbance which threatened Astyochus personally. Most of the Syracusan and Thurian crews were free men, and were consequently all the more outspoken in crowding round Astyochus and demanding their pay. Astyochus, however, answered them arro-

gantly and with threats; and when Dorieus spoke to him on behalf of his own sailors he went so far as to raise his stick against him. When the general mass of the men saw this happening they lost all control, as sailors do, and set on Astyochus to stone him. However, he saw what they were about and took refuge at an altar, and so the incident ended without his being stoned.

The Milesians also surprised and captured the fort built in Miletus by Tissaphernes and drove out the garrison. This action of theirs was approved by the rest of the allies, and particularly by the Syracusans; but Lichas disapproved, and said that the Milesians and all others in the King's territory should acknowledge their dependence on Tissaphernes in every reasonable way and should court his favour, until the war was satisfactorily concluded. The Milesians were angry with him for this and for other things of the same kind, and when he died afterwards of an illness, they would not allow him to be buried where the Spartans at Miletus wanted.

85   It was when things had come to this state of ill-feeling against Astyochus and Tissaphernes that Mindarus, who was to succeed Astyochus as admiral, arrived from Sparta and took over the command. Astyochus sailed back home, and Tissaphernes sent with him as a representative one of his own circle, a Carian called Gaulites, who spoke both the languages. He was to protest about the Milesian action with regard to the fort and to defend the conduct of Tissaphernes, who knew that Milesian representatives were on their way to Sparta mainly in order to attack him, and that they were being accompanied by Hermocrates, who intended to declare that he, with Alcibiades, was ruining things for the Peloponnesians and that he was playing a double game. Hermocrates had been constantly on bad terms with Tissaphernes on the question of supplying the pay in full, and finally, when Hermocrates was declared an exile from Syracuse and new commanders (Potamis, Myscon, and Demarchus) had come out to Miletus to take over the Syracusan fleet, Tissaphernes, now that his enemy was an exile, made still more vigorous attacks on him, accusing him, among many other things, of having once asked him for a sum of money and of only having come forward as his enemy because he failed to obtain it.

So Astyochus and the Milesians and Hermocrates set sail for

Sparta. By now Alcibiades had crossed back again from Tissaphernes to Samos, and it was after his return that the delegates 86 from the Four Hundred who, as already mentioned, had been sent out to explain matters to the army at Samos and to gain their goodwill, arrived there from Delos. An assembly was held, and the delegates attempted to speak. At first the soldiers refused to listen to them and kept shouting out that those who had put down the democracy should be put to death; but in the end, after some difficulty, they quietened down and listened to what they had to say.

The delegates then declared that the object of the change in the constitution was not to weaken the State, but to preserve it; nor was it in order to surrender Athens to the enemy. They had already had, during their period of government, a chance of doing this at the time when the enemy made their invasion. They said, too, that all the Five Thousand in turn would have their share in the government; that, contrary to the slanderous report of Chaereas, no outrages had been committed against the relatives of the forces, nor had they suffered any kind of ill treatment, but were, in fact, all in possession of their own property just as they always had been.

They said much else besides, but the army was no more inclined to listen to them. The soldiers, in fact, were angry and, among many proposals which they put forward among themselves, the most popular one was to sail against Piraeus. It was at this point, it seems, that Alcibiades did his first great act of service to his country, and a very important act it was. For when the Athenians at Samos were all eager to sail against their own countrymen – which would certainly have meant the immediate occupation of Ionia and the Hellespont by the enemy – it was Alcibiades who stopped them.

There was not another man in existence who could have controlled the mob at that time. Alcibiades stopped them from sailing against Athens, and used his tongue to such effect that he diverted them from the anger which they felt against the delegates on personal grounds. It was he who gave the reply to the delegates when they were sent away. He said that he was not opposed to the government being in the hands of the Five Thousand, but he did demand that they should get rid of the Four Hundred and that the original Council of the Five Hundred should be reinstated; he was entirely in favour of any measures of economy which would result in better pay for the armed forces; and, in general, he urged them to hold fast and make no concessions to the enemy, saying that, so long as the city was preserved, there were good hopes of some kind of agreement being reached between the two parties among the citizens, but that if either party, whether the men in Samos or the men in Athens, were defeated, there would be no one left with whom any settlement could any longer be made.

Some representatives from Argos also arrived to offer support to the Athenian democracy at Samos. Alcibiades thanked them and sent them away, asking them to come back when a message reached them to that effect. The Argives had arrived with the crew of the *Paralus*, who, it will be remembered, had been posted to a troop-carrier by the Four Hundred with instructions to sail round Euboea. They were then to carry to Sparta some representatives from the Four Hundred, Laespodias, Aristophon, and Melesius; but when they reached Argos on their voyage, they seized the representatives and handed them over to the Argives as being men who had been largely responsible for overthrowing the democracy, and, instead of going back to Athens themselves, took aboard the Argive representatives and came to Samos in their trireme.

87   In the same summer Tissaphernes made ready to go to Aspendus to fetch the Phoenician fleet, and invited Lichas to accompany him. This was just at the time when, because of his general behaviour, and particularly because of the recall of Alcibiades, he was most unpopular with the Peloponnesians, who thought that he was now quite openly collaborating with the Athenians, and Tissaphernes wanted, or made it look as though he wanted, to to clear himself of these suspicions. He said that he would leave behind his deputy Tamos with instructions to provide pay for the forces during his absence. Different explanations are given, and it is not easy to be sure what his intention was in going to Aspendus and then, when he had got there, in not bringing back the ships. It is certain that 147 Phoenician ships came as far as Aspendus; various conjectures have been made to account for their not coming on from there. According to one view he went away in

accordance with his original plan of wearing down the Peloponnesian forces; and certainly Tamos, whose job it was, paid them worse instead of better. Others say that his purpose in bringing the Phoenicians to Aspendus was to make money out of the crews, whom he never intended to employ in any case, and who would pay to be discharged. Another theory is that it was because of the attacks being made against him in Sparta, and that he wanted to have it said that he was not in the wrong, but had actually set out to fetch a fleet which really did have its full complement of men. I myself feel quite sure that his motives in not bringing up the fleet were to wear down the Hellenic forces and to keep matters in suspense: their efficiency was being impaired during all the time he took going down to Aspendus and waiting about there; and he was keeping the two sides evenly balanced, by not committing himself to either side and so giving it the advantage. Certainly his intervention, so long as there was nothing irresolute about it, could, if he had really wanted it, have put an end to the war. By bringing up the fleet he would in all probability have given victory to the Spartans who already faced the Athenians with a naval force that was equal to theirs rather than inferior. Then there is a most convincing piece of evidence in the excuse he gave for not bringing the ships. What he said was that fewer ships had been collected than the King had ordered; but in that case he could surely have gained all the more credit by not spending much of the King's money and by using smaller means to effect the same result.

However, whatever his real intentions were, Tissaphernes went to Aspendus and met the Phoenicians; and the Peloponnesians sent out at his request, supposedly to fetch the fleet, a Spartan called Philip with two triremes.

88   When Alcibiades heard that Tissaphernes was going to Aspendus, he sailed there himself with thirteen ships, after telling the Athenians at Samos that he was quite certain he would do them a great service: either he would bring the Phoenician fleet to the Athenians himself, or, at any rate, he would prevent it going to the Peloponnesians. It is probable that he knew all along that Tissaphernes had no intention of bringing the fleet from Aspendus and he wanted to prejudice him as much as possible in the eyes of

the Peloponnesians by making them think that he was a friend of himself and of the Athenians, so that in the end this very thing might force Tissaphernes to come over to their side. So Alcibiades set out and sailed eastward straight for Phaselis and Caunus.

89   At the same time the representatives who had been sent out by the Four Hundred returned from Samos to Athens and delivered the message from Alcibiades, saying that he urged them to hold out and make no concessions to the enemy, and that he had great hopes both of bringing them and the army together and of victory over the Peloponnesians. Most of those involved in the oligarchy were, even before this, discontented with it and would have been glad enough to get out of the business, if they could do so safely; and this message made them all the more determined to do so. They now began to organize themselves into an opposition and to criticize the way things were being run. They had as their leaders some of the people who were in the inner circles of the oligarchy and holders of office, such as Theramenes, the son of Hagnon, and Aristocrates, the son of Scellias, and others – men who, though they were holding important positions in the oligarchy, were afraid, they said, of the army in Samos and of Alcibiades (and in his case their fear was quite genuine), and also that those who had gone to Sparta to negotiate might do some harm to the State without consulting the majority of the party. They did not go so far as to suggest getting rid of oligarchy altogether, but they maintained that the Five Thousand should be appointed so that this body should exist in real fact rather than as a mere name, and that the government should be set up on a wider basis. This, in fact, was mere political propaganda: it was for motives of personal ambition that most of them were following the line that is most disastrous to oligarchies when they take over from democracies. For no sooner is the change made than every single man, not content with being the equal of others, regards himself as greatly superior to everyone else. In a democracy, on the other hand, someone who fails to get elected to office can always console himself with the thought that there was something not quite fair about it. But what had the most evident effect in urging on the dissident party was the strength of Alcibiades' position in Samos and the fact that they did not believe that the oligarchy would last.

Each one of them therefore tried to get in first as leader and champion of the people in general.

90   Those among the Four Hundred who were chiefly opposed to the idea of a democracy were led by Phrynichus, the man who had quarrelled with Alcibiades when he was in command at Samos, Aristarchus, who had been for a long time a particularly bitter enemy to the democracy, Pisander, Antiphon, and others belonging to the most powerful families. Even before this time – in fact as soon as they came into power and the army at Samos revolted from them and constituted itself a democracy – they sent representatives of their own party to Sparta and did all they could to make peace; and they had also been building the wall in Eetionia. But now, after the return of their representatives from Samos, they became more active than ever, as they saw that not only the people in general but also members of their own party who had previously been regarded as reliable were turning against them. In their alarm at the position both in Samos and in Athens, they hurriedly sent off Antiphon, Phrynichus, and ten others with instructions to make peace with Sparta on any kind of terms which could be regarded as at all tolerable. At the same time they went on more energetically still with the building of the wall in Eetionia. The idea behind this wall was, according to Theramenes and his party, not to keep the army of Samos out of Piraeus, if they tried to force an entrance, but rather to let the enemy in, with fleet and army, whenever they wanted. Eetionia is a mole of Piraeus directly in the entrance to the harbour. What they were doing now was to build their wall to join up with the existing fortifications on the side of the land, so that it would only require a small force inside in order to control the entrance; for the junction of the two walls (the old one on the side of the land, and the new inner wall now being built on the side of the sea) was at one of the two towers standing at the narrow mouth of the harbour. They also included in the system of their fortifications a warehouse, a very large one, which was quite close to their wall, in fact at the point in Piraeus just next to it. They took over this warehouse themselves, and forced everyone to bring into it their existing stocks of corn and unload there the corn that was brought in by sea, taking it out of this store when they sold it.

91   Theramenes had been going about complaining of all this for
      some time, and now, when the representatives came back from
      Sparta without having succeeded in making any kind of general
      settlement, he went on saying that this wall might well turn out to
      be the ruin of the city. It happened, too, that at this time there were
      forty-two ships from the Peloponnese, including some Italian
      ships from Tarentum and Locri, and also some Sicilian ships,
      which, being invited to intervene by the Euboeans, were already
      anchored off Las in Laconia and getting ready for the voyage to
      Euboea. They were commanded by Agesandridas, the son of
      Agesander, a Spartan of the officer class. Theramenes maintained
      that the idea of this fleet was not so much to bring aid to Euboea
      as to the people who were fortifying Eetionia and that, unless
      measures were taken at once, the city would be lost before they
      knew what had happened. There was more in this than a mere
      attempt to create prejudice, since those whom he accused really
      were contemplating some such action. What they wanted in the
      first place was to preserve the oligarchy and keep control over the
      allies as well; if this was impossible, their next aim was to hold on
      to the fleet and fortifications of Athens and retain independence;
      but if this also proved beyond them, they were certainly not going
      to find themselves in the position of being the first people to be
      destroyed by a reconstituted democracy, and preferred instead
      to call in the enemy, give up the fleet and the fortifications and
      make any sort of terms at all for the future of Athens, provided
      that they themselves at any rate had their lives guaranteed to them.
92   It was for this reason that they were so busy on the building of this
      wall of theirs, with its small gates and entrances and ways of letting
      the enemy in, and were anxious to get it finished before they were
      prevented.

          The agitation against them was at first confined to a few people
      and was carried on in secret. Things changed, however, after a
      man from the militia made a premeditated assault on Phrynichus,
      on his return from the embassy to Sparta, and struck him down in
      the market-place at the time when it was fullest, and not far from
      the Council Chamber, which he had just left. Phrynichus died
      immediately, and the man who had struck the blow escaped. His
      accomplice, however, an Argive, was arrested and put to the

torture by the Four Hundred. He gave nothing away as to the name of his employer, merely saying that he knew that many people met together at the house of the commander of the militia and at other houses. It was at this point, when no further steps were taken in the matter, that Theramenes became bolder and, with Aristocrates and the others who shared their views, both among the Four Hundred and from outside, began to take positive action. By now the fleet had sailed round the coast from Las, come to anchor off Epidaurus, and had overrun Aegina. It was not likely, Theramenes now said, that, if they were sailing to Euboea, they would have come up the gulf as far as Aegina and then gone back again to anchor at Epidaurus; the only explanation was that they were there by invitation and for the reasons which he had always said in the attacks that he had made on the Government; it was therefore, no longer possible to leave things as they were.

In the end, after a number of revolutionary speeches had been made and still more suspicion excited against the Government, Theramenes and his party really took action. The hoplites in Piraeus who were building the wall at Eetionia, among whom was Aristocrates, with the rank of colonel and in command of his own tribe, arrested Alexicles, one of the generals of the oligarchy and a man who had been one of the chief organizers of the political clubs. They took him into a house and kept him there under guard. Among those who supported them in this was Hermon, the commander of the militia stationed in Munychia; but the most important point was that their action met with the approval of the rank and file among the hoplites.

When the Four Hundred, who happened to be in session in the Council Chamber, were informed of what had taken place, all except those who were against the regime wanted to go immediately to the posts where the arms were stacked. Threats were made against Theramenes and his party; but Theramenes defended himself, and said that he was prepared to go at once and help to rescue Alexicles. He took with him one of the generals who shared his own views and set off for Piraeus; Aristarchus and some young men from the cavalry went along too. There was great confusion and a general state of panic, since the people in Athens thought that Piraeus had already been seized and Alexicles put to death, and the people in Piraeus were expecting the troops from Athens to be upon them at any moment. The elder men did what they could to stop those who were running wildly through the city to the places where the arms were kept, and Thucydides the Pharsalian, the representative of Athenian interests at Pharsalus, who was in Athens, threw himself resolutely in their way, crying out to them not to destroy their country, while the enemy was close at hand waiting to take advantage. So, though it took some time, they quietened down and kept their hands off each other.

Meanwhile Theramenes arrived at Piraeus. He was one of the generals himself, and so far as it was a question merely of shouting at the hoplites he appeared to be in a rage; Aristarchus and the opposite faction were genuinely angry. Most of the hoplites, however, went on resolutely with the business in hand and showed no signs of changing their minds. They asked Theramenes whether he thought that the wall was being built for any good purpose and whether it would not be better to pull it down. Theramenes replied that if they thought it was a good thing to pull the wall down, he, personally, agreed with them. After this the hoplites and many of the people in Piraeus immediately climbed up on to the wall and began to tear it down. Their appeal to the crowd was, that everyone should come and help who wanted the Five Thousand to govern instead of the Four Hundred. For they still used this name of the Five Thousand as a cover, and avoided saying straight out 'whoever wants the people to govern', since they feared that the Five Thousand might actually exist and that a man might say something to one of them in ignorance, and so get into trouble. This, in fact, was why the Four Hundred did not want the Five Thousand either to exist or to be known to exist: to have so many people sharing power would amount, they thought, to just the same thing as democracy; but to keep up a state of uncertainty on the whole question would have the effect of making people afraid of each other.

93   Next day, alarmed as they were, the Four Hundred still held a meeting in the Council Chamber. The hoplites in Piraeus released Alexicles, whom they had arrested, pulled down the fortification, and marched to the theatre of Dionysus near Munychia, where they grounded arms and held an assembly at which it was decided

to march to the city. They did so at once, and halted again in the Anaceum. Here they were met by people who had been chosen for the purpose by the Four Hundred, and these people came up and spoke to them individually, trying to persuade those whom they saw to be reasonable persons not to proceed any further themselves and to help hold back the others. They said that they would publish the names of the Five Thousand and that the Four Hundred would be chosen from them in rotation, just as the Five Thousand should decide: they begged them meanwhile not to take any action which might destroy the state or let it slip into the hands of the enemy. After many of these appeals had been made to numbers of the soldiers, the whole body of the hoplites became calmer than they had been and felt chiefly alarmed for the state in general. It was agreed that on a fixed day there should be an assembly in the theatre of Dionysus for settling differences.

94   When the day came for this assembly and the people were, in fact, beginning to come into it, it was reported that the forty-two ships with Agesandridas were sailing from Megara along the coast of Salamis. Everyone believed that this was just the thing that Theramenes and his party had been saying all along, that the ships were sailing up to the fortification, and that it was a lucky thing that it had been pulled down. It is, of course, possible that it was because of some pre-arranged plan that Agesandridas was waiting around Epidaurus and the neighbourhood; on the other hand, in view of the revolutionary situation among the Athenians, it was perfectly natural for him to postpone his departure on the chance that he might be able to intervene at the right moment. In any case, as soon as the Athenians heard the news, they went running down to Piraeus in full force, feeling that more serious than the war among themselves was this war with the common enemy, which was no distant affair, but actually threatened their own harbour. Some manned the ships that were already there, some launched others, some took up position on the walls and at the mouth of the harbour.

95   The Peloponnesian ships, however, sailed past, rounded Sunium, and came to anchor between Thoricus and Prasiae. Later they arrived at Oropus. The Athenians, with revolution inside the city and anxious, as they were, to come quickly to the relief of this

vital point (for, now that they were cut off from Attica, Euboea was everything to them), were forced to act in a hurry and to put on board the ships men who had never been trained together as crews. They sent Thymochares with some ships to Eretria, and when they arrived there they, with the ships already in Euboea, made up the total number to thirty-six ships. They were forced to fight immediately. Agesandridas, after seeing that his men had had a meal, put out from Oropus, which is about seven miles from the city of Eretria by sea. As he sailed up to attack, the Athenians immediately began to man their ships, imagining that the sailors would be standing by ready. However, they were getting food for their meal, not from the market-place, but from the houses at the farthest outskirts of the town. This was because the Eretrians had deliberately seen to it that there should be no food on sale in the market-place, so that the Athenians should not be able to man their ships quickly, should be caught by the enemy's attack before they were ready for it, and be compelled to put out to sea just as they were. And a signal was raised in Eretria to tell the Peloponnesians in Oropus when to put to sea themselves. So, inadequately prepared as they were, the Athenians put out and fought in front of the harbour of Eretria, and, in spite of everything, held their own for a short time. Finally, however, they were put to flight and driven to the shore. Those of them who took refuge in Eretria, in the belief that it was a friendly city, came off worst of all, since they were slaughtered by the Eretrians; others, who fled to the fort held by the Athenians in Eretrian territory, survived, as did those ships which managed to reach Chalcis. The Peloponnesians captured twenty-two Athenian ships and either killed or made prisoners of the crews. They put up a trophy, and soon afterwards made the whole of Euboea revolt (except for Oreus, which was held by the Athenians themselves) and generally reorganized matters there.

96   When the news of what had happened in Euboea came to Athens, it caused the very greatest panic that had ever been known there. Not the disaster in Sicily, though it had seemed great enough at the time, nor any other had ever had so terrifying an effect. And indeed there was every reason for despondency: the army at Samos was in revolt; they had no more ships, and no

more crews for ships; there was civil disturbance among themselves, and no one could tell when it might not come to actual fighting; and now, on top of everything, this disaster in which they had lost their fleet, and, what was worst of all, Euboea, which had been more useful to them than Attica itself. And what disturbed them most greatly and most nearly was the thought that the enemy, after their victory, might venture to come straight on at them and sail against Piraeus, which was now left with no navy to defend it; indeed, they expected every moment to see them coming. And, if the Peloponnesians had been more daring, they could easily have done this. They would then either have produced, simply by anchoring off the city, still greater dissension inside, or, if they stayed there and undertook siege operations, they would have forced the fleet in Ionia, however hostile it might be to the oligarchy, to come to the help of their own people and of the city itself; and meanwhile the Hellespont and Ionia would have fallen into their hands, together with the islands and everything as far as Euboea – the whole Athenian empire, in fact. However, on this occasion, as on many others, the Spartans proved to be quite the most remarkably helpful enemies that the Athenians could have had. For Athens, particularly as a naval power, was enormously helped by the very great difference in the national characters – her speed as against their slowness, her enterprise as against their lack of initiative. This was shown by the Syracusans, who were most like the Athenians in character and fought best against them.

97   When they got the news, the Athenians, in spite of everything, manned twenty ships. They also summoned immediately the first of a number of assemblies. The assembly met in the Pnyx, where they used to meet before. The Four Hundred were deposed and it was voted that power should be handed over to the Five Thousand, who were to include all who could provide themselves with a hoplite's equipment, and that no one, on pain of being put under a curse, was to receive any remuneration for the holding of any office. A number of other assemblies were held later, at which legal advisers were chosen and all the other steps taken for drawing up the constitution. Indeed, during the first period of this new regime the Athenians appear to have had a better government

than ever before, at least in my time.[53] There was a reasonable and moderate blending of the few and the many, and it was this, in the first place, that made it possible for the city to recover from the bad state into which her affairs had fallen. They also voted for the recall of Alcibiades and of others with him, and sent to him and to the army at Samos urging them to take their full part in the war.

98   As soon as the change of government took place, Pisander and Alexicles and their friends and all the most extreme members of the oligarchical party left the city and got away to Decelea. The only exception was Aristarchus, who was also one of the generals, and who quickly got hold of some of the least Hellenized of the archers and marched to Oenoe. This was an Athenian fort on the Boeotian frontier and was now being besieged on their own account by the Corinthians, who had called in the Boeotians also to help them. The reason for this was a loss sustained by the Corinthians when a party of their men returning from Decelea had been destroyed by the garrison of Oenoe. Aristarchus now made contact with the Corinthians, and tricked the garrison of Oenoe by telling them that the Athenians at home had reached a general settlement with the Spartans and that they must hand over Oenoe to the Boeotians, since this was one of the terms of the agreement. The garrison believed him, as he was a general and as they, because of the siege, knew nothing of what had been happening, and they evacuated the place under truce. So Oenoe was captured and taken over by the Boeotians, and at Athens the oligarchy and the civil disturbances came to an end.

ATHENIAN VICTORY AT CYNOSSEMA

99 In this same summer, at about the time of the above events, the position of the Peloponnesians at Miletus was as follows. They were receiving no pay at all from the officers, who, it will be remembered, had been left with this responsibility by Tissaphernes; the Phoenician fleet had not arrived, nor so far had Tissaphernes

53. See Appendix 4, and footnote 10 there, for another possible translation of this sentence.

himself put in an appearance; Philip, who had gone with him, and another Spartan of the officer class, Hippocrates, who was at Phaselis, had written to Mindarus, the admiral, to say that there was no prospect of the ships coming and that Tissaphernes was treating them disgracefully. Meanwhile Pharnabazus continued to ask for their assistance and was very anxious to have their fleet with him, since he, too, like Tissaphernes, wanted to bring about the revolt of the cities in his province that were still subject to Athens and expected to gain great advantages from doing so. Finally, therefore, after careful organization and not giving the order to sail until the last moment, so as to escape the notice of the Athenians at Samos, Mindarus put out from Miletus with seventy-three ships and sailed for the Hellespont. Sixteen ships had already arrived there previously in the same summer and had overrun part of the Chersonese. Running into a storm, Mindarus was forced to put in to Icarus. Bad weather kept him there for five or six days, and he then went on and arrived at Chios.

100   When Thrasylus heard that he had left Miletus, he at once sailed out himself from Samos with fifty-five ships, making all speed so as to reach the Hellespont ahead of Mindarus. But when he found that Mindarus was at Chios he expected that he would stay there, and so he posted scouts at Lesbos and on the mainland opposite so that the Peloponnesians should not move in any direction without his knowledge, and sailed along the coast himself to Methymna. Here he gave orders for stocks of barley and other supplies to be got ready and intended, if Mindarus stayed there longer, to sail out against Chios from Lesbos. Meanwhile he decided to sail against the Lesbian city of Eresus, which had revolted, and to reduce it, if he could. Some of the leading exiles from Methymna had brought across from Cumae about fifty hoplites, who had become members of their party, had hired others from the mainland, making up a force of about 300 altogether, and had given the command to Anaxander, a Theban, because of the racial connection between Lesbos and Thebes. With this force they had first made an attack on Methymna, but had failed in this attempt because of the Athenian garrison in Mytilene, which had come out in time to prevent them. They were then beaten back again in a battle outside the city, and, after crossing the mountains, managed

to make Eresus revolt. Thrasylus therefore sailed against Eresus with all his ships, intending to make an assault on the place. Thrasybulus had already arrived there before him with five ships from Samos, having started as soon as he heard that the exiles had crossed over. He had arrived too late for effective action, but had gone to Eresus and anchored off the city. They were also joined here by two ships, which were on their way home from the Hellespont, and by five Methymnian ships, making a grand total of sixty-seven. With the forces on board they now made a determined attempt, using siege engines and all other means, to capture Eresus, if it could be done.

101   Meanwhile Mindarus and the Peloponnesian fleet at Chios had taken in all their provisions in two days and had received from the Chians three coins of the local currency for each man from Chios who was serving with them. On the third day they put out from Chios as fast as they could and, in order to avoid an encounter with the ships at Eresus, instead of making for the open sea, sailed towards the mainland, with Lesbos on their left. They put in at the harbour of Carteria, in the Phocaeid, for their morning meal, sailed on along the Cumaean coast, and had their evening meal at Arginusae on the mainland opposite Mytilene. From there they went on along the coast some time before dawn and came to Harmatus on the mainland opposite Methymna. They hurriedly took their morning meal there and then, going on past Lectum, Larissa, Hamaxitus, and the towns in that area, reached Rhoeteum, which was already in the Hellespont, just before midnight. Some of their ships also put in to Sigeum and other ports in the area.

102   The Athenians were at Sestos with eighteen ships. Informed by the fire-signals and observing also that many fires were suddenly appearing on the shore held by the enemy, they realized that the Peloponnesians were sailing in, and set off that very night, just as they were and in haste, sailing close in to the shore of the Chersonese along to Elaeus, so as to get out into the open sea away from the enemy's fleet. They were unobserved by the sixteen ships at Abydos, who had already sent a message to their friends who were coming up, telling them to be on the lookout for the Athenians, in case they sailed out; but at dawn they came in sight of the fleet of Mindarus, which immediately sailed in pursuit of them. They

did not escape without some loss, though most of them got away to Imbros and Lemnos. Four ships, however, which were sailing behind the rest were overtaken off Elaeus. One of these ran aground by the temple of Protesilaus and was captured with its crew; two others were captured without their crews; the fourth was aban-
103 doned on the shore at Imbros and burned by the enemy. After this the Peloponnesians were joined by the squadron from Abydos. Altogether they now had a fleet of eighty-six ships. They spent this day in besieging Elaus, but, as the town did not surrender, went back to Abydos.

Meanwhile the Athenians had not received the information they had a right to expect from their scouts and, with no idea that the enemy fleet could have sailed past them without being sighted, were going on with their siege operations as though nothing had happened. As soon as they heard the news they abandoned Eresus at once and hurried to the Hellespont to meet the enemy. They fell in with and captured two of the Peloponnesian ships which had pressed their pursuit during the previous action too boldly and had been carried out into the open sea. Next day they reached Elaeus and anchored there. They brought in the ships that had escaped to Imbros and for five days made ready for the battle in front of them.

104   Afterwards came the battle. It was fought as follows. The Athenians, in column, sailed aong the coast close inshore to Sestos. The Peloponnesians, seeing them coming, put out from Abydos to meet them. It was now obvious that there would be a battle and, realizing this, each side extended its line – the Athenians, with seventy-six ships, along the Chersonese from Idacus to Arrhiani, and the Peloponnesians, with eighty-six ships, from Abydos to Dardanus. On the Peloponnesian side the Syracusans held the right wing, and Mindarus himself with the fastest ships was on the left. On the Athenian side, Thrasylus was on the left and Thrasybulus on the right, with the other commanders variously distributed throughout the fleet. The Peloponnesian plan was to be first into action and, by out-flanking the Athenian right with their own left wing, to cut them off, if possible, from the way out into the open sea, and at the same time to force the Athenian centre on to the shore, which was not far off. Realizing this, the Athenians

extended their own wing in the direction where the enemy was trying to outflank them and succeeded in getting beyond him. By this time the Athenian left had rounded the point of Cynossema, but, as a result of these operations, their centre was weak and dis-organized, expecially so because their fleet was the smaller of the two and the coastline round the point of Cynossema formed a sharp angle so that it was impossible to see from one side what was going on at the other.

105   The Peloponnesians, therefore, bore down upon the Athenian centre, forced their ships on to the shore and, disembarking them-selves, followed them up on land. Here they were having things very much their own way; no help, for the time being, could be given to the centre by the ships of Thrasybulus on the right because of the numbers of the enemy with which he was faced, nor by the ships of Thrasylus on the left, because, owing to the headland of Cynossema, he could not see what was happening and at the same time was being hemmed in by the Syracusans and other enemy ships in numbers quite as great as his own. Finally, however, the Peloponnesians in the confidence of their victory began to scatter in pursuit of individual ships and, over a considerable part of their line, to fall into disorder. Seeing this, Thrasybulus, and his men, instead of continuing to extend their line, turned about immedi-ately and went into action against the enemy ships which were bearing down on them. After routing these, they fell upon that part of the Peloponnesian fleet which had been victorious, driving down upon them in their disorganized state and putting most of them to flight without any resistance being offered. The Syracu-sans, too, were now giving way to Thrasylus and were all the more eager to run for it when they saw that the rest of the fleet also was in flight.

106   The Peloponnesians were routed. Most of them took refuge first at the river Midius and afterwards in Abydos. Though the Athenians captured only a few ships (since within the narrow waters of the Hellespont the enemy had not far to go to reach safety), nevertheless nothing could have been better for them at the time than the winning of this naval victory. Up to now, because of failures in some minor actions and because of the disaster in Sicily, they had been afraid of the Peloponnesian navy; but now

they got rid of their feelings of inferiority and ceased to believe that the enemy was worth anything at sea. The ships which they succeeded in capturing from the enemy were eight from Chios, five from Corinth, two from Ambracia, two from Boeotia, and one each from Leucas, Sparta, Syracuse, and Pellene. Their own losses were fifteen ships.

When they had put up a trophy on the headland of Cynossema, had taken up the wrecks, and given back the enemy dead under an armistice, they sent off a trireme to bring to Athens also the news of the victory. When the ship arrived and the Athenians heard of this quite unlooked-for piece of good fortune, they were greatly heartened after all that they had gone through recently both in Euboea and during the revolution, and they came to believe that, if they did their part resolutely, final victory was still possible.

107   On the fourth day after the naval battle, the Athenians in Sestos, who had worked hard at getting their ships refitted, sailed against Cyzicus, which had revolted. Off Harpagium and Priapus they sighted the eight ships from Byzantium at anchor. Sailing up to them, they defeated the troops on shore and captured the ships. They then came to Cyzicus, which was unfortified, and re-established their control over it, making the inhabitants pay an indemnity. Meanwhile the Peloponnesians also had set sail and gone from Abydos to Elaeus, where they recovered those of their captured ships which were fit for service, the rest having been burned by the people of Elaeus. They also sent Hippocrates and Epicles to Euboea to fetch the ships that were there.

108   About this same time Alcibiades with his thirteen ships returned from Caunus and Phaselis to Samos, with the news that he had managed to prevent the Phoenician fleet from joining the Peloponnesians and that he had made Tissaphernes more friendly to the Athenians than before. He then manned nine ships in addition to those he had already and forced the people of Halicarnassus to contribute large sums of money and fortified Cos. After doing this he appointed a governor for Cos, and, since it was nearly autumn, sailed back to Samos.

Tissaphernes, when he heard that the Peloponnesian fleet had sailed from Miletus to the Hellespont, broke up his camp and hurried back from Aspendus to Ionia.

While the Peloponnesians were in the Hellespont, the Antandrians, an Aeolian people, procured some hoplites from Abydos, took them across by land over Mount Ida, and brought them into their city, considering that they were being ill-treated by the Persian Arsaces, who had been appointed to his post by Tissaphernes. It was this Arsaces who, pretending that he had some quarrel of his own that he wished to keep secret, brought in the Delians who were settled at Atramyttium (after having been removed from their homes by the Athenians because of the purification of Delos) by offering an opportunity of military service to the best of them. After getting them to leave their city as his friends and allies, he watched until they were having their meal and, surrounding them with his own men, had them shot down with javelins. Because of this crime, the Antandrians feared that Arsaces might one day take some such action against them too; he was also putting on them burdens too heavy for them to bear; and so they drove his garrison out of their acropolis.

109 When Tissaphernes heard of this act of the Peloponnesians coming on top of what had happened at Miletus and Cnidus, where his garrisons had also been driven out, he realized that his relations with them were very bad indeed and feared that they might do him more harm still. He was also upset by the idea of Pharnabazus receiving their help, and, at the cost of less time and money, perhaps doing better against the Athenians than he had done. He therefore decided to go and see them at the Hellespont in order to protest against what had happened at Antandros and to clear himself as best he could from what they had to say against him with regard to the Phoenician fleet and other matters. He went first to Ephesus where he made a sacrifice to Artemis. . . .

APPENDIX 1

The Spartan (Peloponnesian) and Athenian Leagues

The treaty concluding the first phase of the war, in 421 B.C., was introduced by Thucydides (v, 18) with the following wording: 'The Athenians, the Spartans and their allies made a treaty and swore to it, city by city, as follows.' The word 'league' does not appear here, nor often in any Greek text; the awkward 'the Spartans (Athenians) and their allies' was preferred. Official Athenian documents occasionally refer to the 'Athenian alliance' and even 'empire' (as does Thucydides), but 'Peloponnesian League' and 'Delian League' are modern coinages.

The obscure prehistory of the Peloponnesian League goes back at least to the middle of the sixth century, when Sparta began to enter into formal alliances with other city-states in the Peloponnese. Roughly speaking these were a combination of defensive alliances and non-aggression pacts, and by the end of the century Sparta had succeeded in securing her position in the Peloponnese by a network of such individual agreements (though Argos, in particular, remained persistently hostile). By no means all were signed voluntarily by the other party, but the fiction was maintained through the word 'ally', much as Rome was to do as she spread her power in Italy in a later period. Formally, too, the alliances with Sparta would not automatically involve individual allies in any relationship with each other.

The situation changed at the end of the sixth century, when the network of alliances became a league in reality if not in name, symbolized by the creation of a league assembly. Although this transformation cannot be dated exactly, it presumably occurred shortly after the fiasco of 506, when the Corinthians discovered at the last moment that Sparta was leading them into battle against Athens in order to restore the tyrant Hippias, and they refused, having marched to Attica in ignorance of Spartan intentions. Not long after, at the first known league assembly, recorded by Herodotus, (v, 90–93), a Spartan proposal to back Hippias once more was voted down. Thereafter the assembly was always summoned whenever there was need for combined military action. Only Sparta, however, could call a meeting; any ally who wished one had first to go to Sparta and persuade her, as is dramatically revealed by the efforts of the Corinthians in much of Book I of Thucydides.

Whether or not the Peloponnesian League had a formal 'constitution' is debated by modern historians, but it may be doubted that the question is of great importance. The reality is that, on the one hand, assembly votes were considered to be binding on all, and secession from the league was prohibited; on the other hand, that states did leave and did not always accept decisions. The Boeotians, Eleans, Megarians and Corinthians voted against the peace of 421, and some of the treaty terms were never carried out. Actual membership in the league fluctuated according to Spartan fortunes and the general political situation in Greece: there was a substantial drop, for example, when Sparta let slip her hitherto accepted leadership of the Greeks after the Persian wars, then a revival as Athenian imperial power grew. Power politics was what counted, not formal constitutional provisions. The league had no finances of its own – the allies paid no tribute – and no permanent executive in the strict sense. Sparta could always summon her allies, she presided at meetings of the assembly and she directed campaigns. At meetings each member had one vote (Sparta herself not voting), but modern experience has proved again what a delusion the one-state-one-vote principle is in practice in international organizations.

The principle proved equally delusory in the first phase of the Athenian alliance (and it was abandoned altogether in due course). Unlike the Peloponnesian League, this one was founded at one go, in 478 B.C., with a formal league structure and a treasury housed on the sacred island of Delos, where meetings were also held. The objective was to mobilize naval resources in order to drive the Persians out of their remaining bases in and near the Aegean Sea, and thereby eliminate, or at least greatly weaken, the threat of yet another invasion. Athens took the initiative and her leadership was welcomed. The Athenian Artistides made the first assessment of the allied contributions, money from some, ships and crews from others; the Athenians provided the ten treasurers, called *Hellenotamiae* ('treasurers of the Greeks'); they also provided the largest naval complement and the command of the league fleet.

Inevitably, a series of successful engagements weakened the interest of some of the members, and there soon began the process whereby a voluntary league was gradually converted into an Athenian empire. Since there is no full, coherent ancient account of those years, we cannot trace the development step by step. For Thucydides, the turning-point was the attempt of Naxos to withdraw from the league (probably in or soon after 470), frustrated by an Athenian invasion: 'This was the first case when the original constitution of the League was broken and an allied city lost its independence' (I, 98). Thereafter, not only were similar moves by other cities forcibly prevented but membership was steadily increased, by force if necessary. No complete list of members is available; the largest number known to have paid the tribute in any one year is about 165, but that is not a very meaningful figure, since it includes insignificant villages in Thrace and Caria and even parts of semi-barbarian states. At its peak, the empire took in virtually all the states bordering on the Aegean Sea to the north-east and east, the Aegean islands and a few cities in mainland Greece itself.

A second aspect of the process was the transformation of the larger member-states from ship-contributors to tribute-payers. Eventually only three – Chios, Lesbos and Samos – remained in the first category, and after the unsuccessful revolt of Samos in 439–8 cost her her fleet, the number of 'independent allies' was reduced to two. Presumably many of the allies made the change willingly, to escape the burden of providing not only ships but also crews for what was becoming a purely Athenian navy. From the Athenian view, the gains were enormous: the allied tribute helped finance the most powerful navy of the time, and simultaneously reduced the capacity for revolt or any sort of independent action.

In 454, all possible doubt about the nature of the alliance was eliminated by the removal of the treasury from Delos to Athens. One-sixtieth of the tribute was dedicated annually to the goddess Athena, and the record was solemnly inscribed on stone stelae for public display. (These are the 'Athenian tribute lists' which have become so basic in modern efforts to reconstruct the history of the empire.[1]) The assessment was revised every four years; exceptionally there were changes in individual cases at other times. Both economic and political considerations entered into the revisions, but the decision was always a unilateral one by Athens. Although the navy was available to pursue defaulters, the amount actually collected varied from year to year. It seems from the inscriptions never to have exceeded 400 talents before 431 B.C., and sometimes it fell substantially

1. Examples of the tribute lists and all the other important epigraphical texts pertaining to the Athenian empire are published and discussed (but only partially translated) in R. Meiggs and D. Lewis, eds., *A Selection of Greek Historical Inscriptions to the End of the Fifth Century B.C.* (Oxford, 1969).

below.[2] When, therefore, Thucydides says (II, 13) that at the beginning of the war, 'the average yearly contribution from the allies amounted to 600 talents', he must be thinking not only of the tribute in the strict sense but also of such income as the annual indemnity imposed upon Samos after the revolt. The war would have created new difficulties in collection. Nevertheless, in 425 the Athenians considered it possible to increase their revenues substantially by trebling (approximately) the tribute assessment. Exactly how much money this measure produced is not known, and the final defeat in 404 of course meant a total cessation of tribute as the empire itself was dissolved on Spartan orders.

The increasingly imperialistic psychology of Athens also expressed itself in other measures, which can merely be listed here. Athens took advantage of her navy to control the corn routes from the Black Sea, with obvious benefits to herself. She ordered a cessation of local coinage throughout the empire, and the exclusive use of Athenian coins. Trials involving Athenian citizens were moved to Athens, as were cases in which conviction led to capital punishment (a measure presumably taken to protect friendly individuals in allied states from political persecution). Every ally was required to contribute a cow and panoply to the Athenian festival known as the Greater Panathenaea.

Above all, Athens intervened to impose or support democratic governments (though a few oligarchies were tolerated, notably in Chios, as well as tribal chieftainships in non-Greek communities). And this is the key point for an assessment of the 'popularity' of the empire. Despite Thucydides' repeated reference to 'enslavement' of the allies, and despite our own assumptions about the desirability of freedom, the pattern among the allies was not a simple one. Many men found and welcomed employment as rowers in the Athenian navy, where they received the same rates of pay and the same conditions as the Athenian citizens doing the same job. Although the Athenians were prudent in levying allied soldiers, they were able to do so effectively on various occasions. Among the 5,100 hoplites and marines in the first expeditionary force sent to Sicily, in 415, there were 2,200 Athenians, nearly as many allied troops, and a contingent of mercenaries. Allied soldiers were still there at the end, and most allowed themselves to be captured rather than desert even when the position had become patently hopeless: 'Gylippus and the Syracusans and their allies then made a proclamation first to the

2. What such a sum as 400 talents means is considered in Appendix 2.

islanders, offering their liberty to any who would come over to them; *and a few cities did so'* (VII, 82).

It appears, therefore, that not all the allied populations felt themselves enslaved, and this conclusion is reinforced by a close scrutiny of the revolts reported by Thucydides. By and large, Athens could count on the support of the lower classes and the hostility of the wealthy and aristocratic families – hence her active backing of local democracies. It is a fair guess, furthermore, that, if we had the evidence, it would show the reverse situation among members of the Peloponnesian League, for, as Thucydides says (I, 19), 'The Spartans did not make their allies pay tribute, but saw to it that they were governed by oligarchies who would work in the Spartan interest.'

APPENDIX 2

Greek Monetary Systems

Like all monetary systems, those of the Greeks were based on weights, and much of the terminology was interchangeable. In Athens the basic unit of weight was the mina, but it was too large to be coined (as was, of course, the talent, 60 minas), though sums of money were frequently expressed in minas and talents for accounting purposes. For coining, the basic unit was $\frac{1}{100}$ of a mina, called a drachma, and the coins most frequently minted were the 4-drachma piece (tetradrachm), the drachma, the 2-drachma piece (didrachm) and the obol ($\frac{1}{6}$ of a drachma). There were also fractions of an obol, for ordinary shopping in the market, whereas the large coins, such as the decadrachm, were jubilee or commemorative issues rather than normal coins.

Since every independent Greek city was free to coin, and many did in the fifth century B.C. (to which this appendix is restricted), the variations were nearly as bewildering as those in the calendar,[3] not only in the engravings on the coins but also in their weights. Thus, in two systems widely used on mainland Greece and in the Aegean islands, the Athenian drachma weighed approximately 4·3 grams, the Aeginetan 6·0. Inter-city exchange was possible only because coins normally circulated by weight, not by 'face value'. That explains why so few clipped Greek coins have been found; it also explains the importance of the money-changers in the society. In international documents, however, it might be necessary to specify the standard to be employed, as in the clause of the treaty of 420 B.C. between Athens and Argos and her allies, quoted by Thucydides:

> With regard to the troops sent out to the help of another city, ... if their services are required for a longer period, the city that sent for them shall be responsible for their supplies at the rate of three Aeginetan obols a day for a hoplite, archer, or light infantryman, and an Aeginetan drachma for a cavalryman (v, 47).

All money was metallic coin, not paper, and essentially it was silver. The Greeks coined in gold only very exceptionally until the time of Philip and Alexander, though Persian gold darics circulated

3. See the Introduction, p. 22.

in Asia Minor and a few travelled further west. Coins of a gold-silver alloy called electrum, minted especially in Cyzicus, were chiefly used in Asia Minor and the regions bordering on the Black Sea. And gradually bronze came to replace silver for the very small denominations, with a strictly local circulation. Conventional ratios existed between gold and ilver, with a certain amount of fluctuation.

No given figure, whether the three Aeginetan obols given to a hoplite as a day's ration allowance, or the nearly 400 talents of annual tribute in the Athenian empire, has any real meaning to a reader today until it is translated into other terms. Some standard of comparison must be established, and it cannot be stressed enough that translation into pounds sterling or dollars according to the weight in silver is the worst possible method. Comparisons must be made within the Greek world itself. The amount of the tribute, for example, begins to take on meaning when it is matched against the regular Athenian public revenue from internal sources at the same time, that is, from harbour dues, sales taxes, rental of state property, court fees and fines, royalties on the silver mined in Attica, and so on. That figure in 431 was 400 talents; in other words, the tribute nearly equalled the rest of Athenian normal revenue. The Parthenon cost more, about 470 talents, but that was an unusually expensive temple, all in marble.[4] About 370 B.C. a substantial, though smaller, temple of Apollo was built at Epidaurus for a total cost of only 23 or 24 talents.

At the other end of the scale, Athens was allowing each hoplite a drachma a day for rations, and another drachma for his batman, a more generous sum than that provided in the treaty with Argos. Athenian jurors received two obols a day until 425, then three (half a drachma). A drachma a day was the average pay for a skilled workman, including the architect on the Erechtheum (another temple on the Acropolis), and that wage enabled him to maintain a small family.

4. See A. Burford, 'The Builders of the Parthenon', in G. T. W. Hooker, ed., *Parthenos and Parthenon* (Supplement to *Greece & Rome*, vol. x, 1963), pp. 23–5.

APPENDIX 3

The Melian Dialogue

The 'Melian Dialogue' (v, 85–113), as it has been called ever since antiquity (see Dionysius of Halicarnassus, *On Thucydides* 37–41), is unique in the *History*. Formally it is set out in the manuscripts like a drama: instead of each 'speech' being introduced by 'the Athenians (or Melians) said (or replied)', each is preceded by the abbreviation, ATH. or MEL., precisely as in the script of a play. Substantively, the dialogue is of an unparalleled abstractness, with virtually none of the concrete details one would expect in such a negotiation.

Nor is the dialogue introduced satisfactorily. Melos, originally a Dorian settlement, was one of the very few Aegean islands that had managed to remain outside the Athenian alliance. She successfully withstood an invasion under Nicias in 426; in the summer of 416 another Athenian fleet arrived and demanded that she become a tribute-paying member of the empire. Thucydides is strangely reticent about the circumstances. Why did Athens decide to force the issue again at this particular moment, while she was formally at peace with Sparta, and then proceed to massacre the male population of the island as a punishment for their resistance to the ultimatum? Had something happened, or was it mere unprovoked viciousness? If the latter, it is surprising that the majority of the fleet consisted not of Athenians but of allied forces, and Thucydides himself makes the point, without comment, that a number of the latter came from other Aegean islands. Finally, why did the Melians refuse to allow the Athenian spokesmen to address the assembly, restricting them to the council and the 'few', presumably the oligarchic leaders? Did they fear popular backing of the Athenians, for the reasons discussed at the end of Appendix 1?[5]

The dialogue takes the following course. The Athenians refuse to discuss either the justice of their demand or any substantive arguments the Melians may wish to offer. They narrow the discussion to hard realism, to expediency. You are too weak, they tell the Melians,

5. We might know a little more if it were possible to date a fragmentary inscription (Meiggs–Lewis, no. 67) listing monetary contributions to a Spartan war-fund, among which are two from the Melians.

to resist effectively. We, on the other hand, cannot allow you to remain outside the alliance, because that may have a bad effect on our subjects.[6] What hope of successful resistance can you have? You cannot count on Spartan assistance. Accept the situation realistically and surrender.

This dialogue thus poses the question of authenticity in a different way from the speeches, and I suggest that, in giving it the formal structure it has, Thucydides was deliberately pointing up the difference.[7] The problem is not, as has sometimes been suggested, about Thucydides' possible informants. That is nearly always an unanswerable question about Thucydides, but it is not difficult to guess several possibilities in this particular instance. The fundamental question is whether such a dialogue is credible at all, under the circumstances. Any answer will necessarily be a subjective one, not subject to decisive proof or disproof. The narrow stress on expediency is equally characteristic of Thucydides' speeches; but the abstractness of the argument here convinces me that, this time, Thucydides has invented more or less everything except the fact that there were negotiations, which broke down, and that Melos was then captured and the male population killed.

This is not the place for an extended discussion, but one small sign deserves notice. Midway in the dialogue, the Athenians warn the Melians that 'hope is an expensive commodity', and conclude this section as follows:

And do not be like those people who, as so commonly happens, miss the chance of saving themselves in a human and practical way, and, when every clear and distinct hope has left them in their adversity, turn to what is blind and vague, to prophecies and oracles and such things which by encouraging hope lead men to ruin (v, 103).

Not only is this Thucydides' personal view, expressed more than once in the *History*,[8] but it is extremely unlikely that an Athenian delegation would have taken such a line even in a secret negotiation, especially when the Melians had themselves made no reference to prophecies and oracles.

The suggestion, in sum, is that the Melian dialogue represents

6. This argument seems particularly out of place in the relatively peaceful year of 416.
7. See the Introduction, pp. 25–9.
8. See the Introduction, p. 20.

Thucydides' own reflections, fairly late in the war (at least later than the Sicilian disaster, to which all the talk about hope and the prophecies that fostered it are an ironic reference⁹), about the moral problems of empire and power.

9. When the news reached Athens of the Sicilian disaster, Thucydides reports (VIII, I), the people 'became angry with the prophets and sooth-sayers and all who at the time had, by various methods of divination, encouraged them to believe that they would conquer Sicily'.

Notes on Book VIII

The sole purpose of this appendix is to provide, on four topics, notes of a length that cannot be conveniently printed at the foot of a page in the text.

1. The revolt of Amorges (chapters 5, 19, 28, 54)

At a date which cannot be determined, one Pissuthnes organized a revolt in Caria against the Persian king, and it was then carried on by his bastard son Amorges, based on Iasus. Amorges had Athenian support, as Thucydides implies (chapter 54) when he reports that Pisander was able to have the Athenians depose Phrynichus as general in 411 'by claiming that he had betrayed Iasus and Amorges'. The support was substantial: Amorges was captured by the Spartans when they made a surprise attack on Iasus by sea, 'the inhabitants never imagining that the ships were not Athenian' (chapter 28). Obviously the Athenian fleet was expected to provide the necessary protection from naval attack. And the revolt was on a considerable scale: Tissaphernes, holding an extraordinary Persian command on the coast of Asia Minor, was now ordered by the king 'either to take alive or put to death Amorges' (chapter 5).

The other new assignment of Tissaphernes was 'to produce the tribute from his province, for which he was in arrears, since he had not been able to raise it from the Hellenic cities because of the Athenians'. This is one of Thucydides' more tantalizing statements and it raises difficult questions. On any interpretation, however, it means that Athens had become openly inimical to Persia at a time when, one might have thought, she was not in a position to invite Persian support of Sparta. Andocides actually says (III, 29) that Athenian backing of Amorges was what led to the Persian alliance with Sparta, and ultimately to the Athenian defeat, and this is one time when Andocides may be accurate. Thucydides does not go so far, even by implication. Yet it does seem that he thought the Amorges affair important, and his treatment of it, together with his earlier neglect of Pissuthnes, is one of the strongest pieces of evidence for the view expressed in the Introduction (p. 13) that Thucydides now came to realize the significance of Persia, which he had largely ignored hitherto. Chapter 5 of Book VIII, dealing with events in the winter of 413–12 B.C., is his first mention of Persia since the report of the embassy of 425–4 (IV, 50), other than an incidental remark in V, I.

As for the thinking in Athens that led to this disastrous shift in policy with respect to Persia, we are without any clues whatever.

2. The Spartan–Persian treaties (chapters 18, 36–7, 57–8)

It is inherently improbable, despite the assertions in the text, that within a space of months Tissaphernes, on behalf of the Persian king, and the Spartans would have concluded and signed three different treaties so widely divergent. Only the third, as quoted in the text, has a proper introductory formula with a date (both Persian and Spartan), and that suggests an explanation, namely, that several drafts were prepared on the spot, in Asia Minor, but that the third document quoted is the finally agreed, and the only genuine, treaty.

Given the incomplete state of Book VIII, one can only conjecture what went wrong. Thucydides had these documents available to him and kept them in his papers. When the work was published after his death, either the editor misunderstood the documents as three genuine treaties and introduced them in that way, or – and this cannot be ruled out – Thucydides himself had an incorrect minute, which he had not got round to checking.

3. The oligarchic coup of 411 B.C. (chapters 47–98)

This detailed account, beautifully interwoven with the war story of the same period, can be partly controlled (unlike any comparable section in the History) because of the very brief, independent version in Aristotle's Constitution of Athens (29–33). Although Thucydides was one of Aristotle's sources – his judgement of the government of the Five Thousand at 33, 2 closely echoes Thucydides VIII, 97 – his main source was the fourth-century annalist (or Atthidographer) Androtion, an oligarchically inclined politician who favoured Theramenes above all the actors in the 411 struggle. Reliance on an annalist gave Aristotle two advantages over Thucydides: he had precise dates, whereas Thucydides had to resort to such vague formulations as 'it was about this time, or even earlier, that the democracy in Athens had been brought to an end' (chapter 63); and he was able to quote the texts of some of the main decrees, which it appears that Thucydides did not have in his possession (otherwise he could have used the dates of the preambles for a more exact synchronization of events).

There are difficulties with Aristotle's documents: at least one is surely not the formal decree it purports to be, but a propaganda document. Nevertheless, one that cannot be challenged is the text of the decree moved by Pythodorus (not named by Thucydides), calling for the election of a board of thirty men (*syngrapheis*) to draft the new oligarchic constitution (29, 2). Thucydides (chapter 67) says the number of *syngrapheis* was ten, and he fails to note that they had to be over the age of forty and that the ten *probouloi*, about whom more will be said shortly, were to be included *ex officio*. These are small details, to be sure, but they cannot be ignored. That is to say, though nothing in Aristotle casts doubt about the sweep of the Thucydidean account, which is inherently consistent and probable, the apparent existence of small inaccuracies at a point at which there is external control must give us pause about the accuracy of other details not subject to independent check.

The chief weakness in Thucydides' account is the abruptness with which the coup is introduced, as a proposal by Alcibiades in chapter 47. It would have helped if he had expanded his meagre statement in chapter 1, that, as a response to the Sicilian disaster, the Athenians appointed 'a body of older men to give their advice (*probouleuein*) on the situation, whenever the occasion arose'. These are certainly the *probouloi*, whom Thucydides does not mention again but who, according to the decree of Pythodorus, were important enough to be automatically included among the draughtsmen of the oligarchic constitution less than two years later. Elsewhere Aristotle offers a broad generalization about *probouloi*: 'A preliminary council or body of *probouloi* is not democratic... but oligarchic' (*Politics* 1299b 30 ff.). Unfortunately we do not know the role they played between 413 and 411, and we are not assisted much by the *proboulos* in Aristophanes' *Lysistrata*, produced early in 411 before the coup, except that there is an implication in the comedy that the *probouloi* were officials with defined duties, not just elder statesmen giving sage advice.

4. *The government of the Five Thousand* (chapters 67, 72, 86, 89–97)

It was not uncommon in Greek states to refer to more or less broadly based oligarchic governments by notional numbers: the 1,000, the 5,000, even the 10,000. In Athens in 411, the 5,000 were in fact those citizens who, as Thucydides says explicitly (chapter 7), had sufficient property to qualify for the heavy infantry, the hoplite class, and there is reason to think that the real number was about 9,000 (Ps.-Lysias xx, 13). Thucydides also makes it clear (confirmed by Aristotle) that most of the leaders of the coup were using the 5,000 as bait to win hoplite support for the overthrow of the democracy, with no intention of allowing the government to slip from their own hands. Nevertheless, a government of the 5,000 came into existence for a period following the fall of the 400. All Thucydides says about it is this (chapter 97):

Indeed, during the first period of this new régime the Athenians appear to have had a better government than ever before, at least in my time.[10] There was a reasonable and moderate blending of the few and the many, and it was this, in the first place, that made it possible for the city to recover from the bad state into which her affairs had fallen.

Thucydides neither describes the 'blending' nor indicates how long the 5,000 lasted. Aristotle merely adds that the régime was short-lived, so much so in fact that he manages to omit it altogether in his summary list of all the constitutional changes Athens had undergone since King Theseus (*Constitution of Athens* xxxv, 1; xli). And that exhausts our knowledge on the subject.

10. An alternative translation of this sentence is a brutal one: 'Indeed, for the first time, at least in my life, the Athenians appear to have been well governed.'

BIBLIOGRAPHY

THUCYDIDES

THE indispensable work for any serious study is *A Historical Commentary on Thucydides*, begun by A. W. Gomme and continued by A. Andrewes and K. J. Dover, which is complete except for Book VIII (4 vols., 1945–70). Even the Greekless reader can learn to use the commentary, in particular the excursuses on special topics. The fact that I have not referred to it in any one footnote or appendix is a sign of my indebtedness throughout.

The most fully rounded book is J. H. Finley, Jr, *Thucydides* (1942), but, as has been pointed out in the Introduction, it adopts the strict 'unitarian' viewpoint; see also his *Three Essays on Thucydides* (1967), and the short work by F. E. Adcock, *Thucydides and His History* (1963).

There is no full-scale study in English presenting the viewpoint expressed in this volume on Thucydides' work, his aims, techniques and methods of composition; for a brief presentation, see H. T. Wade-Gery's article on Thucydides in the *Oxford Classical Dictionary* (second ed., 1970). A. Momigliano, *Studies in Historiography* (1968), chapters 7, 8 and 11, is fundamental on the place of Thucydides in the ancient historiographical tradition. H. D. Westlake, *Individuals in Thucydides* (1968), examines in great detail Thucydides' methods of building up his picture of twelve men, from Pericles, Nicias and Cleon to several rather minor figures.

The following articles explore more fully some of the main questions discussed in the Introduction: A. Andrewes, 'The Mytilene Debate: Thucydides 3, 36–49', *Phoenix*, 16 (1962), 64–85, 'Thucydides and the Persians', *Historia*, 10 (1961), 1–18, 'Thucydides on the Causes of the War', *Classical Quarterly*, n.s., 9 (1959), 223–39; A. W. Gomme, 'Four Passages in Thucydides', *Journal of Hellenic Studies*, 71 (1951), 70–80, reprinted in his *More Essays in Greek History and Literature* (1962), pp. 92–111; A. Parry, 'The Language of Thucydides' Description of the Plague', *Bulletin of the Institute of Classical Studies, London*, 16 (1969), 106–18.

The standard works on ancient calendars and time-reckoning are E. Bickerman, *Chronology of the Ancient World* (1968) and A. E. Samuel, *Greek and Roman Chronology* (1972).

On the place of Thucydides in English education, see M. L. Clarke, *Classical Education in Britain 1500–1900* (1959); R. M. Ogilvie, *Latin and Greek. A History of the Influence of the Classics on English Life from 1600 to 1918* (1964).

THE PELOPONNESIAN WAR

There is no reliable modern book in English on the Peloponnesian War. Longer or shorter accounts appear in every history of Greece, and the following small list of specialized books and articles is restricted to discussions, mostly recent, of a few more important or more interesting aspects of the war and its background.

A. Andrewes, 'The Government of Classical Sparta', in *Ancient Society and Institutions. Studies Presented to Victor Ehrenberg*, ed. E. Badian (1966), pp. 1–20.

D. Blackman, 'The Athenian Navy and Allied Naval Contributions in the Pentecontaetia', *Greek, Roman, and Byzantine Studies*, 10 (1969), 179–216.

I. A. F. Bruce, 'The Corcyraean Civil War of 427 B.C.,' *Phoenix*, 25 (1971), 108–17.

P. A. Brunt, 'Spartan Policy and Strategy in the Archidamian War', *Phoenix*, 19 (1965), 255–80.

G. E. M. de Ste Croix, 'The Character of the Athenian Empire', *Historia*, 3 (1954), 1–41.

G. E. M. de Ste Croix, *The Origins of the Peloponnesian War* (1972).

K. J. Dover, '*Dekatos autos*', *Journal of Hellenic Studies*, 80 (1960), 61–77, on Pericles' constitutional position as one of the generals.

M. I. Finley, *Ancient Sicily to the Arab Conquest* (1968), chapter 5.

M. I. Finley, 'Athenian Demagogues', *Past & Present*, no. 21 (1962), 3–24, reprinted in *Studies in Ancient Society*, ed. Finley (1974).

M. I. Finley, *Democracy Ancient and Modern* (1973).

W. G. Forrest, *A History of Sparta 950–192 B.C.* (1968), chapters 4, 10–12.

J. Hatzfeld, *Alcibiade* (Paris, 1940), the best book available on any individual of the period.

C. Hignett, *A History of the Athenian Constitution to the End of the Fifth Century B.C.* (1952), chapter 12, on the oligarchic coup of 411 B.C.

J. A. O. Larsen, *Representative Government in Greek and Roman History* (1955), chapter 3.

R. Meiggs, *The Athenian Empire* (1972).

R. Meiggs, 'The Crisis in Athenian Imperialism', *Harvard Studies in Classical Philology*, 67 (1963), 1–36.

A. Momigliano, 'Sea Power in Greek Thought', *Classical Review*, 58 (1944), 1–7.

J. S. Morrison and R. T. Williams, *Greek Oared Ships 900–322 B.C.* (1968).

W. K. Pritchett, *The Greek State at War*, Parts I and II (in the press).

H. D. Westlake, 'Athenian Aims in Sicily, 427–424 B.C.', *Historia*, 9 (1960), 385–400.

MAPS

The Aegean

Miles
0   100

Thebes
Plataea
Eleusis   Marathon
Megara   Athens
Sicyon   Piraeus
Corinth   SALAMIS
Cenchreae
AEGINA
Argos
Mantinea   Troezen
Hermione

Miles
0   20

Epidamnus

M A C E D O N I A

E P I R U S

CORCYRA

T H E S S A L Y

Ambracia
Anactorium   Amphilochian
Argos
LEUCAS
ACARNANIA   AETOLIA   LOCRIS
Mt Parnassus   Chalcis O
Oeniadae   Naupactus Delphi Eretria
CEPHALLENIA   RHIUM   PHOCIS
BOEOTIA
ACHAEA   ATTICA
Elis   Corinth
Olympia   ARCADIA   AEGINA
DELOS
Lepreum   T H E
MESSENIA   LACONIA
Pylos   Sparta
P E L O P O N N E S E
Epidaurus
Limera   MELOS

Miles
0   50   100

CYTHERA

Mainland Greece

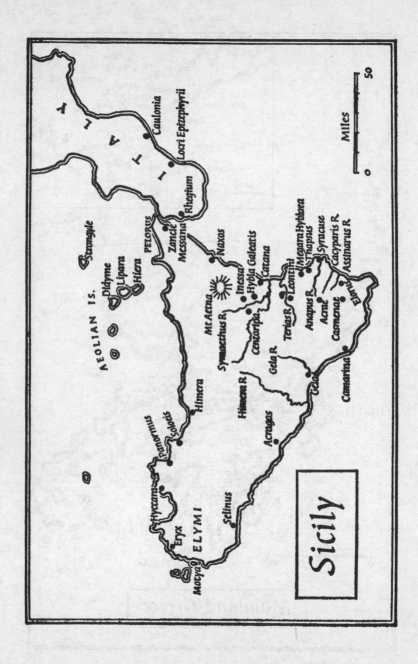

Sicily

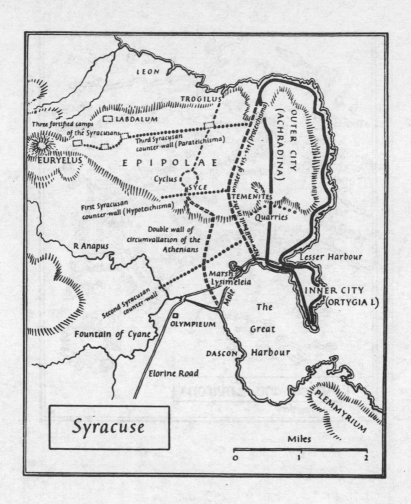

LEON

TROGILUS

LABDALUM

Three fortified camps
of the Syracusans

Third Syracusan
counter-wall (Parateichisma)

EURYELUS

E P I P O L A E

OUTER CITY
(ACHRADINA)

Cyclus

SYCE

First Syracusan
counter-wall (Hypoteichisma)

TEMENITES

Quarries

Double wall of
circumvallation of the
Athenians

R Anapus

Second Syracusan
counter-wall

Marsh
Lysimeleia

Mole

Lesser Harbour

INNER CITY
(ORTYGIA L)

Fountain of Cyane

OLYMPIEUM

The

Great

Harbour

DASCON

Elorine Road

PLEMMYRIUM

Syracuse

Miles

0   1   2

Attica and Environs

········ Frontiers

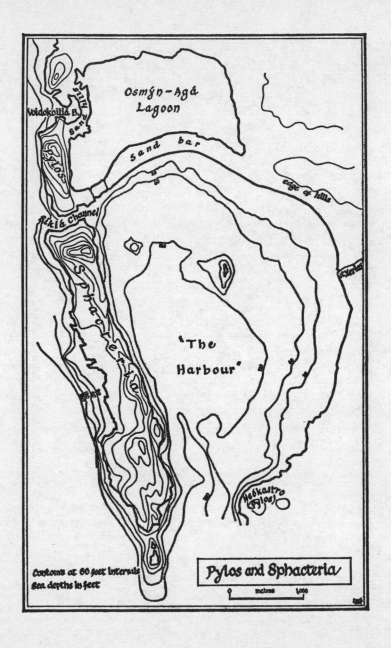

Osmýn-Agá
Lagoon

Voidokoiliá B.

Sand hills

Pylos

sand   bar

edge of hills

Sikiá Channel

Sphacteria

Glóta

'The
Harbour'

Heókastro
(Pýlos)

Contours at 60 feet intervals
Sea depths in feet

Pylos and Sphacteria

0   metres   1,000

INDEX

INDEX

READ MORE IN PENGUIN

In every corner of the world, on every subject under the sun, Penguin represents quality and variety – the very best in publishing today.

For complete information about books available from Penguin – including Puffins, Penguin Classics and Arkana – and how to order them, write to us at the appropriate address below. Please note that for copyright reasons the selection of books varies from country to country.

In the United Kingdom: Please write to *Dept. EP, Penguin Books Ltd, Bath Road, Harmondsworth, West Drayton, Middlesex UB7 ODA*

In the United States: Please write to *Consumer Sales, Penguin Putnam Inc., P.O. Box 12289 Dept. B, Newark, New Jersey 07101-5289.* VISA and MasterCard holders call 1-800-788-6262 to order Penguin titles

In Canada: Please write to *Penguin Books Canada Ltd, 10 Alcorn Avenue, Suite 300, Toronto, Ontario M4V 3B2*

In Australia: Please write to *Penguin Books Australia Ltd, P.O. Box 257, Ringwood, Victoria 3134*

In New Zealand: Please write to *Penguin Books (NZ) Ltd, Private Bag 102902, North Shore Mail Centre, Auckland 10*

In India: Please write to *Penguin Books India Pvt Ltd, 11 Community Centre, Panchsheel Park, New Delhi 110017*

In the Netherlands: Please write to *Penguin Books Netherlands bv, Postbus 3507, NL-1001 AH Amsterdam*

In Germany: Please write to *Penguin Books Deutschland GmbH, Metzlerstrasse 26, 60594 Frankfurt am Main*

In Spain: Please write to *Penguin Books S. A., Bravo Murillo 19, 1° B, 28015 Madrid*

In Italy: Please write to *Penguin Italia s.r.l., Via Benedetto Croce 2, 20094 Corsico, Milano*

In France: Please write to *Penguin France, Le Carré Wilson, 62 rue Benjamin Baillaud, 31500 Toulouse*

In Japan: Please write to *Penguin Books Japan Ltd, Kaneko Building, 2-3-25 Koraku, Bunkyo-Ku, Tokyo 112*

In South Africa: Please write to *Penguin Books South Africa (Pty) Ltd, Private Bag X14, Parkview, 2122 Johannesburg*

READ MORE IN PENGUIN

A CHOICE OF CLASSICS

Aeschylus	**The Oresteian Trilogy**
	Prometheus Bound/The Suppliants/Seven against Thebes/The Persians
Aesop	**The Complete Fables**
Ammianus Marcellinus	**The Later Roman Empire (AD 354–378)**
Apollonius of Rhodes	**The Voyage of Argo**
Apuleius	**The Golden Ass**
Aristophanes	**The Knights/Peace/The Birds/The Assemblywomen/Wealth**
	Lysistrata/The Acharnians/The Clouds
	The Wasps/The Poet and the Women/ The Frogs
Aristotle	**The Art of Rhetoric**
	The Athenian Constitution
	Classic Literary Criticism
	De Anima
	The Metaphysics
	Ethics
	Poetics
	The Politics
Arrian	**The Campaigns of Alexander**
Marcus Aurelius	**Meditations**
Boethius	**The Consolation of Philosophy**
Caesar	**The Civil War**
	The Conquest of Gaul
Cicero	**Murder Trials**
	The Nature of the Gods
	On the Good Life
	On Government
	Selected Letters
	Selected Political Speeches
	Selected Works
Euripides	**Alcestis/Iphigenia in Tauris/Hippolytus**
	The Bacchae/Ion/The Women of Troy/ Helen
	Medea/Hecabe/Electra/Heracles
	Orestes and Other Plays

A CHOICE OF CLASSICS

Hesiod/Theognis	**Theogony/Works and Days/Elegies**
Hippocrates	**Hippocratic Writings**
Homer	**The Iliad**
	The Odyssey
Horace	**Complete Odes and Epodes**
Horace/Persius	**Satires and Epistles**
Juvenal	**The Sixteen Satires**
Livy	**The Early History of Rome**
	Rome and Italy
	Rome and the Mediterranean
	The War with Hannibal
Lucretius	**On the Nature of the Universe**
Martial	**Epigrams**
	Martial in English
Ovid	**The Erotic Poems**
	Heroides
	Metamorphoses
	The Poems of Exile
Pausanias	**Guide to Greece (in two volumes)**
Petronius/Seneca	**The Satyricon/The Apocolocyntosis**
Pindar	**The Odes**
Plato	**Early Socratic Dialogues**
	Gorgias
	The Last Days of Socrates (Euthyphro/ The Apology/Crito/Phaedo)
	The Laws
	Phaedrus and Letters VII and VIII
	Philebus
	Protagoras/Meno
	The Republic
	The Symposium
	Theaetetus
	Timaeus/Critias
Plautus	**The Pot of Gold and Other Plays**
	The Rope and Other Plays

READ MORE IN PENGUIN

A CHOICE OF CLASSICS

READ MORE IN PENGUIN

A CHOICE OF CLASSICS

ANTHOLOGIES AND ANONYMOUS WORKS

The Age of Bede
Alfred the Great
Beowulf
A Celtic Miscellany
The Cloud of Unknowing and Other Works
The Death of King Arthur
The Earliest English Poems
Early Christian Lives
Early Irish Myths and Sagas
Egil's Saga
English Mystery Plays
The Exeter Book of Riddles
Eyrbyggja Saga
Hrafnkel's Saga and Other Stories
The Letters of Abelard and Heloise
Medieval English Lyrics
Medieval English Verse
Njal's Saga
The Orkneyinga Saga
Roman Poets of the Early Empire
The Saga of King Hrolf Kraki
Seven Viking Romances
Sir Gawain and the Green Knight

READ MORE IN PENGUIN

A CHOICE OF CLASSICS